TO
THE MEMORY OF MY
FATHER

PREFACE

IN this volume I have attempted to give a detailed and comprehensive discussion of the system of taxation in Egypt from the beginning of the principate of Augustus until the accession of Diocletian. In 1899 Wilcken published Volume I of his *Griechische Ostraka aus Aegypten und Nubien*, which contained a detailed discussion of the evidence then available concerning taxation in Graeco-Roman Egypt. When the work for the present volume was begun in 1931 there had been no comprehensive treatment published since Wilcken's, although very many new documents referring to taxation, particularly in Lower Egypt, had been made available within that interval. It therefore seemed a service to papyrologists and to students of economic history to reduce the new and old evidence to order, and the results of five years of study are here presented. I wish to express my sincere thanks to the Rockefeller Foundation which, through the Council on the Humanities of Princeton University, gave generous financial assistance that enabled me to devote an entire year to uninterrupted preparation of this volume, and which contributed generously towards the publication of it.

After the preparation was begun, however, the publication by Kiessling of the third volume of Preisigke's *Wörterbuch*, including alphabetic lists of taxes and collectors together with references to the sources, and the appearance of the article *Τέλη* by Schwann in Volume A 9 of Pauly-Wissowa's *Real-encyklopaedie* made easier the access to evidence bearing on the system of taxation in Egypt. Nevertheless, it is hoped that the present study is more complete than any hitherto available, and that a fresh consideration of the evidence has made progress towards the solution of some of the problems involved. In spite of the great increase in the number of published tax-documents, many points in the system of taxation remain obscure. Consequently there will be found a certain unevenness in the following chapters, for I have sometimes been compelled to abandon the systematic treatment of taxation and resort to alphabetic lists of taxes such as are familiar in earlier works.

Our evidence is largely confined to a few districts in Egypt and, since the system of taxation is not uniform, it is more than probable that further publications of papyri may sweep away some of the conclusions now offered as easily as new evidence has disproved solutions presented by earlier students.

This study I have endeavoured to make as complete as the present state of the documentary evidence allows. Experience has indicated, however, that it is practically impossible to control every published document, in spite of the excellence of the Princeton University Library's collection of published papyri where the material for this volume was collected. An effort has been made to make the text of this volume intelligible to students of economic history who are not familiar with Greek, but the attempt has not been wholly successful and was abandoned in Chapter XVII, where the variety of collectors and of their activities could not be represented by translations of their titles or of the taxes which they collected. The index is in Greek, but there is also a brief index of English and Latin terms for which there is no Greek equivalent in this volume. I have not included a systematic bibliography. Most of the significant studies of taxation since Wilcken's *Ostraka* have appeared in connexion with the publication of tax-documents, and references to these and to other discussions will be found in the notes on the various taxes. It seems unnecessary to repeat the select bibliographies which may be found in Volume X of the *Cambridge Ancient History* and in A. C. Johnson's *Roman Egypt*. The abbreviations used in this volume to indicate collections of papyri have been taken for the most part from Preisigke's *Wörterbuch* and his *Berichtigungsliste*.

I wish to express my obligation to the authorities of Princeton University Library and of the Library of the University of Wisconsin for assistance in assembling reference material. I feel a special debt of gratitude to Mr. H. I. Bell and Mr. T. C. Skeat for furnishing transcriptions of unpublished tax-documents in the British Museum, to Mr. H. C. Youtie for supplying excerpts from the then unpublished tax-rolls from Caranis at the University of Michigan Library, to Dr. Edmund H. Kase Jr. for permission to use his transcriptions of tax-documents in the Princeton University Library, and to Professor A. G. Laird

for a photograph of the British Museum's unpublished fragment of the customs-register in the collection of the University
of Wisconsin. Mr. J. G. Tait very generously offered the use
of his transcriptions of unpublished ostraca, but I was unable
to go to England to take advantage of that offer; Mr. Tait, as
reader for the Oxford Press, also made helpful suggestions in
regard to the form and content of the first two chapters of this
volume.

The references have been checked so far as the documents
have been available in the Library of the University of Wisconsin. For assistance in checking these references and in reading
proof I am indebted to Messrs. Eisner, Jenson, Fiedler, and the
late Paul Kennett, students in the University of Wisconsin, and
to my wife. Thanks are due also to Dr. F. M. H. Ould for
reading parts of the manuscript. Professor William Kelly
Prentice of Princeton University gave valuable suggestions for
Chapters VII and VIII, which formed two chapters in the
author's doctoral dissertation presented to the faculty of Princeton University.

My greatest obligation, however, is to Professor Allen Ches-
ter Johnson, who first suggested this study and whose aid and
guidance were generously extended throughout the work. The
special acknowledgements in the succeeding pages do not ade-
quately represent the obligation to his helpful suggestions. He
has read the entire manuscript and the proof of Chapters XVII
and XVIII. Without his encouragement and assistance this
volume could not have been completed. Professor Johnson,
however, is not to be held responsible for matters of opinion
and judgement, which are the author's own.

SHERMAN LeRoy Wallace.

MADISON, WISCONSIN

27 *August* 1937

CONTENTS

I. THE CADASTRE IN ROMAN EGYPT . . 1

II. THE LAND-TAX IN KIND 11

III. FURTHER OBLIGATIONS IN KIND . . 20

IV. COLLECTION OF THE GRAIN-TAX . . 31

V. MONEY-TAXES ON LAND 47

VI. TAXES ON ANIMALS 77

VII. THE CENSUS IN ROMAN EGYPT . . . 96

VIII. THE POLL-TAX IN ROMAN EGYPT . . 116

IX. CAPITATION TAXES 135

X. CAPITATION TAXES LIMITED TO CERTAIN CLASSES OF THE POPULATION . . . 170

XI. TAXES ON TRADES, I. THE STATE MONOPOLIES 181

XII. TAXES ON TRADES, II. CAPITATION TAXES . 191

XIII. TAXES ON TRADES, III. *AD VALOREM* TAXES ON INDUSTRY, SALES-TAXES, OTHER TAXES AND IMPOSTS CONNECTED WITH MARKETS, ETC. . 214

XIV. TAXES PERTAINING TO PRIESTS AND TEMPLES 238

XV. CUSTOMS-DUTIES AND TRANSIT-TOLLS . 255

XVI. MISCELLANEOUS TAXES 277

XVII. COLLECTION OF TAXES IN MONEY . . 286

XVIII. THE REVENUES OF EGYPT 336

APPENDIX 353

NOTES 356

INDEX 495

I

THE CADASTRE IN ROMAN EGYPT

THE conquest of Egypt made ready to Octavian's hand the
great resources of the richest grain-lands of the time. The
conqueror was able to exploit these resources with but few
changes in the system of agricultural economy. His first task
was to restore efficiency in production, which had declined under
the later Ptolemies. To accomplish this the Roman army in
Egypt was used to rebuild the dikes and clean the canals which
had suffered from neglect. But even more important was the
encouragement of the creation of estates by private individuals
who would undertake to maintain land which might otherwise
have become less profitable to the state.[1] To the members of
the imperial family and to favourites, on the other hand, were
granted estates which comprised the most fruitful land in Egypt,
as is evident from the extraordinarily high rents paid by tenants
on the same land after the estates had been confiscated. These
large private estates, like the δωρεαί of the Ptolemaic period,[2]
satisfied a temporary need and later reverted to the Roman
emperors, either through inheritance or by confiscation, when
they were no longer necessary to the most efficient exploitation
of Egypt. Other than the creation of estates no important
changes were required, for the system of land-tenure developed
under the Ptolemies exactly suited the character of an imperial
province. The cleruchic land of the Ptolemaic period became,
within the limits of provincial law,[3] private property. Practically, however, this involved but slight change in the treatment
of the land by the administration of the new province, and hence
there was little change in the system of taxation. In order to
understand why this was so, it is necessary to consider the
classification of the land, for the purposes of administering its
revenue, as expressed in the cadastre.

In the Ptolemaic period legal ownership of all land in Egypt
resided in the king.[4] This conception was an inheritance from
the absolute monarchy of the Pharaohs. For practical purposes
of administration, however, the king upon his own terms ceded

tenure of the land to whomsoever he might wish. Consequently there are found in the records of the Ptolemaic period two great classes of land: βασιλικὴ γῆ, domain land, and γῆ ἐν ἀφέσει, the land whose tenure was ceded to others. The γῆ ἐν ἀφέσει was further divided into ἱερατικὴ γῆ, the land of the priesthoods, and κληρουχικὴ γῆ, the land assigned in allotments (κλῆροι) to various classes of soldiers. These three great divisions of the land correspond to the divisions suggested by Herodotus[5] for an earlier period. The domain land of the Pharaohs was taken over by the Ptolemies without change. When they had attained the sovereignty of Egypt the Ptolemies found the priesthood a powerful organization in possession of a large share of the land. Although it is apparent that the Greek kings made some attempt to curb the grasping ambitions of the native priests, who had profited greatly because of the weakness of the later dynasties of the New Empire, we can believe that comparatively little change occurred in the ἱερατικὴ γῆ.[6]

In the Pharaonic category of land assigned to the warrior-class (μάχιμοι) the Ptolemies made changes at the expense of the important native feudal families which had survived even the Persian conquest. In order to maintain a large standing army the first three Ptolemies assigned a κλῆρος of land to every soldier who agreed to till the soil and pay certain dues to the king. These allotments varied in size according to the military standing of the recipient, and the dues upon the allotments varied slightly according to the rank of the cleruchus.[7] In the Fayûm, where land was reclaimed for the purpose, the allotments were made chiefly to the Graeco-Macedonians who were called catoeci, and their land was termed γῆ κατοικική. Allotments to non-Greek and to native troops seem to have been made chiefly outside the Fayûm.[8] The later Ptolemies made further allotments of land as the occasion arose.[9]

Domain land was leased according to its value, and the average rental paid to the crown for grain-land was between 4 and 5 artabae of wheat for each arura. The land was leased for limited periods, and the length of the lease and rate of rental were subject to change upon the individual plot of land. Upon cleruchic land, on the contrary, were levied dues or taxes[10] at a fixed rate upon the arura and not subject to change, except as the rate might be raised or lowered for the entire class of cleruchi within a nome. The tenure of these cleruchi was indefinite. It was the policy of the Ptolemies to cede κλῆροι, at least in part, from land which could not be leased profitably,[11] so that the rates upon cleruchic grain-land were low, apparently never exceeding 2 artabae upon the arura, and a rate even that high was not common.[12] The land of the priesthoods was sometimes free from taxes and sometimes paid at a low rate similar to that assessed on the land ceded to the cleruchi.[13]

The outlines of the system of land-tenure in Roman Egypt were fixed by Rostovtzeff in his *Studien zur Geschichte des Römischen Kolonates*.[14] As conveniently restated by Wilcken[15] the divisions of the land were:

1. βασιλικὴ γῆ and δημοσία γῆ.
2. προσόδου γῆ.
3. οὐσιακὴ γῆ.
4. ἱερατικὰ ἐδάφη.
5. ἰδιωτικὴ γῆ and οὐσίαι.
    a. Cleruchic and catoecic land.
    b. ἰδιόκτητος and ἐωνημένη γῆ.
6. The land belonging to communities.

The βασιλικὴ γῆ was, of course, the crown-land of the Ptolemies, which was taken over by Augustus as the domain land of the province of Egypt. Δημοσία γῆ is a Roman term for domain land, and the distinction between βασιλική and δημοσία γῆ is not clear;[16] the τυραννικὰ ἐδάφη, probably garden-land, in P. Lond. III. 1157 (p. 61) may have been included in βασιλικὴ γῆ. Domain land was leased to tenants of the crown who were called δημόσιοι γεωργοί or more rarely βασιλικοὶ γεωργοί. Sometimes domain land was sold to private owners and was then taxed like cleruchic or other private land. The sale of this land and the collection of arrears of taxes came under the jurisdiction of the Idiologus. Probably only inferior land was sold at first, but the policy of the government may have been modified to meet changing conditions during the course of three centuries.

There is not yet agreement as to the definition of προσόδου γῆ (or προσοδικὰ ἐδάφη). It was leased like the domain land, but at a very high rental, and the tenants were called προσοδικοὶ γεωργοί.[17] Collart (P. Bouriant, p. 156) suggests that this category represents confiscated lands placed temporarily in this division until they were sold or definitely assigned to some other department of administration. Some of the προσόδου γῆ, however, may have been land sequestrated because dues were in arrears, its income to revert to the treasury until the exactions were fully met.

The οὐσιακὴ γῆ was land belonging to the *patrimonium* of the emperor. It consisted of land formerly belonging to private estates which had been inherited or confiscated by the emperors of the first century. In the second century, as early as the reign of Trajan, usiac land was leased to οὐσιακοὶ γεωργοί or to δημόσιοι γεωργοί, but it was administered in a different manner from the domain land.[18]

Augustus confiscated a part of the land which had belonged to the priesthoods of Egypt.[19] The confiscated portion, called ἱερὰ γῆ ἐν ἐκφορίῳ, was leased like any other domain land; hence it paid rent rather than a fixed tax. The ἱερὰ γῆ (some of which may have been left in the control of the priests[20]) distinguished as ἐπὶ καθήκουσι paid a tax just as it had ordinarily done during the reign of the Ptolemies.[21] This control over the ἱερὰ γῆ ἐπὶ καθήκουσι practically amounted to legal ownership, and the owners could lease the land to their own advantage or perhaps even sell it. Land dedicated to specific gods and called ἀνιερωμένη γῆ was sometimes tax-free in the Ptolemaic period,[22] but it is not likely that this classification of land, which continued into the Roman period,[23] retained its full privileges.

The ἰδιωτικὴ γῆ is the class of land which is most important for the study of the land-tax. This land, other than the great estates, consisted chiefly of cleruchic land, or in the Arsinoite nome and certain other nomes the special class of such land called catoecic. The recognition of private ownership of cleruchic land had its chief effect in that the holders of it were excused from military service under the Romans; the taxes which fell upon the cleruchic land were simply the continuation of the dues which had been assessed in the Ptolemaic period and whose rates had been determined by the military standing of the cleruchi. In many parts of Egypt the ἰδιωτικὴ γῆ was in the minority, especially after the ἱερὰ γῆ was in large part assimilated to the domain land, and in consequence the land-tax on private property did not contribute so largely to the revenue in grain as did the rent from domain land. What privileges the great estates, the οὐσίαι of private individuals, enjoyed in regard to taxation is not known with any degree of precision, and it is probable that the privileges varied with the terms upon which the emperors permitted the creation of the estates.[24]

The ἰδιόκτητος γῆ, confined in the Ptolemaic period to building sites and to vine- and garden-land, was a division of the ἰδιωτικὴ γῆ, but what bearing this had on taxation is not known.[25] Γῆ ἐωνημένη was, of course, land which had been purchased, for the state was accustomed to sell unproductive land, such as had been in the Ptolemaic period ceded as cleruchic land, and confiscated land. After such sale the land was treated as ἰδιωτικὴ γῆ. The βασιλικὴ γῆ ἐν τάξει ἰδιοκτήτου ἀναγρα(φομένη) is obviously domain land which, so far as taxation was concerned, was treated like private property; but we do not know the terms of tenure.[26]

It is known that the corporation of the city (οἶκος πόλεως) of Alexandria owned property near Euhemeria in the Fayûm in the second century. This type of holding became more important in the third century after the reorganization of the municipalities in A.D. 200. In the third century land was owned by Arsinoë and by Hermopolis Magna. These cities leased such land and were responsible for the taxes due to the government of the province, just as were individuals who owned and leased private property.[27]

Certain special categories of lands existed, but they seem to have been less important. Sequestrated lands (γενηματογραφούμενα ὑπάρχοντα) seem to have belonged to owners who were indebted to the fiscus. Until the obligation was discharged the property remained under the supervision of a government agent appointed by the Idiologus. If the debt remained unpaid, the property was confiscated and placed in the category of γῆ προσόδου.

Γῆ ὑπόλογος seems to have been land which was not included in the ordinary account of the administration in reckoning revenues. It included marginal land which was sometimes leased for a nominal sum or was sold at a low price. In P. Kalén 14. 45, however, a parcel of $1\frac{13}{32}$ arurae was assigned for forced cultivation at a rental of $4\frac{1}{5}$ artabae an arura.

A category called marsh land (γῆ λιμνιτική) is found in the

Delta, and such land was administered by a special department of the treasury. Part of this land was devoted to gardens and part to cereals. The rental or tax was generally low (P. Ryl. II. 213, 221; SP. XVII, p. 9).

There were two great divisions of the land of Egypt based upon the type of culture. Grain-land normally paid its tax or rent in kind, whereas vine- or garden-land paid in money. Since the change from one type of cultivation to the other meant an important change in the type of taxation and in the amount of revenue derived by the state from the land, it was necessary to obtain the permission of the government to effect such a change.[28]

To keep an accurate record of this complex system of land-tenure was the purpose of the cadastre, the topographical register of the land of Egypt.[29] In the Ptolemaic period the preparation of the cadastre was the duty of the comogramma-teus.[30] This official was able to furnish upon request exact information as to the area, location, and rate of rent or tax, of any piece of ground in his district by reference to this cadastre. In addition he was required to furnish an annual ἀπολογισμὸς τοῦ ἐδάφους, an account of the land which summarized its yield, brought up to date each year for the guidance of the financial officials of the nome.[31] The information of the cadastre was brought up to date by an annual ἐπίσκεψις, an inspection which was made necessary by the change in some parts of Egypt of the area of cultivable land. This change might be comparatively large or small in any given year, and was caused chiefly by the vagaries of the Nile, which sometimes inundated a given parcel of land, or again left it high and dry, or occasionally left it too long under water. In the latter case the land might remain un-fruitful because encrusted with salt. Sand-storms sometimes left the land covered with sand and so unfruitful.[32] The owner or tenant of the land which so suffered made a report of the facts to the officials in order to secure a reduction in taxation or rent for the year. His report was checked by the episcepsis, a careful official measurement of the land in question. The result of the episcepsis was final and determined whether the claim for reduction of the state's assessment on the land should be allowed, in whole or in part, and the findings were duly reported to the officials concerned in the collection of the revenues. This is precisely the system which Herodotus attributed to Sesostris:[33] 'This king, so they say, divided the land among all the Egyptians, giving to each an equal quadrangular parcel, and from this he derived his revenue by assessing an annual rent. But if the river should take away any part of the parcel of land of any man, he would come to the king and reveal what had occurred; the latter then sent men to inspect and to measure how much the land was diminished, in order that thereafter he might pay an adjusted rental.'

The same system of registration was continued into the Roman period without any significant change. There has been found but one fragment of papyrus which may fairly be called a part of the official cadastre, namely P. Kalén 13. This document is unfortunately incomplete, so that we do not know how the large outlines of the cadastre were fixed, but proceeding from the incomplete description of a given parcel of land, it describes another plot of land as 'South of these (arurae), separated by the afore-mentioned (road, &c.), $2\frac{3}{16}$ arurae of the Dionysodorian estate, paying at the rate of $\frac{7}{120}$ artabae of wheat plus $5\frac{31}{300}$ artabae of barley, through the farmer Pekusis son of Satabous and partners; it is bounded on the south by a road through the fields, on the north by a canal and the above parcel, on the east by a canal and by dry land, on the west by a ποτίστρα (a watering-trough or basin of some kind). Southwest of these (arurae), separated by the canal, are two arurae of domain land paying at the rate of two artabae of wheat, &c.' We must multiply this on the analogy of the Vatican papyrus, published by Norsa and Vitelli in *Studi e Testi*, volume LIII, in order to understand how the entire area of a village was recorded; the village areas must be united to form the toparchy, then the μερίς (subdivision of a nome), and finally the nome.[34] It is not certain that the bureaux of the strategus and the basilico-grammateus had a complete cadastre of the entire nome, but it is not improbable. The comogrammateus was required, however, to present summaries of the areas under cultivation in his district, so that the tax-assessments might be checked without recourse to the complete cadastre. Such summaries were ordinarily prepared after the episcepsis had taken place.[35]

The episcepsis was conducted in the same manner during the

Roman period as under the Ptolemies. There are many examples of the ἀπογραφαί sent in by owners or tenants of land reporting the current state of their property when it (allegedly) deserved a reduction in taxation or rent.[36] The prefect of Egypt (and once the procurator usiacus) in an edict issued instructions for the presentation of these ἀπογραφαί. Such edicts were probably not issued annually, but only in years of exceptional condition of the Nile flood (i.e. low or late). The government did not encourage appeals, because the expense of a survey was great. The ἀπογραφαί, all from the Roman period, contain the same essential clauses, though they differ slightly in details. They are addressed to the strategus, the basilico-grammateus, and the comogrammateus;[37] these officials docketed the returns in the usual manner, and the comogrammateus or the πρεσβύτερος, perhaps the elder of the village peasants, was expected to make an ἐξέτασις, a preliminary investigation.[38] 'The general form and content (of the ἀπογραφή) are as follows: According to the order of the prefect the landowner declares that his land, location given, was unflooded in the present year, usually adding "therefore I hand in the declaration".'[39] If the land became less productive for any other reason, the owner was similarly expected to report the reason: the flooded land might be waterlogged, ἔμβροχος, ὑφ' ὕδωρ, καθ' ὕδατος, or covered with sand, ἐν ἄμμῳ, ὕφαμμος. If there was no change in the normal productive condition of the soil no declaration was required, since no change in the rate of taxation or rent was involved, and the land was therefore called ὁμόλογος.[40]

After the declarations were received, the comogrammateus made up a report listing the unflooded land within his district, in its relation to the flooded land, with the amounts due in taxes and rents from each category; he also gave the names of the owners or lessees of the unflooded land with the amount of rent or taxes due from each.[41]

This report of the comogrammateus served as the basis of the episcepsis carried out by a commission appointed for that purpose. In P. Hamb. 12 an imperial procurator is responsible for the episcepsis, and in P. Brem. 73 (= W. Chrest. 238) a commission of εὐσχήμονες chosen from other nomes, doubtless to secure impartiality, undertakes the task. The comogrammateus did not have a place on this commission, for the investigation of his report served as a check on his activities as well as to determine the amount of land which could not be normally cultivated during the year. The episcepsis consisted of an exact measurement of all the land reported as ἄβροχος: this land was subdivided into quadrangular parcels which could be measured as integers or fractions of arurae.[42] The commission often wrote the result of its findings upon the margins of the report of the comogrammateus,[43] but the members doubtless filed an official report as well. The result of the investigation usually revealed that the wily landholders had over-estimated the amount of ἄβροχος γῆ, and it is significant that the land reported as ἄβροχος was often land which paid at the higher rates of taxes or rent.[44]

The report of the commission on the episcepsis was given to the comogrammateus, who adjusted the data of his cadastre accordingly. From the cadastre and from the corrections given by the report of the episcepsis were compiled the reports of the comogrammateus recording the ὁμόλογος γῆ, the land wrongly reported as ἄβροχος, and the land actually ἄβροχος, and indicating what land could practicably be irrigated.[45] These reports were sent to the strategus and basilico-grammateus in order that the tax-lists might be compiled for the use of the collectors.[46] Summaries of these reports were made for the superior officials of the financial administration to expedite their computation of the taxes on land.[47] We know that the comogrammateus had a copy of the tax-list for his own information and guidance.[48] The same procedure is indicated for the γραμματεῖς πόλεως in regard to the farm-land which might be situated within their competence.[49] Copies of the tax-list, ἀπαιτήσιμον, as well as of the cadastre must have been preserved in the central archives of the nome.[50] Wilcken rightly supposes that a cadastre (in summary form, of course) of all Egypt was in the central archives in Alexandria at the disposal of the high officials charged with the financial administration of the province.[51]

So far as is known the comogrammateus was obliged to depend upon his own investigations to keep the cadastre up to date in regard to changes in ownership or tenancy of the land.[52] Changes in ownership of γῆ ἰδιωτική were reported to the bibliophylaces of the nome, and, after the establishment of that

special archive, to the βιβλιοθήκη ἐγκτήσεων. How the comogrammateus was informed of such changes is not precisely
known, but it is obvious that the officials charged with the
administration of the taxes were interested in such changes
in ownership. Although it has been demonstrated that the
βιβλιοθήκη ἐγκτήσεων had no immediate concern in the cadastre,
it is probable that its records could be inspected directly or indirectly by the comogrammateus in order to check the information as to tenure which was contained in his cadastre.[53] The
bibliophylaces might likewise have access to the cadastre to
verify the rights of any individual to transfer a given parcel of
land.[54] The cumbersome method of keeping records of transfers
of property which prevailed in the βιβλιοθήκη τῶν δημοσίων
λόγων and later in the βιβλιοθήκη ἐγκτήσεων necessitated general
ἀπογραφαί from time to time at the order of the prefect.[55] There
is no evidence that these general ἀπογραφαί occurred at regular
intervals, and there has never been found any document which
was certainly to be identified as an ἀπογραφή sent in for the information of the cadastre.[56] Hence, as we wait in vain for
evidence to the contrary, it becomes clearer that the comogrammateus was dependent upon his own researches for the information necessary to keep his portion of the cadastre up to
date in regard to tenure of land. The soil of Egypt was relatively
stable as compared with the changes in the population brought
about by birth and death and changes of occupation or residence.
Consequently the comogrammateus could build more securely
upon the previous records of the land without a periodic survey
comparable to the census of the population which was taken
every fourteen years.[57]

A cadastre of the buildings erected upon the land was similarly
kept by the scribes of villages and cities.[58] The ownership or
tenancy of all buildings could be checked by reference to the
ἀπογραφαὶ κατ᾽ οἰκίαν, whose primary purpose was to serve the
census.[59] Here, too, a general investigation called a πεδιακὴ
ἐπίκρισις was necessary from time to time as a check on the
ownership of houses and other buildings.[60] What tax was assessed upon the land so built over is not known, but it is known
that a fee, or fine, called πρόστιμον, was exacted for building over
land which had been subject to ἐκφόρια.[61]

II

THE LAND-TAX IN KIND

RENTS paid on domain lands were usually higher than the taxes whose rates were fixed for cleruchic or private land. Voluntary tenants on public lands paid a rental established by the provisions of their individual leases which were renewed from time to time, possibly at intervals of five years, the term stated in many of the leases. Ordinarily domain land was classified according to its worth ($\kappa\alpha\tau'$ $\dot{\alpha}\xi\acute{\iota}\alpha\nu$), and in some cases the wording of the lease provides for a reduction of rent in case the land be un-inundated. Rents of domain land often included barley, beans, and various other products of the soil, although the most important item was almost invariably wheat. The rents were determined with care, as is shown by the minute fractions of artabae used in their calculation. Thus rents on usiac land of a village in the Fayûm were as follows (P. Ryl. II. 207): $5\frac{1}{16}$, $5\frac{1}{5}$, $5\frac{11}{12}$, 6, $6\frac{1}{20}$, $6\frac{3}{40}$, $6\frac{1}{2}$, $6\frac{5}{6}$, $6\frac{51}{60}$, $6\frac{23}{24}$, $6\frac{57}{60}$, $6\frac{109}{120}$, $7\frac{3}{8}$, and $7\frac{11}{18}$ artabae of wheat an arura. In PO. VI. 986 the following rents are recorded: $4\frac{1}{4}$, $4\frac{1}{2}$, $4\frac{171}{1200}$, $4\frac{21}{75}$, $4\frac{68}{120}$, $4\frac{31}{40}$, $4\frac{73}{120}$, $4\frac{33}{40}$, $4\frac{3}{4}$, $4\frac{229}{300}$, $5\frac{7}{25}$ artabae of wheat per arura. Probably the rent in P. Lond. II. 267 (p. 129) at 7 artabae an arura is the highest known for crown-land; the average was much lower. According to P. Lond. III. 604 (pp. 70 ff.) the average rental at Crocodilopolis in a year of low flood was $1\frac{1}{3}$ artabae an arura. Hieratic land at Philadelphia pays rentals of 2, 3, and $3\frac{1}{2}$ artabae an arura in BGU. VII. 1621–2; at Theadelphia a rate of $4\frac{1}{2}$ artabae is found (PO. XII. 1446). In the Mendesian nome rates on hieratic land varied from 1 to $4\frac{1}{2}$ artabae an arura (SP. XVII, pp. 9 ff., lines 11 and 329). Usiac land was ordinarily taxed at a higher rent than crown or hieratic land. According to P. Bouriant 42 *verso* the rent of land on the estate formerly belonging to Lurius averaged $7\frac{5}{6}$ artabae, on that of Seneca $8\frac{1}{4}$ artabae, and on that of Germanicus $9\frac{1}{2}$ artabae, while the highest rate recorded is $14\frac{1}{3}$ artabae an arura. In P. Bouriant 42 part of the estate of Antonia is in the category of land paying at a fixed rate of taxation ($\kappa\alpha\theta\acute{\eta}\kappa o\nu\tau\alpha$). This is the only published example of $\kappa\alpha\theta\acute{\eta}\kappa o\nu\tau\alpha$ on usiac land.

In respect to taxation private land differed from domain land chiefly in that the former paid at a fixed rate determined by the provisions of the original grant of land. We have seen that in the Ptolemaic period a frequent practice of the kings was to assign to their followers allotments (κλῆροι) from land which could not become profitable to the state without the expenditure of considerable labour upon it and hence could not be leased easily. The policy of Augustus and his successors was similar and greatly increased the amount of privately owned land. The concession of large tracts of land to individuals can be inferred from the long list of estates which has been compiled from references to them in the papyri.[1] Many of these estates belonged to members of the imperial family and to their favourites. The land for these grants was obtained by confiscating neglected cleruchic holdings and also ἱερὰ γῆ which had belonged to the temples.[2] Most of these estates, either by inheritance or by confiscation by the various emperors, came into the class of usiac land before the end of the first century after Christ.[3] In the second and third centuries private ownership of land was encouraged because the development of the system of liturgies required large numbers of eligible persons having considerable property. Grants of land to private individuals were not ordinarily made gratis,[4] but we know little about the taxation of estates after they had been acquired. The estates of the members of the imperial family enjoyed ἀτέλεια, either partial or complete exemption from the land-tax.[5] The estate of Julius Asclepiades, a philosopher, likewise enjoyed ἀτέλεια, but that may have been because of his privileges as a philosopher.[6] The conditions of ἀτέλεια (or κουφοτέλεια) were probably determined for individual cases by the terms of the concession of land.[7] We do know, however, that certain private estates paid the usual taxes on garden-land,[8] and there is little evidence for the payment of grain-taxes in kind by the estates because the majority of them were devoted to garden- and vine-culture[9] and consequently paid their taxes in money. Practically all our information, therefore, is confined to the rates of the grain-tax on cleruchic land and on the ἱερὰ γῆ ἐπὶ καθήκουσι.

All land in Egypt devoted to raising grain apparently paid the διχοινικία, a tax of $\frac{1}{20}$ of an artaba of wheat to the arura.[10] Grain-land also paid the tax called ναύβιον, but this was a tax paid in money and levied on garden- and vine-land as well, so that it will be more convenient to consider it in connexion with the taxes on vine- and garden-land.

Private land and ἱερὰ γῆ ἐπὶ καθήκουσι almost invariably paid their land-taxes in wheat, because the revenues were used by the Roman government for the *annona civilis* for the populace at Rome, and there was comparatively little use for the barley, beans, &c., that formed a part of the revenues obtained from the rents of domain lands. The individual receipts for payment of taxes in wheat, unlike those for payment of the taxes in money, give little information concerning the rates of taxation. Most of this information comes from the ἀπογραφαί of ἄβροχος γῆ (and the like), from the surveys made on that account, and from the tax-lists.

The Arsinoite Nome

Most of the ἰδιωτικὴ γῆ in the Arsinoite nome consisted of the κλῆροι which had been granted to the catoeci in the Ptolemaic period.[11] These continued to pay the tax of 1 artaba, μοναρταβία κατοίκων (with supplementary charges which will be considered in Chapter IV), throughout the Roman period.

The editors of P. Ryl. II. 202 consider the ἰδιωτικὴ γῆ in that document, which is designated as μοναρταβίας followed by the name of a village, as different from the catoecic land designated by μοναρταβίας κατοίκων with, or without, the name of a village. This may be correct, for the land sold from the οὐσία ᾿Αντωνίας, which could hardly be catoecic land, is taxed at 1 artaba an arura in P. Bouriant 42.

Other classes of κλῆροι, however, existed in the Fayûm. The κλῆροι of the μάχιμοι in the late first century of our era[12] paid at a rate higher than $1\frac{3}{4}$ artabae to the arura, if the reasoning of the editors of P. Ryl. II. 188. 4, note, is correct.[13] Since we have no evidence that cleruchic land ever paid at a rate higher than 2 artabae an arura, it is probable that the rate for the μάχιμοι was 2 artabae, for κληρουχικὴ γῆ was very rarely assessed at odd fractions of an artaba.[14] This would represent a stiff rise in the rate for this class, since in the Ptolemaic period, at least towards the end of the second century B.C., the ἐπτάρουροι μάχιμοι paid at ¾ artaba an arura.[15]

In the same document a rate somewhere between 1 and 2 artabae is indicated for the cleruchic land of the φυλακῖται. In 112 B.C., however, the φυλακῖται paid at ½ artaba per arura.[16]

A class of land paying at ¾ artaba is mentioned in P. Teb. II. 346, dated shortly after A.D. 16. This was the rate paid by cleruchi who had been granted 7 arurae, at least in 112 B.C. A class of land paying at 2 artabae is also mentioned.[17] The rate paid on land apparently classed in this document as λααρχίας[18] is lost.

A rate of 1½ artabae on the arura is not infrequently found in the Arsinoite nome,[19] and directions for calculating that tax and the supplementary charges are found in the gnomon or standard list of instructions for the collectors and assessors of taxes.[20]

A rate of taxation on ἰδιωτικὴ γῆ at 1¼ artabae (ἷ ωϛ—ad) is found in SP. xx. 62. 10 from the Fayûm. But the recorded payment (ϫ ρλ[.] ιϛ λβ ἷ ρξ), if complete, shows that the tax was actually collected at a rate less than 1¼ and more than 1⅐ artabae an arura. The exact rate cannot be determined because part of the number of arurae is mutilated.

The rate of taxation on γῆ ἀμπελῖτις, former vine-land which, because of the condition of the vines and soil, was no longer profitable as a vineyard, but which if irrigated might be sown with grain, was ordinarily 1½ artabae.[21] The only evidence for the rate on this class of land in the Arsinoite nome is doubtful, but it may have been 1 artaba an arura.[22]

Ἱερὰ γῆ was of two kinds, ἐν ἐκφορίῳ which was leased by the government like the βασιλικὴ γῆ, and ἐπὶ καθήκουσι which paid a fixed tax on the arura. The rate of the tax in the Arsinoite nome may have been 1 artaba on the arura, for the land designated simply as ἱερ(ᾶς) in P. Teb. II. 453. 2 is probably to be regarded as ἐπὶ καθήκουσι, since it seems to be contrasted with that designated as ἱερ(   ) ἐν ἐκφο(ρίῳ). The rate was probably uniform throughout the nome, for there is apparently but one known exception to the rate of 1 artaba per arura on ἱερὰ γῆ in the papyri from all parts of Egypt.[23]

The gnomon published in P. Teb. II, App. I, gives directions for calculating the tax designated as ἀρταβ(ιείας?) ι̇ϡο̇, which may or may not refer to one of the classes of land listed above; the interpretation of the symbol remains obscure.[24]

The Oxyrhynchite Nome

The normal rates for ἰδιωτικὴ γῆ in the Oxyrhynchite nome were 1 artaba and $1\frac{1}{2}$ artabae on the arura.[25]

In PO. XII. 1445 $4\frac{27}{32}$ arurae of private land paid $4\frac{17}{48}$ artabae of wheat. As the editors remark, some part of this land paid at less than the usual rate of 1 artaba on the arura. Unless some part of this land paid at more than 1 artaba (e.g. at $1\frac{1}{2}$ artabae), this would mean that 1 arura paid at $\frac{1}{2}$ artaba, while $3\frac{27}{32}$ arurae paid at the usual rate of 1 artaba (which would total $4\frac{33}{96}$ artabae as against the $4\frac{34}{96}$ artabae of the papyrus); or possibly $1\frac{15}{16}$ arurae paid at $\frac{3}{4}$ artaba, and the rest at 1 artaba. But rates of $\frac{1}{2}$ or $\frac{3}{4}$ artaba are not otherwise attested for the Oxyrhynchite nome.[26]

The Hermopolite Nome

The ἀρταβιεία κατ' ἄρουραν is attested for this nome.[27] This implies a rate of 1 artaba on the arura, although it is possible that the term ἀρταβιεία may cover other rates besides 1 artaba, as Grenfell and Hunt have attempted to prove.[28] Nothing further is known concerning the rates on private land in this nome.

P. London II. 193 (pp. 120 ff.)

This papyrus was republished in SP. XVII, pp. 49 ff., by Martin who assigned it to Middle Egypt. It contains the following classifications of private land (all except the catoecic pay the ναύβιον ἐναφεσίων):

1. Catoecic at 1 artaba per arura.
2. Land designated merely by its rate of $1\frac{1}{2}$ artabae.
3. Γῆ ἀμπελῖτις at $1\frac{1}{2}$ artabae.[29]
4. Ἰδιόκτητος γῆ at $1\frac{1}{4}$ artabae.
5. Land of the μάχιμοι κλη(ροῦχοι) assessed at $\frac{3}{4}$ artaba, with which is combined a tax designated as λααρχίας) συσφ( ) at $\frac{1}{2}$ artaba, so that land of this class paid at a total rate of $1\frac{1}{4}$ artabae on the arura.
6. Land designated by its rate of 2 artabae.

The Apollonopolite Nome

In P. Flor. III. 331 and P. Giss. 60 from this nome are found the following classifications of land:

1. Catoecic land. This forms the largest portion of private land, and presumably pays at 1 artaba.

2. Land with a rate of $1\frac{1}{12}$ artabae, which (if Kalén is right) is really assessed at 1 artaba, since the stated rate includes the διχοινικία.[30]

3. Land designated as αd πολ( ). It is not certain how the abbreviated word is to be restored, but all suggestions relate it to πόλις,[31] so that it is evident that this land received its designation from the fact that the κλῆροι of which the land was composed had been assigned in the Ptolemaic period to citizens of Ptolemais or even of Alexandria, and paid $1\frac{1}{4}$ artabae.

4. Γῆ ἐωνημένη, upon which the rate is not given. It consisted presumably of confiscated κλῆροι, which had been sold, probably before the reign of Nero, in order to bring them into profitable cultivation.[32]

5. Land with a rate of $\frac{11}{12}$ artaba to the arura. This is the only example of a rate of taxation at a fraction other than halves or quarters.

6. Χ(ερσάμπελος) at $1\frac{1}{2}$ artabae. This land has been variously interpreted as 'dry land' which, with proper irrigation and cultivation, was suitable for growing vines, and as former vineland.[33]

7. Κολωνία. This is interpreted as land allotted to a colony of Roman veterans.[34] The rate of tax on the land is not stated.

8. Βασιλικὴ ⟨γῆ⟩ ἐν τάξει ἰδιοκτήτου ἀναγραφομένη or ἰδιωτικ(ῷ) δικαίῳ ἐπικρατουμένη (crown-land administered like private land) was assessed at 1 artaba and at $1\frac{1}{2}$ artabae to the arura.[35]

The Thebaid

From Crocodilopolis, which is presumably near Ptolemais in the Thebaid,[36] comes P. Lond. III. 604 (A and B, pp. 70 ff.), the report of a comogrammateus on the βασιλική, ἱερά, and ἰδιωτικὴ γῆ of the district within his competence.

There are but three parcels of ground which may have been

ἱερὰ γῆ, although the readings are uncertain.[37] One rate may have been the usual 1 artaba to the arura. Two parcels, which may have been temple land, pay at ½ artaba, which is not an impossible rate for ἱερὰ γῆ, since that rate is attested for the Ptolemaic period.[38] These would presumably be the rates on ἱερὰ γῆ ἐπὶ καθήκουσι, although the average rent of the βασιλικὴ γῆ was only 1⅓ artabae an arura.

The following classifications of private land are obtained by combining the data of the two parts of the document:

1. Catoecic land paying at 1 artaba.

2. Land designated as α —ₒ Πολ( ). Part, if not all, of such land had been ceded to citizens of Ptolemais or of Alexandria in allotments of 25 arurae.[39]

3. Land designated as ℰ⁻ πέζων, that is, land which had been ceded to the Ptolemaic infantry and which paid at the rate of ¾ artaba to the arura.

4. Land paying at 2 artabae an arura, but also characterized as αλλεων (or αλτεων), which the editors take as the name of a place.[40] Apparently there was but a small amount of such land in the district, 13⅜ arurae divided among three owners.

5. It is possible that the land first mentioned in the document and designated as Ἰδ( ) was different from any of the land classified above. Ἰδ( ) may be an abbreviation for ἰδιόκτητος rather than for ἰδιωτικὴ γῆ (as the editors have expanded it). The rate on such land must have been well understood, since it is not given.[41] This parcel of land may, however, have belonged to one of the first three classifications in this list.

From the ostraca of the Roman period found at Thebes (as well as at Syene where little grain was raised) we learn but little concerning the rates of taxation on grain-land. O. Tait, p. 75, no. 75, designates certain land as α —ₒ ἱερα(τικῆς), which presumably indicates a rate of 1 artaba an arura on ἱερὰ γῆ ἐπὶ καθήκουσι. If the restoration of WO. II. 1405. 3, given in the Berichtigungsliste, II. 1, is correct, there is evidence for land assessed at 1 artaba an arura. Two ostraca from the late Ptolemaic period (O. Theb. 10–11) apparently indicate rates of 1 artaba and 1¾ artabae per arura; it is probable that the first rate, at least, was continued in the Roman period, since the same rate appears elsewhere in Egypt.

The Mendesian Nome

P. Mendes. Genev., published in SP. XVII, pp. 9 ff. by Martin, gives most valuable information concerning the tax on grain-land in the Delta. The ἱερὰ γῆ ἐπὶ καθήκουσι paid at the usual rate of 1 artaba an arura. Martin found the following classes of private land:

1. $a \overline{}_{o} ἐναφ(εσίων)$, that is cleruchic land paying at 1 artaba to the arura.

2. a (ἀρτάβης) without further characterization, which Martin regarded as different from class 1, although paying at the same rate.

3. Land paying at $1\frac{1}{4}$ artabae, but without any further characterization.[42]

4. Χερσά(μπελος) paying at $1\frac{1}{2}$ artabae.

5. Land of the δεκάρουροι paying at $\frac{3}{4}$ artaba. The δεκάρουροι are frequently further characterized as Ιετηρίτεις.[43]

6. Land of the δεκαπεντάρουροι paying at $\frac{3}{4}$ artaba.

7. Land of the ἑπτάρουροι, whose rate of payment is not given. Martin argues with great probability that the rate was $\frac{3}{4}$ artaba.

8. Land of the ῥαβδο(φόροι), of which the rate has been lost.

9. There are possibly two other classes (Martin's *k* and *l*, p. 43), but the rates are uncertain.

The remarkable way in which these various classes of cleruchic land mentioned in the Mendesian papyrus at Geneva had continued to the end of the second century after Christ indicates with how little change the system of taxation on private land was taken over from the Ptolemies by the Romans. It is not surprising that, once taken over, these classifications should have persisted: they represented privileges in tenure which the landholders were only too eager to maintain. The revolts in Egypt which began as early as the first years of the rule of Augustus apparently taught the Roman administrators that it was more important to maintain the existing system of grain revenues at a high point of efficiency than to attempt to change the assessments to a uniformly higher rate. The salient features of the system are as follows. The ἱερὰ γῆ ἐπὶ καθήκουσι, with but one known exception and that doubtful, was assessed at 1 artaba of wheat an arura. The majority of cleruchic land, including the catoecic whose rate seems never to have varied, was also assessed at 1 artaba. Former vine-land everywhere, except possibly in the Arsinoite nome, was assessed at $1\frac{1}{2}$ artabae. Rates of $\frac{3}{4}$, $1\frac{1}{4}$, $1\frac{1}{2}$, and 2 artabae on cleruchic land are not infrequently found, but there does not seem to be uniformity among the various nomes in the method of assessment upon the different classes of cleruchi.

Partial or total remission of the tax on private grain-land may have been allowed because of impossibility or difficulty of cultivation caused by the vagaries of the inundation of the Nile, but there is no evidence as to the amount or the specific conditions of such remission.[44]

We have little evidence for changes in the rates of the grain-tax during the Roman period. Certain rates on cleruchic land were higher in the first and second centuries after Christ than the rates attested for the same classes of land towards the close of the second century B.C.,[45] but it is more likely that the rise in rates came during the unhappy rule of the Ptolemies in the first century B.C. than that the Roman administration changed the existing rates. In PO. VII. 1044, dated A.D. 173–4 or 205–6, land designated as 'one artaba' land actually pays at the rate of $1\frac{1}{8}$ artabae to the arura; this may represent a temporary or permanent rise in the assessment or an inclusion of some supplementary tax, but nothing is known of a similar assessment elsewhere in Egypt. We have no satisfactory evidence for the third century, when we know that the rates on garden-land were raised.[46] Aurelian boasted that he had added an ounce to the loaves of bread for the city of Rome and that he got this from the revenues of Egypt, but his own words state only that he had improved the transportation on the Nile and on the Tiber.[47] It is possible that he raised the assessment on the grain-land of Egypt, but it is also possible that the increase in the revenue was made feasible by the improvement in the system of irrigation which Vopiscus implies was carried out at that time.[48] These isolated and dubious instances are too little upon which to conclude that there was an increase in the assessments of the grain-tax for all Egypt, and as Milne has aptly said,[49] 'The actual taxes remained practically unaltered in name, scope, and incidence' until the age of Diocletian.

FURTHER OBLIGATIONS IN KIND

IT has often been pointed out that, since the intense cultiva-tion of Egypt was dependent upon irrigation from an elaborate system of dikes and canals, complete exploitation of the arable land required a constant warfare against the unfavourable turns of nature which broke down dikes during inundations and also silted up canals, and against the indifference of the oppressed fellahîn who, when not closely watched, permitted the system of irrigation to fall into decay. Extensive civil disturbances always caused a shrinkage in the area of cultivation, and when such outbreaks had been suppressed the government was obliged to make special efforts to restore the cultivated land to its previous extent. In spite of its efforts the government sometimes failed to obtain voluntary tenants for heavily assessed domain land. Involuntary cultivation of domain land was the answer to the problem, for the Ptolemies and the Pharaohs before them had proved its efficacy. By the Roman administration in Egypt this involuntary cultivation was enforced in two ways, one called ἐπιβολή and the other ἐπιμερισμός.

Ἐπιβολή

By the ἐπιβολή, frequently called ἐπιβολὴ κώμης, small sections of domain land assessed at the usual high rate of rental were assigned for cultivation to the owners of private land. In the Arsinoite nome such assignments fell often upon the holders of catoecic land.[1] O. Mich. 24, presumably from the Fayûm and dated in the second century, records an ἐπιβολή on hieratic land, and to this is added a unique ἱερὰ ἐπιβολή almost a half larger. No principles for the incidence of such ἐπιβολαί have been deduced from our sources; but it is probable that the ἐπιβολή was somewhat like a liturgy, in that theoretically the larger allotments were assigned to those better able to undertake the cultivation of additional land. It is uncertain whether the ἐπιβολή was permanent or imposed only for a limited period of time; but it clearly was an obligation attached to the land with which it was transferred whether by lease, sale, or inheritance. That this burden was unwelcome is revealed by the clauses in conveyances which guarantee that the land is free from ἐπιβολαί. The additions of domain land to various classes of landholdings at Ptolemais in the Thebaid were probably similar to the ἐπιβολὴ κώμης, although they are listed under the heading πλεονασμῶν βασιλ(ικῆς γῆς) in P. Lond. III. 604B (p. 76), line 54. The land in the Mendesian nome denoted by the term χάλασμα (in SP. XVII, pp. 13 ff.) seems to have been land similarly added to private holdings.[2]

Ἐπιμερισμός

The ἐπιμερισμός was organized in a somewhat different manner. When a large proportion of the domain land of a certain town could not be leased in the ordinary way, the officials of the town were directed to divide up the land among the δημόσιοι γεωργοί of the town and to see that the rents were paid therefor. If, because of unfavourable local conditions, the cultivators of the town were unable to assume so large a burden, the area in question might be divided among several near-by villages, whose cultivators became responsible for a share of the ἐκφόρια upon the land so assigned.[3] Such an obligation was not permanent. The ἐπιμερισμός was perhaps at first intended to fall only upon the δημόσιοι γεωργοί, who were able to cultivate such assignments of land with a minimum of difficulty because they were organized in guilds. It appears, however, from the conveyances of private land that the ἐπιμερισμός of domain land had fallen also upon the holders of private land, since the guarantee-clauses of such conveyances state that the land is free from ἐπιμερισμοί.

An ἐπιμερισμός of land in another village must have been a considerable nuisance to the cultivators who had to make arrangements to leave their own land, upon which the usual obligations in rent or taxes were due, or else sub-lease the γῆ ἐπιμερισθεῖσα to some one who could more conveniently care for it. It is perhaps from the ἐπιμερισμοί that most of the payments for διάφορον φορέτρου arise.[4]

The ἐπιβολή and ἐπιμερισμός were two of the drastic measures taken by the Roman government to ensure the cultivation of domain land which found no voluntary lessees. The precedent for such action was found in the involuntary lease of the Ptolemaic period.[5] In spite of these steps the revenues in grain were constantly falling into arrear for various reasons, such as desertion of the tenants, inaccurate assessments, incompetence or peculation of officials, and unforeseen calamities. Although strenuous efforts were made to enforce the collection of arrears, the revenue in grain often did not meet the demands made upon it.

Πυρὸς συναγοραστικός

One of the methods used by the Roman government to meet increased demands was the forced sale of grain termed πυρός (or κριθὴ) συναγοραστικός. Certain cultivators were compelled to sell a part of their crop remaining (ἐπιγένημα) after the payment of taxes at a price set by the government. Such grain was delivered by the cultivators to the state granary, where a separate account of it was kept by the sitologi.[6] Such a forced sale was a hardship, and every effort was made by the great landholders to keep their names off the list of cultivators liable to sell grain εἰς συναγοραστικόν.[7] It is thus evident that this forced sale was a liturgy falling upon landholders and was not a tax whose incidence was fixed upon the arura.[8]

It is probable that the grain so purchased by the government was used chiefly for the subsistence of the army in Egypt.[9] In P. Thunell 1 verso and 4 the amounts of πυρὸς συναγοραστικός are insignificant in comparison with the total receipts of revenue grain, so that it is improbable that the Roman government was engaged in the purchase of grain in Egypt for distribution at Rome. P. Lond. II. 301 (p. 256), however, has a reference to πυρὸς συναγοραστικός shipped to Alexandria, the port of export to Rome, but it is not certain that the purchased wheat formed the whole shipload or that it was not intended for the garrison stationed near Alexandria. It is probable that the government resorted to the forced sale of grain whenever the price of grain rose in the open market to such an extent that the soldiers stationed in Egypt could not afford to purchase it. The great majority of references to forced sale of grain come from the reigns of Antoninus Pius, Marcus Aurelius, and Commodus. It is noteworthy that in P. Goodspeed Cairo 30 πυρὸς συναγοραστικός is mentioned in an account which gives such high prices for the sale of wheat in the open market that a serious shortage in Egypt seems indicated.

Ἀννώνη

Little is known concerning the method of obtaining supplies for the Egyptian legions before the end of the second century. Lesquier[10] has, with reason, held that the requisitions were made upon the various districts of Egypt in a manner analogous to that employed to maintain the entourage of princes and prefects during their journeys through Egypt.

As early as A.D. 185, however, the annona was organized in a more regular fashion, particularly the annona of grain which became a surtax in kind levied upon grain-land. It was collected in such small quantities, however, that it seems to have been used only for the legions stationed in Egypt or in the immediate vicinity. Thus the ἀννώνη of Egyptian tax-documents corresponds to the *annona militaris* as distinguished from the *annona urbis*. Wheat and barley were the grains usually levied for the annona in Egypt. In BGU. I. 336, from Heraclia and dated A.D. 216, a receipt is given by the sitologi for 19⅝ artabae of wheat paid as tax on catoecic land, and in addition there were paid for the annona 2½ artabae of wheat and 2 artabae of barley. Later special collectors of the annona are found, in A.D. 253 an ἀπαιτητὴς ἀννώνης and about A.D. 265 ἐπιμεληταί.[11] Ἀπαιτηταὶ κριθῆς κυριακῆς are found in Garrett Deposit 7669 (in Princeton University Library), a receipt dated in A.D. 217 but whose provenience is not known; the 'imperial barley' was probably intended for the annona of the soldiers. In Garrett Deposit 7687b, from the Oxyrhynchite nome and dated A.D. 255, 100 drachmae are paid to the ἀπαιτητής of the western toparchy for the ἀννώνη στρατιωτῶν.

Vinegar (ὄξος) and wine (οἶνος) were also demanded for the annona.[12] Various other articles were requisitioned for the soldiers' maintenance, but they are hardly to be considered as taxes in kind on land. In PSI. VI. 683, from the Arsinoite nome and dated A.D. 199, steers, calves, goats, and hay are mentioned. This mutilated document is a copy of a communication sent by the epistrategus to the strategi of the Arsinoite nome asking that the strategi furnish a list of available supplies to be found in each village of the nome under their jurisdiction, so that the requisitions could be equably divided (ἐπιμερίζειν) among the various districts of the nome.

Since it was easier to transport money than supplies in kind, it was often permitted that the annona in kind be commuted for a payment of money. An account found at Tebtynis and dated late in the third century records amounts in staters and drachmae paid toward the annona of grain (σῖτος = wheat?), barley, cattle, kids, and pigs.[13] Occasionally receipts for such commuted payments are phrased ὑπὲρ τιμῆς οἴνου εἰς λόγον ἀννώνης, ὑπ(ὲρ) τι(μῆς) κρ(ιθῆς) ἀνό(νης), ὑπ(ὲρ) τι(μῆς) χόρ(του) ἱερᾶς ἀννώνης, or the like.[14] Such payments were collected by the ordinary collectors of money-taxes, the πράκτορες ἀργυρικῶν. Because of the similarity of phrasing, other receipts beginning ὑπὲρ τιμῆς have been associated with the annona. Some of these receipts are earlier than any extant mention of the annona in Egypt, and consequently doubt has been cast upon the connexion of some of them with the annona.[15] Receipts for τιμὴ πυροῦ, for example, are found from 16 B.C. to A.D. 265, but it is unlikely that all of these are to be related to the annona. The editors of PO. XII. 1419, dated A.D. 265, suggested that τιμὴ πυροῦ in that document meant the ordinary land-tax.

In WO. II. 1264 the phrase ὑπ(ὲρ) τι(μῆς) οἴν(ου) γενήματος κβ ⟨ is followed by several letters of which the reading is doubtful. Wilcken first read them as εἰς ἀπόμοι(ραν), then as εἰς ἀννών(ην). The *Berichtigungsliste*, II. 1, asserted that both readings were unsatisfactory. Wilcken is now reported (O. Wilb.-Brk. 40–2 introd.) to have returned to his earlier reading εἰς ἀπόμοι(ραν), so that it is probable that τιμὴ οἴνου in this receipt is equivalent to the ἀπόμοιρα on vine-land. Payments ὑπὲρ τιμῆς οἴνου are attested in receipts from A.D. 90 to late in the third century. At Thebes there were ἐπιτηρηταὶ τιμῆς οἴνου καὶ φοινίκων. Receipts for τιμὴ φοινίκων are found frequently at Elephantine-Syene. Strabo states that an island in the Thebais afforded the best dates in Egypt, and that the revenue therefrom had belonged to the kings, but in Roman times was a perquisite of the prefects. It is probable that the island was Elephantine, and the receipts for τιμὴ φοινίκων from Elephantine-Syene may well represent the collection of the prefect's revenue.[16]

Receipts ὑπὲρ τιμῆς λαχάνου and τιμῆς χλωρῶν have also been found, but it is not at all certain that they are to be connected with the annona.[17]

Jouguet has pointed out that immediately after the organization of the municipalities throughout Egypt (in A.D. 200) the assessment of the annona became one of the duties of the municipal senates.[18]

Ἀχυρικά

The compulsory delivery of straw was a practice which must have dated back into Pharaonic times. Most of the receipts of the Ptolemaic and Roman periods have been found near Thebes. Some receipts for straw state that it was to be used for the making of brick, but its employment for that purpose must have decreased after the Romans introduced the use of burnt brick.[19] Some collection of straw was made for the fuel of public baths,[20] but the majority of the receipts are for straw delivered to divisions of the Roman army to be used as fuel for baths maintained for the soldiers.[21] The straw was also used for bedding and fodder for the horses of the cavalry and for the pack-animals.[22] Milne has pointed out that the receipts for chaff in the first century were normally given by soldiers, while those of the second century are signed by ἀχυροπράκτορες or ἀχυραιοί or ἀπαιτηταί (or παραλῆμπται) ἀχύρου.[23] The 'elders of the village' at Socnopaei Nesus were required to supply the gymnasiarch with chaff for the gymnasium in that village in the second century, but it is not certain that this requisition was levied as a tax.[24] Mention of payments of chaff to the army are found in Lower Egypt only in documents from the end of the third and from the fourth century.[25] It is possible that reimbursement was made for chaff requisitioned for the use of the army, at least in the first and second centuries, although the government probably set a price agreeable to itself. In P. Lond. III. 1212 (p. 90), dated A.D. 255, the payment of chaff seems definitely to be a tax.

Γράστις

The meaning of the tax γράστις (grass) is not clear. Grenfell and Hunt suggested that it might have been exacted for providing better seed in government issues.[26] The tax is rarely found in Roman times.[27] A collection made by ἀπαιτηταί may, like the collections of chaff, have been for military purposes.[28]

Special Assessments

The Roman government sometimes felt obliged to levy special taxes in kind upon both domain and private land. Real emergencies may have dictated some of these special levies, but others were probably caused by the extravagance of officials or of rulers like Elagabalus. Various terms were used to indicate such special levies, but it is not always possible to see wherein the tax designated by one term differs from another.

Ἐπίθεμα

Ἐπίθεμα appears as an interlinear note in a list of lands cultivated by δημόσιοι γεωργοί and the payments of the rents thereon in P. Teb. II. 576. The fragmentary nature of the document makes it impossible to determine the incidence of the tax which was paid in 14–13 B.C.

Ἐπικλασμός

The term ἐπικλασμός was used to designate an extraordinary levy on land, whether in money or in kind. It may have been used loosely to indicate taxes which had other names. In the petition of Apollonarion (PO. VI. 899) the appellant seeks on the score of her sex to be released from the responsibility of cultivating various plots of crown-land in the Oxyrhynchite nome. She states that she had cultivated the land until the ἐπικλασμοί ordered by the prefect Aemilius Saturninus had proved too great a burden. Since the document is to be dated in A.D. 200, it is possible that the ἐπικλασμοί include the extraordinary levies of the crown-tax (στεφανικόν), which was a money-tax, as was the ἐπικλασμός in the Mendesian nome mentioned in PSI. I. 105. 20, dated in the second half of the second century. The ἐπικλασμός in kind levied on domain land is attested in the reign of Trajan (P. Teb. II. 373). Payment of φόρετρα on an ἐπικλασμός assessed in kind is mentioned in P. Teb. II. 470; since the document is dated one or two years after P. Teb. II. 373 this ἐπικλασμός may be the same as that on domain land. Ἐπικλασμοί are mentioned in leases and conveyances of catoecic and other private land from A.D. 180 to 298.[29]

Ἐπιμερισμός

The term ἐπιμερισμός likewise was applied to both money-taxes and taxes in kind.[30] The same term was also applied to the annona and other requisitions of supplies for the soldiers for which, at least in some cases, payment was made by the government.[31] Most of the references to ἐπιμερισμοί occur in the guarantee-clauses of conveyances and leases, dated from A.D. 139 (?) through the fourth century. The only account of the ἐπιμερισμός in kind is in P. Col. I R 6, dated in the reign of Hadrian or of Antoninus. The citizens of Theadelphia subject to the ἐπιμερισμοὶ σιτικοί were obliged each to pay $2\frac{13}{24}$ artabae of wheat, $\frac{13}{24}$ artaba of barley, and $\frac{19}{24}$ artaba of lentils. Wheat might be substituted for the lentils. It is not known what the occasion of these ἐπιμερισμοὶ σιτικοί may have been.

Ἐπινέμησις

A payment of $17\frac{1}{2}$ artabae of wheat occurs for the ἐπινέμησις in BGU. VII. 1610, where it is said to be 'on account' (ἐπὶ λόγου). Other payments of 9 and $8\frac{1}{2}$ artabae follow. In the preceding portion of the receipt occurs a payment on private land (ἰδιωτικὴ γῆ) possessed by the wife of the payer; the amount was $19\frac{1}{4}$ artabae. The receipt was issued in A.D. 259 by the decemprimi. The only other reference to ἐπινέμησις in the third century known to me is in SP. V. 127. ii R iv. 11, where the phrase ἀρχιονηλάται Κουσσων ὑπὲρ ἐπινεμήσεως Κουσσων is followed by 140 drachmae. It seems to refer to the assessment of a money-tax. Elsewhere in the papyri the term seems to be used as equivalent to *indictio*.

Ἐπίτριτον

The name of this tax would indicate that, at least in origin, it was a surtax of one-third. The ἐπίτριτον paid in money is known also, but most of the references are to a surtax paid in kind.[32] The tax was sometimes collected on catoecic land at Tebtynis and, if the restoration of P. Teb. II. 482 is correct, was connected with the γεωμετρία (land-measurement). In P. Teb. II. 561 an artaba of wheat was paid for the ἐπίτριτον κατοίκων. In P. Teb. II. 363 ⅛ artaba of wheat for ἐπίτριτον followed the payment of ⅙ artaba for φόρετρον on ἱερὰ γῆ for which 4⅝ artabae had been paid as tax: the ἐπίτριτον, as the editors remark, is not nearly one-third of any of the amounts there recorded. The tax was collected also in the Ptolemaic period.

Μερισμός

O. Strass. 578 records the payment of $\frac{1}{24}$ (presumably of an artaba) for μερισ(μοῦ) λαχά(νου), and perhaps also for [μερισμοῦ] κρι(θῆς).

Πρόσθεμα

This obviously means a surtax, and it was paid in kind, usually in wheat, but occasionally in beans.[33] In the Roman period this term is confined to receipts from Thebes. Preisigke[34] has suggested that the πρόσθεμα was a fee charged for the use of the tax-collector's account at the public granary, i.e. his θέμα, but this is very doubtful. *Adaeratio* of the πρόσθεμα is occasionally recorded.[35] The occasion for these extraordinary assessments is not known: the only dated examples occur in successive years, A.D. 130–1 and 131–2 and 190–1 and 191–2.[36]

Miscellaneous Taxes in Kind

Payments for ἀναμέτρ(ησις) in P. Bouriant 40 are perhaps for a charge imposed to meet the expense of an official survey, though Kalén suggests a charge for inspection of unflooded land.[37]

The βαλανικόν (bath-tax) was collected in kind at Thebes, apparently for the maintenance of baths owned by the temples.[38]

The ἕκτον (tax of one-sixth) was imposed on γῆ ὑπόλογος. The editors of P. Ryl. II. 221 suggested this tax might be a form of the προσμετρούμενα which were collected at the rate of one-sixth on taxes in kind on private land; but in SB. 4325 the amount collected is not a sixth of the principal tax nor does it bear any obvious relation to the amount of the principal tax or to the number of arurae, so that the nature of the tax is problematical.

A payment of 55 artabae of wheat for ἐπιστατικόν is found in

P. Bouriant 42. It may be a fee for administrative officials, perhaps those in charge of the transport of grain.[39]

An item of $3\frac{5}{24}$ artabae of wheat, with προσμετρούμενα, is recorded as paid for κατακ(ρίματα) in P. Teb. II. 363. Fines paid in kind are rare, and it is impossible to determine from the document whether this fine was imposed in connexion with the land-tax, although that seems probable.

A payment for σύνταξις εἰς Ἴσειν is found in P. Kalén 3 and another εἰς φιλ(   ) Ἀφροδ(   ) in P. Fay. 81. These payments seem to have been accepted by the state for the subvention of the temples of these deities. Perhaps certain lands were designated to provide the annual syntaxis,[40] but the explanation is still uncertain.

The rare tax called τελωνικὴ ἀτέλεια was occasionally paid in kind.[41]

A tax paid in kind on building-sites is found in PO. VII. 1044, where 3 choenices (once 6 choenices) is paid on each plot (οἰκοπ(έδου)). The tax was ordinarily paid in money, if this tax is identical with the impost προσόδ(ων) οἰκοπ(έδων).

Palm-fibre (σεβεννία) was furnished to the army by the villages, and in SP. XXII. 137 an ἐπιμερισμός is mentioned (just as for the annona).[42] Dates and bundles of palm-leaves were also delivered in kind, perhaps for the army.[43] Aromatic nuts (μυροβάλανοι) were delivered in kind at Elephantine-Syene, and the tax was apparently a third of the yield.[44] Olive-oil was also paid in kind in P. Iand. 142; P. Lond. III. 1170 (p. 93). Payments in kind of clothing and the like were liturgies falling upon guilds of workmen, or assumed by the senates of the municipalities after A.D. 200.[45]

In BGU. I. 217 land is taxed at the rate of $\frac{1}{12}$ or $\frac{1}{24}$ artaba of wheat or $\frac{1}{6}$ or $\frac{1}{12}$ artaba of barley an arura. This seems obviously to indicate a surtax of some kind, but it is impossible to identify it with any certainty.

The majority of the special levies in kind, as well as in money, occurred in the reign of Trajan or in the period from Marcus Aurelius through the first half of the third century. It was in these periods that the great military campaigns of the emperors placed a severe drain upon the resources of the Roman empire, and the civil disturbances of the third century were the cause of extra demands upon the production of Egypt. These extra levies in kind were, perhaps, a more serious burden than those in money, for the latter were offset in part by the higher prices caused by the continued depreciation of the currency in the second half of the second century and in the third century.

IV

COLLECTION OF THE GRAIN-TAX

PHILO called Egypt the greatest of the possessions of the emperor of Rome.[1] Nowhere is the special character of this imperial province more clearly shown than in the absolute power of the emperor to levy taxes. We are informed by the edict of Tiberius Julius Alexander[2] that the prefect of Egypt, although representative of the emperor in charge of the financial administration of Egypt, had little legal power to effect changes in the assessment of taxes. The power to raise, lower, or grant exemption from taxes lay with the emperor alone: the power of the prefect was confined to carrying out the regulations of his imperial master, and to him the conscientious prefect referred all major questions concerning taxation.[3] In regard to the taxation of Egypt a *bon mot* attributed to the emperor Tiberius is famous.[4] When Aemilius Rectus, prefect of Egypt, had forwarded revenues in excess of what had been specified, the emperor sent word that he required his sheep to be sheared, not flayed! From this statement it has been supposed that the revenue to be derived from Egypt was fixed annually by the emperor.[5] Recently, however, it has been shown that important modifications in the assessment of taxes might be made at the time when the prefect published his general edict, at intervals of approximately five years.[6] Moreover, the revenue in grain was subject to modification from factors beyond the control of even the emperor of Rome.

Assessment

As is evident from the preceding chapter the grain-tax on private land was determined by the category to which the land belonged, and the owners of that land paid accordingly at from ¾ to 2 artabae an arura. The rent of domain land, on the other hand, was determined by the provisions of the lease granted by the state to the tenant. The maximum revenue in grain to be derived from Egypt was, therefore, fixed at the time of renewing leases of domain land. The *Epitome* of Aurelius

Victor I states that in the time of Augustus twenty million modii of grain were sent to Rome annually from Egypt for the *cura annonae*. We may accept this as the amount of revenue in grain normally expected from Egypt.[7] This probably did not represent a one hundred per cent. collection of the rents and taxes, for arrears constantly accumulated in spite of the vigilance and perseverance of the collectors. Furthermore, in years when there was a low Nile or an excessively high inundation it follows that this amount was substantially decreased, since the reports of un-inundated or of water-logged land were sent to the officials in order to gain a reduction in the assessment of taxes or in the rent due to the state.[8] An approximate estimate of the size of the crop for the ensuing year could be made, without awaiting compilations of the reports of un-inundated land, by referring to the height of the inundation of the Nile recorded on the Nilometer at Elephantine, and Strabo informs us that this measurement was used by the prefects of Egypt to estimate the revenue in grain (προσόδων χάριν).[9] Since the inundation is usually at its height by the 1st of August,[10] it is probable that the estimate of the grain revenue for the ensuing year would be in Rome by the 1st of December at the latest. The purpose of this estimate was not so much to enable the emperor to fix the amount of grain to be derived from Egypt as to indicate about how much he could expect during the coming year, so that the *praefectus annonae* could regulate the import from the other provinces accordingly.[11]

The edict of Tiberius Julius Alexander implies that the annual assessment of taxes was made by the ἐκλογισταί. These officials, one for each nome, had their offices in Alexandria, where they received the reports of the collectors of taxes in kind and in money; and it was their duty to check the reports against the tax-lists to determine whether the demands of the state had been met.[12] Since P. Mey. 3 indicates that the eclogistes had reported a shortage in the account of a single tenant of the imperial estates, it is evident that he had, or could obtain, a completely detailed account of every individual's obligations to the state. It is improbable, however, that the eclogistes in Alexandria often visited the nome under his supervision,[13] and it is consequently unlikely that he superintended the making of the ἀπαιτήσιμον κατ᾽ ἄνδρα, the detailed tax-list for a given district. The material for the compilation of such tax-lists was collected by the comogrammateus and was forwarded by him to the strategus and the basilico-grammateus.[14] It is possible that the actual calculation of the taxes or rent owed by an individual on his holding was made by subordinates of the eclogistes, the γραμματεῖς and βοηθοί in the λογιστήρια, in accordance with a gnomon such as that in P. Teb. II, App. I. From the cadastral reports of the comogrammateus and from the gnomon was made up the annual ἀπαιτήσιμον κατ᾽ ἄνδρα.[15] It was the duty of the eclogistes, I believe, to verify the assessments from duplicate copies sent to him, and to compute from them the total revenues due from the various districts and from the entire nome. The commission charged with the receipt and forwarding of reports to the eclogistes and to the Idiologus[16] perhaps served a useful function by classifying and simplifying the information actually transmitted to Alexandria.

The decree of Tiberius Julius Alexander informs us that the eclogistae during the terms of certain of his predecessors had lined their pockets by neglecting the reports of the inundation of the Nile and assessing the taxes according to the average of the previous years.[17] The normal taxes had consequently to be wrung from the suffering farmers despite the shortage caused by the low Nile, while the actual amounts of revenue in grain delivered (at Alexandria) under the supervision of the eclogistae corresponded to the decreased assessment for the province based upon the estimate obtained by the prefect from the Nilometer and checked against the reports of un-inundated (or of water-logged) land.

Collection of Grain-taxes

The ἀπαιτήσιμον κατ᾽ ἄνδρα for the tenants of the domain land at Socnopaei Nesus was displayed in public by the order of the epistrategus in the third century after Christ.[18] It is probable that the similar ἀπαιτήσιμον κατ᾽ ἄνδρα for the taxes on private land was also posted, and that this had been customary during the previous centuries. As soon as the grain was harvested (April to June, depending upon the district) it was brought to the village threshing-floors. The owner of private land was obliged to transport his sheaves by whatever means he had or could obtain. The use of the government's pack-animals, however, was available to tenants of domain land who had no animals of their own, and for this service a fee called δραγματηγία (transport of sheaves) was assessed. It is not known whether the cultivator of a small plot of private land, who had no pack-animals of his own, could likewise make use of the government transport, for there is no record of payments for δραγματηγία by cultivators other than tenants of domain lands.[19] In Theadelphia in A.D. 158–9 this tax was assessed upon the arura, but it is not impossible that the assessment was made in some other manner if circumstances were different.[20]

At the village threshing-floors, located if possible on land which was conveniently situated near the edge of a village and which was not suitable for cultivation, the ἀπαίτησις took place. Representatives of the government were present when the grain was threshed,[21] and at Oxyrhynchus in the third century the cultivator was not permitted to remove his grain from the threshing-floor until the government's share for taxes or rent had been reserved.[22] The elders of the village, who in this function succeeded the Ptolemaic elders of the cultivators, supported or represented the cultivator to see that the division was made fairly.[23] The reservation of the state's share of the grain at the threshing-floor was not designed to prevent concealment of the grain, as was the case in Sicily where the tithe was collected, but to make sure that the grain paid for taxes and rent was of first quality. Since the threshing-floors were often situated on unleased domain land, it was natural that some fee should have been exacted for the use of the threshing-floor, and 2 artabae of wheat seem to have been paid by a certain Petheus for that purpose (ἀλωνία) early in the first century after Christ in the Fayûm.[24] But evidence for such payments is so rare that it is impossible to determine whether the practice was continued and to learn the incidence of such a fee.[25]

The cultivator was also responsible for the removal of the revenue-grain from the threshing-floor to the granary. The use of the government pack-trains was available to the tenants of domain land, and a tax called σακκηγία (transport of sacks) was exacted from them to cover the cost.[26] Again, however, as in the case of the tax δραγματηγία, there is no evidence that this charge was paid by owners of private land.[27]

Receipt at the Granary

To store its revenues in grain the state was compelled to place a granary in the centre of every community of any importance. Several small villages, however, might be grouped together for the purpose of administering the grain revenue. The granaries (θησαυροί) of small villages were not suitable for storage of large quantities over a long period of time, and consequently the grain was removed from such places to large central granaries in the important towns where the seed-grain could be stored until the next planting and whence the government transport-trains could remove the revenue grain to the harbours for shipment to Alexandria. Such central granaries had in the Ptolemaic period been designated as ἐργαστήρια, but although that term seems to have dropped out of use in the Roman period the system continued.[28] Such central granaries were located in the metropolis of the Fayûm and also in Theadelphia, Caranis, Tebtynis, Apias, and Nilopolis.[29] Concerning other nomes we are not so well informed, but there seems ordinarily to have been a central θησαυρός in the metropolis of each nome.[30] At Thebes, whose great distance from Alexandria made elaborate provision for storage of grain necessary, there was a θησαυρὸς τῆς διοικήσεως, a θησαυρὸς τῶν ἱερῶν, a θησαυρὸς κωμῶν, and a θησαυρὸς μητροπόλεως; in addition there was a granary in most, if not all, of the various quarters and suburbs of the city (Charax, South Quarter, South-West Quarter, Market Quarter, Ceramia, Island, Memnonia).[31]

Upon delivery of the revenue grain at a state granary a receipt was issued to the cultivator or to his representative[32] by the official in charge of the granary, i. e. the sitologus or one of his assistants.[33] This receipt (of which many examples are extant) does not ordinarily specify the rate of taxation, but it frequently states that the payment is for catoecic, cleruchic, hieratic, or domain land, or for a combination of these.[34] The receipt gives the total amount of grain paid for taxes and occasionally specifies the additional amounts collected for the προσμετρούμενα (surtaxes) and for various additional charges. When the cultivator had received his receipt at the granary his specific duties in regard to the revenue grain had been discharged.

The Administration of the Granaries

The granaries belonging to the state were in charge of sitologi. One or more of these officials was assigned to each granary according to its size and importance. There seems, moreover, to have been a hierarchy of sitologi, in which those in charge of small granaries were responsible to the sitologi of the large central granaries. The large granaries received the grain forwarded by the sitologi of the small local granaries. Calderini has advanced the hypothesis that there was a regular progression in the rank of these officials, beginning with the sitologus of the village, then the sitologus of the toparchy, then of the μερίς, and finally of the nome.[35] It is probable, however, that changing conditions in various localities modified such a progression in the hierarchy of sitologi. At Thebes, for example, there were σιτολόγοι ἱερατικῶν (O. Br.-Berl. 6).

The sitologi were aided in the performance of their duties by γραμματεῖς (secretaries) and βοηθοί (assistants), who doubtless were more or less numerous according to the importance of the granary and to the size of the district within the competence of the individual sitologus or college of sitologi.[36] It is not unlikely that additional employees were added to the staff of the sitologus at the time of harvest. Φροντισταί (representatives whose duties are uncertain) of sitologi appear.[37] Connected with the granaries were numerous other functionaries, doubtless subordinates of the sitologi, whose titles indicate but do not define their duties. Σιτοπαραλήμπται (receivers of grain) are found in papyri of the second to fourth centuries; they act as assistants and perhaps secretaries of the sitologi, and Oertel has conjectured that they were special officials in charge of the collection of grain for the military annona, but who were sometimes assigned to the bureaux of the sitologi.[38] A σίτου ἀποδέκτης is mentioned in connexion with the receipt of grain in WO. 1217 from Thebes, dated in the third century; this official is otherwise known only in the fourth century. In the third and fourth centuries reference is made to ἐπισφραγισταί whose duty was to place an official seal upon the grain in storage in the state granary. Θησαυροφύλακες guarded the granaries in the Roman period as they had during the reign of the Ptolemies.[39] Σιτομέτραι (grain-measurers) are mentioned in connexion with the granaries of the metropoleis of the nomes, but not in the χώρα. Kalén has demonstrated that a σιτομέτρης was also engaged as σακκοφόρος (sack-carrier) in the transfer of grain from the granary to the transport-ships.[40] An ἐγμετρητής also is attested for Hermopolis in A.D. 186.[41]

Sitologi are found as the receivers of revenue grain in the Ptolemaic, Roman, and Byzantine periods, but during the second half of the third century their functions were taken over by the δεκάπρωτοι (decemprimi), who apparently conducted the collection in the same manner as had the sitologi.[42] The sitologi superintended not only the measurement of grain as brought to the granary and the issuing of receipts for it, but also the disbursement of grain to be transported to Alexandria, of seed-grain, and of grain issued as a remuneration of the government's employees and for similar purposes. They kept an account of receipts and disbursements by means of day-books, and they issued reports every ten days, every month, and annually to the strategus and the basilico-grammateus.[43] Copies of the monthly reports were forwarded to the eclogistes and to the Idiologus in Alexandria through the commission appointed for that purpose.[44] The reports of the sitologi were made in detail (κατ' ἄνδρα) and also as summaries (μηνιαῖος ἐν κεφαλαίῳ).[45] From these reports it is apparent how carefully the sitologus distinguished the receipts on account of taxes on private land from those for rent on domain land, and further how the surtaxes and additional charges were carefully recorded in making up the total of receipts.

The sitologi received and disbursed not only grain (wheat and barley) but also beans and lentils, sesame and croton, and other products in kind that formed part of the rent of domain land.[46] The vast majority of receipts, however, record the delivery of wheat and barley.

The collection of arrears of taxes and rents in kind was a serious problem. The sitologi were assisted in this by the πράκτορες σιτικῶν who were probably chiefly engaged in getting in over-due payments. It is possible that the κατακρίματα (fines) collected in kind were penalties for failure to pay taxes or rents in grain when due. Many were the complaints of the ruthlessness and brutality of the πράκτορες σιτικῶν and the sitologi in forcing the payment of rents and taxes. In BGU. II. 515 one Syrus son of Syrion makes a formal complaint to the centurion Ammonius Paternus because of the outrage committed by the πράκτορες σιτικῶν. He and his brother had paid all their dues in grain except 1 artaba of wheat, but while he was away in the field the collectors had come to his home and had seized his mother's cloak and had beaten the old lady so that she had become bedridden. But these excesses were probably often provoked by the devices used by cultivators to avoid paying their dues.[47]

Surtaxes on Taxes in Kind

A surtax, called προσμετρούμενα (or occasionally τὰ ἑπόμενα), is prescribed in the gnomon for taxation of land in the Arsinoite nome.[48] This supplement was to be collected on the total of the tax on catoecic land (or other private land) and the dichoenicia. The προσμετρούμενα on payments of rent on domain land made in wheat were assessed at the rate of one-seventh in the Arsinoite nome. These surtaxes appear as early as the reign of Augustus and were apparently established at that time. The purpose of these surtaxes has recently been discussed by Kalén, who believes that they were caused by differences in content of the standards of measures used in the assessment of taxes and rents in the Arsinoite nome. He believes that a still different measure was used for the receipt of wheat at the granary. The προσμετρούμενα, therefore, would represent the difference between the local standard and that which the government used in accepting payments. According to Kalén's view, the surtax on the tax on catoecic land was actually no addition to the assessment, since the artaba of 40 choinices in which the tax was levied in the Ptolemaic period was one-sixth larger than the artaba measure used for measuring receipts at the granary. The προσμετρούμενα on domain land, however, represented a real increase in the rent, since the standard of measure used at the granary for receipt of wheat was larger than that employed in the assessment of rents in the Ptolemaic period; but the addition perhaps absorbed the various extra charges for the 'one twenty-fourth', τριχοινικόν, θησαυροφυλακικόν, and the like, which had been added to the rent on domain land in the Ptolemaic period, but which do not appear in Roman times.[49]

A surtax was charged on rent paid in barley, but the principle upon which it was assessed is not clear, for, as Kalén has shown, the supplement varies from a ratio of 1 : 3·92 to 1 : 6·45. Lentils and beans also were subject to προσμετρούμενα, and the ratios vary from 1 : 4·17 to 1 : 4·29.[50]

The προσμετρούμενα, where preserved in the records of nomes other than the Arsinoite nome, are calculated in percentages rather than in simple fractions of ⅙ and ⅐, as Kalén has pointed out.[51] He has observed that there may be a reference to this practice in CPR. I. 243 (= W. *Chrest.* 367) where the rent of subleased οὐσιακὴ γῆ is given (σὺν ταῖς) ἐθίμοις ἑκατοσταῖς. Furthermore, it appears that outside the Fayûm domain land and cleruchic land often paid προσμετρούμενα at the same rate. This clearly indicates that the problem is different from that presented by the surtaxes of the Arsinoite nome. According to the readings of Kalén for P. Giss. 60[52] the rate of surtax on cleruchic land at Naboö in the Apollonopolite nome was 15 per cent. with an additional charge of ½ per cent. On some classes of domain land this extra ½ per cent may have been included in the rates for προσμετρούμενα of 15½ per cent., 12½ per cent., and 16½ per cent.[53] At Thebes the rate on 1-artaba land in WO. II. 1405 was 15 per cent. or 15½ per cent.[54] At Oxyrhynchus the προσμετρούμενα were 15 per cent on both private land and domain land in PO. XII. 1445. In PO. XII. 1528 (A.D. 266-7) two payments for the surtax at 12 per cent. are recorded. The variation in the rates of προσμετρούμενα in the same nome may be the result of the inclusion or omission of some of the small surcharges which are discussed below.[55]

In repayments of seed-loans the supplementary tax in wheat is approximately a sixteenth of the total and in barley about a seventh.[56] The total repaid included interest on the loan, which might be as high as 50 per cent. (ἡμιόλια) for the year.[57] These supplements are apparently called τὰ ἑπόμενα in PO. VII. 1031.

There is no proof that fees for cleaning and sifting of revenue grain were collected in the Roman period, although an official ὁ ἐπὶ τῆς καθάρσεως τοῦ δημοσίου πυροῦ is mentioned in P. Fay. 23a. ii (second century). Payments for κο( ) appear in a few documents from Upper and Lower Egypt, but it is not certain that the abbreviation should be expanded κο(σκινευτικόν).[58] Rather, as Kalén has pointed out,[59] it was required that revenue grain be delivered clean (καθαρός) at the granary or even at the threshing-floor. Perhaps a fee or penalty for κο(σκινευτικόν) was imposed when a cultivator delivered unclean grain.

The monthly summaries of the sitologi keep an account of payments of πόδωμα (a storage-charge of some kind, possibly a penalty, although the purpose is never stated). At Oxyrhynchus the tax was 2 per cent. and was called διαρταβία. Further supplements of 1 per cent. and ½ per cent., however, were made upon the διαρταβία.[60] At Tebtynis in the Arsinoite nome the same method of calculation was used.[61] At Theadelphia, however, the πόδωμα was calculated as a 2 per cent. charge plus a charge of one ten-thousandth, and upon the total of these two charges a further exaction of 1 per cent. was made.[62] The results of the two systems of calculation are approximately the same. In BGU. III. 897–8 payments for πο( ) appear following small payments on land. The abbreviation is perhaps to be expanded πό(δωμα), although the payment for πο( ) is $\frac{2}{13}$ of the preceding sum, and this is a ratio which bears no apparent relation to the methods of calculation at Oxyrhynchus and Tebtynis and at Theadelphia.[63] Two entries indicate a half of this rate πο( ) τὸ (ἥμισυ). In BGU. III. 977, which may be from the Mendesian nome, a ἡμιαρταβία ποδώματος is found and is evidently a tax of ½ per cent., but it is uncertain whether this was the only charge made for that tax. In the Hermopolite nome the sitologi collected an extra charge of 1 per cent. on wheat and 1½ per cent. on barley, but it is not certain that these charges were for πόδωμα.[64]

In the gnomon for calculating the taxes on catoecic land a charge of 1½ per cent. was added to the total of land-tax, dichoenicia, and surtax (προσμετρούμενα). Kalén has suggested that this 1½ per cent. represents a tax of ½ per cent., called ἐνοίκιον θησαυροῦ in P. Teb. II. 520, and a perquisite of 1 per cent. for the sitologus.[65] So closely connected is this ½ per cent. for 'rent of space in the granary' with the 1 per cent. perquisite (φιλάνθρωπον) that the two are usually treated as a single charge of 1½ per cent., and, in P. Iand. 138, 1½ per cent. (although the document states 1 per cent.) were deducted from payments made to the sitologi by owners of private lands. Evidence for the payment on domain or usiac lands is lacking, unless the extra payment of 1½ per cent. on φόρος ἀπότακτος of barley in BGU. III. 743–4 (Heracleopolite nome, A.D. 261–3) is an instance. In PO. XII. 1445. 9 the payment for φιλάνθρωπον is approximately 3⅓ per cent. of the main charge, but it is possible that it included such small fees as the ½ per cent. for ἐνοίκιον θησαυροῦ. In BGU. III. 835. 15 a payment in wheat for φιλ(ανθρώπου) σὺν ἄλλοις amounts to approximately 3 per cent. of the principal; and in BGU. II. 534. 12 a similar payment in wheat amounts to approximately 3⅓ per cent. of the principal, while a payment in barley, ὑπὲρ φιλανθρώπου only, amounts to 1·4 per cent. of the principal.

A charge of 5 per cent. called πενταρταβία is occasionally found with payments of barley to the sitologi.⁶⁶ Since the occurrences are comparatively rare, it is not certain what the purpose of the tax was or why its appearance is so irregular.⁶⁷

It is difficult to account for the comparatively rare occurrence of these small supplementary fees in kind (other than the προσμετρούμενα). There is a reference to efforts to alter the system of taxation on land in the decree of Ti. Julius Alexander.⁶⁸ Not only did the prefects of Egypt during the reigns of Claudius and Nero attempt to reduce purchased private land to the status of domain land by the exaction of rents instead of the proper taxes (καθήκοντα); new taxes also had been levied upon the land; against these new imposts cultivators all over Egypt had protested. Julius Alexander decreed that all new taxes assessed within the last five years should be abolished. It is not impossible, I believe, that some of these small supplementary fees may have been instituted in a similar manner, since they were usually intended for the benefit of the sitologi and other local officials of the granaries who may have puchased the connivance or the silence of Roman officials. Certainly the accumulation of such supplements and fees was a serious burden upon the cultivators, and protests against them would be expected.

Fees for Transportation from the Granary to the Harbour

The careful analysis by Kalén has shown that the ἐπισπουδασμοῦ φόρετρα (transportation charges for the expedition of grain) are to be distinguished from the charges for δραγματηγία and σακκηγία.[69] The former is a tax, Kalén believes, assessed against all classes of land, but the payments for cleruchic and catoecic land are distinguished in the accounts of the sitologi by being called φόρετρα κληρούχων and φόρετρα κατοίκων. At Theadelphia the charges were assessed by taxing the land at a fixed rate on the arura.[70] Kalén supposes that the charges were heavier for the transport of the tax on cleruchic land than for that of the rent on domain land, because the domain land was already more heavily assessed than private land. But the most important factor determining the incidence of the φόρετρα was undoubtedly the distance of the granary from the harbour. In BGU. III. 802 there seems to be some evidence that owners of private and catoecic lands had to bear the cost of transport from the granary to the Nile boats at Ptolemais Hormos while the government paid for shipments by tenants on public lands. BGU. I. 242 may deal with shipments overland from the Northern Fayûm to the Nile, but the interpretation of the document is uncertain because it is so fragmentary. In the third century private owners were required to pay the cost of transportation (O. Oslo 17 ff.), but there is no evidence from this period in regard to costs of shipments by public tenants.

From the proceeds of the tax for φόρετρα were paid the costs of transport, which included the wages of the employees of the granary engaged in the release of grain, the hire of donkeys and camels and their drivers for overland transport, and the cost of lading at the port. In the φόρετρον was probably absorbed, as Kalén has suggested,[71] the Ptolemaic charge for σιτομετρικόν which appears in a document of the early part of the first century after Christ.[72] Payments in kind to the guild of drivers engaged in the transport were made by the sitologi, who had to account for the disbursements of grain for this purpose, as well as the regular release of the revenue grain, in monthly summaries presented to the strategus and the basilico-grammateus.[73] The strategus was in charge of the entire financial administration of

the nome, and hence was responsible for the collection and forwarding of the revenue, although the transport of government
grain was the immediate concern of the nomarch.[74] Payment
to the transporters was sometimes made in money. In that case
the payments were, of course, not made by the sitologi but by
the state bank.[75] Kalén has suggested that half of the charge for
φόρετρον was assessed in money.[76] Payments in copper drachmae
specified in leases at Tebtynis (P. Teb. II. 373; PSI. x. 1144)
are perhaps to be identified with the 20 drachmae tax in P. Teb.
II. 373. 12, and these payments were made to the nomarch. The
φόρετρα χαλκινά in BGU. I. 166 may be the same tax. Possibly
this tax was imposed on land when it was under hay or clover;
in P. Lond. inv. 1577 verso there is a small charge for καταγώγι(ον)
on τιμὴ χλωρῶν paid in money. The assessment of φόρετρα may
not have been uniform throughout Egypt, however, since the
problem of transportation in the Arsinoite nome was more complicated than in the other nomes, not only because of the greater
amount of grain raised in the Fayûm but also because a large
amount of the arable land in the Arsinoite nome lay farther from
the Nile than was the case in the other nomes. In WO. II 1546
φορικ(   ) should perhaps be read φορέτ(ρου); if so the charge
for transportation at Thebes was $\frac{1}{8}$ artaba on a payment of 16$\frac{1}{2}$
artabae of seed-grain, or less than 1 per cent.

Kalén has offered a reasonable explanation of the phrase
διάφορον φορέτρου.[77] When a cultivator, because of the ἐπιμερισμός,[78] or for some other reason, found it more convenient
to deliver his grain (for taxes or rent) at a granary other than the
one to which the land paying the revenue normally belonged,
he was assessed an extra charge for transport (διάφορον φορέτρου)
if the granary to which the grain was delivered lay farther from
the harbour than the granary ordinarily used. This διάφορον
φορέτρου was assessed against the individual cultivator as a percentage of the number of artabae of grain delivered. This percentage varied with the distance from the harbour of the two
granaries concerned, as Kalén has indicated in his table, and had
to be sufficient to provide compensation for the drivers of donkeys and camels who carried the grain an extra distance.[79]

It is usually assumed that the cost of transport of revenue
grain from the river-ports to Alexandria was paid by the state

from its general revenues.[80] Payments to the ναύκληροι responsible for that stage of the transport were made both in kind and in money. The cost naturally varied greatly, according to the distance of the port from Alexandria. It is not impossible, however, that the tax for φόρετρον was high enough to include the cost of transport to Alexandria. A fee called ναῦ(λον) φο(ρέτρου) was collected from owners of garden-land, although payments in kind on such land appear to have been almost entirely abandoned in the Roman period, and it is possible that the transport of grain to Alexandria likewise fell on the cultivators over and above the amount of their taxes. Against this view may be urged the fact that the first charge for ναῦλον which appears in the grain receipts is dated in A.D. 296, and that the fee which appears (for canal-boats, since it is called ναῦλον διαιρεμάτων) is definitely distinguished from the ὄβολοι which are identified with the usual money-payments for φόρετρον.[81] Further evidence on this point must be awaited before a final decision can be reached. In any case it is not likely that the cultivators during the Roman period made any extra payments to cover the cost of transporting the grain from Alexandria to Rome, since charges for ναῦλον for sea-going vessels out of Alexandria seem to have been a Byzantine innovation of the fourth century after the grain revenues were diverted from Rome to Constantinople.[82]

The sitologi were responsible for the purity of the grain when it reached Alexandria. PO. IV. 708, dated A.D. 188, is a letter from a high official Antonius Aelianus, whose rank is not indicated, to the strategus of the Diospolite nome in the Thebaid; a cargo of 2,000 artabae of wheat had been found to be adulterated with 2 per cent. of barley and $\frac{1}{2}$ per cent. of dirt. The strategus is directed to exact from the sitologi who had shipped the wheat the difference on the whole amount of the wheat, namely $50\frac{3}{4}$ artabae, as well as the extra payments and other expenses involved. The editors note that 50 artabae are exactly $2\frac{1}{2}$ per cent. of 2,000 artabae, and they state that Antonius Aelianus has simply added the $\frac{3}{4}$ artaba. This, however, is an injustice to that official, because it was customary to include an extra amount of wheat in the cargoes shipped to Alexandria. This amount was usually $1\frac{1}{2}$ per cent., but occasionally seems to be $\frac{1}{2}$ per cent.[83] This $1\frac{1}{2}$ per cent. would amount to 30 artabae on the 2,000 artabae of the cargo which had been adulterated, and $2\frac{1}{2}$ per cent. of 30 artabae is $\frac{3}{4}$ artaba. The purpose of this $1\frac{1}{2}$ per cent. is unknown. It is evidently a part of the grain intended for the imperial granaries, since the official takes the trouble to demand that $\frac{3}{4}$ artaba of wheat be exacted from the sitologi responsible in order to compensate for the adulteration; for if the $1\frac{1}{2}$ per cent. had been a part of the pay for shipment by boat, it is unlikely that the Roman official would have so concerned himself about its purity. Furthermore, an additional $1\frac{1}{2}$ per cent. appears in connexion with a cargo out of Heracleopolis, where the cost of shipment down the river would have been less than from Oxyrynchus.[84] Kalén suggests that the $1\frac{1}{2}$ per cent. represents the $\frac{1}{2}$ per cent. ἐνοίκιον θησαυροῦ plus the 1 per cent. perquisite of the sitologus, which in the latter part of the second century and in the third century were required to be sent to Alexandria to cover possible shortages or adulteration in the amounts shipped from the local granaries.[85] If such a practice was adopted on a few occasions to make good losses actually suffered, it may have become a convenient way to swell the income of the state at the expense of the sitologi. It is not impossible, however, that this $1\frac{1}{2}$ per cent. and the earlier $\frac{1}{2}$ per cent. represent a portion of the assessment for πόδωμα, which Kalén has argued was an exaction originally designed to cover such shortages and which from its name was evidently intended to be held as a reserve in the local granaries. It may have become customary to require that a certain part of that reserve be shipped to Alexandria. A final explanation of these supplementary percentages will be possible only when further evidence is available.

At Alexandria the grain was stored in great granaries to await shipment to Rome. These granaries at Neapolis and the Hermeum were under the supervision of Roman procurators who controlled the receipt and disbursement of the revenue grain. These officials were responsible to the prefect who, in turn, was responsible to the emperor alone. It will be remembered that the action of Germanicus in opening the granaries at Alexandria during a temporary and unexpected scarcity in Egypt was regarded as an unwarranted interference, and it is probable that had he lived he would have been called to account by Tiberius.

The transportation of the revenue grain from Alexandria to

Puteoli or Ostia was evidently in the hands of Alexandrians. The shipowners were organized in guilds, and those transporting the grain for the annona enjoyed certain privileges granted by the emperor Claudius. The grain fleet usually sailed as a unit in the spring as soon as weather permitted and may have been convoyed by the *classis Augusta Alexandrina* or another detachment of the naval force.

V

MONEY-TAXES ON LAND

AS is evident from the preceding chapters, the important taxes on grain-land were collected in kind. Taxes assessed in money, however, were sometimes collected on grain-land, for PSI. I 108 mentions ἀργυρικὰ τελέσματα τῶν σιτεικῶν, and one tax paid in money, the ναύβιον, seems to have been paid on all classes of private land.[1] Most of the land-taxes in money, however, were limited to vine-land and garden-land. Some of these taxes on vine- and garden-land had in the Ptolemaic period been collected in kind, but this practice was abandoned, perhaps entirely, before the Romans took over the administration of Egypt.[2] The high incidence of the taxes on vine- and garden-land made it impossible to collect them on land which was not actually yielding fruit (i.e. not φόριμος γῆ), and consequently special surveys of production on this type of land were necessary.[3] A peculiar feature of some of these taxes on vine- and garden-land is that they were assessed in the old Ptolemaic copper drachma, whose value was fixed arbitrarily at a convenient ratio to the silver drachma of 300 : 1.[4] The taxes in money on garden-land and especially on vine-land formed a very considerable part of the cash revenue of the government of Egypt, since in the Roman period, as Rostovtzeff has pointed out,[5] vineyards were the most prominent feature of the culture of private land, especially of the great estates which were developed in the first century and again in the third century.

The evidence concerning the taxes on vine- and garden-land, which had greatly increased after Wilcken published his discussion of them in the first volume of *Griechische Ostraka*, has been ably treated by the editors of P. Ryl. II. 192 b, and to their discussion is due most of our ordered knowledge concerning these taxes. Wilcken had been at some pains to demonstrate that the tax called in the Roman period γεωμετρία and qualified by the addition of ἀμπέλου or φοινίκων (or παραδείσου), according to the type of culture, was the land-tax *par excellence* on vine- and garden-land.[6] He came to this conclusion because the receipts on the ostraca which recorded taxes on vine-land seemed to be inscribed indifferently ὑπὲρ γεωμετρίας ἀμπέλου or ὑπὲρ ἀμπέλου. Since the area in arurae was usually given on such receipts he was able to calculate the tax as 40 drachmae to the arura. He concluded therefore that the γεωμετρία was the land-tax on vine-land, although he expressed his wonder that the land-tax had not been called ἐπαρούριον 'the tax on the arura'.[7] Grenfell and Hunt in the introduction to P. Fay. 41 state that 'the ἐπαρούριον was the land-tax upon those kinds of land which were subject to the ἀπόμοιρα'. The observations of the editors of the Rylands papyri led them to agree with Wilcken that the land-tax on vine- and garden-land was the γεωμετρία rather than the ἐπαρούριον which they did not feel should be considered as the land-tax because the amount paid for ἐπαρούριον was 'less than the tithe' (the ἀπόμοιρα), whereas the γεωμετρία was five times as large as the ἐπαρούριον. This does not seem to be a very cogent reason. Practically all of the taxes on vine- and garden-land were calculated on the arura, at least in the Roman period; but as all of these taxes, except the γεωμετρία and the ἐπαρούριον, are from their names evidently not to be regarded as the land-tax, it is clear that the choice must lie between those two.

New evidence from the great tax rolls from Caranis seems to eliminate the γεωμετρία from the contest. Professor Youtie has observed that the γεωμετρία on beach-land at Caranis was levied at intervals of five years, and payment of the tax might be made in a lump sum or in two or four instalments. The same practice was probably followed elsewhere in the Arsinoite nome, and perhaps in other nomes of Egypt.[8] A tax paid only once in five years could hardly be the land-tax *par excellence*. Furthermore, there is no evidence for the existence of such a tax in the Ptolemaic period. The tax called γεωμετρία in the Ptolemaic period was a charge of ½ artaba of wheat to cover the cost of surveying the land (as the name indicates) and was not assessed according to the arura, so that it obviously has little in common with the land-tax on vine- and garden-land in the Roman period. It seems impossible to nominate for the land-tax proper a tax which may not have existed in the Ptolemaic period, since one would infer that in the Ptolemaic period vine- and garden-land paid no land-tax. The only candidate for designation as land-tax in the Ptolemaic period, equivalent to the Roman γεωμετρία, is the ἀμπελικά; but Tait considers it probably equivalent to the ἐπαρούριον.⁹ References to ἀμπελικά occur only in a few documents of the third century B.C., whereas references to ἐπαρούριον and ἀπόμοιρα are found in the second and first centuries B.C. in several receipts.¹⁰

On the other hand, the ἐπαρούριον is not a wholly satisfactory candidate for designation as the land-tax. If the land-tax on vine- and garden-land is to be judged by the analogy of the tax on grain-land, the ἐπαρούριον does not correspond. It was a tax fixed (at least in the Fayûm) at two thousand copper drachmae to the arura on vine-land and on garden-land of all kinds (except two subdivisions of land producing olives¹¹), both private and domain land.¹² The land-tax on privately owned grain-land, on the contrary, was fixed according to the category of land, at rates ranging from ¾ to 2 artabae to the arura, while the ἐκφόρια or rent on domain land was ordinarily much higher and was fixed by the lease granted to the tenant (δημόσιος γεωργός). Since the ἐπαρούριον is not analogous to the land-tax on grain-land, it must be acknowledged that the system of taxes on vine- and garden-land developed in a different manner from taxes in kind on grain-land. Instead of seeking for a land-tax proper on vine- and garden-land it is better to describe the system of existing taxes.

The Γεωμετρία

The tax called γεωμετρία in P. Teb. I. 93–4 (c. 112 B.C.) was a fee of ½ artaba of wheat charged for the survey of land, irrespective of its area. The same tax seems to have existed under Augustus as late as 11 B.C.¹³ The earliest receipt for the Roman γεωμετρία on vine- and garden-land is WO. II. 13, recording a payment for γεω(μετρία) φοι(νίκωνος), from Elephantine-Syene and dated November 28, A.D. 54. In the following year a receipt from Thebes for γεω(μετρία) ἀμπ(έλου) is found (WO. II. 407). These two receipts are sufficient to indicate that the assessment of the γεωμετρία was not made uniformly at five-year intervals throughout Upper Egypt. At Elephantine-Syene in the reign of Nero a cycle of four years may be indicated (A.D. 54, 58, 66—WO. II. 13, 15, 17), but WO. II. 22, dated in A.D. 72, does not conform

to this arrangement. In the second century a five-year cycle
might be established at Syene (A.D. 131, 141, 146—WO. II. 157,
184, 210). But in the reign of Marcus Aurelius (A.D. 173, 185—
WO. II. 267–8, 275) the receipts are twelve years apart, and the
cycle does not continue that which ended in A.D. 146.

Receipts ὑπὲρ φοινίκωνος are found as early as 19–18 B.C., and
ὑπὲρ ἀμπέλου as early as 9–8 B.C.[14] Since these receipts from the
period of Augustus show the same rate as the later receipts for
γεωμετρία of these two classes of land, Wilcken concluded that
the tax which was later called γεωμετρία was established as
early as the reign of Augustus. Despite the lack of evidence for
such a tax in the Ptolemaic period it is not impossible that the
tax existed in that period and that it was taken over with the
rest of the system of taxation by the Roman administration after
the conquest of Egypt. Thus the word γεωμετρία may have
been applied to a tax already existing and which doubtless had
had another official name. The assessment of the γεωμετρία in
the Fayûm at intervals of five years is consistent with its literal
meaning of 'land-measurement'. Leases of domain land to public
tenants were frequently made for a period of five years, and,
as Professor Reinmuth has pointed out, there is evidence for
a *lustrum* of five years in the decrees of the prefects regulating
the system of taxation.[15] The earliest appearance of the term
γεωμετρία in connexion with vine- or garden-land is in the
guarantee-clause of a conveyance of a vineyard at Tebtynis
(PSI. VIII. 918), dated in A.D. 38–9, where it is mentioned with
δημόσια τελέσματα πάντα and ἐπιγραφαὶ πᾶσαι. The γεωμετρία,
unlike the annual taxes on vine- and garden-land levied on
the arura, was assessed in silver drachmae, and the surtax
(προσδιαγραφόμενα) was fixed at $\frac{1}{16}$ (1$\frac{1}{2}$ obols to the tetradrachm),
the usual rate in the Roman period but different from the rates
of surtax on the taxes assessed in copper drachmae.[16] This may
possibly indicate that the γεωμετρία was entirely Roman in
origin.

At Thebes the amount paid to the διοίκησις for γεωμετρία on
vine-land was ordinarily 40 drachmae to the arura. This is the
rate established in the ostraca published by Wilcken and is the
normal rate in the tax register from Thebes published in P.
Lond. I. 119 and 109A (pp. 140 ff.) and presumably recording

payments for γεωμετρία. Since, however, the rate for γεωμετρία φοινίκων is shown by the latter document to be sometimes 40 drachmae instead of the more usual 20 drachmae found in the same document and in the ostraca, it is possible that there was some variation in the rate on vine-land also. Wilcken supposed that a rate of 20 drachmae was indicated for vine-land by the interlinear notation καὶ ἀνὰ ∫κ above line 33 of P. Lond. I. 119. This is not impossible, but the tax called οἴνου τέλος, which was assessed on all vine-land paying at the rate of 40 drachmae in this document, was not collected on the area assessed at 20 drachmae, so there is some doubt whether the latter was vine-land.[17] A strict interpretation of the phrase ἀνὰ ∫κ ('at 20 drachmae') prevents us from supposing that two instalments of 20 drachmae yielded a uniform rate of 40 drachmae, although the γεωμετρία assessed in the Fayûm could be paid in two or four instalments.

The rate of the γεωμετρία on vine-land paid to the ἱερά (priests' or temple-) account was much higher; 75 drachmae, 150 drachmae, and even 350 drachmae are found in P. Lond. I. 119. Wilcken suggested that the difference in the rate found was caused by the difference in the quality of the land. It is natural that the best vine-land around Thebes should have been at one time in the hands of the priests. In the Pharaonic period wine was comparatively scarce; the common folk drank beer.[18] Even after viticulture became more important, as the demand for wine increased tremendously after the Ptolemaic conquest and its attendant influx of wine-loving Greeks and Macedonians, the powerful priesthood at Thebes doubtless kept in their control the best of the vine-land near that city. Although all of the land described in P. Lond. I. 119 and 109 A is apparently private property, it is possible that the vineyards of the priests were confiscated and sold or allotted by the Roman government and were given rates of γεωμετρία which corresponded to the value of the land and were therefore somewhat analogous to the ἐκφόρια paid on ἱερὰ γῇ ἐν ἐκφορίοις. It is even possible that these small plots which paid their tax to the ἱερά division of the treasury had been attached to tracts of private land by involuntary leases like the ἐπιβολὴ κατοίκων.

The ordinary rate of the γεωμετρία on palm-land was 20

drachmae to the arura. This is the rate given by the ostraca
published by Wilcken and is the usual rate in P. Lond. I. 119.
But in the latter document, as noted above, a rate of 40 drachmae
to the arura is occasionally found on land which pays its tax to
the διοίκησις.[19] Rates of 75 and 180 drachmae are found on the
land which paid its tax to the ἱερά division of the treasury, and
once in line 101 a rate of 180 drachmae is found on land paying
the tax to the διοίκησις. Wilcken noted that in several ostraca the
φοινικῶνες are designated as ἱερατικοί,[20] but in only one of these
is the taxed area indicated (WO. II. 397, corrected on p. 434);
even this reading is doubtful, because the area of $\frac{1}{32}$ arura
pays 4½ obols (exclusive of προσδιαγραφόμενα), which would indicate a rate of 24 drachmae to the arura otherwise unattested
and unlikely. The observations made above in regard to the
rates of γεωμετρία on vine-land paid to the ἱερά division of the
treasury would apply also to the tax on palm-land.

The rate of γεωμετρία on vegetable gardens (λαχανία) is 20
drachmae, so far as it is preserved in P. Lond. I. 119 and
WO. II. 1075.[21] The same rate is found in three instances for
orchards (ἀκρόδρυα).[22] But in one case the rate for παρά(δεισος)
καὶ ἀκρόδ(ρυα) is 30 drachmae. The 30-drachmae rate is also
applied to μυροβάλανοι in the only example preserved in P.
Lond. I. 119 (line 80).

The London papyrus is dated by Wilcken about A.D. 143.[23]
This is important, because it shows that the rates for γεωμετρία
observed in the ostraca from Thebes and from Elephantine-
Syene, dated from 19–18 B.C. to A.D. 66–7 (after the latter date
the area is omitted from the receipts on ostraca, so that the rate
can no longer be calculated), continued into the second century,
when we have evidence for the rates for the same tax in Lower
Egypt.

The evidence collected by the editors of P. Ryl. II. 192 b has
demonstrated two rates of the γεωμετρία in the Fayûm and in
other nomes of Lower Egypt. The rate on vine-land was 50
drachmae to the arura, and on garden-land was 25 drachmae to
the arura. Occasionally the rate on garden-land appears to be
only 12½ drachmae to the arura; but the evidence for instalments
at Caranis makes it more likely that the payment of 12½ drachmae
to the arura was but one of two instalments totalling 25 drach-

mae. Μυροβάλανοι, which paid at 30 drachmae in P. Lond. i.
119, and συ[κ]. ( ) (which may be expanded σύκων or συκάμιναι)
are included in the γεωμετρία ἀμπέλου at 50 drachmae in P. Lond.
ii. 195 (p. 127 = P. Ryl. ii, p. 255) from the Arsinoite nome.
Ἐλαίων and λαχανεία are included in the γεωμετρία παραδείσου
at 25 drachmae (20 drachmae was the rate for λαχανεία at
Thebes).

There is no evidence to show that the rates for γεωμετρία
varied so greatly in the nomes of Lower Egypt as at Thebes,
and it seems safe to conclude that the system of assessment of
the tax was somewhat different in the two parts of Egypt. An
actual difference in the method of assessing the poll-tax in Lower
and in Upper Egypt will also be observed.[24] There is no evidence
to show whether or not the rates of γεωμετρία in the Fayûm were
raised in the third century as were the rates of the ἀπόμοιρα and
of the ἐπαρούριον.[25]

The Ἀπόμοιρα

The ἀπόμοιρα was the 'portion' of the produce of vine- and
garden-land which, first probably in the period of the domination of the priesthood in the time of the Pharaohs,[26] had been
dedicated to the temples. The revenue of the ἀπόμοιρα was
diverted by Ptolemy II Philadelphus in 265–264 b.c. to the support of the newly established cult of Arsinoë Philadelphus.[27]
The diversion of this revenue was a severe blow to the priests of
Egypt, and they made so determined an effort to regain their
'portion', that part, if not all, of the ἀπόμοιρα was restored to their
control by Ptolemy V Epiphanes and again by Ptolemy VIII
Euergetes II.[28] Even after the restoration of this revenue by
Euergetes II, however, the collection and administration of the
impost was in the control of the officials of the king,[29] and in the
Roman period the revenue from this tax was sometimes assigned
to the ἱερατικά department of the treasury and sometimes to the
διοίκησις.[30] It is possible that the ἱερὰ γῆ did not pay the
ἀπόμοιρα, as Otto maintained,[31] since the revenue had been
originally dedicated to the support of the temples, although in
the Ptolemaic period ostraca record payments by priests on
account of that tax.[32] In Roman times a distinction was made
between πα(ράδεισοι) ἱερ(ατικοί) and the παράδεισοι which paid

the ἕκτη, that is, the ἀπόμοιρα (P. Teb. II. 343. 69 f.). But this may be merely the distinction between the two rates of the tax at ⅙ and 1/10, a distinction which survived, in name at least, long after collection in kind had been abandoned and the terms became meaningless, since the tax was assessed *ad aruram*. The name of ἕκτη had clung to the ἀπόμοιρα because this was the 'portion' of the produce which had been fixed by Philadelphus in the Revenue Laws.[33] At some time before the reign of Ptolemy V Epiphanes the ἀπόμοιρα on vine-land of the ἱππεῖς (the catoeci) was set at 1/10.[34] Nevertheless, the tax was usually called ἕκτη in Greek documents of the Ptolemaic period even when the rate is clearly 1/10 of the produce of the land, and occasionally also in Roman times when the tax was assessed at a fixed rate on the arura.[35] In demotic receipts, on the contrary, the tax is designated as the 'tenth', although it is also called the 'portions', just as ἀπόμοιραι in the plural is used in the decree on the Rosetta Stone and in the decree of Euergetes II.[36]

The Revenue Laws of Philadelphus make some provision for an *adaeratio* of the ἀπόμοιρα of wine, but it is not clear under precisely what conditions this was permitted, for ordinarily the ἀπόμοιρα of wine was to be paid in kind, while that of the produce of garden-land was to be paid in money.[37] As Wilcken has pointed out, this was because the wine was not injured by storage, whereas the produce of garden-land could not be successfully kept over any considerable period of time. As the demand of the Greeks and of the Hellenized portion of the populace caused the production of wine to increase constantly with a consequent increase in the revenue from the 'tithe', it became expedient to receive payments for the ἀπόμοιρα of vine-land too in money. The tax on wine is converted into money in BGU. VII. 1561–2, dated in the reign of Philadelphus or of Euergetes I, and Grenfell, indeed, conjectured 'that payment in kind was not allowed after Epiphanes' reign'.[38] By the terms of the Revenue Laws the ἀπόμοιρα was a πρὸς ἀργύριον ὠνή, that is, the tax was to be paid in silver, but if paid in copper a charge for exchange was to be made. As early as 225 B.C.,[39] however, payment for ἀπόμοιρα was accepted in χαλκὸς ἰσονόμος, that is, the tax-farmers were allowed to accept and to turn over payments in copper drachmae without having also to pay the difference of the exchange. Not all classes of vine-land received this privilege, for even in the early part of the third century after Christ in the Oxyrhynchite nome a distinction was made between two classes of ἀπόμοιρα, one termed ὧν ἀλλαγή ('on which a charge for exchange is collected') and the other ἰσονόμου.[40] In BGU. VII. 1561–2 the *adaeratio* of the ἀπόμοιρα of the wine is 300 (copper) drachmae to the metretes; but in the Revenue Laws, col. 31, the price of wine for taxation in certain nomes is established at 6 (silver) drachmae per metretes of 8 choës and in the Thebaid at 5 drachmae. It is probable, therefore, that age and vintage had to be taken into consideration in determining the *adaeratio* of the ἀπόμοιρα of wine.

In the Roman period the ἀπόμοιρα was calculated at a fixed rate on the arura. Nothing is known of the rate of this tax in Upper Egypt; but in the Arsinoite nome, according to the gnomon in SB. 6951, the rate in the second century was 3,000 copper drachmae to the arura of vine-land and 1,500 drachmae to the arura of garden-land. It is interesting to observe that in P. Lond. II. 195 (p. 127 = P. Ryl. II, p. 255) the κάλαμοι Ἑλληνικοί which paid γεωμετρία ἀμπέλου and the arurae producing λάχανος which paid the γεωμετρία παραδείσου do not pay the ἀπόμοιρα. In the tax-rolls from Caranis the γεωμετρία and ἀπόμοιρα are collected on usiac land and on γῆ προσοδική at the same rate as other categories of land; there is no evidence for domain land (γῆ δημοσία or βασιλική). In the third century the rates of ἀπόμοιρα ἀμπέλου and of ἀπόμοιρα παραδείσου were made equal, and the tax was assessed at 3,750 copper drachmae to the arura.[41]

The ἀπόμοιρα was one of the taxes called εἴδη[42] and which, at least when the term was applied to vine- and garden-land, were assessed in copper drachmae. The assessment in copper drachmae was, of course, an inheritance from the Ptolemaic period. When the tax was collected in silver the ratio of copper drachmae to silver drachmae was fixed at 300:1.[43] The προσδιαγραφόμενα were collected at the rate of $\frac{1}{5}$, even when the payment was made in silver drachmae, although the rate of surtax on silver was ordinarily $\frac{1}{16}$. The high rate of $\frac{1}{5}$ or 20 per cent., as Milne has shown,[44] was established in the first century B.C., when it represented a rise over previous charges for exchange. In addition to this charge of 20 per cent. for surtax a fee for exchange called κόλλυβος at the rate of $\frac{1}{60}$ was charged. This small fee was probably intended, at least theoretically, to pay for the service of a money-changer (κολλυβιστής) in converting the copper payment to silver.[45] When paid in silver the rate of the ἀπόμοιρα on vine-land was 10 drachmae an arura, on garden-land 5 drachmae, and when the rate was raised in the third century 12 drachmae 3 obols. In the Oxyrhynchite nome in the third century approximately 12 drachmae 3 obols was the rate of ἀπόμοιρα on which there was a charge for exchange (ἀλλαγή), but the rate of ἀπόμοιρα without ἀλλαγή was 11 drachmae 3 obols.[46] The difference is approximately $\frac{1}{12}$ or $8\frac{1}{3}$ per cent.,[47] which does not correspond to any of the known rates for ἀλλαγή in the Ptolemaic period.[48] The same rate of ἀλλαγή may be observed in BGU. III. 915. 2 on a payment for ἀπόμοιρα at the rate of 5 silver drachmae to the arura; this document, of uncertain provenance, is dated about A.D. 100. In the Oxyrhynchite document cited above it is impossible to relate the sum paid for προσδιαγραφόμενα with the sums paid for ἀπόμοιρα, and there seems to be no clue to the reason for a reduction of approximately 23 per cent. in the amount of the προσδιαγραφόμενα indicated by the enigmatic phrase ὧν σὺν διαφό(ροις).[49]

There is no evidence that the ἀπόμοιρα was ever halved as was the ἐπαρούριον under certain conditions.[50] The rise in the rate of the ἀπόμοιρα at the beginning of the third century may have been due to the necessity of increasing money-taxes to compensate for the depreciation of the Egyptian currency. It is important to notice that the rate on vine-land was increased 25 per cent., whereas the rate on garden-land was raised 150 per cent. The sharp rise in the rate on garden-land as contrasted with that on vine-land was probably due to the fact that there was an oversupply of wine in the Roman empire, and that consequently the productive value of vine-land was no longer so much greater than that of garden-land.[51]

The Ἐπαρούριον

The ἐπαρούριον was, as its name indicates, a tax assessed at a fixed rate on the arura. It was collected on all φόριμος (bearing) vine- and garden-land, both private and domain land.[52] It is therefore an exceptional levy, since few, if any, other dues were collected at the same rate on both private and domain land. In the third century B.C., if the evidence of BGU. VII. 1561-2 is typical, the tax was assessed in kind, but *adaeratio* was permitted at the same rate as for ἀπόμοιρα, that is, 300 copper drachmae for each metretes. In these two documents the ratio of the amount paid for ἐπαρούριον to the amount of the ἀπόμοιρα is 1 : 5·38. Since the ἀπόμοιρα was reckoned as a sixth or a tenth of the produce of vine- and garden-land while the ἐπαρούριον was a fixed charge on the arura, this ratio varies continually in the receipts: from 1 : 1·67 in WO. II. 1234 (dated in 119 B.C.)[53] to 1 : 15·24 in O. Strass. 22 (dated in 121 B.C.). SB. 1096, an ostracon from Syene, gives a ratio of 1 : 4. This is an extremely important document if Milne has dated it correctly. He gives the date as 37 B.C., because the ἀπόμοιρα is paid in bronze (οὖ ἀλλαγή) at an exchange rate of 20 per cent., whereas bronze is accepted ἰσονόμος in payments for ἀπόμοιρα in the other ostraca which are collected in his table in JEA. XI. (1925), pp. 270 ff., the latest of which is dated in 56 B.C. If 37 B.C. is the correct date, a ratio between ἐπαρούριον and ἀπόμοιρα of 1 : 4 would indicate that the change which placed the assessment of the ἀπόμοιρα at a fixed rate on the arura was not made until after 37 B.C., since the ratio in the Roman period of ἐπαρούριον to ἀπόμοιρα ἀμπέλου is 2 : 3 and to ἀπόμοιρα παραδείσου is 4 : 3. Inasmuch as it is unlikely that Cleopatra was able to effect many important changes in the system of taxation on garden- and vine-land between the years 37 and 30 B.C., it would necessarily follow that the change was made by the Roman administration. This, however, is contrary to most of the evidence for the policy of the Roman government regarding the system of taxation in Egypt, so that it is doubtful if Milne's dating will stand. Since PO. XII. 1437 shows that as late as the third century after Christ there were two classes of vine- and garden-land paying ἀπόμοιρα, one with and one without ἀλλαγή, it is not so evident as Milne supposed that the charge for ἀλλαγή was applied to all payments in copper for vine- and garden-land, and that consequently SB. 1096 must be dated after 56 B.C., the date of O. Tait, p. 84, no. 52. Further evidence must be awaited before the date of the change in the method of assessing the ἀπόμοιρα can be determined.

The rate of the ἐπαρούριον in the Ptolemaic period is unknown.[54] Unlike the γεωμετρία and the ἀπόμοιρα the ἐπαρούριον in Roman times was assessed at the same rate for both vine- and garden-land: 2,000 copper drachmae, or in silver 6 drachmae 4 obols, to the arura. The only important exception to this rate was the assessment on land which produced olives. According to the gnomon (SB. 6951) both ἐν κλήρῳ ἐλαιῶν (cleruchic land producing olives) and ἐν ἐκτη(λογουμένη τάξει) ἐλαιῶν (olive-producing land originally assessed at ⅙ for ἀπόμοιρα) paid ἐπαρούριον at 1,000 drachmae to the arura. It is not clear whether all olive-producing land fell into these two classifications. In P. Lond. III. 917 (p. xlv = P. Ryl. II, p. 254) a small part of the area which paid ἐπαρούριον was planted with olive-trees, as is shown by the payment of 120 drachmae for παραγωγὴ ἐλαίας (charge for transport of olives), but the whole area was assessed at 2,000 drachmae to the arura for ἐπαρούριον. The same is true of P. Lond. II. 195 (p. 127 = P. Ryl. II, p. 255) where the area paying παραγωγὴ ἐλαίας was 1 arura. The editors of the Rylands papyri concluded from this that there were three classes of ἐλαιῶνες,[55] one without a special designation which paid ἐπαρούριον at 2,000 copper drachmae to the arura, and the two designated above which paid at 1,000 copper drachmae to the arura. But it is not clear why the ἐλαιῶν in P. Lond. II. 195 cited above had to pay the high rate of ἐπαρούριον and yet paid the low rate of 210 copper drachmae to the arura for παραγωγὴ ἐλαίας, whereas an ἐν ἐκτη(λογουμένη τάξει) ἐλαιῶν paid the low rate of ἐπαρούριον but the high rate of 280 copper drachmae[56] to the arura for παραγωγὴ ἐλαίας. It is possible that the ἐπαρούριον was sometimes reduced to 1,000 drachmae an arura upon land other than that producing olives. In PSI. IX. 1059 a κηπ(οπαράδεισος) pays ἀπόμοιρα at 1,500 drachmae and ἐπαρούριον at 1,000 drachmae to the arura, but there is no mention of παραγωγὴ ἐλαίας.

In the early part of the third century the rate of the ἐπαρούριον was raised to 2,500 copper drachmae per arura.[57] The exact date of this change is concealed in the exceedingly dubious readings of BGU. VII. 1606 (which is dated in A.D. 200–1).[58]

The surtax (προσδιαγραφόμενα) on ἐπαρούριον paid in copper drachmae was assessed at $\frac{1}{13}$, indicating that this tax was among those for which copper was accepted ἰσονόμος, although in BGU.

1561-2 (dated in the third century B.C.) an ἀλλαγή of 13 drachmae per mina was collected on the same tax. This may mean
that there was a class of land paying ἐπαρούριον in copper with an
ἀλλαγή as well as one which did not pay the fee for exchange,
just as there were two classes of land paying the ἀπόμοιρα noted
above. But there is no evidence for the survival of the double
classification for the ἐπαρούριον in the Roman period as there is
for the ἀπόμοιρα. When the ἐπαρούριον was collected in silver
the rate of the προσδιαγραφόμενα was $\frac{1}{16}$ (the usual rate of $1\frac{1}{2}$
obols to the tetradrachm),[58] although προσδιαγραφόμενα at $\frac{1}{8}$ were
ordinarily collected on ἀπόμοιρα, παραγωγὴ ἐλαίας, and ναύβιον
even when paid in silver.

According to the gnomon of SB. 6951 the ἐπαρούριον (and the
ναύβιον), unlike the other taxes on vine- and garden-land, was
assessed on βασιλικὴ γῆ. The rate given is the same as that given
for privately owned vine- and garden-land, 2,000 copper drachmae to the arura. Hombert's revision of the gnomon[59] showed
that, although it stated that the surtax (προσδιαγραφόμενα) on the
ἐπαρούριον on domain land (βασιλικὴ γῆ) was at the rate of $\frac{1}{10}$,
the calculation of this surtax immediately following in the
gnomon proves that this is a mistake for $\frac{1}{13}$. There was, therefore, no difference in the method of assessing the ἐπαρούριον on
domain land and on private land. Nothing is said in the gnomon
concerning halving the rate of the tax on domain land producing
olives, and since the classification of ἐν κλήρῳ ἐλαιῶν (or perhaps
of ἐν ἑκτη(λογουμένῃ τάξει) ἐλαιῶν) could hardly apply to domain
land, it is unlikely that domain land ever received the privilege
of a half rate.

The Ναύβιον

It is safe to assume that the populace of Egypt had been
liable to service in the corvée that dug and cleaned out canals
and built and repaired dikes ever since the irrigation of the left
bank of the Nile was begun in early Pharaonic times. But when
the Ptolemaic kings assigned land to their Graeco-Macedonian
followers it was natural that these should have objected to serving with the native Egyptians in the menial labour of the corvée.
In the Roman period the corvée was so organized in Upper
Egypt that the peasant handled a specific number of cubic ells

of earth used in the maintenance of the system of dikes and canals for each arura of land in his possession.[60] It is apparent that in the Ptolemaic period this organization of the corvée prevailed elsewhere in Egypt, for the Ptolemies permitted the catoeci and also the holders of released land (γῆ ἐν ἀφέσει) in lieu of this service to pay a fixed sum annually on each arura of land. This tax was called χωματικόν, that is the 'dike-tax'. In the second century B.C. this name was displaced by the term ναύβιον, which was the old Egyptian unit of cubic measure used in reckoning the amount of earth to be handled by the peasants in the dike- and canal-corvée;[61] and ναύβιον continued to be used as the name of the tax in the Roman period when χωματικόν was the designation of a capitation tax. In the third century B.C. the rate of the χωματικόν in the Petrie papyri was 1 obol to the arura.[62] In the Roman period there were two rates established for the ναύβιον in the Arsinoite nome. Catoecic land paid at the rate of 100 copper drachmae to the arura, with προσδιαγραφόμενα at $\frac{1}{10}$ and the usual charge of $\frac{1}{60}$ for κόλλυβος.[63] Released land (γῆ ἐν ἀφέσει) paid at the rate of 150 copper drachmae to the arura, with προσδιαγραφόμενα at $\frac{1}{5}$ plus $\frac{1}{60}$ for κόλλυβος. In the gnomon (SB. 6951) the tax on catoecic land is called ναύβιον κατοίκων, and that term frequently appears in receipts and accounts;[64] although the higher rate is designated as ναύβιον ἐναφεσίων in the gnomon, in receipts and accounts the tax usually appears simply as ναύβιον;[65] but it is usually clear that the higher rate applies even when the area of the land taxed is not given, since the surtax is added at the rate of $\frac{1}{5}$.[66] The same rates for the ναύβιον apparently applied elsewhere in Lower Egypt,[67] but in PO. XII. 1434. 25, dated A.D. 107–8, a rate of 200 copper drachmae appears upon which there was apparently a charge for ἀλλαγή. This high rate for ναύβιον is not attested elsewhere. The charge for ἀλλαγή likewise is not elsewhere attested in connexion with this tax, but the difference in the rate of the προσδιαγραφόμενα, $\frac{1}{10}$ for ναύβιον κατοίκων and $\frac{1}{5}$ for ναύβιον ἐναφεσίων, may indicate that originally copper was accepted ἰσονόμος in payments for the tax on catoecic land, whereas an agio was charged for payments in copper for the tax on land ἐν ἀφέσει.[68]

The rate of the ναύβιον did not change in the third century

when the rates of the ἀπόμοιρα and of the ἐπαρούριον were raised, and there is no evidence of any subsequent rise.[69] Nothing is known concerning the rate of the ναύβιον in Upper Egypt, although the tax is attested in a few ostraca.[70]

According to the gnomon in SB. 6951 βασιλικὴ γῆ paid the ναύβιον at 150 copper drachmae to the arura. If the historical origin of the tax is considered, this was unfair to the δημόσιοι γεωργοί, since they had never been exempt from the dike-liturgy for which, as has been indicated above, the payments for the ναύβιον were a substitute. But there is no evidence that the ownership of catoecic land or of γῆ ἐν ἀφέσει gave immunity to the corvée as organized in the Roman period, so that the extension of the tax to include domain land was but natural for an administration seeking to increase its cash revenues. Unlike the other taxes thus far considered in this chapter the ναύβιον was not confined to vine- and garden-land, but included grain-land and probably all other farm-land except the ἱερὰ γῆ.[71] The exceptional position of this class of land was doubtless due to the fact that in the Ptolemaic period the priests had retained their privilege of exemption from the corvée which they had gained during the period of their great power under the Pharaohs.[72] It is evident that the difference in the rates for ναύβιον and the exemption of ἱερὰ γῆ were an inheritance from the Ptolemaic period, since it was of no advantage to the Roman administration to favour the catoeci or to exempt the property of the temples. In Roman times priests who owned catoecic or cleruchic land paid the appropriate ναύβιον.[73]

The ναύβιον was sometimes included with the ἀπόμοιρα and the ἐπαρούριον among the taxes classed as εἴδη, but it was sometimes excluded. No explanation of this inconsistency has been offered.[74] The proceeds of the tax went to the διοίκησις.[75] It is probable that the proceeds of this tax, as well as those from the capitation tax called χωματικόν, were used to pay for the work done on the irrigation system, besides the work of the corvée, for which the government paid wages.[76]

Παραγωγὴ ἐλαίας

The gnomon in SB. 6951 gives a special charge on land producing olives (which, as noted above, was often taxed at a lower rate than other garden-land) called παραγωγὴ ἐλαίας. The editors of the Rylands papyri (II, p. 248) equate this with the ναῦ(λον) φο(ρέτρου) mentioned in PO. VI. 917. 2. Even if this identification should prove to be incorrect, it is evident that a fee for transport of olives is meant. The gnomon gives two rates for this impost: 280 copper drachmae per arura on land designated as ἐν ἐκτη(λογουμένῃ τάξει), that is, land which had originally paid the ἀπόμοιρα at ⅙; 210 copper drachmae to the arura on land ἐν κλήρῳ. The meaning of the latter term is not certain.[77] The παραγωγὴ ἐλαίας is not attested in extant papyri or ostraca from the Ptolemaic period. The charge for καταγώγιον in connexion with the ἐπαρούριον on vine-land in BGU. VII. 1562 is possibly an analogous charge in the third century B.C.

A charge for φόλετρον τῶν ἐλαιῶν in P. Teb. II. 347 is probably to be connected with the παραγωγὴ ἐλαίας. In P. Lond. III. 1157 (p. 61) ναυκληρία seems to be a tax on garden-land inherited from the Ptolemaic period when taxes were paid in kind. Such fees were freely continued after the taxes were universally collected in money rather than in kind, although their continuance was wholly illogical.

The Ὀκτάδραχμος σπονδὴ Διονύσου

In the gnomon of SB. 6951. 47 f. a charge of 8 drachmae 3 obols for σπονδὴ Διονύσου is prescribed in connexion with the payments on vine-land. It is possible to explain the 3 obols as surtax (προσδιαγραφόμενα) at 1½ obols to the tetradrachm. This is confirmed by the tax-rolls from Caranis, in the collection of the University of Michigan, where the σπονδή of 8 drachmae is frequently paid in two instalments of 4 drachmae with προσδιαγραφόμενα of 1½ obols each. It is rather more difficult to explain why the payments for (ὀκτάδραχμος) σπονδὴ Διονύσου in PO. VI. 917 and X. 1283 should be 8 drachmae 4 obols 1 chalcus, unless it is assumed that the extra 1 obol 1 chalcus was (or included) a charge for a receipt (σύμβολον) or for exchange (κόλλυβος). In PO. XII. 1436, a tax account for a village or a toparchy, payments for σπονδή and σπονδὴ Διονύσου are 40 drachmae with προσδιαγραφόμενα of 3 drachmae 2½ obols and 16 drachmae with προσδιαγραφόμενα of 1 drachma 2 obols 2 chalci respectively, just five and two times the rate attested for the Oxyrhynchite nome in PO. vi. 917 and x. 1283. Until Hombert published the revised readings of the gnomon,[78] it was supposed that the rate of the tax was 8 drachmae to the arura.[79] Hombert's reading showed that 8 drachmae 3 obols was a fixed charge without regard to the area of the vine-land. This is quite in accord with the designation σπονδή. In private contracts the σπονδή was the customary gift of tenant to landlord when a lease was drawn up, and presumably it was in origin a sum designated for a libation to 'seal the bargain'. Since this fee is so seldom found in receipts perhaps the σπονδή was collected only every four or five years like the γεωμετρία at Caranis.

It is obvious from the name of the σπονδὴ Διονύσου that the tax was in origin an offering in kind for the benefit of the god and his priests, yet in P. Ryl. ii. 213, from the Mendesian nome and dated in the late second century after Christ, the proceeds of the tax are credited to the διοίκησις, and PO. ix. 1185, which probably refers to the ηʃ σπονδὴ Διονύσου, records that the revenues from the ὀκτάδραχμος were appropriated to the prefect by an imperial ordinance.

The Οἴνου τέλος

The οἴνου τέλος is a tax on vine-land found in papyri and ostraca from Thebes.[80] Its incidence in P. Lond. i. 119 and 109 A (pp. 140 ff.) is 8 drachmae to the arura, and the proceeds are accounted for apart from the γεωμετρία paid to the διοίκησις and to the ἱερά branch of the treasury. This 'wine-tax' does not fall on vine-land that pays its tax to the division of the treasury designated as ἱερά, which probably indicates that the ἱερὰ γῆ was exempt from the tax. It is quite probable, therefore, that the οἴνου τέλος, like the σπονδὴ Διονύσου, was originally intended for the support of the temples or priests. An οἴνου τέλος is known from papyri and ostraca of the second century B.C., when the tax was paid in copper drachmae; a payment of 2,400 copper drachmae for this tax appears in PO. iv. 788, a private account dated early first century B.C., and this sum is equal to 8 silver drachmae at the rate of exchange common for taxation in the Roman period, viz. 300 : 1. A tax whose incidence is 8 silver drachmae to the arura is found in the Ptolemaic period in

P. Petrie III. 70a, and the editors of the Hibeh papyri (112. 13 note) think that the land is vine-land and that the tax may be the ἐπαρούριον, but it was probably the οἴνου τέλος.

It is possible that the οἴνου τέλος and the σπονδὴ Διονύσου were originally the same tax, as suggested by the editors of P. Ryl. II. 216. 128 note. If this be true, it is but one more example of the different way in which taxes in the Thebaid and in Lower Egypt developed during the course of several centuries.

The Ἑξάδραχμος Φιλαδέλφου

In P. Ryl. II. 213. 354 appears a payment for a tax called the ἑξάδραχμος Φιλαδέλφου, an impost of 6 drachmae probably originally collected for the support of the cult of Arsinoë Philadelphus. In this document, however, the proceeds of the tax belong strictly to the treasury department called διοίκησις. The only thing to connect this impost with vine-land is the remotely possible identification with a charge of 6 drachmae an arura which may have been collected from an ἄμπελος in PO. XVII. 2129. 73 ff.[81]

Τέλεσμα

It is impossible to determine to which of the taxes on vine- and garden-land discussed above the receipts refer that record payments for τέλεσμα ἀμπέλου or παραδείσου and the like.[82] The τέλος τῆς τρυγῆς, a tax connected with vintage, is mentioned only in a private letter.[83] In O. Mich. Car. 130 (A.D. 283 or 285) is a puzzling payment of 27 drachmae designated simply ὑπ(ὲρ) ἀρου(ρῶν).

Various taxes in amounts ranging from 10 drachmae down to 1 drachma an arura are found assessed against land. Some of these are assessed against vine- or garden-land; but it is not certain that their incidence was limited to that type of land, since some imposts collected in money fell on grain-land. In general, the evidence in regard to these money-taxes is very limited, so that it is usually impossible to determine whether a given tax was universal throughout the nomes of Egypt or how long it was in force in any district.

Δεκάδραχμος

This tax is known only from P. Ryl. II. 216, where it is incident upon the arura. The document is a survey of land-taxes paid in money in the Mendesian nome, and it is dated second or early third century after Christ. This survey records a number of money-taxes in a system of taxation apparently not duplicated in other nomes. The land is divided into five classes defined by the editors of the document as follows: '(1) land belonging to persons classed as "not paying" (τῶν μὴ τελούντων . . .), (2) land belonging to Alexandrians and assessed at 2 drachmae 3 obols (written β τριωβ( ) Ἀλεξανδρέων . . .), (3) land belonging to citizens and assessed at 3 drachmae (τρίδραχμος μητροπολιτῶν), (4) land at 8 drachmae (ὀκτάδραχμος . . .), and (5) land at 10 drachmae (δεκάδραχμος).' The principle that determined to which of the above categories any given piece of land belonged is not always clear.[84] Although the highest rate of 10 drachmae to the arura coincides with the rate of the ἀπόμοιρα ἀμπέλου in the Fayûm, the taxes are certainly not the same.

Ὀκτάδραχμος

The land in P. Ryl. II. 216 which paid this tax is not distinguished by any designation other than the rate of taxation. The rate is the same as that of the οἴνου τέλος of Upper Egypt, but there is no other evidence that the two taxes are to be related. P. Ryl. II. 186. 5, an official account dealing with several nomes, gives 219 talents 83 drachmae 3 obols under the heading λόγος (ὀκταδράχμου), but it is possible that this sum refers to the crown-tax which was collected at the rate of 8 drachmae to the arura. It is also probable that the ὀκτάδραχμος which, by a decree of Aemilius Saturninus (prefect of Egypt in A.D. 197 and 198), was made incident upon the arura, is to be identified with the crown-tax rather than with the (ὀκτάδραχμος) σπονδὴ Διονύσου or the οἴνου τέλος.[85]

Πεντάδραχμος

This tax is mentioned several times in fragmentary documents, some of which are published in P. Ryl. II. 427 (dated late second or early third century), dealing with garden-land in the Mendesian nome. There is no evidence as to the incidence of the tax, and it may have been connected with the conveyance of the property by auction, to which reference is made in the fragments.

Τετράδραχμος

This tax of four drachmae occurs in PO. XVII. 2129 (line 18 note), where it is apparently subject to a rebate of one-third. It might be supposed that the tax was to be identified with the τέλος καταλοχισμῶν, occasionally collected at the rate of 4 drachmae an arura, if the τετράδραχμος did not appear in P. Iand. 141, where it is exacted upon two parcels of land, one from the estate formerly belonging to Maecenas and the other from the Lurian estate. There is some doubt about the incidence of this tax, since in P. Iand. 141. 13 the amount paid is $1\frac{1}{4}$ drachmae although the amounts paid for the various taxes on garden-land in the lines immediately preceding indicate an area of but $\frac{1}{10}$ arura, and a payment of $1\frac{1}{4}$ drachmae thereon would indicate a rate of $12\frac{1}{2}$ drachmae an arura instead of 4 drachmae. In P. Ryl. II. 213. 157 a τετράδραχμος is mentioned, but it seems to be the price paid per arura for land sold outright or leased in perpetuity, as the editors have suggested.

Τρίδραχμος

The τρίδραχμος is found in P. Ryl. II. 213 among the taxes belonging to the ἱερατικά division of the treasury. This is probably, as the editors point out (p. 297), an indication that the τρίδραχμος was originally established for the support of the temples and the priesthood. Only in the special division of the land whose taxes are classified under λιμνιτικά do the proceeds of the tax go to the διοίκησις. P. Ryl. II. 216 seems to indicate that the 3 drachmae was the rate paid by the privileged citizens of the metropolis (μητροπολῖται) instead of the rates of 8 drachmae and 10 drachmae paid presumably by the native Egyptians and others similarly unprivileged, since the impost is called τρίδραχμος μητροπολιτῶν. Land subject to the τρίδραχμος comprised the larger part of the taxable vine- or garden-land of the nome. If the rates of 8 and 10 drachmae were paid by native Egyptian land-holders in the Mendesian nome,[86] while the τρίδραχμος was the tax paid by the μητροπολῖται, two parcels of land mentioned as paying the 2 drachmae 3 obols of the Alexandrian citizens probably represent a further reduction of a half drachma in favour of land owned by the citizens of the capital of Egypt, whose other privileges in regard to taxation are well known.[87] In the Arsinoite nome the only reference to a similar tax is possibly to be found in P. Teb. II. 500, where γ́ διοικ( ) in connexion with taxes on garden-land might be interpreted as a tax of 3 drachmae (τρίδραχμος); but the abbreviation is perhaps rather to be read τ́ instead of γ́, and so is to be interpreted τ(όκος) διοικ(ήσεως). A tax account of unknown provenience (P. Ryl. II. 376) has repeated entries of 3 drachmae 5 obols 2 chalci, but there is no indication of relation to the τρίδραχμος.

Διδραχμία

A tax designated by β+, which is probably to be explained as διδραχμία, is found in documents of the third century from the Oxyrhynchite and Hermopolite nomes. An example of this tax, which may well have been established no earlier than the third century after Christ, is PO. XVII. 2129, which is dated tentatively in A.D. 205-6.[88] In this document there are two distinct forms of the tax. One is designated simply as διδραχμία, the other as φό(ρος or φόρετρον)[89] at 2 drachmae to the arura; both of them might fall on the same piece of property. The mention of the ἐγκύκλιον and the τέλος καταλοχισμῶν indicates that much of the land in question, which belonged to the family of one Saras of the village of Mermertha, had recently changed hands and was largely catoecic.[90] As in other documents exhibiting this tax of 2 drachmae to the arura it is coupled with a tax of 1 drachma to the arura. In PO. XII. 1442, dated A.D. 252, these taxes at 2 drachmae and 1 drachma are paid by a woman. In P. Lond. III. 1157 (pp. 61 ff.), from Alabastrine in the Hermopolite nome and dated A.D. 226-7, the β+ appears. This papyrus is an official account of the receipts for money-taxes on land. Each section of the document (which is divided into fiscal periods called ἀριθμήσεις) consists of two parts, the first of which deals with the ναύβιον and τέλεσμα παραδείσου and ἀμπέλου and μονόδραχμος ζευγματικῶν, &c., which are called γνήσια τέλη; the

second part records payments for β+ (διδραχμία), which by implication is not one of the 'legitimate' taxes (γνήσια τέλη). A
payment for β+ and ναύβιον at Βοῦναι Κλεοπάτρας, a town in the
Hermopolite nome, is credited to a woman named Tinutis in
P. Lond. III. 1217 A (p. 61) which is dated A.D. 246. Since a second
certificate belonging to the same person (P. Lond. III. 1217 B)
is countersigned by the official in charge of the καταλοχισμοί,[91] it
is possible that the β+ is connected with catoecic land which, as
will be shown later, was subject at times to special assessments
paid in money. In O. Strass. 580, dated in the third century
after Christ, it is possible that a payment for διδραχμία is made
in wheat, for the editor proposed to restore Μεσορὴ ὑπὲρ διδραχ-
[μίας ₹ μίαν ∠d / ₹a ∠d] in order to obtain the stated total: γ(ίνονται)
₹ ιβ∠η̄. If the restoration is correct it means a payment was made
in kind for a tax assessed in money, which is most unusual,
and it also indicates that the διδραχμία was collected in Upper
Egypt as well as in Lower Egypt in the third century after
Christ.

Μονόδραχμος

In BGU. VI. 1344 and 1346 from Apollonopolis Magna and
1350 from Coptos, all dated about the beginning of the first
century B.C., a tax designated simply as δραχμή is found in
connexion with payments for ἀπόμοιρα and ἐπαρούριον, the
taxes on vine- and garden-land.[92] In P. Ryl. II. 427 and
431, from Thmuis in the Mendesian nome and dated late
second or early third century after Christ a tax of 1 drachma
(μονόδραχμος) is mentioned in connexion with garden-land,
but because the documents are so fragmentary it is difficult
to decide whether this is to be regarded as a regular land-tax
or as a charge in connexion with the sale by auction of ὑπόλογος
γῆ (inferior land).[93] In PO. XVII. 2129, cited above, a tax
designated ā (δραχμή) is found assessed on the arura. In
several lines the tax is further defined as ā (δραχμὴ) ζευγμ(ατικῶν)
τελ(ῶν), and it is not certain whether one or two taxes are meant,
since a φόρος seems to be connected with the ā (δραχμή) in line
54.[94] In PO. XII. 1442 the ā δραχμή (without further designation)
is collected in connexion with the β̄ δραχμαί. In P. Lond. III.
1157 (pp. 61 ff.) the α+ ζευγματικῶν is found with the ναύβιον

and τέλεσμα παραδείσου and ἀμπέλου, &c., that is, among the γνήσια τέλη. Because of the connexion with the ναύβιον the editors supposed that the μονόδραχμος ζευγματικῶν was a land-tax assessed to pay for bridges or sluices in the dike- and canal-system. The ζευγματικόν is called a lock-toll in the new Liddell and Scott *Greek Lexicon*, citing this document, but it is difficult to see why a lock-toll should be assessed κατ' ἄρουραν in PO. XVII. 2129. 4, 19, 28, 45. Where ζευγματικῶν appears without ᾱ δραχμή in lines 11 and 65 of the latter document the incidence of the tax cannot be determined, and it is not impossible that a different rate for the impost is to be inferred; it is also possible that ᾱ δραχμή has merely been omitted.

The Πηχισμὸς περιστερεώνων

The πηχισμὸς περιστερεώνων was a tax on pigeon-houses and nests, or rather on the land occupied by them.[95] The rate of taxation was high, 5 drachmae for each ell (presumably a square πῆχυς).[96] This tax is usually found in connexion with payments of the taxes on garden-land, because the pigeon-houses were situated near the gardens for which the pigeon-dung was a valuable fertilizer. In the Ptolemaic period a tax called τρίτη περιστερεώνων was collected, presumably one-third of the profits from the annual increase of the pigeons. This tax was abandoned at Thebes in favour of the land-tax between 114 and 112 B.C.,[97] probably because the tax-collectors found it impossible to obtain accurate figures upon which to base the tax of one-third, since the pigeons (due to their extraordinary fecundity) increased in numbers so rapidly. The tax of one-third persisted in Lower Egypt,[98] but the only examples of its survival into the Roman period are found in P. Ryl. II. 213. 261 from the Mendesian nome and in the great tax-rolls from Caranis in the collection of the University of Michigan. In the documents from Caranis most of the payments are at the rate of 3 drachmae (with surtax of 1¼ obols). Such a uniformity of rate seems to indicate that the tax was not assessed on land occupied by the pigeon-house or on the profits from the increase of the flock, but the term τρίτη περιστερεώνων perhaps survived when the impost had been converted to a licence-fee. It is impossible to tell from the single occurrence in P. Ryl. II. 213 whether this was true in the Men-

desian nome also. At any rate it is clear that the method of
assessing the tax was not the same in Lower Egypt as in the
Thebaid.

Λειτουργικόν

The λειτουργικόν occurs as a tax on land in P. Ryl. II. 213 and
in P. Lond. inv. 1581 recto, col. iii. In regard to this tax one can
hardly do better than to quote the note on P. Ryl. II. 213. 34:
'Wilcken, followed by Lesquier, interprets it as a charge paid by
cleruchs in virtue of their exemption from λειτουργίαι (cf. P.
Tebt. I. 124. 37–40). Perhaps, however, on the analogy of
γραμματικόν, ἐπιστατικόν, δεκανικόν, it was rather a charge for
the support of a λειτουργός, although in effect the two views may
well be the same. In any case the fact that the charge occurs
under λιμνιτικῶν indicates that it was assessed in Roman times
also upon land, though how far it was still restricted to any
special class of cultivators is uncertain, no suffix occurring.' It
was also classed under διοίκησις in P. Ryl. II. 213.[99]

Θωνειτικὰ καὶ λιμνιτικά

Again I quote the note of the editors of the Rylands papyri
(II. 213. 156): 'This tax, or group of taxes, should by its position
be incident upon land . . . . Thonis, however, was a city situated
at the mouth of the Canopic branch of the Nile (cf. Steph. Byz.
sub. Θῶνις; Strabo, 800. 16; Diodor. i. 19), and its connexion
with the Mendesian nome is obscure.' No similar classification
of taxes is attested elsewhere.

Ἐπικλασμοί

The ἐπικλασμοί were apparently extraordinary taxes assessed
to meet a fiscal emergency. PO. VI. 899, a woman's petition to
be released from cultivation of domain land which had become
an impossible burden because of ἐπικλασμοί, extra levies ordained
by Aemilius Saturninus, indicates that they fell on land. In
P. Teb. II. 470 a reference to φόρετρα τοῦ ἐπικλασμοῦ shows that
the extra levy might be made in kind. The collection of the
ἐπικλασμός by the πράκτορες λαογραφίας in P. Teb. II. 391, however, indicates a tax in money, but it is doubtful whether it had
been assessed against land. The ἐπικλασμοί of Aemilius Satur-

ninus mentioned above, however, may have included such measures as transforming the ὀκτάδραχμος to a charge κατ' ἄρουραν, and the ἐπικλασμοί in the guarantee-clauses of conveyances of property may have included money-taxes.[100]

Φόροι

Φόρος literally means yield, and in BGU. I. 8. ii this literal meaning is apparent in the phrase φόρος νομαρχικῶν ἀσχολημάτων ('the yield of the revenues controlled by the nomarch'). Φόρος in leases of domain or private land and in related documents of the Roman period means 'rent'. Land belonging to the state or to the imperial estates was sometimes leased at a cash rental, especially if the land was not to be sown with wheat or barley (crops normally paying ἐκφόρια in kind). This cash rental was termed φόρος,[101] sometimes further defined as ἀργυρικὸς φόρος,[102] for the term φόρος was occasionally used to designate rent in kind.[103] The rate of rental on domain land varied widely because of the great differences in the value of land leased by the state. Ὑπόλογος γῆ or land ἐκ χέρσου was leased on terms as low as 3 obols to the arura per annum.[104]

Vine- and palm- and garden-land naturally paid at a much higher rate, although the rate of the φόρος on such domain land is not stated in the extant documents.[105] There are few extant examples of the φόρος ἀμπέλου, φόρος φοινίκων, or φόρος παραδείσου; probably the government was not anxious to encourage the production of wine on the domain land, since the more profitable vineyards might drive out the cultivation of wheat, which was more necessary to the government for the distributions at Rome and for the commissary of the army. It is possible that the land which paid φόρος ἀμπέλου, for example, was vine-land confiscated for some cause and whose culture was left unchanged inasmuch as the land was not suitable for grain or because vine-land brought in greater immediate returns.

A φόρος φυτῶν was collected occasionally, but what 'plants' or trees were meant is not known.[106] Καταφυτεία is mentioned in the records of the γραφεῖον in P. Mich. 121 R I. xiv and 11. 1. A φόρος ἐλαίνου φυτῶνος is found in the tax-rolls from Caranis in the collection of the University of Michigan, and a φόρος φυῆς is attested in P. Bibl. Giessen 13. It is possible that orchards were leased by the state to its tenants, and that may be the meaning of these φόροι.

Even more obscure is an isolated reference to a φόρος χεσοῦ(   );[107] the context of the document suggests that the φόρος may have been paid by priests or a temple.

Φόρος πλεονασμῶν is probably cash rental paid on land added by involuntary lease to the amount of cultivated domain land,[108] and whose type of culture was unsuited to payment of ἐκφόρια in kind.

The φόρος νόμων was rent paid in money to the government for pasture-land leased from the state.[109] This φόρος must be distinguished from the ἐννόμιον.[110] The supervision and leasing of state or imperial pastures in the marshes, shores, and plains (δρυμοί, αἰγιαλοί, and πεδία) was entrusted to ἐπιτηρηταὶ νόμων,[111] and in P. Lond. III. 842 (p. 141), which is unique, to the πρεσβύτεροι πεδίου Φιλοπάτορος Ἀπίαδος, 'the elders of the plain of Apias'.

A cash φόρος was also paid by hunters and fishermen for the right to hunt or fish in the marshes and waste lands. The terms usually provided for payment of an annual rental for the exclusive right to hunt certain animals or birds within a limited district or to fish in specified waters. The revenue from such concessions is apparently called ὑδατικὴ πρόσοδος in PSI. III. 160.[112]

A φόρος ὑποδοχίου (rent of a reservoir) is mentioned in P. Teb. II. 344. A φόρος φράγμου (rent of a barrier?) is attested in PO. III. 580. Rental for unoccupied land (φόρος ψίλου τόπου ἐν κώμῃ) is found in P. Ryl. II. 215. 27, and a φόρος without further designation in P. Teb. II. 494.

Πρόσοδος ὑπαρχόντων

Πρόσοδ(οι) ὑπ(αρχόντων) are cash payments in P. Ryl. II. 213. 45. Just as land in debt to the treasury for rent or taxes in kind might have its entire produce confiscated,[113] it is logical that land owing debts in money might have a πρόσοδος laid upon it.[114]

Μονοδεσμίαι

An obscure tax called μονοδεσμία χόρτου ('single bundle of hay') is paid in the second and third centuries[115] in the Arsinoite and Hermopolite nomes by δημόσιοι γεωργοί, often through the πρεσβύτεροι κώμης. It is impossible to determine the incidence of this tax paid in silver, because the payment is almost always made ὑπὲρ μονοδεσμίας χόρτου καὶ ἄλλων εἰδῶν, implying that the μονοδεσμία belonged to the class of εἴδη. In P. Fay. 34 a certain Heron from Philagris agrees to act as deputy of the βοηθοὶ γεωργῶν (aides of the farmers) in the collection of the μονοδεσμία χόρτου καὶ ἄλλα εἴδη. He was to pay 560 silver drachmae (in monthly instalments) to be collected on 411$\frac{23}{64}$ arurae of land at Polydeucia. The implication seems to be that the tax was assessed on the arura, although this is not an absolutely necessary conclusion.[116] The sum stated amounts to approximately 1$\frac{3}{7}$ drachmae to the arura, but it is most probable that the tax was collected at a higher rate to provide for the remuneration of the deputy, since there is no mention of salary. If the tax-rate was 2 drachmae to the arura and there were no arrears, the profit of Heron would be 262 drachmae for the year. A payment designated as χαλκοῦ εἰκοσίδραχμος, a tax of 20 copper drachmae, is mentioned in the terms of the sub-leases of crown-land in PSI. x. 1144 and P. Teb. II. 373. It is possible that this payment is included in the ἄλλα εἴδη of the receipts, especially since the εἴδη on garden-land were assessed in copper. The μονοδεσμία χόρτου was one of the taxes within the competence of the nomarch.[117] In a few receipts it is collected with the ζυτηρὰ κατ᾽ ἄνδρα. The beer-tax collected on individuals appears also in receipts for μονοδεσμία ἀργυρικῶν, and the latter tax also appears in receipts with the addition καὶ ἄλλα εἴδη.[118] Μονοδεσμία without further qualification appears with ἄλλα εἴδη in some receipts.[119] It would be tempting to identify the μονοδεσμία χόρτου with the μονοδεσμία ἀργυρικῶν were it not for P. Strass. 60, where payments of 92 and 8 drachmae are made for μονοδεσμία ἐργ( ), which might possibly be a misspelling of the more frequent μονοδεσμία ἀργ(υρικῶν), and another payment of 84 drachmae is made for μονοδεσμία χόρτου, which apparently establishes a distinction between two μονοδεσμίαι. This is confirmed by SB. 5982, which mentions πρακτορία νομαρχικῶν ἀσχοληmάτων ζυτηρᾶς καὶ μονοδεσμ‹ι›ῶν, indicating more than one form of μονοδεσμία. It is unsafe even to assume that ἐργ( ) was mistakenly written for ἀργ( ), since the scribe of P. Strass. 60 is otherwise quite careful; Preisigke restored ἔργ(ων), but the abbreviation is perhaps for the name of some fodder. The name of the tax is always

written in the genitive case in the receipts, so that the exact form
of the nominative is not certain; it is possible that the name of the
tax should be read μονοδεσμία χόρτου (or ἀργυρικῶν) καὶ ἄλλων
εἰδῶν rather than μονοδεσμία χόρτου καὶ ἄλλα εἴδη. In that case
the εἴδη might include μονοδεσμίαι χόρτου (or ἀργυρικῶν) καὶ
ἔργ(ων) and χαλκοῦ εἰκοσίδραχμος.

The name μονοδεσμία χόρτου suggests an original tax in kind
providing that hay-fields of δημόσιοι γεωργοί should pay 'one
bundle' of hay to the arura. In BGU. I. 345[120] a payment of
money is made to the nomarch ὑπὲρ χόρτου ἐν γένει. The
low rate of the tax indicated by P. Fay. 34 may point to one
bundle of hay per arura as the original assessment of this tax
also. There are no receipts before A.D. 100, and it is possible
that Trajan changed the impost from a payment in kind to one
in money; but it is odd that no trace of the tax in kind is found
in the period before Trajan, unless the payments in artabae of
wheat for χο( ) in P. Teb. II. 346 (early first century after
Christ) are connected with χόρτος as the editors suggest.[121] In
SP. V. 119 R v the lessee of land owned by the city of Hermopolis
proposes to plant 6 arurae εἰς σπορὰν πυροῦ καὶ χόρτ(ου). But the
payments for χο( ) in P. Teb. II. 346 are seemingly in connexion
with private cleruchic land, not domain land, and the payments
in wheat would be a substitute for an original payment in hay.

The payments made for μονοδεσμία χόρτου may possibly be
connected with *faenarium*, a deduction from the soldiers' pay to
purchase hay for the use of the army.[122] In that case we might
regard this tax as an innovation of Trajan in connexion with
the increase of the army in Egypt to three legions, which occurred
in or before A.D. 109,[123] and suppose that the tax continued after
the legions had been reduced in number to two and later to one.
If this is correct, it would represent an early effort to systema-
tize the *annona militaris* in Egypt by the *adaeratio* of payments
in kind, which were difficult to collect and to transport.[124]

A δώσις [sic!] χόρτου καὶ ἄλλον [sic!] εἰδῶν occurs in P. Flor. III.
363, but there is no apparent reason for the change in the terminology. Obscure charges for grass, γράστις or χλωρά, appear in
documents of the Roman period as well as the Ptolemaic period,
but nothing is known concerning the conditions under which
such assessments were made.[125]

Ληναῖον

Λιναίου, perhaps equivalent to *ληναίου*, is found in P. Bad. 19 A, and seems to be a tax on a winepress. In P. Lond. II. 195 (p. 127 = P. Ryl. II, p. 255), however, the winepress made up a part of the *κτῆσις* paying taxes for vine- and garden-land.

'Ενοίκιον and πρόσοδος οἰκοπέδων

Wilcken believed that householders paid a tax on the rent received from houses and the land upon which they stood.[126] Such a tax he found in the receipts (*ὑπὲρ*) *ἐνοικίου*, sums paid 'for the rent'. The few extant receipts are for comparatively small amounts, and the payment is said to be for a given year. Such receipts, said Wilcken, could be only for rent paid by the tenant to the government for a house owned by the latter, or for a tax paid by a landlord upon rent paid by a tenant. He preferred the latter interpretation, especially because in WO. II. 292 a payment is recorded *ὑπὲρ ἐνοικίου οἰκιῶν γ̄*, 'denn durch drei Häuser hindurch wird niemand zur Miete wohnen'. In the same category Wilcken placed the *πρόσοδος οἰκοπέδων*, interpreting it as a tax on the income from building-sites. He saw in the phrase in P. Petrie II. xi. 2 (= W. *Chrest.* 223, dated third century B.C.), *ἀπογέγραμμαι δὲ ἐπὶ τελώνιον τὸ οἰκόπεδον φερό-μεν(ο)ν ⊢ ιζϲ ἵνα ἐκ τούτου φέρωμεν τὴν εἰκοστήν*, an indication that the rate of the tax on income from building sites was 5 per cent. This *εἰκοστή*, however, bears a suspicious resemblance to the amount paid for *ἐγκύκλιον*, a tax on sales, and even if line 5 of this document is correctly restored, it is possible that the property had been sold and that the declaration of the income made by Polycrates was to establish the value of the site.

Grenfell and Hunt in editing PO. XII. 1519 state that a payment recorded for *ἐνοίκιον οἰκοπέδων* is rent on property owned by the government and refer to PO. XII. 1461 which records sums paid for rent, &c., on a *λαχανοπωλεῖον* (vegetable stall) belonging to the imperial estate (*κυριακὴ κτῆσις*). If this is correct, we have a reason for the rare occurrence of receipts for *ἐνοίκιον* which should have been extremely common if every landlord paid a tax on house-rent.[127] The receipts would thus be explained on the alternative rejected by Wilcken, namely, that they were issued for rent paid by the tenants of houses owned by the government. The ἐνοίκιον οἰκιῶν γ̄ would represent a payment by a tenant who had leased three houses from the government in order to sublet them at a profit.[128] On this theory, which really implies a 'single tax', we should have a logical explanation of the large payments for ἐπιβολῆς πηχισμοῦ and ἐπιβολῆς πηχισμοῦ οἰκοπέδων (in P. Lond. III. 1157 (pp. 61 ff., lines 111, 113, 150, 152), from Alabastrine in the Hermopolite nome and dated A.D. 226–7); namely, that when φόριμος γῆ was turned into building sites a large sum had to be paid to the treasury as compensation for the loss of revenue from the land previously cultivated, just as a πρόστιμον was exacted in P. Preisigke Cairo 12 (second century after Christ) when land which had paid ἐκφόρια in wheat was built over.

The government apparently confiscated and leased the houses of those who had fled to escape the burden of taxes or liturgies, for the ἐνοίκιον ἀνακ(εχωρηκότων) is mentioned in *Archiv.* v, pp. 170 ff., no. 29; in O. Strass. 293 this amounts to 16 talents.

It would be rather strange, however, if the financial administration of Egypt had overlooked the possibilities of taxing houses and had been committed to the 'single tax'. The sums recorded in the receipts seem rather small for a year's rent, even on property owned by the government. Further, the ἐνοίκια are mentioned with τέλη in BGU. IV. 1117. 29 (from Alexandria and dated 13 B.C.) in the phrase ἀπὸ ἐνοικίων καὶ τελῶν . . . κάθαρον referring to the lease of a bakery, and the ἐνοίκιον seems to be distinct from the φόρος of 2 obols *per diem*. The ἐνοίκιον is described apparently[129] as πρὸς τοὺς μεμισθωμένους, which is a phrase usually used in reference to taxes.

A tax on houses and vacant lots seems to be meant in P. Flor. I. 104 (cf. P. Strass. 31). The rental of camel-stalls by the government is mentioned in P. Iand. 142. (*c.* A.D. 164–5).

Until further evidence is available to demonstrate the lease of houses from the government of Egypt, Wilcken's explanation of the receipts for ἐνοίκιον is the more plausible. Nevertheless, it is noteworthy that the ἐνοίκιον in Wilcken's theory is an income-tax on rent rather than a property-tax on houses for which there is as yet no satisfactory evidence (except perhaps P. Flor. I. 104).

TAXES ON ANIMALS

IN a wall-painting at Sakkara in the tomb of T'y,[1] which dates from the Fifth Dynasty, appears a scene which may throw some light on the vexed problem of taxes on animals in the period of Roman domination. Peasant women, representing the various villages belonging to the deceased, are pictured in procession bringing the yield of his vast estates. The women carry upon their heads baskets filled with the fruits of the field, but more important to us are the ducks and other fowl which they carry in their hands or under the arm and also the donkeys and sheep which walk with them. These animals represent the increase of flocks and herds which the peasants tended for their noble master. This master was not the king of Egypt; but he was one of the powerful nobles who, during the decline of the monarchy which began as early as the Fifth Dynasty, gained control of much of the land and wealth of Egypt. When the power of the monarchy rose at the expense of the feudal nobility with the establishment of the New Empire by the Eighteenth Dynasty, the lands of Egypt were again chiefly owned by the crown and worked by the king's serfs. In his *History of Egypt*[2] Breasted states that upon the re-establishment of the supremacy of the monarchy in the New Empire 'other royal property, like cattle and asses, was held by the people . . . subject, like the lands, to an annual assessment for its use'. These assessments on animals were collected, like those on land, in kind, and the cattle-yards formed a sub-department of the royal treasury. The assessments were, significantly, called 'labour'.

We have seen how the theory that the ownership of all the land of Egypt was vested in the crown was utilized by the Ptolemies in the administration of their kingdom, and how in consequence the system of private tenure of land developed but slowly in the Hellenistic period, so that, when the Roman government took over the administration of the country after its conquest by Octavian, much of the best land of Egypt remained in possession of the crown and played an important role in the exploitation of Egypt by the Roman emperors.[3] Private ownership of domestic animals of all kinds developed gradually, it may be supposed, in a manner analogous to the development of the private ownership of land. That is, possession of animals was granted in perpetuity to private individuals if they agreed to pay a fixed annual assessment corresponding to the καθήκοντα paid on catoecic and cleruchic land. The failure to observe, however, that the ownership of a considerable proportion of the flocks and herds of domestic animals in Egypt remained vested in the state has caused much of the confusion in regard to taxation of animals in the Graeco-Roman period. In the instruction given by the Dioecetes to a subordinate (P. Teb. III. 703. 64–70), dated in the late third century B.C., royal cattle (βασιλικὰ κτήνη) are distinguished from private cattle (ἴδια κτήνη). Now it is a moot point whether the animals used in the cultivation of the crown-lands in Ptolemaic and in Roman times were the property of the state or of the cultivators,[4] but aside from these animals there is ample evidence for the existence of 'royal cattle' in the Ptolemaic period, and there is no proof that the Roman administration did not retain ownership of public cattle (δημόσια κτήνη). Much will become clear if we assume that it did so.

There is no evidence in the Roman period for a φόρος (rent) paid for the lease of donkeys or of camels from the state. In the Pharaonic period it was probably profitable to lease beasts of burden from the state, for the 'labour' was paid in kind, that is, from the increase of the herd (as in the painting in the tomb of T'y) or in occasional service to the state. In the Ptolemaic and Roman periods, however, the predominant importance of the revenue of grain made its transportation to Alexandria a first consideration of the government. The δημόσιοι ὄνοι (public donkeys) were continually engaged in the transport of government grain or in other service to the state. The remuneration for this transport-duty was hardly enough for subsistence, so that the state was obliged to resort to the liturgy of ὀνηλασία (donkey-driving), which was regarded as a most onerous service, to be avoided if possible.[5] The same services *mutatis mutandis* were required of the καμηλοτρόφοι (camel-raisers).

Lessees of animals other than beasts of burden, however, con-

tinued to pay an annual rent for their use. With the introduction
of coinage by the Ptolemies it was no longer necessary to build
stock-yards to receive the 'labour' of flocks and herds, for the
increase of the king's cattle could be assessed and collected in
money. Sheep appear among the animals of the procession in
the tomb of T'y. Their chief value lay in the fleeces which
supplied wool for the weavers thoughout Egypt.[6] In the Ptolemaic and Roman periods the rent paid for the use of sheep and
goats owned by the state was called the φόρος προβάτων.[7] This
φόρος προβάτων was paid by the προβατοκτηνοτρόφοι (herdsmen),
who formed a guild like that of the δημόσιοι γεωργοί who leased
the domain land.[8] In a document from Tebtynis the secretaries
of the δημόσιοι γεωργοί and the secretary of other cultivators of
the village are the parties of the first part in an abstract of a contract of agreement with two προβατοκτηνοτρόφοι, parties of the
second part, who had leased from the former half of the dry
pasture lands (χερσονομαί) of the village.[9] The φόρος προβάτων
is attested from the third century B.C. to the third century after
Christ,[10] but in only one document is the number of sheep given
together with the amount paid to the collectors. In PSI. VII.
817, from Euhemeria and dated in the second century of our era,
a payment of 42 drachmae $\frac{1}{2}$ obol is made for eight sheep—
approximately $5\frac{1}{4}$ drachmae for each animal.[11] Supplementary
charges (προσδιαγραφόμενα) at about one-sixteenth are frequently
recorded in connexion with the payment of this φόρος.[12] Like
the rent of domain land the φόρος προβάτων may have varied
according to the value of the sheep and according to local or
temporary conditions.[13] In BGU. VII. 1712, from Philadelphia
and dated A.D. 165-6(?) or 248-9, a φόρος ἀρνίων (rent paid on
lambs) is mentioned in addition to payments for φόρος προβάτων.

In the third century after Christ the estates of great landholders began to absorb the small holdings of hard-pressed
farmers and also domain land that could no longer be profitably
leased by the state. In the receipts and accounts of this period
the term φόρος προβάτων is applied to the income of these great
landholders from the flocks of sheep and herds of goats which
were leased to their tenants. The owners of such vast estates
leased their cattle in a manner similar to, and on a scale almost
comparable to, the leases made by the state in the previous

centuries. After having practically usurped the function of the state the landholders employed the terminology which had formerly been used only of the revenue of the government from its leases of cattle.[14]

Φόροι paid on other types of domestic animals are more rarely attested.[15] According to the definition of φόρος on animals given above, the φόρος ὀρνίθων should be a rent paid for some variety (or varieties) of fowls leased from the state. The φόρος ὀρνίθων is mentioned in three documents, from Polydeucia in the Arsinoite nome dated A.D. 227, 228, and 230.[16] In those years payments were made by the elders of the village[17] of 135 drachmae, 136 drachmae, and 135 drachmae 2 obols respectively. These ὄρνιθες may have been, or may have included, geese, for the raising of geese was widespread in Egypt, where those who tended geese were formed into guilds;[18] and, moreover, a φόρος χηνῶν is attested for the Ptolemaic period, when the geese were evidently leased from the crown.[19] The payment for φόρος ὀρνίθων in each receipt follows a payment for φόρος προβάτων. In BGU. I. 25 is recorded a payment of φόρος βοῶν.[20] In this document the collectors of money-taxes at Socnopaei Nesus report to the strategus their receipt of 400 drachmae on account of the φόρος βοῶν and of 100 drachmae for the φόρος γενῶν ζωγρ(αφικῶν).[21] Since the craft of the painters at Socnopaei Nesus was probably carried on in connexion with the temple, it is suggested that the φόρος βοῶν was collected from the priests of the temple who were required to pay a φόρος for the use of cattle claimed as the property of the state and therefore subject to lease.

A difficulty with this theory of the lease of domestic animals by the state is the fact that there has not been found any lease, or application for lease, of animals which were certainly the property of the state.[22] There is, moreover, very little evidence to indicate how the government kept account of δημόσια κτήνη (public cattle) when leased. P. Hamb. 34 (A.D. 159–60) is a report addressed to the strategus and the basilico-grammateus from the πρεσβύτεροι προβατοκτηνοτρόφων (elders of the herdsmen) of Euhemeria. A total of 819 sheep and goats is reported, and this is followed by a list of individuals and the number of sheep and goats in the possession of each. Such a report doubtless supplemented the records of leases made to individual members of the guild of herdsmen. That the state did possess the necessary records is demonstrated by PO. IV. 807, dated about A.D. 1, which is a fragment of an official list of sheep and goats in the possession of different persons in a village. The total for the village is given as 4,241 sheep and 336 goats, of which 240 are declared to be Ἀρσινοῆς φορικά. The explanation of the editors of the document is that 'the sheep which were Ἀρσινοῆς φορικά, as contrasted with those that were private property, seem to have been subject to a special impost (φόρος), payable nominally to Arsinoë (i.e. Arsinoë Philadelphus probably), but really of course to the State'.[23] A little more than 5 per cent. of the sheep[24] in one village (presumably in the Oxyrhynchite nome), therefore, had been leased from the government, while the remainder were private property. The large number of references to the φόρος προβάτων from the Arsinoite nome, in contrast to this isolated example from the Oxyrhynchite nome, may indicate that a larger proportion of the sheep in the Fayûm had been leased from the government, but there is no evidence from which any exact deduction may be made. SP. XXII. 81, dated in the third century after Christ, is the conclusion of a list of men with a statement of the number of camels in the possession of each. P. Lond. II. 443 (p. 78), dated in the second century after Christ, is a similar list of animals in the possession of a number of individuals; both full-grown animals and foals are included in this list. It is uncertain whether the document refers to camels or to asses, for the word πῶλοι, by which the foals are designated, may be used of either. Since the heading of each of these documents is lost, the occasion and purpose of their preparation is unknown.

We are much better informed in regard to the records of privately-owned live stock. Annual reports of such domestic animals were required from their owners. In P. Ross.-Georg. II. 13, an ἀπογραφὴ προβάτων (report of sheep) from the Oxyrhynchite nome, there is a reference to a second report, to be made during the same year, of the lambs which were expected. PO. II. 246 is such a supplementary report (δευτέρα ἀπογραφή); and PO. II. 297 is a letter from one Ammonius to his father, requesting him to send information for such a supplementary return of

lambs born since the first report of sheep had been dispatched
to the officials. All of these documents are from the Oxyrhynchite nome and all are dated in the reign of Nero. Since, however, extant returns from other districts of Egypt are rarely to be
dated in Nero's reign, it is uncertain whether the supplementary
return was a temporary or a local peculiarity, and whether the
supplementary return was confined to the reports of sheep.
Diodorus (I. 36, 6), to be sure, states that because of abundance
of pasture sheep in Egypt bore twice a year. If this were true, the
supplementary report would be expected regularly; but in this,
as in many other of his assertions, Diodorus's veracity is open
to question.

Ἀπογραφαὶ προβάτων

Official practice in Egypt followed Attic usage in restricting the meaning of πρόβατα to sheep. The returns of sheep
(ἀπογραφαὶ προβάτων), however, included goats and kids. These
returns are extant in considerable numbers from the Oxyrhynchite, Hermopolite, and Arsinoite nomes, and there is one from
the Heracleopolite nome and another from the Athribitic nome.[25]
They range in date from A.D. 8–9 to 237 or 238. The form was
probably established in the Ptolemaic period or under the administration of Augustus, for the returns exhibit but slight differences that may be attributed to chronological development
during more than two centuries or to local variance.

The majority of the ἀπογραφαὶ προβάτων from the Oxyrhynchite nome are addressed to the strategus. Of the exceptions two
are addressed to the topogrammateus, and the supplementary report (δευτέρα ἀπογραφή) was addressed to the strategus, the basilico-grammateus, and the recorders of the nome (τοῖς γράφουσι τὸν
νόμον). All of the returns from the Hermopolite nome were
addressed to the strategus, while those from the Arsinoite nome
were sent to the strategus, or to the strategus and the basilico-
grammateus. Oddly enough, each of the reports from the Heracleopolite nome and the Athribitic nome is addressed to the
basilico-grammateus only. These addresses indicate that the
chief officers of the financial administration of the nome were
responsible for obtaining information necessary for the collection of the tax assessed on sheep and goats, just as they were

responsible for other taxes. The address on these returns is occasionally preceded by a summary account of the animals reported, e.g. in PO. 1.74 dated A.D. 116, there is written in the first hand Πρό(βατα) ιϛ αἰγ(α) α ἄρν(ας) ϛ, and the address to the strategus is in the second hand; on the verso of this document is the statement: ιθ (ἔτους) ἀπογρα(φὴ) προβ(άτων) ιϛ, αἰγ(ὸς) α ἀρν(ῶν) γ.[26]

In the body of the return the owner of the sheep refers to his report of the previous year (unless he is making such a report for the first time because he has not owned sheep or goats previously), for the animals then reported must be accounted for in the new ἀπογραφή. The lambs of the previous year, if they survived, appear as sheep in the current report, so that it is evident that if lambs were exempt from taxation their exemption did not last for more than a year. Losses by death or other disaster, such as theft, or a statement of sale with the name of the vendee had to be recorded. When the number of sheep and goats was established for the current year, there followed a statement of the district where the sheep were ordinarily pastured; but in addition there was ordinarily a statement that the sheep were pastured throughout the nome, which was an important privilege.[27] The next item of information to be furnished was the name and the address of the shepherd. The latter was seldom the owner of the flock reported, and in fact several flocks belonging to different owners might be under the care of one professional shepherd.[28] The purpose of the ἀπογραφαὶ προβάτων is revealed in the statement in regard to the animals ὧν καὶ ταξόμεθα τὸ καθῆκον τέλος (or ἐννόμιον), and τὸ καθῆκον τέλος seems to indicate a single tax.[29] The usual oath by the emperor[30] is followed by the date of the submission of the document. This date, except for the supplementary return dated in Epeiph (June–July), falls on one of the first five days of Mecheir (January 26–30), when reports of all animals were ordinarily due.

The dockets of the officials indicate that when a return was addressed only to the strategus it might be submitted to other interested offices also. In PSI. 1. 56, for example, the first docket is that of the πράκτωρ ἀργυρικῶν through his secretary, the second that of the basilico-grammateus, and the third is that of the strategus to whom the document is formally addressed. In

P. Cornell 15 the docket of the βιβλιοφύλαξ is included with those of the strategus and the basilico-grammateus. In PO. II. 245 the docket of the toparch is appended to a return addressed to the strategus. The dockets of these officials merely indicate that the number of sheep or goats was duly recorded in their bureaux on a given date and do not, as do the dockets subtended to the returns of camels,[31] state that a representative of the bureau has checked the number of animals against the information in the return.

To test the accuracy of the returns annually made by owners a census of sheep, goats, camels, and other animals (ἐξαρίθμησις προβ(άτων) κ(αὶ) [α]ἰγῶν κ(αὶ) καμήλων κ(αὶ) ἄλλων) was conducted within a nome by the strategus, the basilico-grammateus, and a third member of the commission normally appointed from another nome by the epistrategus. If the epistrategus, for any reason, failed to make an appointment, the third member was selected by the strategus and might be from the strategus's own nome.[32] It is uncertain whether these censuses of animals occurred every year. The extant reports of such ἐξαριθμήσεις are dated about A.D. 156, 159, and 203.[33] In addition returns of camels dated in A.D. 146 and 216–17 refer to the ἐξαρίθμησις of the previous year; but it is unsafe to conclude that these references are necessarily to the census conducted by the commission of three, since P. Lond. II. 328 (p. 75), an ἀπογραφὴ καμήλων dated in A.D. 163, is labelled καμήλ(ων) ἐξαρίθ(μησις), so that the term ἐξαρίθμησις seems to be used to designate the document usually termed ἀπογραφή or to denote simply the owner's count of his camels for his return (ἀπογραφή). It is possible that, like the land-survey, the census of animals was conducted only when deemed necessary because of inadequacy of the returns of the owners or when fraud was suspected by the officials. In any case it is unlikely that the census was intended to include every animal in the nome, but it would rather be limited to suspected districts of the nome. This conclusion is supported by the date of the receipt issued by the keepers of the public records of the Hermopolite nome to the commissioner appointed from Oxyrhynchus which acknowledges the deposit of the enumeration of animals for the year.[34] The receipt is dated in Mecheir, which must mean that the census had been completed within less than a month after the filing of the returns of the animals by their owners: a thorough census must have required longer. A draft of a report on such a census of live stock states that the commissioners proceeded to the middle toparchy of the Oxyrhynchite nome, in accordance with the instructions of the strategus, in Mecheir and found in the locality (ἐπ(ὶ τῶ)ν τόπων) no animals; neither were any animals presented for enumeration.[35] Since it is unlikely that there were no privately owned sheep, goats, or other domestic animals in the entire middle toparchy of the Oxyrhynchite nome, it may be concluded that ἐπὶ τῶν τόπων designated a specific locality or localities within the toparchy which had attracted the attention of the bureaux concerned in the administration of taxation, because no returns of live stock had been received from them. It is evident from this report that the strategus did not go in person to make the census of live stock, but sent one or more representatives to act for him, and the mention of βοηθοί indicates that the commission was supplied with assistants who would have been indispensible if the census was at all extensive.[36] P. Lond. II. 376 (p. 77), an official report of the commission,[37] is dated on the 20th of Mecheir and is a report on the camels and colts of a single individual. This document, too, supports the theory that the census of live stock was held only when and where it was deemed necessary to test the accuracy of the owners' returns. It is not impossible, however, that towards the end of the second century or the beginning of the third century it became necessary to hold the census annually, since the gradual increase of economic distress may have greatly increased irregularities in the owners' returns.

A unique document is PO. II. 244, dated in A.D. 23, which is a report addressed to the strategus by one Cerinthus, slave of Antonia the wife of Drusus,[38] stating his intention of transferring his sheep and goats to the Cynopolite nome, which was opposite the Oxyrhynchite nome, and requesting that the strategus of the former nome be notified of the transfer. Since Antonia possessed an estate (οὐσία) in Egypt[39] it is probable that the sheep and goats were actually her property, and the report of Cerinthus uses the phrase ἃ ἔχω of them. Although Antonia, as a member of the imperial family, may have had exceptional privileges in regard to taxation, it is evident from this document that such a transfer had to be reported in order to keep the records of both nomes in order.

The Tax on Sheep

The tax for the collection of which the ἀπογραφαὶ προβάτων were required is usually referred to, in these documents, as τὸ καθῆκον τέλος (the due or fixed tax), and the term καθῆκον was applied to it in contrast to the variable rate of the φόρος προβάτων. In P. Amh. II. 73. 7, however, which is an ἀπογραφὴ προβάτων from the Hermopolite nome dated in A.D. 129–30, the owner in making the report states that he had sold 47 sheep to a certain Selene who is paying the ἐννόμιον (pasture-fee). From this single occurrence of the word in a return of sheep it has been concluded that the ἐννόμιον is to be identified with τὸ καθῆκον τέλος.[40] It is obvious that the name ἐννόμιον was applied to the tax because payment of it gave the owner of sheep and goats licence to pasture the animals on any available domain land within the nome, a right which is noted in the statement of the ἀπογραφαί that the sheep or goats are pastured in a certain district *and throughout all the nome* (πρόβατα ἃ νεμήσεται δι᾽ ὅλου τοῦ νομοῦ).[41] The ἐννόμιον is attested in documents from the Arsinoite, Hermopolite, and Mendesian nomes.[42] All of these nomes are in Lower Egypt, but it is unlikely that the tax, or even the name ἐννόμιον, was confined to that part of Egypt in the Roman period, since the term ἐννόμιον is found in ostraca of the Ptolemaic period from Thebes.[43] This same tax, indeed, is probably indicated by the payment ὑπὲρ νομῶν in WO. II. 244, a receipt from Syene dated in the reign of Antoninus, which states that 8 drachmae were paid on 6 sheep, a rate of 1 drachma 2 obols each.[44] In P. Lond. III. 1171 (p. 177), lines 14–31, a farm account from Lower Egypt dated 8 B.C., appears a payment of 720 drachmae for ἐννόμιον, with which is combined a payment of 66 drachmae for ἀριθμητικόν. The sum of these two payments amounts to 786 drachmae (corrected by the editors from the 796 drachmae of the papyrus), and this is but two drachmae less than the sum of a tax of 1 drachma 2 obols each on the 566 sheep and 25 goats which the account subsequently states to have been left in the pasture (ἐν ἀγρῷ).[45] This may be sheer coincidence, but it is tempting to assume that the ἀριθμητικόν in the Augustan period was an assessment for the expense of the ἐξαρίθμησις of sheep and other animals, which has been mentioned above, and that in the later period the charge for ἐννόμιον absorbed the smaller fee for ἀριθμητικόν which, in fact, does not appear again in connexion with the tax on sheep and goats.[46] If this assumption is correct, and the rate of 1 drachma 2 obols for each sheep and goat was assessed in the Arsinoite nome as well as in Elephantine-Syene, the payment of 71 drachmae 5 obols for ἐννόμιον in BGU. VII. 1599 may be explained as 66 drachmae 4 obols for ἐννόμιον on 50 sheep (at 1 drachma 2 obols a head) plus 4 drachmae 1 obol for προσδιαγραφόμενα plus 1 drachma for σύμβολον (receipt);[47] other payments may be explained in a similar fashion.[48]

As has been stated above,[49] the name ἐννόμιον was given to the tax on sheep and goats because the licence to find pasture for the animals throughout the whole nome was the most striking characteristic of the tax. It is not at all certain, however, that the ἐννόμιον was originally assessed merely as payment for that privilege.[50] A more consistent theory of taxation suggests that the tax was originally paid for an annual licence to keep sheep and goats, and that it was paid by private owners as contrasted with those who leased such animals from the crown, and finally that the right of pasture was an incidental, although very important, privilege.[51] Consequently the tax called τέλος προβάτων in receipts of the Ptolemaic period from Upper Egypt[52] may well be identified with the ἐννόμιον. Similarly the payment in WO. II. 1369, dated A.D. 10, designated simply as προβάτων, is probably for the tax corresponding to the ἐννόμιον of Lower Egypt and ὑπέρ νομῶν of Syene, and not for the φόρος προβάτων as Wilcken thought,[53] since the amount of the tax is not given but only the number of sheep (i.e. fifteen), which indicates that the rate of the tax was perfectly known to payer and to payee, which would not normally be the case with the φόρος προβάτων, whose rate would hardly be uniform for sheep of different value. Moveover, the payment made in wheat for προβάτω(ν), in *Archiv*, VI, p. 134, no. 13, an ostracon from Tentyra dated A.D. 29, is likewise rather for the tax (ἐννόμιον) than for the φόρος προβάτων, since the probable value of $\frac{7}{12}$

artaba of wheat is nearer to the rate of the tax on one or two sheep than to the rent of even a single sheep.[54]

Ἀπογραφαὶ καμήλων

Animals other than sheep and goats had to be reported by their owners. Of such reports the ἀπογραφαὶ καμήλων are the most numerous. In the Ptolemaic period, at least in Upper Egypt, camels seem to have been in private possession, for there are extant receipts for ἐννόμιον καμήλων which record payments as high as 3,000 drachmae.[55] These receipts are the occasion of some surprise, for the camel is not let out to graze as are sheep and goats, because when kept in pasture it can carry no profitable load. In the Roman period, with the possible exception of P. Hamb. 40,[56] there is no evidence for the ἐννόμιον καμήλων. Indeed, until the second century after Christ there is little evidence that camels were private property. The earliest ἀπο-γραφὴ καμήλων which can be definitely dated is from the year A.D. 136, and the records of sales of camels are all later.[57] Because of the exigencies of the grain transport and because of the profits to be derived from the monopoly of the transport by caravan to the oases and to the Red Sea ports, the government may have maintained a monopoly of the ownership of camels for a time in Egypt. When this monopoly was no longer advantageous it was given up, and thereafter extant returns of camels made by the owners are found from A.D. 136 (or earlier) to 216–17. Of thirty-one ἀπογραφαὶ καμήλων[58] one (BGU. I. 153) is from the village of Dionysias, another (BGU. VII. 1582) is from the city of Arsinoë, one or two are from Caranis, and the rest are from Socnopaei Nesus, the beginning of an important caravan route. It may be possible to account for the scarcity of returns of camels outside Socnopaei Nesus by the supposition that the numerous camels employed in the transport of grain[59] were for the most part δημόσιοι κάμηλοι, still the property of the government.

The ἀπογραφὴ καμήλων was similar in form to the ἀπογραφὴ προβάτων. It was addressed to the same officials, and similar also were the contents including the reference to the report of the previous year, the enumeration of additions to the herd or of its decrease by death or by sale. The dockets, however, are fuller, for they summarize the reports of representatives of the various bureaux who state that they have made a count of the animals reported. It is quite possible that the camels had to be brought, at the time when the ἀπογραφή was filed, to some designated place where the representatives of the strategus, the basilico-grammateus, and the third commissioner from another nome (παρὰ ξένου)[60] could make a check of the number of animals reported. Among the reports of camels are a few which contain the statement of the owner that he is making a report for the first time, and there are other returns which state that, although camels had been reported in the previous year, the owner has disposed of his animals and consequently has none to report for the current year.[61] In P. Lond. II. 328 (p. 75) the owner, although he may have been excused from paying the tax on the animal for the year, reports among his other camels one that had been requisitioned by the government for use on the caravan route from Berenice, the port on the Red Sea, to Coptos.[62] Similarly in BGU. I. 266 an owner declares that one of his camels has been requisitioned for the expedition of Caracalla to Syria. In BGU. III. 762 a camel is said to have been requisitioned for the transport of a porphyry column.

Τέλεσμα καμήλων

The tax on camels (τέλεσμα (or τέλος) καμήλων) is attested from A.D. 141 to 216.[63] In the Arsinoite nome the sums, or the total of the instalments, paid for the tax are always equal to multiples of 10 drachmae. It has therefore been assumed that the tax paid for each camel was 10 drachmae a year.[64] The careful distinction between colts (πῶλοι) and grown camels (τέλειοι κάμηλοι) in the ἀπογραφαὶ καμήλων may indicate that colts were not subject to the tax. Although a colt, at the present time, does not receive its training for service in the caravan until it is four years old, there is no certainty that in the Roman period colts were exempt from taxation for so long a period. In most returns the πῶλοι of the previous year are numbered among the τέλειοι κάμηλοι of the year of the report.[65] The fact that the tax was collected at a uniform rate indicates that it was a licence-tax rather than an ad valorem tax on property, for camels were held at different prices.[66] Προσδιαγραφόμενα at $\frac{1}{16}$ and σύμβολον were sometimes recorded on receipts for the tax which was ordinarily paid in the year when it was due.[67]

P. Lond. II. 468 (p. 81) is a list of payments made by various persons for the τέλος καμήλ(ων). The amounts are very irregular: 11 drachmae (thrice); 5 drachmae 4 obols; 6 drachmae; 2 drachmae (twice); 1 drachma (twice). One payment of 11 drachmae is designated φό(ρος) (δεύτερος), a 'second instalment'.[68] These payments may well be instalments, but inasmuch as it is not known that the provenience of the document is the Arsinoite nome, the total sums on which they are paid are not necessarily multiples of 10 drachmae, and the rate of the tax on camels outside the Fayûm may perhaps not have been 10 drachmae a head. In any case, the instalments recorded in this document are quite different from those found in receipts for τέλεσμα καμήλων from the Arsinoite nome.

Ἀπογραφαὶ ὄνων

The scarcity of ἀπογραφαὶ ὄνων is difficult to explain, for documents not concerned with taxation (such as farm accounts, bills of sale, and the like) indicate that there were large numbers of privately owned donkeys.[69] It is possible that not all of these donkeys were subject to taxation, or perhaps the records of donkeys subject to taxation were ordinarily maintained in some way other than by means of returns made by owners.

Unlike the returns of sheep and goats and of camels, which were addressed to the strategus, the basilico-grammateus, or related officials, the extant ἀπογραφαὶ ὄνων were sent directly to the collectors of the tax on donkeys. In PO. XII. 1457, presumably from the Oxyrhynchite nome and dated 4–3 B.C., these collectors are called οἱ ἐξειληφότες τὴν ἐξαδραχμίαν τῶν ὄνων. The report is of two female asses which were kept at the residence of the owner and were employed in his private business. Unlike the ἀπογραφαί previously considered, this return was filed in the month Tybi. In PSI. VII. 785, from the Hermopolite nome and dated A.D. 93, the editors have restored the title of the officials to whom the return was addressed as οἱ [ἐξειληφότες τὸ τέλος τῶν] ὄνω(ν).[70] This return was made by a tenant or servant of the owner who possessed three female asses and two colts, one male and one female. It is also stated that the owner's son possessed one female ass, which was not hired out but was kept for private use. The place of residence of the person making the return is given, and this is followed by the date, this time in Mecheir as usual. SB. 4516, dated in A.D. 119–20 but of unknown provenience, is a report of donkeys used only for the private business of the owner. It is addressed to οἱ ἐξειληφότες, but a τελώνης εἴδους ὄνων is also mentioned in the document, which unfortunately has not yet been fully published. There seems to be no obvious reason why the ἀπογραφαὶ ὄνων are addressed to the collectors of the tax on donkeys rather than to the officials of the financial administration of the nome as are the ἀπογραφαί of other animals.[71]

Taxes on Donkeys and Horses

The tax on donkeys in PO. XII. 1457 (dated 4–3 B.C.) is called ἑξαδραχμία, which implies an annual rate of 6 drachmae for each of these animals, although the amount actually paid was 5 drachmae 1 obol. In a receipt from Caranis dated A.D. 112–13 (BGU. I. 213) a payment of 8 drachmae is recorded for a δίπλωμα ὄνων for one donkey; the only other payment attested for this tax in the Arsinoite nome is 4 obols, which is obviously an instalment.[72] If the editors of PSI. VII. 785 have correctly restored the title of the collectors of the tax on donkeys in the Hermopolite nome, the tax was there called τέλος τῶν ὄνων. In P. Hamb. 9, from Theadelphia and dated A.D. 143–6, the ἐγλήμπ(τωρ) ὄνων νομοῦ καὶ ἄλλων ὠνῶν (collector of (the tax on) donkeys for the nome and of other contracts) gives a receipt for 8 drachmae 8 obols for the tax on each of three horses.[73] A payment of 8 drachmae 8 obols represents an increase of one-sixth over the payment of 8 drachmae for one donkey cited above, but this slight difference in the rates suggests the possibility that the rates for horse and for donkey were the same, and that the rate for both had been raised from 8 drachmae to 8 drachmae 8 obols between A.D. 112–13 and 143. In fact, so far as the evidence considered up to this point is concerned, it would appear entirely possible that the three different names for imposts on donkeys in the Oxyrhynchite, Arsinoite, and Hermopolite nomes represent that same tax, and that donkeys (like sheep and camels), when privately owned, were subject to one tax only. In the great tax-rolls from Caranis in the collection of the University of Michigan, however, appear payments of 5 drachmae for εʃ ὄνων ... ἀπεργασίας. This seems to be a commutation for the services of donkeys on the dikes (or similar labour). This is not unnatural, for BGU. III. 969 states that it was customary for the owner of donkeys to give the use of them for five days, or else to measure into the government's granary a supply of grain of value equivalent to five days' work. It is known from P. Ryl. II. 195 that a payment of money might be made instead of a payment of grain, but in this document 8 drachmae were paid for πενθημ(έρου) ὄνων. The payments at Caranis, however, seem to give a new name for a tax on donkeys, namely (πενταδραχμία) ὄνων, although a δίπλωμα ὄνων at 8 drachmae is attested for Caranis in BGU. I. 213. Nevertheless, the 8 drachmae at Caranis for δίπλωμα ὄνων is the same amount that was paid for πενθη-μ(έρου) ὄνων in P. Ryl. II. 195. Also the 5 drachmae paid at Caranis for εʃ ὄνων ἀπεργασίας is but an obol less than the amount paid for ἑξαδραχμία ὄνων in PO. XII. 1457. It is difficult to avoid the conclusion that, in spite of the variation in names and even in amounts paid, these taxes on donkeys (and horses) were once the same and were possibly at one time assessed at a uniform rate throughout Egypt.[74] The term δίπλωμα in receipts from the Arsinoite nome implies a licence-tax, but it is not impossible that the δίπλωμα merely stated that the payment of 5 or 8 drachmae exempted the donkey from service in the corvée. There are several points, even supposing this theory to be true, which are not clear. Male and female asses were carefully distinguished in the ἀπογραφαὶ ὄνων, whereas this distinction is only occasionally observed in the returns of sheep and goats and of camels. It is possible that the rate on male asses was higher or lower than that on female asses, or perhaps one of these classes was not liable to taxation or to service in the corvée. Again, donkeys employed in the private business of the owner were carefully differentiated from those which were hired out to others. Perhaps only the latter donkeys were subject to the licence-tax (δίπλωμα ὄνων), if this is not to be identified with the payment for exemption from the corvée (πενθημ(έρου) ὄνων), or the rates for the two classes may have differed. The latter hypothesis would account for the two rates of 5 and 8 drachmae (or 8 drachmae 8 obols). The scarcity of receipts for the tax on donkeys prevents the drawing of positive conclusions in regard to the nature of the licence-tax or to the possibility of difference in rates; but, like the scarcity of the ἀπογραφαὶ ὄνων, it suggests that the majority of donkeys privately owned may not have been subject to taxation, probably because the owners preferred to give their services to the state for the five days' corvée. If this is true it is probable that by the absence of taxation the government encouraged the private ownership of donkeys, for such animals could be requisitioned for government transport when needed.[75]

The Τοκαδεία and the Tax on Pigs

References to the τοκαδεία are found in documents from the Mendesian nome and possibly in an ostracon from Upper Egypt.[76] In P. Ryl. II. 213 the τοκαδεία, the ἐννόμιον, and the ὑϊκή form a class of taxes designated by the ambiguous term εἴδη.[77] It is undisputed that the assessment for τοκαδεία refers to animals, as do the ἐννόμιον and the ὑϊκή. There are no ἀπογραφαί, however, to indicate precisely what animals were subject to the τοκαδεία. In classical Greek the term τόκας, from which τοκαδεία was derived, might be applied to anything having the power of generation, but in the papyri its use seems to be confined to pigs and to fowls.[78] The editors of P. Ryl. II. 213. 9 n. believed that the τοκαδεία referred to an impost on fowls and suggested that it was some kind of licence-tax. This licence-tax would then correspond to the φόρος ὀρνίθων, as does the ἐννόμιον to the φόρος προβάτων.[79] The existing evidence, however, does not yield any information concerning the rate of such a tax, which naturally must have been low, or to its incidence.

P. M. Meyer,[80] on the other hand, proposed to correlate the τοκαδεία with the ὑϊκή and supposed that the former referred to a tax on sows as opposed to a tax on boars. There is no indication of any difference of rates or principles of taxation between male and female animals in the payments for the ἐννόμιον or for the τέλεσμα καμήλων, and there is no proof of such a distinction in the payments of the tax on donkeys, so that Meyer's theory is not supported by analogy. In Chapter IX I shall attempt to demonstrate that the ὑϊκή (pig-tax) in the Arsinoite, Oxyrhynchite, and Hermopolite nomes was not a licence- or property-tax, but a capitation tax (μερισμός). It is not at all certain, however, that the εἶδος (or εἴδη) ὑϊκῆς in the Mendesian nome was a capitation tax.[81] In WO. II. 1031, from Thebes and dated A.D. 31, a τελώνης ὑϊκῆς gives to a woman a receipt for the τέλος δελφακίδος μιᾶς (tax for one young pig). This is the only published evidence for the ὑϊκή in Upper Egypt during the Roman period. Although it might be possible to explain this receipt as a payment of a sales-tax, Wilcken is probably correct in explaining it as a licence-tax[82] whose rate, since well known to payer and payee, is not stated in the receipt.

In the Ptolemaic period ἀπογραφαί of pigs indicate that the tax on those animals was a licence- or property-tax. In the period of Roman administration in Egypt such returns are extant only from the Pharbaithitic nome.[83] These ἀπογραφαί are addressed to the strategus and are of usual form. In one of them pigs belonging to several persons are reported; in another the statement is made that the pigs are being raised for the market in a neighbouring village; in the third the pigs are intended for the εὐθηνία of the city of Alexandria. Although all of these returns were made in the year 187-8 A.D. there is no indication that they were required for some extraordinary census of pigs or of live stock in general. It is probable that the method of reporting the possession of pigs had, in the Pharbaithitic nome, continued without much change from the Ptolemaic period. It is also probable that the tax on pigs in that nome was a licence-tax similar to taxes on sheep and camels in the Arsinoite nome.

At Thebes, in the Pharbaithitic nome, and possibly in the Mendesian nome the tax on pigs seems to have been a licence-tax whose rate and incidence, however, are unknown. This tax would correspond to the φόρος ὑῶν, the rent paid for pigs leased from the government but which is attested only for the Ptolemaic period.[84] The existence of such a tax offers no support to Meyer's attempt to connect the τοκαδεία with the ὑϊκή, but until decisive evidence is available his theory cannot be left out of account.

From the preceding discussion we may safely draw the conclusion that taxes on sheep and goats and on camels were assessed within a given nome at a uniform rate on each type of animal. The same was probably true also of the tax on donkeys and horses. Such taxes are to be regarded as licence-taxes or fees rather than property-taxes. It is true that the fee paid for a sheep was less than that on a camel, and that the amount paid was roughly proportional to the value of each. This proportional difference of rate is, however, to be explained rather as the result of the government's effort to exact the largest possible revenue from these fees on animals than as an attempt to collect some percentage of the average value of a camel or of a sheep. Evidence for the study of the development of private ownership of animals in the Ptolemaic period is even less satisfactory than that for tracing the gradual growth of private ownership of land; but there is nothing in the available documents inconsistent with the theory that these developments were parallel, and that the uniform fees exacted on animals corresponded to the fixed taxes (καθήκοντα) on catoecic and other private grain-land, whose rates were determined by the terms of the original grant from the king to his subject without respect to the productive value of the land, whereas the φόροι were paid on animals leased from the government and may be compared with the ἐκφόρια paid by the tenants on domain land whose rental varied with the value of the land. It is also probable that just as in the third century after Christ the domain land began to pass into the large private estates, so animals which had belonged to the government became the property of the great landholders. It is probable that it had become unprofitable to lease these animals during the period of economic decline in the third century, and that the transfer to private ownership was made in an effort to derive some revenue from them. Because evidence for taxation in this period is so slight, it is impossible to determine precisely how far the treasury was benefited by this change.

VII

THE CENSUS IN ROMAN EGYPT

THE primary purpose of the census in Roman Egypt was the numbering of the population for the efficient collection of taxes. The Egyptian census differed, therefore, from the census taken in most of the modern nations, since the purpose of the census as developed in the last two centuries has been to ascertain the exact number and character of the population of a country for the guidance of its government in determining national policy. I have elsewhere stated my belief that the census was established in Egypt by Ptolemy IV Philopator in order to exact the maximum of taxes when he introduced the poll-tax at the beginning of his reign.[1] The continuation of the poll-tax by the Romans and the increasing importance of capitation taxes as a source of revenue for the efficient administration of the country made the collection of exact information in regard to the population liable to the payment of these taxes a matter of greatest importance to the Roman officials in charge of the province. There are many more documents relating to the census preserved from the Roman than from the Ptolemaic period; hence much more is known about the details of the census under the Romans. But such information as can be derived from the extant Ptolemaic documents indicates that the representatives of the Roman emperor continued the system of taking the census substantially as it had been established and developed by their Ptolemaic predecessors.

The Fourteen Years' Cycle

Unlike the quinquennial census at Rome, the census in Egypt was taken at intervals of fourteen years. This fourteen years' cycle for the census in Egypt was recognized by Wilcken, Viereck, and Kenyon after the publication of the census returns among the Berlin papyri.[2] Further publications have yielded returns from a large number of the nomes of Egypt, and all have confirmed the fourteen years' cycle.[3] No published return can be dated with certainty before the census of the year A.D. 19–20. PO. II. 256, however, according to its editors, is to be dated either in A.D. 6 or 20, or possibly in 34 or 35. In the last lines the document refers to some one as previously enrolled: . .] . προγεγρα(μμεν . .) προαπογραφον τρ εγ[. . . . &c. It is unfortunate that the fragmentary condition of the lines does not admit of a sure restoration and interpretation of these words or of certainty as to the person to whom they refer. In any case, however, if this return is to be dated in A.D. 6, as is likely, it would indicate the existence of the census in 10–9 B.C. Grenfell and Hunt collected the evidence in regard to the census in Egypt under Augustus in the introduction to PO. II. 254. Their discussion maintained that the cycle of fourteen years could not be carried back beyond 10–9 B.C. Consequently they believed that this period of fourteen years was established by the Roman administration under Augustus, and they were willing to admit the possibility of Sir William Ramsay's theory of the connexion of this census of 10–9 B.C. in Egypt with the census which, according to Luke ii. 1–4, was introduced throughout the empire for the first time just before the birth of Christ.[4]

If, however, the fourteen years' cycle was established under the Ptolemies, the first Egyptian census under Roman supervision would have occurred fourteen years before 10–9 B.C., in 24–3, six years after Egypt became a Roman province. There is perhaps confirmation of the existence of this earlier census in PO. IV. 711, dated about 14 B.C. Its last lines refer, as the editors say, 'to a wrong entry in a previous list of some persons "as having . . . before the 6th year". This', the editors continue, 'is too vague to be of much use; but the 6th year (of Augustus, 25–24 B.C.) would seem to be a recognized landmark in the history of the census or of the poll-tax, and some important step in the reorganization of the system may possibly have then been made. The 6th year, however, does not fall in the fourteen years' cycle, being one year too early.' But if any important change or reorganization of the census or of the poll-tax was to be made in Egypt by the representatives of Augustus, it would naturally have been announced in the year before the census was taken, in order that there might be sufficient time to carry out the changes throughout the province.[5] Hence this document may well confirm the existence of a census in 24–23 B.C. The lines, however, are too fragmentary to give any evidence as to the nature of the changes introduced. This is especially unfortunate because there is little evidence in regard to changes in the census during the reign of Augustus. The census in Egypt in 10–9 B.C. probably had no more relation to the census being taken in Judaea at the time of the birth of Christ than the Egyptian census of A.D. 5–6 or 19–20 had to the census which, according to Tacitus, *Annales*, I. 31. 2 and 33. 1, was being supervised by Germanicus in Gaul in A.D. 14.

The Berlin papyri and the papyri from other collections, which have been published subsequently, have yielded returns from every census from A.D. 20 to 258, except that of the year A.D. 62, and there are references to the census of that year in P. Lond. II. 260 (p. 42) and 261 (p. 53). There are no published extant returns later than A.D. 258. It might be supposed that the lack of census returns in the latter half of the third century was merely one of the accidents of survival, were it not that the applications for ἐπίκρισις, examination of a boy for admission into the class of privileged persons who paid poll-tax at a lower rate, are not found after A.D. 250.[6] The disappearance of these two types of related documents indicates a change in the administration of the census. It is possible that a change was introduced by the emperor Aurelian in A.D. 272, when the first census after A.D. 258 would normally have occurred. Kase has shown that the fifteen-year indiction cycle was introduced in A.D. 314–15 and made to date from A.D. 312.[7] The five-year indiction cycle, which Kase believes to have been in use in Egypt before 312, was perhaps introduced in 272 by Aurelian.

The Census Returns

The extant census returns are fairly uniform throughout most of Egypt, although they vary in minor details of expression. Those from the Memphite nome, however, show a considerable variation from the usual type, and the early returns from the Oxyrhynchite and Arsinoite nomes show a less highly developed formula than that of the later returns.[8] The census in Egypt, as in Rome,[9] was taken by houses. The return was called an ἀπογραφή, or more specifically ἀπογραφὴ κατ᾽ οἰκίαν.[10] This was a written report concerning the inhabitants of a dwelling made by the owner of the house. If the owner of the house lived in it, he reported himself and all the other inhabitants of the house. If, however, the owner did not live in the house for which he was making the report, he listed only the tenants of the house, and the document was then called a γραφὴ ἐνοικίων.[11] The only exceptions to this method are found in returns from the Memphite nome, where the tenant made the return for his own family, and in a similar return from Heptacomia.[12] The return made by a tenant in the Memphite nome contained a statement by the landlord that the latter assumed responsibility for the payment of capitation taxes by his tenants.

The owner of a house was obliged to submit copies of his census return to various officials concerned with the census. Ἀπογραφαὶ κατ' οἰκίαν were addressed to the στρατηγός, the official in charge of the financial administration of the nome, to the βασιλικὸς γραμματεύς, the royal scribe who was the assistant of the strategus, to the κωμογραμματεύς, the clerk of the village, and to the λαογράφοι,[13] who were local officials whose sole concern seems to have been the census and the poll-tax. In the capital cities of the nomes the returns were sent to the two μητροπόλεως γραμματεῖς instead of to a comogrammateus and also to the ἀμφοδάρχης or ἀμφοδογραμματεύς[14] who was in charge of the records of a single section of the city. In addition to a copy for each of these bureaux,[15] the owner of the house had to keep for himself one or more copies, which were to receive the dockets of the various officials certifying that a copy of the return had been deposited with each of the bureaux represented in the dockets.[16] This multiplication of copies of the census return was a heavy expense to the landlord, who was obliged to purchase from five to ten sheets of papyrus for these reports and to hire the services of a scribe to draw up the return and to make the several copies. It is probable that the strategus and the basilico-grammateus or their deputies made a circuit of the various villages or districts of the nome in order to facilitate the collection of the returns for their bureaux and to write the required dockets.[17] Such a circuit would have been of advantage to those who made returns, for they would not have to make the trip into the metropolis, which was at a considerable distance from many of the villages. It would also have prevented overwhelming the bureaux with a great mass of returns brought in from many districts at one time: this was important, since the census must have been a very heavy burden upon the bureaux in addition to their ordinary duties.

The extant ἀπογραφαὶ κατ' οἰκίαν may be divided into the following parts:[18]

First, the address to the officials concerned with the census who have been briefly noted above. These officials vary somewhat according to the provenience of the documents. In the Oxyrhynchite nome returns from the rural districts were sent to the τοπογραμματεῖς as well as to the comogrammateus.[19] A return from Oxyrhynchus[20] and one from Hermopolis Magna[21] are addressed to γράμματεῖς πόλεως instead of the more usual μητροπόλεως γραμματεῖς, but this distinction is not important, as is shown by the fact that a return from Arsinoë is addressed to the γραμματεῖς μητροπόλεως, but the officials who appear in the docket sign themselves as γραμματεῖς πόλεως.[22] In returns from Hermopolis Magna[23] the amphodogrammateus appears in place of the amphodarch addressed in the returns from Arsinoë. The two extant returns[24] from Antinoöpolis, whose foundation was late and whose system of government was unique, are addressed to a board of three men from one tribe (φυλή) who were chosen by the council (βουλή) to superintend the census in one district of the city; these men may have corresponded more or less to the λαογράφοι found in the addresses of the ἀπογραφαὶ κατ' οἰκίαν from the Arsinoite nome and elsewhere. It is probable that at Antinoöpolis, as elsewhere in Egypt, copies of these ἀπογραφαί were sent to other bureaux.

The name and local residence of the owner of the house follow the address to the officials. The local residence is designated more exactly when the owner of the house lived in a city than when his home was in a village. The large population in the city made it necessary to give 'street and number' (ἀναγραφόμενος ἐπὶ τοῦ . . . ἀμφόδου). The local address of the owner might be different from the address of the house for which he was making the return as landlord. If the house-owner was a priest or belonged to a similarly privileged class of society he stated that fact.[25] Returns were not always made by the actual owner of a house. If the owner was a minor, the return was made by his guardian.[26] A φροντιστής, or even a slave, in the absence of the owner might make the return.[27] If the house was the property of a woman, she made the return μετὰ κυρίου, that is, with her husband or, if the latter was dead or divorced, her legal guardian; or she might make the return διὰ φροντιστοῦ.[28] Husband and wife make a joint return in P. Lond. III. 946 (p. 31), dated A.D. 230, from Hermopolis Magna. Three brothers make a return in SB. 7460, dated A.D. 142, from Thelbonthon Siphtha in the Prosopite nome.

After the formula of the census returns had become fixed, that is, after the beginning of the second half of the first century, the person making a return stated next that he was doing so in pursuance of the decree of the prefect authorizing the ἀπογραφὴ κατ' οἰκίαν, which had been promulgated in the same or the preceding year.[29] The prefect was directly responsible for the census. Philo implies that the most important duty of the prefect of Egypt was the care of the revenues;[30] it was logical that the census, which provided the information upon which the collection of the capitation taxes was dependent, should have been directly under his charge. The significance of the fact that the census returns from the Arsinoite and Oxyrhynchite nomes and from several other nomes are dated in the year following the decree of the prefect has not been explained. Returns from some of the nomes were made in the same year as the decree of the prefect. Returns from Memphis, Hermopolis Magna, and the village of Ancyra are sometimes dated in the same year and sometimes in the year following the decree. If the direct superintendence of the prefect or of his deputy was required during the taking of the census in every nome of Egypt, it is possible that the census required two years for its completion. But the inconsistency of the returns from the three cities named above makes difficult the assumption of a circuit of the prefect to superintend the census. The solution of the problem requires additional evidence.

The census return proper begins with a description of the house and a statement of its ownership. It was necessary to state the location of the property and to give a general description of the house.[31] Where joint ownership existed through inheritance or purchase, it was necessary to state that the return was being made for the joint owners or to state the fraction of the house owned by the person making the return.[32]

Next in the return come the names and descriptions of the inhabitants of the house. If it is the residence of the owner, the report of his own family usually comes first in this section.[33] With the possible exception of returns from Memphis,[34] the complete household is always reported. The description of the members of the family includes the parentage of the husband and of the wife, and the parentage of the children if the father or mother had been married more than once. The ages of all are given together with their physical descriptions,[35] and in the second century a statement as to the occupation, if any, accompanies each name.[36] Men and women are reported separately in some of the returns from the Oxyrhynchite nome, which was doubtless an attempt to simplify the work of making up tax-lists in the bureaux, since only men were required to pay capitation taxes. Change of residence and deaths are usually recorded.[37] If children had been born since the last census, it is stated whether their births had or had not been included in the registration of births.[38] Slaves are similarly recorded,[39] usually after the members of the family. If relatives lived in the same house their precise relationship to the householder is made clear, e.g. husbands of married daughters, grandchildren, and so forth. If a relative had moved in during the interval after the previous census, the change in residence is made evident. Tenants are grouped by families, with the members of the family and their slaves reported in the same manner as the household of the owner of the house. In the returns from the Memphite nome the statement of the landlord that he will be responsible for the capitation taxes of his tenants follows the list of tenants.[40]

If the householder or any member of his family owned other property this is briefly described with a statement as to whether it was tenanted or empty.[41]

The oath of the owner of the house that his report is true forms the close of his return. The oath varies in different localities: in the Oxyrhynchite nome it is a solemn affirmation by the emperor or is the ὅρκος Ῥωμαίοις ἔθιμος; elsewhere it is by the Τύχη of the emperor. The oath is omitted only in the return from Thelbonthon Siphtha[42] and in one of uncertain provenience of the year A.D. 160.[43] An interesting feature of certain of these oaths is the sworn statement of the landlord that there is in his house no Roman citizen nor citizen of Alexandria.[44] Roman and Alexandrian citizenship seems to have bestowed exemption from capitation-taxes,[45] and those who enjoyed such a privilege were apparently not subject to the ordinary census. It is probable that, when a false ἀπογραφή had been made and suspicion of this had led the officials to make an investigation as to the number of residents in the house, the wily landlord had accounted for some of the extra inhabitants by saying that they were Roman or Alexandrian citizens; and if the suspected persons were conveniently absent at the time, it would have been exceedingly difficult for the officials to ascertain the facts. This provision in the oath would put a stop to such sharp practice. Since the census return furnished to the government the information upon which the tax-lists were made up and was the evidence for the determination of the privileged or unprivileged status of the taxpayer, it was inevitable that attempts to make false returns should have appeared among the hundreds of thousands of ἀπογραφαί made at each census. Severe penalties were provided against such falsifications. The section of the Gnomon of the Idiologus[46] covering these penalties is fortunately preserved. Sections 58 to 63, inclusive, may be translated as follows:

> Those persons who have not reported in the census returns by houses both themselves and those whom they are required to report are to be penalized one-fourth (of their property); and if it is revealed that they have not been reported in two census returns, they are to be fined one-fourth.[47]
>
> Romans and Alexandrians who have not reported those whom they are required to report, whether one or more, are to be fined one-fourth.
>
> Those who have not reported a slave are to be deprived only of their slaves.
>
> The offspring of slaves, who have not been reported, are to be given to their masters, if the latter have no property besides the slaves.
>
> Those serving in the army and not reported in the census are not to be arrested, but their wives and children are to be held to account.
>
> Those who are held to account because they did not report themselves in the previous census, are to be pardoned if the correction is made within three years.

After the oath comes the final statement of the householder, διὸ ἐπιδίδωμι or ἐπιδίδομεν. In SP. ii, p. 27, the similar statement of a μέτοχος of the house is also recorded. Sometimes the signature of one or more persons, apparently witnesses, is added.[48]

The deposition of the scribe, who declares that he has drawn up the document for an unlettered householder, follows. It is not necessary to believe that the householder was in every case entirely illiterate: it was more practical to obtain the services of a scribe to draw up the elaborate return than to run the risk of penalty for an improper return.

The last item of the return is the date. The problem raised by the frequent dating of the census return in the year following the year of the census as decreed by the prefect has been noted above. It is interesting further to observe that the householder often put off to the end of the year the task of making his return.[49]

The docket or dockets of the officials to whom the return is addressed appear, on such copies as were to be retained by the householder,[50] at the end of the document. There is but one exception to this rule: P. Hamb. 7 has the docket of the comogrammateus at the very beginning of the document, just above the address to that official; this is the only extant return from the nome Berenice Trogodytice and is dated A.D. 132.

The Bureaux

The duplication of records caused by the filing of the census returns in four or five different bureaux must have been a heavy expense to the administration of Egypt, but it shows how carefully the officials watched the census to collect information for all types of taxation and for other purposes, and to prevent fraud and connivance with the populace on the part of the lower officials. The receipt of the ἀπογραφαί was but the beginning of the work of the bureaux in regard to the census. The returns from the various householders were received in the bureaux and were then joined together and numbered consecutively. From the rolls thus composed of ἀπογραφαὶ κατ᾽ οἰκίαν there were compiled by the clerks in the bureaux abridgements which are found among the extant papyri.[51] Similar documents are preserved from their Ptolemaic predecessors.[52] Copies of the ἀπογραφαί κατ' οἰκίαν or at least of the abridgements made from them were also preserved in the archives of the nome (δημοσία βιβλιοθήκη or βιβλιοθήκη τῶν δημοσίων).[53] These documents in the archives of the nome were used as a basis for the assessment of taxes and were also kept for reference in case of disputes as to succession of property, claims for privileged civic status, and similar cases.[54]

From the briefs in the bureaux and in the archives of the nome were compiled the lists of those liable to the poll-tax. Separate lists were probably required for the other capitation-taxes, but we do not know whether this was the case at all times in all parts of Egypt. The census rolls and tax-lists had to be kept up to date by the bureaux. Hence it was necessary that new lists should be compiled every year in order that all those attaining the age of liability to taxation during that year should be included in the tax-lists.

Men became liable to the payment of poll-tax at the age of fourteen years. It was because of this that the census was taken every fourteen years. There were three sources of information accessible to the officials whose business it was to enter the names of the fourteen-year-old youths among the tax-payers: the record of the last census, the reports of the birth of children (ὑπομνήματα ἐπιγεννήσεως) sent in by their parents, and the records of the ἐπίκρισις.[55] These last two sources of information seem ordinarily to have applied only to the privileged classes, for the frequent report in the census returns of the unprivileged that their children below the age of fourteen had not been recorded in the registration of births (μὴ ἀναγεγραμμένος ἐν ἐπιγεγενημένοις),[56] and the converse statement that the birth of children of the privileged had been recorded,[57] implies that notices of the birth of children were ordinarily sent in only by the parents who belonged to a privileged class in order to secure the same privileges for their children; this is confirmed by the extant birth-notices.[58]

The removal of names from the tax-lists was an equally important duty. Those who had left the country had to be noted. Reports of these were sent in by members of their families or other interested persons,[59] at least after the establishment of the μερισμὸς ἀνακεχωρηκότων, a capitation assessment to take care of the loss of revenue suffered because of the defaulters who had fled from their homes.[60] The amount collected as the μερισμὸς

ἀνακεχωρηκότων depended upon the number who had de-
faulted; hence the clerks had to keep an accurate check on the
census list, and this may be the reason why the reports of those
who had left the country were apparently sent in annually.[61] It
was necessary also for local officials to compile a list of those
who were resident in their village or district but whose place of
enrolment (ἰδία = origo).was elsewhere.[62] P. Cornell I. 22 is
such a roster kept by the officials of Philadelphia early in the first
century.

Similarly, those who obtained temporary or permanent exemption from capitation taxes because of appointment to high office[63]
or for some other reason, such as a grant of Roman citizenship
by the favour of the emperor,[64] had to be recorded in the files
of the various bureaux concerned with the census or the collection of capitation taxes.

Those who had died during the past year had also to be noted
in the records in the bureaux.[65] Notices of the death were sent
in by members of the family of the deceased to the basilico-
grammateus and to the comogrammateus, or instead of the latter
to the secretaries of the metropolis and to the amphodogrammateus.[66] The notice requested that the deceased be enrolled
among the dead[67] and that his name be stricken from the tax-
lists, if he was liable to payment of taxes. The statement that
all the taxes of the deceased had been paid is sometimes added.[68]
If the deceased was a priest a notice of the death was sent to the
ἡγούμενοι ἱερέων, or if he was a member of a guild subject to
taxes on trades a notice was sent to the collector of the tax.[69]
The copies of the notices sent to the basilico-grammateus usually
have a docket of that official which directs the comogrammateus
or the secretaries of the metropolis to make an investigation of
the facts and, if the report of the death is true, to take the customary steps, which means, of course, to make the necessary
changes in the official records.[70]

Men became exempt from the payment of capitation-taxes in
Egypt, or at least in Lower Egypt where were found all the
documents affording evidence on this point, in their old age.
There is no satisfactory evidence in regard to exemption from
taxation in Upper Egypt, and because of the difference between
the administration of taxes in Upper and Lower Egypt it is un-

wise to assume that an age of exemption which applied to Lower Egypt necessarily applied to the rest of the country. When Wilcken published his *Griechishe Ostraka*[71] he supposed that the testimony of Ulpian[72] as to the ages of liability and immunity to payment of poll-tax in Syria could be applied to Egypt. Ulpian states that men in Syria were liable to payment of poll-tax from fourteen to sixty-five years of age, and women from twelve to sixty-five years of age. Kenyon's publication of the documents relating to census and taxation in P. Lond. II showed that women did not pay the poll-tax and that the age of immunity was less than sixty-five years. But Kenyon's own conclusion that the age of immunity was sixty years must be modified in the light of evidence accumulating from the later publications of tax documents.

Kenyon observed that in a long list of tax-payers in P. Lond. II. 257–9 (pp. 21 ff.), from Arsinoë and dated in A.D. 94, no person is included whose age exceeds sixty years; stating that this can hardly be an accident, he concluded that the age of exemption was sixty years. To support his conclusion he called attention to the phrase, in line 64 of P. Lond. II. 259, $\dot{v}\pi\epsilon\rho$ τ⊙ Lξa ϵ. But this very phrase is the key to the age of exemption, which was sixty-two years at the time of this document, A.D. 94. Eighty-five years later the age of exemption had not changed. In SP. XXII. 93. 12, from Socnopaei Nesus and dated A.D. 179, a man is described as $\dot{v}\pi\epsilon\rho\epsilon\tau\dot{\eta}s$ $\pi\epsilon\pi\lambda\eta\rho\omega\kappa\dot{\omega}s$ $\tau\hat{\omega}$ $\dot{\epsilon}\nu\epsilon\sigma\tau\hat{\omega}\tau\iota$ $\iota\theta$ ($\ddot{\epsilon}\tau\epsilon\iota$) $\ddot{\epsilon}\tau\eta$ $\xi\beta$. A man who has completed his sixty-second year is, as we say, sixty-two years old, or as P. Lond. II. 259. 64 expresses it 'over sixty-one years' of age. In SP. IV, pp. 62 ff., lines 564 ff., men sixty-three years of age are added to the number of $\dot{v}\pi\epsilon\rho\epsilon\tau\epsilon\hat{\iota}s$ from the $\dot{\epsilon}\lambda\dot{a}\sigma\sigma\omega\mu a$ of the preceding year. The $\dot{\epsilon}\lambda\dot{a}\sigma\sigma\omega\mu a$ was the legal reduction of taxes as assessed by the financial officials of the nome. The year that a man reached sixty-two years of age his name appeared in the $\dot{\epsilon}\lambda\dot{a}\sigma\sigma\omega\mu a$ submitted by the local official, if the old man's claim to exemption was upheld. After his right to appear among the names in the $\dot{\epsilon}\lambda\dot{a}\sigma\sigma\omega\mu a$ had been sustained, his name was transferred to the roll of the $\dot{v}\pi\epsilon\rho\epsilon\tau\epsilon\hat{\iota}s$ in the following year, and he was no longer counted among the tax-liable inhabitants when the assessments of his village or amphodon were next fixed by the authorities. It is important to note that a man was not exempt until he had actually passed his sixty-second birthday.

So, in P. Princeton I. 8 vii. l, from Philadelphia and dated A.D. 27–32, a man pays the full tax called συντάξιμον and the pig-tax, although his age is given as sixty-two years. The simplest explanation is that the tax was due before this tax-payer had reached sixty-two, the age of exemption, but he delayed making the payment until after his sixty-second birthday. The fact that the payment was made on the twelfth day of Epeiph, the next to the last month of the year, increases the probability of this explanation. It is unlikely that the age of exemption had not been established by A.D. 27–32, since a mutilated document of the reign of Augustus seems to indicate that in 4 B.C. the age of exemption was sixty years.[73] If the age of exemption was sixty years in 4 B.C., it had been raised to sixty-two years, presumably by A.D. 27–32, and certainly by A.D. 72–3, the date of SP. IV, pp. 62 ff., cited above. It apparently continued at sixty-two years as late as A.D. 179.

It is possible that the age of exemption was raised after the reign of Commodus. In SP. xx. 40, from the Arsinoite nome, we have apparently a list of the citizens of the metropolis who paid the poll-tax at the rate of 20 drachmae per annum. Among the payments (column ii. 5) is one from a man whose age is given as sixty-four years. Upon the evidence of the hand this document is dated by Wessely at the beginning of the second century. If this dating is correct the tax-payer was being subjected to extortion, since the age of exemption at Socnopaei Nesus in the Arsinoite nome was sixty-two years as late as A.D. 179. But it is possible that the date of this document should be placed at the end of the second century or the beginning of the third century, for dating by the style of writing is very uncertain in the second and third centuries. If the document is to be dated in the late second or early third century, it is not likely that this is a case of extortion. It is hardly probable that a record of unjust exaction would be left upon the official report of the collector of the tax, which could have been used as evidence against the collector on a charge of extortion. It is more probable that the age of exemption had been raised in order to secure additional revenue.[74] The age limit may have been raised to sixty-five years, which was the age of exemption in Syria in the time of Ulpian, who died in A.D. 228.

Before the man of sixty-two could be included among the ὑπερετεῖς he probably had to present proof that he had actually attained the age of exemption.[75] Reference to an epicrisis occurs in a passage in P. Lond. II. 258 (p. 38, lines 69 ff.) immediately after the mention of the [ι]γL Lξα οἳ εἰς τὸ ιδL [. . .]; the mutilated condition of these lines does not permit restoration, but the reference is probably to an epicrisis of the claims of men to be included among those classified as ὑπερετεῖς Lξα, that is, sixty-two years of age or older. What proofs had to be submitted is not definitely known, but, as in the epicrisis of youths, records abstracted from the returns of previous censuses should have sufficed.

The Epicrisis

Wessely's opinion that epicrisis meant an examination to determine the civic status of any person, of either sex, slave or free, of any age, conducted by accredited representatives of the government, is now almost universally accepted.[76]

Roman citizens and their families and slaves underwent an epicrisis before the prefect or his representative. The purpose of this examination was in many cases military, but in all cases the result was a permanent record of the proof of Roman citizenship which entitled the holder of it to exemption from payment of poll-tax in Egypt.[77]

The most important epicrisis and the one concerning which we have most information, because of the large number of documents preserved, was the examination of youths applying for admission into the privileged class of tax-payers.[78]

It has long been known that the Romans exacted the poll-tax from different classes of the inhabitants of Egypt at different rates.[79] In this the Romans probably followed Ptolemaic precedent.[80] All Roman citizens, the citizens of Alexandria, and a limited number of priests were certainly entirely exempt from the payment of poll-tax; it has been supposed that the catoeci also were exempt from the poll-tax.[81] Within the remaining populace there were recognized two classes paying at different rates. The Greek inhabitants of the metropoleis in the nomes of

Lower Egypt were assessed poll-tax at a lower rate than the inhabitants of the villages and the country-side. The right of the privileged citizens of the metropolis was an inherited one, and in order to prevent a large increase in the number of privileged citizens, the government hedged about this desirable status with strict regulations. The privileged in the Arsinoite nome were called μητροπολῖται or οἱ ἀπὸ τῆς μητροπόλεως, in the Oxyrhynchite nome μητροπολῖται δωδεκάδραχμοι, in the Hermopolite nome μητροπολῖται ὀκτάδραχμοι.[82]

At the order of the prefect, boys who were eligible for admission to the privileged class were required to present themselves for examination. These boys had previously been registered by their parents by means of birth-notices.[83] Formal applications had to be made by the father or guardian of the boy to the officials in charge of the epicrisis. This application contained a statement of the grounds upon which the application was made: both parents had to belong by descent to the class of οἱ ἀπὸ τῆς μητροπόλεως (this did not mean that the mother paid poll-tax at a lower rate, but that her father had belonged to the privileged class); reference was made to the boy's birth-notice and to his record in the last census, if he had been born then. PSI. x. 1109 gives the report of a φροντιστής who had searched the records for proof that a boy was entitled to become a μητροπολίτης. The father presented the documentary evidence of his son's inherited right at the epicrisis. Witnesses (γνωστῆρες) could probably be called if necessary, as in the similar examination for entrance of youths into the gymnasium.[84] The officials who made the decision were called ἐπικριταί and were, in the Oxyrhynchite nome, apparently identical with the βιβλιοφύλακες who were in charge of the records which would furnish evidence upon which the final decision could be made; these petitions were also addressed to the officials in charge of the census (except the λαογράφοι) and to the gymnasiarchs. In the Arsinoite nome one or more ex-gymnasiarchs were appointed ἐπικριταί. If the examination was sustained, the boy entered the privileged class of persons who are often called ἐπικεκριμένοι, in contrast to the unprivileged λαογραφούμενοι.[85] So far as we know, the decision of the ἐπικριταί was final. It is probable that a boy automatically reverted to the class of λαογραφούμενοι, if he was absent from the epicrisis held at the duly appointed time.[86] In case of absolute error appeal probably could be made to the basilico-grammateus, as in the case of a catoecus who had not yet come up for epicrisis but had nevertheless been enrolled among the λαογραφούμενοι, and whose claims were subjected to a special inquiry (ἐξέτασις) and were upheld.[87] Once admitted to the ranks of the μητροπολῖται a citizen probably retained this privilege of a lower rate of poll-tax no matter where he might live subsequently.[88] Conversely we may assume that no change of residence could improve the status of those who had not inherited the privilege of metropolitan citizenship.

Applications were also made for the epicrisis of slaves to determine their civic status.[89] Slaves of the male sex had to pay poll-tax, or rather their masters had to pay it for them. It would have been a heavy burden for a μητροπολίτης with a large number of male slaves if he had to pay the full rate for all his slaves. As a favour to the μητροπολῖται and to the other privileged classes, the rate of poll-tax paid for the slave depended upon the status of his master. The proof of the privileged status of the master alone was sufficient to sustain the epicrisis of a slave, and in some instances the evidence offered for one slave consisted simply in showing that another of the master's slaves had sustained the epicrisis and enjoyed the lower rate of poll-tax. Freedmen or freedwomen could transmit their privileged status to their children.[90]

Jews also were required to undergo an examination called epicrisis, but for a far different purpose. Beginning in the reign of Vespasian the Jews, both male and female, were required to pay a special tax called the 'Ιουδαίων τέλεσμα. Consequently the Jews had to submit to an epicrisis in infancy to determine when they should begin the payment of this tax, and again in old age to ascertain when they had reached the age of exemption which was sixty-two years.[91]

It will be readily understood that it was necessary for the bureaux concerned with the census to keep full records regarding the status of the μητροπολῖται in order to segregate them in the tax-lists. Copies of the documents relating to the epicrisis were certainly kept in the archives of the nomes. The epicrisis of youths ordinarily was held once a year. In the first year of

Nero a general epicrisis of the whole population was held as a proving of the civic status of all classes.[92]

The Amphodarch

Final responsibility for an accurate account of the population in a given district seems to have rested with the local official. In the villages this was the comogrammateus, in the cities the amphodarch, and the following observations in regard to the latter may probably be applied *mutatis mutandis* to the former. Wessely in SP. IV. (1905), pp. 58 ff., has published three parts of a great papyrus roll which contained the official report of the amphodarch of the ἄμφοδον Ἀπολλωνίου Παρεμβολῆς in the capital of the Arsinoite nome; two parts of the roll had been published by Kenyon as P. Lond. II. 260 and 261. The valuable information concerning the census, epicrisis, and poll-tax contained in it make this document a most useful source to which we shall turn many times, but in addition it gives a unique insight into the clerical duties of a local official. The three parts of the roll are all written in the same hand, presumably that of the amphodarch himself. The sheer amount of manual labour in the writing of the complete document with its many repetitions and recapitulations is astounding, especially when it is observed that the first column preserved is numbered thirty-one. Furthermore, it is recorded that most, if not all, of the document was represented by a copy sent to the office of the basilico-grammateus, and that part at least had likewise been duplicated in a report to the secretaries of the metropolis.[93] How much of this work had been independently duplicated in these offices from the notices of birth, death, epicrisis, &c., and how much these notices were used merely as a check on the accuracy of the amphodarch's report we do not know. If we multiply this report by all the amphoda in Arsinoë, and then remember that Arsinoë was but one of the hundreds of cities and villages in Egypt, we may get some idea of the gigantic bureaucracy which the Romans had taken over from the Ptolemies and had developed for their own uses.

The following account of this report is but little more than an expansion of Wessely's analysis. He has shown that the correct order of the fragments is P. Lond. II. 261, the Rainer fragment,

and P. Lond. II. 260. The first thirty-two columns contained
an account of the 385 men residing in the amphodon and the
amount of the poll-tax paid by them. Of the total number 330
paid at the rate of 20 drachmae a year, 3 at 40 drachmae, 5
(deceased) had paid one-half of the tax at the 20-drachma rate,
and 47 were exempt from the payment of poll-tax. This section
ends with the statement that a copy had been deposited with
the basilico-grammateus through his deputy, the δημόσιος βιβλιοφύλαξ.

From the second section of P. Lond. II. 261, which preserves
its heading in full, we learn the author of the document. To
whom this copy of the report was addressed we do not know;
it is possible that it was to be retained by the amphodarch,
although the formula is that of a report sent to a higher official: 'From Heraclides, amphodarch of Ἀπολλωνίου Παρεμβολή.
Register of minors, sons of men liable to payment of poll-tax,
of the year A.D. 72–3, reported as between two years and one
year of age in the census of the A.D. 61–2.' In the list which
follows the boys are initially divided by the years in which they
were born, but within each year there is a further division according to the year in which they were officially registered. Those
who had died are, of course, separately noted. The sons of
catoeci are listed separately, since their civic status was different
from that of the sons of the λαογραφούμενοι. The slaves are
listed separately, and a further distinction is made between the
slaves of the λαογραφούμενοι and the slaves of the catoeci. Column
15 is a supplementary report of those whose registration apparently occurred after the closing of the records. This preserved
portion of the report reaches sixteen columns before it breaks off.

The contents of the Rainer papyrus are more varied. It begins
with a list of slaves and freedmen of the amphodon. These
follow, as the tax assessment shows, the status of their masters
or mistresses, and they are accordingly differentiated. Column
4 contains the list of the Roman and Alexandrian citizens who
lived in the amphodon and who were tax-free. Column 5 lists
the slaves of two Alexandrian women, and column 6 gives the
names of these two women of Alexandria who had not been
included in the list of Roman and Alexandrian citizens, because
women did not pay poll-tax. This section ends with a statement

that copies had been deposited with the basilico-grammateus and the secretaries of the metropolis, and the date.

Columns 7–10 give an account of the taxes on trades, in this case on potters and weavers. There is an elaborate account of the effect on collection of taxes which had been produced by the fact that one potter had left the place (presumably to avoid payment of his taxes), whereupon his tax apparently had to be made up by the guild of potters; another potter had died, and his place was taken by another with the due adjustment of taxes. Κατακρίματα (fines) play a mysterious part in the report of these taxes on trades.

Columns 11 ff. contain the important and interesting section on the taxes of the Jews. With elaborate care the tax-liability of each Jew is stated, since liability to the 'Ιουδαίων τέλεσμα and to the poll-tax were not coincident.[94]

With column 14 begins a new topic, the list of aged and decrepit.[95] These persons are again treated in the section of the report dealing with ὑπερετεῖς in P. Lond. II. 260.

P. Lond. II. 260 contains in columns 1–5 a report on 173 male residents and their relation to the epicrisis. The starting-point is the epicrisis of the first year of Nero (A.D. 54–5). Whoever was fourteen years of age or more at that time is described in this list of A.D. 72–3 as ἐπικ(εκριμένος) πρώτῳ ἔτει. If one was fourteen years old after the first year of Nero, the year is noted in which he underwent ordinary epicrisis as a boy about to come of age at fourteen years and so liable to taxation. The census in the eighth year of Nero (A.D. 61–2) included an epicrisis of all males over ten years of age, and this epicrisis and also the year in which the younger persons reached their fourteenth year are noted. Those who at the time of the last census were not included, because they were not residing in the amphodon of 'Απολλωνίου Παρεμβολή, were designated as ἀναπόγραφοι; as ἀπαράστατοι were designated those whose entry into the lists had been made without their appearance; four persons are listed as ἀνεπίκριτοι, since their examination had not occurred, because at the time three were in Italy and one was in India.

Columns 6–13 offer a list of sons of catoeci who are thereby contrasted with the sons of λαογραφούμενοι in P. Lond. II. 261, col. 3 ff. The most interesting item concerns a lad whose registration was irregular, since he had been admitted to epicrisis for entrance into the class of catoeci, because his father had been made a catoecus after a victory, probably in the games at a festival.[96]

How much of the whole report of this amphodarch may have been lost is unknown. Forty-five columns are preserved and thirty are known to be lost. The whole with its duplicate copies was a prodigious work. It is no wonder that the offices of local secretaries were difficult to fill. If the other liturgies were as burdensome, we can readily understand why men chose to leave their property and flee from the country rather than stay to be ruined by undertaking an office in the city or village where they had lived and achieved sufficient means to become liable to liturgies.

THE POLL-TAX IN ROMAN EGYPT

IN the Roman period the poll-tax was called λαογραφία, that is, 'census-tax'. This word is not found in the Ptolemaic period as the name of a particular form of taxation. The reason for the introduction of this term for poll-tax is obscure. It may have been an official recognition of popular usage in applying the word for census to the poll-tax whose collection was based on the census. A close parallel would be the use of the word κῆνσος, a transliteration of the Latin *census*, in Matthew and Mark to denote the poll-tax in Judaea which is called φόρος by Luke.[1] Or the term may have been introduced by the Roman government to mark the change in the administration of the poll-tax after Egypt became a Roman province. There are more receipts for payment of λαογραφία extant than for any other tax paid in money.[2] Yet receipts for poll-tax have been preserved from only a few of the nomes of Egypt. This circumstance, however, is no reason for supposing that the tax was not universal throughout Egypt (except for the citizens of Alexandria). Census returns, which by chance have been preserved from parts of Egypt where no receipts for poll-tax have yet been found,[3] support the view that the tax was universal.

In my opinion the λαογραφία was imposed in the seventh year of the reign of Augustus as a reform of the poll-tax collected under the Ptolemies which was called σύνταξις. The earliest extant receipt for λαογραφία is dated in 22–21 B.C., two years after the census of 24–23 B.C., the probable date of the change in the tax.[4] We have but little information concerning the changes in the financial administration of Egypt introduced by Augustus, but it is probable that the most important change consisted in making the poll-tax more universally applicable among the inhabitants of Egypt. Before Egypt became a Roman province the Macedonian and Greek subjects of the Ptolemies held a favoured position in regard to taxation. It is clear from the epicrises that they retained some portion of their privileges during the period of Roman control. Nevertheless, in broadening the basis of taxa-

tion it is possible that Augustus compelled the descendants of the Graeco-Macedonian catoeci to pay a poll-tax.

Heretofore it has been generally supposed that the catoeci of the Roman period were exempt from the poll-tax. Kenyon, in the introduction to P. Lond. II. 260 (pp. 42 ff.), argued that the catoeci applied for epicrisis, and were thereafter called ἐπικεκριμένοι to distinguish them from the λαογραφούμενοι who paid the poll-tax, and were therefore free from the payment of poll-tax.[5] To confirm the argument he cited lines 124 ff. (of P. Lond. II. 260), 'where a boy is said to be transferred ἐνθάδε (i.e., to the list of κάτοικοι) ἀπὸ υἱῶν λαογραφουμένων ἐπὶ τῷ τὸν τούτου πατέρα ἀπὸ λαογραφίας κεχωρίσθαι διὰ τὸ ἐπικεκρίσθαι τῷ αL, and since the same boy is described, a few lines farther on (line 136), as υἱὸς κατοίκου, there is no doubt that his father, by this process of ἐπίκρισις, had become a full κάτοικος'. Kenyon's argument has been generally accepted.[6] There is in the same document, however, strong evidence against this view. In the Ptolemaic period λαογραφία did not mean poll-tax, but census, or more specifically 'the list of those liable to the payment of poll-tax'. The latter meaning was not lost in the Roman period, as Henne has demonstrated,[7] and it is probable that the meaning in the passage quoted above is not 'poll-tax', but 'the list of those paying poll-tax', i.e. the λαογραφούμενοι. Persons applying for entrance into the class of those who paid poll-tax at a lower rate in the Arsinoite nome made a formal application for epicrisis.[8] If they sustained the examination they were called ἐπικεκριμένοι. The lower rate of poll-tax in the Arsinoite nome was 20 drachmae a year. Yet the persons living in the amphodon of Ἀπολλωνίου Παρεμβολή who paid the tax at the rate of 20 drachmae are λαογραφούμενοι, since the boys listed in lines 28 ff. as sons of λαογραφούμενοι are far too many in number to be the offspring of the three men living in the amphodon who paid poll-tax at the rate of 40 drachmae a year.[9] Hence the 330 men who paid at the rate of 20 drachmae per annum, or at least a part of them, were called λαογραφούμενοι and yet they were certainly ἐπικεκριμένοι. In this apparent paradox may lie the explanation of the troublesome description of certain men listed in the ἀπογραφαὶ κατ' οἰκίαν as λαογραφούμενος ἐπικεκριμένος or λαογραφούμενος ἰδιώτης ἐπικεκριμένος : such a man is λαογραφούμενος, because he pays the poll-tax; but he is ἐπικεκριμένος, bcause he pays at the privileged rate granted to the citizens of the metropolis.[10] Consequently the fact that a catoecus is designated as ἐπικεκριμένος would not necessarily mean that he was exempt from the payment of poll-tax. What, then, was the advantage of being a catoecus? Bickermann has made a study of the different classes of inhabitants of Roman Egypt, and he identifies the catoeci with the men designated as οἱ ϛ̄ υοε ἐν ᾿Αρσινοείτῃ ῞Ελληνες and asks if they correspond to the class known as οἱ ἀπὸ γυμνασίου in the Oxyrhynchite and Hermopolite nomes.[11] I believe that they do correspond and that, just as οἱ ἀπὸ γυμνασίου in Oxyrhynchus were μητροπολῖται δωδεκάδραχμοι and in Hermopolis Magna were μητροπολῖται ὀκτάδραχμοι, the catoeci in the Arsinoite nome were μητροπολῖται and paid poll-tax at the rate of 20 drachmae a year. The distinction between οἱ ἀπὸ γυμνασίου and the μητροπολῖται in Oxyrhynchus was social and was connected with the privileges accruing from the ephebia.[12] I believe that the distinction between the catoeci and οἱ ἀπὸ τῆς μητροπόλεως in the Arsinoite nome was similar.[13] The catoeci of the amphodon of ᾿Απολλωνίου Παρεμβολή were not necessarily included among the 47 ἀτελεῖς mentioned in the summary in line 20 of the amphodarch's report. Those 47 men included 13 men exempt because of age (ὑπερετεῖς), a man who had just received Alexandrian citizenship, 2 Romans, and 3 slaves belonging to Alexandrian women, 19 in all.[14] The remaining 28 ἀτελεῖς may have included priests, officials, and other exempt persons whose descriptions were in the missing portion of the papyrus. I do not believe that they were catoeci.

There are two reasons for this disbelief. First, Nicanor, called Pappus, who was son of Heraclides and grandson of Heraclides, and whose mother was named Myrtis, received Alexandrian citizenship in the year 71-2 and was included in the ἐλάσσωμα of that year together with two men who had reached the age of sixty-two years.[15] He had previously been a 'catoecus of the 6475', as is stated in another part of this document.[16] If the catoeci paid no poll-tax and Nicanor had been a catoecus previous to the year A.D. 71-2, what was the purpose of including him in the ἐλάσσωμα with the new ὑπερετεῖς, when he became an Alexandrian citizen? Transfer from one tax-exempt class to

another should not give rise to an ἐλάσσωμα.[17] Second, sons
born to slaves of catoeci are included in the list of the sons of
the λαογραφούμενοι.[18] It is well known that the civic status of
slaves and freedmen and of their sons in respect to payment of
the poll-tax followed that of their masters.[19] If the catoeci paid
no poll-tax, why are the sons of their slaves listed with the sons
of the λαογραφούμενοι? In the Oxyrhynchite nome the slave of a
μητροπολίτης δωδεκάδραχμος could receive epicrisis for entrance
into the class of privileged taxpayers. There is nothing, however,
to indicate that the slave of a man of the gymnasium class (ἀπὸ
γυμνασίου) could apply for epicrisis for entrance into the gymnasium which was undoubtedly reserved for free-born Greeks;
but he could enjoy the privileges of his master in regard to
taxation. The slave of a catoecus in the Arsinoite nome could
not hope to become a catoecus, but he was qualified to enter
the class of the λαογραφούμενοι, who are evidently the same
as οἱ ἀπὸ τῆς μητροπόλεως of the Arsinoite nome who paid
poll-tax at the rate of 20 drachmae a year. If there was any
logical system of taxation in Egypt it follows that, if the sons
of the slaves of catoeci paid a poll-tax, the catoeci also paid
the tax.

Augustus also curtailed the privileges of the priests in regard
to the poll-tax, but not in the same fashion.[20] The priests of
Egypt had retained under the Ptolemies many of the privileges
which they had received from the Pharaohs; not only had they
enjoyed freedom from the exactions made upon the Egyptian
populace, but they had often made successful claims for support
by the state.[21] Under the Roman administration only a limited
number (usually fifty) of priests were exempt from the poll-tax.[22]
Those exempted were presumably confined to the higher orders
of priests, and perhaps to the priests of the most important
temples: those not exempted paid the poll-tax, or it was paid
for them by the temple.[23]

Roman citizens, of course, enjoyed complete exemption from
the poll-tax in Egypt. Citizens of Alexandria were exempt in
the Ptolemaic period, and their privileges seem to have been
continued by the Roman administration.[24] It is possible that the
privileges of the citizens of Alexandria in respect to the poll-tax
were abrogated after the massacre and the partial destruction

of the city by the soldiers of Caracalla,[25] but there is no evidence from this period to indicate their status.

Certain officials in Egypt ordinarily did not have to pay the poll-tax. PO. IX. 1210, dated in the reign of Augustus or of Tiberius, states that the basilico-grammateis of the Tentyrite and Cynopolite nomes, the topogrammateis and comogrammateis of the Oxyrhynchite and Cynopolite nomes, and the comogrammateis of the Oasis by the Oxyrhynchite nome were among those usually exempt. The same document, which was intended to give the total number of men in the Oxyrhynchite and Cynopolite nomes paying the poll-tax (the numbers were never written in), also has a space left for the number of men chosen by their parents from their sons to support them in their old age. Full or partial exemption from the poll-tax was allowed in the case of such men. Unfortunately there is no further information on this subject from later documents. Hunt suggests that these immunities of officials and of sons chosen for the support of their aged parents were an inheritance from the Ptolemaic régime. Some of these immunities may have been abolished by the successors of Augustus, since there is no evidence for them in later documents concerned with census or poll-tax.

'Ατέλεια, which presumably means exemption from taxes when applied to persons as it does when applied to land, was enjoyed by members of the world society of victors in the games, at least in the second and third centuries after Christ.[26] An official record of the society shows that privileges (δίκαια) of the society went back to the emperor Claudius or even earlier, but ἀτέλεια is not specified among these privileges, although it may have been included among them without being named. It is consequently impossible without further evidence to determine precisely when freedom from taxes was granted to members of the society.[27]

The scholars (φιλόσοφοι) of the museum in Alexandria, if they were not already exempt from poll-tax as Alexandrian citizens, also enjoyed ἀτέλεια.[28] Rhetoricians enjoyed partial, if not complete, freedom from poll-tax in the cities of Egypt, as is indicated by the special classification of a ῥητορικὸς δοῦλος in line 289 of SP. IV, pp. 62 ff.[29] The limitation of the privileges of rhetoricians established by Antoninus Pius at a later date presumably applied to Egypt.[30]

The receipts and other documents referring to the poll-tax indicate that there were considerable differences in the rate of assessment and in the method of collection of the λαογραφία between Upper and Lower Egypt and among the various nomes within those two divisions.[31] It has been necessary to refer to the special privileges of the Greek inhabitants of the capitals of the nomes of Lower Egypt in the discussion of the civic status of the catoeci above and also in the discussion of the census in Chapter VII.

The rate for the privileged μητροπολῖται in the Arsinoite nome was 20 drachmae. This is known from SP. IV, pp. 62 ff., which states that of the 385 men living in the amphodon of Ἀπολλωνίου Παρεμβολή 330 paid at the rate of 20 drachmae per annum. Receipts for λαογραφία found in considerable numbers in many parts of the Arsinoite nome show that an additional fee of 10 obols called προσδιαγραφόμενα was charged.[32] Why the receipts for payment of poll-tax at the rate accorded to citizens of the metropolis should be found in so many of the villages and towns of the nome is a puzzle. The majority of these receipts which preserve a local designation refer to some one of the amphoda at Arsinoë;[33] only seldom is a receipt for 20 drachmae found which is actually signed by the collectors of one of these villages.[34] We know that many persons were ἐπὶ ξένης, that is, living in a town other than their ἰδία,[35] and that these ἐπίξενοι paid poll-tax at the rate assessed at their ἰδία.[36] Yet the number of receipts (for the 20 drachmae rate) found in the villages seems very large. It is probable that citizenship in the metropolis could be merely nominal for those who had inherited it, and that μητροπολῖται could retain their citizenship, if they made the proper census returns, although they resided in one of the villages.[37] It may also be possible that the same rate of poll-tax enjoyed by the citizens of the metropolis was granted to certain inhabitants of the villages under circumstances as yet unknown.[38] Perhaps catoeci, who enjoyed the metropolitan rate, did not have to be residents of the metropolis.

Inhabitants of the Arsinoite nome who were not citizens of the metropolis paid poll-tax at the rate of 40 drachmae per annum.[39] This view has not always been accepted, because receipts for poll-tax with different amounts found in Tebtynis tended to obscure this fact.[40] Moreover, as Keyes has pointed out,[41] there are but few receipts for λαογραφία at the rate of 40 drachmae. SP. xx. 62, whose exact provenience is unknown, but which is undoubtedly from the Arsinoite nome and is dated late second or early third century, states that 146 ὁμόλογοι paid poll-tax at the rate of 40 drachmae,[42] together with certain minor taxes and additional charges. P. Ross.-Georg. iii. 24, from Philadelphia and dated between A.D. 198 and 211, is a receipt for 40 drachmae for λαογραφία. P. Bouriant 32, from Apias and dated early in the third century, has instalments for λαογραφία totalling 40 drachmae (or possibly 44 drachmae). A receipt in the collection in the Library of Princeton University (A.M. 8932 *verso*) records a payment of 44 drachmae made at Philadelphia in the second century; the payment may be for λαογραφία, although the reading is doubtful. P. Teb. ii. 635, dated in A.D. 180–92, amounts to about 40 drachmae. No other similar receipts have been found. On the other hand, as Keyes states, the publication of P. Princton i. 11, 12, and 14 and of P. Cornell i. 24 seemed to show a rate of 45 drachmae 2 obols for λαογραφία in the first century after Christ. P. Col. i R 2 shows rates of 44 drachmae 6 chalci[43] for a tax in Theadelphia in the second century, and a marginal note in the papyrus may mean that the tax was the λαογραφία.

The suggestion has been made by Wilcken and Kenyon that the tax called συντάξιμον, paid at the rate of 44 drachmae 6 chalci, which was found on a number of receipts from various parts of the Arsinoite nome, might be equivalent to the λαογραφία.[44] Keyes published in 1931 his careful study of the two taxes and presented strong arguments in favour of the identification of the συντάξιμον and the λαογραφία. But since the identification of the tax in P. Col. i. 1 R 2 as λαογραφία depends upon a marginal note απ( ) λαο( ) in the manuscript and not upon an official statement in the text of the document, there was room for the argument that the συντάξιμον was always paid at the rate of 44 drachmae 6 chalci, and that the λαογραφία was always 40 drachmae or 45 drachmae 2 obols (or 20 drachmae), and that the two could therefore hardly be the same tax.[45] The publication of PSI. x. 1133 in 1932, however, gives a receipt for συντάξιμον for the year A.D. 71–2 at the rate of 44 drachmae,[46] and for the following year at 45 drachmae 2 obols. This entirely confirms Keyes's argument for the identification of the two taxes.

Keyes explained the amount of the σύνταξιμον as 40 drachmae for λαογραφία, 4 drachmae for extra charges, the 2 chalci for an unknown purpose, and the ½ obol possibly for a receipt. In a note on O. Tait, p. 87, no. 79, published in 1930, Tait gives a much more ingenious solution of the relation between the σύνταξιμον and the λαογραφία. He suggests that the key to the σύνταξιμον lies in SP. xx. 62, where the amount paid by each ὁμόλογος is λαογραφία 40 dr. + προσδιαγραφόμενα 2½ dr. + συμβολικά 2½ ob. + ἁλική and συμβολικά 4½ ob.[47] + ἱερ( ) γεφ( ) and προσδιαγραφόμενα 2 ob. 6 ch. equals 44 dr. 6 ch., which is the usual payment for the σύνταξιμον in the receipts.[48] The σύνταξιμον, therefore, was a method of paying the extraordinarily high poll-tax of 40 drachmae (in the Arsinoite nome) plus certain minor taxes, which went to the central government of Egypt,[49] and the additional charges. The σύνταξιμον, I believe, received its name from the σύνταξις, the poll-tax of the Ptolemaic period, and means 'like the σύνταξις'.[50] The σύνταξιμον was occasionally paid in a lump sum, but more often it was paid in instalments of 4, 8, or 12 drachmae, if necessary in eleven monthly instalments of 4 drachmae each. The extra chalci were paid with any instalment, in Theadelphia usually with the first, in Philadelphia usually with the last. The records of payment of the σύνταξιμον were kept in ledgers, which have become more familiar since the publication of the Princeton papyri.[51] The official ledgers among the Princeton papyri show that the pig-tax called ὑϊκή was often paid with the σύνταξιμον, and the day-book of arrears (P. Princeton I. 1) shows that the pig-tax and the 6 chalci were often left in arrears at the end of the year, at least in Philadelphia. The pig-tax in the Arsinoite nome amounted to 1 drachma 1 obol,[52] which brought the total paid to 45 drachmae 1 obol 6 chalci. No συμβολικά or other additional charge is ever recorded for the pig-tax in the ledgers. Yet when the σύνταξιμον or λαογραφία is in arrears, the amount against each name is 45 drachmae 2 obols, which is 2 chalci more than the sum of the σύνταξιμον plus the pig-tax. The missing 2 chalci may be συμβολικά for the pig-tax, since 2 chalci is the amount charged for συμβολικά on ἁλική in SP. xx. 62.[53] The total amount of arrears, 45 drachmae and 2 obols, may have been posted in P. Cornell I. 24 to save book-keeping. If the full amount of delinquent taxes owed to the central government was posted it was easy to compute the total amount of arrears and to inform the taxpayer the amount of his arrears. Λαογραφία is thus used loosely to designate the total amount of taxes due to the central government, including the supplementary charges.[54] The pig-tax was kept separate from the συντάξιμον, except in accounts of arrears, because it belonged to the class of taxes known as εἴδη,[55] and, as P. Ryl. II. 213[56] shows, the εἴδη belonged to a department of the finances separate from the λαογραφία. It is possible that the 2 chalci were not recorded when the pig-tax was paid, because that tax was the last tax paid under the general head of λαογραφία, and it saved book-keeping to omit writing in a separate charge for the receipt; it was understood that the extra fee had been paid with the tax itself.

In all cases where the συντάξιμον is over 44 drachmae 6 chalci (or 45 drachmae 2 obols), e.g. 48 drachmae,[57] it is most likely that the payments include arrears. People did not habitually go about overpaying their taxes, nor did tax-collectors leave records of overpayment on their books to serve as evidence in prosecutions for extortion.[58]

There is one difficulty with the theory of the συντάξιμον as stated above. In the ledgers among the Princeton papyri and the Columbia papyri the total payment of the συντάξιμον (not including the pig-tax) is sometimes 44 drachmae 6 chalci and sometimes only 44 drachmae 2 chalci. This discrepancy was one of the problems for which Keyes was unabl to find a satisfactory solution in his theory, although he suggested that the ½ obol might have been the payment for a receipt which was optional. One-half obol seems to be too small a charge for a receipt for the whole συντάξιμον, but it may have been the charge for an optional receipt for ἁλική, which was included as a separate item in P. Lond. III. 1235 (p. 35), and ἱερ( ) γεφ( ).

It is interesting to note that the tax was not remitted if the tax-payer died.[59] If the death took place within the first five months of the year the estate of the deceased owed one-half, or approximately one-half, of the συντάξιμον. If the tax-payer died in the sixth month of the year he paid somewhat more, and if he died in the last half of the year the entire sum was due. There is no indication that the government made any return to the estates of those tax-payers who had paid their poll-tax in full and had died in the first half of the year, although the payment in full was obviously an overpayment. A member of the privileged class of tax-payers in the Arsinoite nome likewise paid one-half of the λαογραφία, if he died within the first five months of the year, as is shown by the collection of 50 drachmae credited to five men (in SP. IV, p. 70, line 394) who had died.

It is possible that the system of collection of the poll-tax called the συντάξιμον was abandoned at the end of the second century. As early as A.D. 180–92 there is a receipt for λαογραφία from Tebtynis totalling approximately 40 drachmae.[60] Two receipts for λαογραφία at 40 drachmae are known from the beginning of the third century, one from Apias and the other from Theadelphia.[61] A series of receipts from Tebtynis (O. Oslo 8–11) gives total payments of 44, or possibly 48, drachmae for λαογραφία in the nineteenth year of Septimius Severus (A.D. 210–11).[62] The only receipt for συντάξιμον which can certainly be dated after A.D. 174 is BGU. III. 791, col. i, which is probably to be dated in A.D. 205. But it is not entirely certain that this receipt is for συντάξιμον. It states that the payments are for συνταξ( ) of the town of Caranis, and these total 40 drachmae for one year, but there seems to be one payment missing. The second column of this papyrus continues with payments for the previous year which total 60 drachmae. Keyes notes that the payment in col. i for the year A.D. 204–5 is incomplete, and he states that there is no reason for supposing that the payments in col. ii refer to the συντάξιμον. The reason for thinking that the payments in the second column refer to the same tax as those of the first column is this: the payments in the second column continue exactly as if they referred to the same tax, for there is no statement of a different tax in the second column but merely a change in the year for which payments are made. It is possible that the receipts in both columns are for σύνταξις, payments for which are occasionally mentioned in the papyri of the Roman period.[63] Even if this receipt from Caranis is for συντάξιμον, it is possible that the συντάξιμον had been abandoned in Tebtynis, Apias, and

Theadelphia in favour of a direct collection of the λαογραφία at the rate of 40 drachmae; and it is also possible that the minor taxes had been remitted at the end of the second century as not worth the trouble of collection, for the regular imposition of the crown-tax in this period would more than have made up for the loss of that insignificant revenue.[64]

The privileged class in the Arsinoite nome paid λαογραφία at a rate half that of the unprivileged. It might be supposed that this proportion in the rates was the same in the other nomes of Lower Egypt, and this seems to be true in the Memphite nome. P. Flor. I. 12, dated A.D. 186–7 to 189, records the payment of 8 drachmae for λαογραφία in three successive years. P. Lond. III. 1216 (p. 34), dated A.D. 192, also is a receipt for 8 drachmae for this tax. This seems to be the privileged rate.[65]

The privileged rate in the Hermopolite nome is known from the applications for epicrisis for entrance into the class of μητρο-πολῖται ὀκτάδραχμοι[66] to have been the same as the rate deduced for Memphis, and this is confirmed by P. Ryl. II. 193 (A.D. 132–5), a receipt which records payments of 8 drachmae for λαογραφία during successive years. There is but one other receipt for λαογραφία from the Hermopolite nome, SB. 5677 (A.D. 222), and this shows a payment of 12 drachmae. This may or may not be the full amount of the tax for the year, since partial payments of poll-tax are common in other parts of Egypt, and the higher rate in the Hermopolite nome may have been 16 drachmae a year.[67] There is no proof, however, that the unprivileged rate of poll-tax was always twice that of the privileged, since this does not seem to be the case in the Oxyrhynchite nome.

The applications for epicrisis for entrance into the privileged class of μητροπολῖται at Oxyrhynchus show that their rate was 12 drachmae a year.[68] PO. II. 289, dated A.D. 65–82, given to a member of the privileged μητροπολῖται,[69] contains receipts for λαογραφία at the rate of 12 drachmae, regularly paid in two instalments of eight and four drachmae. PO. II. 288, dated A.D. 22–5, and referring to members of the same family as the preceding document, has receipts for ἐπικεφάλαιον at the rate of 12 drachmae a year, and the ἐπικεφάλαιον here is probably to be identified with the λαογραφία.[70] PO. II. 389, early first century after Christ, is an official account recording one payment of 12 drachmae for λαογραφία and also one of 16 drachmae. The latter sum may be the higher rate, since PO. II. 313 (A.D. 47) records instalments of 12 and 4 drachmae for λαογραφία. PO. XII. 1438, late second century, includes 16 drachmae for λαογραφία in a list of arrears, but arrears are frequently unsatisfactory in determining the rate of a tax. The other receipts are for instalments and are incomplete, and so are also unsatisfactory as evidence for the rate.[71] We may tentatively conclude that the higher rate for poll-tax in the Oxyrhynchite nome was 16 drachmae a year.

The λαογραφία is attested for the Mendesian nome in the totals of an account of taxation,[72] but I have not been able to deduce the rate from the various sums given; and it is hardly possible that the rate can be deduced, since the account seems to be one of arrears. In BGU. IV. 1198 a formal complaint is lodged that 16 drachmae annually had been illegally exacted for λαογραφία from each of four priests at Busiris in the Heracleopolite nome; the priests complain also of exactions for the dike-tax (χωματικόν); the document is dated in 5–4 B.C. With this rate of 16 drachmae should be compared the payment of 16 drachmae 4 obols for κατοίκων ἐπικεφάλαιον at Busiris and Bubastus in SP. xx. 67 verso (dated in the second or third century); but these towns may have been in the Fayûm, and the tax may be equivalent to the ἀριθμητικὸν κατοίκων rather than to the λαογραφία.

It appears that the rate of poll-tax at 40 drachmae for the unprivileged inhabitants of the Arsinoite nome was much higher than that of the tax-payers of the other nomes of Lower Egypt.[73] This is to be explained by the fact that the system of irrigation developed in the Fayûm by the Ptolemies had made it the richest agricultural district in Egypt, and the inhabitants were expected to pay a heavier poll-tax. Furthermore, the great number of Macedonians and Greeks settled in the Fayûm by the earlier Ptolemies had probably prevented the natives in the region from joining in the revolts in the reigns of Philopator, Epiphanes, and Soter II, which had as their object relief from oppressive taxation.[73] It is surprising, however, to discover that the favoured μητροπολῖται of the Arsinoite nome paid more than the unprivileged natives of the other nomes of Lower Egypt and much of Upper Egypt. The Arsinoite μητροπολῖται received some compensation in freedom from other capitation-taxes which were paid by the μητροπολῖται of other nomes of Lower Egypt.[74] No other taxes ever appear on the receipts for λαογραφία paid at the rate of 20 drachmae 10 obols, and no receipts for μερισμοί (assessments) can with certainty be assigned to Arsinoë. This does not absolutely prove that capitation taxes other than λαογραφία were never collected in the Arsinoite metropolis, but it shows that the citizens of Arsinoë did not ordinarily pay the pig-tax, dyke-tax, and guard-tax, commonly paid by the μητροπολῖται of the other nomes.

There is no real evidence for the existence of a privileged class of tax-payers in Upper Egypt.[75] As in Lower Egypt, however, the rate of assessment varied among the different towns in Upper Egypt and, surprisingly, among the various subdivisions of Thebes. There is no evidence for exemption from taxation because of old age in Upper Egypt. There were slight rises in the assessments for poll-tax at many of the towns of Upper Egypt, for which there is no parallel in Lower Egypt.

Ostraca bearing receipts for λαογραφία published since 1899, the date of Wilcken's *Griechische Ostraka*, have for the most part confirmed his conclusions in regard to the rates of assessment in the various sections of Upper Egypt. In addition the later publications have given information in regard to towns whose rates of taxation were unknown to Wilcken.

The rates established by Wilcken for Elephantine-Syene have been confirmed.[76] From A.D. 19 to 92–3 the λαογραφία was paid at the rate of 16 drachmae a year; from 96–7 to 112–13 at 17 drachmae; from 114–15 to 170–1 at 17½ drachmae, and if Tait's dating of O. Tait, p. 66, no. 21, is correct, the last rate continued to A.D. 194. Receipts from the other periods have not been found. A payment of ½ obol for δεσμοφυλακία was frequently included in the amount paid for poll-tax in this last period, so that the amount stated to be paid for λαογραφία is 17 drachmae 1 obol. This need not cause any difficulty, since in the receipts from Upper Egypt the payment for λαογραφία frequently includes a payment for another tax without mention of the name of the other tax. The poll-tax at Elephantine-Syene was frequently paid in two instalments, of which one was usually 8 drachmae.

The rates in the subdivisions of the old city of Thebes varied. The earliest receipt from Thebes comes from the division of Charax and is dated 22–21 B.C. The amount paid is 10 drachmae, and this continued to be the rate until at least A.D. 97.[77] Wilcken observed that from the year A.D. 113–14 onwards the λαογραφία included the payment for the bath-tax and that the total payment was 12 drachmae. Since the bath-tax had previously been 1½ drachmae, it was obvious that one or both of the taxes had been slightly raised, or that some other payment was also included. O. Theb. 81 gives a receipt for two instalments of the λαογραφία of 8 and 4 drachmae, so that the change in the rate must have come as early as this receipt which is dated in A.D. 107. It is therefore impossible to connect the rise in the rate with that which was made at Elephantine-Syene in A.D. 113–14 or 114–15, as Wilcken tried to do.[78] Neither was there any connexion with the earlier rise at Elephantine-Syene, which occurred at least as early as A.D. 96–7, since the payments of 10 drachmae occur at Charax as late as A.D. 97. Inasmuch as the rate for λαογραφία at Charax was low, there are but few extant receipts showing payments in instalments.

The receipt for λαογραφία from Ophi published in PSI. VIII. 993 does not conform exactly to the receipts published by Wilcken.[79] The two receipts from the first century given by Wilcken record 10 drachmae for poll-tax. His receipts from the second century begin with A.D. 113–14 and record 10 drachmae 4 obols. The new receipt is for 11 drachmae, from the year A.D. 117. Since there are but six receipts for λαογραφία from Ophi, any deductions in regard to the fluctuation of the rate for poll-tax in that village are hazardous. It is probable that the increase in the poll-tax known to have begun by A.D. 133–4 was in effect by A.D. 117. It remains to account for the differences of two obols in the amounts recorded in 117 and 133–4. Since there is no evidence for a lowering of the poll-tax at any time during the first two centuries of Roman rule, it is unlikely that the 11 drachmae recorded for the year 117 are all for the poll-tax, but the payment may contain 2 obols for an unnamed tax or charge, as did the amounts for λαογραφία in many of the receipts from Elephantine-Syene and Charax.

The receipts from the North Market Quarter confirm the con-

clusions which Wilcken was able to draw from the two ostraca
known to him in 1899.[80] The poll-tax was paid in the same way
as at Charax. In the first century the rate was 10 drachmae a
year (payments for 11 drachmae 1½ obols presumably include
a payment for the bath-tax). In the second century, at least as
early as A.D. 106,[81] the receipts for λαογραφία show a payment of 12
drachmae, which probably includes the payment for bath-tax.[82]

Wilcken's estimate of the poll-tax at Ceramia as 10 drachmae
4 obols, which was disputed by Milne,[83] is probably correct.
Wilcken concluded that the annual rate was 10 drachmae
4 obols, because he had two ostraca which each gave a payment
of 5 drachmae 2 obols. Tait has suggested that O. Strass. 101
should read δέ(κα), that is 10 drachmae, instead of δ (= 4) drachmae, and if this is correct the rate in Ceramia as late as A.D. 96
was 10 drachmae a year as in Ophi and elsewhere. The parallel
between Ceramia and Ophi is exact for both the first and the
second centuries.

Milne's observations in regard to the rate at Memnonia are
more important. Wilcken had concluded, from the four ostraca
from Memnonia known to him, that the annual rate was 16
drachmae. But the large number of receipts subsequently published show instalments, usually of 4 drachmae, reaching various
totals, but most often 16, 20, or 24 drachmae.[84] Except for the
unpublished receipts cited by Milne the total is never higher
than 24 drachmae. Milne states that there is one receipt for
λαογραφία from Memnonia with payments amounting to 32
drachmae, and another whose instalments total 28 drachmae.
Since there is no indication of two rates for poll-tax in any part
of Upper Egypt, it is safest to conclude that the rate for Memnonia was 24 drachmae per annum, which was also the assessment in the South-West Quarter. The receipts quoted by Milne
probably include arrears, which are sometimes included without
designation in receipts, or they may include instalments for the
following year as in O. Strass. 103 and 105 and other receipts.[85]
The receipts range in date from A.D. 44 to 160. Tait has attempted to date O. Strass. 118 in the sixth year of Gordian, and if
he is correct this is the latest extant example of a payment for
λαογραφία.[86]

Wilcken's conclusion that the rate of the poll-tax for the South-

West Quarter was 24 drachmae a year is confirmed by the new examples,[87] if in SB. 4334 the payment of 11 drachmae in Hathyr is the initial payment for the following year, although this is not stated in the receipt.[88]

A district called the Market and distinct from the North Market Quarter has been recognized since Wilcken published his work on the ostraca. From it there are three receipts for λαογραφία.[89] Two are instalments of 4 drachmae each from the same man for the year A.D. 198–9. The other receipt is for 8 drachmae paid for λαογραφία καὶ ἄλλα. It is not safe to conclude on the basis of three receipts that the poll-tax was as low as 8 drachmae a year, and therefore the rate for the Market Quarter remains uncertain.

Pacerceësis is also a new division of Thebes.[90] The highest total on any ostracon from this place is 20 drachmae, but it is unwise to conclude that this was the annual assessment. It was possibly 24 drachmae as at Memnonia and the South-West Quarter.

Φωτρ( ) is likewise new. The total on the only receipt from that district is 24 drachmae.[91]

Ταυρ( ), Milne's reading of the name of the village in O. Theb. 86, is also new.[92] The amount paid for λαογραφία καὶ ἄλλα is 12 drachmae, which is similar to the rate in Charax and the North Market Quarter.

The amounts for the poll-tax at Thebes may be tabulated as in Wilcken's *Griechische Ostraka*, I, p. 238:

Charax	.	.	10 dr.	From A.D. 104 on slightly more.
Ophi	.	.	10 dr.	Later 10 dr. 4 ob.
North Market	.	.	10 dr.	From A.D. 106 on slightly more.
Ceramia	.	.	10 dr.	Later 10 dr. 4 ob.
Memnonia	.		24 dr.	
Southwest Quarter	.		24 dr.	
Market Quarter	.		8 dr. or more.	
Pacerceësis	.		20 dr. or more.	
Φωτρ( ).	.	.	24 dr.	
Ταυρ( ).	.	.	Perhaps slightly more than 10 dr. in the third century.	

Looking over this table it is tempting to conclude that there were but two rates for poll-tax in the subdivisions of Thebes, 10 drachmae (later 10 drachmae 4 obols) and 24 drachmae.

The custom of combining the payments for λαογραφία and βαλανευτικόν in one sum has obscured the amount of the rise in the rate for poll-tax made early in the second century at Charax, the North Market Quarter, and perhaps Ταυρ( ), but it is not improbable that the rise amounted to 4 obols as in Ophi and Ceramia. This would mean that the rise in the rate of the bath-tax was ½ obol, bringing it up to 1 drachma 2 obols. It is also evident that the rise in the rate applied only to those villages enjoying a lower assessment, and that it was made quite independently of the rises in the rate at Elephantine-Syene, since it occurred after the earlier rise there and before the later rise. The districts which paid at the higher rate of 24 drachmae a year would be Memnonia, the South-West Quarter, Φωτρ( ), and Pacerceësis. The districts which paid at the rate of 10 drachmae in the first century and at 10 drachmae 4 obols in the second century would be Charax, Ophi, North Market Quarter, Ceramia, Ταυρ( ), and perhaps the Market Quarter.

There are a number of receipts from Thebes or its environs, dating from 19 B.C. to A.D. 147 or later, which cannot be assigned to any of the villages or subdivisions noted above.[93] These include a payment of 4 drachmae for λαογραφία καὶ ἄλλα collected by the πράκτορες of the Ἄνω τοπαρχία, according to Milne's reading, which is a division of the nome but does not appear on other receipts of the Roman period from Thebes. Three receipts[94] for poll-tax at the rate of 15 drachmae plus προσδιαγραφόμενα perhaps cast some doubt upon the conclusion suggested above that there were but two rates of poll-tax for Thebes. It is possible, however, that the 15 drachmae plus προσδιαγραφόμενα (equal approximately to 16 drachmae) are but an irregular instalment on the higher rate of poll-tax at Thebes. O. Tait, p. 158, no. 44, which Tait thinks may contain instalments for λαογραφία totalling 32 drachmae, may be explained as including arrears;[95] but it is not certain that the payments are for poll-tax.

A number of ostraca from other cities and villages of Upper Egypt have come to light since Wilcken published his collection. One receipt comes from the village of Papa in the Coptite nome, but it is impossible to determine the rate of the poll-tax, since the payment of 16 drachmae is for λαογραφία καὶ χώματα.[96]

Three or four receipts for poll-tax have been found coming from Hermonthis.[97] The highest amount recorded is 8 drachmae, but it is possible that this is an instalment on a higher rate. The earliest receipt, which may be from Hermonthis, is dated 8 B.C., the latest in the reign of Marcus Aurelius.

Five receipts from Coptos range from A.D. 2 to 53.[98] The amount in each is 8 drachmae.

Seven receipts from Apollonopolis Magna are dated from A.D. 96 to 180.[99] Of these two are for 4 drachmae and the rest are for 8 drachmae. One of the two ostraca picked up by Sayce at Elkab, the ancient Ilithyiaspolis, records a payment of 16 drachmae for poll-tax.[100] Tait notes that the formula is the same as that of ostraca from Apollonopolis Magna. Since the towns are not far distant it is possible that the rates were the same in both, and that the 8 drachmae payments at Apollonopolis Magna are for half of the annual poll-tax, as are the contemporary payments of 8 drachmae at Elephantine-Syene.

A large number of demotic receipts for poll-tax found at Tentyris, dating from the first to the twenty-third year of Tiberius, indicate that the poll-tax was assessed at 16 drachmae, and that it was usually paid in instalments of 4 drachmae.[101]

It is not impossible that the rate in all of these towns, which (except Papa) lie not far to the north or south of Thebes, was 16 drachmae per annum, the early assessment at Elephantine-Syene. It is hazardous, however, to make such an assumption, since the rate for the privileged tax-payers in Hermopolis Magna was 8 drachmae, and the lower rate in the subdivisions of Thebes was only 2 drachmae higher than the payments of 8 drachmae so frequent on the receipts from these towns. There is no evidence for any rise in rates for poll-tax in these towns as there was at Elephantine-Syene and parts of Thebes, but the number of ostraca found is too few to permit a final conclusion on this point.

When Caracalla promulgated the *constitutio Antoniniana* conferring Roman citizenship on all citizens of the provinces except the *dediticii*, he seems to have made but little change in the civic status of the inhabitants of Egypt. Keyes states that 'the συντάξιμον as well as the λαογραφία appears to go out of existence at the time of Caracalla's extension of the Roman citizenship'.[102] There are, however, three receipts for λαογραφία which are dated after A.D. 212, the date of the *constitutio*; the last one of these is dated in A.D. 243.[103] P. Ross.-Georg. IV. 20 is a collector's detailed report of collections of the poll-tax (κατ' ἄνδρα λαογραφίας) dated A.D. 223; it comes from Corphetu in the Heracleopolite nome, and it included the tax-payers who were temporarily absent (τοῖς ἐκτὸς ὁμολ(όγοις)); unfortunately only the heading is preserved. It is hard to explain why only three receipts should be extant from this period (one from Lower Egypt and two from Thebes), if the poll-tax continued without change. The census, however, continued unchanged through A.D. 257–8, and the epicrises for admission into the favoured class of μητροπολῖται continued until A.D. 250. Although the *constitutio Antoniniana* filled Egypt with Aurelii, it appears that it did not remove all the distinctions between the classes of the population, nor did it immediately relieve the Egyptians from the crushing burden of the poll-tax. It is possible that the ἑξηκοντάδραχμος μερισμὸς εἰς τὸ κατ' οἰκίαν τῆς πόλεως, a house-tax at the rate of 60 drachmae, found in a third-century document (after A.D. 212) from Hermopolis Magna,[104] is a late development of the poll-tax: the high rate may be explained as a temporary assessment, or perhaps the depreciation of the currency in the third century made the high rate necessary. We cannot be sure that the poll-tax was abolished throughout Egypt in the third century, even after the change in the census in the second half of the century. The poll-tax was but one of the taxes which had caused a large part of the populace to flee from their homes and abandon the cultivation of the soil; but the steady drain of wealth from Egypt caused by the collection of the poll-tax, for which there is no evidence that the Romans gave anything in return, must have played an important part in the economic decline which became so severe in the third century.

IX

CAPITATION TAXES

CAPITATION taxes formed one of the most important
sources of revenue of the Roman government, especially for
the internal administration of Egypt. The term 'capitation taxes',
as distinguished from the poll-tax (λαογραφία), is used in this
chapter to designate those taxes which, in the period of Roman
domination of Egypt, were often called μερισμοί. As applied to
taxation[1] μερισμός ordinarily meant a tax 'distributed', that is,
assessed in equal amounts over the entire tax-paying populace
of a given district, or a tax similarly assessed upon a specific
class of persons liable to that form of taxation.[2] The term
μερισμός is common in the Roman period, especially during the
second century. Its use as a designation for taxes was continued
in the Byzantine period, and finally in the Arabic period it became the general name for a tax of almost any kind.[3] The meaning of the term in the Ptolemaic period is not clear. Only two
examples are listed in section 11 of the third volume of Preisigke's
Wörterbuch, and the specific application of either of these examples
to taxation is somewhat doubtful.[4] Since receipts for capitation
taxes seem not to have been given after the beginning of the
reign of Ptolemy IV Philopator,[5] it is but natural that the development of a term for capitation taxes cannot be traced during
the Ptolemaic period.

Capitation Taxes for the Central Administration

The λαογραφία itself could be called a μερισμός, as was evident
from the definition of the latter term established by Wilcken,
but it is not so called in the extant documents except by implication in P. Col. I R I a–b in the phrase δι[οί]κ(ησις) λαογ(ραφίας) καὶ
ἄλλω(ν) μερισμ(ῶν).[6] A strict interpretation of the term μερισμός
as applied to the λαογραφία would mean that a specific sum was
due from a given community on account of the poll-tax, and that
this sum was divided by the number of persons liable to taxation who were residing there to obtain the rate of the poll-tax in
that community. Actually the process was reversed. The rate

of the poll-tax was fixed for a given community, and that rate was multiplied by the number of tax-paying inhabitants to obtain the total sum owed to the central government of Egypt. But once obtained, that sum of the annual payment for the poll-tax remained fixed during each census period of fourteen years.[7] Perhaps some variation occurred because of loss by death or because of increase by the adding of new names to the rolls of tax-payers, but these changes were supposed to balance each other.

In a country like Egypt under the Romans, where an accurate census is taken, the poll-tax is comparatively easy to collect so long as the rate of taxation is low. In Roman Egypt, however, the rate of the λαογραφία paid by the less favoured classes was as high as 40 drachmae a year, and possibly higher.[8] That alone was a very high tax for a poor man to pay, and since the poll-tax was combined with a number of other capitation taxes, it was inevitable that a certain percentage of the total sum due for poll-tax should fall in arrear. The prosperity of Egypt depended upon the Nile river, whose vagaries were only partly under control in antiquity. Because of an occasional unfavourable Nile and for other reasons the economic fortunes of individuals naturally varied from time to time, and to such an extent that they were sometimes unable to meet the exaction of the poll-tax. The irrigation projects of Augustus and the improvements in administration introduced by him had led to increased efficiency in the agricultural economy of Egypt,[9] and yet as early as the middle of the first century after Christ we find reports of tax-collectors who complain that they are unable to collect the taxes, because the villages were deserted by their inhabitants.[10] To flee from one's village was a favourite method of escape from over-burdensome taxation or liturgies. Men left their homes and sought refuge in the deserts or the swamps or tried to lose themselves in the crowded cities. Such escape was made possible through the connivance of friends and relatives. Leaving home and property was indeed a desperate device for escaping the tax-gatherer, but it was effective. In fact the unfortunate tax-collectors, who were held responsible,[11] threatened to throw up the collection unless they were granted some relief.[12]

What immediate steps were taken by the government to relieve this situation we do not know—perhaps none. Tax-farmers are liable to find the collection more difficult than they have anticipated, and are prone to seek a remission of a part of the total sum which they have contracted to pay. Nevertheless, by the latter part of the reign of Trajan the administration was obliged to attend to the complaints of its tax-gatherers or lose their services. It was simplest to collect additional taxes from those who were able to pay.

The Μερισμὸς ἀνακ(εχωρηκότων) and Μερισμὸς ἀπόρων

The new taxes designed to relieve the tax-farmers from the impossible burden of accumulating arrears of the poll-tax were called μερισμὸς ἀνακ(εχωρηκότων), 'assessment for those who have fled', and μερισμὸς ἀπόρων, 'assessment for the destitute'. The former of these taxes was collected in Upper Egypt and was but recently explained by J. G. Tait.[13] The latter tax is frequently found in receipts from the Arsinoite nome. This circumstance leads to the suspicion that the two taxes are identical, and this hypothesis is strengthened by the wording of SB. 7462, which states that . . . ἀπόρους ἀνακεχωρηκέναι, and especially by the list of ἄποροι ἀνεύρετοι in P. Cornell 1. 24. But the presence of one ostracon bearing a receipt for μερισμὸς ἀπόρων and definitely coming from Charax, from which in the same year we have a receipt for μερισμὸς ἀνακ(εχωρηκότων), casts some doubt upon this identification.

If, however, the receipts from Charax are followed in chronological order from A.D. 133 to 150, it will be observed that the amount paid for μερισμὸς ἀνακ(εχωρηκότων) is very small in the first years after a census, and then rises rapidly until a few years before the next census, when the assessment begins to fall gradually until the first year after the new census, when the amount drops to almost nothing.[14] This phenomenon is easily explained on the assumption that the amount of the poll-tax was fixed at the time of the fourteen-year census and remained constant during the years until the next census. Previous to the establishment of the μερισμὸς ἀνακ(εχωρηκότων) any deficiency in the amount of the poll-tax collected in a given year had to be met by the tax-farmers, unless a special remission was granted to them. These collectors acting in self-defence had probably been guilty of extortion to make good their losses. The μερισμὸς

ἀνακ(εχωρηκότων) was designed to stop such abuses and to ensure the full collection of the revenue. The annual deficiency
was assessed *per capita* upon the remaining tax-payers who had
been sufficiently prosperous or conscientious to pay their own
poll-tax. In making this adjustment the government was not
endeavouring to establish an ideal state in which the strong
should bear the burdens of the weak, but was recognizing the
hard fact that a tax-payer suffering under such an additional
burden as the μερισμὸς ἀνακ(εχωρηκότων) would not readily connive with a fellow citizen who sought to escape his taxes by
taking leave of his community. We have a sworn statement made
by a shoemaker that a certain person was ἀνὰ πόλιν, that is,
apparently had fled and was in hiding; but it is not certain that
this is merely a case of tax-evasion.[15] The number who fled because of inability to pay taxes, or because of the burden of the
liturgies, seems to have been about the same each year; this led
to a progressive rise in the assessment of the μερισμὸς ἀνα-
κ(εχωρηκότων). Why the assessment declined slightly in the last
years before the census of A.D. 145–6 is not obvious. Perhaps
the number of youths reaching the age of fourteen years, when
they began to pay the poll-tax, happened to exceed the losses
caused by men who died or reached the age of exemption, or
possibly the peasants were returning to the land.[16] Possibly
also there was a greater diligence in the collection of arrears.[17]

In the year 142, however, there is an exception to this rule of a
progressive rise in the rate of assessment of the μερισμὸς ἀνα-
κ(εχωρηκότων). In A.D. 138 the rate was 4 drachmae; in 139 (if
WO. II. 585 has been read correctly)[18] it was 6 drachmae; and
in 143 7 drachmae 2 obols. In 142, however, there are two receipts for this tax at the rate of 1 drachma 6 obols, and the
appearance of two receipts makes it unlikely that this amount
represents an instalment. The unique ostracon WO. II. 613
bearing a receipt for μερισμὸς ἀπόρων is dated in A.D. 142; and
if the amount paid in this receipt, namely, 2 drachmae 3 obols,
be added to the assessment for μερισμὸς ἀνακ(εχωρηκότων), the
total is 4 drachmae 2 obols, which, though still short, is nearer
to the expected rate for that year. It appears, therefore, that in
the year 142 at Charax the officials decided to divide the μερισμὸς
ἀνακ(εχωρηκότων) into its component parts and to collect one

tax for the deficit caused by those who had fled and another for those whom the state recognized as absolutely unable to pay the poll-tax, that is, the ἄποροι.[19] It is not impossible that there was still a third division of the tax in that year, whose name has not been preserved to us,[20] which brought the total up to the level expected for A.D. 142. It is important to observe that the amount paid on behalf of the ἄποροι was larger than that paid for the ἀνακεχωρηκότες as late as ten years after the census. The experiment of collecting two (or more) μερισμοί in place of one seems to have found no favour, for no more ostraca are found with receipts for μερισμὸς ἀπόρων. The assessment for μερισμὸς ἀνακ(εχωρηκότων) is at the expected high level in the following year, A.D. 143.

We may, therefore, conclude that the μερισμὸς ἀνακ(εχωρηκότων) of Upper Egypt includes the assessment for the ἄποροι. Conversely it may be supposed that the μερισμὸς ἀπόρων in the Arsinoite nome includes the assessment for the ἀνακεχωρηκότες. That there were ἀνακεχωρηκότες in Lower Egypt is shown by the complaints of the collectors of taxes in the Arsinoite, Oxyrhynchite, and Mendesian nomes.[21] If the two taxes are substantially the same, it is quite likely that Kenyon and Bell were correct in their contention that P. Lond. III. 911 (p. 127) is a certificate of poverty, presumably entitling the holder to complete or partial exemption from taxation, rather than a list of ἄποροι similar to P. Cornell I. 24. What calamities or disabilities suffered entitled a man to be included among the ἄποροι is unknown. Official recognition of a class of ἄποροι unable to pay taxes must have been the source of temptation to practise deception on the part of the populace and to receive graft on the part of officials. It was largely up to the tax-payers to prevent such fraud, since the cost of any abuses fell upon them.

The difference between the μερισμὸς ἀπόρων and the rare ἐπιμερισμὸς ἀπόρων[22] is not clear. The two may be identical, or the latter may have been an additional assessment like the μερισμὸς β̄ of O. Strass. 212 and 219.

In the years when the μερισμὸς ἀνακ(εχωρηκότων) is at its maximum it is very high, about seven-tenths of the rate of the poll-tax at Charax. If the tax were levied to cover the deficit of the poll-tax only, this would mean that in the year A.D. 143

approximately 42 per cent. of the populace did not pay the poll-tax. It is not unlikely, however, that this additional levy was intended to cover the deficit of all capitation taxes owed to the central government of Egypt, especially the most important of these, the χωματικόν, a tax for the maintenance of dikes and canals. P. Cornell 1. 24, the list of ἄποροι ἀνεύρετοι of Philadelphia, indicates that those individuals were in arrear with both the συντάξιμον (poll-tax)[23] and the χωματικόν. If at Charax the μερισμὸς ἀνακ(εχωρηκότων) was intended to cover the deficit in both λαογραφία at something over 10 drachmae and χωματικόν at 6 drachmae 4 obols per annum, the number of persons from whom these taxes had not been collected in A.D. 143 would be about 30 per cent. of the tax-paying population. If other taxes were included, the percentage would be smaller.

The Χωματικόν

The dike-tax, which may have had its deficit thus made up, was a tax of great importance. The place of the system of dikes and canals in the agricultural economy of Egypt is too well known to require comment here. One of the most important duties of the administration of Egypt was the development and maintenance of that system. Taxes were collected by the Ptolemies for the dikes and canals. One of these called διάχωμα[24] does not appear in the receipts of the Roman period. The tax called χωματικόν in the third century B.C. seems to have been a tax of 1 obol per arura,[25] which indicates that those persons directly benefited by the system of irrigation paid for it. No examples of this tax have been found after the third century B.C.; this may be an accident of survival, or it may mean that the tax was made a capitation tax in the reign of Ptolemy IV Philopator or of one of his successors, and so was no longer recorded in receipts. Such information as we possess from the Byzantine and Arabic periods indicates that the taxes for maintenance of dikes and canals again fell chiefly, if not wholly, upon the interested property-owners.[26]

In the Roman period, on the contrary, the χωματικόν was clearly a capitation tax. It was paid by the ὁμόλογοι of the Arsinoite nome and apparently by all citizens of other nomes (except the specially privileged)[27] at a uniform rate of 6 drachmae

4 obols a year. The dike-tax is the only capitation tax, so far as I know, collected at a uniform rate throughout Upper and Lower Egypt. In special cases, however, the rate in a particular locality might be temporarily altered. In Philadelphia the rate was doubled in the year A.D. 35,[28] and in the villages of Thebes there are several receipts for abnormally high payments for the tax, though not so high as at Philadelphia. The examples from Thebes all fall in the latter part of the reign of Trajan.[29] It is possible that extensive repairs on, or development of, the dike- and canal-system around Thebes necessitated raising the rate of the χωματικόν which was paid by those whom such construction would primarily benefit. Some such emergency must certainly have been the occasion for doubling the dike-tax at Philadelphia in the time of Tiberius. It was probably not his policy to increase taxes without cause.[30] According to BGU. IV. 1198 (5–4 B.C.) a dike-tax was paid by priests at Busiris in the Heracleopolite nome apparently at the rate of 6 drachmae $4\frac{1}{2}$ obols (an increase of $\frac{1}{2}$ obol over the rate common elsewhere in Egypt), for four priests had paid 108 drachmae on that account in the course of four years. Amundsen (O. Oslo. 7 note) has attempted to demonstrate a decline in the rate of the χωματικόν from 6 drach- mae 4 obols to 5 drachmae 2 obols between A.D. 86–7 and 91–2 with a slow rise to 6 drachmae 4 obols again in A.D. 97–8. This is not an impossible interpretation of the evidence in the ostraca cited by Amundsen, but it is not a necessary conclusion, since receipts for less than 6 drachmae 4 obols may represent partial payments.

Kenyon first suggested that the χωματικόν of 6 drachmae 4 obols was paid as an *adaeratio* of the πενθήμερος, the five days of manual labour annually required of every unprivileged person in the Arsinoite nome for the maintenance of the dikes.[31] Oertel has collected evidence to show that this period of labour could, if necessary, be increased, or even be doubled, which cor- responds to the doubling of the tax at Philadelphia in A.D. 35. In fact the number of days of labour required was doubled at Philadelphia, but in the year A.D. 209.[32] Kenyon's suggestion has been attractive, although the *adaeratio* is rather high, since the wage of an unskilled workman was probably under 1 drachma a day.[33] There is, however, not one shred of actual evidence that the χωματικόν was an *adaeratio* of the πενθήμερος, as scholars have pointed out.[34] Kenyon's theory is, moreover, embarrassed by the complete lack of evidence for a πενθήμερος in Upper Egypt where, however, the χωματικόν was regularly collected. In Upper Egypt liturgic work on the dikes was not a matter of five days of labour, but a specified amount of earth thrown up on the embankments fulfilled the liturgy. It might be urged that the χωματικόν of 6 drachmae 4 obols was an *adaeratio* of this liturgy; but this is most improbable, because the number of *naubia* of earth put in place by each individual varies in the certificates so greatly at different times that Oertel was unable to classify the receipts in any satisfactory manner.[35] Consequently an *adaeratio* of the ἀναβολὴ χωμάτων would not be the χωματικόν at a practically uniform rate of 6 drachmae 4 obols. The ἀναβολὴ χωμάτων may have been assessed upon landholders in proportion to the extent of their holdings, doubtless with the usual exemptions for Romans and other favoured classes. This was the principle employed at Caranis in the assessment of the dike-liturgy. In O. Mich. Car. 272-94, which are receipts for work done on the embankments, the number of *naubia* recorded in individual receipts is 1, 3, 4, 5, 10, and 100. O. Mich. Car. 273 makes it evident that the number of *naubia* transferred depended upon the amount of land owned, for the phrase used is: παρέδ(ωκεν) ὑπὲρ ἀρουρῶν ναύβια δ'.

If the ἀναβολὴ χωμάτων in Upper Egypt was likewise assessed in proportion to the extent of holdings of land, the ναύβιον κατοίκων and ναύβιον ἐναφεσίων found commonly in Lower Egypt, although rarely at Thebes, as a land-tax paid in copper seem more like an *adaeratio* of the ἀναβολὴ χωμάτων. Since the χωματικόν was uniform in Upper and Lower Egypt, it could hardly be an *adaeratio* of the πενθήμερος which, so far as we know, did not exist in Upper Egypt. The πενθήμερος might possibly be considered a way for the heavily taxed peasant of Lower Egypt to work out his dike-tax. This, however, is improbable. The corvée existed in Egypt from the time of the Pharaohs of the Old Kingdom. It undoubtedly continued in the Fayûm and elsewhere in Egypt in the time of the Ptolemies. In the Ptolemaic period, I believe, holders of catoecic land and of land ἐν ἀφέσει were allowed an *adaeratio* of their obligations to work on the dikes, and the *adaeratio*, which varied with the size of their holdings, was in the third century B.C. called χωματικόν but later was named ναύβιον.[36] The corvée in the Fayûm, since work on the dikes in that nome was especially important, was systematized by the Ptolemies or by the Roman administration into the πενθήμερος. All ὁμόλογοι were liable to the corvée. Augustus, as Suetonius relates,[37] found the dike- and canal-sytem in bad repair as a result of the neglect of the later Ptolemies. He used the labour of the soldiers of the army in Egypt to put the irrigation-system into proper condition. To finance this work, I believe, he exacted the Roman χωματικόν, the capitation tax of 6 drachmae 4 obols per annum throughout Egypt. This money, in addition to the revenue from the ναύβιον, went to the central treasury of Egypt at Alexandria, and it was disbursed as needed for the upkeep or enlargement of the system of irrigation. The government, therefore, recognized that all Egypt owed its prosperity to the successful management of the irrigation-system, although it also exacted special rates from specific communities to provide for special local needs. The treasury doubtless found its own good use for any excess of revenue from the χωματικόν.

It is my belief that the unprivileged inhabitant of the Fayûm had not the choice of χωματικόν or of πενθήμερος. I believe that he was liable to both. This may seem hard on the peasants of the Arsinoite nome; but, as in the case of the poll-tax, it must be remembered that the Fayûm was rich and that the development of that region had received the special care of the Ptolemies and probably of the Roman government. The peasants of the Arsinoite nome had, therefore, to pay heavily for benefits received, as usual more heavily than the natives elsewhere in Egypt.[38]

The Ὑϊκή

To the native Egyptians, as to the Jews, the pig was anathema. It is, therefore, highly improbable that a tax on these animals brought any great revenue to the Pharaohs. In the eyes of the Greeks, however, and later of the Romans, the pig was valuable for food and as a desirable offering to the gods. The Ptolemies, therefore, introduced a tax on pigs. In the third century B.C., as extant receipts indicate, this was a property-tax.[39]

In the Roman period there is but one published receipt for a tax on pigs from Upper Egypt: WO. II. 1031 is a property- or, perhaps, a sales-tax collected on a single pig by a τελώνης ὑϊκῆς. The scarcity of receipts for a pig-tax in Upper Egypt is only natural, since the pig was raised for the benefit of the Greeks and other foreign inhabitants of Egypt who for the most part had settled in Lower Egypt. Many examples of the tax on pigs have been found among the documents from Lower Egypt, but it has only recently been suggested that this tax might be a capitation tax.[40]

H. Comfort has pointed out that the ὑϊκή is among the taxes covered by the phrase δι[οί]κ(ησις) λαογ(ραφίας) καὶ ἄλλ(ων) μερισμ(ῶν) in P. Col. I R I. a–b. iv, 5. An examination of the evidence from the Arsinoite nome reveals that the rate of the pig-tax is there invariably 1 drachma 1 obol from about A.D. 20 to 134–5, and that it was paid by all of the ὁμόλογοι, including, probably, even the unhappy Jews. The only exception to this rate is found in the great tax-rolls from Caranis in the collection of the University of Michigan, where the ὑϊκή is everywhere recorded as 5 obols 2 chalci, and this may indicate a local or temporary variation in the rate of pig-tax in the Arsinoite nome. There is a receipt found at Tebtynis in which the payment for this tax is 1 drachma 4 obols.[41] It is possible, of course, that the rate of the ὑϊκή in the Arsinoite nome was higher at the time when this receipt was issued (A.D. 186); but there is some reason for thinking that this receipt, like some other receipts found at Tebtynis, was originally issued at some place outside the Arsinoite nome. The rate of the λαογραφία, for which also payment is made in this receipt, is 8 drachmae, which is the rate of the poll-tax at Hermopolis where the pig-tax in A.D. 132–5 was 1 drachma 4 obols. The receipts from Πεενσάκοι, another town which was probably not in the Arsinoite nome, also show a pig-tax of 1 drachma 4 obols towards the end of the second century.[42]

It is not so evident that the ὑϊκή was a μερισμός in the Oxyrhynchite nome, since there the rate seems to vary. At the beginning of the first century after Christ the ὑϊκή is 2 drachmae $1\frac{1}{2}$ obols.[43] In A.D. 45–50 the payments for the tax were 1 drachma 4 obols, and thereafter receipts give that same amount but also 1 drachma $4\frac{1}{2}$ obols and 1 drachma $5\frac{1}{2}$ obols. PO. III. 574, dated in the

second century, may indicate that one obol of the payment of
1 drachmae 5½ obols mentioned above was for προσδιαγραφόμενα.
If in PO. XII. 1520 ½ obol was accidently omitted after the 1
drachma 4 obols (the 4 obols is questioned by the editors), it is
probable that the rate in the Oxyrhynchite nome was, after
A.D. 47, kept at 1 drachma 4½ obols. In PSI. I. 106, from Mendes
and dated in the second half of the second century after Christ,
the total of the pig-tax is ∫μθ, and 49 drachmae is exactly divisible
by 1 drachma 4½ obols; but it is not safe to accept this as the rate
for the Mendesian nome, since none of the totals of the ὑϊκή in
P. Ryl. II. 213 (to which PSI. I. 106 belongs) can be divided
evenly by 1 drachma 4½ obols. PO. XII. 1518, furthermore, indicates that barbers (κουρεῖς) and key-makers (κλειδοποιοί) in the
Oxyrhynchite nome paid a μερισμὸς ὑϊκῆς.⁴⁴

Despite some variations in the rate in the Oxyrhynchite nome,
I think it has been shown that the pig-tax in a part of Lower
Egypt was a μερισμός. In the Ptolemaic period the pig-tax was
clearly a tax on property, but all examples are from the middle
of the third century B.C. There is no evidence as to when the
tax was changed into a μερισμός, or whether this was done by the
Ptolemies or by the Roman administration, but it is possible to
hazard a guess as to why the change was made. The pig is the
most fecund of the domestic animals,⁴⁵ which makes the taxing
of its offspring a rather difficult matter. A brood-sow usually
has two litters a year and may have as many as three litters within
the limits of a fiscal year, and the number of pigs in each litter
may be ten or twelve and occasionally more. An owner of a pig,
in seeking to evade taxation on young porkers which he had
already eaten or marketed, could cheerfully lie to the tax-collector
concerning the number of young born to his pigs during the
fiscal year, and unless his neighbours betrayed him it is hard to
see how the collector of the ὑϊκή could disprove his statement.
Difficulties caused by lying owners and conniving neighbours
must have caused the somewhat surprising change of the property-
tax on pigs into a capitation tax, either by the Ptolemies, which
would explain the disappearance of receipts for the tax during
the second and first centuries B.C., or by the Romans when they
undertook to adapt the tax-system of Egypt to their own purposes.

Μερισμοί for the Support of Local Government

Much of the burden of expense for local government was lifted from the tax-payers by the system of 'liturgies' which compelled the competent citizens of an Egyptian community to assume the various offices of local government, often without pay.[46] Not all functions of government, however, could be fulfilled in that simple manner. It was necessary, therefore, to provide revenue by taxation to ensure the continued performance of these necessary functions. The collection of these local taxes was in the hands of the governmental agencies, that is, the official collectors of taxes and the state-banks,[47] but it is probable that these agencies turned the money over to local officials for disbursement under the supervision of the financial administration of the nomes—the strategus and his staff. There is no reason to believe that the money realized from such taxes was sent to Alexandria and then sent back to various communities in the nomes, or even that the elaborate system of banking was utilized for paper-transfer of such funds.

Φύλακες

The safety of life and property required the continuous presence of a police force. In the Ptolemaic period, or at least in the third century B.C., taxes for the support of guards had fallen upon the cleruchi who paid, sometimes in money and sometimes in kind, a tax called φυλακιτικόν.[48] In addition to this tax special φυλακιτικά, taxes with descriptive names, such as λείας (of the flock), γῆς (of the land), ἀμπελίτιδος (of the vine-land), προβάτων (of the sheep), &c., were levied for the protection of farms and herds, and presumably these were paid by the persons immediately concerned for the safety of their possessions.

In the Roman period the pay of the various types of guards or police was provided through μερισμοί which bore varying names according to the particular branch of the *gendarmerie* for which they were intended. The capitation tax was assessed by the Roman government either because it was supposed that the protection of the police extended equally to each tax-payer or because it was easier to collect the revenue in that way.

A tax (ὑπὲρ) φυλάκων (for the guards) or (ὑπὲρ) ὀψωνίου φυλάκων (for the salary of the guards) was collected from the inhabitants of the North-West Quarter at Thebes from A.D. 58–93, according to the extant receipts on ostraca, and from other districts of that city during the first half of the second century. In the North-West Quarter the tax paid at various times varied from 1 to 2 drachmae a year; in other divisions of the city it is impossible to determine the rate because the payments for the police-tax were combined with those for other μερισμοί, but the rate can hardly have been much higher, since the total paid for several capitation taxes was 4 drachmae 5 obols at most.[49] From the rest of Upper Egypt there are but few receipts: one from Elephantine-Syene, dated A.D. 91, for 1 drachma; one from Coptos, dated A.D. 102, whose amount is lost; two from Edfu, dated A.D. 97 and 99, for 1 drachma 1½ obols and 1 drachma 3 obols respectively; and finally O. Strass. 113, whose provenience is unknown, whose date is lost, and whose rate cannot be determined because the payment for φυλ(άκων) is combined with that for the bath-tax.

In the Arsinoite nome receipts for guard-tax from several of the villages have been found, ranging in date from A.D. 110 to the reign of Commodus.[50] The lowest amount recorded is 4½ obols; the highest 2 drachmae 5 obols, except that for Philadelphia BGU. VII. 1625 seems to record a payment of 4 drachmae, and P. Hamb. 85 records two instalments of 8, totalling 16, but whether drachmae or obols is not stated in the document.

There is little evidence for the tax in Lower Egypt outside the Arsinoite nome. The tax designated as (ὑπὲρ) φυλάκτρου at Memphis and Oxyrhynchus, and perhaps elsewhere, may have been the same tax.[51] The rate seems to be higher for this tax at Memphis and Oxyrhynchus than for the ὀψώνιον φυλάκων in Upper Egypt and the Arsinoite nome: possibly the guards were not separated into so many specialized subdivisions at these two cities as elsewhere. In P. Goodspeed Cairo 10 a house-owner at Memphis makes a payment of 400 drachmae for the poll-tax and φύλακτρον of the residents (ἔνοικοι) of his house. The tax was levied on house-owners in PO. III. 502, and it is evident from that document that special guards were assigned to the various blocks (ἄμφοδα) throughout the city of Oxyrhynchus. It is possible that this was an emergency measure, and that the tax was not ordinarily assessed against the house-owner, but the same organization of police is found at Apollonopolis Magna, according to *Archiv*, VI, p. 427, which gives a διάταξις παραφυλακῆς πλατειῶν καὶ ῥυμῶν ('organization of the watch of squares and streets'). There the watch was divided into ten districts with an ἄρχων and two εὐσχήμονες assigned to each. There were from 125 to 130 houses in each district. PO. I. 43 is a list of police available for assignment to various districts in the city of Oxyrhynchus in A.D. 95.

A tax called στατ(ίωνος) seems to take the place of φυλ(άκων) in P. Col. I R 2. ii. 3, &c. As the editors point out, it occupies the same position as φυλ(άκων) in the similar report, P. Col. I R 1 a–b. These documents are separated in date by only five or six years, and yet it is possible that the official terminology had changed meanwhile, or that a new board of collectors preferred to write the Greek φυλ(άκων) rather than to transcribe the Latin *statio*. Στατ(ίων) is elsewhere found only in ostraca from Elephantine.[52]

Μερισμὸς σκοπέλων

A tax designated as μερι(σμὸς) σκοπ(έλων) or simply σκοπ(έλων) is found at Elephantine-Syene from A.D. 89 to 91 and again in A.D. 162 and 189–90.[53] The comparative rarity of this tax for look-out places at Elephantine-Syene suggests that this may have been a special capitation tax to provide funds for building such look-outs, and this is confirmed by WO. II. 249 (A.D. 162) which records payment of a μερισμὸς οἰκοδ(ομίας) σκ(ο)π(έλων). The amounts range from 2¾ obols to 4 drachmae (the latter sum is attested only once).

Three ostraca from Edfu record payments for σκοπ(έλων): 4½ obols in A.D. 97, ½ obol in A.D. 98, 2 obols in A.D. 99. These are too few to determine whether the purpose of the payments was for building or for the remuneration of the sentinels.

If the payments (ὑπὲρ) σκοπ(έλων) at Elephantine-Syene were for the construction of look-outs this was certainly not the case at Thebes. Receipts from Charax record the tax from A.D. 104 to 167 continuously, so that it was obviously a tax for ὀψώνιον (salary). Receipts for this tax are found from other districts at Thebes, expecially from the North Market Quarter. It is impossible to follow the changes in the rate, because the payment is so often combined with that for another tax or taxes. It is worth noting that the South-West Quarter, where payments for ὀψώνιον σκοπ(έλων) were collected, has yielded no receipts for σκοπ(έλων). The districts from which receipts for σκοπ(έλων) are found yield none for φυλ(άκων) until A.D. 122, and thereafter payments are recorded for σκοπ(έλων) καὶ φυλ(άκων) καὶ ἀλ(λων). There is one exception: two receipts from Charax dated A.D. 107 record payments (ὑπέρ) σκοπ(έλων) φυλ(άκων) καὶ ἀλ(λων), which Wilcken[54] took as the full name of the tax. It is more probable, however, that καὶ has been omitted and that the payment was for σκοπ-(έλων) <καὶ> φυλ(άκων) καὶ ἀλ(λων) as in the ostraca of later date, or that this represents a special assessment for building, as in the ostraca from Elephantine-Syene.

No receipts from Lower Egypt for taxes (ὑπέρ) σκοπ(έλων) have been published.

Μαγδωλοφυλακία

At Thebes the district of Memnonia yields receipts for a tax abbreviated μαγδ( ) which may be resolved as (ὑπέρ) μαγ-δ(ώλων) or as (ὑπέρ) μαγδ(ωλοφυλακίας).[55] The amount paid in A.D. 95 was 2 drachmae 3 obols, and in A.D. 111 3 drachmae; 1 drachma 3 obols paid in A.D. 109 may have been an instalment. If Viereck's reading[56] of WO. II. 1284 and 1285 is correct, this tax for the watch-towers was also paid by the inhabitants of the South-West Quarter in A.D. 87, but the 1 obol recorded in each receipt is rather small for this tax.[57]

A single receipt[58] from Coptos testifies to the existence of the tax for watch-towers in that city, where 6½ obols were paid for it in A.D. 110.

This tax is frequently found in receipts from many of the villages of the Arsinoite nome (where no receipts for σκοπ(έλων) have been found). At Euhemeria and Theadelphia 2½ obols were paid in the early part of the second century; the rate was higher in Socnopaei Nesus, especially in the later part of the second century, where payments of 5½ obols and of 1 drachma are recorded. At Apias at the end of the third century 8 drachmae seem to have been paid for the tax. At Peënsaci, which was in Lower Egypt but probably not in the Arsinoite nome,[59] 7 drachmae and also 6½ drachmae are found as payments which include the μαγδ(ωλοφυλακία) among other capitation taxes.[60]

Tait has pointed out[61] that the μερισμὸς μαγδώλων is probably synonymous with the μερισμὸς σκοπέλων. The receipts from the Arsinoite nome for ὀψώνιον μαγδώλ(ων) φυλ(άκων)[62] indicate that the tax was intended for the support of the guards rather than for the construction of the towers.

Δεσμοφυλακία

This tax, whose abbreviation δεσμο( ) (the fullest form on the extant ostraca) gave trouble to Wilcken and his predecessors,[63] was elucidated by the publication of the Fayûm papyri by Grenfell and Hunt. It was a tax for the support of the guards of the local prisons, and although it was usually collected in connexion with the λαογραφία, and indeed was sometimes included in the payment for λαογραφία without mention of that fact,[64] it was probably a local assessment whose rate was determined by local needs and whose disbursement was controlled by local officials under the general supervision of the strategus and his aids.

Receipts from Elephantine-Syene record the collection of this tax from A.D. 116 to 145 and possibly to 168.[65] The amount of the assessment was uniformly ½ obol. The tax is not mentioned on extant ostraca from Thebes, while a single example from Coptos shows a payment of 1½ obols.[66]

The rate of this tax in Lower Egypt varied among the nomes, and in the Fayûm varied greatly among the different towns and villages of the nome.[67] The lowest amount recorded is ½ obol at Socnopaei Nesus in A.D. 115-17, and the highest is 2¾ obols at the same town in A.D. 174. In Theadelphia the tax was ¾ obol in A.D. 110-11 and again in A.D. 122-3, but it was increased to 1½ obols in A.D. 134-5. Other examples from Lower Egypt, but outside the Arsinoite nome, are from Oxyrhynchus, Nebo, Hermopolis, and perhaps Memphis. The sums paid in the receipts from these towns are 1 obol or 1 obol 2 chalci.

Φύλ(ακτρον) ἀπόρων

If the reading φυλ(άκτρου) ἀπόρων[68] in BGU. III. 881. 9 is correct, it is probable that a kind of 'debtors' prison' was supported by the tax, for the ἄποροι were those who could not meet their financial and liturgical obligations to the state because of extreme poverty. The fact that such a tax and such an institution are elsewhere unattested casts some doubt upon the reading and upon Preisigke's expansion of the abbreviation φυλ( ). It is possible that even if the reading is correct the scribe made some error here, since the document records two payments for ἐπιμερισμὸς ἀπόρων and several payments for guard-taxes of various kinds. Perhaps the phrase should be read φυλ(ακίας) ⟨καὶ⟩ ἀπόρων.

Ποταμοφυλακίς

Many receipts for the payment of the tax for the support of the fleet of the river-guards have been found, as we might expect, from Elephantine-Syene. The most usual annual payments found there are 1 drachma 3 obols and 1 drachma 4 obols (the latter after A.D. 128). Other payments of smaller amounts may be instalments, and larger sums may include arrears or, as frequently occurs, may include the payment for another tax or fee.[69]

At Thebes no satisfactory information can be derived in regard to the rate of the tax, except perhaps in the South-West Quarter, where the assessment seems to have been 4 obols in A.D. 76. At Charax and Memnonia and in the receipts where the district is not specified the amounts vary greatly, but charges for κυνη(γίδων), (hunting-boats) &c., are found, and payments of larger sums (e.g. 10 drachmae) are made by, or perhaps to, δέκανοι.[70]

In the Fayûm the payments are small in the first half of the second century: 1 obol, 1½ obols, 1 obol 2 chalci at Socnopaei Nesus, Euhemeria, and Theadelphia. In A.D. 174, however, a receipt from Socnopaei Nesus for 1 drachma 4¾ obols is found. At Apias the tax is attested early in the third century when 4 drachmae were paid ὑ(πὲρ) . . . ποταμῶν ἐκ τοῦ τέλ(ους).[71]

Μερισμὸς ἐρημοφυλακίας

PO. XII. 1436 mentions in column ii a payment for μερισμὸς ἐρημοφυλακίας which is not otherwise attested.[72] *Ad valorem* tolls for the maintenance of the desert-guard (ἐρημοφυλακία) were exacted at the borders of the Arsinoite nome, but that method of collection bears no relation to this μερισμός. It is possible that this document, although unique, was typical of the method used by the financial administration of the Oxyrhynchite nome to provide the revenue for the support of guards for the caravans through the roads of the desert, and that it must be assumed that the collection of tolls for this purpose was not the practice in this nome as it was in the Fayûm. It is possible, however, that this μερισμός was an extraordinary measure called for by unusual circumstances. The second column of PO. XII. 1436 is dated by the editors in A.D. 153. It is evident from the edict of M. Sempronius Liberalis, which is dated in A.D. 154,[73] that Egypt had been troubled by bands of brigands, whose depredations had become so serious that soldiers had been assigned to police-duty in order to suppress them. Such conditions may have demanded the employment of additional men for the desert guard of the Oxyrhynchite nome for whose support the regular funds of the nome's treasury were insufficient and had to be supplemented by the revenue from a capitation tax. If the revolt in Egypt, which occurred under Antoninus Pius, is correctly dated in A.D. 153–4,[74] it is evident that additional safeguards had to be provided at that time.

Πορθμοφυλακία

Two documents from the Hermopolite nome and dated in the second century (P. Ryl. II. 185, 193) include payments for what seems to be a tax for the maintenance of guards of a ferry. The payments are marked προ( ) or (once) προθ( ), and the editors have expanded the abbreviation as πορθ(μοφυλακίας). In P. Ryl. II. 193, which is definitely from Hermopolis Magna and is dated A.D. 132–5, the amount of each payment is 1 obol 2 chalci. In P. Ryl. II. 185, whose provenience and date are less certain, the amount of the payment is doubtfully read as 1½ obols. Since the items for προ( ) or προθ( ) are found among payments for other guard-taxes, the editors may well be right in considering the payment of 1 obol 2 chalci as a μερισμός for the support of guards for a ferry at Hermopolis.

It may be well to note here that the rates of taxes for the support of guards of all kinds rose in the second half of the second century and in the third century. The rise in these taxes apparently outstripped the rise in other taxes. This may have been caused in part by the increase in the cost of living which occurred during this period and which necessitated an increase in the wages paid to the guards. It is more probable, however, that the economic difficulties of Egypt in this period led more men to seek a living by robbery, brigandage, and smuggling, and this made necessary larger forces of guards and police to combat this lawlessness.

Μερισμὸς διπλῶν

This tax has puzzled many editors of papyri. It is found in receipts from Elephantine-Syene, Coptos, Thebes, and the Fayûm, and it is mentioned in a list of arrears from the town of Nebo, apparently in the Oxyrhynchite nome.[75] The amount of the tax recorded in the receipts from the Arsinoite nome is always small, 4 obols or less; but in Upper Egypt the rate of the tax varies from 2 obols 2 chalci to 4 drachmae. The name of the tax is abbreviated as δι( ), μερισμ( ) διπλ( ), or the like, and once at Theadelphia the payment is indicated by δαπ(ανῆς) διπλ( ). In WO. II. 1477 the payment for διπλῶν is curiously combined with a μερισμός for the guard (φυλακή) and the receivers of ships (ναυλοδόκοι) in a single payment. The following explanation of the μερισμὸς διπλῶν is suggested.

The tax was imposed to provide for the billeting of soldiers who, sent on missions away from their military organizations, had to be cared for by the various communities along their route. An edict of the prefect L. Aemilius Rectus,[76] dated A.D. 42, provides that στρατευόμενοι and μαχαιροφόροι are forbidden to press any one into service, demand supplies for travelling or any gift, unless they bear the certificate, δίπλωμα (or διπλῆ), of the prefect. A decree of a few years later,[77] found inscribed at Girgeh in the Great Oasis, is of the same tenor, but mentions officers among the offenders. The decree provides that shelter (στέγη) alone may be provided even soldiers having the required διπλώματα. A tenfold punishment is promised to offenders, and a fourfold reward to an informer. It appears, however, that billeting became a serious burden in the second century, and that a tax was assessed to cover this expense, which no longer fell upon unlucky individuals but upon all tax-payers of the community. In P. Ryl. II. 214 a from Thmuis an excess of 400 drachmae collected from the μερισμὸς διπλῶν is allotted to another μερισμός.

Making the billeting of soldiers a public charge, however, did not stop the illegal exactions made by the soldiers, and in fact it opened the way for collusion between them and unscrupulous officials in the nomes. PSI. v. 446, dated in A.D. 133–7, is an edict of M. Petronius Mamertinus stating that soldiers ἄνευ διπλῆς[78] had demanded boats, animals, and men. The warning is given, this time to strategi and basilici, not to furnish anything to anybody afoot or afloat; the prefect promised punishment to him who gave without authorization as well as to him who received. It is evident, therefore, that the placing of revenue from the capitation tax at the disposal of the officials of the nome had opened the way to graft, since those officials could connive with soldiers travelling without authorization to pay their expenses, on condition that the officials received a share of the alleged expense-money, or could even appropriate sums to their own use and charge it off the books to payments to imaginary soldiers.

It would be natural to suppose that after the establishment of the tax to provide for the billeting of itinerant soldiers the amount needed for a given year would be estimated on the basis of past experience. Thus we could account for the excess from the μερισμὸς διπλῶν at Thmuis mentioned above. If the tax was not assessed until after the close of the year, when the rate of the μερισμός was based on the actual monies expended, we can account for the excess noted above only on the assumption that the collections of the tax for the year had exceeded normal expectation, or that monies wrongfully expended from the fund had been recovered from the guilty officials, which is rather unlikely. It is possible, of course, that the method of arriving at the annual assessment may have varied among the different nomes.

Μερισμὸς ἀννώνης

The annona, transcribed in the Greek documents as ἀννώνη, was collected, as a surtax in kind upon the produce of the land, for the support of the legionaries stationed in Egypt.[79] An adaeratio of this impost in kind was permitted and is indicated frequently in the receipts. It is possible that an occasional deficit in the *annona* was made up by the exaction of a capitation tax paid by all persons not specially exempted.[80] Such an exaction may be compared with the unique reference to a μερισμὸς ἐρημοφυλακίας noted above and with the μερισμὸς τελέσματος καμήλων (SP. XXII. 145) which was probably imposed to make up a deficit in the estimated income from the τέλεσμα καμήλων (the familiar tax on camels). Three receipts for μερισμὸς ἀννώνης have been found: WO. II. 674, from Thebes and dated in the late second or early third century, records a payment of 1 drachma 5 obols ὑπ(ὲρ) μερισ(μοῦ) ἀννώ(νης); O. Strass. 161, from Upper Egypt and of about the same date, is a receipt ὑπ(ὲρ) μερισ(μοῦ) [αν]ρο( ) ἀννώ(νης);[81] P. Lond. III. 944 (p. 53), from Hermopolis Magna and dated A.D. 233, records a payment of 3 drachmae 2¾ obols for μερ(ισμὸς) παραλείμ(ματος) εἶδ(ους) ἀννώνης ā.[82]

The Bath-Tax

When the Macedonian and Greek followers of the Ptolemies settled in Egypt they established a social life similar to that to which they had been accustomed in their native lands. Prominent in that life was the gymnasium, which usually had a bath in connexion with it. Public baths owned by private individuals also were established, and in them the financial agents of the Ptolemies found a source of revenue, for the profits, or perhaps even the gross receipts, were taxed at the rate of one-third, the τρίτη βαλ(ανείου). This tax was continued under the Roman administration, but it could not have played a very important part in the revenues of the state, for there are but few extant receipts from the Roman period. The great tax-rolls from Caranis in the collection of the University of Michigan show a large number of payments always made in billon (ῥυπαραί) drachmae; a certain Gemellus, for example, paid 264 drachmae between December 24 and the following August 26. P. Ryl. II. 213. 474 attests the tax in Thmuis, PO. XII. 1436 shows that the tax was collected at a village in the Oxyrhynchite nome, and BGU. II. 362 records the payment of a tax on the bath at the village of Philagris in the Fayûm, but it is not certain what the rate was.[83]

When the Romans took over the administration of Egypt they established public baths supported by taxation. In Lower Egypt, however, the government was apparently content to continue the system of baths as they had existed in the Ptolemaic period, for the dearth of evidence for the bath-tax ($\beta\alpha\lambda\alpha\nu\epsilon\upsilon\tau\iota\kappa\acute{o}\nu$) in that region seems to indicate that there was no great need for tax-supported baths in that portion of Egypt where the Greeks had lived and developed their social institutions. Public baths supported by taxation, however, did exist in the Fayûm, certainly at Euhemeria and Caranis[84] and probably at Theadelphia[85] and Tebtynis.[86]

In Upper Egypt, however, the situation was quite different. The native Egyptians probably made no sustained demand for state baths, which simply meant more taxes to support a public convenience for which they themselves had no use, and the Greeks had not settled in sufficient numbers to develop the institution of the gymnasium throughout Upper Egypt. Consequently the Roman government was obliged to collect taxes for the support of public baths, which were a necessity of Roman civilization. The collection of a $\phi\acute{o}\rho\sigma\varsigma$ $\beta\alpha\lambda(\alpha\nu\epsilon\acute{\iota}\sigma\upsilon)$ by a $\beta\alpha\lambda(\alpha\nu\epsilon\upsilon\tau\acute{\eta}\varsigma)$ in A.D. 6–7[87] may indicate that privately owned public baths existed at Thebes or that private individuals were encouraged at the beginning of Roman administration to rent public baths built by the state.[88] Whatever that receipt may mean it is clear that by A.D. 23, and probably even earlier, the public baths in and around Thebes were supported by a tax. The method of assessment and collection seems quite clear at Thebes. At Charax, the North Market Quarter, Market Quarter, and South Quarter, and in many receipts which do not designate the place of origin, the annual assessment was 2 drachmae; this was undoubtedly a capitation tax paid by every tax-payer whether he used the baths or not. For the convenience of the tax-payers and of the collectors the tax was often paid in two instalments. The first instalment of 1 drachma $1\frac{1}{2}$ obols was paid with the $\lambda\alpha\sigma\gamma\rho\alpha\phi\acute{\iota}\alpha$ of 10 drachmae, making a total of 11 drachmae $1\frac{1}{2}$ obols which was paid with three billon tetradrachmae without any necessity for making change;[89] this was usually paid between January and May. The second instalment of $4\frac{1}{2}$ obols was paid with the $\chi\omega\mu\alpha\tau\iota\kappa\acute{o}\nu$ of 6 drachmae 4 obols, making a total of 7 drachmae $2\frac{1}{2}$ obols.[90] Inclusion of unknown charges makes the total payment vary up to 7 drachmae 5 obols 1 (or 2) chalci.[91] The second instalment (with the χωματικόν) was paid within the period from July to December.

The amount of the tax paid at Ceramion is unknown. Apparently only one receipt for the bath-tax is definitely known to come from that quarter. The amount recorded is 4 obols, which is probably an instalment (the second instalment mentioned above was sometimes 4 obols instead of 4½ obols). It is unsafe, however, to assume that the annual assessment was therefore 2 drachmae.

At Memnonia and the South-West Quarter (where the rate of the λαογραφία was higher) the rate was perhaps 4 drachmae, the highest amount recorded on the receipts from those places. Ostraca from Thebes, whose quarter of origin is not indicated, which record payments of 4 drachmae for the bath-tax are probably to be assigned to one or the other of these two quarters. Similarly, ostraca from Upper Egypt recording a rate of 2 drachmae for the bath-tax should probably be assigned to one of the quarters noted in the preceding paragraphs.[92]

The βαλανευτικόν was regularly collected by the officials of the state, in the first century by the πράκτωρ βαλανείου and in the second century by the πράκτορες ἀργυρικῶν.

There are also from Thebes many receipts issued by the τελώνης (or τελῶναι) θησ(αυροῦ) ἱερῶν or by the ἐπιτ(ηρηταὶ) θησ(αυροῦ) ἱερῶν or by the τελ(ῶναι) θησ(αυροῦ) ἱερῶν διὰ ἐπιτ(ηρητῶν) θησ(αυροῦ) ἱερῶν.[93] The receipt is given almost invariably during one of the summer months, and it states that the officials mentioned above have received the βαλ( ) of a given year. The amount of the tax is almost never given. The word θησαυρός should mean a granary and suggests payment in kind. Scholars doubted, however, that the payment for the bath-tax was actually in wheat, especially since all payments where the amount is actually recorded are in money and for 1 drachma; and Otto, pointing out that where it is written out ἱερῶν is invariably in the plural, suggested that θησαυρὸς ἱερῶν was equivalent to the ἱερατικά department of the state financial system. O. Strass. 440, recording payment of 1/12 artaba of wheat for βαλ(ανευτικόν), gave the solution of the payments made to the τελῶναι and ἐπιτηρηταί. The thesaurus was a granary, and the payments were normally in wheat. The expansion of β( ) as β(αλανευτικόν) in WO. II. 1587, where 1 drachma is paid ὑπ(ἐρ) τι(μῆς) (ἀρτάβης) κδ ($\frac{1}{24}$), suggests that the 1 drachma paid to the τελῶναι in other ostraca was likewise an *adaeratio* of the payment in kind. The fact that 1 drachma should normally have purchased three times as much grain as $\frac{1}{24}$ of an artaba does not alter this conclusion. It becomes evident that temples, presumably in Thebes, owned a bath or baths in some part of the city, and that the bath-tax was paid to the temples in kind at a fixed amount so well known that it was almost never recorded. In the two ostraca where the amount is preserved there was doubtless some special reason for the departure from the usual formula, but there is not sufficient evidence in the two examples to determine what that reason may have been in each case. There is no evidence to determine what temples received the revenue from the tax or where the baths were situated. It is unlikely that baths owned by the temples were rival establishments in the same districts as the public baths owned by the state and supported by the capitation tax paid in money. Memnonia, the South-West Quarter, Ceramion, Charax, the Market Quarter, the North Market Quarter, and the South Quarter were all assessed a bath-tax in money. Ophi is the only quarter from which no such receipts have been found. It is possible that the bath for which a tax in kind was collected for the temples was located there; but to assign all receipts issued by the τελῶναι and ἐπιτ(ηρηταὶ) θησα(υροῦ) ἱερῶν to Ophi makes too many receipts from such an obscure district. The solution of the problem requires further evidence. In any case the situation in Thebes was entirely different from that in the Fayûm where privately owned baths were the rule and where a temple as the owner of a private bath paid a tax to the state.[94] How large the revenue from the tax in kind paid to the thesaurus of the temples was cannot be determined, nor do we know what circumstances led the Roman government to permit the collection of a tax for the support of baths owned by temples. It is possible, however, that the powerful priests had built a bath during the Ptolemaic period and had maintained it through a tax in kind, and that the Roman administration did not care to antagonize the priesthood by disturbing their privilege.

The τέλ(ος) βαλ(ανευτικόν) is attested for Elephantine in O.

Mey. 13–14 (6 and 5 B.C.). The tax, which is obviously for a government-owned public bath, was at least 5 obols a year and probably more.[95] From a later period are the ostraca recording the tax published by Viereck, but the annual rate cannot be determined without further evidence.[96]

One ostracon from Coptos (WO. II. 501) attests the existence of the tax in that city. The payment of 6 drachmae 4 obols is larger than that known at Thebes, but since the amount may have included arrears it is impossible without further evidence to accept that as the annual rate.[97]

The payments of 40 drachmae for the bath-tax at Denderah, in the demotic ostraca published in *Archiv*, IV, pp. 125 ff., are almost incredibly large.

O. Strass. 262–3 are unusual in that they apparently mention a particular bath for which the tax is collected. They record receipts issued by the πράκτωρ Θεαγῶν for payments for the βαλανείου Μακ(εδώνων) in the years A.D. 26 and 29.

Although the βαλανευτικόν was obviously a capitation tax, it is not ordinarily designated as a μερισμός in the receipts. It is possible that WO. II. 617 and 1061 recording receipts issued by the ἀπαιτηταὶ μερισμοῦ βαλ( ) indicate a special assessment to cover the cost of building a bath or of extraordinary repairs.

Μερισμὸς ἀνδριάντος

From time to time special capitation taxes were assessed to cover the expenses of erecting statues of the reigning emperor in the cities of Egypt. Receipts for such assessments have been found in considerable number at Elephantine, where the presence of a Roman garrison made the erection of such a tribute to the emperor important. Receipts have also been found at Thebes. The formula for the payment in the receipts varies at different times according to the nature of the dedication and the ideas of the scribes.[98] At Elephantine about A.D. 114–15 there is recorded a payment ὑπ(ὲρ) τιμῆ(ς) καὶ δαπανή(ματος) ἀνδ(ριάντος) Τραιανοῦ, and in P. Bad. IV. 101 this expression is supplemented by the location of the statue, which was erected in the Caesareum: ἀνατεθέντος ἐν Καισαρίῳ; the whole expression may be translated 'for the cost and expense of a statue of Hadrian erected in the Caesareum'. An ostracon published in *Archiv*. VI, p. 219, no. 4, dated A.D. 117–18, records payment for συνεισφορᾶς ἀν-δ(ριάντος) χαλκ(οῦ) καὶ προτομῆς ἀργυρᾶς ῾Αδριανοῦ τοῦ κυρίου, a 'contribution for a bronze statue and a silver bust of Hadrian the Lord'. Somewhat similar is the expression found in A.D. 141 ὑπ(ὲρ) μερισ(μοῦ) ἀνδριάντ(ος) καὶ προτομ(ῆς), and again in A.D. 161–2 μερισμ(οῦ) ἀνδριά(ν)τ(ων) β̄ καὶ προτομ(ῶν) β̄ τῶν κυρίων Καισάρων. The formula in WO. II. 1430, from Thebes and dated A.D. 138–9 is ὑπ(ὲρ) ἀνδ(ριάντος) Καίσαρος ῾Αδριανοῦ.

Three receipts published by Wilcken (WO. II. 559, 603, 604) for μερισμὸς ἀνδ( ) were left unexplained by him.[99] Milne published another in O. Theb. 42, and suggested that the contracted word be expanded ἀνδ(ριάντος), just as Wilcken had expanded the similar contraction in receipts from Elephantine. He pointed out that the three receipts published by Wilcken and O. Theb. 42 all fell in two years, the eighteenth of Hadrian and the fifth of Antoninus Pius, although it was difficult to explain why funds for statues should have been collected in those particular years. Further receipts, from Thebes, however, were published in O. Strass. 108, 118, 159, of which the first two were dated in 103 and 122 (?) respectively. Viereck expanded the abbreviation in each case as ἀνδ(ριάντων). From Elephantine Wilcken had published a series of receipts which differed in formula from those previously noted, and which are dated from A.D. 128–9 to 139–40, also one dated 143–4; O. Tait, p. 66, no. 21, dated A.D. 194 is similar. These receipts record payments for μερισμ(οῦ) ἐπικεφαλί(ου) ἀνδ( ) ἀνακεχ( ). The last two words were expanded as ἀνδ(ριάντος/ων) ἀνακεχ(ρυσαμένου/ων). Now it is, of course, possible that the statues of the emperors were gilded and that they required regilding from time to time, and that for this a capitation tax was collected. But it is difficult to see why a series of μερισμοί should have been collected to cover that expense in every year from A.D. 128–9 to 139–40, and also why that assessment should increase slightly from year to year. It is significant that the μερισμὸς ἀνακ(εχωρηκότων) behaved in precisely this manner at Thebes, as has been noted above; and this phenomenon combined with the fact that very few receipts for μερισμὸς ἀνακ(εχωρηκότων) have been found at Elephantine suggests the possibility that these receipts should be expanded to read ὑπ(ὲρ) μερισμ(οῦ) ἐπικεφαλί(ου) ἀνδ(ρῶν) ἀνακεχ(ωρηκότων); ἐπικεφαλί(ου) in this case is an objective genitive instead of being a redundant adjective, and the phrase should be translated 'for the capitation tax (to cover the non-payment) of the poll-tax of men who have fled'. O. Strass. 284 has the phrase ὑπ(ὲρ) μερισμοῦ ἐπικεφαλιο(ῦ) ἀνακεχ( ), and Viereck expanded ἀνακεχ(ρυσωμένου) and stated in his note that ἀνδριάντος is to be supplied; but, remembering the common formula μερισμὸς ἀνακ(εχωρηκότων), it is much easier to expand ἀνα-κεχ(ωρηκότων), since it is not even necessary to supply ἀνδρῶν in order to make sense. Unfortunately for this theory, however, Wilcken read in WO. II. 183 ἀνδρια( ) ἀνακ( ). It is just possible that he misread the first word, and the same thing may be true of WO. II. 151 which was read as ὑπ(ὲρ) μερισμο(ῦ) ἐπι-κεφαλί(ου) ἀνδριάντ(ος); perhaps the latter should rather be read ὑπ(ὲρ) μερισμο(ῦ) ἐπικεφαλί(ου) ἀνδ(ρῶν) ἀνακ(εχωρηκότων).[100] If this be true, it is possible that some, or even all, of the receipts for μερισμὸς ἀνδ( ), when not clearly to be expanded ἀνδ(ριάντος) because of an unmistakable reference to bronze or silver sculpture or the like, should be expanded ἀνδ(ρῶν) ⟨ἀνακεχωρηκότων⟩.

If the expansion of ανδ( ) and of ανδ( ) ἀνακεχ( ) suggested above is correct, the occasions on which capitation taxes were collected for defraying the cost of erecting statues in honour of the Roman emperors are somewhat reduced. At Thebes the only reference regarded by Wilcken as certain is to a statue of Hadrian for which a μερισμός was collected in the second year of the reign of his successor Antoninus Pius (A.D. 138–9); a statue at that date might be regarded as a pious memorial to the late emperor who had honoured Egypt with a visit some years earlier and had been pleased to grant some favours in regard to taxation and to tenure of domain land.[101] Possibly O. Strass. 108, dated in A.D. 103, recording a payment of 3 obols for μερισμ(οῦ), ἀνδ( ), refers to a statue of Trajan, since the μερισμὸς ἀνα-κ(εχωρηκότων) is not attested until later in his reign, although the reason for erecting a statue of Trajan as late as the fourth or fifth year of his reign is not known. O. Theb. 42 and WO. II. 559 are dated in A.D. 133, the eighteenth year of Hadrian; and if the payment for μερισμὸς ἀνδ( ) actually refers to a statue, it must, as Milne suggests,[102] represent 'a collection for a rather belated statue of the emperor, put up to celebrate his visit to Thebes over two years previously'.[103] WO. II. 603 and 604, recording a payment for μερισμὸς ἀνδ( ) of the fifth year of Antoninus Pius, are, as Milne admits,[104] still more difficult to explain on the supposition that the ἀνδ( ) is to be expanded as ἀνδ(ριάντος). O. Strass. 118 and 159 are of uncertain date.[105]

At Elephantine WO. II. 71–3 record payments ὑπ(ὲρ) ἀν-δριάντ(ος) made in the seventh year of Trajan, the year after the payment recorded at Thebes.[106] Payments for a statue of Trajan are also recorded in the year A.D. 114–15, and, presumably for the same statue, in A.D. 116; the statue is perhaps to be explained as a symbol of loyalty expressed during or after the Jewish revolts in Alexandria which later spread throughout Egypt and Cyrenaïca.[107] In 117–18 Hadrian was honoured at his accession by a statue of bronze and a silver bust. The statue and bust, for which payment was made in A.D. 141, were possibly a belated recognition of the accession of Antoninus Pius. An exceptionally high capitation tax of 10 drachmae was collected in A.D. 161–2 for busts and statues of the two emperors, Marcus Aurelius and Lucius Verus, set up promptly after their accession.

Μερισμὸς ᾿Αδριανείου

Several ostraca and papyri from Elephantine, Hermopolis Magna, and perhaps from Thebes,[108] record receipts for a tax called μερισμὸς ᾿Αδριανείου. Since temples dedicated to the emperor Hadrian are known to have existed in Alexandria, Memphis, the Fayûm, Oxyrhynchus, and Hermopolis, it was but natural to assume that such payments were to defray the cost of such temples. The receipt from Elephantine (WO. II. 227), however, is dated in A.D. 155 and so could hardly be for the construction of a temple so many years after the death of Hadrian, although it might be interpreted as a payment for the maintenance of the temple and its cult. The fact that in the accounts of the μερισμὸς ᾿Αδριανείου from Hermopolis (P. Lips. 93–6) the tax is associated with the ναύβιον led Professor A.C. Johnson to suggest that the payment was not for the construction or maintenance of a temple, but for the construction or repair of a canal named in honour of the emperor. Further evidence is necessary to establish this view.

Μερισμὸς πλινθευομένης

O. Strass. 245, from Thebes and dated A.D. 139, records the payment for which a receipt is given by the ἀπαιτη(τὴς) μερισμοῦ πλινθ(ευομένης) καὶ . . . , and Tait conjectured Ἁδριανείου to fill the lacuna. If this conjectural reading is correct, it is possible to reconcile it with either of the theories quoted above, since brick-work could be used for a dike as well as for a temple. The nature of the tax for brick-work is not clear, although it is found in a number of receipts from Thebes and Oxyrhynchus.[109] Grenfell and Hunt[110] suggested that the tax was paid in lieu of providing so many bricks to the government,[111] and they further suggested that it may well be a variant for the tax called ναύβιον. The fact that the tax was frequently called a μερισμός tells against this theory, since the ναύβιον was not a capitation tax but was a tax assessed in money on land. Wilcken, Grenfell and Hunt, and Tait assume that WO. II. 1421, from Thebes and dated in A.D. 118–19, proves that the μερισμὸς πλινθ( ) recorded in that receipt was assessed and collected on the arura.[112] The ostracon is so mutilated, however, that it is not at all certain that the payment calculated upon the arura was the μερισμὸς πλινθ( ) of line 2; there is room in the broken lines for another tax.

In WO. II. 592 the bricks were apparently intended for the construction or repair of a military building, πραι(τωρίου). In PO. III. 574 the bricks are for the construction of Παμμέ(νους) Παραδί(σου) βαθμοῦ ᾱ Ἑρμαίου βαθμ(οῦ) ᾱ Δρόμ(ου) Θο[ήριδος . . .]; a payment of 11 drachmae 4 obols for βαθμῶν ε̄ (2 drachmae 2 obols per step) is recorded at the mutilated beginning of the document.

Μερισμοί for other Public Works

In P. Teb. II. 352, dated A.D. 158, a receipt is given for the payment of the μερισμὸς ἔργ(ων) Κρίου, which in line 10 is shortened to μερισμο(ῦ) Κρίου. The editors of the document suppose that Κρῖος is a proper name, 'and the mention of ἔργ(ων) suggests that the tax was levied for public works under the direction of Crius'. But since the levy is made in connexion with the ναύβιον, whose proceeds were devoted to the maintenance of the dike- and canal-system, it is possible that κρῖος should be understood in the sense in which it appears in BGU. I. 14. iii. 9, 23 as a part of the structure of canals or sluices, rather than as a proper name. Similarly, the payments for τιμὴ θυρῶν collected with the ναύβιον are probably to cover the cost of new sluices in the irrigation-system.[113]

On the other hand, the μερισμὸς Ζοίλου and the μερισμὸς Κάμπωνος may well be taxes for public works, and perhaps Ζόιλος and Κάμπων were the superintendents of these projects,[114] which may have been canals. A payment for the 'canal of the Divine Julius' is found in O. Tait, p. 70, no. 41, and a μερισμὸς διώρυγος in WO. II. 259 from Elephantine and in WO. II. 577 from Thebes.[115]

Μερισμὸς ὠνίων ἐνλείμματος τελωνικῶν

A tax similar in purpose to the μερισμὸς ἀνακ(εχωρηκότων) was the μερισμὸς ὠνίων ἐνλείμματος τελωνικῶν found in receipts from Thebes dating from A.D. 126–7 to 159–60.[116] The editors of the Rylands papyri[117] supposed that the phrase represents two separate taxes and should properly be written μερισμὸς ὠνίων ‹καὶ μερισμὸς› ἐνλείμματος τελωνικῶν. Their reason for this is that in the year A.D. 140 the same company of collectors (ἀπαιτηταί) at Thebes were collecting a tax called μερισμὸς ἐνλείμματος τελωνικῶν and also a tax called μερισμὸς πεντηκοστῆς which they identified with the πεντηκοστὴ ὠνίων.[118] They desire always to read μερισμὸς τελ( ) ὠνίων as μερισμὸς τέλ(ους) ὠνίων and distinguish between it and the μερισμὸς ἐνλείμματος τελωνικῶν. Wilcken,[119] on the other hand, had supposed that the latter tax was always to be associated with ὠνία, and that various expressions found in the ostraca were merely variants. I agree with Wilcken's view. There are several flaws in the arguments presented by the editors of the Rylands papyri. First, the πεντηκοστὴ ὠνίων may very properly be referred to as τελωνικῶν, since the tax on sales was collected by a τελώνης.[120] Second, the πεντηκοστὴ ὠνίων is quite specifically designated in the two ostraca, which give receipts therefor, whereas the μερισμὸς πεντηκοστῆς without further specification might be referred to the customs collected by the τελῶναι (πεντηκοστῆς). Third, the distinction between the two taxes is unsound because the ἀπαιτηταὶ Χά(ρακος) [μερισμ(οῦ)] τελ( ) ὠνίων in A.D. 131–2 collect 12 obols for the tax, and the ἀπαιτηταὶ μερισμοῦ τελ(ωνικῶν) in the same year collect 12 obols, which rather indicates that the two expressions denote the same tax, which is merely designated in a different way by different scribes attached to the company of ἀπαιτηταί. In the following year, moreover, 2 drachmae are collected for the tax at Charax where it is called ὑπ(ὲρ) ὠνίων or ὑπ(ὲρ) μερισμοῦ ὠνίων, at Ophi (?) and in the South-West Quarter (?) where it is called μερισμὸς ὠνίων ἐνλείμματος τελωνικῶν, and at the South Quarter where it is called μερισμὸς τελωνικῶν. This is, I think, sufficient to establish Wilcken's contention that the different terms are simply variants for the same tax.[121]

It seems evident that the μερισμός was collected to make up a deficit in a tax on sales, but the variation in the formula used makes it difficult to determine what tax on sales was meant. The ὠνία of πεντηκοστὴ ὠνίων might be called τελωνικά, since that tax was collected by a τελώνης; the customs collected by the τελῶναι (πεντηκοστῆς) might likewise be called τελωνικά; and also the τέλος ἀγορανομίας ὠνίων might be included in τελωνικά, since it, too, was often collected by τελῶναι.[122] It is possible that the editors of the Rylands Papyri are right in supposing that a καί should be supplied in the complete formula for the tax, even though they are probably wrong about there being two separate μερισμοί involved, and thus the deficit may have been in other taxes besides the πεντηκοστὴ ὠνίων. On the basis of the present available evidence, however, it is impossible to determine what other taxes, if any, were involved.

It is also uncertain whether this μερισμός was assessed upon the whole population of Thebes or whether it was limited to a specific class or classes connected with the trades which paid the tax on sales and perhaps the tolls. The buyer was ordinarily responsible for the payment of the tax on sales[123] and the shipper for the customs-tolls.[124]

The occasion for the establishment of this μερισμός was doubtless the same as that of the μερισμὸς ἀνακ(εχωρηκότων). PO. I. 44 (= W. Chrest. 275) is a letter, dated at the end of the first century after Christ, from the strategus in Oxyrhynchus to the basilico-grammateus complaining of the difficulty of finding a publican (δημοσιώνης) to bid on the ἀγορανομεῖον and the ἐγκύκλιον, both taxes on sales. It is evident that the populace had found a way to avoid payment of market-taxes and that the tax-farmers were unable to make a profit on the collection. A similar condition in the second century doubtless led to the establishment of the μερισμὸς ὠνίων ἐνλείμματος τελωνικῶν.

This μερισμός is attested elsewhere than Thebes only in a statement in a document from Thmuis[125] of a balance after allocation of the excess from a μερισμός of the fifth year and from the μερισμὸς ἐνδεήματος τελωνικῶν (capitation tax for the deficit in farmed taxes).

Μερισμὸς τελέσματος καμήλων

The only reference to this μερισμός of the familiar tax on camels is found in SP. XXII. 145 from Heraclia and dated A.D. 191. It is probably to be explained as a rare assessment made necessary by a deficit in the expected collections of the tax on camels. Again it is uncertain what portion of the populace was liable to this tax, but the high rate of 8 drachmae attested probably indicates that only a small percentage of the tax-paying citizens paid this levy, perhaps only the owners of camels.

Μερισμὸς διοικήσεως

This is the heading for one of the totals in a list of taxes in P. Teb. II. 500, and it may indicate a supplementary capitation tax exacted to supply a deficit in the revenues of the financial department called Διοίκησις.[126] The payment of $3\frac{1}{2}$ obols collected by the ἀπαιτ(ηταὶ) μερισμ(ῶν) πρακτορίου in WO. II. 517 is probably to be placed in the same category, for the πρακτόριον is to be understood as the bureau of the tax-collectors called πράκτορες.

Other Μερισμοί for the Army

Μερισμοί of the eighteenth year (A.D. 117–18) ὑπ(ὲρ) προυρίου (sic!) περὶ Φοινίκ(ην) καλο[ύ]μενον Σανδάντην were collected at Elephantine in the following year. The high amount, 14 drachmae $1\frac{3}{4}$ obols, probably represents a special assessment to cover the cost of a military post at the place named. The tax is attested only in WO. II. 271.

Similar is the μερισ(μὸς) πρεσιδί(ου) attested in WO. II. 621 from Thebes and dated in A.D. 145.

A μερισμὸς στόλου στρατιωτῶν was collected in A.D. 222, although the money had been needed two years previous to that date.[127] It is attested in SB. 5677, perhaps from Hermopolis. The payment of 85 drachmae seems very high, although the depreciation of the currency may have begun to make itself felt in the rates of such extraordinary levies more quickly than in the ordinary taxes. The payment is said to be ἀπὸ προχρείας, and this 'previous need' probably explains why the payment of this μερισμός for the cost of an expedition was exacted at a time when there was no important military activity. A μερισμὸς προχ(ρείας) also is attested in WO. II. 549 and 551, from Thebes and dated A.D. 131–2.

Unexplained Μερισμοί

P. Lond. III. 844 (p. 54), from Socnopaei Nesus and dated in A.D. 174, includes among other capitation taxes a payment for μερισμὸς θηρίων which, although it has something to do with wild animals, is not explained as to purpose or occasion. Perhaps it is to be connected with the payment to the account of the chief huntsmen (εἰς λόγο(ν) ἀρχικυν(ηγ)ῶ(ν)) and with the μερισμὸς κυνη(γετικῶν) δορά(των) at Thebes (WO. II. 1545, 579, 1247, 1248). Even more obscure is μερισμὸς διθ( ) in O. Strass. 232 from Thebes, dated A.D. 147. If it were possible to read μερισμὸς λιθ( ) we might suppose that a capitation tax had been exacted to pay for the stone used in constructing a military camp or some public building, for a payment ὑπὲρ λίθ(ου) appears in SB. 5677 where the phrase ἀπὸ προχ(ρείας) shows that the construction had taken place before the tax was levied. Quite obscure also are μερισμὸς να( ) and μερ[ι]σ(μὸς) μη( ) καὶ Σύρσεως in SB. 5677, perhaps from Hermopolis; the document is dated in A.D. 222. A receipt (BGU. VII. 1605 from Philadelphia and dated A.D. 182) from the νομάρχαι to a farmer for 100 drachmae for μερισ . .( ) Φιλ. τοπ( ) is likewise unexplained. In O. Tait, p. 69, no. 35 (from Charax and dated A.D. 141), the nature of the μερισμός, for which four billon drachmae were paid to the collector of money taxes along with the payments for χω(ματικόν) and βαλ(ανευτικόν), is lost in the lacuna.

At Elephantine-Syene from A.D. 115 to 179, and perhaps even to 227–8, receipts are found for a μερισμός or for μερισμοί without further designation. It is, of course, not impossible that this levy is equivalent to the μερισμὸς ἀνακ(εχωρηκότων) found at Thebes and so far but seldom attested for Elephantine-Syene, although the fixing of the assessment at 4 drachmae a year from A.D. 146 to 152 makes this unlikely.[128] The receipts in other years vary in amount from 3½ obols to 8 drachmae 2½ obols and even 19 drachmae ½ obol in A.D. 227–8, although it is quite probable that some of these represent instalments and others may include arrears.[129]

Other localities at which similar μερισμοί are attested, although far fewer receipts have been found, are Ophi (as early as A.D. 75), Charax, the South-West Quarter and the South Quarter at Thebes, Coptos, Apollonopolis Magna (Edfu); a μερισμός at Thmuis (P. Ryl. II. 214 (B)) has been noted above. SP. v. 101 contains a memorandum to the βουλή of Hermopolis Magna concerning an ἀργυρίου μερισμός of 60 drachmae per person.[130]

In the third century other towns and cities apparently sought to meet deficits in general revenues, after the municipalities had become responsible for the collection of revenues of the state, by the levying of capitation taxes. In SB. 7596 there is reference to a μερισμὸς ἐπιβολῆς in which the total amount exacted at Elephantine was 1 talent 38 drachmae, or 7½ drachmae per man; there were, therefore, 813 tax-payers. At Thebes (WO. II. 1472) in A.D. 255 4 drachmae were paid by one man for an ἐπιβολή of 2 talents, and (according to O. Wilb.-Brk. 43) 2 drachmae were paid in the same year at the Market Quarter ὑπ(ὲρ) ληfor(μάτων), that is, for the deficit in the receipts for the year. At Caranis (O. Mich. Car. 134) in A.D. 290 a single payment of 400 drachmae was made for ἐπιβολὴ καταγ(ωγῶν) ὀρ(ιοδεικτίας) Καρ(ανίδος). With these levies may be compared the 60 drachmae μερισμός at Hermopolis (SP. v. 101) and the ἐπιβολὴ τοῦ ἱεροῦ ἀποτάκτου in PO. XIV. 1662.

The multiplication of capitation taxes in the second century was probably caused by the reluctance of the government to invite trouble by raising the rates of existing taxes. The tax-payers would pay a new tax for new police, from whose protection they benefited directly, with less complaint than would be made if the existing police-tax were doubled. The high rates of the μερισμοί in the third century may reflect the depreciation which had begun in the second half of the third century, but it also shows how the government grasped the easy means of raising revenue by large capitation taxes. The patent injustice and economic unsoundness of such taxes which hastened the complete impoverishment of the native Egyptians may well have contributed to the economic decline of Egypt in the third century.

X

CAPITATION TAXES LIMITED TO CERTAIN CLASSES OF THE POPULATION

The Ἰουδαίων τέλεσμα

THE Ἰουδαίων τέλεσμα or, as it was called in the Arsinoite nome, Ἰουδαϊκὸν τέλεσμα was a capitation tax paid by the Jews in Egypt. Although it was probably assessed throughout all Egypt, it is attested only in receipts from Apollonopolis Magna (Edfu) dating from A.D. 71–2 to 116,[1] and in a report from an amphodarch of the city of Arsinoë dated A.D. 72–3.[2] From the evidence of the latter document it is clear that the tax fell upon both males and females over the age of three years, and that a Jew had to pay the tax upon his slaves as well as for the members of his own family. The age of exemption from the tax is not stated in the report, but it was probably sixty-two years, as it was for the poll-tax.[3]

The amount of the annual assessment of the tax at Apollonopolis Magna and at Arsinoë was the same, 8 drachmae 2 obols, which were often paid in two instalments of about one-half.[4] In addition to the Ἰουδαίων τέλεσμα each Jew was obliged to pay 1 drachma annually for the ἀπαρχή. The payment of 1 drachma for ἀπαρχή was occasionally included, without naming it, in receipts for the Ἰουδαίων τέλεσμα, so that a payment of 9 drachmae 2 obols was apparently made for the latter tax.[5] From ostraca found at Apollonopolis Magna[6] we learn that 8 drachmae 2 obols was regarded as the equivalent of 2 *denarii* (τιμὴ δηναρίων δύο) which may well be an indication that the rate of the tax had been fixed at Rome, for such an expression is not found elsewhere in the records of Egyptian taxation[7] whose terminology was largely an inheritance from the Ptolemaic administration.

After the fall of Jerusalem (September 2, A.D. 70) Vespasian ordered that the tax of ½ shekel, formerly paid by the Jews to the temple of Jehovah at Jerusalem, should be paid into the treasury of Jupiter Capitolinus.[8] In Greek this temple-tax was called the δίδραχμον, since the Jewish shekel was approximately equivalent to the Attic tetradrachm. The Attic drachma was considered equivalent to the Roman *denarius*, so that when Vespasian confiscated the temple-tax the rate of payment in Roman coinage was 2 *denarii*. Wessely, therefore, concluded that the Ἰουδαϊκὸν τέλεσμα was the same tax as the confiscated δίδραχμον or temple-tax.[9] In this he was followed by P. M. Meyer.[10] Schürer, however, doubted this identification on two grounds: first, because the Ἰουδαϊκὸν τέλεσμα was collected from all Jews of both sexes over three years of age, whereas the old temple-tax had been paid only by males over the age of twenty years; second, the Ἰουδαϊκὸν τέλεσμα seemed to him to have existed before A.D. 70, as he interpreted the amphodarch's report.[11] This passage of the report of the amphodarch Heraclides states that in his district (Ἀπολλω(νίου) Παρε(μβολή)) there were fifteen Jews who paid the Ἰουδαϊκὸν τέλεσμα, among whom were eleven adults and four minors. Of the minors one was five years old, two were four years old, and one was three years of age. The name of the last one had been added to the rolls only in the current year (A.D. 72–3). The two four-year-old children were added to the rolls in the preceding year, after an epicrisis had been held to determine their age and their consequent liability to payment of the tax—for, as the report states, they were *one year old in the second year of Vespasian*.

In answer to Schürer's first objection Wilcken[12] explained that Vespasian in confiscating the temple-tax (and apparently also the ἀπαρχή) simply extended the basis of taxation, thus making the burden heavier. This is probably somewhat similar to the policy of Domitian, of whom Suetonius[13] says 'Judaicus fiscus acerbissime actus est'. Wilcken declares that Schürer's second point is not pertinent.[14] Schürer may have gained his false impression that the tax had been collected before A.D. 70 from the elaboration of technical terminology in which the amphodarch Heraclides revelled throughout his report. The fact that in lines 440 ff. of the report it is stated that in the preceding year children of three years had been added to the rolls from a supplementary report based upon a formal inquiry (καὶ διὰ προσγρά(φου) ἀ[ναλαμβ(ανόμενοι)] ἐκ τῆς γενομέ(νης) ἐπικρίσ[εως]) means simply that epicrisis was necessary to determine the age of the child before affixing its name to the roll of tax-payers;

it does not necessarily mean that the tax had been collected before the fourth year (A.D. 71–2), although the rolls for the collection of the tax had probably been compiled in the previous (third) year upon receipt of Vespasian's order that the collection of the tax be begun (in A.D. 71–2). No mention is made in the report of the epicrisis of the child who was five years old in A.D. 72–3, because apparently no epicrisis had been necessary two years before to determine whether a child so old was liable to the payment of the tax. The liability was self-evident.

It is necessary to ascertain, if possible, why the second year of Vespasian is mentioned in the report, for that is one of the objections raised by Schürer, and why liability for payment of the Ἰουδαϊκὸν τέλεσμα began at the age of three years rather than some other age such as fourteeen years, the age when payment of the poll-tax was begun both in Egypt and in Syria,[15] or twenty years, the age when the young men of Israel began to pay the old δίδραχμον to the temple in Jerusalem. A child of three years was certainly not able to earn the money for the payment of the tax, and yet if the selection of that age was purely arbitrary, why did not Vespasian select one year of age for the beginning of liability to the tax, since that would have added thousands of *denarii* paid for children under three years old? It may be possible to find the reason for the beginning of liability at three years of age in the chronology of the events which led to the confiscation of the temple-tax.

During the fighting at Rome between the followers of Vitellius and of Vespasian the great temple of Jupiter Capitolinus was destroyed by fire. It was, of course, necessary for the victorious Vespasian to restore that religious symbol of the state whose sovereignty he had just gained. Dio Cassius[16] states that Vespasian began the reconstruction immediately (εὐθύς), and in Tacitus[17] the ceremonies attending the laying of the foundation stone of the temple are related among the events of the year A.D. 70. Yet Hieronymus states that in the fifth year of his reign (A.D. 73) 'Vespasianus Capitolium aedificare orsus'.[18] If the information in Hieronymus is accurate, it is clear that some time elapsed between the ceremonies described by Tacitus and the actual rebuilding of the temple. It is probable that Vespasian was deterred from immediately beginning actual construction

of the new temple by that incubus of the early part of his reign—
the exhaustion of the imperial treasury. An unexpected source
of revenue, however, soon came to hand.

When Vespasian went to Rome after his elevation to the principate, he left unfinished the suppression of the rebellion in
Judaea. He assigned to his son Titus the command against the
Jews, who had withdrawn into Jerusalem in great numbers to
make a last stand against the forces of Rome. Titus began his
famous siege of Jerusalem in the spring of A.D. 70, and on the
second of the following September the last stronghold of the
upper city fell. The Jews had obstinately rejected the terms presented by Titus before and also during the siege,[19] and they
reaped their reward in the destruction of their holy city and the
burning of the temple of Jehovah, which was never restored
thereafter. The Jewish rabbis then concluded that the duty of
paying the temple-tax ceased when the temple no longer existed,[20]
but Vespasian decided otherwise and was able to put the income
from the tax to good use. He decreed that the tax should be
exacted from every Jew at the rate of 2 *denarii* per annum, and
should be paid into the treasury of Jupiter Capitolinus in Rome.
If we may make universal the regulations deduced from the
report of the amphodarch of Arsinoë, the decree must have
provided that the tax be collected from every Jew, male or
female, one year of age (or older) in the second year of the
reign of Vespasian (A.D. 70), the year when the Jews had defied
the Roman army of Titus before the walls of Jerusalem. This
included almost every Jew alive at the time of the siege. It is
probable that the decree ordering this confiscation of the temple-
tax was promulgated shortly before or after the triumph over
the Jews celebrated by Vespasian and Titus in the summer of
A.D. 71.[21] The old temple-tax had been due by the month of
Adar (approximately March),[22] and it was probably the intention
of Vespasian to make the first collection in the following (fourth)
year of his reign, in order to give the bureaux throughout the
empire time to compile the tax-lists and make the necessary
arrangements for the systematic collection of this tax. Considerable time was required for this, because of the extension of
liability for payment of the Ἰουδαϊκὸν τέλεσμα to include women
and children.

In the fourth year of Vespasian,[23] therefore, we find the first evidence of payment of the tax on Jews both at Apollonopolis Magna and at Arsinoë, where the roll of the amphodarch dated in the fifth year of Vespasian is stated to have been checked against the records of the fourth year: σ[υ]νοψισμένον [πρὸς τὸ (τέταρτον) (ἔτος)]. Every Jew who was one year of age in the second year of Vespasian was three years old in the fourth year of his reign, and three years consequently was taken as the age at which all Jews thereafter became liable to the tax.

When the collections of the tax on Jews made in the fourth year of Vespasian were sent to Rome, it was possible to use the revenues to make a real beginning at rebuilding the temple of Jupiter Capitolinus. It is in the fifth year (A.D. 73), Hieronymus states, that Vespasian began the rebuilding of that temple.

In Egypt, however, there was an unforeseen difficulty in the confiscation of the temple-tax which soon had to be taken into account. In the second century B.C. Onias IV, of the family of high priests at Jerusalem, had been forced to flee for his life. He found refuge in Egypt and asked Ptolemy to permit him to build a temple of Jehovah which should be a centre of loyalty for the many Jews in Egypt. The king of Egypt was persuaded that a sanctuary rivalling the temple in Jerusalem would draw the interests of his Jewish subjects away from Judaea, which was no longer under Egyptian control, and so the temple was built in the Heliopolite nome. To it the Jews of Egypt, I believe, had paid the temple-tax down to the time of Vespasian, instead of paying the δίδραχμον to the temple in Jerusalem. Therefore not only was the extension of that tax in Egypt to include Jewish women and children and even slaves of Jews a heavy burden upon a class of inhabitants who had hitherto enjoyed many privileges under Roman rule in Egypt, but its confiscation was also a severe blow to the revenues of a temple still in existence after the destruction of the temple in Jerusalem.[24] The results may be seen in the Jewish disturbances, during the prefecture of Ti. Julius Lupus, which are described by Josephus.[25] The Zealots, σικάριοι Josephus calls them, who escaped from the war in Judea (which had not entirely ceased with the capture of Jerusalem) fled to Egypt and there turned their hands to new mischief. For they persuaded many of the Egyptian Jews 'to assert their liberty, to consider the Romans to be no better than themselves, and to regard God as their only ruler'. Although Josephus relates that the better class of Jews had no part in this sedition and, indeed, turned the agitators over to the Roman authorities, it is clear that he has not told the whole story. Reading between the lines of Josephus it is evident that the attempted rebellion centred in the temple of Onias, and that the Zealots' injunction to the Jews 'to regard God as their only ruler' meant to pay the temple-tax to the temple of Jehovah and not to the Roman government. Lupus, striving to be discreet in dealing with the ever-troublesome Jewish problem in Alexandria, wrote to the emperor for instructions, and Vespasian sent orders to take the drastic step of demolishing the temple of Onias. Lupus obeyed the order only in part, for he merely carried off some of the dedications and closed the temple. It is not clear whether he felt it unsafe to destroy the temple or thought his action sufficient to halt the movement of sedition among the Jews. Lupus died shortly after, and his successor Q. Paulinus was in office in the year A.D. 72–3.[26] It is evident that the measures taken by Lupus were insufficient and that the disorders continued among the Jews, for Paulinus was obliged to close the temple permanently so that worship there was stopped forever. Hieronymus dates a *seditio* (στάσις) at Alexandria in the fifth year of Vespasian (A.D. 73). This uprising, I believe, was caused by the confiscation of the temple-tax and led to the final closing of the temple of Onias by Paulinus. It is not likely that the *seditio* of Hieronymus is to be limited to the disturbance described by Josephus who, in his anxiety to present the Jews in a favourable light to the Greeks and Romans, has related an incident illustrating the loyalty to Rome of the better class of Jews (like himself). It is probable that the στάσις was more serious than the impression given by Josephus in that it involved the Jewish priesthood of Egypt and lasted a longer time than his narrative implies.[27] Only the severe measures of Vespasian in ordering the destruction of the temple around which the rebellion centred brought resistance to an end. Thereafter no temple of Jehovah existed either in Jerusalem or in Egypt to serve as an excuse for refusal to pay the tax.

No receipts for the tax on Jews have been found to date later than the year A.D. 116. No certain conclusion can be drawn from this, but it is not impossible that the 'Ιουδαίων τέλεσμα was abolished by Hadrian.

The 'Απαρχή

Nothing definite is known of the origin of the payment of the ἀπαρχή by the Jews in Egypt in connexion with the 'Ιουδαϊκὸν τέλεσμα. The 'First-Fruits', translated by ἀπαρχή in the Septuagint version of the Old Testament, were offerings in kind made to Jehovah by the Israelites.[28] The *Priestly Code* interpreted the offering to Jehovah to mean that the 'First-Fruits' should be brought to the priests. In two tracts of the Mishnah 'a distinction was finally drawn between *bikkûrîm* and *tᵉrû-môth*. . . . The latter was a payment in kind for the support of the priesthood, an impost levied upon every species of fruit, whether of the ground or of trees. The amount to be given was not fixed, but the person who gave $\frac{1}{40}$ was counted liberal, while he who gave $\frac{1}{60}$ was thought somewhat stingy.'[29] The small capitation tax of one drachma per annum in Egypt can hardly be equated with the important offering in kind of the 'First-Fruits', but it is not impossible that in Egypt some portion of the 'First-Fruits', such as the *tᵉrûmāh* of the Mishnah, was devoted to the priests of the temple of Onias. Payment of such a tax in kind may have at some time been transformed into a small annual payment in money, and this may have been confiscated by the Roman government in Egypt when the temple-tax (δίδραχμον) of the Jews was renamed the 'Ιουδαίων τέλεσμα and diverted to the treasury of the Capitoline Jupiter in Rome.

The 'Αριθμητικὸν κατοίκων

The ἀριθμητικὸν κατοίκων ('tax for the numbering of catoeci') is attested in the Roman period from 9 B.C. to the end of the second century after Christ.[30] It has been called a land-tax,[31] and in PSI. VIII. 906, a document from Tebtynis dated in A.D. 45–6, it is called ἀριθμητικὸν κατοικικῆς γῆς. The character of the payments recorded in receipts for the tax, however, indicates that it may, with limitations, be considered a capitation tax falling upon all owners of catoecic land.[32]

In O. Tait, p. 67, no. 24, from Thebes and dated 9 B.C.,

the amount of the tax is not given, but it is stated that the payment is for 14½ arurae and is made 'through Ampheion'. This is the only example of the tax at Thebes as yet published, and the statement of the number of arurae suggests that the receipt is for a genuine land-tax assessed *ad aruram*. Although further evidence is necessary to confirm this impression, it is entirely possible that the method of assessment of this tax at Thebes, where there was comparatively little catoecic land, may in the reign of Augustus have differed from that later employed in the Arsinoite nome.

P. Teb. II. 361, dated A.D. 132, recording a payment of 28 drachmae 3 obols for ἀριθμ(ητικὸν) τέλει(ον), is the only extant receipt from the Arsinoite nome before the second half of the second century.[33] Other payments range in date from A.D. 164 to 195–6 in amount and from 5 drachmae 2½ obols (plus προσδια-γραφόμενα) to 20 billon drachmae, but the usual payments are 16 drachmae, 16 drachmae 1½ obols, and 18 drachmae. There is, indeed, a slight variation in the rate of the tax, but since the rate of 16 drachmae 1½ obols is found seven times, of 18 drachmae five times, and of 16 drachmae twice, out of twenty payments for the tax where the amount is preserved, it is clear that the method of assessment is *per capita* upon classes of holders of catoecic land. The rate of the ἀριθμητικὸν κατοίκων is clearly not assessed *ad aruram* in SP. XXII. 112 and 113, since Panephremes pays 18 drachmae for ἀριθμητικόν and 500 (copper) drachmae for ναύβιον κατοίκων (which was assessed at 100 copper drachmae for each arura) on 5 arurae, whereas Stotoëtis paid 20 billon drachmae for ἀριθμητικόν but 1,000 (copper) drachmae for ναύβιον κατοίκων on 10 arurae. It is possible that the slight variation in the rate of the tax depended upon the size of the holdings of each man, even though the tax was not assessed *ad aruram*, but this cannot be proved without further evidence. It is also possible that the slightly higher rate included charges (such as προσδιαγραφόμενα) which are not specified, and hence that the variation in the rate of the tax is more apparent than real.

A further complication is introduced by the phrases τέλειον ἀριθμητικόν and ἡμιτέλειον ἀριθμητικόν. BGU. I. 330 is an answer from a comogrammateus to the collectors of money-taxes at Caranis who had inquired as to who owed the ἡμιτέλειον ἀριθμητικόν on a parcel of pasture-land which had been posted against a certain Satabous. Information obtained by the comogrammateus from one Ptolemaeus the fishmonger revealed that the tax was to be collected from a certain Deius and his sons. Evidently some title or equity in the land had changed hands, but the tax-lists had not been corrected accordingly. Nothing is said about catoecic land, although that is presumably involved, and the relationship of Satabous, Ptolemaeus, and Deius to the land for which the tax was collected is left quite obscure. SB. 4415, from Nilopolis and dated A.D. 144, sheds a little light on the ἡμιτέλειον ἀριθμητικόν. A certain Statia Petronia writes to the basilico-grammateus and states that she is paying the τέλειον ἀριθμητικόν at Nilopolis on a parcel of land at Memphis (in the Fayûm) which had come into her possession in the preceding year through legal foreclosure of a mortgage. Yet, according to her complaint, the mortgager Aphrodisius, in the name of Thamunius, is paying the ἡμιτέλειον ἀριθμητικόν at Memphis, although he possesses no catoecic land in the nome. She therefore requests that his name be stricken from the κατοικικὴ γραφή (official list of catoeci). It is evident that Statia Petronia made this request not from any misgiving because the government was collecting a tax not rightfully due, but because the presence of the name of Thamunius in the κατοικικὴ γραφή and the continued payment of the ἡμιτέλειον ἀριθμητικόν prejudiced her title to the land obtained by foreclosure. It is possible that, when a parcel of catoecic land was mortgaged, the mortgager paid, instead of the τέλειον ἀριθμητικόν, the ἡμιτέλειον ἀριθμητικόν, and the mortgagee likewise paid a ἡμιτέλειον ἀριθμητικόν. When the mortgage was paid off the owner resumed payment of the τέλειον ἀριθμητικόν or when the mortgagee foreclosed he assumed the payment of the τέλειον ἀριθμητικόν, as Statia Petronia has done in this document.

Such an explanation of the ἡμιτέλειον ἀριθμητικόν, however, casts no light upon the payments in BGU. I. 342 (from Caranis and dated A.D. 181), where Apion son of Polynices pays 16 drachmae 1½ obols for ἀριθμητικὸν κατοίκων of the preceding year (plus προσδιαγραφόμενα of 1 drachma 2 chalci) which is followed by the statement: καὶ εἰς Πεθέα Ἀτρείους ὁμοίως ἀριθ(μητικοῦ) κ(ατ)οί(κων) 5 drachmae 2½ obols (plus προσδιαγραφόμενα of 2

obols 2 chalci). This is followed by an identical receipt from
A.D. 184. Apion apparently paid τέλειον ἀριθμητικόν at 16
drachmae 1½ obols, and for Petheus he paid 5 drachmae 2½
obols, which is exactly one-third of 16 drachmae 1½ obols. There
is no information given concerning the relationship of Apion and
Petheus or as to what equity each held in catoecic property or
how they obtained it. Furthermore, there is no extant example
of a term τριτητέλειον ἀριθμητικόν.

The simplest explanation of both ἡμιτέλειον ἀριθμητικόν and
'τριτητέλειον ἀριθμητικόν' would be to assume that these represent instalments of one-half or one-third of the τέλειον ἀριθμητικόν. BGU. 1. 342 cited above records payments of the ἀριθμητικὸν
κατοίκων made at an interval of four or five years,[34] and it is
possible that this fee, like the γεωμετρία (which could be paid in
two or four instalments) was levied only every fifth year. It is
necessary, however, to assume that Petheus was in A.D. 184 in
debt to the treasury for two-thirds of his ἀριθμητικὸν κατοίκων
which had been due five years before, or that he had paid the
balance, but the receipt (or receipts) was not recorded on this
papyrus (BGU. 1. 342) and has not survived. In either case it is
not clear why the payments of Apion and Petheus appear on the
same receipt and why Apion made the payment for Petheus.

The purpose of the tax is as uncertain as the principles of
assessment. Wilcken[35] supposed that the ἀριθμητικόν was collected to pay for the services of ἀριθμηταί employed by the
government to check the reports of the landholders, as for
example the ἀπογραφαί of cattle, &c.[36] Grenfell and Hunt[37]
asserted that Wilcken's explanation was unconvincing. Von
Woess[38] modified Wilcken's view slightly, inasmuch as he declared that the ἀριθμητικόν was paid for the maintenance of
the γραφὴ καταλοχισμῶν (register of transfers of catoecic land)
and of the special cadastre of catoecic land. Von Woess also
assumed the existence of a register of the owners of catoecic
land and a register of catoeci. The separation of the last two
lists could have occurred only after the development of the right
of transfer of catoecic land as private property, which did not
occur, at the earliest, until late in the Ptolemaic period.[39] The
register of owners of catoecic land may well correspond to the
κατοικικὴ γραφή mentioned in SB. 4415. The ἀριθμητικὸν

κατοίκων may have been intended to cover the cost of maintenance of this register of owners of catoecic land, as well as of the γραφὴ καταλοχισμῶν and of the special cadastre as suggested by Von Woess. If this be true we have an explanation of the equal or nearly equal assessment of the tax upon owners of varying amounts of catoecic land. It must be remembered that payments of the poll-tax were made ὑπὲρ λαογραφίας, literally, 'on account of the enrolment of the λάος.' Ἀριθμητικὸν κατοίκων, then, may have been originally a tax for the 'numbering' (i.e. the registration) of the catoeci, since in the Ptolemaic period they were identical with the owners of catoecic land. In the Ptolemaic period, therefore, when the catoeci paid no λαογραφία,[40] they may have paid instead the ἀριθμητικόν, a capitation tax for which they received some return in the maintenance of records securing their property-rights and their political and social position. This would account for the lack of evidence for the ἀριθμητικὸν κατοίκων in the Ptolemaic period, when receipts for capitation taxes were ordinarily not given.[41] In the Roman period, when the catoeci as a class were no longer exempt from payment of the λαογραφία,[42] the ἀριθμητικόν, which provided useful revenue for the maintenance of records of catoecic land, was made a tax upon the ownership of catoecic land payable by any one who owned land of that category. In the Arsinoite nome it retained, at least in part, its characteristic as a capitation tax.

The Ἀριθμητικὸν φυλακιτῶν

The ἀριθμητικὸν φυλακιτῶν is attested in P. Ryl. II. 213, a document from Thmuis dated late second century, and in the great tax-rolls from Caranis in the collection of the University of Michigan. In the latter documents the amount of the levy is $5\frac{1}{4}$ obols (with προσδιαγραφόμενα of $\frac{1}{2}$ obol). Its occurrence sheds no light on the problems of the nature and purpose of the ἀριθμητικὸν κατοίκων, although they may have been practically the same; but the holders of land once assigned to φυλακῖται paid a fee so small that it is difficult to compare the two taxes. The existence of the ἀριθμητικὸν φυλακιτῶν confirms the theory that the ἀριθμητικόν was a Ptolemaic tax, since the categories of κάτοικοι and φυλακῖται were of political significance only in the Ptolemaic period.

TAXES ON TRADES, I. THE STATE MONOPOLIES

THE soil of the Nile valley, constantly enriched by the annual inundations of the river, was the great resource of Ancient Egypt, and from it the Pharaonic and Ptolemaic rulers, and after them the provincial administrators of the Roman emperors, drew their largest revenue. Agriculture was not, however, the only industry which paid tribute to the treasury of the Ptolemaic and Roman governments. It may be considered certain that every trade and occupation of any consequence was in some way made to yield revenue to the central administration of the country. When the Ptolemies succeeded to the throne of Egypt they regarded the soil of Egypt as theirs, because the possessions of the Pharaohs which had fallen into the hands of the Persians had been wrested from them in turn by the arms of the Macedonians. Included in the spear-won property of the Ptolemies were many places for the manufacture and sale of various commodities. The profits from the production and distribution of these goods belonged to their owner, the king of Egypt, and were a source of no little revenue for his treasury.

To secure the maximum profit from such enterprises, moreover, the first Ptolemies developed state monopolies of the manufacture, import, and sale of certain products.[1] By strict regulation of the production of such monopolized commodities and by a prohibitive tariff against their importation by private traders the Ptolemies were able to set an artificially high price, whether wholesale or retail, and so to secure an increased revenue for their treasury. To protect themselves against possible loss, however, the Ptolemies farmed out state monopolies to the highest bidders. The successful bidders had to be closely watched to protect the treasury from fraud and the public from extortion, and this required officials to supervise the farmers of the monopolies. So at best the regulation and supervision of such monopolies was often an exceedingly complicated problem and an onerous task. Consequently the officials charged with the financial administration of the Ptolemaic kingdom made little effort to maintain a complete monopoly of an industry where unfavourable local conditions made it unprofitable. To derive the greatest possible revenue under circumstances unfavourable to a full state monopoly two courses were open to the king's financial agents. They could lease the right of the king to a private individual, who would pay for the exclusive privilege of conducting a certain business in a given district, or they could give up the monopoly entirely and let an unlimited number of men engage in an industry and assess a tax upon the profits of each businessman or a capitation tax upon each person employed in a particular trade. In the latter case the number of persons engaged in a business in a given locality would be determined by the ability of the community to support them. This number, however, was further limited by the development of trade-guilds, which restricted the number of persons engaged in the trade under the control of the guild. The existence of such guilds made the administration of taxation on trades much easier, since the guilds were responsible organizations able to furnish information concerning their members to officials charged with the assessment or collection of taxes.[2]

Full monopoly, leased monopoly, and taxes on free industry were all used by the financial administration of Egypt in the Ptolemaic period, and indeed were often combined in the treatment of a single industry. These methods were continued by the Roman officials; but by the time that the Romans took over the administration of Egypt some modifications had become necessary if industry was to yield the greatest profit to the government. Chronological data for such changes are lacking; the extant documents merely show that important features of the state monopolies of the Ptolemies were often absent in the Roman period. It is not improbable, however, that conditions in the later years of Ptolemaic rule, when the kingdom suffered a decline from its early prosperity and power, had already brought about many of these changes in the administration of government revenue from industry.

In the Roman period many of the state monopolies had been wholly or partially abandoned. Of nineteen state monopolies listed by Heichelheim[3] for the Ptolemaic period but eleven are in his list for Roman times, and the dearth of evidence for the organization of monopolies in the latter period may well indicate that their importance had suffered a decline.[4] Such monopolies had not been favoured at Rome, but the fact that a number of the Ptolemaic monopolies were retained in the Roman period shows that in Egypt expediency rather than moral or legal principle determined their survival. Strabo (XVII, C. 798), indeed, writing at the beginning of the period of Roman rule states that Egypt had monopolies, but the context indicates that he was thinking of natural monopolies gained through an advantageous situation on the trade-routes rather than artificial state monopolies.

A curious feature of the Ptolemaic system of state monopolies was that many of them were accompanied by a capitation tax upon the consumer. Such capitation taxes were continued, in some cases, into the Roman period, and for this reason the monopolies are important for the study of the taxation in Egypt during that period.

The Salt-Monopoly

Little is known concerning the production of salt in Egypt, which was obtained from sea-water, salt lakes, and probably from mines (as at the present day, although Strabo (XVII, C. 822) speaks of salt as being quarried only in Ethiopia and Arabia), but it is generally agreed that production was monopolized by the state. There is more evidence concerning the retail distribution of salt which was closely regulated by the government. In the Roman period salt-sellers presented bids for the privilege of selling salt in a district protected against competition, and they promised to pay a rental ($\phi \acute{o} \rho o s$) to the government for the concession (P. Mich. Car. 1. 123 R. and 128). In P. Fay. 23, also dated in the Roman period, there appears in a list of officials a former superintendent of brokerage of salt-dealers ($\dot{\epsilon} \pi \iota \tau (\eta \rho \eta \tau \grave{\eta} s)$ $\dot{\epsilon} \rho \mu \eta \nu \acute{\iota} \alpha s \, \dot{\alpha} \lambda o \pi \omega (\lambda \hat{\omega} \nu))$ whose duties are not entirely clear, but who was undoubtedly employed by the government in its regulation of the monopoly of trade in salt. Private dealers sold salt at retail at a price fixed by the government and paid a trade-tax to the state treasury.[5] Privileged institutions such as the army, the bureaucracy, and the temples were permitted in the Ptolemaic period to purchase salt directly from the government, presumably at a price under that set for the market. SB. 6967 is possibly to be understood as meaning that the army enjoyed the same privilege in Roman times.

In the Ptolemaic period all adult men and women, whether slave or free, were required to pay a capitation tax called ἁλική, 'salt-tax', unless they were specially exempted.[6] The rate of the tax for free men was from 4 obols to 1 drachma a year; women paid much smaller amounts; and for slaves the tax was normally one-half the rate for free men. The extant ostraca and papyri show that the tax was wide-spread in Egypt in the Ptolemaic period. After the Roman conquest, however, the tax is attested only in documents from the Arsinoite nome, and it is not impossible that the tax had been abandoned elsewhere in Egypt.[7] Even in the Arsinoite nome the tax rarely appears in receipts.[8] In P. Teb. II. 482, dated 11 B.C., 3 obols are recorded as payment for ἁλικ(ῆς) in a receipt which includes payments for various taxes. In P. Lond. III. 1235 (p. 35) 5 obols are paid for a tax which was read by Grenfell[9] as ἁλικ(ῆς), but the reading is doubtful;[10] the receipt is from Theadelphia and is dated A.D. 176–7. The salt-tax is mentioned more often in tax-accounts. In BGU. VII. 1613, an account of arrears of the Heraclides district, dated A.D. 69–70 or later, ἁλ(ικῆς) occurs twice. The tax also appears in an account, probably of arrears, in P. Fay. 42 a, a return from the πράκ(τορες) ἀργυρικῶν κώμης Φαρβήθ(ων) to the strategus of the Heraclides district, which is dated late second century. SP. XX. 49 recto, a tax-account dated second or third century, includes payments for ἁλικ(ῆς) at the rate of 4 obols, a man. In SP. XX. 62, a somewhat similar account, the tax is paid by the ὁμόλογοι of the Arsinoite nome (who paid poll-tax (λαογραφία) at 40 drachmae a year) apparently at the rate of 4 obols a year,[11] a rate found also in the Ptolemaic period. It is probable that the tax was confined to that class of tax-payers in the Roman period, so that women were no longer required to pay it. It has been suggested by Tait[12] that the ἁλική was included with other small charges in the συντάξιμον, and this is not unlikely, since the tax appears so seldom in receipts but is mentioned in tax-accounts.

The Oil-Monopoly

Thanks to the famous Revenue Papyrus of Ptolemy II Philadelphus and to the recently published P. Teb. III. 703 more is known concerning the oil-monopoly in the Ptolemaic period than about any other state monopoly. The whole production of oil from the growing of the plants from whose seeds it was obtained to the sale of the finished product was closely supervised and regulated by the farmers of the monopoly and by the official bureaucracy. The number of oil-plants set out each year and the number of arurae devoted to their culture were limited annually by the estimate of the needs of Alexandria and the rest of the country. The production of olive-oil, however, was not limited in the Ptolemaic period, because the cultivation of olive-trees had not become widespread in Egypt much before Roman times. Failure to carry out the plan of the authorities at Alexandria meant severe punishment for the officials in the nomes. The seeds of oil-yielding plants were issued to the cultivators by the government and had to be repaid at the time of the harvest; repayment was in kind or was sometimes compounded for a payment in money at a price set by the government. The price of the harvested oil-plants was set by the government, and the entire crop was purchased for the government's oil-factories (ἐλαιουργεῖα), which were managed by the Oeconomus. The temples, which were among the largest consumers of oil, were granted special privileges of manufacture for their own use, but even these privileges were strictly limited, so that the state monopoly should not suffer. The workmen in the state's factories served under a liturgy if it was impossible to obtain voluntary workmen, and when once the work was begun in the factory the employees could not leave the nome until the production for the year had been completed. When production was ended for the year the ἐλαιουργεῖα were closed and sealed in order that they should not be surreptitiously used for private production. The retail trade was closely supervised. Specific amounts were assigned to the retail dealers (ἐλαιοκάπηλοι) each month under the supervision of the farmers of the monopoly. It is possible that a capitation tax upon the consumers was collected by the farmers of the monopoly. A duty of 50 per cent. was laid on imported oil, which had to be sold at a price set by the state, and transport of imported oil into the interior of the country was forbidden.

The oil-monopoly continued in Roman times, but its development in that period is not yet fully known. The monopoly of sale in particular towns or districts could be granted by nomarchs, or similar officials, to an individual who paid a φόρος for that privilege, but it is uncertain how far the monopoly of production was maintained in the Roman period.[13] There is no evidence after the Ptolemaic period for the allotments of limited quantities of oil to the retailers, and there is no evidence for a capitation tax on consumers in the later period.

The oil-industry in Roman Egypt was, however, subject to several imposts. First, the ἐλαϊκή or εἴδη ἐλαϊκά was collected in the Arsinoite nome and in the Delta, but the nature of the tax is not clear.[14] Second, payments ὑπὲρ ἐλαίου are found among the receipts for taxes at Thebes, but the principle of assessment and the rate of this charge are likewise unknown.[15] It is not impossible that the payments ὑπὲρ ἐλαίου at Thebes were for the same purpose as the ἐλαϊκή of Lower Egypt. Third, there are receipts for payments ὑπὲρ τιμῆς ἐλαίου, which are discussed in another chapter.[16] Fourth, manufacturers of oil had to pay taxes called τέλος ἐλαιουργικῶν ὀργάνων, a tax on the presses used in the production of oil, and τέλος θυιῶν, a tax on the mortars used in the equipment of the oil-factories. The τέλος ἐλαιουργικῶν ὀργάνων is mentioned in a tax-account from the Mendesian nome dated late second century; 60 drachmae were paid for the tax, and its presence among taxes on land suggests that the place of manufacture was on a farm. The τέλεσμα τῶν ὀργάνων and the payment ὑπὲρ τῶν ὀργάνων τελουμέ[νων] mentioned in administrative documents of the same date and provenience may be for the same tax.[17] The receipts for the τέλος θυιῶν are probably all from the Arsinoite nome; the amounts range from 15 to 185 drachmae, but the incidence of the tax cannot be determined.[18] There was at least a partial monopoly of retail distribution of oil in the Roman period, but the details of its administration are not clear. In PO. XII. 1517 (A.D. 272 or 278) an oil-broker (ἑρμηνεὺς ἐλαίου) apparently pays a tax of 60 drachmae. The exclusive right to sell oil at retail (κοτυλίζειν) in a certain village is sought in P. Amh. II. 92, and the lessee offers to pay for a certificate δίπλωμα ιπ[. . .]; the restoration of the second word is uncertain.[19] In the similar clause of a lease in SP. XXII. 177 the lessee offers to pay a tax which Wessely read as τέλεσμα διπλώματος εἰερῶν (ϵι corr. ï), and he agrees to pay it on the following condition: ἐφ' ᾧ οὐχ ἕξωι πρὸς τοῦ κοτυλισμοῦ τελέσματος. It is evident that each certificate is connected with the concession of a monopoly of retail sales, and it is probable that the word following δίπλωμα in each case is the same, but Wessely's reading is not much more enlightening than the suggestions made in regard to the restoration of the word in P. Amh. II. 92. Διπλώματα are mentioned in the lease of a flour-mill in PSI. VII. 787, but each certificate was apparently required for the privilege of making a different type of flour or bread, and so does not throw any light on the δίπλωμα in the concessions of monopolies to retail oil.

The Beer-monopoly

The monopoly of the brewing and sale of beer of the Ptolemaic period seems, as Heichelheim points out,[20] to have developed into a system of leases of concessions to private individuals or to temples whose industries were scattered all over Egypt. This relinquishment of concessions to brewers had existed under the Ptolemies, for the φόρος of the ζυτοποιοί is mentioned in the Ptolemaic papyri as well as in the documents of the Roman period.[21] There is no evidence for the continuation in the Roman period of the allotments (συντάξεις) of barley to the state's brewers, which were a feature of the monopoly of the Ptolemaic period, so that it may be concluded that the once strict regulation of the production of beer had been considerably relaxed. The capitation tax called ζυτηρά, or ζυτηρά (or ζυτοποιία) κατ' ἄνδρα, persisted in the Roman period. The question was raised by Reil[22] whether this was merely a consumers' tax or was an impost designed to take toll from the home-brewing so prevalent in Egypt. Reil favoured the latter theory, but Heichelheim[23] defended the former view for the Ptolemaic period, since he had demonstrated that consumers' taxes were commonly assessed in connexion with state monopolies. Heichelheim admitted,[24] however, that home-brewing was common in the Roman period, and the tax may well have been developed in that period to recover revenue which might otherwise have been lost through the growth of that home-industry. The amount of the capitation tax cannot be determined for the Roman period, but it was evidently high in the third century.

Partial payments of 4 and 8 drachmae are recorded early in that century, and in A.D. 228 a payment of 28 drachmae occurs, and in 238 payments of 40 drachmae. One of these payments of 40 drachmae is made by the heirs of a certain man, and the other seems to be a joint payment by a man and his wife. The payment by the heirs and a joint payment by husband and wife can hardly be taken as evidence for a capitation tax at the rate of 40 drachmae. Amundsen[25] connects the high rate in the third century with the depreciation of the currency; but the depreciation had not caused similar increases in other taxes in the first half of the third century, and it is more probable that a change in the method of levying the tax had occurred. Except for the joint payment noted above, the beer-tax in the Roman period seems to have been collected from men only, a change similar to that in the collection of the ἁλική which, however, remained more purely a consumers' tax than did the ζυτηρὰ κατ' ἄνδρα. The capitation tax collected from sellers of beer will be discussed in Chapter XII.

The Bath-monopoly

The baths are considered a state monopoly by Heichelheim, although private baths were permitted to exist. The important capitation tax βαλανευτικόν collected for the maintenance of the public baths has been considered in Chapter IX. The βαλανευτικόν differed, indeed, from the ἁλική, for example, in that the latter was not collected to maintain an institution directly serviceable to the tax-paying public, or to a portion of it, as were the public baths.

Other monopolies listed by Heichelheim for the Roman period are not important for the study of taxation. There was at least a partial monopoly of perfumes (ἀρώματα), and the sellers of these luxuries were subject to a high capitation tax.[26] The agents of the Roman government leased concessions for the exclusive right to carry on the dyer's trade and also the fuller's trade, but it is not probable that the government attempted to maintain a full monopoly in the Roman period;[27] taxes on these trades are discussed in Chapter XII.[28] The manufacture of kiln-dried bricks was perhaps a full monopoly in the Roman period. When in SP. XXII. 35 two men lease a brick-works they agree to pay a fee to the government for the privilege of carrying on the manufacture. In PO. III. 502 πλινθευομένη as a capitation tax is assessed with the police-tax (φύλακτρον), but the πλινθευομένη seems ordinarily to have been levied only on the occasion of erecting some government building. In Egypt, as elsewhere in the Roman empire, the mines and quarries were a government monopoly, and a payment for lead is recorded in O. Tait, p. 126, no. 310 (A.D. 212?). Transport-boats, for which receipts ὑπὲρ πορθμίδων[29] are found, were at least a partial monopoly for which concessions in certain districts were let by the government; in BGU. IV. 1188 the rent (φόρος) for the concession of a ferry is paid to tax-farmers (τελῶναι). Heichelheim considers this monopoly a Roman innovation, since he could find no evidence for a government monopoly of the business in the Ptolemaic period; he rather considers payments to the government in that period a rent for the use of the waters which naturally belonged to the state. It seems unlikely, however, that the Roman government should have introduced a monopoly when the tendency was rather to eliminate state monopolies in Egypt; further evidence may show that the business was at least a partial monoply of the Ptolemaic government. A monopoly of trade in alum (στυπτηρία) existed in the Roman as well as in the Ptolemaic period; a tax on the import of alum from the Small Oasis is probably to be regarded as a customs-toll,[30] and the tax on peddlers of alum is discussed in Chapter XII. A state monopoly of the production of paper from the papyrus of Egypt was undoubtedly continued into the Roman period; receipts from this monopoly were sometimes included in the lists of taxes,[31] but there is no evidence for a capitation tax on consumers; it is probable that an artificially high price was maintained, and the charges for official receipts are sufficiently high to include an exorbitant price for the papyrus on which they were written.[32] The trade of the goldsmith (χρυσοχοική) was a state monopoly in the Ptolemaic period and was continued as such in the Roman period, when it was leased in concessions covering single villages; this monopoly apparently was unimportant from the standpoint of taxation. PSI. v. 459 (A.D. 72) records the offer to pay a φόρος of 60 drachmae for the privilege of selling wool by the fleece or by measure in

Caranis. According to Strabo[33] a trade monopoly existed for a number of wares imported from India by way of the Red Sea. Strabo does not specify what products were monopolized, but, as Heichelheim suggests, it is probable that the monopoly was organized in a manner similar to that of perfumes in the Ptolemaic period. Although the trade with India was not so highly developed in the Ptolemaic period as later, some at least of the products referred to by Strabo may well have been the subject of a monopoly before the Roman period. The regulation of the Red Sea trade will be treated in the discussion of customs-tolls in Chapter XV.

There is no way by which we can estimate the income from the monopolies which accrued to the treasury in the Roman period. It was undoubtedly less than the income which the Ptolemies derived from their carefully organized and more elaborately extended monopolies. Even this comparison is not very enlightening, because we do not know how much of the Ptolemies' cash revenues were derived from the monopolies and how much from other sources.

TAXES ON TRADES, II. CAPITATION TAXES

TO replace the revenue from the waning monopolies the Roman government in Egypt resorted to taxes on trades, and these taxes became increasingly important to the treasury of the province. Of the two types of taxation on trades the Roman administration favoured capitation taxes on all persons engaged in an industry rather than taxes set at a percentage of the profits or of the gross income from a business. Capitation taxes, as we have seen, were characteristic of the Roman financial policy in Egypt, probably not as the result of a definite economic theory but because they were the simplest solution to the immediate problem of securing needed revenue. They were particularly attractive as applied to trade because of the ease of collection, for the development of trade-guilds made it easy for government officials to gather the necessary information concerning persons engaged in the organized trades, so that the assessment of the trade-taxes could be made and a comparatively steady revenue assured. At best taxes on profits or gross income of business varied from year to year because of fluctuations in national prosperity. Furthermore, since the information regarding the amount of taxable income from a business had to be supplied by a report from the tax-payer, fraud and deceit at the expense of the government might be expected in the income-tax report of the tradesmen. To prevent fluctuations in revenue from such causes the capitation tax on trade was made in part an income-tax, for the rates on different trades varied, presumably in accordance with the probable incomes to be derived from them. In some cases the two principles of taxation seem to have been combined for a single trade, since the capitation taxes were assessed at different rates upon different classes of handicraftsmen in that trade, and it may be assumed that the rate was roughly proportional to the income possible from the exercise of a particular branch of it.

The capitation taxes on trades were usually called χειρωνάξια[1] 'taxes paid by handicraftsmen', or sometimes ἐπικεφάλαια 'head-taxes'.² The latter term was used for any taxes assessed *per capita*. In many receipts, however, the word χειρωνάξιον is not employed, and the payment is said to be for (ὑπέρ) some trade.³

The rates of capitation taxes on various industries were probably formulated at Alexandria by the financial agents of the central administration. The rates were based on the evidence of past experience in regard to the income which might be expected from each trade; the knowledge of industries in which the government had previously exercised a monopoly formed a fair guide to the expected profits of private enterprise. The rates were published in γνώμονες, which were sent to the local officials. An excellent example of such a γνώμων for the businesses at a small market is the unpublished P. Lond. inv. 1562 *verso*, a tariff for the market at the Serapeum in Oxyrhynchus in A.D. 135–6. The expected revenue from any trade in a given locality could be quickly determined by multiplying the rate for the tax in the gnomon by the number of persons engaged in the trade. The amphodarchs in the cities and the κωμογραμματεῖς in the towns and villages were required to prepare a report of all persons in their districts engaged in any trade.⁴ Lists of persons engaged in business have been found, and, if it cannot be proved that their purpose was always the assessment of taxes, similar lists could as readily have been prepared for that purpose.⁵ PSI. VIII. 871 (from Oxyrhynchus and dated A.D. 66) is a notice of a change in residence sent by a father on behalf of his son apprenticed to a bronze-caster and is addressed to the basilico-grammateus, topogrammateis, and comogrammateis; it was undoubtedly required for the records of the officials charged with the collection of taxes on trades. Besides their own investigations the local officials could refer to the census-returns, which often gave the occupation of all men resident in a house, and they could also demand information from responsible guilds.⁶

Women as well as men were liable to the payment of taxes on trades in which they were engaged, for in PSI. IX. 1055 (from Oxyrhynchus and dated in A.D. 66) a female weaver (γερδίαινα) pays the tax to the nomarch's account. Minors practising trades were exempted from the payment of the taxes thereon, according to SB. 5678 (from Oxyrhynchus and dated A.D. 118), an appeal to the prefect which cites a decree of Vibius Maximus, who had

held the office of prefect a few years earlier. In PO. II. 275
(A.D. 66), a contract for apprenticeship, the taxes of a minor who
was apprenticed for a year are to be borne by his father; the
nature of the taxes is not specified in the document, but since
a minor was not liable to the poll-tax and μερισμοί it is probable
that trade-taxes are meant. In PO. XIV. 1647 (dated late second
century), a similar contract, the trade-taxes (χειρωνάξια τῆς
τεχνῆς) are to be paid by the διδάσκαλος (instructor) of a female
slave who is a minor, but since the apprenticeship was to last
for four years it is possible that the girl may have become of
age during that period. Neither of these documents actually
prove that χειρωνάξια were exacted from minors, but that is not
an impossible interpretation, particularly since the appeal to the
prefect (in SB. 5678) would not have been made if Vibius Maximus' ruling had not been disregarded by officials at Oxyrhynchus.

Taxes on Weaving, Dyeing, and Fulling

Far more receipts for taxes on weavers have been found than
for the tax on any other trade (not including, of course, agriculture). Yet the principles of taxation in this industry are still a
matter of dispute and will doubtless remain so until further
evidence solves some of the problems.[7]

At Elephantine-Syene many receipts for χειρωνάξια have been
found, but unfortunately they do not often specify the particular
trade for which the tax is paid.[8] A few of the ostraca from that
site published by Wilcken, however, reveal that in the second
half of the first century after Christ and in the early part of the
following century weavers of linen (λινόϋφοι) paid χειρωνάξιον
at 12 drachmae a year, often in two instalments of 8 and 4
drachmae.[9] The rate of their tax may have been raised later,
for in O. Wilb.-Brk. 33 (dated A.D. 188) the μισθωτὴς χειρωναξίου
μηνιαίου καὶ ἑταιρικοῦ collects 4 drachmae for the months Thoth
and Phaophi from a [λινύ]φος. Sellers of linen (λινοπῶλαι) also
paid at the rate of 12 drachmae a year.[10] This rate is confirmed
by SB. 7274 (A.D. 113), a receipt for 12 drachmae paid for
χειρω(ναξίου) λι(νύφων) βυσσ(ουργῶν).[11] Chwostow has suggested that the low rate of the tax on linen-weavers (as compared
with the weavers of wool) is a characteristic of the narrow
specialty of these handicraftsmen.[12] WO. II. 16 is a receipt for

4 drachmae paid by a woman ὑπὲρ χειρωναξίο(ν) μη(νιαίου?) ζι
Θὼτ Φαῶφι ʿΑθὺρ μη(νῶν) γ̄.[13] It appears as if this woman paid a
χειρωνάξιον of 16 drachmae a year, but that payments were
assessed at the rate of 1 drachma 2 obols a month, and that payments were made every three months because payment in tetradrachmae was more convenient both for the tax-payer and for the
collector. It is tempting, therefore, to assume that the linen-
weavers' tax, amounting to 12 drachmae per annum, was actually
assessed at 1 drachma a month, but was paid in tetradrachmae for
convenience. Other payments for χειρωνάξιον at Elephantine-
Syene, however, show an annual rate of 20 drachmae 2 obols,
which cannot be divided into twelve equal monthly instalments,
so that it becomes doubtful if the linen-weavers' tax, which was
never paid in monthly instalments, was assessed at 1 drachma
a month rather than by the year.

If O. Strass. 58 is from Elephantine-Syene,[14] it is the only receipt for the ordinary weavers' tax (τέλος γερδικ(όν)) from that
place. The amount of the receipt is 18 drachmae 4½ obols, but it
is uncertain whether this was the full payment of the tax for a
year. If this sum is the full payment it is unlikely that it represents an assessment made by the month, for one-twelfth of
18 drachmae 4½ obols is 1 drachma 3 obols 3 chalci.[15]

At Denderah (Τέντυρα) a single ostracon written in demotic
attests the weavers' tax.[16] It is curious, as Milne pointed out,
that the name of the tax is transliterated from the Greek γερδιακόν as krtyaqe. The receipt is given for a payment of 1 kite
(= 2 drachmae) 4 obols paid in Pachon of the sixth year of
Tiberius; it is not stated whether the amount paid covered the
tax for the year, but that is unlikely since the amount paid
is so small; if it represents a monthly rate the annual total was
30 drachmae.

O. Tait, p. 109, no. 213, dated A.D. 16, is a unique receipt
for the tax from Coptos; again, the amount of the payment, 2
drachmae 2½ obols, seems too small for an annual rate; if it was
the monthly rate, the payments for a year amounted to 29 drachmae. At Apollonopolis Magna (Edfu) a weaver is recorded
among a list of Jews,[17] and at Ombos weavers (γέρδιοι) are mentioned in a decree concerned with taxation.[18]

There is an abundance of receipts for the weavers' tax from

Thebes, where the payments are clearly stated to be collected by τελῶναι (or ἐπιτηρηταὶ) γερδ(ίων or -ιακοῦ). These receipts ordinarily state that payment is made for a particular month or for two months, and often the amount of the payment is not recorded because it was too well known to tax-payer and collector. Wilcken believed that all persons engaged in the same trade paid the tax on that trade at the same rate, and that the capitation tax on a trade was, in effect, a licence-tax.[19] When Milne published his collection of Theban ostraca, however, he found that payments of 2, 4, 6, 8, and 10 drachmae for γερδιακόν were each stated to be the payment for a specified month, and that 20 drachmae, for example, was stated to be paid for two months. Milne, therefore, concluded that there were five classes of weavers at Thebes each assessed at a different rate.[20] Presumably the rate rose approximately in proportion to the income possible from the sale of products of a given class of weaving. From the contracts between apprentice and master-weaver in the Arsinoite and Oxyrhynchite nomes it is known that apprenticeship might continue for almost any period of time from one to five years.[21] It might be assumed that it required different lengths of time for an apprentice of average aptitude to qualify for the practice of different classes of weaving, and this might confirm Milne's theory. Three ostraca, however, should be considered: WO. II. 660 is a receipt for 7 drachmae 1 obol paid to the ἐπιτ(ηρηταὶ) τέλ(ους) γερδ(ίων) for ἀριθ( ) Φαμενὼθ καὶ Φαρμοῦθι τὸ τέλος; WO. II. 680 records a payment of 1 drachma 5 obols for the τέλος μηνὸς Μεχείρ made, according to Wilcken's restoration,[22] to the τελ(ῶναι) [τέλ(ους) γερδ(ίων)]; Archiv, v, p. 176, no. 23, is a receipt for 2 drachmae 1 obol paid to the τελ(ῶναι) γερδ(ίων) for the τέλ(ους) Πάχ(ων). If the sums given in these receipts represent full payments for the months specified, and there is nothing in the receipts to prove the contrary, it is necessary to add three more classes of weavers to the five assumed by Milne, or else to assume a change in the assessments of the tax for which there is no evidence at this period. A theory of eight classes of weavers presents a system of trade-tax so complicated as to be highly improbable, because of the difficulty of maintaining records sufficiently complete and accurate to ensure efficient collection of the tax.[23]

Chwostow recognized the difficulty inherent in the theory of so complicated a system and sought to simplify it by assuming two rates of γερδιακόν at Thebes. The most usual instalments paid there were 4 and 8 drachmae a month which, multiplied by twelve, give yearly rates of 48 and 96 drachmae. Chwostow maintained that any monthly payments at other rates (i.e. 2, 6, 10, &c., drachmae) represented partial payments or included arrears for a previous month, despite the explicit statement of the receipts that the payments were made for specific months.

Chwostow believed that his theory of two rates for the weavers' tax at Thebes was strengthened by an analogy from the tax in the Arsinoite nome. In the latter district the rate of the γερδιακόν in the second half of the first century after Christ was 38 drachmae, which was raised to 38 drachmae 2 obols by the middle of the second century.[24] Chwostow further noted that in P. Lond. III. 846 (p. 131) (= W. *Chrest.* 325) a weaver in Socnopaei Nesus states that he pays 76 drachmae 'annually into the public treasury'.[25] Wilcken[26] had stated that 76 drachmae represented the annual rate of the weavers' tax. Seventy-six drachmae is just twice 38 drachmae, and Chwostow concluded that there were two rates of γερδιακόν in the Arsinoite nome at those figures. This conclusion has been strikingly confirmed by the publication of BGU. VII. 1616, dated in the first half of the second century A.D., an official abstract of the taxes paid by weavers at Philadelphia. The payments of fifteen weavers are recorded; of this number two had paid only 16 and 8 drachmae respectively, but their payments are evidently incomplete; of the rest all but one had paid 76 drachmae for the year, and the total of 64 drachmae credited to that one probably represents merely an incomplete series of payments rather than another annual rate.[27] The rate of 38 drachmae (or 38 drachmae 2 obols) in the Arsinoite nome corresponded to Chwostow's rate of 48 drachmae at Thebes, and the rate of 76 drachmae with that of 96 drachmae. In the Oxyrhynchite nome the known rate of the γερδιακόν was 36 drachmae a year,[28] and Chwostow might have assumed a high rate of 72 drachmae, double the lower rate.

There are, however, some possible objections to Chwostow's theory that the rates of the γερδιακόν at Thebes were 48 and

96 drachmae. First, why was the rate of the tax on weavers in the Arsinoïte nome more than 20 per cent. less than that paid at Thebes? A higher rate of taxation generally prevailed in the Fayûm, which was a richer district than Thebes; the poll-tax at 40 drachmae (or more) per annum, for example, in the Arsinoïte nome is considerably higher than 24 drachmae, the highest rate recorded at Thebes.[29] It is rather difficult to explain why an attempt to equalize the burden of taxation at Thebes and in the Arsinoïte nome should have fallen upon the unfortunate weavers of Thebes. Moreover, the products of the looms in the Arsinoïte nome were an important article of commerce in the Red Sea trade, which must have been a valuable source of income to the weavers of that district, whereas nothing is heard of Theban cloth in international commerce.[30] Second, if the dates of the receipts issued by the collectors of the tax on weaving at Thebes are examined, it will be found that none of the receipts are for the tax of the month of Μεσορή, the last month of the year, but one receipt for Παῦνι and one for ᾿Επείφ (the tenth and eleventh months of the year), although two were issued for Παχὼν καὶ Παῦνι and one for Παχὼν καὶ ᾿Επείφ, whereas thirty-one receipts are scattered through the months of the first three quarters of the year. This suggests the possibility that we have to do not with twelve uniform monthly payments, but rather with payments usually of 4 or 8 drachmae, similar to the payments in the Oxyrhynchite and Arsinoïte nomes, and paid on account towards an unknown total. Since payments in the last three months are rare, it might be supposed that the norm was nine monthly payments of 4 drachmae each, totalling 36 drachmae, which would agree rather closely with the amounts paid in the Oxyrhynchite and Arsinoïte nomes,[31] and similarly nine monthly payments of 8 drachmae each totalling 72 drachmae. The difficulty with such an explanation is to account for the explicit statement of the ostraca that the various payments recorded are the τέλος of a particular month or months, but the same objection may be raised against the theories of Wilcken and Chwostow.[32]

The problem cannot be called solved by this suggestion that the rate of the weavers' tax at Thebes may have been 36 drachmae as in the Oxyrhynchite nome. I have raised the points above in order to show that the correct solution is not necessarily so simple as it appeared to Chwostow.

The low rate of the tax on weavers (and on sellers) of linen at Elephantine-Syene has been noted above. Nothing is known concerning the rate of this tax in Lower Egypt. It is, however, very probable that the tax on linen-weaving was separate from the γερδιακόν in the Oxyrhynchite and Arsinoite nomes, for λινοϋφικόν appears in a list of arrears in PO. XII. 1438 dated late second century after Christ, and an obscure reference to λινική is found in an account of deposits of taxes in a bank in P. Teb. II. 347, dated second century. At Thebes in A.D. 134 the tax on linen-weavers was apparently 20 drachmae a year.[33] O. Strass. 277, dated A.D. 111, reveals that the τέλος λινοπλόκ(ων) (tax paid by makers of linen thread) was received by the collectors of money-taxes at Memnonia (πράκ(τορες) ἀργ(υρικῶν) Μεμνο-(νείων)) at the rate of 2 drachmae a month[34] for successive months from Phaophi to Thoth, a total of 24 drachmae for twelve months. In SB. 4364, from Thebes and dated A.D. 148, the τέλος [[ο]]λίνου is collected in Phaophi by the τελώνης γερ(διακοῦ). The collection of the tax in O. Strass. 277 (and also in O. Strass. 280) by the πράκτορες ἀργυρικῶν rather than by the special collectors of the weavers' tax may indicate that at Thebes, as in the Arsinoite nome, linen-spinning and weaving was regarded as quite separate from other weaving and that the tax was administered separately. SB. 4364, however, indicates that by the middle of the second century the busy πράκτορες ἀργυρικῶν had shifted the collection of taxes on linen-weaving to the collectors of weavers' taxes.

If Wilcken's reading in WO. II. 1395 of δαπ(ιδύφων) = ταπ(ιδύφων) is accepted,[35] a still lower tax was paid by the weavers of carpets. One drachma was apparently paid for the τέλος of two months, so that the tax may have been assessed in Thebes in A.D. 66–7 at 3 obols a month or 6 drachmae per annum. PO. XII. 1517 includes among its list of artisans' payments 184 drachmae paid by a carpet-weaver (ταπιτᾶς). The document is to be dated in A.D. 272 or 278; and, whether or not the 184 drachmae are to be regarded as a monthly instalment or the annual rate of the tax, it is clear that the depreciation of the currency had caused a tremendous rise in the carpet-weavers' tax.

A broiderer or pattern-weaver (ποικιλτής) is listed in PO. XII. 1519 among those owing arrears of taxes in A.D. 247–8 or 257–8, but the amount due is lost.

In the unpublished P. Lond. inv. 1562 *verso* the κασσοποιοί, makers of thick garments, of the market at the Serapeum in Oxyrhynchus apparently paid their tax at an annual rate of 4 drachmae. In PSI. x. 1154, a day-book of the collectors of the γερδιακόν at Tebtynis in the second century,[36] a payment of 16 drachmae is made by a κασο(ποιός), one of more than 10 drachmae by another, and possibly one of 12 drachmae by a third.[37]

Owners of large weaving establishments were thought by Reil and Chwostow[38] to have paid a special tax called ἱστωναρχικόν. The restoration ἱστωναρχ(ικοῦ), however, in BGU. III. 753. iv. 4 is probably wrong, and the word should be expanded ἱστωναρ-χ(ίας), for the payment is certainly the total of the τέλος paid by the γέρδιοι of Cerccësis and Lysimachis and other villages whose names are lost.[39] The ἱστωναρχία was the superintendence of the looms in a certain district, and in P. Ryl. II. 98 (from Arsinoë and dated A.D. 172) a bid of 300 drachmae a year was presented to the ten ἐπιτηρηταὶ μισθοῦ βαφικῆς (superintendents of the lease of the dyeing monopoly in the Arsinoite nome) for the concession of the ἱστωναρχία at Archelais. At Thebes the ἱστωνάρχης could grant or refuse permission to set up a loom and exercise the weaver's craft.[40]

The weaving industry in the temples, which had developed rapidly in the Ptolemaic period, continued under the Romans. The temples engaged in the weaving of wool, as well as the byssus-cloth in the weaving of which they had enjoyed a monopoly in the earlier period. Chwostow believed that in Roman times the temples lost the monopoly of byssus-cloth and that the weaving of it consequently suffered a decline in the temples, for in the third century the temple in Socnopaei Nesus was obliged to buy byssus-cloth for the raiment of the statues of the gods.[41] The temples had few, if any, privileges as manufacturers in the Roman period, and they paid the trade-tax like any other craftsmen.[42] As Chwostow pointed out, this was in full accord with the policy of the Roman government in regard to the temples, whose power was curtailed by limiting their sources of revenue and by taxing the revenue which remained to them.

The fulling of cloth in the Ptolemaic period was a state monopoly, and there is evidence that this monopoly continued, at
least in part, in the Roman period.⁴³ Chwostow has demonstrated, furthermore, that fulling, unlike weaving, demanded a
rather large establishment to carry on its processes and consequently the outlay of a considerable amount of capital.⁴⁴ This
was favourable to the continuance of the monopoly and also
to the development of this industry in the temples of Egypt
which engaged actively in the business or leased their establishments to others.⁴⁵ In the Roman period temples paid the
fullers' tax.

In the Arsinoite nome in A.D. 276 seven fullers (γναφεῖς) out
of eight paid their tax at the rate of 16 drachmae a month; the
other paid 12 drachmae. Wilcken supposed that all were assessed
at the same rate,⁴⁶ apparently assuming that the 12 drachmae
represented only a payment on account. Chwostow, on the
other hand, supposed that the 12 drachmae were a full payment
for the month and indicated two rates of the tax on fullers
similar to the system which he attempted to prove for the tax
on weavers.⁴⁷

The rate of a tax in the second half of the third century is not
a safe guide to the rate in the previous century, yet Wilcken
attempted to show that the same rate for the fullers' tax prevailed in the reign of Marcus Aurelius. In P. Teb. ii. 287 (= W.
Chrest. 251) certain fullers and dyers in the Arsinoite nome
make an appeal to the prefect(?) Severianus 'against the exaction by a minor official of what they held to be an undue amount
for the tax upon their respective trades. The affair was practically a repetition of a previous case which, after having been
referred by the prefect to the epistrategus, had ended in a
verdict in favour of the fullers and dyers. A fresh attempt at
augmentation had now occurred, and this trial was the result. On
the first day the judge Severianus ordered an adjournment in
order to enable the eclogistes, the financial inspector or auditor
for the nome, to appear. The trial was resumed on the following day, but at this point the papyrus becomes too fragmentary
for complete comprehension.' According to the ῥήτωρ Longinus
the fullers paid annually 1,092 drachmae and the dyers [. .]88
drachmae κατὰ τὸν [γν]ώμονα καὶ τὴν συνήθειαν, and had paid

at that rate, according to the report of the eclogistes, for the twenty years before the earlier trial and, since their previous claim had been upheld, had continued to pay at the same rate until the occasion of the new appeal against the exactions of the ἐπιτηρητὴς [τέλους χειρωναξίο]υ. The editors of the Tebtynis papyri supposed that the fullers and dyers of the Arsinoite nome were organized into guilds, which were represented in this suit by the ῥήτωρ Longinus, and that the guilds paid collectively a fixed amount to the state for the right to exercise their trades. They, therefore, supposed that 1,092 drachmae was the collective payment of the guild of fullers, and that the number of the fullers remained constant or the sum paid by them individually varied from year to year.[48] Consequently they wished to restore 1,088 drachmae as the annual payment of the dyers. Wilcken,[49] on the other hand, wished to restore the amount paid annually by (each of) the dyers as 288 drachmae, since in BGU. iv. 1087. iv. they paid at the rate of 24 drachmae a month; and, therefore, to emend the payment of the fullers to 192 drachmae a year, since in A.D. 276 the rate of the tax paid by the fullers was 16 drachmae a month.[50] Reil[51] properly pointed out that a rate of taxation established some time before the reign of Marcus Aurelius would hardly have remained unchanged until A.D. 276, unaffected by the great depreciation of the currency which had occurred and the greatly changed economic conditions. It may also be noted that the trade-taxes at the Serapeum in Oxyrhynchus in the first half of the second century A.D. were assessed by the year and not by the month; and, although this does not prove, it tends to support Reil's contention.

The only other evidence for the tax on fullers in the second century is WO. ii. 1487, which Wilcken discusses among the trade-taxes in the Thebais,[52] although in the text of volume ii it is stated that the provenience of the ostracon is unknown. The text reads: εἰς λόγο[ν . . .] τὴν κναφικ[ὴν τοῦ μη]νὸς ʿΑθὺρ ϛβ[. . . .]. Wilcken thought it unlikely that this was a payment for a month; hence he assumed an annual assessment of 24 drachmae. The document is dated late in the second century.[53]

The rates of taxation noted above applied to fulling in the narrow sense of the word. Washing and treating the cloth was

the work of στιβεῖς who paid at a lower rate than the γναφεῖς
—in A.D. 276 at 8 drachmae a month.[54] There were workmen
even more narrowly specialized in the processes of the fulling-
industry, such as ἐριοραβδισταί or γερδιοραβδισταί, whose tax was
assessed, apparently, at 12 drachmae a year in A.D. 72–3 and
13 drachmae a year in A.D. 135–7 in the Arsinoite nome.[55]

It is probable that weaving and fulling were sometimes combined in the same establishment. The tax paid by the proprietor
was doubtless raised accordingly. Chwostow suggested that
perhaps the payments designated κοπῆς ⟨καὶ⟩ τριχὸς καὶ χειρωναξίου referred to such establishments.[56]

As has been noted above, the dyers in the city of Arsinoë in
A.D. 276 paid at a rate higher than the fullers, namely 24 drachmae
a month. The rate of the tax in Lower Egypt earlier than that
is unknown.[57] Two ostraca of the Roman period attest the tax
at Thebes, but they do not reveal the rate of taxation: WO. II.
1068 merely indicates a monthly rate (τὸ καθ(ῆκον) τέλ(ος) μηνὸ(ς)
Θώθ), while WO. II. 700 records two instalments totalling 8
drachmae 4 obols; both ostraca are dated in the second half of
the second century.

Taxes on Tailors and Clothiers

Tailors, according to Chwostow,[58] played an insignificant
role in the Graeco-Roman world. Nevertheless, as he notes, professional tailors existed in Egypt and paid a tax which at Elephantine and Thebes was apparently due monthly.[59] O. Mey.
34, from Elephantine(?) and dated A.D. 35, reveals that two
brothers together paid to the τελῶναι ἤπη(τῶν) 4 drachmae, τὸ
τέλος τοῦ Μεχείρ. In O. Theb. 74 (dated A.D. 44) two instalments
totalling 11 drachmae 3 obols were paid in Pharmouthi, while
O. Theb. 76 (second or third century) records the payment of
10 drachmae 5 obols for the τέλος τοῦ Παχών. In the last two
examples it is somewhat doubtful whether the sums recorded
actually represent monthly rates for the tax.

The tax on clothiers ἱματιοπωλικόν is attested only in P. Leipzig (Wessely, 'Die gr. Papyri Sachsens' in Ber. Sächs. Ges. d.
Wiss. 1885, p. 245) 5. 7, a list of miscellaneous taxes at Memphis.
At Thebes, however, the ἐπιτηρηταὶ τέλους ἱματιοπωλῶν (superintendent of the tax on clothiers) or τελῶναι ἱματιοπωλῶν

collected a tax of 2 drachmae for each burial (τέλος ταφῆς).[60] Wilcken has suggested that the clothiers provided the garments for the laying-out of the dead as a part of their business and that a special tax, besides the regular licence-tax, was assessed for each burial.[61]

The Potters' Tax

The potters' tax in Arsinoë in A.D. 72-3 was 17 drachmae ½ obol 2 chalci a year. This is revealed in an important section of the report of the amphodarch Heraclides published by Wessely in SP. IV, pp. 62 ff.; the section dealing with the χειρωνάξιον comprises columns vii to x inclusive. The report of the χειρωνάξιον for the fifth year of Vespasian's reign was composed by the amphodarch with reference to the report of the previous year (συνοψισμένος [πρὸ]ς τὸ (τέταρτον) (ἔτος) = A.D. 71-2). Normally there seem to have been in the district four potters, who doubtless formed a guild or the subdivision of a guild. These four potters were Tryphon son of Colluthus, Theogiton son of Theogiton and grandson of Tyrannus, Heraclides son of Didas and grandson of Ammonius, and one other. In the year A.D. 71-2 one of the potters, Heraclides, had died before the middle of the year and so paid (or his heirs paid) but 8 drachmae 3½ obols 1 chalcus, approximately half of the annual tax. To replace him a new potter, Ammonius son of Antonius and grandson of Heraclides, was admitted to the guild.[62] Although he could have entered the guild only after the death of Heraclides,[63] Ammonius son of Antonius had paid the full tax for the fourth year (A.D. 71-2). In the fifth year (A.D. 72-3), however, half of the χειρωνάξιον of the deceased potter and the first half of the tax of the new potter were the subject of a formal remission (ἐλάσσωμα), for the deceased no longer owed his tax and his name was to be stricken from the tax-rolls, whereas Ammonius son of Antonius had apparently overpaid in the previous year.[64] The payment of the potters' tax had been further complicated by the fact that in the year A.D. 70-1 one of the potters had absconded (ἀνακεχωρ(ηκέναι)). His tax, nevertheless, had to be paid, for flight from the burdens of taxation (or of liturgies) could not be condoned by a formal ἐλάσσωμα. Apparently this additional burden had to be assumed by the remaining potters, for their payments in the year A.D. 72–3 are introduced by the phrase ἀπὸ μὲν αἰρούντων κατακριμ(άτων) which seems to mean 'from the fines due'.[65] In the year A.D. 71–2 the place of the potter who had absconded in the previous year was apparently filled by a new potter, Ammonius son of Sambas and grandson of Ammonius, and the total of 51 drachmae 2 obols 2 chalci received in 71–2 from Tryphon, Theogiton, and Ammonius son of Sambas was introduced by the phrase (γίνονται) ἀπὸ αἰρούντων κατα[κριμ(άτων)]. What the fines were exactly or how they affected the rates of χειρωνάξιον paid by the potter is not clear. In the year 71–2 the report of the payments (or perhaps merely the assessments) of the potters had been subject to some delay, for it is introduced not by the phrase ἤχθησαν εἰς ἀπαίτησιν, as were the 60 drachmae paid by the five ἐριοραβδισταί, but by the phrase καὶ διὰ προσγράφου ἀνελήμφθησαν ('added in a supplementary report'). Whether this delay in submitting the report was caused by difficulty in arranging to replace the absconding potter, or by the death of Heraclides and the subsequent addition of Ammonius son of Antonius, is uncertain.[66]

A τέλεσμα κεραμέων of 30 drachmae (with προσδιαγραφόμενα of 2 drachmae) is found in the tax-rolls from Caranis in the collection of the University of Michigan. Nothing further is known concerning the rate of the χειρωνάξιον paid by the potters in Egypt. It seems unlikely that κεραμοπ(οιοί) in P. Lond. inv. 1562 verso (line 26) paid an annual tax as low as 1 drachma, so that the basis of their taxation must have been other than an annual rate.[67]

Taxes on Building-Trades

It is not absolutely certain that the following imposts paid by persons engaged in the building-trades were all capitation taxes, but that seems the most probable explanation of the payments. The receipts are few in number; further examples may confirm or disprove this view.

A tax on builders, ὑπ(ὲρ) οἰκοδ(όμων?), for which 18 drachmae 2 obols (and προσδιαγραφόμενα) were paid, is recorded in a receipt from Thebes dated A.D. 39–40; an earlier ostracon from Diospolis Magna, dated A.D. 15, gives a receipt for 22 drachmae for the same tax.[68] O. Wilb.-Brk. 31, dated in A.D. 128 and perhaps

from Elephantine, shows that the apprentice of an οἰκοδόμος paid
1½ drachmae a month. Various payments in silver drachmae for
δημόσια, which the editors explain as χειρωνάξιον, are made
by carpenters (τέκτονες) of Tebtynis to the ἐπιτηρηταὶ κοπ[ῆς . . .]
in P. Teb. II. 455.

P. Fay. 44, from Theadelphia and dated in 6 B.C.,⁶⁹ records
the payment of τὰ λαξικά by a λάξος (stonemason). The total
amount paid apparently was 5 talents of copper.

The monopoly of making and selling brick in the village of
Cercethoesis was let by the government for 80 drachmae annually. At Elephantine-Syene in A.D. 118, however, a tax of 2
drachmae a month was paid for πλινθευτική, apparently χειρωνάξιον of a brick-maker.⁷⁰

In WO. II. 672 from Apollonias in the Thebaid the collectors
of money-taxes give a receipt to two men for the tax on ship-
wrights (ναυπηγοί). One of these men paid 20 drachmae and the
other 8 drachmae. An addition to the receipt (in another hand)
states that the collectors had received from the two men 40
drachmae 4½ obols.

Service-trades

A tax on smiths seems to be attested in an ostracon from Syene,
dated A.D. 120–1, published in *Archiv*, v, p. 175, no. 20. Twenty
drachmae two obols were paid ὑπ(ὲρ) χειρω(ναξίου) σιδη(ρουρ-
γῶν?). Previous to the publication of this ostracon it was not
known what handicraftsmen at Elephantine-Syene paid at this
rate which is found in several receipts. Of course, there may have
been other crafts besides that of the smiths that paid at the same
rate.

Four tinsmiths (κασσιτερᾶτες)⁷¹ are recorded in BGU. IV.
1087. iv among the artisans of Arsinoë paying χειρωνάξιον towards the end of the third century. Two of them pay 36 drachmae, one 32 drachmae, and one 64 drachmae. Most of the other
payments in this document are for monthly instalments of the
various trades, but it is not certain that any of the amounts just
noted is to be accepted as the normal monthly rate of the tinsmiths' tax.⁷² The κασσι(τερᾶτες) paid at the rate of 20 drachmae
a year in the γνώμων of the market at the Serapeum in Oxyrhynchus,⁷³ but since this payment was made in the first half of the

second century after Christ, it does not throw any light on the rate of the tax more than one hundred years later.

The barbers (κουρεῖς) of Thebes paid their tax in the first century after Christ normally at the rate of 3 drachmae 4 obols. If this was a monthly instalment,[74] the annual rate was 44 drachmae. In BGU. I. 9. iv the barbers of Arsinoë are apparently called κορσᾶτες, but the amount of their monthly assessment is lost. In PO. XII. 1518 barbers in the Oxyrhynchite nome in the reign of Hadrian or of Antoninus Pius were assessed at the rate of 6 drachmae. The editors of the document supposed that 6 drachmae was a monthly rate, but this is very uncertain.[75]

The locksmiths (κλειδοποιοί) who also are mentioned in PO. XII. 1518 apparently paid at the same rate (6 drachmae) as the barbers.

In the accounts of the temple at Socnopaei Nesus occurs an item of 16 drachmae apparently for the tax paid by the ταριχευταί. This was the name of those who prepared pickled or salted fish, but it was also applied to the embalmers of mummies. Which is meant here is uncertain. A recent study of unpublished ostraca recording the tax paid by the ταριχευταί maintains the view that they are mummifiers.[76]

Owners of donkeys and wagons for hire paid a trade-tax, but the widely variant amount paid (ranging from 150 drachmae, plus προσδιαγραφόμενα, in A.D. 47 down to 2 drachmae 1 obol at the end of the second or beginning of the third century) makes it difficult to discover what principles determined the rate of taxation.[77] It may well have been based upon the number of animals and vehicles owned rather than been a capitation tax, since in WO. II. 1054 the tax is said to be paid 'upon a wagon'. WO. II. 684, however, seems to be a payment of a donkey-driver for the capitation tax on his occupation. In PO. XII. 1517, dated A.D. 272 or 278, 60 drachmae are perhaps the monthly tax paid by an ὀνηλάτης.

The uncertainty of the restoration of WO. II. 1563 makes it difficult to decide what occupation connected with sacks is meant. This ostracon from Thebes, dated A.D. 87, records a payment of 4 drachmae (plus προσδιαγραφόμενα) for σακκο( ) which may be expanded to mean the tax paid by the sack-carriers (σακκοφόροι) or the sack-makers (σακκοποιοί).[78]

A fragmentary document, P. Ryl. II. 374, includes in a list of artisans paying taxes a κηριοελκός (maker of wax lights), a στιππουργός (hemp-worker), and an ὑελουργός (glass-worker); the amounts of their payments are lost.

Dealers

According to PO. XII. 1519 a merchant or importer (ἔμπορος) was 8 drachmae in arrear with his trade-tax in A.D. 247–8 or 257–8.

Bakers (ἀρτοκόποι) at Arsinoë in the late third century paid their tax at the rate of 8 drachmae a month, a low rate at that time.[79] A bakeshop (ἀρτοστάσιον) is named in the mutilated fragments of what may be an account of χειρωνάξιον at Tebtynis.[80] Every workman in the bakery of fine bread (καθαρουργεῖον) at the Serapeum in Oxyrhynchus paid a tax of 24 drachmae a year.[81]

Sellers of oil (ἐλαιοπῶλαι) in Arsinoë in A.D. 276 paid a tax at the rate of 8 drachmae a month. Those at the Serapeum in Oxyrhynchus in A.D. 135–6 paid only 6 drachmae a year.[82] For the payment by an oil-broker (ἑρμηνεὺς ἐλαίου) see Chapter XI, p. 186.

The temple at Socnopaei Nesus in A.D. 138(?) paid for its vegetable-dealer (λαχανοπώλης)[83] 12 drachmae, according to SP. XXII. 183; the same amount was paid, perhaps somewhat later, by the same temple, as recorded in BGU. I. 337 (= W. Chrest. 92). At the Serapeum in Oxyrhynchus in A.D. 135–6 the payment of the λαχανοπῶλαι was 108 drachmae, but this amount seems to have been the total assessment paid by a guild or corporation (λαχανοπ(ωλῶν) κοιν(όν)); if perchance the rate was the same as at Socnopaei Nesus, nine dealers made up the guild. In P. Teb. II. 360 (A.D. 146) 8 drachmae 8 obols are paid apparently for a vegetable-seller's licence (δίπ(λωμα) λαχα-(νοπωλῶν)) at Tebtynis.

In PO. XII. 1432 (A.D. 214) 80 drachmae were paid into the bank at Oxyrhynchus, as the collections of the month of Payni, by the contractor for the collection of the tax on pulse-sellers (ἀθηροπῶλαι) and vetch-sellers (ὀρβιοπῶλαι). P. Bouriant 13 records the lease of the right to sell vetch (ὀρβιοπωλία) at Memphis in A.D. 98; this was apparently a monopoly, and the lease was obtained from the ἐγλήμπτορες β ἀγορανομίας καὶ ἑτέρων εἰδῶν, and the lessee agreed to pay for his concession a φόρος ὀρβιοπωλίου of 160 drachmae per annum plus a half-artaba of vetch for the ἀγορανόμοι.

According to PSI. VI. 692 a general retail store was leased from the superintendents of the monopoly (οἱ ἀσχολούμενοι τὴν παντοπωλικήν).

A tax upon, or a monopoly of, the sale of rice (ὀρυζιοπωλική) is mentioned in the mutilated P. Teb. II. 612, but apparently the trade was extinct at Tebtynis, as the editors suggested, for the name of the tax is followed by the phrase ἐάν τι περιγίνεται which is followed by a blank space.

A dealer in lentils (φακινᾶς) in Arsinoë in the latter part of the third century paid at the extraordinarily high rate of 100 drachmae a month (BGU. IV. 1087). There seems nothing in the nature of lentils which warrants such a high tax, for the rate is twelve and a half times that paid by the bakers (ἀρτοκόποι) in the same document, and more than half again as much as that paid by the dealer in perfumes (ἀρώματα), and the perfumes were luxuries which commanded high prices and justified a correspondingly high tax upon the dealers. It is because of this, presumably, that Schwahn[84] has suggested that a φακινᾶς was a seller of fine clothing.

Sellers of small wares, γρυτοπῶλαι, paid at the rate of 12 drachmae a month in BGU. I. 9 (= W. Chrest. 293), also from Arsinoë and dated late in the third century. One dealer, however, had paid only 8 drachmae, but it is uncertain whether this was his normal rate, or whether he was 4 drachmae in arrears for the month.

Two ἀρτυμᾶτες, sellers of condiments, in Arsinoë were taxed at the rate of 36 drachmae a month in BGU. IV. 1087 (late third century), although another had paid but 8 drachmae in the same month. In PO. XII. 1517, of approximately the same date, these tradesmen paid 40 drachmae a month. Such a rate, high even in the last quarter of the third century, was caused by the fact that their wares were luxuries. At the Serapeum in Oxyrhynchus in the year A.D. 135–6, according to the gnomon in the unpublished P. Lond. inv. 1562 verso, a dealer had to pay a tax of 2 obols (?) upon each package of condiments which he sold.[85]

The sellers of perfumes or unguents (ἀρώματα), mentioned above, paid at Arsinoë in the late third century 60 drachmae a month.[86]

The beer-sellers at the same time paid only 16 drachmae a month, and one of them paid only 8 drachmae.[87] According to PO. XII. 1519, of approximately the same date, an οἰνοπώλης (wine-merchant) was 32 drachmae in arrears with his tax. The rate of taxation on liquor-dealers is not otherwise known, although in P. Teb. II. 612 there is a reference to a tax paid by tavern-keepers through the wine-sellers (καπήλων διὰ τῶν οἰνοπρατῶν).

WO. II. 1449 is a receipt for the tax of the month of Hathyr collected at Thebes by the ἐπιτ(ηρητὴς) τέλ(ους) μεταβολ(ῶν) ἁλιέων, which Wilcken[88] interpreted as a tax paid by fishermen who sold their catches at retail in the public market. The amount of the tax is not given in this receipt, but in WO. II. 647 the amount of the tax stated to have been paid for the month of Pharmuthi is 74 drachmae. Wilcken explained this high amount as the payment of a company of fishermen (Πικὼς Ἀμμωνᾶτος καὶ μ(έτοχοι) μεταβολοὶ ἁλιεῖς). In PO. XII. 1517, dated in A.D. 272 or 278, the fisherman (ἁλιεύς) paid monthly (?) 56 drachmae for his tax. A tax called δεκανικόν of 60 drachmae was paid by the ἰχθυομεταβολ(οί), who were evidently a guild.[89] The nature of the tax is uncertain.[90] SB. 4345 (from Thebes and dated A.D. 49) gives a payment of 12 drachmae εἰς λόγον μεταβολῶν ὑπὲρ μηνῶν τριῶν. An ἰχθυοπώλης is mentioned several times in connexion with payments in P. Lond. II. 266 (p. 234), but the payments are not necessarily related to taxation. Smuggled fish are mentioned in PSI. VII. 798, and we may assume that the purpose of smuggling was to avoid payment of taxes.

Bankers

According to Schwahn[91] a tax paid by private bankers in the third century is attested in Pap. Berl. Bibl. 21, 10. The document is inaccessible to me.

The Ἑταιρικόν

The tax levied on prostitutes seems to have been paid by the year in Elephantine-Syene, according to WO. II. 83 in which the τελώνης ἑταιρικοῦ gives a receipt to Thipsansnos for 1 drachma, the balance of the tax for the fourteenth year of Trajan. Payment by the month was made at Thebes in A.D. 31 and 112, if WO. II. 1030 and 504 are correctly interpreted by Wilcken as payments for ἑταιρικόν.[92] In an ostracon from Elephantine[93] dated in A.D. 144–5 a τελώνης ἑταιρικοῦ gives to a certain Aphrodite a permit to ply her trade for one day. WO. II. 1157 is a similar permit from Thebes dated in the second or third century. In P. Lond. inv. 1562 verso a tax on brothels (κοινεῖα) is mentioned, but the amount of the tax is lost; this is the only one of the trade-taxes in this document which was reckoned by the month (ἐκ τοῦ κατὰ μῆνα). The tax is not otherwise attested in Lower Egypt,[94] although PSI. IX. 1055 (a) (from Arsinoë and dated A.D. 265) apparently refers to the lease of a city brothel.

If WO. II. 1030 has been correctly interpreted by Wilcken as a receipt for ἑταιρικόν, that tax in Egypt was older than the introduction of the tax on prostitutes at Rome by Gaius.[95] According to Suetonius the tax was: 'ex capturis prostitutarum quantum quaeque uno concubitu mereret.' The same was true of the tax at Palmyra.[96] The amount of the tax, therefore, depended on how often it was paid. Wilcken attempted to apply the system of monthly payments found in the receipts from Thebes to Rome and Palmyra, and assumed that the tax-payments were made by the prostitutes at Rome and Palmyra twelve times a year. It is not improbable, however, that the system of assessment in Egypt was different from that at Rome and Palmyra. In WO. II. 83 (from Elephantine) Thipsansnos had paid her tax in full for the year by Payni, the tenth month of the year. This suggests that the tax at Elephantine was assessed on an annual basis, and it is most probable that, like other trade-taxes, the tax on prostitutes was a capitation tax at a fixed rate.[97] The tax at Thebes probably differed only in that it was assessed on a monthly basis. Perhaps the reference in P. Lond. inv. 1562 verso to the monthly report of the collectors implies a principle of assessment of the tax on brothels at Oxyrhynchus similar to the assessment of the ἑταιρικόν at Thebes.

The permits good for one day only are most probably to be explained as given to ἑταῖραι who had come into a town for a brief stay during a festival or some similarly profitable occasion, and who paid a special tax for one day's permit. Such a tax, of course, bore little relation to the trade-tax upon the stable business of the ἑταῖραι resident in the town.

Miscellaneous Trades

In the unpublished P. Lond. inv. 1562 *verso*, frequently cited above, there are given annual rates of the capitation tax on various trades whose taxation has not been hitherto attested in published documents:

κακιοπ(ῶλαι?)	sellers of cakes[98]	12	drachmae
θρυοπῶλ(αι)	sellers of rushes	6	,,
ξυλοπῶλ(αι)	sellers of wood	6	,,
κηπ[οῦροι?]	gardeners	6	,,
στεφανοπλόκ(οι)	weavers of garlands	12	,,
καρπῶ(ναι?)	dealers in fruit[99]	30	,,
ἐρι‹ο›κάππ(ηλοι)	dealers in wool	48	drachmae
σιτοκάπ(ηλοι)	dealers in grain	40	,,
σκυ[.]ποιμ( ) κοιν(όν)	guild of shoemakers (?)[100]	4	,,
τῶ(ν) κατὰ πόλιν πολο( ) ἰδιω( ) τό(ν) στ[ύπ]τη- ρο(ν)	peddlers of alum[101]	1½ (?)	obols
στημονο(ποιεῖον)	thread-mill, each man	6	drachmae
μαγειρῶ(ν) κοιν(όν)	guild of cooks	12	,,

In the great tax-rolls from Caranis in the collection of the University of Michigan the wool-dealers (ἐριοπῶλαι) pay ὑπο-κείμενα at 12 drachmae, as do the wool-shearers (ἐριοκάρται). In P. Mich. Teb. 123 R vi. 25 and 124 ii. 15, however, merchants make affidavits of sales of wool, which would most naturally be interpreted as reports to enable officials to assess an *ad valorem* tax.

PO. XII. 1519 is a list of arrears of taxation probably of the year A.D. 247–8 or 257–8. Since the trades of the persons named were generally stated, it is possible, as the editors suggested, that the tax was the χειρωνάξιον. The sums are not large, despite the comparatively late date, and it is possible that they represent arrears of monthly payments. The occupation of certain men is omitted, but it is not improbable that it is the same as that of the man preceding in the list:

γέρδιος	weaver	8	drachmae
—		8	,,
κωδᾶς	seller of fleeces (?)[102]	20	,,
—		4	,,
βαφεύς	dyer	5	,, 5 (?) obols
πορτᾶς	seller of calves (?)[103]	20	,,
ἔμπορος	merchant or importer	8	,,
οἰνοπώλης	wine-seller	32	,,

PO. XII. 1517 is a list of money-payments in which again the trades of most of the persons named are stated. If the payments are for χειρωνάξιον[104] the rates should be compared with those of BGU. I. 9 and IV. 1087, for all three documents are dated about the middle of the second half of the third century. The rates in the Berlin papyri from Arsinoë were assessed on a monthly basis, but those in the Oxyrhynchite document may have been annual assessments:

ταπιτᾶς	carpet-weaver	184	drachmae
—		120	,,
ἤπατιν (= ἠπητής?)	tailor	120	,,
ἑρμηνεὺς ἐλαίου	oil-broker	60	,,
—		60	,,
ὀνηλάτης	donkey-driver	60	,,
—		60	,,
ἁλιεύς	fisherman	56	,,
—		52	,,
μολυβάτης	dealer (or worker) in lead	48	,,
ἀρτυματᾶς	dealer in condiments	40	,,

Taxes on Unknown Trades

In the receipts from Elephantine-Syene for χειρωνάξιον the usual practice was to omit the name of the tax. Consequently it is impossible to tell what trades paid some of the rates attested in the receipts. The rates found in these receipts are 8, 12, 16, and 20 drachmae per annum. By A.D. 83–4 the rate of 20 drachmae was raised to 20 drachmae 2 obols. It is known that weavers and sellers of linen paid at the rate of 12 drachmae a year at Elephantine-Syene, and apparently a smith paid at the rate of 20 drachmae 2 obols; but it is possible, of course, that other trades also were assessed at these same rates.[105]

In BGU. I. 9 (from Arsinoë, dated late third century), which has been mentioned many times in this chapter, a man who worked with his hands (χειρητής), perhaps without skill in any trade, paid a monthly tax; but the rate has been lost. In the same document a man whose trade has not been deciphered (οτου . κυ . . . υ)[106] paid at the rate of 40 drachmae a month; similarly, two classes of artisans or dealers whose occupation is not preserved paid at the rate of 8 drachmae a month. In the related papyrus BGU. iv. 1087 a class of persons pays trade-tax at the rate of 8 drachmae a month, and for another class payments of 16, 12, and 8 drachmae a month are recorded.

In P. Teb. ii. 579 (A.D. 129–30) receipts are recorded for χειρωνάξιον at the rate of 6 drachmae (plus προσδιαγραφόμενα) for successive years. In P. Bouriant 31, also from the Arsinoite nome and dated in the second or third century, χειρωνάξιον τε . . . ων is mentioned in an account of money-taxes; it is tempting to restore τεκτόνων.

Capitation taxes on trades were one of the most important sources of revenue exploited by the Roman administration in Egypt. It is, therefore, a significant fact that no general large increase in the rates of these taxes can be proved to have been made before the reign of Probus. The depreciation of Roman coinage in Egypt, as well as elsewhere in the empire, had begun in the second century, and the emperors of the third century resorted to it continually and increasingly. The increase in the price of commodities which was inevitable, though not great in Egypt before the last quarter of the third century, should have benefited the artisans of Egypt. Yet their income was not sufficiently increased to attract the attention of the financial administration of the province. It is probable that the great decrease in the trade with India in the third century and the general impairment of commerce caused by the civil disruption in that century diminished the volume of Egyptian exports and offset any increase in prices of commodities. Consequently the great increase in the rates of these taxes appears in documents of the last quarter of the third century when uncontrolled inflation of prices had come suddenly but nevertheless as the result of the gradual and continual depreciation of the currency during a period of more than a hundred years.

TAXES ON TRADES, III. *AD VALOREM* TAXES ON INDUSTRY, SALES-TAXES, OTHER TAXES AND IMPOSTS CONNECTED WITH MARKETS, FEES, ETC.

MONEY was apparently used but little in Egypt before the Ptolemaic period. The Pharaohs, therefore, took their toll of the land by requiring that a portion of its produce be delivered into the royal granaries and storehouses. Without doubt industries other than agriculture were similarly required to pay a percentage of the wares, which they produced or handled, to the kings of Egypt. Such imposts in kind upon industry and trade, however, were generally compounded for a payment in money after the Ptolemaic system of coinage was established and the use of money had become more common throughout the country. Imposts upon a few industries, however, continued to be levied in kind for special purposes, such as the support of the army or of government officials, where collection in kind was more expedient than collection in money.[1] As has been shown in the previous chapter, capitation taxes were preferred and developed by the Roman financial administration because they offered an easy method of collecting a comparatively steady revenue from industry, since they were less immediately affected by fluctuations in business; yet on certain industries *ad valorem* taxes both in kind and in money were continued in the Roman period.

The ʾΑναβολικόν

Rostovtzeff's explanation of the ἀναβολικόν (Latin *anabolicum*) as a tax in kind collected in Egypt upon the principal products of industry is quite generally accepted by scholars.[2] He has explained the *anabolicae species* mentioned by Vopiscus[3] as the types of products subject to the *anabolicum*. The action of the emperor Aurelian, described by Vopiscus in the phrase 'Vectigal ex Aegypto urbi Romae Aurelianus vitri, chartae, lini, stuppae atque anabolicas species aeternas constituit', is interpreted to mean that this emperor regularized the levy and reserved it for the city of Rome; mention of the ἀναβολικόν in papyri of the first and second centuries and the discovery of leaden seals with the legend ANABOLICI dating from as early as the reign of Septimius Severus prove, as Rostovtzeff has pointed out, that Aurelian was not the first to make such levies. Reil properly objected, however, to Rostovtzeff's suggestion that products comprised in *anabolicae species* were subject to state monopoly in Egypt, since monopolies of none of the articles mentioned by Vopiscus can be definitely proved for the Roman period.[4]

No satisfactory explanation of the term ἀναβολικόν has as yet been given.[5] The correct explanation is to be discovered, in my opinion, by a close observation of the dates of the documents which attest this tax. The earliest reference is in O. Fay. 49, from Euhemeria and dated in A.D. 19 (?), a receipt including an item of 18 drachmae paid ⟨ὑπὲρ⟩ τιμῆς ἀναβολικ(οῦ). The expression τιμῆς ἀναβολικ(οῦ) indicates an *adaeratio* of a tax in kind, although there is no information as to the products subject to the levy. The edict of Ti. Julius Alexander,[6] which is dated A.D. 68, contains a reference to τισὶν ἀναβολικὰ εἰληφόσι ἐκ τοῦ φίσκου (the treasury department's collectors of ἀναβολικά). P. Amh. II. 131 is a letter, dated early in the second century, in which a man reproves his wife for supposing that he had appropriated τὸ ἀναβολικόν; since a few lines later he states that 54 drachmae had been paid for taxes (τέλη) and boat-fare, it seems not impossible that the discharged τέλη may have included a payment for ἀναβολικόν.[7] The leaden seals, mentioned above, bearing the inscription ANABOLICI date from the time of Septimius Severus on, and Rostovtzeff thinks that the seals found at Lyons had been placed upon goods intended for the use of the Rhine army, as the goods so imported at Rome were used for the praetorians as well as for the populace.[8] This importation was revived especially by Alexander Severus, but Rostovtzeff thinks that the custom may have been begun by the Antonines.

In the third century PO. VIII. 1135 records the receipt issued by the ἀπαιτηταὶ ἱεροῦ ἀναβολικοῦ (collectors of the imperial ἀναβολικόν) for 56 drachmae, which may be assumed, on the analogy of the payment in O. Fay. 49, to be an *adaeratio* of a levy in kind. In PSI. VII. 779, however, which is probably to be

dated in the third century, the tax is collected in kind: 14 litres
of flax is collected on 100 arurae of land subject to the tax (λίνου
ἀναβολικοῦ τῶ(ν) ἑκατὸν ἀρουρῶν λ ιδ); the tax was, therefore,
an assessment on the land which produced flax. P. Thead. 34.
iii is a similar receipt dated A.D. 324 (?) for 50 litres of flax
collected by two ἀποδέκται λίνου τοῦ ἱεροῦ ἀναβολικοῦ, one of
whom was a woman. PO. VIII. 1136, dated A.D. 420, records the
collection of four cloaks (στιχάρια) to meet the ἀναβολικόν of
the fourth indiction.

PSI. VII. 779 and P. Thead. 34. iii are especially important,
inasmuch as they mention λίνον, because linum was specified
by Vopiscus among the four products from Egypt connected
with Aurelian's establishment of the anabolicae species. Since
PO. VIII. 1135 records the receipt of a money payment for the
tax, and since the later receipts all specify payment in kind, it
is possible that one of Aurelian's measures was to stop the adaeratio of the ἀναβολικόν in Egypt. Prices had been kept moderate
in Egypt during the second half of the second century and the
first half of the third century in spite of the depreciation of the
currency.[9] In the second half of the third century, however,
the high rates of the trade-taxes in Arsinoë are fair evidence
that the continued and reckless depreciation of the Egyptian
currency had caused sufficient inflation of the prices of commodities and services to warrant a very high rise in the rate of
the money-taxes on trade and industry.[10] On the other hand,
the adaeratio of levies in kind became unprofitable for the
government, since prices of commodities might rise appreciably
between the time when the collection of money was made and
the time when the supplies were purchased by the agents of the
government. For that reason, I believe, Aurelian insisted upon
payment in kind, especially since the products of the tax were
to be used directly for the city of Rome.

It is my opinion that the ἀναβολικόν, before the changes introduced by Aurelian, was a special levy made for the Roman
armies engaged in actual warfare. The term ἀναβολικόν was used,
I believe, to distinguish such a special levy from the collection
in kind for the legions stationed in Egypt, which was called the
ἀννώνη.[11] Ἀναβολικόν designated goods for export overseas.[12]
The earliest receipt for this tax in Egypt, O. Fay. 49, is dated

early in the sixth year of the reign of Tiberius, but the payment
was made for the tax of the previous year. It was in that year
(A.D. 18) that Germanicus planned an invasion of Armenia at
the head of the legions of Syria.[13] Although his plan was frus-
trated by Piso's refusal to permit the Syrian legions to go, it is
not improbable that Germanicus had ordered a special levy in
Egypt for supplies for the expedition; his campaigns in Germany had been characterized by elaborate preparations wholly
out of proportion to the results which he attained in the field.[14]
The next extant reference is in the decree of Ti. Julius Alexander, the prefect of Egypt, which is dated in A.D. 68. In this case
the levy may have been for the campaign of Vespasian against
Jerusalem, which had begun in the previous year.[15] If τὸ ἀναβολικόν in P. Amh. II. 131. 15 refers to the tax, the date early
in the second century may coincide with the Parthian War of
Trajan (A.D. 114–16). It is probable that the continuous over-
taxing of the resources of Egypt during Trajan's campaigns, as
well as the brigandage and pillage following the Jewish revolt
of A.D. 114, necessitated the concessions to the Egyptian peasants
made by Hadrian in the first year of his reign.[16]

If, as Rostovtzeff suggests, the *anabolicum* was developed
under the Antonines, the wars of Marcus Aurelius would have
been the logical occasion for its assessment. The Parthian War
of A.D. 197–9 and the war in Britain in 208–11 could account
for the revival and further development of the tax by Septimius
Severus. The campaign against the Persians or the Germanic
campaign may well have caused the assessment of the *anabolicum* by Severus Alexander. There is no evidence that the
ἀναβολικόν assessed in Egypt was used for the Rhine army before
the time of Septimius Severus, from whose reign date the earliest
seals found at Lyons, and it is not impossible that previously
the special levies were made in Egypt only upon the occasion of
campaigns in the East. On the other hand, O. Fay. 49, dated
in A.D. 19, which (as suggested above) was connected with the
proposed expedition of Germanicus into Armenia, states that
the ἀναβολικόν is of the fifth year of the reign of Tiberius. Since
such specific statement regarding the year of assessment is common in regard to taxes which were collected annually over a
number of years, it is possible that the ἀναβολικόν had been

assessed during one or more of the preceding years of Tiberius'
reign. If that were true, the obvious explanation would be that
the tax had been assessed in order to ensure supplies for the
campaigns of Germanicus in Germany during the years A.D.
14–17. Such tenuous evidence, however, cannot be regarded as
demonstrating such a conclusion.

In the statement of Vopiscus, in regard to Aurelian's reservation of the tax for the benefit of the city of Rome, four articles are
specifically designated as the *vectigal ex Aegypto*: glass, paper,
flax, and hemp. How these products of the tax were administered
for the benefit of the population of Rome is not stated by Vopiscus. Certainly, distributions of these articles, similar to the distributions of grain, would have aided the populace but little. It
is possible that the proceeds of the sale of such materials by the
government may have been used for the direct relief of the people
of the city, but I am inclined to think that the benefit lay rather
in a lowering of commodity-prices brought about by the government's importation of these articles, which could be sold to manufacturers and dealers at a very low cost, and the competition in
the market of these materials (whose only cost was that of transportation) may have reduced commodity-prices which had perhaps risen unduly on account of the depreciation of the currency.
Rostovtzeff has noted that these products formed the chief
articles in Egypt's export trade. Aurelian, therefore, took from
Egypt those products which were of value in commerce and
which Egypt produced in abundance, rather than articles which
the Roman urban populace especially needed. In the previous
centuries, when the ἀναβολικόν was assessed for the aid of the
Roman armies, the products upon which the levy in kind was
made in Egypt may not have been the same as those specified
by Vopiscus. If they were the same, it may be that the articles
not used directly by the army were bartered for supplies or
simply sold at a huge profit to obtain revenue for the purchase
of supplies and for the pay of the soldiers.

Similar levies in kind may have been made in the Ptolemaic
period, although there is no evidence for them. The term ἀναβολικόν, however, naturally belongs to the development of the
tax in the Roman period, since the Ptolemies had few occasions
to support their armies overseas. The tax seems to have been

continued in the Byzantine period substantially as it was re-organized by Aurelian.

Taxes on Fishing

A complete monopoly of the fishing-industry on the Moeris Sea in the Fayûm was held by the Ptolemies.[17] Elsewhere in Egypt, since all waterways belonged to the king, fishermen were obliged to pay as a licence-tax 25 per cent. of their catch.[18] The τετάρτη, 25 per cent., was a common rate for taxes in kind in the Ptolemaic period, and it is quite probable that the rate was an inheritance from the Pharaonic system of taxation in kind. The tax on fishing was commuted to a payment of money in the Ptolemaic period after the system of coinage was established.

Evidence in regard to the imposts on the fishing-industry in the Roman period is limited to the Arsinoite nome, where the monopoly of the Ptolemaic government was continued only in concessions to fishermen in certain districts. There is no proof that any of the payments made in the Fayûm in the Roman period corresponded to the τετάρτη of the earlier period; they seem rather to be derived from the pre-Roman monopoly.[19] It is possible, however, that the tax of 25 per cent. of the catch was continued elsewhere in Egypt, but evidence is as yet lacking.

In the accounts of the temple of Socnopaeus at Socnopaei Nesus, which are to be dated in the second century, 625 drachmae 4 obols are recorded as an annual (?) payment to the nomarch for fishing-boats [ὑπὲρ . . . .] προκειμένων ἁλιευτικῶν πλ[οίων].[20] In a similar document, from the reign of Antoninus Pius, 625 drachmae 1½ obols are paid for the same purpose, and in this account the payment is designated as ὑπὲρ ἀποτάκτου τῶν ἐναποσημαι[ομέν]ων ἁλιευτικῶν π[λ]οίων.[21] Φόρου is certainly to be supplied with ἀποτάκτου, but it is uncertain whether this represents rent upon boats leased from the state or a payment for an exclusive concession to use boats (owned by the temple) for fishing on the waterways of the state, in this case Lake Moeris.[22] A tax of 60 drachmae was paid on the same boats for δεκανικόν, a tax evidently for the support of δέκανοι, who seem to be police officials supervising the waterways of the state and who may have acted as fish-wardens, since fishing must have been forbidden to those who had not leased concessions from the state or paid licence-taxes. Ἁλιευτικὰ πλοῖα are mentioned also in the reports of ἐπιτηρηταὶ τελωνικῶν in BGU. i. 10 and 277, but nothing can be determined from them in regard to the rate or method of assessment.

Boats belonging to the Ἀντωνιανὴ οὐσία were leased, and the receipts to the extent of 540 drachmae were reported to the strategus by the collectors of money-taxes at Socnopaei Nesus in A.D. 207–8.²³ It is not certain in this case, however, that the boats were used for fishing, although this is not improbable.²⁴

Fishing in the marshes (δρυμοί) belonging to the state was subject to an impost of some kind. In A.D. 126, according to P. Teb. ii. 359, five persons paid a total of 336 (billon) drachmae to the (ex-)ἐπιτηρητὴς ἰχθυ‹η ›ρᾶς δρυμῶν Τεβέτνυ καὶ Κερ[κή]σεως Πολέμωνος μερίδος (superintendent of fishing in the marshes of Tebetnu and Cercesis in the division of Polemon); a second receipt on the same papyrus and issued by the same official mentions a φόρος and ἀπο[.]ιτησ[ ], but this does not necessarily refer to the same impost. Ἐπιτηρηταὶ ἰχθυηρᾶς δρυμῶν are attested also in P. Fay. 42 (a) verso, a tax-collector's report from Theadelphia dated late second century. P. Teb. ii. 329, a document dated A.D. 139, states that the security posted by the two persons to whom had been farmed²⁵ the right to collect the τέλος ἰχθυηρᾶς δρυμῶν Τεβέτνεως καὶ Κερκήσεως καὶ τῶν συνκυρουσῶν κωμῶν (the tax on fishing in the marshes of Tebetnu and Cercesis and the villages of the same district) was set at 1 talent 100 drachmae, which had been placed to the account of the nomarch. Thus the nomarch appears to be responsible for the tax on fishing in the marshes as well as for the fishing on Lake Moeris. It is possible that the impost paid by the five men cited above was the τέλος ἰχθυηρᾶς δρυμῶν of this document. The use of μίσθωσις in line 27 of P. Teb. ii. 329 may indicate that the two collectors (later one) of the tax were called μισθωταί, as were the collectors of the τέλος ἰχθυηρᾶς δρυμῶν in BGU. ii. 485; the latter, however, were concerned also with the τέλος λυχνίτιδος θρυίτιδος (= τρυείτιδος), which Grenfell and Hunt explained as a tax on a kind of mullein which produced lamp-wicks and grew in the marshes.²⁶ PSI. iii. 160 is a report to the basilico-grammateus from the ἐπιτηρηταὶ . . . . . . ων καὶ δρυμοῦ Θεαδελ-

(φείας) καὶ [Πο]λυδ(ευκείας) which, while mentioning other possible sources of revenue, contains the account of monthly receipts from the θηρ(ᾶς) ἰχθυ‹ί›(ας). Since this reference to fishing is found, and fishermen (ἁλιεῖς) are mentioned in line 21 of the account, it is possible that ἁλιευτικῶν is to be restored after ἐπιτηρηταί, as suggested by the editors.[27]

P. Teb. II. 347, dated in the second century, contains a puzzling reference to ἁλιευ(τικά) collected or assessed by one Trebius Justus. The assessment seems to have been based on mysterious units of 50, 75, and 25. Two units of 50 at a town designated as Λαμπ( ) and assessed at 38 drachmae 3 obols each were leased (presumably) to a certain Ζω[. . .]ας Διοσκόρο(υ) for 77 drachmae. Ἀρθ[ο]ῶνις of Hypsele leased three units of the 75 at Καινή, assessed at 69 drachmae each, for 207 drachmae. At Κο[. . .]-ξο( ) ἐποί(κιον) a certain Nemesion leased one unit of 25 for 78 drachmae. If the units referred to the length or burden of fishing-boats, the rate of assessment ought to bear a closer relation to the size of the units, whereas the recorded figures show that one unit of 25 at Κο[. . .]ξο( ) ἐποί(κιον) is assessed at more than twice as much as a unit of 50 at Λαμπ( ). It is suggested, therefore, that this account represents leases of riparian rights to fish along a canal (Καινή is supposed by Grenfell and Hunt[28] to have been situated on the south side of the Bahr Yusuf), and that the units of 50, 75, and 25 were units of linear measure. The reason for the difference between the rates of assessment on units of different length would be that the fishing at Καινή was four times as good in the small part of the canal available as in the waterway at Λαμπ( ) and three times as good as in that at Κο[. . .]ξο( ) ἐποί(κιον). Perhaps the unit of linear measure was the cubit (πῆχυς). In any case fishermen who did not use boats formed a special class for the purpose of taxation. In BGU. III. 756 the ἁλιεῖς ἀπὸ ποδός of Socnopaei Nesus paid 80 drachmae for the seventh year of Septimius Severus (A.D. 198–9) to the nomarch through the βοηθός; the amount paid for the following year was 163 drachmae.[29] The term ἀπὸ ποδός indicates that the fishermen waded out into the lake near Socnopaei Nesus or fished along the bank of the canal at the village; but since the payment was made for the guild of fishermen through a representative, it is impossible to determine the rate of the tax.

Taxes paid by Millers and Bakers

A tax which preserves the favourite rate of assessment on trades in the Ptolemaic period is the τετάρτη ἀρτοπωλῶν, an impost of 25 per cent. paid by sellers of bread. In P. Ryl. II. 167 this tax is assumed by the lessee of a privately owned mill, which evidently combined the businesses of both miller and baker.[30] The lessor of the mill agrees to pay the δημόσια τοῦ μυλαίου, a term further qualified by τοῦ πελωχικοῦ. The πελωχικόν is attested in other documents, and it is evident that it was a tax on flour-mills, but its incidence is not revealed in the extant papyri and the derivation of the word is unknown.[31] The δημόσια are further defined in a lease of a mill in PSI. VII. 787 as [πελ]ωχικοῦ [καὶ δ]ιπλωμάτων [. . . ἀρτο]ποιίας καὶ νομαρχικῶν πάντων,[32] all of which are in this case to be paid by the lessee of the mill. A σιτικὸν τέλεσμα is mentioned in the lease of a mill in BGU. IV. 1067: the lessee states that he will deliver the loaves of bread to be paid as a part of the rent of the mill ἄνευ σιτικοῦ τελέσματος. The connexion is not clear; possibly the tax is to be related to the Ptolemaic τετάρτη σιτοποιῶν.[33] In this lease also it is stated that δημόσια are to be paid by the lessor. These δημόσια are perhaps to be regarded as property-taxes on the mill as well as professional taxes.

A tax called καθαρουργ(ία) is mentioned in a municipal account from Oxyrhynchus dated late second century.[34] Since the tax was collected in connexion with the πελωχικόν, it is probably a tax on the baking of fine bread (ἄρτοι καθαροί). There is no evidence in the account, however, to show whether this tax was or was not similar to the capitation-tax on the workmen in the καθαρουργεῖον at the market at the Serapeum in Oxyrhynchus.[35]

Painters

The products of painters were assessed a tax of 25 per cent. according to BGU. I. 25: δ′ (= τετάρτη) ὑπὲρ φόρου γενῶν ζωγραφικῶν, and the amount of the payment was 100 drachmae. The significance of φόρος is not clear in connexion with an *ad valorem* tax on the works of painters. The tax is called a τέλος in BGU. I. 199 *verso*, but φόρος τελέσματος in BGU. II. 652. It appears also in the reports of ἐπιτηρηταὶ τελωνικῶν in BGU. I. 10 and 277.

As Wilcken has pointed out,[36] the famous Fayûm portraits were the work of the painters of the villages of the Arsinoite nome, whose profits or gross receipts were thus taxed at the rate of one-fourth. All of the published documents attesting the tax on painters come from Socnopaei Nesus, which was evidently a centre of the practice of the art.

The γυψική in P. Fay. 23 a (introd.) was collected together with the ἐπιστατικὸν ἱερέων, a tax paid by priests. The γυψική may have been levied on a shop producing terra-cotta images for votive offerings at a temple, rather than a plasterers' tax.[37]   In BGU. II. 471 the γυψική at 8 drachmae[38] follows taxes paid by priests, so that again the shop was probably in connexion with a temple.

Τέλος τῆς τετάρτης

This tax, without further designation, is attested in a single receipt from Thebes dated 27–26 B.C.,[39] before many changes in the administration of the taxes of Egypt had been introduced under Augustus. It may, therefore, have referred to any of the various 25 per cent. taxes on industry found in the Ptolemaic period.[40]

Τρίτη βαλανείου

The privately owned public baths established in the Ptolemaic period for the Graeco-Macedonian population, especially in Lower Egypt, continued their existence under the Roman administration.[41] The tax of one-third on the profits or gross receipts of such baths was established by the Ptolemies.[42] It is attested for the Roman period in an account of village taxes from the Oxyrhynchite nome dated A.D. 153–6 and in a tax-account from Mendes, dated late second century, where it appears among the taxes classed as belonging to the διοίκησις, a subdivision of the department of the same name (*ΔΙΟΙΚΗΣΙΣ*).[43] For the Arsinoite nome the τρίτη βαλανείου is attested in the great tax-rolls from Caranis in the collection of the University of Michigan. There the tax is always paid, for some unknown reason, in billon (ῥυπαραί) drachmae.

Ἑκτὴ τεμάχων

This tax of a sixth, for which 2 drachmae 4 obols were paid, appears among the δημόσια in a farm account dated 8 B.C.[44] The editors suppose this tax, which is not otherwise attested, to be assessed on salt-fish, but this seems an odd item to be found in a farm account. Perhaps it was a tax on *slips* cut in the garden.

Ἑβδομή

A payment for this tax of one-seventh appears in P. Mey. 10. 5 from Theadelphia and dated A.D. 144. There is nothing to indicate upon what the tax was assessed. Meyer considered it a tax on land, but his arguments are not cogent,[45] and no tax on land at the rate of one-seventh is otherwise attested. The tax was collected by an ἐπιτηρητής and may have been a tax on a trade.

Sales-Taxes

In the unpublished P. Lond. inv. 1562 *verso* there appears a type of taxation not hitherto attested in the documents of the Roman period. A special tax on the sale of oil, dates, cucumbers, pumpkins, and vegetables was paid by the importers (?)[46] at the rate of 2 obols[47] on each package (μανδάκ(η) or μάνδακ(ον)). Condiments (ἀρτύματα) and beans were assessed at the same rate.[48] The μανδάκη is a unit of measure usually found applied to trusses of hay, but in this document it must mean a cubic measure of capacity, or at least a container, whose content may have been fixed for this particular market. A tax on the sale of washing-soda (νίτρον), which in the Ptolemaic period was a monopoly of the government, was paid at the rate of 6 drachmae a hundred artabae. This seems a very low rate, especially when it appears that the women who sold salt were required to pay a tax of 2 drachmae on a unit designated as πλ.[49] Whatever may be the correct expansion of that abbreviation, the high rate of the tax was undoubtedly caused by the complete or partial monopoly of the production and sale of salt maintained by the Roman government. Another high tax is that of (apparently) 6 drachmae on each κόιξ (palm-leaf basket) of dates; the reason for the difference between the rate on dates sold by the κόιξ and by the μανδάκη is not certain; but different measures may have been used for pressed dates and fresh dates. The potters (κεραμοπ(οιοί)) and carters of hay (χλωραγ(ωγοί)) are grouped together as paying a tax of 1 drachma. Similarly, the carters of wood (ξυληγ(οί)) paid a tax of 2 drachmae. The next group also paid a tax of 2 drachmae and includes the κοπροπ(ῶλαι), dung-sellers, the βολ-βιτω(πῶλαι?), cow-dung sellers, and the λ[. . .]μ( ).[50] It seems unlikely that any of these tradesmen would have paid a capitation tax so low as 1 or 2 drachmae a year.[51] Since the tax on these men follows the sales-tax on units of measure in the gnomon, it is probable that the tax of 1 drachma or of 2 drachmae is to be applied to some unit of measure. Most of these men were engaged in hauling something or in selling something that had to be carted into the market, or perhaps to the purchaser's dwelling or land, so that it may be possible to consider the unit of measure as a cart-load or a donkey-load. This would be a satisfactory unit of measure for the products of each of these tradesmen, except perhaps that of the potter. If, however, the potters at the market at the Serapeum in Oxyrhynchus were engaged in the manufacture of tiles or of rough cheap pottery,ʼ their wares may have been sold by the donkey-load or by the cart-load.[52]

Although this type of sales-tax paid by the dealer at a fixed rate on units of sale is attested only for the market at the Serapeum in Oxyrhynchus, it is not improbable that a similar system was in use elsewhere in Egypt.

In P. Genf. 77, from Philadelphia and dated A.D. 211, a wine-seller (οἰνοπώλης) pays 244 drachmae and 52 κέρματος drachmae, and later 400 drachmae, ἀπὸ τιμῆς οἴνου γενήματος ιηL. It is possible that this is the familiar tax ὑπὲρ τιμῆς οἴνου,[53] but the use of ἀπό makes this somewhat doubtful. If ἀπό is correctly used, this is a tax collected on the wine purchased by, or sold by, a wine-dealer in a given year. In the case of a commodity like wine it was far more satisfactory to assess a tax on the wholesale purchase of the dealer than to attempt to collect a tax on retail sales;[54] moreover, if the tax had been on retail sales, the tax-collector would have had no interest in the year in which the wine was produced and probably no means of ascertaining the vintage after the dealer's supply was gone.

(Πεντηκοστὴ) ὠνίων

A tax on purchases made in the public market was collected at Thebes by special τελ(ῶναι) ν̄ ὠνί(ων) ὑποτελ(ῶν). The tax was assessed at the rate of 2 per cent. and was paid by the purchaser. In WO. II. 1056 the tax is collected on the sale of a cow, or of some article connected with cattle.[55] WO. II. 1076 is a similar receipt for the tax on the purchase of wood. The importance of this tax and also the difficulty of collecting it are shown by the large number of receipts for the $\mu\epsilon\rho\iota\sigma\mu\dot{o}s$ $\dot{\epsilon}\nu\lambda(\epsilon\dot{\iota}\mu$-$\mu\alpha\tau os)$ $\tau\epsilon\lambda(\omega\nu\iota\kappa\hat{\omega}\nu)$ $\dot{\omega}\nu\dot{\iota}\omega\nu$ which was assessed to make up the deficit in the expected collection of this tax.[56]

A tax on the purchase of a cow ($\tau\dot{\epsilon}\lambda os$ $\beta o\dot{o}s$) is also attested at Cercesucha in the Fayûm.[57] The price is given as 44 drachmae, but the rate of the tax was not stated, because it was well known. The editors supposed that this $\tau\dot{\epsilon}\lambda os$ was identical with the $\dot{\epsilon}\gamma\kappa\dot{\upsilon}\kappa\lambda\iota o\nu$, which was assessed in the Roman period at the rate of 10 per cent. In P. Lond. II. 305 (p. 79), moreover, the $\dot{\epsilon}\pi\iota$-$(\tau\eta)\rho(\eta\tau\alpha\dot{\iota})$ $\dot{\epsilon}\kappa\langle\sigma\rangle\tau\dot{\alpha}\sigma(\epsilon\omega s)$ $\kappa\alpha\dot{\iota}$ $\delta\epsilon\kappa(\dot{\alpha}\tau\eta s)$ $\dot{\alpha}\gamma o\rho\hat{\alpha}s$ $'A\lambda\epsilon\xi\dot{\alpha}\nu\delta\rho o\upsilon$ $[N\dot{\eta}\sigma o\upsilon]$ collect a tax from the purchaser of a mule colt. The implication of the title of the collectors is that the tax was assessed at the rate of 10 per cent., but this is not an absolutely necessary conclusion. The rates of taxes often differ between Upper and Lower Egypt, but since the tax on the purchase of a cow at Thebes was apparently only 2 per cent. it is rather doubtful whether the identification of the $\tau\dot{\epsilon}\lambda os$ $\beta o\dot{o}s$ on the sale at Cercesucha with the $\dot{\epsilon}\gamma\kappa\dot{\upsilon}\kappa\lambda\iota o\nu$ at 10 per cent. is correct. This in turn casts doubt upon the rate of 10 per cent. on the sale of the mule colt. Purchasers of donkeys (in P. Hamb. 33. ii) paid a tax of 4 drachmae on each donkey; it is doubtful if the rate there was 10 per cent., for 40 drachmae was extraordinarily little to pay for a donkey. At a rate of 2 per cent., on the other hand, a tax of 4 drachmae would mean a purchase price of 200 drachmae, which is not too high for the second half of the second century (cf. Segré, *Circolazione monetaria*, pp. 126–7). P. Hamb. 33 comes from Arsinoë, and thus it is possible that the tax on the sale of a donkey in the Fayûm was collected at the same rate as the tax on the sale of a cow at Thebes.

In *Archiv*, VI, p. 130, Milne published a number of demotic receipts for what is apparently a market-tax. His remarks are as follows: 'The demotic name of this tax has not hitherto occurred elsewhere: but, as it is a feminine form of the word which in the masculine is the equivalent of $\delta\rho\dot{o}\mu os$ in the inscription of Canopus, it is presumably a market-tax: since no similar tax occurs on Theban ostraca, the tax or the name may have been a local one at Tentyra. The amounts vary irregularly from 2 drachmae to 2 drachmae 1 obol and 2 drachmae $1\frac{1}{2}$ obols. Possibly the payments were instalments. . . .'

The only receipt from Thebes which may be at all similar to the demotic receipts from Tentyra is SB. 4346 (dated A.D. 50). This ostracon records a series of payments ὑπὲρ τέλους ἀγορανομίας ὠνίων. Two payments of 4 drachmae are recorded in the month Mecheir and one payment of 4 drachmae in each of the following five months, a total of 28 drachmae. WO. II. 1419 (from Thebes and dated A.D. 113) is a receipt given by the τελ(ῶναι) ἀγορ(ανο)μ(ίας) ὠνίων for a payment, whose amount is not stated, ὑπὲρ τέλ(ους) Τύβει. If the collection of the χειρωνάξιον was under the administration of markets (ἀγορανομία) at Thebes, these monthly payments could be explained as instalments of χειρωνάξιον paid by artisans. The ἀγορανομία, however, ordinarily confined its activities to superintendence of transfers of property and the assessment of taxes thereon and to the lease of certain concessions in the market. These monthly payments might be considered rent for such concessions leased from the government, but φόρος, not τέλος, is the proper term for rent. Perhaps the nature of some forms of business was such that it was more expedient to collect a tax in monthly instalments than to attempt the exaction of an *ad valorem* tax on sales.

Τέλος μισθώσεως

This obscure tax appears in WO. II. 1053 (from Thebes and dated A.D. 105) where it is collected by the τελ(ῶναι) ἀγο(ρανομίας?). If the reading is correct a tax was collected upon the lease of a part of an island (τέλ(ος) μισθ(ώσεως) μέρο(υς?) νήσου).

The Ἐγκύκλιον

The ἐγκύκλιον was a tax on transfers of real property and of certain other types of property. According to tradition the tax on real property had been established by Psammetichus I at the rate of one-tenth (δεκάτη).[58] In the Ptolemaic period the rate of the tax seems to have varied from 5 to 10 per cent.[59] The

10 per cent. rate of the ἐγκύκλιον on sales of real property continued through the first two centuries of Roman rule.[60]

In several of the ostraca from Thebes the reference to the ἐγκύκλιον does not specify the type of property subject to the tax. The amount paid in some of these receipts is so small that, unless an instalment is intended, it is unlikely that real property was transfered.[61] In certain ostraca the payment is made ὑπὲρ ἐγκυκλίου καὶ ἄλλων. The taxes or fees designated by ἄλλων are not further specified in the receipts from Thebes. In the Ptolemaic period a tax of 1 per cent. (ἑκατοστή) was added to the ἐγκύκλιον on the sale of slaves;[62] in addition, a fee for handling (προπωλητικόν or προπρατικόν) was charged.[63] Other fees were charged in the compulsory sales by auction.[64] Some of these fees or taxes may be intended by the ἄλλων of the ostraca, since they were sometimes indicated in Ptolemaic documents by the phrase τὰ τέλη πάντα.[65] In P. Teb. II. 351, dated in the second century, the amount of the tax on the sale of the half-share of a small bakehouse was 66 drachmae, although the price of the property sold is stated to be 600 drachmae. The editors explained the amount of the tax as 60 drachmae for ἐγκύκλιον and 6 drachmae for προσδιαγραφόμενα. It is more likely, however, that the surcharge is the ἐπιδέκατον mentioned as an extra charge on the ἐγκύκλιον of the sale of a house in PO. I. 99 (dated A.D. 55).[66] The rate of this ἐπιδέκατον is the same as that of the ἑκατοστή added to the ἐγκύκλιον on the sale of slaves in the Ptolemaic period, and it is not impossible that the taxes are to be identified. P. Lond. III. 933 (p. 69) gives the price of purchase of an olive-orchard as 300 drachmae; the ἐγκύκλιον, however, is stated to be 40 drachmae 1 obol instead of the 30 drachmae expected. Grenfell[67] suggested that the phrase ἀχρὶ συντ{ε}ιμή-[σεως] may refer to something unusual in the sale. In PO. x. 1284, dated A.D. 250, the amount of the sale was 3[.]5 drachmae 5½ obols, on which taxes called διαγραφή amounted to 73 drachmae 5½ obols. In their introduction the editors remarked that these charges certainly included an unknown amount for σπονδή as well as the ἐγκύκλιον. Ordinarily, however, the σπονδή is a relatively small item, and the editors suggested that unless it is to be regarded here as practically as large as the ἐγκύκλιον, it is necessary to conclude that in the course of the third century the rate of the latter tax rose considerably. It is possible, how-ever, that other charges were included under διαγραφή suffi-cient to bring the total of fees and taxes to an amount almost double that of the normal ἐγκύκλιον.[68]

There are several documents which mentioned taxes that seem to be connected with the ἐγκύκλιον, although they are not so named. In Mey. J. P. 60. 29 appears a τέλος τάφου καὶ ψιλῶν τόπων collected on property which had changed hands (δι' ἐγκ(υκλίου)); this is the only example of a tax on the sale of a cemetery-lot and, since the amount of the tax is not given, it is impossible to determine the relation of this tax to the ἐγκύκλιον. In P. Lond. III. 1158 (p. 151 = M. *Chrest.* 256), from Hermopolis and dated A.D. 226-7, the ἐγκύκλιον is apparently called τέλος ἀγορασμοῦ. In BGU. I. 156. 9, 250 drachmae are paid for a fee called βεβαιωτικόν[69] on a purchase-price of 1,200 drachmae; this is a rate slightly over 20 per cent. The new Liddell and Scott *Greek Lexicon* defines βεβαιωτικόν as a tax paid to the government as warrantor of sales, apparently following P. M. Meyer (in *Διοίκησις und ῎Ιδιος Λόγος* in *Festschrift für Otto Hirschfeld*, p. 151).

It is interesting to note that Hadrian granted to citizens of Antinoë immunity from the payment of ἐγκύκλιον on sales of houses. SB. 7601 records a suit brought to establish the applica-tion of this immunity to sales of property outside the city of Antinoë, since an ἐπιτηρητὴς ἐγκυκλίου (superintendent of the tax on sales of real property) had attempted to collect the ἐγκύκλιον on such property from a citizen of Antinoë.

A tax called the τέλος ἐκστάσεως was assessed on gifts of property (*cessio bonorum*), and was associated with the tax of one-tenth on sales of property.[70] In BGU. III. 914 the cession seems to have been made to cancel a debt, while in P. Teb. II. 351 a mother gave a house to her daughter. In neither example is the rate ascertainable, but the payment of only 4 drachmae for the tax on the cession of a house in P. Teb. II. 351 would indicate that the rate was less than the 10 per cent. ἐγκύκλιον on sales, unless the 4 drachmae represent an instalment of which there is no indication in the wording of the document.

The ἐγκύκλιον was also collected on mortgages, but at the rate of 2 per cent., payable by the mortgagee.[71] A tax was again paid if the mortgage was renewed.[72] PO. III. 511 records the loan of 16 drachmae borrowed in order to pay the tax on a mortgage.[73] A tax was also collected on the foreclosure of a mortgage: in PSI. VI. 688. 72 a τέλος of 58 drachmae (together with other fees) was made for ἐμβαδεία on a mortgage whose capital sum was 4,500 drachmae. The same tax is possibly represented in the τέ(λος) ἐμ(βαδικόν) for which 2 drachmae 1 obol were collected in 16 B.C. (WO. II. 358), but the reading is declared uncertain by Wilcken; the tax ἐμβαδικόν is found in several ostraca of the Ptolemaic period.[74]

The ἐγκύκλιον was collected also in the Roman period on the purchase of slaves. The rate of the tax on such transactions is not given in extant papyri of the Roman period, but it is generally supposed that it was 10 per cent.[75] This tax is probably to be identified with the τέλος δούλου paid upon the purchase of a slave in P. Hamb. 79, an Oxyrhynchite document of the second century. A tax on public auctions, the κομακτορία, is associated with the ἐγκύκλιον in PO. XII. 1523, a document concerned with the purchase of two slaves.[76] The term ἐγκύκλιον implies a tax paid upon the manumission of a slave in SB. 6293, from the Arsinoite nome and dated A.D. 195-6. Again the rate is unknown. There was evidently more than one tax paid upon the manumission of slaves, for the expression καὶ ὧν ἄλλων [καθήκει] follows ‹δι'› ἐγκυκλίου[77] in that document, and the plural τέλη τῆς ἐλευθερώσεως is used in P. Strass. II. 122 and P. Teb. II. 407. The tax at Rome of 5 per cent. on manumissions was paid by Roman citizens resident in Egypt, as is demonstrated by the expression εἰκοστὴ . . . ἐλευθερ(ιῶν) in BGU. I. 326. ii. 10,[78] the will of a Roman veteran, but it is very uncertain whether this rate can be applied to the ἐγκύκλιον or to the other tax (or taxes) included in τέλη τῆς ἐλευθερώσεως paid by persons who were not Roman citizens.[79]

The purchase of boats was likewise subject to the ἐγκύκλιον. This is attested, however, only for Elephantine and Thebes.[80] At the latter place the collectors of the ἐγκύκλιον on boats collected that on slaves also: in WO. II. 1454, for example, the collectors are called ἐπιτηρηταὶ τέλο‹υ›ς ἐνκυκ(λίου) ἀνδραπ(όδων) καὶ πλοίων. The rate cannot be ascertained from the two published receipts.

Among the demotic ostraca from Denderah published by Milne in *Archiv*, VI, pp. 130 ff., are several recording payments of a tax of one-twentieth. The receipts do not state of what sums the payments are one-twentieth, or what was the occasion of the payment; but the editor was inclined to think that the tax was one-twentieth of the profits or receipts of some transactions during a year, for the tax was always paid at the beginning or at the very end of the year. The payers were all members of the same family and may have traded in common and shared profits, which would account for the fact that the payments made by different men are the same amount in any given year, although the amounts vary from year to year for each man. Milne, there-fore, suggested that the tax may be the same as the ἐγκύκλιον. If that suggestion is correct, it is not impossible that the rate of the tax was 10 per cent., as it was in Lower Egypt, despite the demotic designation of 'one-twentieth', for the ἀπόμοιρα was termed ἕκτη (one-sixth) in Greek documents and 'one-tenth' in demotic receipts, although these terms bore no relation to the assessment κατ᾽ ἄρουραν of the Roman period.[81] The ἐγκύκλιον was assessed at 5 per cent. during a part of the Ptolemaic period, and it might be argued that the anachronistic term 'one-twentieth' was retained in demotic receipts of the Roman period to distin-guish the tax on transfers of property (or on business) from the ἀπόμοιρα which was called the 'one-tenth'. A τέλος εἰκοστόν is mentioned, however, in a letter (BGU. IV. 1207. 19) dated in 28 B.C., but there is no way of identifying the tax.

Ἑκατοσταί

In BGU. I. 156 (= W. *Chrest.* 175), from Hephaestias and dated A.D. 201, a soldier of the legion directs his bankers to pay to the οἰκονόμος of the emperors 1,200 drachmae for a plot of land which he had leased (probably in perpetuity). The land had formerly belonged to the estate of Tiberius Gemellus, but had passed into the possession of the *fiscus*,[82] and had been offered at auction. The purchaser authorizes also the payment of 48 drachmae ὑπὲρ ἑκατοστῶν τεσσαρῶν, a charge of 4 per cent. In P. Fay. 36, a lease of the monopoly to manufacture and sell bricks at the village Cercethoëris dated A.D. 111–12, the ἑκατοσταί are mentioned and also the κηρυκικά, the auction expenses. The κηρυκικά are attested also in an official account (P. Ryl. II. 215. 44, 51) from the Mendesian nome dated in the second century and in PSI. I. 105. 22 also from that nome. In line 51 of P. Ryl. II. 215 the charge for κηρυκικά is 14 drachmae, exactly one-sixth of the charge for ἑκατοσταί (84 drachmae); approximately the same ratio is found in line 44 of the same document. In the latter case, however, the main sum upon which these charges were made is given, and the payment for ἑκατοσταί is only 1 per cent., i.e. an ἑκατοστή. The ἑκατοσταί are mentioned also in line 40 of the same document, but the previous line, which probably contained the charge for κηρυκικά, is lost. Both charges appeared in Fragment 1 cited in the introduction to P. Ryl. II. 215. A fee for the herald (κηρυκεῖον) was collected in connexion with the sale of slaves by auction in the Ptolemaic period.[83]

Τέλη καταλοχισμῶν

Special taxes, the τέλη καταλοχισμῶν, were charged for transfer, by cession or inheritance, of catoecic land. These charges were justified, at least in part, by the extra work involved in recording such transfers in the special records of catoecic land.[84]

The plural τέλη καταλοχισμῶν is used in BGU. I. 340 and perhaps in BGU. I. 328. Included among these charges on the inheritance of catoecic land, which were collected by the δημοσιώνης τέλους καταλοχισμῶν, was the τέλος γνωστείας,[85] evidently a tax for the services involved in searching the records and calling witnesses to establish the identity of an heir. The rate of this tax is not known, but it must have been quite high, since 25 drachmae is merely the final instalment of the tax paid on an inheritance of 2 arurae. The singular τέλος καταλοχισμῶν also occurs in P. Teb. II. 357, where 40 drachmae are paid as an instalment on the tax on 1 arura, which had probably been inherited, since the tax-payers were three minors.

A most valuable addition to our knowledge of the τέλη καταλοχισμῶν has recently been made by the publication of a gnomon for the collection of such taxes in the Arsinoite nome. In this gnomon (P. Iand. 137) catoecic land is divided into two classes according to its culture: grain-land (σιτική) and land devoted to (fruit) trees (δενδρική). Taxes on the latter class of land are invariably twice as high as the rates on the former. Furthermore, the rate of the tax to be paid by women gaining possession of catoecic land was twice or sometimes three times as high as the rate paid by men. Thus the tax paid by a man for each arura of grain-land was 4 drachmae, for each arura of 'wooded' land 8 drachmae, but for the same classes of land a woman paid 8 and 16 drachmae respectively. During the first five years that catoecic grain-land was owned, a tax of 8 drachmae an arura was collected from a male owner, with the corresponding increases if the land was 'wooded' or was owned by a woman. A male child duly enrolled and inheriting catoecic grain-land from his father paid a tax of 2 drachmae an arura and double for 'wooded' land. A girl, however, paid 6 drachmae for an arura of catoecic grain-land under the same circumstances. If the reports were delayed the amount of the tax was doubled. A tax of 1 drachma was made for each arura of catoecic grain-land which was mortgaged, and the same amount was collected when the mortgage was cancelled. The gnomon concludes with a list of fees for declarations, recording of reports sent up from Alexandria, publication of names, seals, &c.[86]

Receipts for the collection of these taxes on catoecic land are infrequent. P. Fay. 56 is certainly to be regarded as such a receipt, for it records a payment of 300 copper drachmae for ναύβιον κατοίκων, the tax on 3 arurae of catoecic land, and 12 drachmae (ὑπὲρ) κατοίκων, or 4 drachmae an arura—a rate found in the gnomon above on catoecic grain-land. A payment of 4 drachmae for the same kind of tax is found in P. Hamb. 13, and BGU. VII. 1587 is apparently another similar receipt. A payment of 40 drachmae to the πράκτορες κατοίκων in P. Goodsp. Cairo 30. xxi is possibly another example.

Fees for the transfer of catoecic property by sale (μετεπιγραφή) were collected in the Ptolemaic period,[87] but it is probable that the rates were different from those collected in the Roman period.[88] The collector of the transfer-taxes on catoecic land was called the δημοσιώνης τέλους καταλοχισμῶν 'Αρσινοείτου καὶ ἄλλων νόμων. The Arsinoite nome is thus emphasized, as the editors of P.Teb. II. 357 have pointed out, because most of the catoecic land was in the Fayûm.[89]

Inheritance-Taxes

The tax on inheritances paid by Roman citizens in Egypt was the *vicesima* (5 per cent.) as paid at Rome.[90] There are no certain references to inheritance-taxes paid by citizens of Egypt, except in connexion with the inheritance of catoecic land.[91] An inheritance-tax called ἀπαρχή is attested in the Ptolemaic period in P. Turin I. 7. 10, and it is most unlikely that the Egyptians paid no similar tax in the Roman period. The ἀπαρχή mentioned in Mitteis *Chrest.* 372. iv. 7, however, seems to be the *vicesima* paid by a Roman soldier. Lumbroso suggested[92] that Augustus introduced the *vicesima hereditatum* into Rome modelled upon the tax in Egypt, but there is no proof of this, since the rate in Egypt is not known either for the Ptolemaic or for the Roman period.

Fees of the Official Bureaux

Various supplementary fees were charged by the official bureaux in connexion with transfers of property or similar transactions, whenever deeds or other legal documents were recorded or posted at the request of private citizens.

PO. XIV. 1697 records the sale of the courtyard of a house at Oxyrhynchus in A.D. 242 for 200 drachmae. The document includes the stipulation that the καταγραφῆς τέλη were to be paid by the vendor. The editors believed these charges to consist of the 'twelve drachmae', a fee charged for the recording (δημοσίωσις) of deeds and similar documents, which was set aside for the city of Alexandria,[93] and the τιμήματος τέλη. These are apparently the same taxes as are designated by the word τέλη in PO. XII. 1473. 17. The plural τιμήματος τέλη is found in P. Lips. 10. ii. 21, but the same impost is apparently indicated by the singular τιμήματος τέλος of PO. IX. 1200. 45. This was apparently an *ad valorem* tax,[94] like the ἐγκύκλιον, and might be mistaken for it, were it not that the latter tax is invariably paid by the purchaser of property, while the τιμήματος τέλος (or τέλη) is paid by the person applying for the registration of a deed or bill of sale, usually the vendor.[95]

A fee of 12 drachmae appears in the gnomon of transfer-taxes (P. Iand. 137) for the 'recording of each name' (χρημα-

τισμ(ῶν) ἑκάστ(ου) [ὀνόματος]). Perhaps this fee is to be identified with the charge of 12 drachmae for recording deeds (δημοσίωσις) noted above, although it is not impossible that the same
amounts are merely a coincidence. The same gnomon records
a fee of 2 drachmae paid by a man making a declaration
(ἀπογραφή) of catoecic land and 4 drachmae paid by a woman.
A charge of 4 obols for ἀγράφου may have been made for signing
the name of an illiterate person to a transfer of catoecic land.
One drachma was charged for the seal on such documents. Two
drachmae had to be paid by a man for the recording of papers
sent up from the central record-office in Alexandria, and 4 drachmae were paid by a woman. Another charge of 4 drachmae is
found in the last line of the gnomon, but the reason for the
charge is lost in the lacuna.

P. Goodsp. Cairo 30. xxxviii records a payment to the νομο-
γράφως for the registration of a house (ὑ(πὲρ) οἰκ(ίας) ἀν[α-
γρ(αφομένης)]), but the occasion of the registration is unknown,
and the amount of the fee is lost.

Another fee of 12 drachmae was charged in SP. xx. 14 for
διανομή, that is for the execution of a will.[96] A tax of 12 drachmae is mentioned in P. Fay. 43 (28 B.C.), but the amount of the
payment is given as $\overline{\mathcal{L}ιβ}$ χα(λκοῦ) which the editors were unable
to explain; the occasion of the collection of the tax is not suggested in the text of the receipt.

A fee was charged for the application by a woman for a legal
guardian. This fee, called αἰτήσεως τέλος, is recorded in two
documents from Oxyrhynchus dated in the third century.[97]
The amount paid for the application is not stated in either of
these documents, but in P. Ryl. II. 120, from Hermopolis and
dated A.D. 167, $9\frac{1}{2}$ obols were ordered to be paid as a fee for
filing a similar petition.

In PO. XII. 1474. 6, payment of 14 drachmae is recorded in
an application concerning a loan. The editors in their note on
the line suggest that the 14 drachmae may have included the
12 drachmae regularly paid to Alexandria (mentioned above) or
more probably the τιμήματος τέλος, or perhaps γραμματικά
(which are discussed below). They regard the payments of 16
drachmae $1\frac{1}{2}$ obols and 12 drachmae [.] obol(s) in PSI. I. 109,
which were paid apparently for the δημοσίω(σις) of contracts

and included σπονδαί, as of the same nature as the payment of 14 drachmae in PO. XII. 1474.

A tax upon the division of property (τέλος διαιρέσεως) was collected, but there is no evidence as to the rate.[98] A fee for distraint (τέλος ἐπικαταβολ(ῆς) ὑποθήκης) was also collected.[99]

A fixed charge was made for giving notice (ἐπίσταλμα ὡρισμένον), but the nature of the fee is not clear, and the variety of documents in which it appears (settlement of long-standing claims and liabilities of estates, a receipt for a nurse's wages, &c.) is such that the only conclusion that can be drawn is that a fee was charged when certain types of formal notices were filed.[100]

The Γραμματικά

Some of the various charges listed above were probably included in the fees called γραμματικά. Under the Ptolemies a tax called γραμματικόν seems to have been exacted from cleruchi to pay for clerical work in the government bureaux made necessary by the special character of cleruchic land.[101] If P. Teb. II. 345 is correctly dated in 28 B.C., this tax may have survived into the beginning of the Roman period, for a tax abbreviated γρ( ) is found in this account of taxes paid by several persons from villages in the division of Polemon in the Arsinoite nome. The tax may have been abolished by Augustus or one of his successors, for there is no later evidence for a special tax for the support of the bureaux. In other documents of the Roman period the γραμματικόν appears as a fee charged for services rendered in preparing and filing documents for private citizens. Much new light has been thrown on the nature of the γραμματικά charged in the γραφεῖα (official writing-bureaux) by the publication of P. Mich. II by A. E. R. Boak. According to the evidence there presented in the registers and accounts of the γραφεῖον at Tebtynis, fees were charged for the preparation of public and private documents for citizens who required the services of the bureau. The price charged apparently depended on the length of the document prepared and the number of copies required, for the amounts vary from a single obol to as high as 40 drachmae. The fee for this service fell upon the person who requested the preparation of the document; if more than one person was interested, the cost might be shared. BGU. II. 568 is a fragment of a similar record of fees collected at a γραφεῖον. The γραμματικά are mentioned in several documents and accounts of the Roman period.[102] In the accounts of private individuals, however, it is often difficult to determine whether the payments were made to official γραφεῖα or to scribes for strictly private services.

The lessees of the γραφεῖον at Tebtynis were charged with the collection of the tax on papyrus, the χαρτηρά.[103] Nothing is known concerning the incidence of this tax. Boak follows Wilcken in supposing the χαρτηρά to be a tax levied on papyrus used for documents prepared at the γραφεῖον and paid by the person who requested the execution of the document.[104]

In P. Grenf. ii. 41 the payment for καταχωρισμός seems to be a fee for filing documents in the state archives which was paid by the lessees of a γραφεῖον, although without doubt the concessionaire was able to pass the charge along to the person who requested that documents be filed in the official bureaux of records.

The γραφεῖον at Tebtynis seems to have had some connexion with the collection of the ἐγκύκλιον, for the collectors of that tax had to have access to the records of the γραφεῖον, and γραμματικά were collected for recording transfers of property which were subject to payment of the ἐγκύκλιον.[105] Professor Harmon has recently pointed out that the purpose of the elaborate records of the βιβλιοθήκη ἐγκτήσεων was not to serve 'private interests in a purely altruistic spirit', but by its control of transfers of property to relieve the courts.[106] The local γραφεῖα, like that of Tebtynis, whose purpose was to relieve the central record office of much of the burden of the preparation of documents to be filed, were no more purely altruistic in spirit. The lease of a γραφεῖον was a purely commercial venture, and the multiplicity of fees for its services was necessary if the lessees were to make their business at least self-supporting.

TAXES PERTAINING TO PRIESTS AND TEMPLES

WHEN, after his conquest of Egypt, the prefects of Augustus assumed the administration of that country, they found the native priesthood exercising powers which had been increasing steadily for more than a century. From the time of the Middle Kingdom, indeed, the priests had enjoyed an exalted position in the political, social, and economic life of Egypt. Their power reached its greatest height when the monarchy declined in the Twentieth Dynasty and the high-priest of Amon-Ra was able to seat himself upon the throne of the Pharaohs. During the period of Persian domination the priests, like the rest of the Egyptians, were severely repressed; but, thanks to superior organization, the priesthood emerged from that period of national servitude with strength greater than that of any other class in the state. In the Ptolemaic period the earlier kings attempted to limit the income and privileges of the temples and their priests; but taking advantage of the period of confusion and distress, caused by political and economic crises confronting the later Ptolemies, the priests secured additional privileges and grants of land. Consequently the Roman conquest found the priests again occupying a position of vast importance in the state—a position supported by the great wealth of the temples.[1]

The successful administration of Egypt required that the power of the priesthood be subordinate to the civil government. The steps taken by the prefects of Augustus to secure that subordination were similar in principle to the measures employed by the first three Ptolemies; but the limitations set upon the privileges of the priests and temples by the representatives of the Roman emperor were more drastic than the Ptolemaic kings had cared, or dared, to enforce. The whole hierarchy of native priests, as well as the priests of Greek and Roman temples, was made subject to the authority of the High-Priest of All Egypt (ἀρχιερεύς . . . Αἰγύπτου πάσης), who was not an ecclesiastic but a Roman procurator.[2] This attempt to control the personnel

of the priesthood might easily have failed had it not been accompanied by an attack directed against the economic foundation upon which the independence of the Egyptian priesthood
was based. The first step taken by the government was to assume
control over the finances of all temples—this control was eventually concentrated in the bureau of the Idiologus.[3] The second
step was taken by definitely diminishing the revenues of the
temples. Otto[4] has described the sources of revenue for priests
and temples as follows: endowments in property, particularly of
productive land; ownership of industries, some of which were
monopolies, and of various commercial enterprises (including
banking); ownership of slaves; special gifts from individuals and
from the government; regular taxes collected directly from the
people and subventions from the government. We have seen
in previous chapters[5] that the Roman government, to secure the
dependence of the priests, retained in the hands of its officials
the administration of the temples' endowments of land ($\iota\epsilon\rho\grave{\alpha}\ \gamma\hat{\eta}$)
and that much of the temple-land was confiscated and its yield
added to the revenues of the civil government. We have observed also that the exemptions of the priests from personal
taxation, and of the temples from trade-taxes, were severely
limited or entirely withdrawn. In addition special taxes were
assessed by the Roman administration upon the priests and upon
the temples.

The Ptolemies developed, and perhaps had introduced,[6] a
system of subventions granted by the government to the temples
for the maintenance of the priests. Such a subvention was called
a $\sigma\acute{\upsilon}\nu\tau\alpha\xi\iota\varsigma$, and it might be made in money or in kind (grain,
oil, wine, or the like).[7] These subventions assured to the priests
a steady annual income which compensated, in part, for the loss
of revenues suffered when the administration of their endowments and tithes was appropriated by the government. Under
a weak civil administration such subventions might become an
almost intolerable burden upon the state treasury, when the
demands of the priests increased as their power mounted at the
expense of the government; but under the firm control of the
prefects of the Roman emperors the subventions, as Bell has
recently pointed out,[8] became an instrument for maintaining a
strict control over the priests and their property. By limiting

the income of the temples the subvention checked the ambitions of the priests; by assuring their subsistence it made the clergy fairly content, and the fear of the loss of such assured income was a powerful deterrent to revolt.

Receipts issued by the priests in acknowledgement of the delivery of the σύνταξις, and their complaints of failure to receive it, date from 13–12 B.C. to A.D. 233–4.[9] Payments in the Roman period were made both in money and in kind, but most of the συντάξεις granted to the priests probably were in kind, since it seems to have been the policy of the Roman government to reduce rather than to increase the monies available to the temples. The grain for these payments in kind to the priests probably came, at least originally, from the yield of the ἱερὰ γῆ. Our information concerning the administration of this revenue is deficient. It is probable that the methods of administration differed in the various nomes, and that the method was determined in each section of the country by local conditions, difficult to define in the present state of the evidence, and was modified by agreements made by the government with individual temples. At Thebes there was a temple granary (θησαυρὸς τῶν ἱερῶν) whose officials bore the titles σιτόλογος ἱερατικῶν, ἐπιτηρηταὶ θησαυροῦ ἱερῶν, τελῶναι θησαυροῦ ἱερῶν.[10] Into this granary were measured the payments for the bath-tax (βαλανευτικόν) which, as a tax in kind, seems to be unattested elsewhere.[11] Granaries connected with temples are mentioned in many documents from Lower Egypt also.[12] There is no evidence at Thebes or elsewhere, however, to indicate that the priests had any control over the assessment or collection of the taxes whose yield filled the temple granaries. In P. Teb. II. 302, dated A.D. 71–2, the priests of Socnebtynis address a petition to the prefect in regard to the rent to be paid on 500¼ arurae of land which, originally the property of the temple but confiscated (apparently in the reign of Augustus), had been leased to the priests in lieu of a syntaxis. The rent paid by the priests was probably quite low, although an effort on the part of the comogrammateus to increase it, by requiring an additional 200 artabae of barley, is represented by the priests as endangering their subsistence and consequently the performances of the services and ceremonies of the temple. In BGU. IV. 1197, from Busiris in the Heracleopolite nome and dated 12–11 B.C., the complaint of the priest and prophet of Harpsentesis and Sarapis in regard to his failure to receive the annual σύνταξις of 150 artabae of wheat, states that the payment was to have been made ἐκ τῆς Ἀρπήσεως προσόδου, and the editor of the document suggests that the payment was made from an endowment given by Harpesis, a private individual.[13] A complaint from another temple in the same town in 2–1 B.C. (BGU. IV. 1200) states that the σύνταξις of its priests was derived to the extent of 100 artabae from the ἐδάφη of the temple, which had been confiscated, and another 100 artabae from a πρόσοδος[. . . . . .]. In both cases the cause of the failure to receive the subvention was its illegal transfer to the priests of another village or villages.

A fragment of the Hawara papyri (*Archiv*, v, p. 387, no. 188 *recto* (b)) records the release from the state granary of 162 artabae of lentils for the syntaxis of the priests (εἰς ἱερατικ(ὰς) συντάξεις). Such a payment may have been drawn against the receipts from ἱερὰ γῆ booked as ἱερατικά in the granary accounts of grain received.[14] This may have been the usual way of administering the subventions of the priests, for in BGU. III. 707, from Caranis and dated A.D. 151, the subvention in money (ἀργυρικὴ σύνταξις) is said to have been assigned from the funds of the state bankers (δημόσιοι τραπεζῖται). This payment in money was probably charged against the collections of taxes which had once been levied exclusively for the benefit of priests and temples, but whose administration had been taken over by the civil government.

P. Ryl. II. 213 and certain related documents[15] reveal that, in the Mendesian nome at least, such money-taxes were booked in a separate account called ἱερατικά. The editors' Table II (p. 294) lists the following taxes under that rubric: ἀπόμοιρα, εἰκοστή, θησαυρικ(όν), λύτρωσις αἰγῶν, μόσχου τέλος, [. . . . .] πανηγύρεως, [. . . . . .] ποιμένων, τρίδραχμος. The ἀπόμοιρα[16] had been a tithe of the produce of vine- and garden-land collected by the priests from the landholders; this tax was, however, appropriated to the cult of Arsinoë Philadelphus; but since that cult had been discontinued in the Roman period the government had, at least in the Mendesian nome,[17] restored the revenues of that tax to the general account of the ἱερατικά.[18] The εἰκοστή, a tax of one-twentieth, seems to have been connected with land in P. Ryl. II. 213, and it may have been an *ad valorem* tax on transfers of property which, like the διδραχμία Σούχου at Arsinoë in the Fayûm,[19] had once been assigned to the revenues of the priests and temples in the Mendesian nome. The θησαυρικόν, according to the editors, was probably 'a priestly charge levied in connexion with certain taxes paid to the Διοικησις'.[20] The λύτρωσις αἰγῶν is a charge which occurs only in this document; the goat was the sacred animal in the Mendesian nome, and the word λύτρωσις means *ransoming, redemption*, or *release from an obligation*, but nothing is known concerning the incidence[21] or rate of the tax, although the fact that the item amounts to only 2 drachmae ½ obol 1 chalcus in one instance and 2 drachmae 4 obols [plus?] in the other suggests that the rate cannot have been high. The μόσχου τέλος was undoubtedly related to the τέλος μόσχου θυομένου collected on sacrifices in the Arsinoite nome, which is discussed below. The two taxes whose titles are mutilated, but the second words of which were, respectively, πανηγύρεως (*of an assembly*) and ποιμένων (*of shepherds*), are not attested elsewhere, and nothing is known concerning their nature. The τρίδραχμος was apparently a tax of 3 drachmae assessed *ad aruram* on one of the classifications of land in the Mendesian nome. Since it was a low rate of land-tax paid by the privileged residents of the metropolis (μητροπολῖται), it is probable that the revenues of this tax were granted to the temples of the Mendesian nome during the Ptolemaic period at a time when the king was unable otherwise to satisfy the demands of the priests. The farming of the sales- or market-tax is sometimes called ἱερατικὴ ὠνή,[22] possibly because it too had once been assigned to the revenues of the priests, or perhaps the farming of the market-taxes had originally belonged to the temples, since the markets were so often located on the δρόμος that led up to the temple and which may have been included within its precinct.

Receipts and accounts of the Roman period include payments for ἱερατικά or ἱερατικόν, with or without some further term of definition. A large payment, 81 drachmae 4 obols, was made to the bank of Cephalus at Thebes for ἱερατικ(ῶν) by one Osoroeris in 9 B.C., according to O. Strass. 52. An item for ἱερατικοῦ is recorded also in a mutilated list of payments dating from the reign of Hadrian in O. Strass. 298.[23] The large amount of the payment in O. Strass. 52 is surprising, for the payments in Lower Egypt for ἱερατικόν, ἱερευτικόν, and the like, are generally quite small: 5 obols in P. Ryl. ii. 187 (first century after Christ), and 4½ obols in P. Fay. 54 (Euhemeria, A.D. 117–18). Such payments may be related to the payments of 5 obols for the mysterious ἱερ( ) γεφ( ) in SP. xx. 49, 62 (dated by the editor in the second or third century after Christ).[24] A larger sum appears, however, in P. Teb. ii. 354 (A.D. 188), where 57 drachmae are paid for δω( ) ἱερευτικῷ(ν); but this is the only example of the exaction of so large a sum found in the documents from Lower Egypt, and it may have been a special gift to the temple or a special levy assessed for repairs to a sacred building or even for the construction of a new one.[25] A sum of 4 drachmae 1 obol for ἱερατ(ι)κ(ῶν) and one of 21 drachmae 4 obols for ἱ[ε]ρῶν are included in a report from the collectors of money-taxes of the village of Pharbetha in the Arsinoite nome (late second century after Christ);[26] but the summary statement of payment in such reports does not reveal the incidence or rate of the tax or taxes so named. In general the evidence is insufficient to determine the exact nature or purpose of payments for ἱερατικόν. It is quite possible that some of them were entirely different from others. The editors of P. Teb. ii. 354 have suggested that the payments for ἱερατικόν may have been collected from the priests rather than levied for their benefit, although the latter had been their earlier explanation,[27] in which they were followed by Otto.[28]

A similar difficulty exists in determining whether the priests were the payers or the beneficiaries of a tax called the τέλος ἱεροῦ Βουκόλων. This tax is mentioned in P. Fay. 39, which is a reply from the elders of Theadelphia written in A.D. 183 to the farmer (μισθωτής) of the tax. The latter had inquired from whom the 'aforementioned sum' (προκείμενον ἀπότακτον) was to be demanded, and the answer named one man, a certain Chaeremon, son of Iemouthes. The editors remark that ἀπότακτον means the prescribed sum, and they suppose that προκείμενον refers to a statement in the letter of the μισθωτής, for 'it can hardly be supposed that Chaeremon was responsible for the whole of the τέλος'. The collection of the whole τέλος of the village from the one man would be possible, however, if the tax was collected from priests and if Chaeremon was the priest, or chief priest, of the temple at the village of Boucolon. The Egyptian priests, however, seem ordinarily to have refrained from the prevalent habit of adopting Greek names, so that it is more likely that, as the editors suggest,[29] the use of the term ἀπαιτεῖται may imply that the payment was in arrear.[30] Since Chaeremon does not seem to be a priest, and there is no indication that the elders of the village were naming him as another official connected with the collection of taxes, it is probable that the τέλος ἱεροῦ Βουκόλων was an impost, probably local, for the benefit of the temple and perhaps was collected only upon this special occasion.[31]

Four drachmae (without supplementary charge) recorded in SB. 4340 as a payment ὑπὲρ Ἄμμωνος θεοῦ μεγίστου seems to be an example of an impost collected for the benefit of a temple, especially if the receipt was given by the προφήτης, as has been suggested.[32] The receipt is from Thebes and is dated in A.D. 255. The fact that the collector of the tax was a δεκάπρωτος (whether or not a prophet) indicates that this was an official tax assessed by authority of the government and not merely a voluntary offering by a pious votary.

Such voluntary offerings are not unknown, however, for an item called λογεία (collection) occurs in the report of priests at Tebtynis and their revenues, dated A.D. 107–8 (P. Teb. II. 298. 34, 36). It is probable that in the late Ptolemaic period this λογεία had been a quasi-compulsory tax, since in P. Teb. II. 554, dated late first century B.C., there appears a list of persons under the heading 'Street of the Shepherds: Those Paying the Collection' (Ποιμένων λαύρα· οἱ τελοῦντες τὴν λογείαν). The editors state that the σιτικὴ λογεία in P. Teb. II. 298. 34 was practically a compulsory tax for the benefit of the temples, and levied by the priests, which may be contrasted with the voluntary contributions (τῶν ἐξ εὐ[σεβ(είας) δι]δομέν[ω]ν). Lack of other evidence makes it impossible to determine how long the compulsory character of this tax persisted or how far the priests were permitted by the civil officials to press their demands.

From Hermonthis, above Thebes, comes a series of fourteen receipts (10 in Greek and 4 in Demotic) given between the years A.D. 52 and 68 to Pibuchis son of Peteêsis, who is sometimes designated as a ὁμόλογος.[33] The receipts are issued by a succession of priests who, in those years, held the office of 'Prophet of Isis' (Φέννησις)[34] or 'Intercessor of the god (Mont)' (προστάτης τοῦ θεοῦ), and are for the λογεία (or λειτουργεία), the 'collection' of one or the other of the two divinities. In the receipts written in Greek the amount of the contribution for Isis was 4 drachmae 2 obols (four times), 4 drachmae 1 obol (once), 4 drachmae 5 obols (once); for the god, 4 drachmae 10 obols (once, but the same amount was paid also by another ὁμόλογος), 4 drachmae 2 obols (once, in the year when the contribution to Isis was only 4 drachmae 1 obol), 5 drachmae 3 obols (once). In the four Demotic receipts the amount of the collection of Isis is always 5 'Silver-Stater-Kite', a term which Spiegelberg hesitantly equated with drachmae.[35] These amounts are often stated to *be* the λογεία with the additional description περὶ (or ὑπὲρ or ὑπερὶ) τῶν δημοσίων, to which sometimes is appended the further description τῆς Φεννησίας. Despite the use of the word δημόσια, which ordinarily is used to designate state-taxes, I am not inclined to believe that these 'collections' were recognized by the state as generally compulsory, for the term δημόσια may here mean 'public ceremonies'.[36] PSI. III. 262 is another receipt for λογεία at Hermonthis, but it is not issued to Pibuchis, but to another ὁμόλογος. The word ὁμόλογος, I believe, contains the clue to the explanation of these charges paid so regularly by Pibuchis. Wilcken's explanation of ὁμόλογος, hitherto generally accepted, was that the term had here a common significance, namely, 'a worker attached to the soil by a contract or lease'.[37] I believe, however, that Pibuchis was ὁμόλογος (literally, 'confessed' or 'agreed'), because he was on his own admission a votary of the cults of Isis and of the god Mont.[38] Such votaries were, in my opinion, required by the priests to pay an annual assessment fixed by the latter according to the requirements of the public ceremonies (δημόσια) of the temples. The list of persons in P. Teb. II. 554 designated as οἱ τελοῦντες τὴν λογείαν would correspond to these ὁμόλογοι of the Thebaid. There is no evidence available, however, to enable us to determine how far the priests could rely upon the co-operation of the civil officials to enforce the payment of the λογεία by the ὁμόλογοι.[39] It is not impossible that the degree of co-operation afforded by the civil officials depended upon the policy of the Roman government respecting the priests and temples, which may have changed in the course of three hundred years.

The Roman government continued the policy of the Ptolemies in seeking to control the income of priests and temples by the rigid supervision of their finances, but it resorted also to direct taxation of priests and temples. In some of these exactions the Roman administration may merely have followed or revived measures of the Ptolemies, but so far as can be judged from the extant evidence these taxes were more frequent and more severe in the Roman period.

The τέλος μόσχου θυομένου is evidently, from its name, a tax levied by the government upon the sacrifice of a calf. This name for the tax is found, however, only in receipts from Socnopaei Nesus in the Arsinoite nome. BGU. III. 718, dated in A.D. 102, is the earliest receipt for the tax which has yet been published; the amount of the payment is not stated, but the tax was paid on the same day that the sacrifice was made.[40] BGU. II. 463 is a similar receipt, dated in A.D. 148, which gives the amount of the tax as 24 drachmae, paid by the person offering the sacrifice[41] to the nomarch, under whose jurisdiction this tax seems to have fallen. An unpublished papyrus in the Library of Princeton University[42] records a payment for τέλος μόσχου θυομένου, and the amount seems to be 20 drachmae. The other receipts, the latest recorded date of which is A.D. 188, do not state the amount of the tax.[43] BGU. I. 250 (= W. Chrest. 87) is the reply of a priest to the strategus of a μερίς of the Arsinoite nome. The priest had sacrificed an animal in the year A.D. 120–1, and the strategus had written, some time after A.D. 130, to inquire why no official report of the μοσχοσφραγιστής (the official who affixed the seal upon sacrificially clean calves) had been submitted upon that occasion.[44] The priest replied that the Idiologus had not issued his order requiring the filing of such a report on the occasion of a sacrifice until the year A.D. 122–3. The interest of the strategus, the chief financial official of the nome, in what was apparently only a matter of the sacrificial cleanliness of a calf sacrificed about ten years previously can be most plausibly explained by the assumption that such a report was instituted by the Idiologus in order that the tax upon the sacrifice might be collected

promptly. BGU. I. 356 (= W. *Chrest*. 88), from Philadelphia
and dated A.D. 213, is a receipt for a payment by one Aurelius
Didymus of Alexandria ὑπὲρ σφραγισμοῦ ('for the sealing') of a
sacrificial calf. The payment at Philadelphia, as in the documents
from Socnopaei Nesus, was made by the person offering the
animal for sacrifice, and it is possible that this tax 'for sealing'
is but a different name for the τέλος μόσχου θυομένου found at
Socnopaei Nesus. The tax ὑπὲρ σφραγισμοῦ, however, was paid
to the nomarch through the official in charge of the toll-gate of
Philadelphia (πραγ(ματευτὴς) πυλ(ῆς) Φιλαδελ(φίας)).[45]

A τέλος μόσχου is attested also in the Hermopolite nome in
P. Ryl. II. 193, dated A.D. 132–5; but the amount paid, 14 obols,
is so small that it is doubtful whether this was the same tax as
the τέλος μόσχου θυομένου at Socnopaei Nesus.[46] A tax called
τέλος μόσχου appears eleven times in P. Ryl. II. 213, a great tax-
account from the Mendesian nome dated in the second century,
and the amounts recorded range from 1 drachma 1 obol 2 chalci
to 35 drachmae 3 obols.[47] Such various amounts are probably
due to the fact that instalments are recorded, or several payments
of the entire tax may have been lumped in the larger items; but
either explanation precludes a determination of the rate of taxation. This tax is included in the division of the treasury called
ἱερατικά, and this may be an indication of kinship with the
τέλος μόσχου θυομένου of the Arsinoite nome.

At Tebtynis in the Arsinoite nome were found receipts for
a tax called δεκάτη μόσχων. Grenfell and Hunt pointed out that
this differed from the τέλος μόσχου θυομένου in that the former
was paid by the priests of the temple, and that the amount paid
to the nomarch was always 20 drachmae (although in one example
the payment is stated to be made on account), except in P. Teb.
II. 572 where 84 drachmae were paid 'for the period of two
years' (ὑπὲρ διετίας) which may represent a biennial festival. A
tax called δεκάτη μόσχων is known from the third century B.C.
(P. Hib. 115). The rate of 10 per cent. *ad valorem* suggests that
the δεκάτη μόσχων is probably to be regarded as a variety of the
sales-tax or ἐγκύκλιον which may have been collected on sacrificed animals, because the ceremony of sacrifice involved the
transfer of ownership of the animal—from the worshipper to
the deity. The repetition of the amount of 20 drachmae may

merely be the result of a conventional valuation of a bullock at 200 drachmae. Since the δεκάτη was paid by the priests, rather than by the worshipper, it is clear that it cannot be completely identified with the τέλος μόσχου θυομένου paid by the worshipper; but the amount of the latter tax, 24 drachmae in BGU. II. 463, is not too far from 10 per cent. of the price of the μόσχος recorded in BGU. III. 986, namely something over 300 drachmae.[48] The amount paid in the document in the Library of Princeton University is identical with the ordinary amount of the δεκάτη μόσχων, and the 20 drachmae probably represent an assessment of 10 per cent. of the value of the sacrificed animal. The τέλος μόσχου θυομένου at Socnopaei Nesus probably was, therefore, a sales-tax in origin.[49] Since the δεκάτη μόσχων had its origin as early as the third century B.C. the variation in the method of collection may be explained by the varying degrees of influence exerted by the priesthoods of the two villages, Socnopaei Nesus and Tebtynis, during the intervening centuries.

The tax called λύτρωσις αἰγῶν mentioned in P. Ryl. II. 213 may have been of a similar nature, that is, a form of ἐγκύκλιον, but since the goat was a sacred animal in the Mendesian nome, it is quite possible that it was not sacrificed, and the similarity of the λύτρωσις αἰγῶν and the τέλος μόσχου may be more apparent than real.[50] In P. Iand. 29 payments ὑπὲρ κριοτάφων are collected by πράκτορες for the expenses of burying a sacred ram.[51]

Not only were the sacrifices of bullocks taxed by the Roman government, but a rental was exacted from the priests for certain altars in the sacred enclosures of the precincts of their temples. This rental was called the φόρος βωμῶν. This was exacted on each altar, as is indicated by SP. XXII. 183, from Socnopaei Nesus and dated A.D. 171, where payment was made to the Idiologus for two enclosed altars, one of Isis Nepherses and the other of Isis Nephremmis, at Nilopolis (ὑπὲρ σηκωμά(των) ἐπικαλουμ(ένων) [β]ωμῶν δύο κώμης Νειλουπόλεως ἐν[ὸς μὲν] Εἴ[σι]δος Νεφέρσητος ἐτέ[ρου] δὲ [Ε]ἴσιδο[ς] Νεφ[ρ]έμμιδο(ς) θεᾶς μεγιστῆς ‹Βρ προσδ(ιαγραφομένων) ‹ρλα ϝϲ/‹Β σ[λ]α ϝϲ). This payment is included in the accounts of the priests of Socnopaei Nesus, who evidently were in charge of precincts of Isis at the village of Nilopolis situated close by. From these altars or precincts the priests at Socnopaei Nesus themselves received a φόρος, however:

from the first 500 drachmae and from the latter 400 drachmae. It is evident, therefore, that unless the φόρος derived by the priests from those altars was augmented (which is probable) by other income not preserved in the mutilated account, their annual loss for the two altars was 1,331 drachmae 4½ obols. All receipts and accounts mentioning the φόρος βωμῶν are dated in the second half of the second century after Christ, or later, and all are from the Arsinoite nome.[52] The amounts range from 320 to 2,100 drachmae. The προσδιαγραφόμενα, where given, are at the usual rate of one-sixteenth of the principal; but in two receipts the supplementary charges are recorded as two separate items one of which is 4 per cent. of the principal. No explanation of this peculiarity has been suggested.[53]

According to P. Ryl. ii. 196 the representatives (ἡγούμενοι) of the priests paid to the account of the nomarch 124 drachmae for a tax or rent of boats used in the sacred processions (πλοίων θεαγῶν). The same document records payments (by the same ἡγούμενοι) of 80 drachmae for ζυτηρὰ κατ᾽ ἄνδρα and of 60 drachmae for δεκανικὸν ἰχθυομεταβολ(ῶν).

The significance of the payments by the priests of Socnebtynis of more than 100 drachmae for κατακρίματα ('fines') in P. Teb. ii. 298 (= W. Chrest. 90) is unknown.

Εἰσκριτικόν and ᾽Επιστατικόν

The elaborate hierarchy, into which the priests of the temples of Egypt were organized, was placed under the rigid control of the Roman official entitled the High-Priest of All Egypt. At Thebes there occur payments for πεντεφυλία, evidently a tax connected with the priestly order of five tribes, but the occasion of such payments is uncertain.[54] Eligibility to serve as a priest of the native religion depended upon birth into one of the priestly families. But those thus eligible for the priesthood were not permitted to enter the ranks of the priests until certain fees had been paid to the government. The fee for entrance into an office of the hierarchy was called the εἰσκριτικόν, or the payment of the fee was designated as ὑπὲρ εἰσκρίσεως.[55] The first payment of an εἰσκριτικόν probably occurred after the initiatory rite of circumcision had been performed (at the age of seven to eleven years) upon an applicant whose birth and other qualifica-

tions had been approved by the local priests and had been confirmed by an official letter from the High-Priest of All Egypt.[56]
Each advance in the hierarchy, moreover, was accompanied by
an additional fee which rose in amount as the importance of the
office increased. Such a fee is known to have been called
τελεστικόν in the Ptolemaic period.[57] In the Roman period the
assessment and collection of such fees was a function of the
bureau of the Idiologus, whose office seems ultimately, for
reasons of convenience, to have been combined with that of
the High-Priest of All Egypt.[58]

The lowest amount attested for the εἰσκριτικόν is 8 drachmae[59] paid at Elephantine by *pastophori*, who formed one of the
inferior ranks of the hierarchy.[60] The payment of the same
sum by a *pastophorus* in PO. XII. 1435 was probably likewise for
the εἰσκριτικόν, although it is actually designated as ὑπὲρ ἱεροῦ.
Eight drachmae are also found as the amount paid by a priest
(ἱερεὺς γ̄ φυλ(ῆς)) for ‹ε›ἰσκρίσεως ἱεροῦ Ἑρμαίου, that is for a
priesthood of Hermes at Socnopaei Nesus.[61] The shrine of
Hermes, however, was under the control of the priests of the
temple of the god Socnopaeus at Socnopaei Nesus, and in three
other receipts the fee of 8 drachmae for the priesthood of
Hermes is combined with a payment of 20 drachmae for εἴσκρισις
(entrance) into the priesthood of Socnopaeus.[62] These fees of 8
and 20 drachmae paid for εἴσκρισις into the priesthoods of
Hermes and Socnopaeus respectively were probably not the fee
paid for the initiation into the ranks of the priests immediately
following circumcision, since a report from the same temple
of Socnopaeus gives a list of priests who had paid for their
hereditary priesthood εἰσκριτικόν at the rate of 12 drachmae
each.[63] The initial εἰσκριτικόν of the priests (ἱερεῖς, who are carefully distinguished from the *pastophori* in the Gnomon of the
Idiologus[64]) at Socnopaei Nesus may have been this fee at the
rate of 12 drachmae, and the fees of 8 and 20 drachmae may
have been εἰσκριτικά for particular priesthoods in the temples of
Hermes and Socnopaeus, which were filled only upon the occasion of a vacancy created by death, promotion, or some other
cause. The scale of fees was apparently different at the temple of
Socnebtynis in the village of Tebtynis. There the various priests
are reported to have paid 52 drachmae each for their priesthood.[65]

The term εἰσκριτικόν was not usually applied to the sums paid for entrance into the higher ranks of the hierarchy. Some of the higher priesthoods were hereditary, while others were sold to any eligible priest. Of the latter type some were sold at a fixed price and others to the highest bidder. The office of Feather-Bearer (πτεραφόρος) of Socnebtynis was purchased for 50 drachmae.[66] The στολισταί of the temple of Socnebtynis at Tebtynis had each paid 100 drachmae for their office,[67] and the same amount (plus προσδιαγραφόμενα) was offered by each of two priests at Panopolis as τιμὴ στολιστείας for the two vacancies in that rank at some temple in their city.[68] In the latter case the imperial procurator acting as High-Priest of All Egypt directed the imperial oeconomus to offer these priesthoods at auction, and if no higher bids were made to let the offices go to the priests who had made the original offer, but not to permit the offer to be reduced if no other applicants appeared.[69] The largest amount attested for εἰσκριτικόν is 200 drachmae, suggested as a proper sum to be paid upon entrance into the rank of prophet of the temple of Socnebtynis at Tebtynis.[70] The office of prophet was very lucrative, for its perquisites included one-fifth of the revenue (πρόσοδος) of the temple.[71] In this case an offer of 2,200 drachmae was made for the post of prophet, but only on condition that the office be thereby made hereditary and that the heirs of the applicant be entitled to enter upon the rights and privileges of the office upon payment merely of an εἰσκριτικον of 200 drachmae. The εἰσκριτικόν is here clearly the fee paid upon entrance into an office for which there was to be no competitive bidding.[72] It is probable that the term εἰσκριτικόν was used loosely by the priests and by officials of the Roman administration, and usage may have differed in various parts of Egypt, so that the word may have been applied to all payments of fees upon entering hereditary offices, from the lowest[73] to the highest, and it may have been extended to cover ordinary payments for offices which were for sale, such as the στολιστεία; but it probably did not apply to the purchase-price of offices actually obtained by competitive bidding, particularly when the value of the perquisites of the office made the bidding keen and brought a high price.[74]

Despite Otto's view that the payment ὑπὲρ εἰσκρίσεως was an

annual charge, it is probable that the annual payments of the priests to the government were not so named. Annual payments by the priests are known, however, but the method of making such payments differed among the temples in various localities even within the same nome. In the Ptolemaic period the government kept the administration of the revenues of the temples under its own supervision by the installation of its own comptroller in each temple of importance, an official called the ἐπιστάτης ἱεροῦ. The administration of the finances of several temples was united under a superior comptroller with the title ἐπιστάτης ἱερῶν.[75] To provide for the maintenance of these government officials the priests were required to pay certain sums from the income and perquisites of their respective priesthoods.[76] Some time after the Roman government took over the administration of Egypt the finances of the priests and temples were placed under the jurisdiction of the Idiologus, and in the various nomes the representatives of that official displaced the ἐπιστάται ἱερῶν, who are not attested in the Roman period, while the reports of revenues and disbursements of the temples were made directly to the strategus of the nome.[77] It is far from certain that the payments of the priests in the Ptolemaic period for ἐπιστατικόν were merely for the salary of the ἐπιστάται; probably the government even then was able to collect and use for its own purposes something in excess of the amounts required to maintain the ἐπιστάται ἱερῶν.[78] At any rate in the Roman period, although the office of ἐπιστάτης ἱεροῦ seems to have been abolished, the tax was still collected for the benefit of the government. Perhaps its proceeds were applied to the support of the bureau of the Idiologus and of the High-Priest of All Egypt. In several temples of the Arsinoite nome it was customary for the temple to pay the ἐπιστατικὸν ἱερέων for its priests in a lump sum.[79] At Socnopaei Nesus an annual payment of 5,500 drachmae is attested for the temple of Socnopaeus, and in addition the temple paid 64 drachmae for the προφητεία καὶ λεσωνεία καὶ θεαγεία of a shrine at Nilopolis under its control.[80] Lower amounts attested for temples or priests at Hexapotamus, Tebtynis, and elsewhere may have been instalments.[81]

Some of the temples, however, did not pay the ἐπιστατικόν for their priests, and the tax was collected from individuals. At Caranis the great tax-rolls indicate that the rate of the tax varied with the rank of the priests liable to pay the charge.[82] One of these, a priest of a first class temple,[83] paid 87 drachmae 3 obols with προσδιαγραφόμενα of 12 drachmae 3 obols (a rate of $\frac{1}{7}$, which is abnormally high), or a total of 100 drachmae. Other priests paid at the rate of 24 drachmae, with προσδιαγραφόμενα of 3 drachmae 3 obols; but to this was added a tax upon their perquisites (γέρα), usually at the rate of 4 drachmae with προσδιαγραφόμενα of $2\frac{1}{2}$ obols and an additional charge for exchange (κόλλυβος) of $\frac{1}{2}$ obol, a total of 4 drachmae 3 obols.[84] The combined payments for ἐπιστατικόν and γέρα with their supplements total 32 drachmae.[85] The presence of the charge for κόλλυβος indicates that the exaction for perquisites had its origin in the Ptolemaic period, when γέρα was the term used to designate the perquisites of priests below the rank of prophet.[86] Origin in the Ptolemaic period is probably the explanation of the extraordinarily high charge for προσδιαγραφόμενα on the ἐπιστατικόν.[87] The payment for ἐπιστ(ατικόν) ἱερέων was combined with that for the poll-tax (λαογραφία) in a receipt from a village in the Arsinoite nome, dated A.D. 186;[88] the sum of 16 drachmae paid for the two taxes by two brothers doubtless represents an instalment on account, since the lowest attested rate for the poll-tax is 8 drachmae a year.[89] At Theadelphia the ἐπιστατικόν seems to have been collected from the individual priests, for in P. Lond. III. 1235 (p. 35) the payments for ἐπιστ(ατικὸν) ἱερέω(ν) are found among the payments for capitation taxes which probably include the poll-tax.[90]

The ἐπιστατικόν is the best example of a specific tax designed to curb the power of the priests by reducing their wealth. It made up, at least in part, for exemption from the poll-tax granted to many of the priests. It is important to observe, however, that none of these taxes definitely known to have been exacted from the temples or priests is attested in the Roman period before the second century. This does not necessarily mean that all of these taxes were introduced in the second century, since many of them were known in the Ptolemaic period. It is possible that a change in the method of collecting and recording these taxes accounts for their sudden appearance in the second century. But this change in the method of accounting was certainly not without cause. I believe that the necessity for increasing the revenues of the empire, caused by the prodigious outlays required for the campaigns of Trajan, led the Roman administration in Egypt to seek increased revenues from the class best able to bear the taxes. The income of the priests from temple-lands had been seriously curtailed by the measures of Augustus, but their revenues in money had not been greatly affected by his reforms. The peasants and bourgeoisie were already being assessed at the limit of their capacity to pay,[91] and the priests consequently were the only class of the native population from whom a substantial increase in payments could be expected. I am inclined to think that the change in the method of collecting and recording taxes paid by the priests, which has been suggested above, marked not so much the introduction of new taxes or even the revival of certain Ptolemaic exactions from the priests, but rather the increase of the rates of existing levies and a policy of making universal some assessments whose incidence had theretofore been only partial. The differences in the method of collecting these assessments in various temples must have caused no little trouble in the bureaux of records in the nomes and in Alexandria; but differences among the temples in regard to their privileges and obligations were probably encouraged by the civil government, in spite of the resulting complications in administration, because those differences tended to foster jealousy between the temples and so to break the solidarity of the priesthood in Egypt, which in the second century had less cause to be grateful and loyal to the Roman government. Such precautions were not unnecessary, as is shown by the fact that the Bucolic revolt, which took place in the reign of Marcus Aurelius and assumed a national and religious character, was led by a priest.[92] The ideals which inspired Isidorus in this revolt are perhaps suggested by the grants of land and other privileges gained by the priests of the Ptolemaic period as the result of similar revolts. The prompt military aid and diplomacy of Avidius Cassius were perhaps all that prevented the Egyptian priest from wringing similar concessions from the Roman government.

XV

CUSTOMS-DUTIES AND TRANSIT-TOLLS

COMMERCE in and through Egypt was subject to three known types of customs-duties—one external and two internal. External customs were collected at the borders of the province, while internal customs were collected at the north and south boundaries of the ἐπιστρατηγία of the Heptanomia and Arsinoite nome, and on imports and exports of several of the separate nomes.

External Customs-Dues

Through the valley of the Nile passed the most important single trade-route between the Roman empire and the Orient.[1] Pliny makes the statement that the trade with India, China, and Arabia drained the Roman empire of one hundred million sesterces annually.[2] The source of Pliny's information was probably the contracts for the collection of customs-duties at the Red Sea ports and perhaps at the termini of the other great trade-routes as well.[3] One hundred million sesterces did not represent the total volume of imports from the East, since Egypt, according to Pliny,[4] purchased her eastern goods by means of flax, and it is evident from other sources that a considerable volume of goods was exported to the East.[5] A major share of the empire's trade with India was probably carried by the route through Egypt, favoured because overland transport was thereby reduced to a minimum; and Egypt also imported and processed much of the spices and other luxuries brought into the empire from Arabia. It has been suggested that the figure of fifty million sesterces, which in another passage Pliny gives as the value of the commerce with India alone, represents the amount on which customs were levied *at the Red Sea ports* and includes the trade with Arabia and Ethiopia as well as with India.[6] Strabo indeed states that Alexandria had a monopoly of trade (with India and Trogodytica).[7]

In consequence the revenue derived by the Roman emperors from the customs-duties of Egypt was very large. Strabo, writing during the reign of Augustus, informs us that double duties, import and export, were levied on goods entering and leaving Egypt.[8] He speaks of the 'most valuable freights' brought in from India and Ethiopia, and he states that 'the most expensive wares pay the heaviest duties'. Strabo is undoubtedly describing *ad valorem* duties assessed according to a sliding scale that increased in proportion to the value of the particular type of merchandise. This interpretation of his words is confirmed by the fact that a sliding-scale of duties was applied to imports into Alexandria in the Ptolemaic period. In 259 B.C. duties on goods received at Pelusium for transfer to Alexandria were assessed at rates of 20, 25, 33⅓, and 50 per cent.[9] It is possible, however, that this sliding-scale of duties inherited from the Ptolemies did not apply to imports entering through the Egyptian ports on the Red Sea, i.e. Myos Hormos and Berenice Trogodytice, or had been abandoned for a fixed rate *ad valorem* not long after Strabo wrote his statement.

The duty on imports into Leuce Come, a port on the coast of Arabia opposite Myos Hormos, was fixed at 25 per cent. according to the author of the *Periplus Maris Erythraei*,[10] whose date is disputed but is certainly later than A.D. 50.[11] To Leuce Come was dispatched a collector of the 25 per cent. duty on imported cargoes, and for protection the φρούριον there was in the charge of a centurion with a detachment of troops.[12] Nowhere else in the Roman empire, before the Byzantine period, do attested duties on imports exceed 5 per cent. It has, therefore, been doubted whether so high a duty on imports was ever collected by the Romans, and Hirschfeld even suggested that the τετάρτης (25 per cent.) of the *Periplus* should be emended to τεσσαρακόστης (2½ per cent.), a rate found in Gaul and Asia.[13] Rostovtzeff, however, regarded the toll of 25 per cent. at Leuce Come as a protective tariff inherited from the Ptolemies, who had sought thereby to divert trade from the overland route (from Leuce Come to Petra and thence to Syria) to the Red Sea ports of Egypt, and he supposed that the income of the tariff had been assigned by the Romans, with crafty diplomacy, to the dependent king of the Nabateans, while the amount of the tariff drove ships to the Egyptian ports.[14] According to the Periplus, however, the harbour of Leuce Come was crowded with the small boats of the

Arab traders,[15] and Strabo states that the caravans went up
from Leuce Come to Petra 'like an army'.[16] Charlesworth has
pointed out that it is unlikely that the Roman emperors had
failed to reserve 'to themselves the collection of the dues from
so profitable a region'.[17] The amount of the duty, moreover,
requires neither emendation nor the elaborate explanation of
Rostovtzeff. The special status of the province of Egypt as the
private estate of the emperor makes it improbable that its rate
of import-duty was made to conform to rates found elsewhere
in the empire, especially since a higher rate brought more revenue
into the *fiscus* of the emperor. Furthermore, the imports from
the East consisted almost wholly of articles of luxury which
could easily sustain a duty of 25 per cent. Indeed, Pliny tells
us that goods were sold (presumably at Rome) for one hundred
times the cost of their purchase in India.[18]

There is no proof that the rate of 25 per cent. on imports
collected at Leuce Come applied also to cargoes landed at the
Egyptian ports on the Red Sea, although this is not unlikely,
since the collection of the *vectigal Maris Rubri* was farmed as a
whole to the Roman corporations in the reign of Claudius,[19]
and in the reign of Augustus, or a little before, the strategus of
the Ombite nome and the district about Elephantine and Philae
was also collector (of customs-dues) of the Red Sea (παραλήμπτης τῆς 'Ερυθρᾶς θαλάσσης).[20]

There is no evidence in regard to the rate of duty on goods
imported into Egypt from the West or on exports to the East. If,
however, the Roman government was disturbed by the loss of
gold and silver caused by the excess of imports over exports in
the eastern trade, the rate of duty on imports into Alexandria
and the other seaports of the Delta and on exports from Myos
Hormos and Berenice Trogodytice may have been somewhat
lower than the duties on products from the Orient. Such a
policy would have encouraged the exchange of commodities instead of the purchase of Oriental luxuries with specie, and thus
would have helped toward a more favourable balance of trade.

The παραλήμπτης τῆς 'Ερυθρᾶς θαλάσσης mentioned above
may have supervised also the collection of duties on goods
exported and imported through Elephantine and Syene in the
trade with the Ethiopians directly to the south beyond the First

Cataract, but nothing definite is known about this branch of the provincial customs. Information concerning customs-duties on the trade with the nomadic tribes about the Great and Little Oases is similarly lacking. Alum brought from the Little Oasis to the Fayûm paid a duty of $1\frac{1}{2}$ drachmae per light talent, which was exacted at the gate of Nynpou, but this was probably an internal customs due.[21]

Customs-barriers at Hermopolis Magna and the Harbour of Memphis

Strabo mentions in passing that traffic from the Thebaid was examined at the guard-house (Φυλακή) at Hermopolis Magna situated at the southern boundary of the Heptanomia.[22] This is probably the station attested for the Ptolemaic period by Agatharchides, who mentioned the Φυλακή, also called Σχεδία.[23] This toll-station is not mentioned in the published papyri, so that nothing is known concerning the rates of duty. It is not known whether goods shipped up the river were subject to toll at Hermopolis; Strabo may have failed to mention it merely because the trade down the river was much more important.[24]

Papyri from the Arsinoite and Oxyrhynchite nomes attest a toll connected with the harbour of Memphis situated at the northern boundary of the Heptanomia a short distance above the point where the Nile divides into the branches which form the Delta. This toll seems to have been collected on both imports and exports passing through Memphis.[25] On goods transported overland between the Fayûm and Memphis the tax was paid at toll-stations in the villages situated near the boundary of the Arsinoite nome. The receipts for exports issued by these toll-stations may have been presented to the harbour-master at Memphis.[26] Little is known concerning fees collected at the harbour of Memphis itself. The purpose of collecting these duties before arrival at Memphis was undoubtedly the desire to avoid delay and consequent congestion at the harbour, through which had to pass practically all of the traffic between Upper and Middle Egypt and the Delta.

The extant receipts for the tax for the harbour of Memphis (λιμένος Μέμφεως) from the Fayûm were issued to drivers of camels and donkeys which formed trains for transport over the short roads across the desert to Memphis.[27] Most of the extant receipts were issued at Socnopaei Nesus and Bacchias, but Philadelphia and Caranis also had toll-stations which issued several. All of these villages were situated on the northern border of the Arsinoite nome. The rate of the toll for the harbour of Memphis is stated in none of these receipts. The amount of the tax on various articles, however, is found in collectors' reports, which were made up periodically.[28] Fiesel, in an elaborate study of this toll and the related customs-duties of the Arsinoite nome, attempted to demonstrate that the rate was 3 per cent. *ad valorem*.[29] There are several flaws in Fiesel's argument,[30] and Clauson pointed out that, in the long register of payments of customs-dues in the collection of papyri at the University of Wisconsin (published in *Aegyptus*, IX. (1928), pp. 240 ff. = SB. 7365), 'any attempts at establishing the ratio between the duty and the cost are unsatisfactory because of our limited sources'. Some of the items in SB. 7365, however, seem to indicate that a sliding-scale of duties was used in the assessment of the tax 'for the Harbour of Memphis'.[31]

This register (SB. 7365) is a monthly report of the customs at Bacchias.[32] Since the report was audited by the harbour-master and the toll-gate is said to be 'subordinate' to the 'Harbour of Memphis', it is probable that the tax recorded is the toll λιμένος Μέμφεως, or at least that the tax for the harbour of Memphis is included in the total receipts for the month which include charges for χειριστικόν and ἀλλαγή.[33] The report was submitted by one Chaeras who was in charge of the toll-station. What assistance he had in clerical work is not revealed by the text. Two guards (ἀραβοτοξόται) kept order at the station; for their services each received 16 drachmae a month, and their salary was deducted from the receipts before the money was forwarded to the treasury (δημόσιον). In P. Lond. III. 1169 (p. 43) a single ἀραβοτοξότης (who received the same salary of 16 drachmae a month despite the fact that he was serving nearly a century later than the guards of SB. 7365) was employed at the toll-station, and to him was entrusted the task of forwarding the receipts of the tax. In this document, however, a scribe (γραμματεύς) assisted in the preparation of the report (λόγος).

At this station the total receipts for five months amounted to only 1,213 drachmae, whereas in SB. 7365 the receipts of one month amounted to nearly 1,000 drachmae. If these two documents are confined to reports of the receipts from the tax for the harbour of Memphis, this will explain the large number of days on which there were no receipts and which are indicated by the word 'Hermes', apparently an ironical dedication to the god of trade.[34] It is quite possible that local customs had been collected on some of the days designated by the name of Hermes.

P. Amh. 77 (= W. *Chrest.* 277), dated A.D. 139, is one of the most interesting of the documents dealing with the customs in Egypt. It is the complaint of the ἀραβοτοξότης at the customs-station of Socnopaei Nesus made to the epistrategus. The station was in charge of two men, Polydeuces and Harpagathes, the former of whom had served (contrary to law) for four successive years. These officials had, according to the guard, defrauded the government of a portion of the receipts of tolls. Harpagathes had, however, kept an accurate record of the exports and imports for his own use; but the guard had in some manner secured this autograph copy. He had given a copy of Harpagathes' secret record to the overseers of the nomarchy (τῆς νομαρχίας ἐπιτηρη-ταί) with a request that an investigation of the alleged embezzlement be made. Apparently no steps were taken against Polydeuces and Harpagathes, but the action of the ἀραβοτοξότης was reported to those worthies, who had him assaulted and beaten on three separate occasions. The last of these beatings occurred at the counting-house of the overseers of the nomarchy, when the unfortunate guard refused to restore the autograph copy to Harpagathes. The overseers must have been accomplices of the guilty customs-collectors. The honest but unhappy ἀραβο-τοξότης then appealed to the epistrategus to summon Polydeuces and Harpagathes in order that the proof against them might be presented and the protection of the epistrategus might be granted to the informer, who appended a copy of Harpagathes' autograph record. It seems probable that the tax which had suffered the peculations of Polydeuces and Harpagathes was that for the harbour of Memphis. Possibly the local tax of 3 per cent. (ρ καὶ ν), which was under the supervision of the overseers of the nomarchy,[35] had been paid over in full by the collectors, for this would account for the apathy (or connivance) of the overseers who were not concerned with the income of the toll of the λιμένος Μέμφεως. It this is correct, the guard appealed to the epistrategus for an investigation not merely because of the latter's police power, as Martin suggested,[36] but because the tax for the harbour of Memphis was one of the chief imposts of his province, and any diminution of the toll through peculation was of peculiar concern to the epistrategus.

The tax for the harbour of Memphis collected on cargoes moving over the canals to the Nile is perhaps represented by P. Lond. III. 1107 (p. 47). This document of the third century after Christ lists payments for λιμένος Μέμφεως from the metropolis Arsinoë and from Apias and various other villages situated in the Themistes division of the Arsinoite nome. From some of these places donkey- or camel-trains may occasionally have started overland to Memphis, but their merchandise undoubtedly was far more often shipped to Memphis by canal- and river-boats. These payments for λιμένος Μέμφεως are recorded together with sums designated for ἐπιστατείας καὶ (πέμπτης), i.e. for 'superintendence and the tax of one-fifth'. The payments for the harbour of Memphis present curious sums:

Apias	.	.	.	.	.	.	40 drachmae 6 chalci.
Arsinoë	.	.	.	.	.	.	81 „ 6 „
Alexandri Nesus	.	.	.	.	40 „ 6 „
Hermopolis	.	.	.	.	40 „ 6 „
Theoxonis	.	.	.	.	47 „ 3¾ obols.
Magais	.	.	.	.	.	80 „ 1½ „
Philagris	.	.	.	.	.	80 „ 1½ „

I make the hesitant suggestion that these amounts represent the tax collected on cargoes of ships from these places during some limited period of time.[37] The payments for ἐπιστατείας καὶ (πέμπτης) from the villages of Theogonis and Philagris are larger than their payments for λιμένος Μέμφεως; in all other cases the sum of ἐπιστατείας καὶ (πέμπτης) is approximately seven-tenths of the payment for λιμένος Μέμφεως. I believe that the (πέμπτη) is a surcharge of 20 per cent. collected on the payment for λιμένος Μέμφεως on the cargoes, and that the ἐπιστατεία is a fee for the maintenance of an ἐπιστάτης of the customs who, perhaps, was stationed at a point on the canal through which ships from all of these places passed. If the πέμπτη was 20 per cent. of the λιμένος Μέμφεως, the ἐπιστατεία was ordinarily about one-half of the rate of the λιμένος Μέμφεως, but in the case of shipments from Theoxonis and Philagris was multiplied 4½ and 6½ times respectively. This multiplication of the rate of ἐπιστατεία may have resulted from an infraction of the regulations for customs. Such infraction, when discovered, may have necessitated the unloading of the cargo and its minute inspection, so that the fee for ἐπιστατεία was naturally increased to the proportion of a penalty.[38] It is also possible that the rate of fees for examination of different types of merchandise varied.

P. Fay. 104, dated late in the third century, seems to be an account of, or possibly regulations for, the collection of customs-dues. The papyrus is unfortunately broken in such a manner that only the figures of the first column and the names of the second column remain. The names are those of various articles, some quite strange, upon which duty was paid as well as certain fees. The payments to inspectors (ἐραυνηταί) are familiar in other accounts of customs, but the frequent repetition of this item suggests that the fees may have varied with the type of goods to be inspected.[39] The charges for receipt (σύμβολον) may be compared with the fees for συνβολικά, χειρογραφία, and πιττάκιον in the accounts of customs-payments from the Oxyrhynchite nome which are discussed below. The payment for ξυλικοῦ occurs also in the Oxyrhynchite account, which is dated in the third century. An item ἐπιστατεία suggests that this document deals with the tax for the harbour of Memphis, and perhaps confirmation of this hypothesis may be found in the fact that the papyrus was found at Theadelphia, which, like the villages listed in P. Lond. III. 1107 (p. 47), was situated in the Themistes division. The payment for σχεδίας which immediately follows ξυλικοῦ in the document probably refers to a customs-barrier, at some point in the Fayûm, like the Σχεδίαι at Alexandria and at Hermopolis Magna.[40]

The tax for the harbour of Memphis is attested for the Oxyrhynchite nome in PO. XIV. 1650, 1650(a), 1651, and VI. 919. In the last of these documents the sum of 160 drachmae is advanced to a ship's pilot to be used for the payment of the τέλη Μέμφεως on 90 measures of olives (and possibly also on a private consignment of honey). The olives were to be transported from the Arsinoite nome, where, presumably, the 160 drachmae were to be paid to the local collectors.

In PO. xiv. 1650, dated in the first or second century after Christ, the λόγος Μέμφεως is probably not a private account of freight to Memphis, as the editors believed, but a statement of the various customs- and harbour-dues assessed upon cargoes shipped down the Nile. The account for two shiploads of wheat is given in two columns: the first cargo amounting to 550 artabae paid 44 drachmae; the second paid 43 drachmae, although the sum was erased, for 540 artabae. This rate was very low, hardly more than 2 per cent.,[41] but there were various other fees. All of these additional fees, except three, were identical for both shiploads. The payment for πηδαλίου, probably a fee for the service of a pilot,[42] made for the larger shipload was 14 drachmae 4 obols; for the smaller shipload it was a trifle higher, 14 drachmae 5 obols. In the first column (that of the larger shipload) there appears a payment of 4 obols for φύλαξ ἀπὸ γ(ῆς) καὶ κυδ(άρῳ?), which the editors doubtfully translated as 'a guard from the land and for a boat', and also a payment of 2 drachmae for ἐραυνητικ(οῦ) εἰς λ(όγον) σπονδ(ῆς), apparently a *pourboire* for the customs-examiner,[43] neither of which appears in the second column. Probably payment of these items was made for both vessels at the same time and was listed only in one column of the account. The other (identical) supplementary charges were as follows: νέων, probably a wharf-fee,[44] 6 drachmae; γένους, a tax, 4 drachmae; ἐραυνητικ(οῦ), fee for customs-examination, 4 drachmae; τραπεζίτῃ fee to the banker, 1 drachma; χειριστικοῦ, commission(?), 5 drachmae; ἀλλαγῆ(ς), exchange, 1 drachma; ἑρμηνεῖ{ς}, fee for a broker,[45] 2 drachmae; γραμματεῦσι, fee for the scribes, 4 drachmae; 'Αρτεμεῖτι, fee for a sacrifice to Artemis,[46] 1 drachma; χειρογρα(φίας), affidavit, 1 drachma; πιττακίου, a pass or receipt, 4 obols. It is possible that some of these fees are to be classed as private expenses of the shippers, but it is clear from the parallel document, PO. xiv. 1651, that the majority of them were government charges.

PO. xiv. 1650(a) is a portion of a similar account of a shipment of beans, on which a payment of 119 drachmae was made.

The charge for νέου is 5 drachmae 5 obols; that for πηδαλίου 14 drachmae 5 obols; τραπεζ(ίτη), 1 drachma; γένους, 8 drachmae; χ‹ε›ιριστικοῦ, 14 drachmae; ἀλλαγή, 2 drachmae; γραμματέων, 4 drachmae; πιττακίου, 2 obols. The amounts paid for ἐραυνη- τικοῦ and for χ‹ε›ιρογραφίας are lost. Three additional charges appear: ταμίου, storage, 10 drachmae; συνβολικά, receipt-charges, 2 drachmae; and 4 drachmae to a soldier (στρατιώτη) who per- haps corresponds to the φύλαξ ἀπὸ γ(ῆς) of PO. xiv. 1650, but since the payment of the στρατιώτης was so much higher, perhaps he was (as the editors suggested) the ἐπίπλοος who commonly accompanied cargoes of grain.[47]

A similar account from the third century is found in PO. xiv. 1651. According to this document a cargo of 400 ceramia of wine paid at the rate of 4½ obols a ceramion, a total of 300 drachmae. Unless the value set upon the wine was extraordinarily great, the rate of the toll was much higher than that upon the wheat in PO. xiv. 1650.[48] In addition 36 drachmae 3 obols were paid for ἀναλώματος οἰνηγ(ίας), which in proportion to the principal charge approximately corresponds to the fee for νέου in PO. xiv. 1650.[49] Ἐραυνητικόν was again 4 drachmae. The payment of 24 drachmae for τ[έ]λους may be compared to the payment for γένους in PO. xiv. 1650 and 1650 (a).[50] The fee for πηδαλίου was 12 drachmae 4½ obols, less than in the other accounts; but the payment to the scribes was 8 drachmae, twice that for the other cargoes. The total of these payments is given as 385 drach- mae 2 obols, and upon this 30 drachmae were paid for προσδια- γρα(φόμενα) at the rate of one-thirteenth, which certainly in- dicates that the preceding charges were collected by the govern- ment. These προσδιαγραφόμενα perhaps correspond to the charges for χειριστικόν in the earlier accounts.[51] The charge for χειρογρα(φίας) is 3 obols, only half of that charge in each column of PO. xiv. 1650. A fee of 4 obols for κυδάρῳ appears. The charge for πιττακίου, 1 drachma 1 obol, is higher than that found in the earlier accounts. A supplementary payment of 1 drachma 1 obol made to the customs-examiner (ἐραυνητῇ) may be com- pared with the ἐραυνητικ(οῦ) εἰς λ(όγον) σπονδ(ῆς) of PO. xiv. 1650. The fee for the soldier on guard ([σ]τατιωναρίῳ) is 2 drachmae 2 obols. Additional payments not found in the earlier accounts are: 14 drachmae 2 obols for ξυλικοῦ, a payment for timber;[52] 4 drachmae to a *beneficiarius* ($\beta(\epsilon\nu\epsilon\phi\iota\kappa\iota\alpha\rho\iota\omega)$);[53] and 4 obols for a mutilated item .[.]τει.

In PO. XIV. 1650 the total of the charges in (column i) on the shipload of 550 artabae of wheat is 91 drachmae, on the shipload of 540 artabae (in column ii) is 87 drachmae 3 obols, in each case a little more than twice the amount of the initial charges of 44 and 43 drachmae for the respective cargoes. In PO. XIV. 1651 the total of the charges is 492 drachmae 2 obols, so that the additional charges amount to approximately 64 per cent. of the initial tax of 300 drachmae. If the initial charges in these documents correspond to the toll for $\lambda\iota\mu\acute{\epsilon}\nu$ος $M\acute{\epsilon}\mu\phi\epsilon\omega$ς in P. Lond. III. 1107 (p. 47), the total of some or all of the supplementary fees and exactions in the documents from Oxyrhynchus may correspond roughly to the assessments for $\acute{\epsilon}\pi\iota\sigma\tau\alpha\tau\epsilon\acute{\iota}\alpha$ καὶ ($\pi\acute{\epsilon}\mu\pi\tau\eta$) added in the account from the Arsinoite nome. If this suggestion is correct, the difference in these accounts affords another example of the striking variation in the method of assessment and collection of the same or analogous taxes in the different nomes of Egypt.

Customs regulations which exhibit some points of resemblance to the fees found in the accounts from Oxyrhynchus (PO. XIV. 1650–1) are in P. Lond. III. 928 (p. 190), a fragmentary document of unknown provenience which is dated in the third century after Christ. The first item in the list of dutiable goods is cotton, but its rate is lost, and the same is true of the rate of the second item, something made of hemp. Third in the list is $\lambda\acute{\alpha}\chi\alpha\nu$ος-seed which paid 1 drachma $1\frac{1}{2}$ obols an artaba. This is followed by a charge for $\tau\alpha\mu\epsilon\acute{\iota}ο\nu$ (storage), found also in PO. XIV. 1650 (a) on a shipload of beans, which is here assessed in kind at the rate of 1 artaba (per shipload?). The charge for 'expense of a boat' ($\acute{\alpha}\nu\alpha\lambda\acute{\omega}\mu\alpha\tau$ος $\pi\lambda$οίου) is new, for the fee of 9 drachmae can hardly be compared with the charge of 4 obols for a skiff ($\kappa\acute{\upsilon}\delta\alpha\rho$ος) found in the Oxyrhynchus accounts.[54] The charge of 4 drachmae for the scribes ($\gamma\rho(\alpha\mu\mu\alpha\tau\epsilon\tilde{\upsilon}\sigma\iota$)), however, is familiar. The next item is either a tariff for a toll on sacrificial animals or a fee for a sacrifice corresponding to the drachma paid to Artemis in PO. XIV. 1650. The charge varies with the size of pig: for a sow ($\tilde{\upsilon}$ς) the charge was 4 drachmae $1\frac{1}{2}$ obols, for a $\delta\acute{\epsilon}\lambda\phi\alpha\xi$ 2 drachmae 3 obols, for a χοῖρος 1 drachma $1\frac{1}{2}$ obols.

The next item is mutilated but ends in]ελτων, and it was assessed at 3 drachmae 5 obols for a dry measure called ψίαθος. Unguents[55] of various scents (lily, narcissus, rose, palm, myrtle, rose, almond) were assessed at 9 drachmae 1 obol the μετρήτης. Painters' colours paid at the rate of 7 drachmae 1 obol the ξέστης. Various other items—some at least pigments—at different rates follow.[56]

Customs regulations (νόμος τελωνικός) are found also in PO. I. 36 and *Archiv* III, pp. 185 ff. (republished by Wilcken in *Chrest.* 273), a papyrus of the second or third century. Most of the rates given are for spices and other objects imported from Arabia and the Trogodytic coast. Wilcken compared these items with the imports from the Orient subject to *vectigal* which are listed in *Dig.* 39, 4, 16, §7,[57] and Rostovtzeff maintained that the νόμος τελωνικός from Oxyrhynchus was but a part of a copy of general regulations governing the assessment and collection of the *vectigal Maris Rubri*.[58] There are serious objections, however, to such a view. It is difficult to see why a copy of the general regulations governing the assessment and collection of the *vectigal Maris Rubri* should have existed at Oxyrhynchus. Moreover, Rostovtzeff's assumption that the Oxyrhynchus papyrus is a fragment of such general regulations is not well founded. Although the majority of the items listed were imports from Arabia and Ethiopia, the oil κύπρος was probably a product of Egypt. Pliny states that Egypt produced the best quality of κύπρος and names Ascalon and Cyprus as the next best sources.[59] I believe that the inclusion of κύπρος among the items points to a tariff on traffic by way of the Nile river.[60] The provisions of the second column of this νόμος τελωνικός also suggest that the duties were those collected upon goods transported on the Nile rather than those collected at the ports on the Red Sea. Provision is there made for the unloading and examination of cargoes of the merchants (ἔμποροι), if the tax-farmer (τελώνης) is not satisfied with the declaration of the merchant. If the τελώνης discovers anything not declared, it is to be confiscated. If, however, the declaration prove correct, the τελώνης must reimburse the merchant for the cost of unloading his vessel. Such a procedure suits exactly the character of the tax for the harbour of Memphis, since the tax apparently was paid in advance and the

receipts were kept to present to the officials at Memphis. Thus
if the customs-agents stationed at Memphis itself suspected that
a ship was carrying undeclared or contraband articles and an
attempt was being made to smuggle into the Delta articles upon
which the payment for λιμένος Μέμφεως had not been made, the
shipper could be forced to unload the cargo, and the agents
could inspect it to their own satisfaction. This seems much more
likely than Rostovtzeff's supposition that the provision for unloading applied to ships entering the Red Sea at Bab-el-Mandeb or
lying over at Berenice Trogodytice on their way to Myos Hormos.
The third column of the νόμος τελωνικός directs the toll-payers
to obtain an affidavit (χειρογραφία) from the collectors for protection against informers.[61] The shippers may have been careless
about obtaining the affidavit because of the charge made for it
(1 drachma in PO. xiv. 1650 and 3 obols in 1651). In the same
column appears the word ὅπλα (arms), but the space below it is
blank. Evidently regulations in regard to traffic in weapons were
intended. Such regulations were necessary within Egypt itself
because of the danger of revolt.

BGU. iii. 812, dated in the second or third century, is a record
of customs-duties for goods transported by water. The provenience is unknown. The units of measure are unusual in customs documents, perhaps because the shipments were by water.
Pentadia, whatever measure that may have been, were assessed
at 3 obols each. Wool was taxed at 40 drachmae a bale (σάκκος),
and barley at 20 drachmae a *litra*. Barley shipped by a certain
Φεῖτις was immune from the toll. The name Φεῖτις probably
stands for Festus, and the immunity may have been granted to
him because he was a veteran, since a rescript of Domitian
granted exemption from *portoria* to Roman veterans.[62] There
is nothing in this report to prove that it records collections of the
tax for the Harbour of Memphis, but the document seems most
closely to resemble the reports of that tax found in SB. 7365
and P. Lond. iii. 1169 (p. 43).

The view that the tax for the harbour of Memphis represents
an internal customs collected at the northern boundary of the
ἐπιστρατηγία of the Heptanomia and Arsinoite nome differs from
previous theories.[63] I believe that Memphis played a role analogous to that of Hermopolis Magna, where Strabo mentions the

collection of duties at the Φυλακή. The Φυλακή at Hermopolis is attested for the Ptolemaic period by Agatharcides, who states that it was also called Σχεδία (a customs-barrier in the river).[64] Cagnat pointed out that the toll-station at Hermopolis separated the ἐπιστρατηγία of the Heptanomia and Arsinoite nome from that of the Thebaid.[65] Memphis is, of course, not mentioned as a customs-barrier in the Ptolemaic period, because the ἐπιστρατηγία of the Heptanomia and Arsinoite nome was not established until the Roman period. Perhaps Memphis is not mentioned by Strabo as a toll-station because at the time of his visit to Egypt the Roman administration had not yet taken advantage of the establishment of the new ἐπιστρατηγία to collect customs at Memphis.[66]

Local Customs-dues

The collectors of the tax for the harbour of Memphis in the villages on the edge of the Arsinoite nome also collected the ρ καὶ ν, a customs-duty of 3 per cent., and the ἐρημοφυλακία, a tax for the maintenance of the desert-guard employed against the brigands that frequently troubled the country. The ρ καὶ ν is attested in a large number of receipts from the Arsinoite nome. It does not, at least under the same designation, appear elsewhere in Egypt. In P. Grenf. II. 50 (b) the tax is indicated more fully as ρ καὶ ν νομ(αρχίας) 'Αρσινο(ίτου), which seems to mark it as one of the taxes within the competence of the nomarch.[67] This definitely distinguishes it from the tax for the harbour of Memphis and designates it as an export- and import-toll for the Arsinoite nome.

The principal exports carried by donkey- and camel-trains from the Fayûm were oil, wool, wheat, vetch, dates, and λάχανος. The chief import was wine. Various other articles appear in the receipts and customs-registers, but it is not always possible to determine from the latter documents whether exports or imports are recorded.[68] Presumably the grain subject to the customs-dues was exported by private individuals, for it is hard to see what purpose the Roman government could have had in placing a toll upon the grain which it collected as taxes and rents in kind and transported to Rome.

The rate of the ρ καὶ ν was obviously 3 per cent. *ad valorem.*

It is probable, however, that the duty was assessed by means of a tariff which stated the tax upon specific measures of articles without regard to slight variations in value. This may be deduced from the receipts which almost never state the amount of the tax collected, but ordinarily give the number of donkeys or camels passing through the toll-gate and what they carried, usually measured in artabae or ceramia or metretae. The ρ καὶ ν was collected on many of the same articles which paid the tax for the harbour of Memphis, and in two cases separate receipts have been found for ρ καὶ ν and λιμένος Μέμφεως upon the same shipments.

Wilcken suggested that the ρ καὶ ν represents two taxes, one of 1 per cent. and the other of 2 per cent, which had been combined.[69] He explained the tax of 2 per cent as an export- or import-duty upon the produce carried by the donkeys and camels, and the tax of 1 per cent. as an impost upon the animals. Grenfell and Hunt argued conclusively against the latter hypothesis,[70] and maintained their previous theory that the ρ καὶ ν was simply a 3 per cent. tax upon the produce. The extant evidence does not permit of proof that the ρ καὶ ν represents two combined taxes, but the receipts for the internal customs found in the Oxyrhynchite nome lend some support to such a view. In PO. XII. 1439 a customs-toll of 1 per cent. is designated as διαπύλιον, a fee paid for passing the gate (πύλη); the payment was for an ass-load of barley and one of garlic, apparently exported.[71] PO. XII. 1440 is a receipt for the payment of the duty of 2 per cent. levied upon produce exported, probably from the Hermopolite to the Oxyrhynchite nome. Perhaps the ρ (1 per cent.) of the ρ καὶ ν in the Fayûm is also to be regarded as διαπύλιον.

In Upper Egypt the farmers of the 2 per cent. tax collected tolls on imported and exported goods. At Thebes and Hermonthis those collectors are titled in the receipts τελῶναι ν̄ (= πεντηκοστῆς),[72] while in one receipt from Syene they are called πεντηκοσ(τῶναι) λ[ι(μένος)] Σοήνης, and in another τελ(ῶναι) πεντ(ηκοστῆς) [λι(μένος)] Σοήνης.[73] These receipts are obviously parallel to the duty of 2 per cent. levied in PO. XII. 1440, and perhaps also to the 2 per cent. of the ρ καὶ ν of the Arsinoite nome. In the absence of receipts for an additional 1 per cent.

toll in Upper Egypt it is uncertain whether a διαπύλιον was collected there. One of the receipts from Hermonthis (WO. II. 801) is particularly important. It records the payment of toll on 150 artabae of wheat and 8 artabae of vetch exported in A.D. 107. The striking thing, however, is that the payment was made by a veteran Longinus Crispus, whereas in A.D. 87–8 Domitian had granted to Roman veterans immunity from *portoria*.[74] There is no reason to believe that this grant of immunity was repealed, for it is repeated in the *Codex Theodosianus*.[75] Consequently it is necessary to consider whether the 2 per cent. toll was really a *portorium*. I believe that the tax of 2 per cent. collected on exports and imports was not a *portorium* but an extension of the πεντηκοστὴ ὠνίων, a sales-tax of 2 per cent., attested for Thebes in WO. II. 1056 and 1076. This leaves only the 1 per cent. διαπύλιον to be regarded as a *portorium*, and even that is doubtful, because a Roman veteran named Κολλοῦθος is said to have paid the ρ καὶ ν in a receipt described, but unfortunately not published, in P. Teb. II. 557, dated second or third century after Christ.

A toll of one-twelfth (2 obols per tetradrachm) is attested in P. Lond. III. 856 (p. 91), which is dated late in the first century after Christ. This rate, which is different from any found in other documents, was assessed on exported pickled fish of all kinds. This rate follows a section on the regulation of the purchase and export into other villages, into the metropolis, and even into other nomes, and in the latter case there is a provision requiring satisfaction of the claims of the ἀγορανομίας ὠνίων καὶ πελωχικοῦ (or πυλωγικοῦ)[76] καὶ μνημονείου καὶ τῶν ἄλ[λω]ν εἰδῶ[ν] καὶ γραφείου ὅρμου μητ[ρο]πόλεως.[77] This is quite consistent with the view that the customs-dues collected at the boundaries of the nome were but extensions of the market-tax, and if the older reading πυλωνικοῦ is correct, its connexion with the ἀγορανομίας ὠνίων may confirm the suggestion that the ρ καὶ ν consists of a 1 per cent. tax for διαπύλιον and a 2 per cent. sales-tax (πεντηκοστὴ ὠνίων). The rate of one-twelfth, which applied to all articles imported into the metropolis except wine and vinegar, seems to indicate a type of local customs not found elsewhere. Another unusual stipulation provides for the collection of samples (ὀψολογία) of oil, &c. The mention of πλοίου indicates a toll upon river- or canal-traffic, and the strange names of villages in the first column suggest some nome in the Delta.[78]

The first column of the same document gives rates of toll or sales-tax on calves or steers (μόσχοι) which vary with the age and provenience of the animal, and which presumably were assessed *ad valorem*. The rates range from 2 drachmae to 4 drachmae 4 obols. For some unknown reason καθήκοντα (taxes assessed at a fixed rate) of 1 obol are added once to a rate of 2 drachmae. The resulting total of 2 drachmae 1 obol is duplicated in another rate where, however, there is no mention of καθήκοντα. Καθή-κοντα of $1\frac{1}{2}$ obols are once added to a rate of 4 drachmae, but the resulting total of 4 drachmae $1\frac{1}{2}$ obols is not duplicated in the other rates that are preserved in the fragmentary first column. If the value of the μόσχοι averaged 200 drachmae,[79] the rate of toll at 4 drachmae was 2 per cent. *ad valorem*, which is a more familiar rate for local customs than the rate of one-twelfth on pickled fish and other articles mentioned in the second column, and is the rate of the τέλος βοός in P. Fay. 62.

In O. Strass. 258, dated A.D. 146, the tax for import and export (εἰσαγωγίου καὶ ἐξαγω(γίου)) in the Apollonopolite nome appears. This tax was collected at the rate of 5 drachmae a month, which indicates a licence to import and export rather than a toll assessed *ad valorem*. Such a tax is unattested elsewhere in Egypt, but if the local customs of 2 per cent. in Upper and Middle Egypt was an extension of the 2 per cent. tax on sales, as suggested above, the tax of the Apollonopolite nome may be compared with the Dromos-tax (apparently a market-tax) found in demotic receipts from Tentyra and collected in quite regular amounts or instalments.[80]

Strabo mentions Schedia, the toll-station of the city of Alexandria, where the duty on merchandise transported up and down the river was collected. The city of Alexandria formed an independent unit for administration, and it is not surprising that it had customs-dues of its own, and these must have yielded a great revenue because of the tremendous importance of Alexandria in the commerce of the ancient world. Unfortunately no papyri amplify the statement of Strabo so that nothing is known concerning details of the local customs-dues of Alexandria in the Roman period.[81]

The ᾽Ερημοφυλακία

A tax for the support of desert-guards (ἐρημοφυλακία) was
exacted at the border of the Arsinoite nome by the same officials
who collected the tax for the harbour of Memphis and the
ρ καὶ ν.[82] The payments for ἐρημοφυλακία and for ρ καὶ ν have
been found in receipts for identical shipments.[83] Fiesel therefore supposed that the ἐρημοφυλακία was a surtax of 3 per cent.
assessed in addition to the ρ καὶ ν upon traffic between the
Arsinoite nome and the oases of the Libyan desert.[84] It is quite
true that guards would have been necessary for the protection
of caravans travelling between the Fayûm and the oases, and the
ἐρημοφυλακία was undoubtedly collected for the maintenance
of the government's desert-police.[85] There is not the slightest
proof, however, that the ἐρημομοφυλακία is to be regarded as a
surtax on the ρ καὶ ν, or that it was assessed at 3 per cent.[86]
No published receipts show payments of ἐρημοφυλακία, ρ καὶ ν,
and λιμένος Μέμφεως all on the same shipment. It is not
impossible, however, that in times of revolt and increase of
brigandage desert-police may have been required to guard
donkey- and camel-trains between the Fayûm and Memphis,
but an inspection of the dates of the receipts for ἐρημοφυλακία
does not indicate that they were more common at such times.

The ἐρημοφυλακία is the only one of the three taxes assessed
at the toll-stations on the border of the Arsinoite nome which
we know was levied on camels and donkeys which were not carrying loads and were not themselves objects of import.[87] The
ἐρημοφυλακία on an unloaded donkey was 1 drachma, and on a
camel 2 drachmae.[88] In SP. XXII. 140, however, 4 drachmae
were collected on an entering camel. Although the fee is not
named in the receipt, it is probable that the usual 2 drachmae for
ἐρημοφυλακία had been doubled by the addition of another fee of
2 drachmae. This other fee was, I believe, the παρόδιον.

The παρόδιον is mentioned in σύμβολα καμήλων (camel-
receipts) in connexion with the ἐρημοφυλακία.[89] Camels travelling between Prosopis in the Delta and Socnopaei Nesus in the
Fayûm had to have these receipts, which were obtained from
the μισθωτὴς ἐρημοφυλακίας καὶ παροδίου Προσοπίτου καὶ Λητοπολίτου.[90] The amount for each camel was 6 or 8 drachmae.

Since the borders of three nomes had to be crossed on the journey, it is probable that the ἐρημοφυλακία was collected at the rate of 2 drachmae for each nome, and that the extra 2 drachmae were for παρόδιον, a transit-toll of unknown nature.[91] The payment of 2 drachmae for ἐρημοφυλακία of each nome is interesting because two of the nomes were not in the same ἐπιστρατηγία as the Arsinoite nome. This must mean that the ἐρημοφυλακία was a toll assessed by the central administration of Egypt, and so distinguished from such local tolls as the ρ καὶ ν and from the toll for the Harbour of Memphis at the border of the ἐπιστρατηγία.

The Coptos Tariff

A pass (πρόσταγμα or ἀπόστολος) was required for emigration from Egypt, both in Ptolemaic and in Roman times, as Strabo informs us,[92] but concerning the payments for such passes nothing is known. Roman citizens were required, when leaving Egypt, to carry documents (γράμματα) either in addition to the ἀπόστολος or as a substitute for it.[93] The granting of ἀπόστολοι apparently had once been within the competence of the Idiologus, but the prefect had taken over that function by the date of the publication of the Gnomon of the Idiologus in the second half of the second century after Christ.[94] Penalties for the emigration of various classes of persons without such passes (ἀναπόστολοι) are, however, recorded in the Gnomon.[95]

Uxkull-Gyllenband has found in the famous Coptos tariff an example of fees for passes, rather than a transit-toll or transportation charges, as it had previously been interpreted.[96] The pass purchased at Coptos did not entitle its recipient to leave Egypt, but to travel over the road from Coptos to one of the ports on the Red Sea. The tariff had, so far as we can judge, nothing to do with customs-dues internal or external. Every animal or vehicle used in transport over the roads from Coptos to the coast, which were maintained by the government,[97] was required to have a πιττάκιον, the written permit to use the road, for which a fee was collected. For a camel the πιττάκιον cost 1 obol with an additional charge of 2 obols for affixing an official seal (σφραγισμός), a total of 3 obols. This fee for πιττάκιον is not to be connected with the fee paid in the Fayûm and the

Delta for ἐρημοφυλακία or σύμβολον καμήλων, for both of which
the payments were much higher; but it is similar to the fee
for πιττάκιον exacted for ships in the λόγος Μέμφεως in PO.
XIV. 1650. The fee for an ass was 2 obols, apparently including
σφραγισμός, and for a wagon with a tilt 4 drachmae. Each
traveller[98] was required to purchase a πιττάκιον, for which men
paid 1 drachma each, and women 4 drachmae each. These fees
were uniform for all persons.[99]

The principal fee exacted from all travellers on the road varied
greatly. Men were required to pay from 5 to 10 drachmae.
Women paid at a much higher rate than men, 20 drachmae
ordinarily, but 108 drachmae for prostitutes. A fee of 20
drachmae had to be paid for a mast transported over the road,
and 4 drachmae for a yard-arm. A cortège passing out to the
cemetery in the desert and returning paid a fee of 1 drachma
4 obols.[100]

The fees were termed ἀποστόλιον, a diminutive of ἀπόστολος,
and they fell within the competence of the Arabarch,[101] whose
jurisdiction evidently included toll-roads from Coptos to the
ports of Myos Hormos, Berenice Trogodytice, and perhaps
Leucos Limen. The fees were collected by tax-farmers (μισθωταί). The decree containing the tariff was set up, at the
order of the prefect of Egypt, by the prefect of Mons Berenice,
who was the military commander of the district and probably
responsible for maintenance of order therein.

The purpose of the fees of the ἀποστόλιον was, at least in
part, to provide funds for the maintenance of the roads from
Coptos to the Red Sea ports with the stations (ὑδρεύματα) thereon,
and for the sustenance of the guards at those stations and the
guards who may have accompanied caravans en route. At the
same time it must be borne in mind that the fees were tolls and
not merely payments for services rendered by the government,
for it cost no more to guard an artizan than a sailor, although the
former paid 3 drachmae more than the latter. It may have been
more trouble to assure the safety of women on the long and
sometimes dangerous journey, but again the differential in the
fees is too great to be accounted for in that way alone. The
principle determining the rate of the charges seems to have
been to assess the maximum feasible amount.[102] Presumably

similar fees were collected at the ports on the Red Sea when a
caravan started inland, but there is no extant evidence concerning this.[103]

The 'Ενόρμιον

Somewhat similar in purpose to the fees collected for use of
the roads from Coptos to the Red Sea was the charge made for
the use of harbours and collected from ships. In P. Fay. 104,
which has been mentioned above, appears an item for ἐνόρμιον
which is perhaps related to the charge for πηδαλίου in PO. XIV.
1650–1. The amount of the fee in this document is lost. A
payment for [ἐν]όρμιον appears also in P. Flor. III. 335, an
account of expenses (dated in the third century). At Syene the
ἐνόρμιον was collected by the officials of the harbour-watch
(μισθωταὶ εἴδους ὁρμοφυλακίας or ὁ ἀσχολούμενος τὴν ὁρμοφυλακίαν).[104] The shippers who resided at Syene or in the vicinity
had an account at the office of the harbour-watch, and their fees
were paid periodically—for one, three, or four months. The
tax seems to have been assessed according to the number of
shiploads and their value.[105] In WO. II. 262 three shiploads
(ἀγώγια) during the month Thoth were assessed 2 drachmae
1 obol.

Fiesel has suggested that the Coptos tariff was descended
from a Ptolemaic institution.[106] This is probable because the
roads had been maintained by the Ptolemies who doubtless
exacted fees to meet that expense. It is also probable that the
Roman administration took over the customs-duties, external
and internal, from the Ptolemaic system without many changes.[107]
The addition of the toll-station at Memphis after the establishment of the ἐπιστρατηγία of the Heptanomia and Arsinoite nome
was a consistent development of the Ptolemaic duties which
were collected at Hermopolis Magna. The theory of Ptolemaic
origin of the customs-dues of Roman Egypt accounts for the
lack of precise information concerning the external customs of
the country, since the Roman governors had little occasion to
change well-known established principles. It accounts also for
the variation of the internal customs in the different nomes.[108]
The Ptolemies, however, could never have collected so great a

revenue from the customs-dues of Egypt as did the Roman administration, since the great development of commerce with India took place within the Roman period.[109] The income from these revenues was greatly increased, moreover, by the added value given to imports from the Orient which were processed in the factories of Alexandria.

XVI

MISCELLANEOUS TAXES

IN this chapter must be grouped those taxes and fees of various kinds about which there is some information available but which as yet cannot be fitted into an ordered analysis of taxation in Roman Egypt. Our information about some of these taxes is considerable, but about the majority it is very slight. Consequently it has seemed best to list them in alphabetical order and to give such data concerning each as seemed pertinent.

Ἀπαρχή

The ἀπαρχή seems to be a tax in BGU. I. 30, but its nature is not clear. In P. Teb. II. 316, P. Flor. I. 57. 81, and PSI. v. 464 ἀπαρχή seems to be a payment by an ephebe for enrollment in a deme at Alexandria. The same term ἀπαρχή is used of a tax paid at the time of reporting the birth of a house-born slave (οἰκογένεια) in SB. 6995–6, and according to PSI. VI. 690 this tax had been dedicated (in Ptolemaic times) to Berenice Euergetis. The term was also used to refer to the inheritance-tax and to a tax paid by Jews.[1]

Βικαρίου

In PO. XII. 1436, an account of village-taxes, βικαρίου thrice appears in the list of payments. This may represent a fee paid for the benefit of a *vicarius*, although the editors suggest that the *vicarius* was engaged in tax-collecting.

Γραμματικὸν φυλακιτῶν

In the Ptolemaic period γραμματικά were charges made upon various classes of cleruchi, including φυλακῖται, for the support of the secretaries who kept the records of the cleruchi and their land. These charges were collected in kind.[2] In P. Teb. II. 345, however, the γρ(αμματικόν) in 28(?) B.C. was collected in copper drachmae, and the change to a money-tax may have taken place earlier in the first century B.C. before the Roman conquest of Egypt. In the Roman period the γραμματικὸν φυλακιτῶν is attested for the Fayûm and the Mendesian nome.[3] The method of assessing the tax is unknown, although its occurrence under the classification λιμνιτικά in the latter nome led the editors of the Rylands papyri (II. 213. 334 note) to assume that the tax fell upon land. The tax may, however, like the ἀριθμητικὸν κατοίκων[4] have been assessed upon the ownership of land (γῆ φυλακιτῶν) rather than on the land itself. In the tax-rolls from Caranis in the collection of the University of Michigan a charge for γραμματεία φυλακιτῶν is collected together with the ναύβιον; the payments amount to 1 drachma 1 obol 2 chalci, 4½ obols, and 2 obols. The variation in amount suggests that the assessment was based upon the amount of land (γῆ φυλακιτῶν) owned, although this is not certain.

Εἰσιτήριον

This payment in P. Ryl. II. 77. 37 was apparently a fee paid for a sacrifice by an exegetes upon entering office. It may have been a municipal tax.

Ἑκατοστή

According to the Gnomon of the Idiologus (BGU. V, § 29) an unmarried Roman woman or freedwoman having an estate of 20,000 sesterces or more was required to pay an annual capital tax of 1 per cent. (ἑκατοστή). A ἑκατοστή (as well as πεντηκοστή) is mentioned in P. Bouriant 31, but it was probably a different tax. In P. Teb. II. 297 (ἑκατοσταί?) αἰπ.[   ] appears in the mutilated beginning of proceedings concerning the purchase of a priestly office, and the editors listed it in the index as a tax.

Τέλος ἐπιξένων

Persons residing outside their places of origin (ἰδία = origo) were sometimes required to pay a tax to the authorities of their place of temporary residence.[5] In O. Theb. 87 the collectors are called ἐπιτηρηταὶ τέλους ἐπιξένων. The rate of the tax varies, perhaps with the social or economic status of the person subject to it, for rates of 2 drachmae and of 1 drachma a month are found in O. Mey. 31 and 32, receipts issued by the same collector at Thebes for the same year.

Ἐπιστατεία φυλακιτῶν

In P. Ryl. II. 213. 29 and PSI. I. 106. 15 appear payments for ἐπιστατεία φυλακιτῶν. Nothing is known concerning this tax in the Ptolemaic period, although it doubtless originated then. It is probably to be related to the γραμματικὸν φυλακιτῶν above and so was a payment for an ἐπιστάτης φυλακιτῶν who may have survived in the Mendesian nome where the cleruchies of φυλακῖται seem to have been common. A payment from Upper Egypt (O. Strass. 158) of 4 drachmae ὑπ(ὲρ) ὑποκ(ειμένων) ἐπιστα(τεία) may, if the reading is correct, be similar.

Ἐπιστολικόν

This seems to have been a fee charged for the dispatch of official documents to Alexandria. The amounts of the payments range from ½ to 4 obols in P. Teb. II. 355, 544, 638, and BGU. III 898, but a payment of 20 drachmae is recorded in BGU. II. 653. A payment for ἐπιστολ( ) is also recorded in PO. XII. 1438, where the amount is 4 drachmae. The termination of ἐπιστολ( ) has not occurred written in full: in BGU. II. 653 the editor has expanded ἐπιστολ(ῶν); in PO. XII. 1438 the editors doubtfully suggested ἐπιστολ(ικοῦ). The latter expansion seems more probable since the payments are evidently for fees.

Ἐπίτριτον

The term ἐπίτριτον was applied to a tax in kind.[6] When the ἐπίτριτον was collected in money, the amount was usually 4 drachmae, but this is sometimes stated to be a payment on account.[7] The name of the tax should mean a surtax of a third, but it is not clear what the unit was upon which the third was levied. The ἐπίτριτον is mentioned twice in articles of apprenticeship to a weaver, but this may be a mere coincidence.[8] The editors of PO. XIV. 1647, which contains articles of apprenticeship to a weaver, suggested (in their note on line 45) that the ἐκδόσεων τελέσματα, 'taxes on apprenticing', found in that document may be identical with the ἐπίτριτον.

Ἐρετικόν

The ἐρετικόν seems not to be an actual tax but the payment of wages of a substitute by a man liable to the occasional liturgy of rowing in a state barge.⁹ Probably the κωπηλασία mentioned in PSI. IV. 289 was similar.

Ζευγματικόν

Ζευγματικόν appears in P. Lond. III. 1157 (p. 61) and PO. XVII. 2129. The new Liddell and Scott *Greek Lexicon* defines the word as a lock-toll; but since it is found among the land-taxes, it is more probably a tax for sluices in the irrigation canals, as suggested in PO. XII. 1438. 21 note.¹⁰ Ἡρακλεοτικ( ) ζευγ( ) in PO. XII. 1438 may be related to this tax, although the editors believe that it refers to double loaves of bread (ζευγή).

Μέλι καὶ κηρός

A collector of honey and beeswax (ἐγλήμπτωρ μέλιτος καὶ κηροῦ) appears in P. Lond. III. 1171 *verso* (p. 106). This apparently refers to a requisition made at Hermopolis in A.D. 42. Such a requisition would naturally require a special collector.

Τέλος κορμῶν τριῶν

This tax has appeared only in WO. II. 1055. Preisigke (WB. I, *s.v.* κορμός) gives a definition of this tax as an impost for the κορμοί (blocks of wood used in the hand-sluices of the irrigation canals), which was paid by the cultivators to the state.

Λιθικόν

In P. Princeton 13. V. 2 (from Philadelphia and dated *c.* A.D. 35) payments of 2 to 14 drachmae are indicated on account of this tax (εἰς τὸν λόγον τοῦ λιθικοῦ) which is otherwise unknown. The editors suggest that 'perhaps the state had undertaken some public work for which the individuals who benefited therefrom were assessed in a special levy which was collected through the same agency as the λαογραφία and the ἀριθμητικόν'. In PSI. III. 263, an ostracon from Thebes, there is recorded a payment of 4 obols ὑπ(ὲρ) λιθίνου ὀφρίου, 'for the stone embankment', and this may have been a similar assessment.

Παραζυγὴ ζυγῶν

The παραζυγὴ ζυγῶν is found in three documents from the Arsinoite nome dated in the middle of the first century after

Christ.[11] Perhaps these payments represent the *adaeratio* of the liturgy of furnishing a team for service to the state. Another possibility is that they were made for a license, like the τέλος ἁμαξῶν.

Προστατικόν

One-half artaba of barley for this charge appears in a lease of land (PO. III. 590; A.D. 112). It may have been a survival of a fee for the support of a προστάτης.

Πλεῖθος

In P. Strass. I. 66 the elders of the village of Polydeucia pay to the μισθωταὶ πλείθου νόμου 48 drachmae ὑπὲρ ἀποτάκτου πλείθου. If the reading is correct there seems no solution.

Πρόστιμον

Πρόστιμον may be a tax rather than a fine (its ordinary meaning) in PSI. VII. 797, a mutilated document from Alexandri Nesus dated A.D. 232.

Στεπτικόν

In PO. XII. 1413 the στεπτικόν is a fee paid by a municipal official for the right to wear a crown (cf. the εἰσιτήριον above).

Στεφανικόν

The crown-tax (στεφανικόν) is by far the most important tax listed in this chapter, and it is placed in this miscellany only because the occasions for levying it and the method of assessment varied. The στεφανικόν had its origin in the Ptolemaic period, although it was not confined to Egypt. Like other monarchs the Ptolemies had upon their accession received gold crowns which were ostensibly the voluntary offerings of their loyal subjects. The voluntary character was largely theoretical, and moreover, as time went on, cash offerings became more acceptable to the rulers than actual crowns. Roman emperors found the acceptance of such gifts from their provincial subjects agreeable; and the *aurum coronarium*, levied as a tax, became an important source of revenue for the *fiscus*.[12]

Certain emperors—Augustus, Hadrian, Antoninus Pius, and Severus Alexander—are known to have granted to the provinces full or partial remission of the *aurum coronarium*, and this must have applied to Egypt. If none of the other emperors remitted the crown-tax at their accession, the occasions of its payment must have been frequent, yet documentary evidence from Egypt for payment of this tax is relatively scarce before late in the second century. Payments for the crown-tax are first attested in ostraca from the reign of Claudius, and the payments amount to 2½ drachmae.[13] To the same year are perhaps to be assigned receipts from Tentyra where amounts of 1 drachma 2 obols and 2 drachmae 4 obols are recorded.[14] The next definitely dated example of the crown-tax in Egypt is P. Hamb. 81 (A.D. 188), although an ἐπιτηρητὴς στεφανικῶν is mentioned in a list of land-tax payers dated first or second century.[15] Since it was not the policy of the Roman government in Egypt to increase the rates of the regular taxes, the financial stress which began with Marcus Aurelius made the additional revenue from the crown-tax particularly welcome. Other occasions than the emperor's accession seem to have been found for levying the *aurum coronarium* in Egypt. Triumphs, anniversaries, and similar festivities may have been deemed sufficient excuse for assessing the tax, and it is a striking fact that scarcely any of the dated Egyptian receipts or accounts of the tax can be made to coincide with the year of an emperor's accession.[16] Late in the second half of the second century, the theory of the crown-tax was so far forgotten that the στεφανικόν became an annual exaction. As such, however, it lost its agreeable character as a source of extraordinary revenue. Consequently such emperors as Caracalla and Elagabalus demanded the *aurum coronarium* on every conceivable occasion and in addition to the annual crown-tax.

PO. XIV. 1659 is an account of the crown-tax from the Oxyrhynchite nome dated in the reign of Elagabalus. It lists receipts from the six toparchies of the Oxyrhynchite nome during a period of five days during which a total of 12 talents 5,890 drachmae 4 obols 1 chalcus was received.[17] In addition there is a comparatively small amount recorded from the Hermopolite nome to which a village formerly on the border of the Oxyrhynchite nome had been added, apparently after the assessment for the nomes had been fixed. It is interesting to note that an excess of 206 drachmae over the assessment had been collected in three villages, and that an arrangement for abatement had been made by an official with the title ὁ πρὸς παραδοχῇ; but the paragraph recording this abatement was cancelled by the scribe.

Such exactions could not be continued indefinitely, and it is to the credit of Severus Alexander that he promised to remit the crown-tax.[18] Receipts from the latter part of his reign, however, indicate that the tax was collected at least twice.[19] Either the emperor's generosity failed him, or he may never have intended to remit the annual στεφανικόν.[20]

There is evidence that the crown-tax was collected on land in the third century, both at Thebes and in the Oxyrhynchite nome.[21] In the Oxyrhynchite nome private land (γῆ ἰδιωτική) paid at the rate of 8 drachmae an arura; the rate on domain land is not given. The edict of Aemilius Saturninus providing a levy of 8 drachmae an arura probably refers to the crown-tax.[22] In the only extant receipt from Thebes 4 drachmae were paid as the tax on $\frac{1}{6}$ arura, which appears to indicate a levy of 24 drachmae an arura, a rate three times that at Oxyrhynchus.[23] It is not certain that this levy on land was the annual στεφανικόν, but this seems probable.[24]

Special collectors were appointed to assess and collect the crown-tax. The vote of the senate of Oxyrhynchus to provide a further appropriation of 12 talents for a gold crown for the emperor Aurelian indicates the responsibility of the senate in raising the local levy.[25] The ease of collecting large sums by means of this tax led to its abuse by the emperors during the financial stress at the end of the second century and in the third century. The large amounts collected indicate that the στεφανικόν was a burden which fell heavily on the moderately well-to-do, and the repetition of such a tax at too frequent intervals amounted to confiscation of a large part of their capital.[26] Since the instability of the Roman government in the third century seriously interfered with commerce, it became impossible to restore the fortunes of the upper middle-class after such depredations on the part of the treasury, for the economy of Egypt was dependent upon the sale of its exports to obtain money to meet the taxes paid to Rome. Furthermore, the rich booty in cash from the crown-tax (and later in goods from special taxes in kind) seems to have been a factor in the neglect of ordinary sources of revenue and to have led to the abandonment of parts of the system of dikes and canals with attendant deterioration of cultivable land. From this decline in agriculture, despite the valiant efforts of Aurelian and Probus to restore the irrigation system,[27] Egypt never fully recovered.

Σωματικόν

WO. II. 1052 is a receipt issued apparently by the laographi ὑπὲρ σωματικοῦ. Wilcken supposed that it was a tax connected with the λαογραφία, or possibly a tax on slaves (σώματα).[28] Grenfell and Hunt in commenting on an occurrence of σο( ) in P. Teb. I. 95. 10 (Ptolemaic period) denied that the tax could refer to slaves.

Τέλος ταφῶν (?)

A tax in connexion with a burial is mentioned in a document, concerned with the consignment of a mummy, published by Spiegelberg in *Archiv*, I. 340. Wilcken in a note (p. 342) suggested that this tax was identical with the τέλος ταφῆς, found in the Theban ostraca, which was collected by the ἐπιτηρητ(αὶ) τέλ(ους) ἱματιοπωλ(ῶν).[29] It is probable, however, that the tax in the document published by Spiegelberg was paid for the burial itself, for such a tax is known from demotic ostraca of the Ptolemaic period.[30] P. Ryl. II. 95 indicates the farming of the collection at Oxyrhynchus of fees of 4 drachmae and of 5 obols in connexion with burials. O. Tait, p. 160, no. 51, records a tax for burial (τέλος νεκροτάφων) for which at least 5 drachmae were paid.

Τόκ(ος) διοική(σεως)

This item is included in a list recording payments of taxes and dues (PO. VII. 1046). It does not seem to be a tax, however, but it is perhaps interest on credits borrowed from the government for the purchase of land from the public domain. In P. Iand. 141 (and in the tax-rolls in the collection of the University of Michigan, of which P. Iand. 141 is a column) there are records of payments made for land purchased from the διοίκησις as well as from the account of the Idiologus. This land had been confiscated by the treasury, for the names of the previous owners were used to identify the plots of land.

$$Τραπ(εζιτικόν)$$

In an account of various assessments (μερισμοί) in PO. III. 574 two obols are paid for τραπ(εζιτικόν). The editors suggested that it was perhaps a tax for the support of an official bank.

COLLECTION OF TAXES IN MONEY

FARMING of taxes seems to have been introduced into Egypt by the Ptolemies.[1] Their officials continued direct collection of the grain-taxes, as had been the practice under the Pharaohs; but after the introduction of Ptolemaic coinage taxes assessed in money and even the tithe (ἀπόμοιρα) paid in kind were farmed to contractors. The finance ministers of the Ptolemies were not content, however, to allow these contractors to make their collections without any supervision or control. To each contractor was assigned an ἀντιγραφεύς who supervised the collections, prevented extortion (so far as possible), and made sure that the revenues were paid into the treasury in accordance with the provisions of the contract. Because of this close regulation by the agents of the government and also because of the nicety with which the revenues had been calculated by the financial administration, it was difficult for the tax-farmer to make a large profit, even under favourable circumstances. The decree of Ti. Julius Alexander reveals that in the first century of Roman rule tax-farmers were obliged to accept contracts against their will, although the officials of the province had no legal right to compel contractors to submit bids.[2] Rostovtzeff has conjectured that in the last century of Ptolemaic rule a similar condition existed, and that under Roman administration the widespread practice of direct collection by πράκτορες and similar agents was the inevitable development of the system of compulsory contracts.[3] The Roman practor, Rostovtzeff maintained, was forced to assume a liturgy, since he could not hope to make a reasonable profit from the collection of taxes and, indeed, more often faced a deficit in the revenue—a deficit for which he was responsible with his personal fortune.

The practor had existed in the Ptolemaic period. His duties in connexion with taxation, so far as is known, were then confined to the collection of fines and arrears, although he stepped in to collect taxes when, because of exceptional circumstances, the contract of the tax-farmer had been suspended or cancelled. Wilcken, arguing against Rostovtzeff's theory of a gradual decline in tax-farming in Egypt, has remarked that in the rest of the empire there occurred a definite change in the policy of the Roman government in regard to tax-farming.[4] Mommsen[5] dated this change in the second half of the reign of Tiberius: at that time the collection of the majority of taxes was put in the hands of official collectors, and only the taxes on auctions, inheritances, and emancipation of slaves, and the customs-dues (*portoria*) were farmed. After the reign of Trajan only the *portoria* were farmed. Wilcken pointed out that in the reign of Tiberius ostraca from Thebes show that the bath-tax, introduced as a capitation tax by the Romans and at first collected by a tax-farmer ($\tau\epsilon\lambda\dot{\omega}\nu\eta s$), was collected by a practor.[6] Yet the shift from $\tau\epsilon\lambda\dot{\omega}\nu\eta s$ to $\pi\rho\dot{\alpha}\kappa\tau\omega\rho$ in the collection of the bath-tax was but a minor matter, and Wilcken has perhaps attached too much importance to it, for the extant tax-receipts do not indicate very great activity of the practors until the end of the first century after Christ. There was not in Egypt so pressing a need for reform of tax-collection as in the other provinces, for Ptolemaic Egypt had never experienced the extortion and corruption of provincial administration under the Roman Republic. Furthermore, both Rostovtzeff and Wilcken seem to have underestimated the importance of the state banks in the collection of taxes in Egypt.

It was once believed that the Ptolemaic $\beta\alpha\sigma\iota\lambda\iota\kappa\alpha\grave{\iota}$ $\tau\rho\dot{\alpha}\pi\epsilon\zeta\alpha\iota$ were tax-offices and that the $\tau\rho\alpha\pi\epsilon\zeta\hat{\iota}\tau\alpha\iota$ were tax-collectors.[7] Wilcken and Lumbroso, however, were able to show that the $\tau\rho\dot{\alpha}\pi\epsilon\zeta\alpha\iota$ were established in the third century B.C. as depositories for state revenues, and that their primary function was the receipt and disbursement of such funds upon the order of competent officials. But in his anxiety to emphasize this primary function Wilcken seems to have disregarded the possibility that the banks could gradually have acquired the secondary function of receiving the payments of taxes. Many receipts for various taxes issued and signed by the state bankers are extant from both Ptolemaic and Roman times.[8] Wilcken maintained that in the Ptolemaic period the banks received tax-payments only from collectors;[9] but the ledgers and day-books of the Roman period show that taxes were paid directly to the banks, and that the collectors' deposits often formed but a small portion of the entries of tax-payments.[10] The practice of paying taxes directly to the banks probably developed during the Ptolemaic period, for it is not likely that Augustus would have introduced such an unnecessary innovation in financial administration, when he avoided all changes so far as possible. There is no evidence that the state banks underwrote the collection of taxes, as the tax-farmer did and the practor was later compelled to do, but even this is not an absolute impossibility.

After the system of collection in Egypt became fairly well established, as Wilcken has observed,[11] the direct taxes were collected by agents of the government and only the indirect taxes (customs-dues, market- and sales-taxes, income-taxes on trades, and the like) were farmed by the Roman administration. Wilcken[12] considered collectors designated by the terms τελῶναι, μισθωταί, δημοσιῶναι, ἐγλήμπτορες, ἐξειληφότες, πραγματευταί, and ἀσχολούμενοι, to be tax-farmers. Πράκτορες, ἀπαιτηταί, and the μισθωταὶ ἱερᾶς πύλης Σοήνης were official collectors. Ἀπαιτηταί, however, also collected arrears of taxes farmed to publicans, as Wilcken recognized; and Rostovtzeff maintained that the μισθωταὶ ἱερᾶς πύλης Σοήνης, like the other μισθωταί, were tax-farmers.[13] Ἐπιτηρηταί (supervisors), whose title ought to indicate officials of supervision and control like the ἀντιγραφεῖς of the Ptolemaic period, engaged in actual collection and issued receipts for taxes which were ordinarily collected by both publicans and practors (i.e. taxes which were farmed and taxes which were collected directly).

Little is known about tax-farming in Egypt under Roman rule. It is generally assumed that the system was similar to that of the Ptolemaic administration concerning which much more documentary evidence has survived.[14] Perhaps the most illuminating document from the Roman period is PO. i. 44 (dated late in the first century of our era), a letter from Paniscus the strategus of the Oxyrhynchite nome to his assistant, the basilico-grammateus. Paniscus states that the contract for collecting the ἐγκύκλιον and the ἀγορανομεῖον, although offered at auction several times, had attracted no bidders. The previous contractors (δημοσιῶναι) had lost money and when pressed to bid again had threatened to abscond. In this emergency the prefect had been consulted by the strategus and had advised that the terms of the previous contracts be examined and that, so far as possible, the burden of the tax-farmers be lightened. There is no indication that any of the officials contemplated a resort to force to secure bids, a practice which had prevailed earlier in the century, although contrary to law, and against which Hadrian later was obliged to direct a rescript.[15] A little light on the sureties of the tax-farmers, so well attested in the Ptolemaic period, is secured from P. Teb. II. 329 (dated A.D. 139), a petition from a woman who had acted as surety for a lessee of the fisheries-tax on marshes at Tebetnu, Cercesis, and associated villages in the Arsinoite nome. In this capacity she had deposited in the state bank for one of two lessees the sum of 1 talent 1,100 drachmae. After the other lessee assumed sole management of the tax for one year he reimbursed his former partner's surety, and she sought from the strategus a formal release from further responsibility for the collection. P. Ryl. II. 95 seems to be the contractors' formal acceptance of a farmed tax on funerals; unfortunately the document is so fragmentary that the addressee is unknown, and the terms of the contract are quite uncertain.

Men who were nominated as collectors and served under liturgic compulsions were sometimes permitted to delegate the tax-collecting to others. In BGU. IV. 1062 those nominated by the amphodogrammateus to the superintendence of the tax on fine flour (ἐπιτήρησις ὠνῆς πελωχικοῦ) of the city of Oxyrhynchus delegated the task to two others who undertook faithfully to perform all the duties of collection. The new collectors agreed to act as securities for each other.

A curious delegation of tax-collecting is found in P. Fay. 34, from Polydeucia and dated A.D. 161. A certain Heron purchased from the βοηθοὶ γεωργῶν (assistants in connexion with taxes upon cultivators) the right to collect the tax on hay (μονοδεσμία χόρτου) and other taxes of the nomarchy. These taxes are not known to have been farmed, but were ordinarily collected directly. The document, therefore, attests a combination of direct collection with sub-letting to a tax-farmer. Heron agreed to pay 560 drachmae in five equal monthly instalments during the last five months of the year, with an allowance for any amounts paid up to the date of the contract. The collection was to be made on $411\frac{27}{64}$ arurae of land, at the village of Polydeucia, assigned to cultivators from the village of Philagris. It is to be assumed that Heron made some profit on the collection. Such sub-letting of a tax supposed to be collected directly seems not to have been uncommon, for Heron refers to the customs of former years as precedent for the terms of his offer; but no similar contract for collecting any other tax has been found. Presumably the tax was sub-let because of the inconvenience and expense of collecting from residents of another village.

In the first century after Christ the practors seem to have been liturgical officials who were responsible for deficits in their collections but who did not share the publican's opportunity for reasonable profit if the collections were successful.[16] Most of the practors of this period were assigned to collect specific taxes and bore such titles as πράκτορες λαογραφίας, πράκτορες χειρωναξίου γερδίων, and πράκτορες κατακριμάτων.[17] According to P. Teb. II. 391 (dated A.D. 99), the four collectors of the poll-tax (πράκτορες λαογραφίας) at Tebtynis agreed to divide their duties, two of them undertaking the collection at the village, while two concerned themselves with persons registered at the village but who were away from home. The second pair became responsible for the collection of 1,100 silver drachmae each month, and the first pair agreed to make up the monthly balance of the quota for poll-tax and to pay the salary of the armed guard (μαχαιροφόρος). These same collectors were also responsible for the collection of an expected special levy (ἐπικλασμός). Violation of the covenant by any one of the four parties was penalized by a fine of 1,000 drachmae, half to be paid to the party abiding by the provisions, and half to the public treasury. The liturgical character of the πρακτορία is apparent, for a certain sum was to be paid to the treasury each month whether the amount was collected from the tax-payers or not. The difficulties of collectors in exacting taxes from non-residents is illustrated in P. Graux 1 (= SB. 7461), a letter from the strategus of the Arsinoite nome to the strategus of the Heracleopolite nome, who is requested to furnish Nemesas, collector of the poll-tax at Philadelphia, with men to accompany him in order to facilitate collections from Philadelphians residing in the villages of the Heracleopolite nome. This document is dated A.D. 45. About ten years later six πράκτορες λαογραφίας of six villages in the Fayûm appealed to the prefect of Egypt for relief from the responsibility for the collections in their particular villages, inasmuch as the villages had become depopulated 'because some have become impoverished and left and others have died without kin'.[18] Unless relief was granted the collectors threatened to desert their office. This represented a serious condition, for important villages were included among the six named: Philadelphia, Bacchias, Nestus's district, Socnopaei Nesus, Philopator, and Hiera Nesus. In P. Cornell 24, dated A.D. 56, forty-four citizens of Philadelphia were recorded as impoverished tax-payers who could not be found.

There is no evidence that the appeal of the practors was heeded immediately. In fact it is probable that the exactions were somewhat increased during the second half of the first century. In the same fifty years, however, the increasing prosperity of Egypt, which resulted from the development of trade with India, must have relieved the pressure upon the unfortunate tax-payers and rendered collection less difficult. Yet the prosperity of the cities of Egypt attracted peasants away from the land, and so probably increased the collectors' troubles in the country-districts. Philo vividly describes the tortures inflicted by a desperate collector on the relatives and neighbours of a defaulter.[19] Philo's account is open to a charge of rhetorical exaggeration, but the almost impossible task of maintaining tax-collections among the peasantry of Egypt and the spectre of bankruptcy as the result of failure must have frayed the nerves of many a collector. Philo implies that whole villages were deserted because of such exactions.[20]

Trajan was finally obliged to introduce important modifications into the system of tax-collection in Egypt in order to relieve both the publicans and the practors. In his reign were introduced the πράκτορες ἀργυρικῶν, who were charged with the collection of all direct taxes (i.e. the poll-tax, other capitation taxes, fixed taxes in money on land and on live stock, temple-taxes, and licence-taxes on trades).[21] Responsibility for deficits in collection was transferred from the practors to the inhabitants of the various communities. This was accomplished by the introduction of the μερισμὸς ἀνακ(εχωρηκότων) and μερισμὸς ἀπόρων, assessments levied on the more prosperous members of a community to pay the taxes of those who had fled or were incompetent.[22] The publicans who leased the market-tax, at least at Thebes and the vicinity and in the Mendesian nome, were relieved from responsibility for deficits by the introduction there of the μερισμὸς ἐνλείμματος τελωνικῶν ὠνίων.[23] In the reign of Trajan there appear at Elephantine-Syene for the first time μισθωταὶ ἱερᾶς πύλης Σοήνης and ἐπιτηρηταὶ ἱερᾶς πύλης Σοήνης, who collected both direct and indirect taxes, and whose exact status as tax-gatherers, therefore, is a matter of dispute.[24]

In the second century it was customary for the collectors of taxes to be nominated by the village or ward officials, who submitted names to the strategus or to the prefect, and the selection was made by lot. By the beginning of the third century, however, it had become customary for a retiring collector to nominate his successor. It was possible to avoid such service only by ceding one's property to the treasury.[25] In the third century, after the organization of the municipalities, collectors again became responsible for deficits in collections. In a letter, dated by the editor between A.D. 250 and 284, an official threatens a suspected collector and his sureties (ἀπεύθυνοι) with confiscation of their property, if the official finds upon his arrival in the collector's district that the treasury has been deprived of its due revenue.[26] Similarly an official communication, dated A.D. 248, refers to the sequestration of the property of nomarchs and their associates (καὶ τῶν λοιπῶν τῶν ἐνεχομένων, either the nomarchs' sureties or the collectors of nomarchic taxes) and the prytanis who nominated them.[27] Since nominations to office were made by the prytanis in the municipal senate it is probable that the senatorial order as a whole was involved in the responsibility for collections. Certainly the village elders and the citizens shared this responsibility in the villages, for in P. Ryl. II. 219 they are specifically stated to be responsible for the payment of certain charges.[28]

Administration

The general administration of the revenues of Egypt was in the hands of the prefect.[29] This was his most important single function, and Philo states that the prefect spent the greater part of his time each year in the inspection and audit of the accounts of the various nomes, for the task of mastering the details of the financial system was most arduous.[30] The Roman prefect thus assumed the function of the powerful διοικητής, the finance minister of the Ptolemies.[31] His duties in administering the revenues included responsibility for formal announcement of the census every fourteen years, formal requests for extraordinary registration of land, and all similar registrations. He was also responsible for the assessment of taxes, issuing of tax-schedules (gnomons which were made public), supervision of the strategi, who were directly responsible to the prefect for the collection of taxes in their respective nomes, receiving of appeals from tax-payers, and granting of abatements or exemption from taxation to individuals, but ordinarily only after a dispensation from the emperor.[32]

The prefect was not without assistance in the general administration of the revenues, but little is known concerning the bureaucracy at Alexandria. Besides the procurators in charge of the granaries at Neapolis and the Hermeum, there was a *procurator usiacus* who managed the imperial estates in Egypt and who superintended their revenue both in kind and in money.[33] There are also attested an ἐπίτροπος προσόδων Ἀλεξανδρείας and a καθολικός, but their duties are not precisely defined.[34] A Roman διοικητής seems to have been almost wholly confined to judicial functions.[35] The income from property reverting to the treasury because of confiscation and escheat was under the care of the Idiologus. This official also supervised the collection of fines and other irregular income, and so important were his functions that his bureau formed a separate department of the treasury.[36] After his office was combined with that of the High Priest of All Egypt (perhaps under Hadrian) the Idiologus relieved the prefect of the burden of supervising the revenues of the temples.[37]

The three epistrategi were not directly concerned with the collection of taxes except, possibly, with the internal customs-dues collected on goods crossing the boundaries of the nomes.[38]

The strategi were responsible to the prefect for the payment in full of the quota of taxes assigned to their respective nomes.

It was to the strategi that the prefect addressed requests for reports concerning various matters connected with taxation, and the strategus in turn demanded the information from the collectors or other subordinate officials.[39] The basilico-grammateus acted as assistant to the strategus in all such phases of administration. Under the strategus was the army of tax-collectors immediately responsible for the collection of taxes in the local districts.[40] The strategus, with the approval of the prefect or his representative, selected practors from the lists of those liable to such liturgical offices and leased to tax-farmers various indirect taxes.[41] To the strategus (and the basilico-grammateus) the various tax-gatherers made formal reports of their collections.[42]

The nomarch had under his supervision those taxes whose yield could not be accurately determined in advance.[43] He was a subordinate of the strategus, but he was allowed to select the πράκτορες νομαρχικῶν ἀσχοληµάτων who collected taxes under his supervision.[44] Officials of subdivisions of the nome, the µεριδάρχης and the τοπάρχης, were also concerned with the collection of taxes, but evidence is lacking for a precise definition of their competence.[45]

Assessment

In the assessment of taxes the prefect of Egypt exercised control. The emperor at Rome determined the total amount of the annual revenues to be exacted, probably basing his estimate on reports furnished by the prefect, and communicated this amount to the prefect.[46] Adjustment of the assessment was ordinarily made at the issuing of the prefect's edict every five years.[47] The emperor himself was the only court of appeal from the decision of the prefect in regard to partial or full exemption from taxes paid by individuals, although in some cases the prefects dared to ignore the exemptions granted by the emperor.[48] Some of the prefects even levied extra assessments without the consent of the emperor.[49] On the other hand, the prefect could, in time of emergency, reduce the assessment for a whole district,[50] although abatements materially affecting the total revenues from a district ordinarily could be authorized only by the emperor.

The assessment of taxes in Egypt was based upon a highly

developed system of records and accounting. The exact quota for each nome was assessed by a board of eclogistae of the several nomes. The bureau (λογιστήριον) in Alexandria of the eclogistes of each nome has been mentioned in the chapter on collection of taxes in kind.[51] There the eclogistes, with a corps of subordinates, carried on the preliminary work of assessment. A strategus apparently had some power, perhaps only delegated by the prefect, to modify unreasonable exactions of the eclogistes of his nome.[52] Since it was in the bureaux of the eclogistae that peculation and extortion were most feasible, Reinmuth has well remarked, 'The prefects apparently tried to moderate the exactions of the eclogistae to that fine point at which the people paid all that they could without growing restless or rebellious, always mindful of the disturbance caused by the coming of the Roman tax-collectors to the Thebaid and of the fact that political unrest diminished the revenues'.[53]

The numerous records sent from the various villages and towns supplied the information necessary for the assessments. For the taxes collected in money upon land the cadastre, prepared from the reports of the comogrammateus, formed the basis of the assessment, and the taxes were reckoned in accordance with tax-schedules which were issued by authority of the prefect.[54] Such a schedule, or gnomon, for taxes on garden-land is found in P. Ghent 1 which establishes the rate for each of the various taxes on land divided into several categories according to culture, and the rate only requires multiplication by the number of arurae reported under cultivation in the cadastre to give the total of the tax.[55] Indeed, examples of such calculations are included in the text of the gnomon for the enlightenment of the functionaries in the local λογιστήρια. The assessment of the taxes on animals required reference to the ἀπογραφαί submitted annually by their owners, and there were doubtless gnomons setting forth the rates of taxes on the different kinds of animals. For the collection of the poll-tax and various other capitation taxes the census, taken every fourteen years by order of the prefect, furnished the necessary data concerning the classes of people liable to taxation, and from the records of the census could be quickly prepared the ἀπαιτήσιμα for these taxes.[56] The capitation taxes limited to certain classes of people, such as the ἀριθμητικὸν κατοίκων and the Jewish tax, required reference to special registers.[57] The assessment of capitation taxes on trades may have been based in part on the census returns, but the officials of the various guilds must have been required to report the names of the members of the guild, and the amount due from each was determined by reference to a gnomon. The *ad valorem* taxes on trades, which could not be exactly determined in advance, were assessed by reference to gnomons (such as P. Lond. Inv. 1562 *verso* cited in Chapter XIII above) and must have required a report of individual transactions. Similarly the market-taxes and customs-dues, which were farmed to publicans or assigned to ἐπιτηρηταί, were set down in tax-schedules such as the νόμος τελωνικός in PO. 1. 36 (= W. *Chrest.* 273) and P. Lond. iii. 928 (p. 190) and iii. 856 (p. 91 = W. *Chrest.* 274).[58]

Collection of Taxes in Money

On the basis of the ἀπαιτήσιμα produced in the λογιστήρια were made the collections. Payments were made in full or by instalments, and the privilege of making partial payments was particularly used in the taxes whose amounts were large, such as the poll-tax, the χειρωνάξιον, and the γεωμετρία, or when it was desirable to combine a partial payment of one tax with the full payment of another in order that the amounts given to the collector might be in even tetradrachms.[59] When the tax-payer had paid his tax he received a receipt, possession of which freed him from further obligation.[60]

In many localities of both Upper and Lower Egypt the tax-payer could make his payment at the local bank, usually a state bank but sometimes apparently a private bank.[61] This was a convenience to the tax-payer, who thus had some opportunity of making the payment when it suited him, and if he paid his tax in good time he was not hounded by the collector. Payment at the banks was a greater convenience to the government, however, since it was not necessary for the tax-collectors to search out every individual tax-payer. It is possible that the tax-collectors were present at the bank in a given locality on specified days to receive taxes,[62] and that the rest of their time was devoted to locating the more reluctant payers and extracting taxes from them. Thus in practice the practors may have continued for some time to be what they had been in the Ptolemaic period—collectors of fines, arrears, or payments that were merely slow.

Conditions varied widely in the different sections of Egypt, and it is improbable that the system of collecting taxes remained uniform throughout the country during the centuries of Ptolemaic rule. The Roman government was slow to introduce changes that did not seem necessary, and consequently the system of collection does not reveal a uniform development in the various nomes during the three centuries of Roman rule. This lack of uniformity may be seen by a study of the methods of collecting various taxes in the different nomes of Egypt.

1. Elephantine-Syene

There is, unfortunately, some uncertainty about the collectors of taxes and the role of the bank in collection at Elephantine-Syene during the first hundred years of Roman rule. O. Strass. 58, dated A.D. 8, is a receipt issued by a τραπεζίτης named Asclas for the weavers' tax (τέλος γερδικ(όν)). WO. II.2, dated A.D. 13, is signed by the τραπεζίτης, but the name of the payment is lost, so that it is not entirely certain that the payment was made for a tax. Viereck lists a number of receipts (O. Strass. 120–40), for poll-tax and other capitation taxes, as issued by the state bank; but this is only a deduction, though probably correct, from the formula of the receipts,[63] since they were not signed with the title of the τραπεζίτης or of the collector. No practor is named in receipts from Elephantine-Syene before A.D. 83–4 when the name of Socrates is found, and even then his title does not appear on the ostracon; but it is assumed that he is identical with the Socrates who signed himself πράκ(τωρ) in an ostracon of the year A.D. 91–2.[64] It is possible that receipts issued by collectors without title prior to A.D. 83–4, as well as later, were given either by practors or by banks. Such receipts are common from A.D. 18 to 118.[65] More of them record payments of poll-tax than of all other taxes combined, but among the taxes named on these receipts are χειρωνάξιον, γεωμετρία φοινίκων, ἐννόμιον, and assessments for river-guards, embankments, a statue of Trajan, and undesignated purposes. Some receipts were issued after A.D. 118 by collectors who did not name their title; but the number is so small that it is impossible to determine whether the omission of the title is mere accident or the idiosyncracy of a few collectors, or has some meaning now obscure.[66]

Collectors who signed themselves simply πράκτωρ appear from A.D. 91-2 to 140.[67] Their chief duty was the collection of the poll-tax down to the reign of Hadrian, but during that reign only one extant receipt for λαογραφία was issued by a practor at Elephantine-Syene.[68] The practors also collected the χειρωνάξιον. In one receipt a practor is associated with the ἐπιτηρηταί in collecting the μερισμὸς ἀνακ(εχωρηκότων).[69] When the μερισμὸς ποταμοφυλακίδος (assessment for the river-guard) was introduced in the reign of Trajan the practors became active in collecting it, and they collected the other assessments for guards, and ὑπὲρ ἀνακ(εχωρηκότων), ὑπὲρ διπλῶν, ὑπὲρ φρουρίου περὶ Φοινίκην, and the general assessments (μερισμοί without special designation). They also issued a few receipts for τιμὴ δημοσίων φοινίκων and a single receipt for εἰσκριτικόν.

In the reign of Trajan, as has been noted above, the πράκτωρ ἀργυρικῶν was introduced, and the earliest appearance of that official in Upper Egypt is found in an ostracon from Elephantine or Syene (WO. II. 1268), a receipt for τιμὴ δημοσίων φοινίκων, dated A.D. 104. A few other receipts have been found that were issued by πράκτορες ἀργυρικῶν without a statement of the particular place from which they came (i.e. whether Elephantine or Syene).[70]

In A.D. 110 collection in Elephantine and Syene seems to have been united, for in WO. II. 1609 a πράκ(τωρ) ἀργ(υρικῶν) Σοή(νης) καὶ Ἐλ(εφαντίνης) issued a receipt for τιμὴ δημ(οσίων) φοι(νίκων). Within a few years, however, the practorship was divided and πράκτορες ἀργυρικῶν Ἐλεφαντίνης (and twice πράκ(τορες) Ἐλεφ(αντίνης)) and πράκτορες ἀργυρικῶν Σοήνης are found. The latter, however, appear in but few receipts. Two πράκτορες ἀργυρικῶν καὶ σιτικῶν Σοήνης issued a receipt for an unknown tax, and three similar officials with their associates (μέτοχοι) at Elephantine issued a receipt for μερισμὸς ποτ(αμοφυλακίδος) καὶ στατ(ίωνος) καὶ πλοίου πραιτωρίου; the dates of both receipts are lost, so that it is impossible to know precisely when the practorships of money-taxes and grain-taxes were combined in this district.[71] The πράκτορες ἀργυρικῶν Σοήνης issued receipts for μίσθ(ωσις) ποταμοφυλακίδος, τιμὴ δημοσίων φοινίκων, and assessments (μερισμοί). At Elephantine the receipts are usually signed by a single practor, but two practors acting together are not uncommon. It is a surprising fact that the πράκτορες ἀργυρικῶν at Elephantine and Syene issued no receipts for λαογραφία, although the collection of the poll-tax was the chief duty of practors at Thebes and in Lower Egypt. The πράκτορες ἀργυρικῶν Ἐλεφαντίνης seem to have been chiefly engaged in the collection of μερισμοί (without any further designation), for they issued 49 receipts therefor, as compared with 23 receipts for all other taxes combined. Of the latter receipts 6 were for μερισμὸς ποταμοφυλακίδος, and at least 2 others were for capitation taxes; 8 were for τιμὴ δημοσίων φοινίκων. Others include payments ὑπὲρ προσόδων φοινίκων, for ἀννώνη, φόρος διώρυγος, ἐνοίκιον οἰκίας, δημόσια, and εἰσκριτικόν.[72]

During the reign of Hadrian and later, when the practors at Elephantine and Syene were busy with the collection of μερισμοί, the poll-tax was collected by the μισθωταὶ ἱερᾶς πύλης Σοήνης, whose receipts for poll-tax are found from A.D. 117 to 164, and by the ἐπιτηρηταὶ ἱερᾶς πύλης Σοήνης, mentioned in receipts for poll-tax from A.D. 121–2 to 171. These officials appear in ostraca first in the reign of Trajan and are found issuing receipts for other taxes from A.D. 114 to 208.[73] The Lessees of the Sacred Gate of Syene and the Overseers occasionally appear on the same receipt.[74] Ordinarily, however, each college issued receipts separately for various taxes, but apparently without any distinction in their sphere of duties. These colleges of collectors also undertook the collection of the χειρωνάξιον. In addition they issued receipts for the different assessments, particularly the δεσμο(φυλακία), which at Elephantine-Syene was regularly collected with the λαογραφία. Furthermore they, or their representatives, issued receipts for γεωμετρία φοινίκων, τιμὴ δημοσίων φοινίκων, and ἡ νομ( ) (or εἰκ-( )) μυροβαλάνων which was collected in kind.[75] An ἐπιτηρητής without further designation is found in WO. II. 85, dated A.D. 113, the earliest appearance of an ἐπιτηρητής at Syene, but since the receipt which he issued was for λαογραφία and διπλῆ, it is probable that he is to be identified with the later ἐπιτηρηταὶ ἱερᾶς πύλης Σοήνης. The receipts issued by the Lessees and Overseers of the Sacred Gate of Syene were frequently signed by assistants (βοηθοί).[76]

Other ἐπιτηρηταί are found at Elephantine-Syene. A college of ἐπιτηρηταὶ πεντηκ(οστῆς) λιμένος, who collected the harbour-tax of 2 per cent. on the value of shipments, is found in O. Strass. 250, dated in the first or second century. These are probably not much different from the two ἐπιτηρηταὶ εἴδους ὁρμο[φυλακίας].[77] The latter probably bore the same relation to the μισθωταὶ εἴδους ὁρμοφυλακίας (who appear in five receipts)[78] as the ἐπιτηρηταὶ ἱερᾶς πύλης Σοήνης do to the μισθωταὶ ἱερᾶς πύλης Σοήνης. Officials called οἱ ἀσχολούμενοι τὴν ὁρμοφυλακίαν Σοήνης also issued six receipts for ἐνόρμιον.[79] The πεντηκοσ(τῶναι) ἱερᾶς πύλης Σοήνης issued a receipt for the tax on exports, and these officials are probably identical with the τελῶναι πεντηκοστῆς.[80] The customs-dues of the Roman empire were ordinarily farmed, and so all these officials connected with the collection of the ἐνόρμιον at Syene may well have been tax-farmers or their overseers.

One receipt for the tax paid by prostitutes (ἑταιρικόν) was issued by a τελώνης ἑταιρικοῦ at Elephantine-Syene in A.D. 111, but a μισθωτὴς χειρωναξίου μηνιαίου καὶ ἑταιρικοῦ signed a receipt for the weavers' tax in A.D. 188.[81]

An ἀπαιτητής is found at Elephantine-Syene in A.D. 173 and 186, but he acts as assistant to the ἐπιτηρηταὶ ἱερᾶς πύλης Σοήνης in the collection of the γ´ νομ( ) μυροβαλάνων in kind.[82] The ἀπαιτητής appears in the place usually occupied by the βοηθός, and in WO. II. 291 the same Marcus Annius Nemonianus, who was ἀπαιτητής (in WO. II. 1460), signs himself βοηθός in a receipt for χειρωνάξιον.

The title of the collectors who issued SB. 4355 (dated A.D. 116), a receipt ὑπὲρ παικίσωνος [καὶ] ὑπὲρ χω( ) ὀψω(νίου), is lost.[83]

2. Thebes

In the Roman period taxes in money, as attested in published receipts, were collected at Thebes from 22–21 B.C. to A.D. 258 by the public bankers who issued the receipts.[84] Since similar receipts are found from the fourth century, it is probable that the practice was followed in the intervening decades. Nowhere in Egypt do the banks seem to have played a more important part in the collection of taxes than at Thebes in both Ptolemaic and Roman periods. The bankers at Thebes gave receipts for various taxes during the first one hundred and fifty years of Roman rule, especially for the poll-tax, bath-tax, dike-tax, taxes for river-guards and for other guards, and similar capitation taxes. They also collected various land-taxes assessed in money (γεωμετρία and ναύβιον) and the various payments for the 'value' of products (τιμὴ πυροῦ, κριθῆς, ἐλαίου, φοινίκων, and χόρτου) whether the latter were intended for the *annona militaris* or the tithe of garden-produce. The trade-taxes of barbers, weavers, builders, and the guild of merchant-fishermen and the tax of donkey-drivers and that on carriages or wagons were occasionally paid to the banks. Other receipts for miscellaneous taxes indicate that the bankers at Thebes were accustomed to receive payments for practically any tax assessed in money.[85] After the first few years of the reign of Trajan the banks seem seldom to have issued receipts for capitation taxes until the end of the second century and the beginning of the third when three receipts for poll-tax signed by bankers are found.[86]

Throughout the greater part of the second century the collection of capitation taxes was carried on at Thebes by the πράκτορες ἀργυρικῶν. The practors at Thebes had previously confined their efforts to the collection of the bath-tax.[87] After the introduction of the πράκτορες ἀργυρικῶν various districts of Thebes were assigned to colleges of varying number or to a single practor. We find one πράκτωρ ἀργυρικῶν μητ(ροπόλεως) or one πράκτωρ καὶ μέτοχοι, one πράκτωρ Μεμνονίων, one or two πράκτορες ἀργυρικῶν Χά(ρακος), two at the South Quarter, one or two at the South-West Quarter, &c. The principle determining the distribution of practorships among the several districts of Thebes is not evident. The number of practors may have depended in part upon the number of tax-payers in a district, or perhaps on the number of men able to act as collectors or as sureties, or possibly the government sometimes attempted to make the πρακτορία more tolerable by dividing the burdens and responsibilities of the practors. It is not impossible that idiosyncrasies of various collectors in signing receipts make the system of distribution of practors seem more complicated than it actually was.

Beginning at least as early as A.D. 107 the πράκτορες ἀργυρικῶν at Thebes collected the poll-tax, bath-tax, dike-tax, and the various assessments (for guards, διπλῶν, ἀνακ(εχωρηκότων), πλινθ( ), and the undesignated μερισμοί). They also collected certain land-taxes (γεωμετρία, τιμὴ φοινίκων, and τιμὴ πυροῦ). They occasionally collected a few of the trades- and market-taxes (τέλος λινύφων, τέλος [λινοπλ]όκ(ων), τέλος ναυπηγῶν, τέλος ἀγορα(νομίας) ὠνίων, and the ἐγκύκλιον), and a few miscellaneous taxes.[88]

Special practors at Thebes included the πράκτωρ τοκ( ), the πράκτωρ βαλανείου, and the πράκτωρ Θεαγῶν who collected the bath-tax in the quarter of the Macedonians, if that was one of the districts at Thebes.[89]

Collectors without titles are not uncommon at Thebes before the introduction of the πράκτορες ἀργυρικῶν in the time of Trajan, but it is difficult to classify them, for they collected the land-taxes in kind, the bath-tax, the τιμὴ πυροῦ and φοινίκων, and the monthly trade-tax (χειρωνάξιον).[90]

The introduction of ἐπιτηρηταί at Thebes was a part of the reorganization of the system of collection in the time of Trajan. The chief purpose of these ἐπιτηρηταί was the collection of the χειρωνάξιον, particularly the weavers' tax (τέλος γερδίων or γερδιακόν) and related taxes (τέλος ἠπητῶν and τέλος ἱματιο-πωλῶν).[91] The ἐπιτηρηταὶ τέλους ἀγορανομίας collected the tax on sales, but the extant receipts show chiefly the tax paid by fishermen. For the latter there were even special ἐπιτηρηταὶ τέλους μεταβολῶν ἁλιέων.[92] There were also special ἐπιτηρηταί of the ferry-tax (πόρθμιον), of the tax on transients (τέλος ἐπιξένων), and of the sales-tax on slaves and boats (τέλος ἐγκυκλίου ἀνδραπόδων καὶ πλοίων).[93]

There are also found at Thebes special ἐπιτηρηταί of certain land-taxes: ἐπιτηρηταὶ νέας ἀμπ(ελίτιδος), ἐπιτηρηταὶ τιμῆς οἴνου, ἐπιτηρηταὶ τιμῆς οἴνου καὶ φοινίκων, ἐπιτηρηταὶ οἴνου καὶ φοινίκων, ἐπιτηρηταὶ κτημάτων γενηματογραφουμένων, and ἐπιτηρηταὶ κατακ( ).[94]

The ἐπιτηρηταὶ τέλους θησαυροῦ ἱερῶν and the τελῶναι τέλους θησαυροῦ ἱερῶν seem to have confined their collection to taxes in kind, except that one payment for βαλανικόν, which one of the latter collected, was compounded for 1 drachma.[95]

Τελῶναι are found at Thebes in receipts dating from A.D. 14 to 178.⁹⁶ Τελῶναι γερδίων (or γερδιακοῦ) collected the weavers' tax before the introduction of the ἐπιτηρηταί and also continued to collect it afterwards. The τελῶναι ἱματιοπωλῶν always collected the τέλος ταφῆς, and there were also special τελῶναι ἠπητῶν. The bath-tax in kind was collected at Thebes and in the vicinity by τελῶναι before the introduction (apparently in the time of Domitian) of the ἐπιτηρηταί and τελῶναι θησαυροῦ ἱερῶν.⁹⁷ Earlier still there was a special τελώνης βαλ(ανείου) who collected the bath-tax assessed in money, but who was displaced by the πράκτωρ βαλ(ανευτικοῦ) in the reign of Tiberius.⁹⁸

Τελῶναι ṽ collected the export and import dues, and also the 2 per cent. tax on sales, for a τελώνης πεντ(ηκοστῆς) issued a receipt for the tax on wood which had been purchased.⁹⁹ A τελώνης ὠνί(ων) ὑποτελ(ῶν) and a τελ(ώνης) ἀγο(ρανομίας?) are also found. Other special τελῶναι were the τελώνης ὑκῆς (pig-tax), τελώνης νή(σου), τελῶναι λαχ(ανικοῦ?), τελῶναι ἀμαξικοῦ, τελῶναι ὀνηλατικοῦ, and the τελῶναι ρ καὶ ιᵏ who issued a receipt for what may have been an inheritance-tax.¹⁰⁰

There is little evidence for μισθωταί at Thebes. O. Strass. 251, which Viereck states is from Upper Egypt, is a receipt issued by the μισθωταὶ τέλους ἀγ(ορανομίας) ὠνίων. In his index to WO. II Wilcken lists Ammonius of Thebes among the μισθωταί, although his title is lost from the ostracon; he collected the ἐγκύκλιον.

'Απαιτηταί at Thebes are found in receipts of the Roman period from A.D. 62 to 216.¹⁰¹ The only tax regularly collected by them was the μερισμός for the deficit of the sales-tax, and at least half of the published receipts issued by ἀπαιτηταί at Thebes record that tax.¹⁰² The majority of the remainder are for special assessments of various kinds, especially for the repair or construction of public buildings, canals, statues of the emperors, and similar projects.¹⁰³ Three receipts issued by ἀπαιτηταί record the collection of the μερισμὸς προχ(ρείας).¹⁰⁴ An ἀπ[αιτ(ητὴς)] τέλ(ους) ἐγκυ(κλίου) appears in A.D. 154–5, and two ἀπαιτηταί collected the dike-tax and bath-tax.¹⁰⁵ Once (in A.D. 194) the τιμὴ οἴνου καὶ φοινίκων was collected by ἀπαιτηταί, but this looks like a special collection for the *annona militaris* in Egypt; in A.D. 192 an ἀπαιτ(ητὴς) κυ(άμων) is found and he was probably also making a special collection for the military annona.[106]

Several special collectors at Thebes are listed by Wilcken in the index to the second volume of *Griechische Ostraka* (p. 465 f.): προστάτης θεοῦ (or φέννησις), λαογράφοι (?), οἱ ἐπὶ τῶν παρα-κ(αταθηκῶν), οἱ ἐπὶ τοῦ καθ( ), βαλανεῖς, and a στρατιώτης. Three village elders (πρεσβύτεροι Μεμνονίων) collected an assessment of 4 obols for λιθινοῦ ὀφρίου in PSI. III. 263, and a γραμματεὺς θησαυροῦ issued a receipt for χω(ματικόν?) in O. Theb. 98.

3. *Other Towns in Upper Egypt*

At Hermonthis near Thebes there is evidence for practors of money-taxes (πράκτορες ἀργυρικῶν) who collected the λαογραφία in A.D. 158,[107] but in another payment of the same tax the βοηθός of the λαογράφος seems to have given a receipt in the reign of Marcus Aurelius.[108] Τελῶναι ν̄, as usual, collected the tax of 2 per cent. on exports and imports.[109] Many receipts for taxes at Hermonthis issued by other tax-farmers in the Ptolemaic period are listed in Wilcken's index in the second volume of *Griechische Ostraka*, but these tax-farmers are not attested for the Roman period in the comparatively few extant receipts from that site.

From Coptos there are but few receipts for taxes paid in money during the three centuries of Roman rule. Most of these were issued by the banks at Coptos where the bank of Hermias received payments for τιμὴ πυροῦ διοικήσεως and τιμὴ κρότωνος in 4 B.C., while the state bank (βασιλικὴ τράπεζα) of Apollonius[110] and his partner Macron issued receipts for λαογραφία, χωματικόν, and ὑπὲρ φυλάκων.[111] A receipt for various assessments (μάγ-δωλοι, δεσμοφυλακία, and διπλῆ) was issued by a γραμματεύς presumably of the πράκτορες ἀργυρικῶν.[112] In O. Strass. 780 from Papa in the Coptite nome a practor of Memnonia issues a receipt for λαογραφία and χωματικόν in A.D. 29; this ostracon is stated to be a copy of a receipt for a payment made through the exchange-bank (κολλυβιστικὴ τράπεζα) in Papa. Special τελῶναι γερδιακοῦ collected the weavers' tax in A.D. 16.[113] Other tax-farmers are attested at Coptos in the Ptolemaic period, but have not been found in Roman receipts.

The extant receipts from Apollonopolis Magna (Edfu) were probably issued by the state bank. Some of the receipts include the phrase διέγρα(ψε), which is similar to the phraseology of ostraca bearing receipts issued by the state banks at Thebes and elsewhere.[114] The receipts include payments for poll-tax, various assessments (φύλακες, σκόπελοι, χωματικόν, βαλανευτικόν, διλ (?)), undesignated μερισμοί, Ἰουδαίων τέλεσμα, and the φόρος προβάτων.[115]

Of the ostraca from Tentyra (Denderah) only one gives any indication of the agency of collection, and it records a payment for μυροβάλανοι which was made at the bank in Tentyra (τέτα(κται) ἐπὶ τὴν ἐν Τεντύ(ρᾳ) τρά(πεζαν)).[116] The formulae of the other receipts written in Greek is consistent with the supposition that all of them were issued by the bank.

A company of practors gave a receipt at Pselkis about A.D. 217, but the tax has not been preserved.[117] At Τωῦτ the τελῶναι ῡ collected the toll on a donkey-load of bones and dates.[118] Τελῶναι and δημοσιῶναι are mentioned in a decree concerned with taxation in the first century after Christ and found at Ombos.[119] A receipt for poll-tax found at El-Kab gives no indication of the agency of collection.[120]

Among the receipts from Upper Egypt, but for which no definite provenience has been recorded, a payment for πηχισμός was made to practors in the first or second century.[121] Πράκτορες ἀργυρικῶν collected the dike-tax and also the bath-tax in O. Strass. 202 and 214. Ἐπιτηρηταὶ ἀγορανομίας and μισθωταὶ τέλους ἀγορανομίας ὠνίων collected the market-tax in Upper Egypt, but it is probable that many of the receipts actually came from Thebes.[122] Ἀπαιτηταί collected the μερισμὸς ὠνίων and also some special assessment for which 1 drachma 2 cermata were paid in A.D. 62.[123] O. Strass. 291 suggests by its formula (τετελ(ώνηται)) that the collectors of the mysterious κιθ( ) ἀργυρίου Σε( ) were tax-farmers (τελῶναι). On the basis of formulae Viereck assigned to the state bank many ostraca from Upper Egypt recording payments for poll-tax, dike-tax, bath-tax, crown-tax, a payment for palm-land, several assessments (μερισμὸς καˡ, ἀννώνης, α.τ( ) λη(μμάτων)), and a few miscellaneous taxes.[124] Similarly many receipts, judging from their formulae, were certainly issued by practors or other collectors, but the titles are lost or were never included; these receipts include payments for the rent of a bath (βαλανικὸς φόρος), bath-tax, τέλος ἐπιξένων, γεωμετρία, μερισμὸς ἀνακ(εχωρηκότων), and a φόρος of some kind.[125]

4. The Arsinoite Nome

We are not well informed about the methods of collecting taxes in the Arsinoite nome during the first century of Roman rule because of the scarcity of receipts as compared with Upper Egypt. The day-books and registers of the poll-tax and other capitation taxes from Philadelphia and Theadelphia found in the Princeton and Columbia papyri, which were evidently prepared by banks, testify to the activity of the bankers in the collection of those taxes in the first and second centuries.[126] Similarly P. Fay. 335 is a list of payments of some tax, probably the poll-tax, to the bank.[127] The ἐγκύκλιον and the τέλος ἐκστάσεως were frequently paid directly to the bank and credited to the account of the nomarch, and in one receipt the bank is called τράπεζα νομαρχίας.[128] In two receipts the internal customs-dues seem to have been paid at the bank.[129] The state banks also served as the repositories for collections made by practors and other collectors.[130]

A practor is mentioned in A.D. 3 at Theadelphia in a petition of a δημόσιος γεωργός, but the competence of the practor is not revealed (SB. 7376). A practor's assistants (χειρισταί) are mentioned in a register of collections of poll-tax (συντάξιμον) in P. Princeton 8, from Philadelphia and dated A.D. 27–32,[131] although the register seems to have been prepared by the bank at Philadelphia. Practors were also active in connexion with an assessment on (or an assignment of) land in the first century.[132] Practors without any qualifying title are mentioned in receipts and registers and various other tax-documents from A.D. 106 to the end of the second century, and they collected almost every variety of direct taxes; but these practors are probably to be identified with the πράκτορες ἀργυρικῶν, who were introduced into the Fayûm at least as early as A.D. 103–4,[133] for they collect about the same taxes.

When the πράκτορες ἀργυρικῶν were introduced in the reign of Trajan, the same variation in the number of practors issuing

receipts may be found at the different villages of the Fayûm
as was observed in the various districts of Thebes.[134] The
πράκτορες ἀργυρικῶν collected the poll-tax, dike-tax, and the
various assessments for guards and the like, the land-taxes in
money, the nomarchic taxes, the taxes on animals, taxes paid
by priests and temples, various φόροι, the σύνταξις, ἀριθμητικὸν
κατοίκων, general assessments, occasionally certain trade-taxes,
and sundry miscellaneous taxes.[135]

Special practors are found in documents from the Arsinoite
nome. A single collector of the poll-tax at Philadelphia (πράκτωρ
λαογραφίας Φιλαδελφίας) is mentioned in official correspondence
concerned with arrears of that tax in A.D. 45 (SB. 7461). About
ten years later the πράκτωρ λαογραφίας of the same town and
those of five other towns· appealed to the prefect to protect
them against losses from the decrease in population caused by
death and by the flight of the tax-payers.[136] At the end of the
century four πράκτορες λαογραφίας of the town of Tebtynis
made an agreement as to the division of the collection of the
poll-tax in their district and of an expected special assessment
(ἐπικλασμός).[137] A hundred years later a possible reference to a
πράκτωρ λα(ογραφίας?) is found in a daybook of receipts of
taxes.[138] In A.D. 204, if the reading in P. Teb. II. 595 is correct,
a πράκ(τωρ) λα[ο(γραφίας)] gave a receipt for 100 drachmae.[139]
A πράκτωρ λαογραφίας is mentioned in BGU. VII. 1617, dated
in A.D. 198 (or possibly 227).

The increasing use of the extraordinary levies of the crown-
tax required special collectors in the Fayûm, and πράκτορες
στεφανικῶν are found at Theogonis in A.D. 181–2 (or 213–14),
at Socnopaei Nesus in A.D. 199, Ptolemais Nea in the same
year, and at Nilopolis, Bacchias, Caranis, and the village of
Nestus at the beginning of the third century.[140] The office
must have existed at Euhemeria also, since it is included
in a γραφὴ λειτουργῶν, dated early in the third century, where
it appears that a πόρος of 1,000 drachmae was required for
the office.

A special practor sometimes collected the taxes under the
supervision of the nomarch, for a report of a comarch to
the nomarch mentions the πρακτορία νομαρχικῶν ἀσχολημάτων
ζυτηρᾶς καὶ μονοδεσμιῶν καὶ ἄλλων εἰδῶν.[141] This is confirmed

by the appearance of a πράκτωρ νομαρχικῶν in BGU. III. 711, from Bacchias and Hephaestias and dated A.D. 211.

A πράκτωρ τῶν προσόδων is mentioned in connexion with the στέφανος paid for transfer of property in the reign of Augustus (BGU. IV. 1123). Two πράκτορες δερμάτων χωρούντων εἰς κατασκευὴν ὅπλων are found in the third century; they collected 8 drachmae for one skin.[142] A πράκτωρ οὐσίας received from the village elders a payment of 700 drachmae for φόρος προβάτων.[143]

Ἀπαιτηταί are not commonly found in the Fayûm. At Caranis ἀπαιτηταί gave a receipt for ἀριθμητικὸν κατοίκων in A.D. 179–80, but on the same papyrus the receipt for the next payment made five years later is signed by the πράκτορες ἀργυρικῶν.[144] In P. Grenf. I. 50 an ἀπαιτητής gave a receipt for a tax which is not certain, but has been read as δίδραχμον γερδίων; the receipt was issued in A.D. 260.

The collection of taxes on trades in the Arsinoite nome was under the supervision of ἐπιτηρηταί.[145] At Philadelphia there was an ἐπιτηρητὴς γερδιακοῦ who collected the weavers' tax. An ἐπιτηρητὴς λεσ(ωνείας) is attested at Apias, but the tax which he collected is not understood. The carpenters (τέκτονες) at Tebtynis paid their trade-tax (δημόσια) to the ἐπιτηρητὴς κοπ[ῆς . . .], and at the same town was an ἐπιτηρητὴς . . . ἐλαικῆς καὶ ἄλλων προσόδων. An ἐπιτηρητής in BGU. I. 199 verso seems to be connected with the collection of a tax paid by painters (εἴδη γενῶν ζωγραφικῶν) at Socnopaei Nesus, and there the ἐπιτηρηταὶ τελωνικῶν collected various dues apparently in connexion with government leases (φόρος γενῶν ζωγραφικῶν, φόρος πλοίων ἁλιευτικῶν, &c.). At Socnopaei Nesus also the ἐπιτηρηταὶ κοπῆς ⟨καὶ⟩ τριχός collected the trade-tax from the fullers and dyers. At Tebtynis the ἐπιτηρητὴς ἱερατικῶν ὠνῶν collected the trade-tax of the γερδιοραβδιστής.

Leases of government property and monopolies were superintended by ἐπιτηρηταί in the Fayûm. Hunting and fishing rights in the marshes were leased by ἐπιτηρηταί in the various districts.[146] The superintendence of the weavers' trade (ἱστωναρχία) was leased from the ten ἐπιτηρηταὶ μισθοῦ βαφικῆς (superintendents of leasing the dyers' business).[147] At Ptolemais Nea the rent for government property (ἐνοίκιον) was paid to ἐπιτηρηταί.¹⁴⁸ The government's monopoly of alum (στυπτηρία) was under the care of ἐπιτηρηταί.¹⁴⁹ There were also super-intendents of the writing-bureau of Arsinoë (ἐπιτηρηταὶ γραφείου μητροπόλεως).¹⁵⁰ Other ἐπιτηρηταί in the Arsinoite nome included those supervising confiscated property (γενηματογρα-φούμενα ὑπάρχοντα), revenues from imperial estates (οὐσιακά), estates belonging to the corporation of the city of Alexandria, the public steelyard at Ptolemais Harbour (σταθμὸς Πτολε-μαΐδος Ὅρμου), brokerage (ἑρμηνία), &c.¹⁵¹

In the Arsinoite nome the ἐπιτηρηταί were assisted in their collection of trades-taxes by ἐγλήμπτορες, who were particularly employed in lifting the taxes paid by the weavers. At Phila-delphia in A.D. 123 the ἐγλήμπτορες γερδίων καὶ ἄλλων received the tax paid by the weavers, although the actual collection was made by an assistant (χειριστής) to the ἐγλήμπτορες.¹⁵² Ἐγλήμ-πτορες χειρωναξίου κοπῆς καὶ τριχός, collectors of the taxes paid by those who prepared the wool for weaving, are attested at Theadelphia and Socnopaei Nesus in the second half of the second century.¹⁵³ At Philadelphia from A.D. 143 to 146 an ἐγλήμπτωρ διπλώματος ὄνων νόμου καὶ ἄλλων ὠνῶν (collector of the license of donkeys in the nome and of other farmed taxes) issued the receipts for the license of horses.¹⁵⁴ At Caranis in A.D. 72 a request for a license to sell wool was directed to the ἐγλήμπτωρ ζυγοστασίου μητροπόλεως καὶ νόμων καὶ ἄλλων ὠνῶν (collector of the weigh-station of the metropolis and of the nomes and of other farmed taxes).¹⁵⁵

According to P. Teb. II. 287 an ἐξεταστὴς τέλους χειρωναξίου had once demanded too high a tax from the fullers and dyers in the Arsinoite nome, and an appeal by the injured tradesmen to the courts had been successful. Since the official who simi-larly made a higher exaction from them at a later date was called ἐπιτηρητὴς τέλους χειρωναξίου, it is probable that the duties of the two officials were similar.

Ἐπιτηρηταί collected the internal customs-dues in the Arsi-noite nome in the second century. One served at the toll-gate in Bacchias and one at that in Socnopaei Nesus.¹⁵⁶ They were assisted by secretaries and by armed guards.¹⁵⁷

At Socnopaei Nesus μισθωταὶ κοπῆς καὶ χειρ(ωναξίου) issued a receipt to a priest for a trade-tax (χειρωνάξιον) and for rent of

some kind (φόρος βL).¹⁵⁸ In receipts from the Fayûm μισθωταί
are attested in connexion with the tax for desert-guards (δεσμοφυλακία) when the caravan route through the Prosopite and
Letopolite nomes was used; these μισθωταί issued the pass for
camels (σύμβολον καμήλων).¹⁵⁹ A μισθωτὴς διπλώματος ὄνων
(farmer of the licence-tax on donkeys) issued a receipt for the
tax on one donkey paid by a mechanic.¹⁶⁰ A μισθωτὴς τέλους
ἱεροῦ βουκόλων (an obscure tax for a temple) is attested in a
receipt found at Theadelphia and dated A.D. 183.¹⁶¹ The payment of the πρεσβύτεροι (κώμης?) for the obscure πλείθου νόμου
is made to two μισθωταί at Polydeucia in A.D. 227–8.¹⁶² A
μισθωτὴς εἴδους ἐγκυκλίου καὶ ὑποκειμένων βασιλικῷ γραμματεῖ
is found in P. Paris 17. 22; this combination of dues is unique,
and the official is not attested in other documents.

Τελῶναι are attested in the Arsinoite nome in the Ptolemaic
period, but not many receipts or accounts prepared by them
have survived from Roman times. A τελώνης collected 2 obols
for an unknown tax in A.D. 1, for he is mentioned in one of two
receipts, recorded on a single ostracon, issued by the state
bank.¹⁶³ Several payments to τελῶναι are recorded in the great
farm-account in P. Goodspeed Cairo 30; most of the items give
only the number of drachmae paid to a τελώνης, but in one the
payment of 48 drachmae is stated to be ὑπὲρ οἴνου καινοῦ καὶ
κάρρου, and in another the payment is made from the sale of
myrrh (ἀπὸ μυρρῶν τιμῆς).¹⁶⁴ An appeal to the epistrategus
against a double exaction of taxes on the inheritance of catoecic
land (τέλη καταλοχισμῶν) attempted by τελῶναι is found in
BGU. I. 340. The collectors of these taxes were more usually
called δημοσιῶναι τέλους καταλοχισμῶν Ἀρσινοίτου καὶ ἄλλων
νόμων.¹⁶⁵

In the Arsinoite nome the collectors of the ἐγκύκλιον (tax
on transfers of real property) were ordinarily called πραγματευόμενοι or πραγματευταί.¹⁶⁶ A πραγματευτής also collected the
τέλος μόσχων θυομένων in BGU. II. 383. A πραγματευτὴς
ἐρημοφυλακίας issued a receipt for σύμβολον καμήλων (P. Grenf.
II. 58).

Χειρισταί have already been mentioned as assistants to the
practors in the collection of poll-tax, capitation taxes, land-
taxes in money, and the like. A χ(ε)ιριστὴς κώμης is mentioned

in a register of taxes on land from the village of Hermopolis in the Fayûm and dated early in the second century.[167]   A χειριστής collected the ἐπίτριτον in Tebtynis in A.D. 105, according to PSI. x. 1137. A tax-receipt issued by the nomarch to the ἡγούμενοι of priests in the Arsinoite nome records that the payment was made through a χειριστής of Heron, but it does not specify what office Heron occupied.[168]

The γραμματεὺς πέζης Ἀνουβίου issued a receipt for the toll-gate at Socnopaei Nesus in the third century.[169] A λογευτής signed a receipt for συντάξιμον at Philadelphia in A.D. 6–7, and another λογευτής apparently collected the τέλος μόσχου [θυομένου] at Socnopaei Nesus for the nomarch in A.D. 161–9.[170] The νομογράφος of the village of Philadelphia gave a receipt to a farmer (γεωργὸς ἴδιος) for the tax on a gift which consisted, apparently, in a half-interest in two slaves. The οἰκονόμος οὐικάριος (a steward of the imperial estates) issued a receipt to the elders and comogrammateus of Socnopaei Nesus for φόρος προβάτων in A.D. 161; the large payment of 443 drachmae 3 obols perhaps indicates that a portion of the sheep owned by the imperial estates had been leased to the village of Socnopaei Nesus, perhaps by an involuntary lease.[171]

Βοηθοί have been mentioned above as the assistants of practors in the collection of taxes assessed in money.[172] The βοηθὸς ἁλιέων seems to have been a collector of the tax paid by fishermen of Socnopaei Nesus, for the payment is said to have been made 'through' (διά) him; his title makes his exact status doubtful, for it should mean that he was a representative of the fishermen; possibly he was an officer of the guild of fishermen and was held responsible for the collection of the tax and for turning it over to the officials of the state.[173] If that is correct, it is probable that the elders (πρεσβύτεροι) of the priests occupied a similar position, for it is to them that the receipt for taxes of the priests and of the temple is given.[174] In P. Lond. II. 345 (p. 113) the two πρεσβύτεροι παστοφόρων present to the basilico-grammateus a report of the παστοφόροι of the temple, as well as an inventory. In P. Ryl. II. 196 taxes paid by the priests are collected διὰ ἡγουμένων, and it is probable that the ἡγούμενοι were those of a temple rather than of a village.[175] A series of receipts for φόρος προβάτων issued by the ἡγούμενοι of a village is described in P. Lond. III. 849 (p. xl). In BGU. I. 63 (dated A.D. 201) the πρεσβύτεροι of the First Estate of Theoninus seem to have paid the φόρος προβάτων of 443 drachmae 3 obols. In P. Genf. 42, however, the payments of the farmers (γεωργοί) seem to have been made to πρεσβύτεροι at Philadelphia in A.D. 224–5.

The elders of the villages seem to have been made responsible for the collection of certain taxes at least as early as the reign of Hadrian. In P. Lond. II. 255 (p. 117) the elders of the village of Caranis had appointed one of their number to the collection (πρακτορεύειν καὶ χειρίζειν) of the beer-tax (ζυτηρὰ κατ' ἄνδρα) and of the φόρος προβάτων, and their representative had faithfully paid his collections of the former tax into the state bank (δημοσία τράπεζα) and of the latter tax into the bank established for that purpose (ἡ ἐπὶ τούτοις τράπεζα). A payment of φόρος προβάτων to the οἰκονόμος οὐικάριος made by the elders and comogrammateus of Socnopaei Nesus has been mentioned above, and another payment by the elders of the village of Caranis for the same tax was made to a practor in A.D. 206.[176] At Apias in A.D. 178 the beer-tax (ζυτηρὰ κατ' ἄνδρα) was paid to the elders of the village.[177] The nomarchic taxes were paid through the elders of the villages of Philadelphia, Bubastus and Socnopaei Nesus, Caranis, and Tanis.[178] A payment for φόρος νόμων also was made through the elders of Tanis. The payment 'through' the elders apparently means that the elders of the village were responsible for the payment of the tax by the villagers from whom it was due. A payment of 40 drachmae for the dikes seems to have been made by two elders of the village of Socnopaei Nesus in A.D. 152; this may have been a special assessment which the two undertook as a personal obligation, for there is no record of a village treasury from which the sum could have been appropriated by vote.[179] A payment of 22 drachmae 3 obols was made for φόρετρον by the elders of the village to the credit of one individual at Tebtynis in A.D. 170–5.[180] According to P. Bouriant 29, from Socnopaei Nesus and dated A.D. 211, a sum of 443 drachmae was collected from the elders of the village for the 8-drachmae tax (probably the crown-tax assessed κατ' ἄρουραν). BGU. III. 772 is a curious memorandum of two payments of money for an unknown tax credited to the ἀρίθμη(σις) of Pachon; the payments were made by (or possibly to) the γρ(αμματεὺς) πρεσβ(υτέρων) καὶ οἱ (μέτοχοι).

When the βουλευταί of the metropolis were made responsible for taxes after the establishment of the municipal senates under Septimius Severus, they sometimes delegated specific tasks of collection to some of their members, just as earlier (in the reign of Hadrian) the πρεσβύτεροι κώμης Καρανίδος had appointed one of their number to collect taxes for which they were responsible. According to BGU. VII. 1588 the τέλος γνωστείας (a tax connected with inheritance of property) was collected by βουλευταί appointed to collect such taxes (ἐπὶ τῆς τῶν καταλοχισμῶν εἰσπράξεως).

In the third century soldiers sometimes assisted or protected the tax-collectors (BGU. i. 8, ii. 9; PO. ix. 1185).

5. The Oxyrhynchite Nome

In Oxyrhynchus also the banks were actively engaged in the collection of taxes. In the first century after Christ the poll-tax and dike-tax were paid to the bank; in the second century the tax of the pastophori, in the second and third centuries the sales-tax (ἐγκύκλιον) and the crown-tax, and in the third century the tithe (ἀπόμοιρα) were collected by banks.[181]

The early practors at Oxyrhynchus usually appear with special titles.[182] In A.D. 45 a citizen of Oxyrhynchus declared on oath that he would appear before the strategus at the next reckoning (ἀρίθμησις) of taxes; the declaration was addressed to the πράκτωρ δημοσίων.[183] In PO. II. 285 Apollophanes, a former collector of the tax on trades (γενόμενος πράκτωρ χειρωναξίου), is accused of extorting 16 drachmae from a weaver in A.D. 47–8; the weaver addressed a petition for redress to the strategus about the year A.D. 50. The same Apollophanes, called simply γενόμενος πράκτωρ, is found in another petition to the strategus from a weaver who accused the collector of extorting 4 drachmae and a linen tunic worth 8 drachmae in A.D. 48–9.[184] Extortion is also charged against Damis, an ex-collector, in a petition from a weaver; the extortion occurred in the years 47–8 and 48–9, and the petition was submitted in the following year.[185] Since Damis and Apollophanes were both charged with extortion in the same years, it is evident that there were at least two practors collecting the weavers' tax at Oxyrhynchus in the middle of the first century after Christ. Complaints of extortion were ordinarily made when taxes had fallen into arrear, and it is probable that at Oxyrhynchus as late as A.D. 50 the practors were chiefly occupied in exacting arrears. Πράκτορες λαο(γραφίας) are found at Oxyrhynchus in A.D. 102, the year before the πράκτορες ἀργυρικῶν appear in receipts from Elephantine-Syene and from the Arsinoite nome; the πράκτορες λαογραφίας collected the poll-tax and also the pig-tax.[186] After the introduction of the πράκτορες ἀργυρικῶν under Trajan, they are found in the metropolis and in the villages of the nome from A.D. 113 to 254, and a πράκτωρ πολιτικῶν is found in a document dated A.D. 265.[187] The simple title of practor continued to be used, but only occasionally. The πράκτορες ἀργυρικῶν in the Oxyrhynchite nome collected the poll-tax and other capitation taxes, various trades-taxes, land-taxes, and the ὑποκείμενον ἐκλογιστείᾳ.[188] In the second century a πράκτωρ ἀργυρικῶν reported to the strategus his collections from Roman citizens and from those who did not make declarations (ἀνεπίκριτοι). In A.D. 208 the φόρος ἐδάφων was to be paid to the elders of a village *through* the πράκτωρ ἀργυρικῶν.[189] In A.D. 265 the πράκτωρ πολιτικῶν was ordered to pay the τελωνικά of the nome to the prytanis of the senate of Oxyrhynchus. Such control of the revenue by the senate of the metropolis is not unusual in the third century, but to find that the τελωνικά had been collected by a practor is surprising, since we should expect τελωνικά to be exacted by τελῶναι.[190] A χειριστής is attested as assistant to the πράκτορες ἀργυρικῶν in the Oxyrhynchite nome.[191]

When the irregular collections of the crown-tax became frequent, special πράκτορες στεφανικῶν were appointed to collect the tax, just as in the Arsinoite nome. In one example the tax was clearly collected on land.[192] The crown-tax was collected also by practors who had no special title.[193]

Ἐπιτηρηταὶ ἐγκυκλίου (superintendents of the tax on transfer of property) are found in the Oxyrhynchite nome.[194] The two receipts, however, record the collection of the tax on the sale of slaves; in one the ἐπιτηρητὴς ἐγκυκλίου authorizes the bank to receive the tax of 52 drachmae. The sales-taxes assessed at the market at the Serapeum in Oxyrhynchus were collected by ἐπιτηρηταί.[195] An ἐπιτηρητὴς φόρου φράγμου is found in a list of persons eligible to hold office.[196]

Τελῶναι seem to have farmed the taxes on funerals in the Oxyrhynchite nome in the first century after Christ.[197] There were also τελῶναι χειρωναξίου to collect the trades-taxes.[198] Τελῶναι leased the ferries at Oxyrhynchus and at certain villages, for they issued a receipt for two payments (of 200 and 100 drachmae) for the φόρος πορθμειός made by two men who were probably ferrymen. A τελώνης is mentioned in the customs regulations (νόμος τελωνικός) found in the Oxyrhynchite nome (PO. I. 36 = W. Chrest. 273). A νομοφύλαξ, however, was the agent of collection of the 2 per cent. tax on exports from the nome.[199]

The collectors of the licence-tax on donkeys were known as οἱ ἐξειληφότες τὴν ἐξαδραχμίαν τῶν ὄνων and an ἀπογραφὴ ὄνων was addressed to them.[200]

The notice of the death of a slave who was a weaver was sent to the ἐγλή(μπτωρ) γερδ(ιακοῦ) at Oxyrhynchus in A.D. 61, according to PO. II. 262.

Officials charged with the leasing of government monopolies and properties in the Oxyrhynchite nome were called οἱ ἀσχολούμενοι, and they are found leasing the general store (παντοπωλική), fish-pickling, &c., market-supervision and the record-office, and the tax on the transfer of property (although τελῶναι more commonly leased this tax).[201] In a letter from the strategus to the basilico-grammateus in the first century the farmers of the sales-tax and supervision of markets are called δημοσιῶναι.[202] A ὑποσχεσάριος ὠνῆς ἀθηροπωλῶν καὶ ὀρβιοπωλῶν (contractor for farming the tax on sellers of pulse and of vetch) in A.D. 214 reported that his collections in the month of Payni amounted to 80 drachmae (PO. XII. 1432).

An ἐπεικτὴς χρυσοῦ στεφάνου καὶ Νίκης (collector of the golden crown and Victory of Aurelian) is mentioned in the report of the proceedings of the senate of Oxyrhynchus.[203] An ἐπεικτής who collected taxes in kind is also attested in the Oxyrhynchite nome in the third century.[204]

Ἐπιμεληταὶ ἀννώνης, whose duty was to see that sufficient supplies were available for the Roman army in Egypt, are attested at Oxyrhynchus in the second half of the third century.[205] The eutheniarch is also attested for Oxyrhynchus.[206]

In the Oxyrhynchite nome ἀπαιτηταί are found in documents of the third century. Ἀπαιτηταὶ ἱεροῦ ἀναβολικοῦ are found in PO. VIII. 1135–6, ἀπαιτηταὶ ἀννώνης in PSI. VII. 795 and PO. IX. 1192, and an ἀπαιτητὴς τιμῆς πυροῦ in PO. XII. 1419.

A payment to the κοσμητὴς φόρου κήπων Σαραπείου is found in a document from Oxyrhynchus dated in the third century. It is not certain, however, that this supervisor of the rent of the gardens of the Sarapeum was a government official.[207]

6. Other Nomes in Lower Egypt

It is a fair assumption that the banks served as agents of collection throughout Lower Egypt just as they did in the Arsinoite and Oxyrhynchite nomes. At Hermopolis Magna the banks received payments of rent of domain-land, of poll-tax and other capitation taxes, and of the catoeci's contribution to the temple of Aphrodite (Ἀφ(ροδίτης) σ(ύνταξις) κ(ατ)οί(κων)).[208]

The πράκτορες ἀργυρικῶν seem to have been introduced everywhere in the nomes of Lower Egypt early in the reign of Trajan. They are found at Hermopolis from A.D. 107 to 222; they collected the direct taxes as elsewhere.[209] A practor without further title is attested at Hermopolis as late as A.D. 233.[210] In Memphis πράκτορες ἀργυρικῶν of the third and fifteenth amphoda are found collecting the poll-tax and guard-assessment in A.D. 180.[211] A report from a πράκτωρ ἀργυρικῶν of Tamauonesus in the Memphite nome is addressed to the commission appointed to receive and forward the accounts concerning the procurator of the ἴδιος λόγος. Practors are attested also for Ancyra and the vicinity, Naboö and the metropolis in the Heptacomia, Abusir, and Tanis, and they are mentioned in documents whose provenience in Lower Egypt is not exactly known.[212]

An ἐπιτηρητὴς στεφανικῶν is attested at Hermopolis Magna in the first or second century after Christ; this is surprising because the ἐπιτηρηταί were apparently introduced to serve as control-officers for the tax-farmers, while the crown tax seems ordinarily to have been collected by practors.[213] Ἐπιτηρηταί of the ξενικὴ πρακτορία in the Athrebitic nome are mentioned in a document concerned with the collection of debt but which also refers to taxes (τέλη);[214] corresponding μισθωταὶ ξενικῆς πρακτορίας receive a report from the πραγματευτής of Memphis in PO. IV. 825 (dated second century after Christ). The ἐπιτηρηταί of the sales-tax (ἐκστάσεως καὶ δεκάτης ἀγορᾶς) at Alexandria were active in A.D. 144; and other ἐπιτηρηταί were serving about the same time.[215] Another μισθωτής from Lower Egypt was a lessee of hunting rights (μισθωτὴς ἀγριῶν θηρᾶς ζωῶν καὶ ὀρνέων) who sublet the rights and collected θηρατικοὶ φόροι and τὰ τεταγμένα τέλη at Heracleopolis Magna at the end of the third century.[216] He complained to a peace-officer that not only had he been unable to collect the φόρος due from the hunter at each of two villages, but those worthies had inflicted upon him the most contumelious and outrageous treatment.

The collectors of the licence-tax on donkeys in the Hermopolite nome were called οἱ ἐξειληφότες τὸ τέλος τῶν ὄνων τοῦ Ἑρμοπ(ολίτου) in an ἀπογραφὴ ὄνων from Hermopolis Magna.[217] A ταβουλάριος (a transliteration of the Latin title) is mentioned in a register of receipts from Alabastrine dated A.D. 226–7, but the part which he took in collection is unknown.[218] A ὑπηρετὴς ἐποχῆς ἐμβαδείας is mentioned in accounts of unknown provenience.[219]

The ἐγλήμπτορες ἀγορανομίας καὶ ἄλλων εἰδῶν let the right to sell vetch at Memphis in A.D. 98 (P. Bouriant 13), and an ἐγλήμπτωρ is mentioned in a schedule of import-duties in P. Lond. III. 856 (p. 91).

Two τελῶναι collected the ἐγκύκλιον in the Mendesian nome, according to PO. XVII. 2111. A τελώνης is mentioned in a document regarding the selling of fish in the market, a τελώνης εἴδους ὄνων occurs in an ἀπογραφὴ ὄνων, and another τελώνης is found in a document of the time of Severus and Caracalla.[220]

The decemprimi (δεκάπρωτοι), who collected taxes in the third century after the establishment of the municipal senates, were almost wholly engaged in the collection of grain, according to the testimony of extant receipts; but in PO. XII. 1442 money was paid to them for the land-tax in A.D. 252. In P. Lond. III. 1157 (p. 61) δεκάπρωτοι make payments on behalf of landowners in their villages. Since all these documents deal with land-taxes it is possible that the δεκάπρωτοι collected only land-taxes, and consequently the various practors and tax-farmers were still necessary for the collection of other taxes.[221]

Nothing is known concerning the system of collecting taxes at Alexandria, just as almost nothing is known concerning taxes paid by citizens of Alexandria. Rostovtzeff (following Ruggiero) believed that the *fiscus Alexandrinus* established at Rome was organized for the receipt of the poll-tax of Alexandrian citizens, whether residing at Alexandria or elsewhere in the Roman empire. This is very dubious, for although Dio Cassius states that Vespasian, before he left for Rome, exacted 6 drachmae from every Alexandrian citizen, Alexandrians in the fifth year of his reign were exempt from poll-tax.[222]

Collectors of taxes issued receipts to individual tax-payers, to representatives of guilds or other corporations (such as priest-hoods), to elders of villages, and to other tax-collectors.[223] Receipts issued to individuals far outnumber all other types together. The value of the receipt to the tax-payer is obvious, and its importance is emphasized by the marginal annotations in tax-registers where the payment of an individual is incomplete, for we find the imperative ζή(τη) σύμβ(ολον) which literally translated is 'look up the receipt' but which probably meant 'make the tax-payer produce his receipt'.[224] That the tax-payers could produce their receipts is indicated by the notations ἀπὸ συμβ(όλου) and πλ(ήρους), which mean that payment in full was verified from the tax-payer's receipt.[225] The edict of the prefect M. Petronius Mamertinus requiring that, when any payment was made to the government, payer and payee should mutually give receipts seems either not to have applied to payments for taxes or to have proved impractical of enforcement, for no receipts for taxes signed by the payer have been found.[226] Payments for several taxes might be included in one receipt, and several instalments of the same tax were likewise recorded on one receipt. A temporary receipt was sometimes given by collectors, and when the permanent receipt was issued it contained a clause enjoining the recipient from using the former receipt which was cancelled by the new one (cf. P. Fay. 64, 54. 3 note; WO. I, p. 79). Ostraca were used for tax-receipts in Upper Egypt, while in Lower Egypt most receipts were written on papyri; in the Fayûm receipts were sometimes written on ostraca, although the majority of these were not for taxes but for transport of government grain. The fully developed formula of a tax-receipt included the following items: (1) the year in which the receipt was issued, (2) the names and title of the tax-collectors, (3) the name of the tax-payer (or payers), (4) the description of the tax or taxes paid (the name of the tax and sometimes the town where it was assessed and the year of its assessment) (5) the date and amount of each payment. The formulae of the receipts varied with the time of issue, the place of payment, the kind of tax, and the type of collector (bank, tax-farmer, practor, or other official collector). It is not necessary to discuss here the different formulae, which have been treated by Wilcken and elaborately classified by Viereck, who has promised a full discussion of them in the second volume of the Strassburg Ostraca.[227]

Although the tax-payer's responsibilities were over when he was given his tax-receipt, the work of the collector was only half done. The collectors were required to keep an accurate record of all monies received and to present reports of their collections to the strategus or to some other official of the financial administration. The facilities of the banks were undoubtedly of great convenience to the practors engaged in the collections, not only because they provided a safe place and responsible care for large sums of money, but also because the banks could offer competent and experienced clerks and accountants to keep the records of payment and to assist the practors in the preparation of their monthly reports. The bank kept day-books of collections, such as have been preserved at Philadelphia in P. Princeton 1-6 and 10, from which were prepared such ledgers as P. Princeton 8-10 and the Columbia papyri from Theadelphia, and such a register as P. Princeton 14.[228] The practors must have kept accounts of their personal collections, but no accounts have survived which can certainly be identified as such; perhaps P. Princeton 13 is such an account, but it too may have been prepared at the bank, for it begins with a notation τρ(απέζης) πινακίδ(ια) and is written on the verso of a ledger of the συντάξιμον probably prepared at the bank. After the introduction of the πράκτορες ἀργυρικῶν in the reign of Trajan the bureaux of the collectors may have become more independent of the banks; a large number of tax-accounts have been found whose loss of title makes it impossible to know in what bureau they were prepared.[229]

From the day-books and registers kept at the banks supplemented by their own accounts the practors made up their reports to the strategus of the nome wherein the collections had been lifted. These reports, like those of the sitologi described in Chapter IV, were of two kinds: detailed reports (κατ᾽ ἄνδρα) listing the payments of individuals, and monthly summaries (μηνιαῖος ἐν κεφαλαίῳ).[230] For some taxes reports were made at longer intervals of three or four months, and probably annual reports also were required.[231] Special reports were frequently demanded of collectors, such as the return addressed to the strategus of the Heraclides division of the Arsinoite nome by the πράκτορες ἀργυρικῶν of Pharbetha, giving a list of arrears of taxes at the end of the first six months of the year.[232] Tax-farmers were likewise required to submit reports of their collections.[233] The reports of the collectors of internal customs-dues were quite detailed, and in SB. 7365 the statement is found that the accounts had been audited by the harbour-master.[234]

From the reports of the practors and other collectors the strategus (or his assistant, the basilico-grammateus) made up his reports, which were sent directly to the bureaux of the financial administration in Alexandria. Special reports were required for the revenues under the jurisdiction of the Idiologus. In the second century a commission undertook to forward monthly reports to the eclogistes of the nome and the Idiologus in Alexandria. To this commission the πράκτορες ἀργυρικῶν, as well as the sitologi,[235] directly presented reports addressed to the Idiologus, perhaps because reports of the irregular revenues under the control of the Idiologus were outside the competence of the strategus of the nome. The ἐπιτηρητὴς ὑπὲρ καταπομπῆς μηνιαίου mentioned in BGU. II. 362 (dated A.D. 215) may have served as a member of the commission or may have replaced it in the third century.

The prefects set definite days when the reports of the strategi were due at Alexandria, and a fine awaited the strategus who was late with his monthly reports of collections in grain and in money or with his summaries (ἀπολογισμοί), as we learn from a letter from the procurator of Neapolis admonishing the strategi of the Delta. He points out that the reports of one strategus for the month Epiph had been recorded by the ἐπιτηρητὴς τῶν ἐπιστολῶν by the 8th of Thoth (within a little more than a month after the close of Epiph). The procurator's letter was forwarded by the acting-strategus of Nesyt to the basilico-grammateus.[236] In PO. 1. 61 a strategus is found to have paid into the bank 2255 drachmae for a fine imposed by the dioecetes for failure to send reports at the proper time.[237]

A letter of a tax-collector speaks of the difficulty of collecting taxes (δημόσια) in the Oxyrhynchite nome in the first century.[238] The problem of arrears was ever vexing, as much or more so for money-taxes as for taxes in kind. Every effort was made to collect arrears, but no penalty for overdue payment is mentioned in any of the receipts.[239] The edict of Ti. Julius Alexander states that debtors of the government could be legally imprisoned, but it is uncertain whether the general term for debts (δημόσια) includes taxes.[240] Considerable sums for fines (κατακρίματα) are included in the tax-collectors' reports, and some of these fines may have been exacted for late payment of taxes.[241] A daybook of payments of arrears of συντάξιμον is found in P. Princeton 1, and payments of arrears of poll-tax and dike-tax were recorded on the backs of discarded daybooks (P. Princeton 11). The special reports of practors to the strategi concerning arrears in their districts have been mentioned above. A list of delinquent tax-payers (ἄποροι ἀνεύρετοι) who owed for poll-tax and dike-tax was compiled by the λογευτὴς λαογραφίας (P. Cornell 24). A statement of arrears of various taxes at several villages is found in BGU. VII. 1613 which is addressed to the toparch; this official is also found in connexion with a payment of arrears of dike-tax at Philadelphia in A.D. 69–70 (BGU. VII. 1614), but what particular function he performed in exacting arrears is not evident. We have noticed above that Trajan introduced assessments to cover deficits caused by defaulting tax-payers, but it is not to be assumed that their introduction and collection freed the defaulter from his obligations if the tax-collector ever located him.

Forcible collection of overdue taxes by the strategus was forbidden by imperial ordinance and was rebuked by the prefect.[242]
Even worse, and not uncommon, was the practice of peculation
and extortion by officials and collectors. The very number and
complexity of the taxes and other demands made upon the inhabitants of Egypt by the government gave many opportunities
for illegal exactions. Prohibitions of extortion go back to Ptolemaic times, and Reinmuth has noted that the Roman prefects
'found it necessary to make official pronouncements concerning
this subject more often than about any other'.[243] Instances of
extortion and peculation have received notice in the various
chapters of this book, and the subject has received detailed
treatment elsewhere.[244] In the great number of documents
which have survived from Roman Egypt there are comparatively few which complain of illegal exactions, but the variety
of officials and collectors accused is ominous. The prefect
L. Aemilius Rectus sent to Tiberius a greater revenue than had
been assessed and was doubtless surprised at the emperor's
rebuke.[245] The decree of the prefect Ti. Julius Alexander
admits that his predecessors in office had been guilty of unauthorized exactions and had disregarded the exemptions
established by the emperors.[246] Philo Judaeus accused Lampo,
who was perhaps the *a commentariis* for the prefect Avilius
Flaccus, of 'perverting the record for pay'.[247] The eclogistae
were accused by Ti. Julius Alexander of extortion by disregard-
ing the abatements due the peasants because of variations in the
Nile flood, and he commanded the strategi not to accept gifts
from the eclogistae without the consent of the prefect.[248] PO.
1. 57 reveals that in the third century the former eclogistes of
the Oxyrhynchite nome had failed to pay over to the treasury
the sum of 3,187 drachmae 3 obols which had been received
towards the completion of the dikes and canals in a certain year,
but it is not certain that he had been guilty of embezzlement.[249]
The strategus and basilico-grammateus of the Tanite nome
were reprimanded for peculations by Plautius Italus, a high
functionary who may have been an epistrategus.[250] Practors of
the trade-tax were accused of extortion by weavers at Oxyrhynchus, and the ἐξεταστής and ἐπιτηρητὴς τέλους χειρωναξίου in
the Arsinoite nome made illegal attempts to raise the assess-

ments of the guilds of fullers and dyers.[251] Reinmuth cites an unpublished papyrus containing the edict of a prefect commanding the τελῶναι to cease from their πλεονεξία 'which took the form of imposing fines, collecting them with the use of violence, and in some way not clearly ascertainable making their victims pay for freedom from molestation'.[252] The collectors of customs at Socnopaei Nesus were accused by the guard (ἀραβοτοξότης) at the customs-house of defrauding the government by keeping two sets of records, an official record which reported smaller collections than those actually made and a private register which was correct. The two collectors of customs were evidently acting in collusion with the overseers of the nomarchy and the superintendent of the domains.[253] The village secretaries were also guilty of extortion: a certain Psais falsified his records in reporting an assessment on land, and by threatening to falsify his reports still further he succeeded in extorting varying sums of money from different tax-payers as well as a total of 200 artabae of wheat.[254] Probably the most frequent and flagrant extortions were those practised by soldiers and travelling officials, who exacted money in addition to supplies, billets, and transportation, although taxes had been assessed to pay such expenses and heavy penalties were provided for illegal exactions.[255]

The temptation to peculation and extortion was aggravated by the liturgical character of the practorships and of the offices of the nome. The expenses of the offices must often have been inadequately compensated by the salaries, even when salaries were paid. A second letter of Plautius Italus to the strategi and basilico-grammateis rebuked certain of them for paying themselves salaries for some period on their own responsibility, and ordered that the imperial monies were not to be touched without leave.[256]

Little information is available concerning the cost of collecting taxes. Clerical expenses were at least partly compensated by the charge made for receipt (συμβολικά) which, like the charges made by the γραφεῖον for the preparation of official documents, varied with the number of items in the receipt and consequently with the amount of writing necessary; the usual amount was 2 or 3 obols.[257] The collectors of customs deducted the wages of the guards of the custom-house from their monthly payments into the treasury. P. Teb. II. 542, probably a collector's report submitted by his clerk (in the second century), gives a total for the month of Choiak of 625 drachmae from which deductions were made as follows: salary of the clerk 28 drachmae, salary of the guard 20 drachmae, allowance for paper used in issuing receipts 9 drachmae, allowance for exchange (κόλλυβος) 6 drachmae 3 obols; and allowance of 3 obols for a receipt; the balance was turned over to the bank.

A fee called πρακτορικόν is found occasionally in tax-accounts. Wilcken supposed that it was collected to pay the salary of the practors, but Rostovtzeff explained it as a charge for late payment. Fees called πρακτορικά collected in connexion with foreclosures for debt are consistent with either interpretation.[258]

Surtaxes

It is not impossible that some of the cost of collection was met by the exaction of surtaxes (προσδιαγραφόμενα), but much remains to be learned concerning the nature of these extra charges. Various extra charges for exchange and other purposes had been collected in the Ptolemaic period, although for the most part they throw little light on the surcharges collected by Roman practors, banks, and other collectors.[259] These agents of collection frequently added the surtax in some form to the taxes which they collected; but a surtax is rarely mentioned in receipts for taxes farmed to τελῶναι and μισθωταί, such as trade- and market-taxes (except the ἐγκύκλιον) and customs-dues.[260] At Thebes the extra charges were introduced, according to Tait, between the forty-first and forty-third year of Augustus,[261] although the term προσδιαγραφόμενα seems to have been used as early as 11–10 B.C.[262] At Thebes the surcharges appear in receipts in three forms: προσδιαγραφόμενα, αἳ κ(αἱ), and ῥυπαραί δραχμαί.[263] All of these mean a surcharge of $\frac{1}{16}$ added to the principal of the tax.[264] The first of these formulae was used by the δημοσία τράπεζα in the metropolis of Thebes; the τράπεζαι in Memnonia and the South-west Quarter used the second; and the third formula was employed by the πράκτορες ἀργυρικῶν μητροπόλεως. In the extant documents from other towns in Upper Egypt and from Lower Egypt the only common formula is the first, the addition of προσδιαγραφόμενα, which was used by banks, practors, and other collectors.[265] In some documents, however, the surtax seems to be included in the main sum paid and is not separately indicated.[266]

The purpose of the προσδιαγραφόμενα remains uncertain. Tait quotes Revillout (*Mélanges*, 216, 225) who stated that in demotic ostraca the προσδιαγραφόμενα are said to be paid 'pour la versement à Alexandrie'. But this statement is not very enlightening. Does it mean that the surtax was collected for transportation charges on monies sent to Alexandria, although the rate of $\frac{1}{16}$ (or $6\frac{1}{4}$ per cent.) seems to have been uniform throughout Egypt? In PO. II. 288 payments for poll-tax (ἐπικεφάλιον) are accompanied by the phrase σὺν καταγωγίῳ; the payments for trade-tax, dike-tax, and pig-tax are not so accompanied. The editors point out that the phrase does not occur in other documents from Oxyrhynchus, and state that while in Louvre Pap. 62. v. 17, 21 καταγώγιον means the 'expenses of transport' (of copper), that sense does not suit in PO. II. 288. Since, however, the receipts of the poll-tax were forwarded to Alexandria, it is far from certain that 'expenses of transport' does not suit. In P. Teb. II. 345 a supplementary payment designated by the abbreviation κ( ) or κα( ) is possibly to be expanded κα(ταγώγιον), a charge for the transportation of the principal tax paid in copper; its rate of $\frac{3}{40}$ or $7\frac{1}{2}$ per cent. is close to the rate of the προσδιαγραφόμενα.[267] In the report of customs-dues in SB. 7365 charges for χειριστικόν and ἀλλαγή were added to the total receipts at the rate of $8\frac{1}{2}$ per cent., which is approximately equivalent to the total of προσδιαγραφόμενα and ἀλλαγή in the customs-account in PO. XIV. 1651. The term χειριστικόν, instead of προσδιαγραφόμενα, is found in the customs-accounts in PO. XIV. 1650–1650 (a), and the editors connect the charge with transport. The payments in PO. XIV. 1650–1 show that the ἀλλαγή (fee for agio) was very small in comparison with the payment for χειριστικόν or προσδιαγραφόμενα.

The problem is complicated, however, by the division of προσδιαγραφόμενα into two separate charges in certain documents which include payments for φόρος βωμῶν and the tax on sheep.[268] One of these two charges is 4 per cent. and the other is $2\frac{1}{4}$ per cent. The 4 per cent. is approximately equivalent to 1 obol per tetradrachm, and Tait observed that the surcharge on the Ἰουδαίων τέλεσμα was at the exceptional rate of

1 obol on each tetradrachm.[269] The extra obol would seem to have been collected for the express purpose of paying the exchange on a Roman *denarius*, since 8 drachmae 2 obols are stated in a receipt to be the *price* of two *denarii* (τιμὴ δηναρίων δύο). If the 4 per cent. was used for agio it may still have included a fee for transportation to Alexandria, if the other 2¼ per cent. was not used for that purpose when the usual προσδιαγραφόμενα was collected on other taxes. Or the 2¼ per cent. may have been a fee collected to reimburse the banks for their care of tax-funds and their preparation of accounts. It may be noted that when the banks at Thebes issued receipts for trades-taxes, the charge for προσδιαγραφόμενα was collected, while it does not appear in receipts issued by τελῶναι or ἐπιτηρηταί.[270]

In Upper Egypt προσδιαγραφόμενα were not added to the payments for poll-tax assessed at rates higher than 10 drachmae per annum. Either tax-payers assessed at higher rates were excused from paying the surtax, or it was included in the principal sum, as it seems to have been in payments of συντάξιμον in the Fayûm, or it was not recorded. In receipts for the minor assessments (μερισμοί) the προσδιαγραφόμενα are not mentioned. In the tax-registers from Theadelphia (P. Col. I R 1–2) the surtax is usually omitted with these assessments, but in SP. xx. 62 the surtax is recorded with them. It is, therefore, unsafe to assume whenever the surtax does not appear in the tax-receipts or even in the registers that it had not been exacted.[271]

There were a number of rates for προσδιαγραφόμενα other than ¹⁄₁₆. Certain taxes on garden-land were called εἴδη (perhaps because they were once paid in kind) and were calculated in copper drachmae. They were subject to surcharges at various rates, which were tabulated by the editors of P. Ryl. II. 192 (b) (p. 245). The προσδιαγραφόμενα were collected at the rate of ⅛ on ἀπόμοιρα ἀμπέλων and παραδείσων, παραγωγὴ ἐλαίας, and ναύβιον ἐναφεσίων. On ναύβιον κατοίκων the rate of the surtax was ¹⁄₁₀, and on ἐπαρούριον it was ¹⁄₁₃.[272] These rates had their origin in the Ptolemaic period when assessments for taxes were made in Ptolemaic copper, and the difference in the rates is explained by Milne as resulting from the date in the first century B.C. when the assessments of these taxes were fixed, for the

rate of surtax varied during that century.[273] On these payments
of taxes assessed in copper an exchange-fee (κόλλυβος) of $\frac{1}{60}$ was
collected.[274] The official rate of exchange between copper
drachmae and 'silver' drachmae in tax-payments in Roman
times was 300 : 1.[275] In addition to the extraordinary rates
of surcharges on the εἴδη assessed on garden-land, there are
other rates of προσδιαγραφόμενα which do not admit of so ready
an explanation. In BGU. II. 471 the surtax paid for taxes on
γέρδιοι, γυψική, πρακτορικόν, and ἱερεῖς Δήμητρος is exacted at
the rate of 6½ per cent. instead of the usual $\frac{1}{16}$ (or 6¼ per cent.).
In SP. XXII. 183 the rate of surtax on τέλος θυιῶν and ὑποκείμενον
κωμογραμματείᾳ is again 6½ per cent., and it is the same on all
items under ὑποκείμενα ἐπιστρατηγίᾳ, except ὑπὲρ γναφέων Νειλο-
πόλεως where it is slightly more. In BGU. I. 342 the surtax
on the ἀριθμητικὸν κατοίκων is at the rate of 6½ per cent. In
BGU. II. 471, cited above, the προσδιαγραφόμενα on ἐπιστατικὸν
ἱερέων are at the rate of 14 per cent., while in the tax-rolls from
Caranis in the collection of the University of Michigan they
are assessed on ἐπιστατικὸν ἱερέων and γέρα ἱερέων at the rate
of $\frac{1}{7}$. In P. Teb. II. 306 the rate of the surtax on payments of
ἐπιστατικὸν ἱερέων is usually at the rate of 8½ per cent.[276] Other
taxes paid by priests are usually accompanied by προσδιαγραφόμενα at the normal rate of $\frac{1}{16}$.[277]

In a single receipt from Caranis dated A.D. 154 and in two
receipts from Socnopaei Nesus dated A.D. 172 and 174 the
προσδιαγραφόμενα are 1 drachma 2 chalci on the dike-tax paid
at the usual rate of 6 drachmae 4 obols.[278] This is a rate of $\frac{5}{32}$,
2½ times the usual rate of surtax assessed on the dike-tax at
Thebes (2½ obols on 6 drachmae 4 obols). In BGU. I. 359 the
payment for dike-tax is made in ῥυπαραί drachmae at the rate of
7 drachmae 4 obols 2 chalci which, as the editors of P. Lond. III.
844. 9, note (p. 55) explain, includes the προσδιαγραφόμενα of 1
drachma 2 chalci. There is no apparent reason for this exceptional rate, which is attested at two different places in the
Fayûm nearly twenty years apart. The amount of the προσδιαγραφόμενα is too large to be explained as merely including a
charge for receipt (σύμβολον). In Upper Egypt the payment for
dike-tax sometimes included the assessment for bath-tax, but
the προσδιαγραφόμενα were assessed on the sum of the payment

for the two taxes. It is, however, not impossible that the payment of 1 drachma 2 chalci for surtax included another fee, but
further evidence is necessary to support such an hypothesis.
There is no evidence that the unusually large surtax was a
penalty for late payment. In other receipts and registers of the
dike-tax definitely known to come from the Arsinoite nome the
προσδιαγραφόμενα are not mentioned at all or the amount paid
for them is not given—the receipt usually reads χω( ) ∫ϛϝ
πρ( ) συμβ( ). This perhaps means that the προσδιαγραφό-
μενα were collected at the usual rate of $\frac{1}{16}$. But it might be argued
that the normal rate of surtax on χωματικόν in the Arsinoite
nome is the only one attested, namely $\frac{5}{32}$. Whether exceptional
or normal for the payments of dike-tax, the rate of $\frac{5}{32}$ for
προσδιαγραφόμενα is the highest attested in the Roman period.

In the Fayûm, as is indicated in SP. xx. 62, the rate of προσδιαγραφόμενα on the pig-tax was $\frac{1}{13}$; according to this document
the pig-tax was one of the εἴδη. In the Oxyrhynchite nome in
the second century the rate of surtax on the pig-tax was even
higher. In PO. III. 574 one obol was paid for surtax on a pig-
tax of 1 drachma $4\frac{1}{2}$ obols, a rate of exactly $\frac{2}{21}$. In PO. XII. 1436,
an account of village taxes dated A.D. 153–6, the pig-tax totalled
481 drachmae 3(?) obols 2 chalci upon which 55 drachmae $2\frac{1}{2}$
obols 2 chalci were paid for προσδιαγραφόμενα. This would
indicate a rate of surtax slightly higher than $\frac{1}{8}$. There seems to
be no obvious explanation for the difference in the rate of surtax
on the pig-tax in this nome.[279] A surtax at the rate of $\frac{2}{21}$ is again
found in P. Iand. 143. ii, where the editor suggests that the tax
is the ἐξ(αδραχμία ὄνων) paid at the rate of 5 drachmae $1\frac{1}{2}$ obols.

An item of 30 drachmae for προσδιαγραφόμενα appears in
PO. XIV. 1651, an account of wine-transport. If this surtax was
calculated on the immediately preceding total of 385 drachmae
the rate was approximately $\frac{1}{13}$. If it was exacted, as Professor
Johnson suggests,[280] only on the item of 300 drachmae which
heads the list of payments, the rate was 10 per cent. If, however,
it was exacted on all of the preceding items except that for
ἀναλώματος οἰνηγ(ίας)—an item not found in other similar accounts—the rate was approximately $8\frac{1}{2}$ per cent., the rate found
in PO. XIV. 1650 and 1650 (a) for χειριστικόν, which is apparently
equivalent to προσδιαγραφόμενα. In the customs-account from

the Fayûm (SB. 7365) an allowance of 8½ per cent. was made for χειριστικὸν καὶ ἀλλαγή. The ἀλλαγή (charge for exchange) is recorded separately in the Oxyrhynchus accounts, but it is very small in every one of them.[281] In P. Amh. 11. 115, from Hermopolis Magna and dated A.D. 137, προσδιαγραφόμενα on an unknown tax are calculated at the rate of 8½ per cent.

Several records of προσδιαγαφόμενα give amounts which do not seem to permit easy correction and yet seem impossible. For example, in PSI. 1. 103, from the Mendesian nome and dated in the second century after Christ, an item of 148 drachmae [.] obols is recorded for τοκαδεία and immediately thereafter 8 drachmae [.] obols for προσδιαγραφόμενα; a payment of 8 drachmae [.] obols for φόρος νόμων is followed by 4 drachmae [.] obols for προσδιαγραφόμενα. The first amount for surtax is less than ¹⁄₁₆, while the second amount is about 50 per cent., unless another payment followed in a lacuna after φόρος νόμων. Some correction seems necessary, for the succeeding total of 286 drachmae 2 chalci is followed by 17 drachmae [.] obols for προσδιαγραφόμενα which is calculated at the usual rate of ¹⁄₁₆.[282]

The term τὰ ἑπόμενα seems to have been used occasionally instead of προσδιαγραφόμενα. It is found in PO. XIV. 1633, a bid for the purchase of land from the state. Τὰ ἑπόμενα were assessed at the rate of ¹⁄₁₆ in a receipt for the sale of confiscated property (PO. III. 513 = W. Chrest. I. 183) and at the same rate on the price of acacia trees sold by the government (PO. VIII. 1112). Presumably the same rate was applied in P. Amh. II. 97. 14, an application for the purchase of confiscated buildings at Socnopaei Nesus, although the amount of τὰ ἑπόμενα is not stated.

The ἐπιδέκατον, a supplementary charge of 10 per cent., is found assessed upon the sales-tax (ἐγκύκλιον).[283] The ἐπιδέκατον mentioned in PO. III. 609–10, two orders for payment, may have been the same; but the brevity of the documents leaves the meaning uncertain. A supplement of approximately 10 per cent. called ἐρήμων is assessed on taxes at Oxyrhynchus (PO. XIV. 1652; see Chapter XV, note 82); Professor Johnson (in Roman Egypt, p. 563) has suggested that in the third century the surtax was increased because of the difficulty or danger in transporting funds to Alexandria.

A supplementary tax was sometimes called καθήκοντα. In

P. Lond. III. 1171 (p. 177) the καθήκοντα amount to 68 drachmae on a total of 796 drachmae paid for pasture-tax (ἐννόμιον καὶ ἀριθμητικόν), a rate of approximately 8½ per cent. It is not impossible that the supplement of 7½ per cent. abbreviated κ( ) or κα( ) in P. Teb. II. 345 is to be expanded as κα(θήκοντα), instead of κα(ταγώγιον) suggested above. Καθήκοντα appear as a surcharge on a tax paid on cattle, but in two items the rate is 2 obols a tetradrachm and in one it is 1½ obols a tetradrachm; the latter rate is $\frac{1}{16}$, the usual rate for προσδιαγραφόμενα.[284] Καθήκοντα appear as a small charge with taxes on garden-land at Caranis, but the principle of assessment is not clear.[285]

A charge of 1 drachma ½ obol or 8½ per cent. for ἀλλαγή (exchange) is found in BGU. III. 915 on a payment of 12 drachmae 3 obols for ἀπόμοιρα. This is the same rate as the χειριστικὸν καὶ ἀλλαγή in SB. 7365, and several other surtaxes mentioned above were assessed at the same rate. Ἀλλαγή at 8½ per cent. on ἀπόμοιρα assessed in silver drachmae seems to have no relation to the προσδιαγραφόμενα at ⅕ plus κόλλυβος at $\frac{1}{60}$ found with payments of ἀπόμοιρα assessed in copper drachmae.[286] As PO. XII. 1437 indicates, it is rather a survival in Roman times of a Ptolemaic distinction between ἀπόμοιρα upon which a charge for exchange was made (ὧν ἀλλαγή) and that upon which no charge was made (ἰσονόμος).[287] In P. Flor. III. 335 the rate of ἀλλαγή is lost.

The similarity of rates of the variously named surtaxes probably indicates that some of them were identical. The variety of rates found in surtaxes of the same name, such as the προσδιαγραφόμενα, is not yet fully understood. The name προσδιαγραφόμενα was first applied to a definite surtax during the reign of Augustus, although surtaxes were collected in the Ptolemaic period, and the term προσδιαγραφόμενα had been used for surcharges in general (e.g. in P. Amh. II. 31, dated 112 B.C.). The different rates of surtax probably had some reasonable explanation when they were established, but the explanation is not evident now. The Roman administration seems to have accepted the various rates as a part of the system of taxation inherited from the Ptolemies and to have preserved them long after the monetary or other conditions which gave rise to them had ceased to exist.

Administration of Revenue

Three great divisions of the treasury in Egypt are familiar from references in the papyri. These are the διοίκησις (department of administration), the ἱερατικά (department of hieratic income), and the ἴδιος λόγος (the separate account).[288] Almost all taxes, including the taxes in kind on grain-land, were paid into one of these three divisions of the treasury, which were an inheritance from the Ptolemaic organization. Down to the time of Hadrian the διοίκησις and the ἱερατικά were under the supervision of the prefect, who was, of course, assisted by various subordinate officials.[289] The ἴδιος λόγος was administered by the Idiologus, a Roman procurator who took his title from the department, and in the reign of Hadrian the department of ἱερατικά was transferred to his jurisdiction when the office of Idiologus was combined with that of High Priest of Alexandria and All Egypt.[290] After the majority of the great estates which had been formed at the beginning of Roman rule had come into the control of the emperor through inheritance or confiscation, a new department was organized under Nero or the Flavians to handle these imperial estates, and its administration was in the hands of a *procurator usiacus*; thereafter, rents of usiac land in kind or in money were carefully distinguished by the collectors.[291] In addition, many assessments were collected for purely local purposes and so were never paid into any of these departments.

The most illuminating document in regard to the administration of the various taxes collected in money is P. Ryl. II. 213, a tax-account from the Mendesian nome dated late second century. Only a summary can here be given of the editors' excellent analysis of the document in their introduction, particularly Tables I and II. The collections were divided into two main categories, the first and far more important called πρακτορία, and the second the ἀριθμητικὸν φυλακιτῶν. The latter was a single tax and was of comparatively slight importance; it was separated from the taxes of the πρακτορία perhaps because it was not collected by the practors—the similar ἀριθμητικὸν κατοίκων in the Fayûm was sometimes collected by special ἀπαιτηταί—or because, like the ἀριθμητικὸν κατοίκων, it was levied but once in every five years and so did not form a part of the practors' regular annual collection.[292]

The heading πρακτορία is subdivided into three divisions: (1) Διοίκησις, (2) Ἱερατικά, (3) Εἴδη. The first two divisions are familiar and have been noted above. The third division, the Εἴδη, which in this document consists of three taxes on animals (ἐννόμιον, τοκαδεία, and ὑϊκή), is not found as a separate department in other accounts, although the pig-tax is listed as εἰδῶν ὑϊκῆς in SP. XXII. 62. It has been observed that the taxes classified as εἴδη differ in documents from different nomes, that the classification may go back to the Ptolemaic period when the taxes were paid in kind, and that the classification was preserved by the Romans, although practically all of the taxes so designated had been converted into payments of money.[293] It is hardly safe to conclude from this solitary document that the Εἴδη formed a separate department of the treasury at Alexandria, although that is not an impossibility.[294]

The first division of Διοίκησις is further subdivided into four heads: (a) διοίκησις, (b) λιμνιτικά, (c) λαογραφία, and (d) χωματικόν. The subdivision διοίκησις included various rents and taxes on land or connected with the tenure of land, revenues from the sale of land and perhaps from the sale of livestock,[295] two trade-taxes probably connected with government monopolies, two taxes on animals, the crown-tax, and taxes collected for the support of the comogrammateus and the toparch.[296] The second subdivision, λιμνιτικά, consists of taxes on land recovered for cultivation from the marshes of the Delta; it probably owes its separation from the first division only because taxes on γῆ λιμνιτική were assessed on a different basis from those on other land.[297] The third and fourth subdivisions, the poll-tax and dike-tax respectively, were the two most important capitation taxes collected from the whole population of Egypt.

The taxes assigned to the Ἱερατικά division of the treasury include the ἀπόμοιρα on garden-land (a tax which in the Fayûm was sometimes given to the διοίκησις[298]), the εἰκοστή, which the editors suggest was a tax of 5 per cent. on transfers of real property, the τρίδραχμος, which was perhaps a tax assessed on land at the rate of 3 drachmae an arura, taxes or fees connected with sacrifices and ceremonies, and the θησαυρικόν, which was a surcharge of some kind collected with some of the land-taxes and sometimes with the poll-tax.[299]

There are several categories of taxes, however, which are not found in the great account in P. Ryl. II. 213. The editors suggest that the document is an account of arrears, and consequently some taxes may have been omitted because they had been paid in full. But the document is so comprehensive in scope, apparently including payments from the whole nome, that it should include most of the taxes collected by practors. Some categories of taxes we should not expect to find, because they were not collected by practors, but others are missing for perhaps less obvious reasons. Customs-dues, trade- and market-taxes were collected by tax-farmers. None of the assessments (μερισμοί) used for purely local purposes or to make up deficits in collections appear in an account of taxes forwarded to the central treasury in Alexandria. Rents of usiac land are not included because they were administered separately by the *procurator usiacus*.

In P. Ryl. II. 213 taxes collected for the office of como-grammateus (κωμογραμματείας, ὑποκειμένων κωμογραμματείας) and the toparch (ὑποκειμένων τοπ(αρχίας?)) and topogram-mateus (ὑποκειμένων τοπογραμματείας) are included under διοί-κησις.[300] Martin argued that charges called ὑποκείμενα were assigned to the maintenance of various public offices.[301] The following ὑποκείμενα are found in documents from different nomes of Upper and Lower Egypt: for the basilico-grammateus, topogrammateus, comogrammateus, grammateus (perhaps of a practor), epistrategus, eclogistes, meridarch, toparch, guard of watch-towers, epistates, administration of the pasture-tax, and priests.[302] The taxes so assigned for the support of officials are known only for the epistrategus: in W. *Chrest.* I. 92 (= BGU. I. 337 plus BGU. I. 1) the taxes paid by industries owned or controlled by the temple—fullers, embalmers, vegetable-sellers, and public weigh-station—are listed under ὑποκείμενα ἐπιστρα-τηγίᾳ. These taxes in the Arsinoite nome also belonged to the διοίκησις, as is evident from SP. XXII. 183.

In SP. XXII. 183, however, nomarchic taxes are distinct from the taxes paid to the διοίκησις. In P. Ryl. II. 213 the tax on sacrifices (μόσχου τέλος) and the 5 per cent. tax (εἰκοστή) are listed among the Ἱερατικά. In the Arsinoite nome the taxes on sacrifice and the ἐγκύκλιον (10 per cent. tax on sales made through the record office) were among the nomarchic taxes (designated by λόγος νομαρχίας, νομαρχικά, νομαρχικὰ ἀσχολήματα, or the like). Other taxes controlled by the nomarch were: beer, fishermen, fishing-boats, trades, bread, customs (ῥ καὶ ν́), paper, rent of pastures, *monodesmia* of hay and other taxes once paid in kind, and certain phases of transport of government grain, including the δραγματηγία when paid in money; in the third century the meridarchic taxes came under the supervision of the nomarch, but what taxes were so classified is not known.[303] P. M. Meyer[304] observed that the nomarchic taxes included the contingent taxes whose yield could not be accurately foreseen— taxes for the most part collected by tax-farmers. The yield of the nomarchic taxes was quite large in the Arsinoite nome, where total collections were reported as 17 talents 4,660 drachmae on the 11th of Mesore in A.D. 248 (BGU. I. 8. ii. 23-4). On an earlier date in the same month the collections were recorded as 15 talents 1,660 drachmae, so that within a period of not more than ten days 2 talents 3,000 drachmae had been collected and reported. We cannot, however, assume that collections were so large in every similar period throughout the year; perhaps the sum of 31 talents 4,790 drachmae in BGU. III. 753. vi represents the total collections of nomarchic taxes from the Arsinoite nome in some year of the third century.[305] In that century the officials collecting these taxes were named by the prytanis and the municipal senate (BGU. I. 8. ii. 23-4).

We know little concerning the transfer of the collected taxes from the various nomes of Egypt to the treasury in Alexandria and thence to Rome. Since the tax-payers made payments directly to the banks, and the practors and other collectors deposited their collections in the same banks, it is probable that payments of collections were made at Alexandria by means of bills of exchange. Yet a good deal of currency or bullion must have been shipped to Alexandria from the metropoleis of the nomes, although we have no evidence concerning the method of shipment or the officials responsible for it.

Egyptian currency was not shipped to Rome from Alexandria,

since the Egyptian drachma was fiat money, and the Egyptian tetradrachm, although for practical purposes equated with the *denarius*, had a lower silver content. Furthermore, there would have been little point in shipping silver from Alexandria to Rome because of its weight and the consequent expense. We know nothing of how the prefect and his treasury staff handled the flow of currency from the nomes to Alexandria or of how sufficient foreign credits were accumulated to make the annual payments to Rome. P. Baden 37, however, states that officials at Alexandria were chosen by lot to administer the public revenues, and it is evident that their task was to purchase foreign exchange in gold. They had contracted to purchase gold at a high price during the Dacian war, and they had not fulfilled their obligations to the treasury, although the term of settlement had expired. Meanwhile the war had ended, the booty of Trajan was thrown upon the market, and the price of gold fell from 15 drachmae to 11 drachmae. The contractors were in danger of sustaining a heavy loss, and they appealed to the prefect to stabilize the price which he promised to do.[306]

Before the organization of the imperial fiscus the revenues of Egypt flowed into the aerarium, as is stated by Velleius.[307] Later there was a *fiscus Alexandrinus* at Rome with a *tabularium* at Puteoli, but its functions are a matter of dispute.[308] It was probably organized by Vespasian in order to segregate the revenues of Egypt for exclusive administration by the emperor, just as the *fiscus Iudaicus* was a separate department to collect the Jewish tax which was devoted exclusively, at least for the first years of its collection, to the temple of Jupiter Capitolinus. The lead tesserae bearing the stamp *fisc(i) Alex-(andrini)* are believed to have been affixed to the bags of money brought to the harbour at Puteoli and thence transferred to Rome.[309]

THE REVENUES OF EGYPT

AURELIUS VICTOR states that the annual shipments of grain from Egypt to Rome in the time of Augustus amounted to 20 million *modii*.[1] This is the only evidence for the total revenues in grain from Egypt during the Roman period. Josephus, indeed, informs us that in the reign of Nero Egypt supplied Rome with corn for four months of the year, but the requirements of the city at that time are not known.[2] Official reports giving the total yield of a village, toparchy, or some larger district, are occasionally found among the papyri, but it is quite impossible to estimate from such fragmentary evidence the total yield of a nome, much less the revenues of the whole province. We do not even know whether Aurelius Victor's figure represents the revenue at the beginning of the reign of Augustus, when the yield was comparatively low because the later Ptolemies had allowed the irrigation system to fall into disrepair, or the increased revenue after Augustus had rebuilt the dikes and cleaned the canals, by using the labour of the army in Egypt, and also had confiscated the greater part of the lands belonging to priests and temples. Twenty million *modii*, indeed, may represent the average annual yield during the forty-four years of the reign of Augustus; it would necessarily be an average over some period of years, for we know that the tribute varied somewhat from year to year according to the flood of the Nile river.

Twenty million *modii* is a yield far greater than the tribute in grain ascribed to Ptolemy Philadelphus by Hieronymus.[3] The commentator on Daniel states that Egypt annually contributed to Philadelphus $1\frac{1}{2}$ million artabae of grain, and that the artaba was equivalent to $3\frac{1}{3}$ *modii*. Thus the yield in the time of Philadelphus calculated in Roman *modii* would have been 5 million *modii*. Wilcken has pointed out that it is much more likely that the artaba in the time of Philadelphus contained $4\frac{1}{2}$ *modii*, and that the total tribute was $6\frac{3}{4}$ million *modii*.[4] Various attempts have been made to explain the discrepancy between the yield in the time of Philadelphus and in the reign of Augustus, but no

theory has received general acceptance. Wilcken rightly depre-
cated Mommsen's suggestion that the Romans exacted a greater
proportion of their total revenues in kind and less in money than
had the Ptolemies, as contrary to the available evidence.
Wilcken himself sought to explain the increase by the exaction
of the annona and by a general increase in the rates of taxation
on land. H. A. Thompson has pointed out, however, that the
annona was drawn from the general revenues of the province
and that no special assessment for annona can be found in the
time of Augustus, and further that no great increase of the rates
of taxation or rent on land can be observed between the time of
Philadelphus and the reign of Augustus.[5] Tenney Frank
suggested that 20 million *modii* included shipments of grain by
private individuals for sale in the Roman market, in addition to
the government grain for the annona.[6] This may be true; but it
is unlikely that private shipments formed a really considerable
proportion of the total, for the remainder of the crop after the
government had withdrawn its share was hardly more than
enough to support the farmers in the country and the non-
agricultural population of the towns and cities of Egypt—the
requirements of the city of Alexandria must have been almost as great as those of Rome. Augustus confiscated much
of the hieratic land and the estates which the later Ptolemies had
granted to their favourites, and it is probable that an increase in
revenue resulted when those lands were added to the domain
land; but most of the confiscated lands seem not to have been so
added, but were granted or sold to private individuals to form
the great estates which paid no rents to the treasury and probably but little in taxes. Strabo asserts that Roman administration had restored the agricultural prosperity of Egypt,[7] but this
was the result of the rehabilitation of the irrigation system, and
there is no reason to believe that the system was much more
efficient in the time of Augustus than in the prosperous days of
the great Philadelphus. Thompson has demonstrated that the
yield of the Arsinoite nome in the third century B.C. was so great
that Hieronymus' figure for all Egypt must be rejected.[8]

Twenty million *modii* did not, indeed, represent the maximum
annual tribute from Egypt, for in the time of Justinian 8 million
artabae, or 26⅔ million *modii* were sent annually from Egypt to

Constantinople.[9] The return of the great private estates to the crown, a process which had probably been completed by the time of Vespasian, naturally increased the revenues of the province. Nero or Vespasian established the department of the imperial estates (οὐσιακὸς λόγος) to administer the revenues of the inherited or confiscated estates which were no longer lightly taxed or wholly tax-free, but whose tenants paid unusually high rents in kind. It is not improbable that in the second half of the first century and in the second century the average annual tribute of Egypt was higher than in the reign of Justinian. Professor Johnson has pointed out that 20 million *modii* mean an average tax and rental on the cultivable land in Egypt of about $1\frac{1}{2}$ artabae an arura.[10] This is probably slightly higher than the average tax on private land (which varied from $\frac{1}{2}$ to 2 artabae an arura, although but little land was assessed at less than 1 artaba an arura); but the average rental of domain- and usiac-land, particularly in the second century, was much higher than $1\frac{1}{2}$ artabae an arura, and the amount of such land in Egypt was certainly great enough to raise the average of tax and rental well above $1\frac{1}{2}$ artabae an arura. The deductions for stipends of minor officials and clerks, who received part of their remuneration in kind, had to be taken from the general revenues of grain, but they did not reach a very large total. Consequently for 150 years the average tribute in grain was probably considerably higher than 20 million *modii* a year.

In some years the Nile flood was too low or too high, and a shortage of grain resulted in spite of the improvements made in the system of irrigation. Native revolts occasionally caused the devastation of grain-lands in parts of the country. During such years the yield of the province decreased, and in A.D. 100 famine in Egypt was so great that Trajan ordered the grain-fleet to return from Rome to Egypt in order to relieve the suffering of the Egyptians. Low Niles in successive years preceded the edict of Hadrian in A.D. 136, and apparently occurred again at the end of the second century. Although there is evidence for poor crops in other years,[11] such conditions were exceptional in Egypt. Even in time of scarcity the revenues from private land were uniform, for the taxes (καθήκοντα) were not remitted or adjusted because of a low Nile as were the rents (ἐκφόρια) upon domain land.

Numerous extra charges on grain-land, intended to reduce the various grain-measures to uniformity and to pay the expenses of collection of grain and transport to Alexandria, were inherited, at least in great part, from the Ptolemaic administration. Such new levies as were introduced by Augustus were probably intended to increase the returns from catoecic and other private land. The system of grain revenues developed by the Ptolemies required little change when adopted by Augustus, and as fixed by him was continued with few changes until the reign of Diocletian. The most important innovations were the establishment of the οὐσιακὸς λόγος, when the great estates were recovered by Nero and Vespasian, the organization of the *annona militaris* as a separate charge upon land at the end of the second century or the beginning of the third century, and Septimius Severus' transfer of responsibility for collection of taxes to the municipal senates. There is some indication also that the rate of rentals paid for domain and usiac lands rose gradually throughout the three centuries of Roman rule.[12]

The lack of flexibility in the system of taxes and rents in kind, which would seem to preclude raising the rates to meet emergencies, was no obstacle to the Roman government. The emperor or his prefect did not hesitate to make special levies for the support of the army of occupation, for the expenses of travelling officials and soldiers and of visiting princes, or for the use of armies campaigning in other parts of the empire (the ἀναβολικόν [13]). These special levies must have caused great suffering among the poorer peasants who could not buy immunity from unjust exactions. In addition, the government forced the cultivators to sell their wheat to it at a low price during emergencies, when the market-price was high, and this was a serious annoyance even when it did not work a very real hardship upon the peasants. Furthermore, the prosperity brought to Egypt by the benefits of Roman rule did not reach all of the populace. The poorest class of peasants had never been anything but poverty-stricken, and their share in the economic recovery of Egypt did not suffice to meet the increased demands of the tax-collectors. By the middle of the first century the peasants had begun to leave the land, and tax-collectors complained that they were unable to make their collections because the villages were deserted.

The cultivable land of Egypt, however, was not allowed to stand idle. The Roman government found a ready answer to the loss of its tenants in resorting to the old Ptolemaic device of forced cultivation of domain land both by freeholders and by the remaining state-tenants. The attractions of life in the cities and towns of Egypt, where the prosperity brought by increasing commerce with Arabia and India made industry and trade more attractive than agriculture, doubtless accounted in part for the urban movement.[14] But that was not the only cause; it is evident that the over-rigorous exaction of taxes described by Philo drove many peasants to flee from their holdings.[15]

The system of taxation on land established by Augustus and maintained under Tiberius was severe; but it seems unlikely that it would have caused so much distress, if it had been equably administered under the officials appointed by succeeding emperors. It is clear, however, that efforts to satisfy the demands of the spendthrift Caligula led officials in Egypt to impose new burdens of taxation, and that the efforts of Claudius to relieve the Egyptians were thwarted by unscrupulous officials. Nero's extravagance again caused the exaction of unauthorized taxes. The edict of Ti. Julius Alexander (A.D. 68) acknowledges that the chief causes of complaints by the Egyptian farmers were forced cultivation of domain lands at high rentals, imposition of unauthorized taxes by the prefects, disregard of immunities granted by the emperors, and illegal exactions of assessors who demanded a normal tax in years when the Nile flood was low. The new prefect promised relief from these intolerable conditions, but how far he was able to make good his promise is not known. Vespasian had greater need for cash revenues than for an increase in the tribute in corn, and there is no evidence for an increase in the amount of grain collected by the government or for higher taxes or rents on grain-land in his reign or in that of Domitian.

Trajan by an act of expedient generosity relieved the distress of famine in Egypt in A.D. 100. In his Panegyric of Trajan, however, Pliny read a little sermon to the Egyptians on the necessity of their submissive payment of the tribute to Rome, for it was the manifest destiny of the province to serve the head of the empire. It is probable that Trajan increased his demands upon

Egypt to support his great campaigns against the Dacians and the Parthians, and that as a result the capacity of Egypt was over-strained. The condition was aggravated by a series of low Niles in the reign of Hadrian, and that emperor was finally obliged to grant an extension of time for the payment of land-taxes and to agree to reduce the rentals upon domain land in accordance with their productive value.[16] Later in the second century the peasants again fled from the land; but the cause is unknown. It may have been a combination of unfavourable circumstances. Professor Johnson has suggested 'either that the productivity of Egypt was declining because of overcropping and defects in the canal system, or that the burden of the tribute in kind had been increased'. The plague in this period, more-over, was particularly devastating in Egypt, and Wilcken once traced the disappearance of the peasants from the villages to that cause.[17] In the reign of Commodus some anxiety is said to have been felt at Rome that Egypt would be unable to furnish its quota of the annona of the city, and steps were taken to insure a supply from Africa.[18]

The transfer by Septimius Severus of responsibility for the collection of taxes to the municipal senates probably had little effect upon the revenues in grain. Similarly the grant of citizen-ship to the inhabitants of Egypt by Caracalla, although it seems to have relieved them of payments of poll-tax and many other capitation taxes, did not affect the principle of taxation in kind on land. It is certain, however, that the revenue in kind declined during the first half of the third century. It was a period of general anarchy in the empire and of revolt and invasion in Egypt. Neglect of the irrigation system led to the decline of the villages in the Fayûm, which was particularly dependent upon irrigation for its productivity. This neglect of the system of dikes and canals may have resulted from the fact that the need in Rome for the grain of Egypt was somewhat less on account of the increased yield of the province of Africa, and perhaps because the population of Rome, particularly the poorer classes sustained by the dole, had been reduced by the plague brought by the soldiers of Verus returning from the East. There is evidence that in the third century an attempt was made to secure a greater yield from the usiac land by direct management instead of leasing it, but the experiment was a failure.[19] In the second half of the third century Aurelian and Probus took steps to drive the invaders from Egypt and to restore the productivity of Egypt after this period of decline, and their efforts were similar to measures once used by Augustus to restore the efficiency of the irrigation system. Aurelian is said to have added an ounce to the loaves of bread distributed to the people of Rome, and to have appointed additional boatmen on the Nile in order that this increase (of a twelfth?) in the tribute might be made perpetual.[20] Probus used his soldiers in Egypt to clean the canals and restore the dikes.[21] There was a temporary revival of many of the villages in the Fayûm towards the close of the third century, which doubtless reflects the benefits of Probus' work. It is significant that the effort to restore the productivity of Egypt coincides with the time when the depreciation of the coinage had resulted in an inflation which made taxes in kind more valuable than taxes in money.

Although the amount of grain exacted in tribute from Egypt by Augustus is at least three times as great as that which Hieronymus attributes to Ptolemy Philadelphus, the revenue in money obtained by the Roman conqueror was much less than that which flowed into the treasury of the Greek king. Hieronymus states that the annual income of Philadelphus from Egypt was 14,800 talents, or 88,800,000 drachmae, which is equivalent to 355,300,000 sesterces.[22] Caesar's conquest of Gaul added 40 million sesterces annually to the income of Rome, and Velleius Paterculus states that Augustus by his conquest of Egypt added almost as much revenue to the Roman treasury as his father had done by the conquest of Gaul.[23] Therefore the income from Egypt at the beginning of the reign of Augustus was a little less than 40 million sesterces a year. Velleius says, however, that in his own day Gaul contributed just the same tribute to the treasury as the rest of the whole empire, an amount vastly greater than the 40 million sesterces obtained from it in 49 B.C.[24] It is evident from the same statement that Egypt contributed much less than Gaul in the reign of Tiberius when Velleius was writing. The revenue obtained from Egypt increased, however, during the reign of Augustus, as is attested by Strabo, who declares that the revenue after Augustus had restored the agricultural prosperity of Egypt and had developed the foreign commerce of the province was greater than that of Ptolemy Auletes which, according to Cicero, amounted to 12,500 talents annually.[25] Because of the doubtful value of the talent when the drachma was depreciated, it is uncertain how many sesterces should be set as the equivalent of the sum; it may have varied from 75 million to 300 million sesterces.[26] It is as natural that the tribute of Egypt should have increased during the forty-four years of Augustus' reign as that the tribute of Gaul should have increased during the seventy-eight years intervening between the conquest in 49 B.C. and A.D. 29 when Velleius was writing his history. During the reorganization of the province of Egypt Augustus probably increased the rate of the poll-tax and widened liability to it and he probably introduced the dike-tax. If the latter tax was paid at the same rate as in later reigns it amounted to about 20 million sesterces annually. Strabo tells us that the prefect Gallus had to engage in suppressing armed revolts in the Thebaid arising from the increased demands of Roman tax-gatherers.[27]

There are two reasons for the great difference in the revenue immediately available to Augustus and that attributed to Auletes. In the time of Auletes Egypt was still essentially sound, as Milne has pointed out.[28] But Egypt was in a sorry condition when Augustus completed his almost bloodless conquest of the country. The neglect of the system of irrigation could not have been without its deleterious effect on the whole economy of the country based, as it was, on agriculture. Cleopatra, in her effort to finance Antony's war against Octavian and in her desperate attempt to salvage something after the battle of Actium, had confiscated an enormous amount of capital, even robbing the temples of their precious dedications and their hoards of gold.[29] Cleopatra's treasure became the booty of Octavian, and accounted for a portion of the vast spoils of the conquest which Tenney Frank has estimated at about a billion sesterces.[30] Even though a part of this great sum may have been realized by the sale of confiscated land to Roman citizens, Octavian's booty meant the withdrawal of a very great amount of the liquid capital of Egypt. That must, for at least a few years, have retarded the recovery of the country, and it is not surprising that the initial tribute was small.

In the second place there was great overhead expense in the administration of Egypt. The bureaucracy had undoubtedly grown in the three hundred years that had passed since the reign of Philadelphus, for the birth-rate among bureaucratic offices is always higher than the death-rate. There is no evidence that the bureaucracy was reduced in Roman times, and it probably grew.[31] The salaries of the five highest officials at Alexandria totalled more than a million sesterces a year.[32] This does not include all of the high-salaried officials, and there was in addition a small army of clerks and minor officials in the various Alexandrian bureaux. The higher officials in the nomes were also paid a salary and each had a staff of clerks and assistants. Part of the stipend of minor functionaries was probably paid in kind, but the total charge in money against the provincial budget must have been enormous. Something also was spent on maintaining public buildings in Alexandria, such as the museum, the libraries, the record offices, the mint, and the great granaries and docks. The cost of the army of occupation has been estimated at about $11\frac{1}{3}$ million sesterces a year down to A.D. 81.[33] Some of the provinces were held at a loss, and it was only the phenomenal productivity of Egypt which enabled it to provide so much as 40 million sesterces at the beginning of the reign of Augustus. Through the three centuries of Roman rule the most important changes in the system of taxation seem to have been made with a view to reducing the overhead expense of administration, or rather to transferring the cost from the imperial budget to the tax-payers of the province.

The cash revenues of Augustus were derived from the taxes on garden-land, taxes on animals, the poll-tax, the ἐγκύκλιον on sales of real property, licence-taxes and *ad valorem* taxes on trades, the income from state monopolies and external customs-dues specially mentioned by Strabo, and various miscellaneous taxes which, however, are not well attested. The market-taxes and internal customs also contributed to the revenues, but their organization in the reign of Augustus is not known. The income collected by the department of the Idiologus from such items as fines and *bona vacantia* falling into the treasury also swelled the total receipts, but such income was by nature highly variable.

The bath-tax introduced for the maintenance of the baths built by the Roman conquerors was used for a specific purpose and could hardly affect the net revenue of the province. One of the great items of expense in the budget in Egypt was the outlay for maintaining dikes and canals. Augustus used the army in Egypt, in addition to the usual *corvée*, for the restoration of the irrigation system, but it is probable that he introduced the dike-tax to remove the cost of maintenance of the rehabilitated system from the charges against the general revenues. Similarly his development of the surcharges ($\pi\rho o\sigma\delta\iota\alpha\gamma\rho\alpha\phi\delta\mu\epsilon\nu\alpha$), whether they were intended to pay the cost of shipping tax-monies to Alexandria or to defray the cost of monetary exchange, or both, was designed to remove such expenses from the charges against the general budget. These two items alone would account for a considerable increase in the net revenues available to Augustus by the end of his reign. The general increase in the prosperity of the province and particularly the development of commerce with Arabia and India and with Rome, which was heavily taxed at the customs-barriers, necessarily meant a great increase in the net revenue by the early part of the first century after Christ.

There is no evidence for the introduction of new taxes in the reign of Tiberius. He apparently was content to maintain the efficiency of the system established by Augustus, and we may recall the tradition that he rebuked one of his prefects for exacting and forwarding a greater tribute than had been assessed. The displacement of the tax-farmer collecting the bath-tax at Thebes by a practor was consistent with the policy of Tiberius for the whole empire; in Egypt it was but a minor change, however, and the complete development of this policy in that province had to wait until the reign of Trajan.

The illegal levies under Gaius and Claudius, which are mentioned in the decree of Ti. Julius Alexander, are not attested in the extant receipts. The crown-tax was collected in the reign of Claudius, and the peculiar nature of that tax, as an ostensibly voluntary offering of the provincials to the emperor at his accession, may have provided officials with an excuse for unauthorized exactions. In the reign of Nero the first receipts for assessments ($\mu\epsilon\rho\iota\sigma\mu o\iota$) for guards are found.[34] It is possible that these were at first occasional levies for special guards, but the continuation of the collection of assessments indicates that the government was seeking to eliminate the salaries of guards and police from the general budget. Commerce with Arabia, Trogodytica, and India was well developed by the reign of Nero, and manufacture consequently expanded in the cities, especially in Alexandria, and by virtue of the taxes on trades contributed heavily to the increasing revenues. The cash rentals from estates confiscated by Nero added to the income from the province. At this time the revenues from Egypt in a month are stated by Josephus to have been more than the tribute of the whole province of Judaea in a year, and it has been estimated that Egypt paid approximately 400 million sesterces annually.[35] This is ten times the tribute obtained at the beginning of the reign of Augustus and more than the annual revenue of Ptolemy Philadelphus. We may recall that the province of Gaul seventy-eight years after its conquest showed a similar increase in its tribute. Despite the great prosperity of Egypt in this period, the peasants, as has been indicated above, were finding it impossible to meet the exactions of the collectors of such taxes as the poll-tax and were leaving the land. Tax-payers had fled from their responsibilities before,[36] but the trouble seems to have become especially acute in the decade after A.D. 50.[37] Philo's harrowing description of the desperate efforts of the tax-collectors to exact payments of arrears may be rhetorical exaggeration, but it certainly was not without a basis of fact. Rostovtzeff has pointed out that the collectors' attempts to force the relatives and neighbours of the delinquent to pay his taxes imply a collective responsibility for payment of taxes which later on was officially recognized not only in Egypt but throughout the empire.

Dio states that Vespasian made innumerable exactions in Egypt in his effort to raise funds for his western campaign. There is little trace of this, however, in the extant receipts and accounts, and it is probable that the levies were only temporary. The tax of 6 drachmae, which he demanded from every Alexandrian citizen, seems to have been remitted, for citizens of Alexandria were exempt from poll-tax in the fifth year of his reign.[38] The only new tax which appears in the receipts of Vespasian's reign is the undesignated μερισμός at Ophi, unless

the uncertain διλ(   ) ε Ούεσπασιανοῦ, for which 8 drachmae
were paid by a Jew in A.D. 78, was a special levy.[39] Vespasian
confiscated the temple-tax of the Jews, and those in Egypt, who
are said to have numbered a million,[40] must have paid about
8 million sesterces a year into the treasury of the temple of
Jupiter Capitolinus. The earliest extant receipt for customs-
dues (ρ καὶ ν́) in the Arsinoite nome is dated in the reign of
Titus (A.D. 80).[41] It is probable that the internal customs were
reorganized during the reign of Vespasian and probably contributed thereafter to increase the total revenues of Egypt.
The establishment of the customs-barrier at Memphis (for
which were made the payments ὑπὲρ λιμένος Μέμφεως), when
the epistrategia of the Heptanomia and Arsinoite nome was
inaugurated about this time, must have greatly increased the
yield of the internal customs.

In the reign of Domitian occurs the first extant receipt for the
assessment for watch-towers (μαγδωλοφυλακία), and this is an
indication that the practice of making assessments for the support
of the guards and police of Egypt was being extended.[42] In
A.D. 91 a receipt from Elephantine-Syene records payments for
both guards (φύλακες) and watches (σκόπελοι).[43] In the year
A.D. 96–7, the first year of Nerva, the rate of the poll-tax at
Elephantine-Syene was raised from 16 to 17 drachmae, but it is
possible that the increase is more apparent than real, for the 1
drachma is exactly equivalent to the surcharge (προσδιαγραφόμενα) at $\frac{1}{16}$ which may have been collected at Elephantine-
Syene ever since its introduction in the reign of Augustus, but
appeared first in the receipts in the reign of Nerva because of a
change in the method of book-keeping.

The reign of Trajan brought considerable change in the
system of taxation. The collectors seem to have been given a
semi-official status, and assessments were made to relieve them
of their responsibility for the uncollectable arrears of taxes.
This was official recognition of the practice of holding the community responsible for the sum of the taxes assessed upon its
individual inhabitants. At the same time assessments for various
purposes—guards of all kinds, travelling-expenses of soldiers,
buildings, statues—multiplied and increased, and were collected
regularly until the issuing of the Edict of Caracalla. This again

was an attempt to reduce the overhead expenses of administration and so increase the net revenue, for Trajan needed funds for his great campaigns. The poll-tax in Upper Egypt seems to have been increased slightly towards the end of his reign.[44] Hadrian, on the other hand, seems to have abolished the special tax paid by Jews, for receipts are not found after the reign of Trajan, and Hadrian's efforts to relieve the tenants of domain lands have been mentioned above. His visits to Egypt, however, meant that the inhabitants were subject to extra burdens in furnishing proper conveyance and entertainment for his retinue and also for statues of the emperor to be placed in temples dedicated to him.

The Antonines continued the system of taxes without important revision. P. Fay. 26, dated A.D. 150, is a significant bit of official correspondence referring to the establishment of a commission to investigate the diminished $\phi \acute{o} \rho o \varsigma$ from the Arsinoite nome. Late in the second century began the pernicious habit of exacting the crown-tax on every possible occasion. This extraordinary levy was soon made into an annual tax and was assessed on land; thereupon an additional crown-tax was added as an extraordinary levy. Rises in the rates of local capitation taxes which may have begun as early as the reign of Hadrian, were frequent in the latter half of the second century. New revenues were needed, for the coinage had been depreciated throughout the empire, and the ease with which vast sums could be obtained in Egypt by exaction of the crown-tax proved too tempting to be resisted. At the same time the government began to seek immediate revenues from the sale of land; but since the major portion of this was probably land confiscated for non-payment of taxes, it may have yielded no increase in the average annual income.

The inflationary effect of the continued depreciation of the coinage is probably reflected in the rise in the rates of taxes on garden-lands under Septimius Severus. The rise amounted to 25 per cent., except for the 'tithe' ($\mathring{a}\pi \acute{o} \mu o \iota \rho a$) on gardens which was raised 150 per cent. Land could best be made to pay increased rates because the value of its products tends to show an increase most nearly parallel with the inflationary effect of depreciated currency. The depreciation of the coinage begun by Marcus Aurelius and continued by his successors was not immediately reflected by an inflation of prices in Egypt because of the rigid control over Egyptian currency maintained by the government. Except for the rise in taxes on garden-lands at the beginning of the third century, the rates of money-taxes do not seem to have been increased until the reign of Probus. Then the taxes on trades were mightily increased when the inflation of the currency was felt with great suddenness in Egypt after a century of depreciation of the coinage. Aurelian's establishment of the *anabolicae species* as an annual tax paid in kind shows that inflation was making itself felt before the rates of taxes were raised.

Septimius Severus' transfer of responsibility for collection of taxes to the municipal senates is best understood as an effort to eliminate entirely the overhead expenses of collections from the provincial budget and to stop the losses from arrears. It was a natural and probably inevitable extension of the principle of collective responsibility for the tribute which in the time of the Ptolemies had found expression in forced leases of crown-land, which had violent and unauthorized application in extortion practiced by tax-collectors in the days of Philo, and which finally had been officially recognized in the assessments introduced under Trajan. How well this new collecting agency would have functioned, had not Caracalla's edict granting Roman citizenship to the inhabitants of the provinces practically abolished the poll-tax and other capitation taxes in Egypt, cannot be known. The immediate loss in revenue which the abolition of those taxes would mean was compensated by the continued exaction of the crown-tax. This unhealthy levy upon the capital of the middle-class was abused in the third century, particularly by Elagabalus, until Alexander Severus promised to put an end to the exactions. A crown-tax was, however, collected twice during his reign.[45] It was necessary to replace in some way the revenue formerly obtained by the crown-tax, and budgetary stability seems to have been attained during the rest of the third century by the imposition of an annual assessment on each community.[46] This often amounted practically to a restoration of the poll-tax, although in some communities the burden may have been divided among the citizens more in accordance with their ability to pay. But there were fewer and fewer inhabitants of Egypt who could be said to possess an ability to pay.

The system of taxation developed by the Ptolemies was curiously fitted to the capacity of an isolated country. Theoretically, at least, Egypt was the property of the king. Part of the land he retained and leased to state tenants who paid rents (ἐκφόρια) varying in accordance with the productivity of the land; the rest he ceded to his subjects on condition that they paid small fixed taxes (καθήκοντα). This distinction between ἐκφόρια and καθήκοντα was consistently extended to money-taxes on land and to other sources of revenue. Lessees of flocks and herds paid φόρος or rent; owners paid the license-tax which in the Roman period was called ἐννόμιον and τέλεσμα καμήλων. Industries were maintained as monopolies of the government and might be managed directly or leased to parties who paid a φόρος; but, on the other hand, licence-taxes were paid by persons engaged in trade and industry not monopolized by the government, or some tithe of the products of industry or the profits of trade was demanded by the government. The customs-dues, external and internal, were but a logical extension of the sales-tax upon trade. This system was adopted by Augustus with a minimum of change.[47] So long as the rents and tithes were but a fair share of the yield of land and industry, and the licence-taxes and other fixed taxes were not exorbitant, the system yielded a rich, if somewhat variable, revenue to the government and was not too oppressive to the vast majority of the populace. But across this system cut capitation taxes and special levies. Both of these devices for increasing the revenue had been employed by the Ptolemaic administration, but they seem to have been used sparingly and not to have crippled the country, except perhaps under the last of the Ptolemies.

The exploitation by the Romans and the consequent ruin of Egypt have been analysed and condemned by historians.[48] Milne has cited evidence to show that Egypt was comparatively prosperous during the last century of Ptolemaic rule. Rostovtzeff has taken pains to show that the exploitation by the Roman government was having its vicious effects in the first century after Christ—results, he maintained, of the defects in the system established by Augustus. But if Augustus erred in his reorganization of the taxation of Egypt, it was in the extension of the poll-tax and the introduction of new capitation taxes. Reducing exemptions of priests and catoeci to payment of the poll-tax merely meant that there were fewer privileged persons exempt although quite able to pay the tax, and this could have injured the province only on the doubtful assumption that all taxation is destructive. If, however, Augustus raised the rates of the poll-tax, it is probable that the increased burden fell upon those least able to pay, for he continued to recognize privileged classes who were exempt from poll-tax or paid at a lower rate than the native peasants. The introduction of the dike-tax and bath-tax as capitation taxes and the conversion of the pig-tax into a capitation tax were additional burdens upon the less privileged classes. Nevertheless, I believe that it was abuse by unscrupulous officials rather than defects in the system which caused the bankruptcy of peasants in the middle of the first century. As soon as the abuses were halted the increased prosperity of Egypt, caused by the development of its foreign commerce, enabled it to bear the burdens of taxation without too great difficulty, even after Trajan introduced additional assessments. After all, when the products of Egypt were sold at Rome or elsewhere in the empire, the purchaser indirectly paid the tax of the Egyptian artisan and the customs-dues as well, for they were all included in the price of his purchase.

The exaction of the crown-tax, at the end of the second century and in the third century, was a much more serious strain upon the economy of Egypt, for it drained away the capital of the middle-class and of the moderately well-to-do. The petition of Apollonarion shows that as early as A.D. 200 a woman of considerable wealth and extensive landholdings had been reduced to comparative poverty largely because of the extra levies ordained by the prefect Aemilius Saturninus.[49] The decline of trade with India in the third century was also a heavy blow to the province, and since the anarchy of that century injured Egypt's trade with the western Mediterranean her external commerce no longer sufficed to carry the burden of taxation. It is not surprising, therefore, that Egypt declined in the third century. We cannot trace the effects of this decline upon the tribute with any precision because of the scarcity of receipts and accounts. We have no information at all regarding the total revenues from Egypt during this period, but it is probable that they varied greatly. BGU. 1.8 shows that considerable sums were realized from nomarchic taxes in the Arsinoite nome during the fourth year of the emperor Philip, and yet we are told that Philip was compelled to make peace with the Goths on the Danube because the government was unable to collect the revenue in the Eastern provinces.[50] In the reign of Gallienus Egypt was the scene of revolt and of invasions by desert tribes, and in the reign of Claudius II all Egypt, with the exception of Alexandria, fell under the control of the Palmyrenes. The latter were defeated by Aurelian; his general and successor Probus succeeded in driving out the Blemmyes and the Libyans.[51] When he had succeeded in bringing peace to Egypt, Probus increased the rates of taxes in an effort to keep pace with the inflation of the currency, but this increase must soon have become lost in the uncontrolled inflation which immediately followed.

The moderate inflation of the currency earlier in the third century may at first have benefited the landholders of Egypt who were able to obtain better prices for their grain and other products. But this benefit could only have been temporary, even if the exactions of the crown-tax, constant pressure of high capitation taxes, and the crushing liturgies had not immediately wiped out its effect. Soon the small farmers and eventually the well-to-do were compelled to sell their lands to the rich, who were often able to avoid their own obligations to the treasury by bringing influence to bear upon venal officials.[52] Great estates, which had evidently swallowed up the small holdings, appear in the third century, and the very rich were able to take advantage of the government's policy of selling land and add to their vast possessions. Thus the way was prepared for the reforms in taxation inaugurated by Diocletian and for the quasi-feudal system in Egypt under Byzantine rule.

APPENDIX

In this appendix are listed alphabetically the taxes and abbreviations for taxes concerning which it has been impossible to make any very helpful suggestions.

α . . . P. Flor. I. 105: ὑπὲρ α . . .

ακκ( ). SB. 4355.

τέλ(ος) ἀληθικ( ) μνομ(εν). O. Strass. 224, 226.

ἀναλ(ώματος) χρόνων . . ακ ( ). O. Strass. 110.

απ^{αι}(?). PSI. IV. 281. 64.

ἀπομ( ) πολ( ). O. Tait, p. 110, no. 217, from Coptos and dated 18 B.C. Possibly this is a receipt for ἀπόμ(οιρα), since that tax may once have been paid to a *thesaurus*, for it was originally assessed and delivered in kind.

ἀποχ( ). WO. II. 847-8. Possibly a variant of πρόχρεια and therefore to be restored ἀπόχ(ρεια), or perhaps a repayment of a loan in wheat.

αρ . . ρ(.) BGU. VII. 1599. Perhaps ἀρ[γυ]ρ(ίου).

α . τ( ) λη(μμάτων). O Strass. 164. Perhaps α[ὑ]τ(ῶν) λη(μμάτων) or ἄ[ρ]τ(ων) λη(μμάτων).

ἀφ( ) and ἀφ( ) σ( ) κ(ατ)οί(κων?). P. Ryl. II. 185. Perhaps Ἀφ(ροδίτης) σ(ύνταξις). Cf. P. Fay. 81, where a payment of 22½ artabae of wheat by catoeci (or for catoecic land) at Theadelphia is stated in the interlinear note to be for the Σύντ(αξις) εἰς Φιλ.( ) Ἀφροδ( ).

βα( ). P. Teb. II. 463. Possibly this should be read κα(θήκοντα).

β . . το( ). O. Mey. 25.

γλυ( ). PO. IV. 734.

γρ( ) τ( ). P. Lond. II. 166 a (p. 116). The editor doubtfully suggested that the name of the tax might be found in this abbreviation, but it seems more likely that a single payment was made to the secretary of the collectors of money taxes (γρ( ) πρ( ) αργ( )) by Longinus, the secretary of the toparchy—γρ(αμματεὺς) τ(οπαρχίας).

δ( ) or δα( ). P. Teb. II. 345.

δασμ( ). SP. XXII. 110, 117. Possibly δεσμ(οφυλακία) should be read.

δεσδ( ). P. Fay. 42 (a).

διλ( ) ε Οὐεσπ(ασιανοῦ). SP. XIII, p. 8, no. 5. Possibly δι(έγραφεν) ﬅε Οὐεσπ(ασιανοῦ) should be read, or perhaps διδ(ράχμου).

διογ[ ]. P. Fay. 42 (a). Perhaps διαγ(ραφή) should be read.

δο( ). P. Ryl. II. 375. It is not certain that this is a tax.

ὑπ(ἐρ) δ[. .]α^σ κορα^κ in line 4 of the *verso* of P. Mich. inv. no. 5766, published by H. C. Youtie in *Aegyptus*, XIII (1933), pp. 569 ff. The editor doubtfully suggested δ[ρ]άσ(σεσθαι) κοράκ(ων), a tax for the protection of the crops against crows.

ε( ). O. Mich. Car. 121–5, second or third century after Christ, record payments of 2 to 4 drachmae.

ε . ( ) . . ω( ). O. Strass. 98. Perhaps (ὑπὲρ) ἐγ(οικίου) . . ω( ).

ε . . . ου μυρ( ). P. Fay. 42 (a).

εδ( ). P. Kalén 3–4. Kalén (p. 99) reads ἐδ(αφῶν) and regards this as a tax on cleruchic fields. It was paid in money (cf. P. Teb. II. 477; BGU. I. 20).

εξ( ). P. Teb. II. 277, introd. (early third century). This was collected on οὐσιακὴ γῆ.

επ( ). PO. XII. 1518; P. Teb. II. 638. Perhaps for ἐπ(ιστατικόν) or ἐπ(ιστολ . . .).

επ( ) χ( ). P. Teb. II. 353.

ἐπικαρσίου. WO. II. 64, 67.

θησο( ). P. Teb. II. 347.

ἰδιω( ). P. Flor. III. 387.

. ικογγ( ) [.]οργ( ). P. Ryl. II. 213. 444.

ιλ( ). P. Fay. 57.

. . . . κ( ). O. Strass. 240. Possibly this should be restored [μερ(ισμοῦ) ἀνα]κ(εχωρηκότων).

κ( ). P. Teb. II. 345; P. Hamb. 40, 51; P. Fay. 42 (a).

κα( ). SB. 441. A list of names with amounts of 2 to 4 drachmae (?). Perhaps this should be expanded κα(θήκοντα).

κιθ( ). O Strass. 291. Possibly this should be expanded κιθ-(αροίδου). Viereck has promised an explanation of this word in the second volume of O. Strass.

κλεινεντ( ). WO. II. 185, 187; cf. WO. I, p. 225. Possibly it is a place-name.

λογ( ). O. Tait, p. 90, no. 89; WO. II. 472. There is a λόγος προσ-θήκης in SB. 7583, and a λόγου καυ . [. .] in O. Tait, p. 104, no. 182, where 6¾ artabae of wheat are collected on land (ἐδάφη).

λελμ( ). PO. XII. 1438. Perhaps this should be read δεσμ(οφυλακία).

λου( ). P. Fay. 42 (a).

]μερῶ Σούχ(ου?). P. Lond. III. 1235 (p. 35).

μυρ( ). P. Fay. 42 (a).

νε[ ] seems to be a tax in P. Columbia 1 R 1 a–b. iii. 18, since προσδιαγραφόμενα of 4 drachmae 5¼ obols were paid on it.

π—( ). SP. XXII. 111–13. Perhaps this is not a tax.

π[. .] ρ( ) εἰδῶν. P. Flor. I. 16.

παικίσωνος. SB. 4355.

πατ( ). BGU. III. 897, 898.

πε( ) μηχ( ). BGU. III. 771. Perhaps this should be expanded πε(λωχικοῦ) μηχ(ανῆς); see Chapter XIII, p. 222.

. . πραμ Διὸς πόλεως. PSI. VIII. 990.

σ( ) and συ( ). P. Teb. II. 345. συ( ) occurs also in PO. IV. 734.

σλ( ). WO. II. 760, 761, 1539, 1546. κ(ατ)οί(κων) σλ( ) occurs in P. Ryl. II. 188. Perhaps this should be read σπ(ερμάτων).

στοιχή(ματος). O. Strass. 152.

τοκ( ) τυ( ). P. Teb. II. 358. Perhaps this should be read τόκ(ος) διο(ικήσεως).

τρ( ). BGU. VII. 1613B. Perhaps this is the τρ(απεζιτικόν) mentioned by Schwahn in PWRE. A 9, Sp. 286.

. . υ. O. Mey. 21.

[. . . .]υ BGU. III. 789.

. [.]υ[. . . . . . .] P. Strass. 62.

φ( ). PO. II. 289.

φ . . Θεαδελ( ) and φι̃( ) νι̃( ) Θεαδ( ). PSI. VIII. 925–6.

χ( ). BGU. VII. 1599.

χάλκινα. P. Hamb. 85. Cf. the tax of 20 copper drachmae in P. Teb. II. 373.

χο( ). P. Teb. II. 346.

χρυ . . .( ). O. Strass. 73.

χω( ) ὀψω(νίου). SB. 4355 (cf. BL. II. 1).

ψυγμοῦ καὶ διαψειλῶν. BGU. I. 10. 8.

The names of the taxes in the following documents have been lost: PO. II. 386; O. Tait, p. 174, no. 2; O. Strass. 241, 242, 216, 137, 139; P. Lond. II. 164 (p. 116) (?); BGU. VII. 1625; O. Strass. 114; P. Lond. II. 182 (a) (Plate 83); O. Mey. 74; O. Strass. 70; BGU. I. 346; O. Strass. 154; O. Tait, p. 108, nos. 206–7; P. Ryl. II. 195. 3, 7; BGU. I. 222; WO. II. 1418 (?).

A large number of accounts recording payments of 4 drachmae or multiples thereof may be for poll-tax, crown-tax, or possibly τέλος καταλοχισμῶν on catoecic land; examples are: BGU. VII. 1600, III. 761; P. Ryl. II. 373; BGU. VII. 1708, 1709; P. Lond. II. 156 (p. 249); BGU. II. 392, 639; P. Lond. II. 166a (p. 116); BGU. I. 42; P. Gron. 4, 7; O. Mich. 7.

Wilcken suggested that the following payments for τέλος, since each is stated to be the τέλος of a certain month (or months), might be receipts for χειρωνάξιον: WO. II. 504, 1030, 1048, 1050, 1078, 1386, 1394, 1412. A μερισμὸς τέλους is found in WO. II. 554, 624, 670, 1586. All these ostraca are from Thebes.

NOTES

CHAPTER I

1. Rostovtzeff, *Social and Economic History of the Roman Empire*, Oxford 1926, pp. 266 ff., and chapter vii, notes 42–7 (the German edition of 1929 has a different pagination, but the numbering of the notes is the same), and the material there cited; T. Kalén, *Berliner Leihgabe griechischer Papyri*, Uppsala Universitets Årsskrift, 1932, pp. 67 ff.

2. Rostovtzeff, *A Large Estate in Egypt in the Third Century B.C.*, University of Wisconsin Studies in the Social Sciences and History, VI (1922), esp. pp. 143 ff.

3. Wilcken, *Grundzüge*, p. 287 f. and the material there cited.

4. Rostovtzeff, op. cit., pp. 257 ff., chapter vii, note 35, and the material there cited.

5. II. 109, 168. Diodorus, I. 21. 7; 73 implies that the land of Egypt was divided into three equal parts belonging respectively to king, priests, and soldiers, but the equality of the divisions is very doubtful; cf. Otto, *Priester und Tempel*, Leipzig and Berlin, 1905–8, I, pp. 262 ff.

6. The fact that the Ptolemies settled their soldiers on the land reclaimed in the Fayûm and in the Delta (cf. Rostovtzeff, op. cit., chapter vii, note 47) indicates that comparatively little change was made in the existing tenure of land.

7. Lesquier, *Les Institutions militaires de l'Égypte sous les Lagides*, Paris 1911, p. 221.

8. Ibid., pp. 162 ff. Cf. the data collected in the next chapter.

9. Ibid.

10. These dues were called καθήκοντα in contrast with the ἐκφόρια, the rental on domain land. Cf. Kalén, op. cit., pp. 59 ff., and the literature there cited.

11. Rostovtzeff, *Large Estate*, pp. 136 ff., and the literature cited in notes 99–101.

12. Lesquier, op. cit., p. 221. The tax of two artabae is found in P. Teb. I. 5. 15, 99; BGU. VI. 1238, where the note based upon P. Teb. II. 346. 14 n., is wrong. Cf. next chapter, note 16.

13. In P. Teb. I. 5. 57–61 it is directed that no assessment be made upon property dedicated to the gods, ἀνιερωμένη γῆ, but that concession may have been only temporary and perhaps not even universal in application throughout Egypt. The famous Rosetta Stone (OGI. I, 90) records the praise of Ptolemy Epiphanes by the priests because of his remission of the tax of 1 artaba to the arura on temple-land, but in P. Teb. I. 98. 27–40 the temple-land pays at ½ artaba.

14. This work has not been superseded.

15. *Grundz.*, pp. 287–309. The statements of this chapter are based upon Wilcken's presentation of the material.

16. Ibid., pp. 288 ff.

17. Cf. Jouguet in *Rev. ét. gr.* XXXIII (1920), pp. 392 ff., and the material there cited; Rostovtzeff, *Soc. and Ec. Hist.*, chapter viii, note 13; Collart, P. Bouriant, pp. 156 ff.; Schmidt, GGA. 1928, 4, p. 162; Kalén, op. cit., p. 68, note 2.

18. Δημόσιοι γεωργοί were strictly the tenants of δημοσία γῆ, but the term was used loosely of the tenants of any class of domain land of the Roman period.

19. Rostovtzeff, GGA. 1909, pp. 606 ff., *Soc. and Ec. Hist.*, chapter vii, note 44.

20. The complete confiscation of the land of the temples did not occur until Christian influence became dominant in the fourth century; cf. Wilcken, *Grundz.*, p. 313.

21. Cf. notes 10 and 13.

22. Cf. Wilcken's introd. to *Chrest.* 65 (= P. Teb. I. 5); *Grundz.* pp. 279 ff.

23. For the Roman period ἀνιερωμένη γῆ is mentioned in SB. 5280. 9 and, if Wilcken's suggestion is correct, in P. Lond. III. 604 A (p. 70), lines 115 and 118. (Cf. *Archiv*, IV, p. 536; Plaumann, *Ptolemais*, Leipzig 1910, pp. 88 ff.)

24. Rostovtzeff, *Soc. and Ec. Hist.*, chapter vii, note 44.

25. See Chapter II, p. 15 f. and note 35.

26. Ibid., p. 16, section 8, and cf. Meyer's introd. to P. Giss. III. 60, pp. 27 ff., and the material there cited. Cf. also Kalén, op. cit., pp. 240 ff., who is, I think, mistaken.

27. Cf. Wilcken, *Grundz.*, p. 308 f.; SP. xx. 38 (cf. Kalén, op. cit., p. 244). The οἶκος πόλεως Ἀλεξανδρείας had land at Anubis in the Fayûm; cf. O. Tait, p. 180, H.

28. Kalén, op. cit., pp. 183 ff., and the material there cited; SB. 7360.

29. Wilcken, *Grundz.*, pp. 176-9, 205-8, and the literature there cited; Von Woess, *Münch. Beitr. z. Papyrusforsch.* &c., vol. VI (1924), pp. 63 ff.

30. Wilcken, *Grundz.*, p. 206.

31. P. Teb. I. 30. 25; 61 a. 164; 61 b. 216.

32. Cf. Wilcken, *Grundz.*, pp. 177 ff.

33. Herodotus, II. 109. But cf. Genesis xlvii. 24-6. Cf. WO. I, pp. 175 ff., 485 ff.

34. Egypt was divided into a number of districts called nomes. We have information concerning the taxes of comparatively few of these. Within a nome the taxation is ordinarily uniform; but the rate on the same tax may differ between neighbouring nomes. The nome might be divided into two or more μερίδες, depending on the size of the nome. The μερίς was divided into toparchies; the toparchies were subdivided into comogrammatiae, each under a comogrammateus whose competence might include one or more villages. The land embraced within a comogrammatia was divided into σφράγιδες or κοιταί (cf. Martin, SP. XIII, pp. 30 ff.) for the convenience of the cadastre. In the Vatican papyrus published by Norsa and Vitelli in *Studi e Testi*, vol.

LIII, the villages are grouped into παρατομαί, which are in turn grouped
into larger unnamed divisions of which there are several; but a comarch
of one of these larger divisions is named in the document, so that it is
evident that the system of subdivisions of the nome of Marmarica was
somewhat different from that common in Egypt proper (cf. the remarks
of the editors, pp. xviii ff.). Σφράγιδες and τόποι also appear as small
local subdivisions, but of varying and often indeterminable size.

35. As P. Lond. III. 604 (pp. 70 ff.) shows, such summaries might
be drawn up in two ways, κατ' ἄνδρα and κατ' εἴδη σωματισμοῦ
(according to the types of tenure). P. Lond. II. 192 (p. 222) is somewhat similar to P. Lond. III. 604; cf. P. Teb. II. 344. Many of the
extant lists are so fragmentary that it is hard to tell what arrangement
was followed: PSI. VII. 793 has a list of names of landholders arranged
alphabetically, each name followed by a number of arurae; the arrangement is by τόποι in BGU. II. 426, VII. 1639; P. Ryl. II. 383.
Numerous other lists are so fragmentary that it is impossible to
tell what the arrangement is: SP. XXII. 178 recto; BGU. VII. 1632; P.
Bouriant 38; P. Ryl. II. 382, 397; P. Lond. II. 175 b (p. xvi); P. Ryl.
II. 385, 387, 400 verso; P. Bad. IV. 90; SP. XX. 49 verso, 62 verso; SB.
7633; P. Iand. 135. Cf. BGU. VII. 1636.

36. The ἀπογραφαί of uninundated land are listed by S. Avogadro
in Aegyptus, xv (1935), pp. 134 ff., and her important article (ibid., pp.
131–206) Le ἀπογραφαί di proprietà nell'Egitto greco-romano should be
consulted. Of the ἀπογραφαί listed P. Oslo II. 26 a and PO. VIII. 1113
show that the ἀπογραφαί were joined together as a portion of a roll
in the office of the comogrammateus. SB. 5342 is a report of land which
was left under water; BGU. I. 108 (= W. Chrest. 227) is an ἀπογραφή
of land covered by sand. It had always been assumed that ἄβροχος γῆ
paid rent or taxes at a lower rate than land normally inundated until
Westermann (CP. XVI. (1921), pp. 169 ff.) pointed out that the rates of
rents on domain land and of taxes on private land were stated to be
higher on uninundated land than on the inundated. Westermann
supposed that the rates were raised because the government wanted to
force the artificial irrigation of uninundated land. His conclusions
apparently were accepted by Rostovtzeff, Soc. and Ec. Hist., chapter
ix, note 52. Kalén, op. cit., p. 323 f., has rightly questioned Westermann's statistical method and points out that a difference in rates on
different classes of land rather than a rise in the rate of the προσμετρούμενα can account for the higher rates noted by Westermann. It
might be added that it seems difficult to explain why, if Westermann
were right, the Egyptian peasants almost invariably returned far more
land as uninundated than was recognized by the official episcepsis,
and why the Roman government so conscientiously corrected their
over-estimates to its own disadvantage. Professor A. C. Johnson has
suggested that some γῆ ἄβροχος was perennially irrigated, since it
lay outside the basins, and could produce two crops in a year and so paid
a higher rent.

37. Cf. Westermann, CP. xv. (1920), p. 133. Cf. the similar address of the ἀπογραφαὶ κατ' οἰκίαν discussed in Chapter VII.

38. The preliminary ἐξέτασις probably consisted of verifying the ownership or tenancy of the parcel of land mentioned in the return. Cf. Wilcken, *Grundz.*, p. 207. The nature of the ἐξέτασις by the πρεσβύτερος is not known.

39. Quoted from Westermann, op. cit., p. 133 f.

40. Cf. Martin, op. cit., p. 38 f.; Wilcken, ibid.; P. Ryl. ii, pp. 287 f.

41. The episcepsis has been discussed in the works cited in notes 35–8; cf. the material cited by Kalén, op. cit., pp. 163 ff. The important reports of comogrammateis preparatory to the episcepsis are: P. Brux. 1 (= SB. 4325 = W. *Chrest.* 236); P. Gron. 2; PO. vi. 918; P. Ryl. ii. 207a; P. Hamb. 12 (= W. *Chrest.* 235); P. mend. Gen. (= SP. xvii, pp. 9 ff.); *Bull. dell'Ist. Dir. Rom.* lvi (1904), pp. 193 ff.; P. Ryl. ii. 426. P. Bouriant 42 is a very elaborate account of the land in seed with reference to the uninundated land.

42. Cf. P. Lond. ii. 267 (pp. 129 ff.); with which cf. P. Teb. i. 87 for the Ptolemaic period.

43. Cf. P. Brux. 1 (cf. note 41 above) and P. Ryl. ii. 426.

44. Cf. ibid.; P. Lips. 105.

45. Cf. P. Lond. ii. 604 A. 1–9; P. Giss. iii. 60; P. Flor. iii. 331; P. Bouriant 41 b; BGU. vii. 1621–3; PSI. v. 448 (report of a commission on episcepsis to the basilico-grammateus); P. Ryl. ii. 378; P. Ross.-Georg. ii. 42 (report of commogrammateus and ὁριοδείκτης); P. Ryl. ii. 87 (report of ὁριοδείκτης concerning land part of which was under sand); P. Flor. iii. 326 (report of ἐπιμεληταὶ λιμνασμοῦ κώμης Ναβοώι to the strategus concerning land which could be ready for ploughing and sowing within three days. P. Flor. iii. 327–9 seem similar). SB. 4518 is a letter of a strategus to the ἐπισκέπται, the commission on the episcepsis.

46. For the ἀπαιτήσιμον κατ' ἄνδρα, the tax-list, see Chapter IV.

47. P. Ryl. ii. 216 is a survey of the land of a whole nome, arranged by toparchies and by villages; it is, however, apparently confined to garden-land; P. Ryl. ii. 384 is a similar document. Such surveys were prepared in the bureau of the basilico-grammateus.

48. BGU. iv. 1047. ii. 4–9.

49. *Archiv*, v, p. 245; P. Giss. 4–7.

50. Cf. Wilcken, *Grundz.*, p. 206, 210; BGU. i. 175.

51. Wilcken, op. cit., p. 206.

52. Cf. Eger, *Zum Ägyptischen Grundbuchwesen in Römischer Zeit*, pp. 190 ff.; Von Woess, *Untersuchungen über das Urkundenwesen und den Publizitätschutz im römischen Ägypten* (Münch. Beiträge z. Papyrusforsch. usw., vol. vi), pp. 63 ff.

53. On the βιβλιοθήκη τῶν ἐγκτήσεων cf. Flore, *Aegyptus*, viii (1927), pp. 43 ff., and the material there cited.

54. This is only a natural assumption. I know of no proof of it.

55. Cf. Flore, op. cit.; Harmon in *Yale Classical Studies*, IV, pp. 153–230; Avogadro, op. cit. (note 36 above).

56. Cf. Wilcken, *Grundz.*, p. 203, and his references.

57. Cf. Chapter VII.

58. Cf. Von Woess, op. cit. BGU. I. 186 is perhaps such a cadastre.

59. Cf. Eger, op. cit., p. 183; Von Woess, op. cit., p. 75.

60. PSI. v. 450; Von Woess, op. cit., p. 71; cf. the ἐπίσκεψις . . . οἰκοπέδου in BGU. III. 870.

61. P. Cairo Preis. 12.

CHAPTER II

1. Rostovtzeff, *Kolonat*, pp. 119 ff.; *Soc. and Ec. Hist.*, chapter vii, note 43; P. Thunell, pp. 72 ff. and 87; P. Kalén, pp. 67 ff.

2. Cf. P. Teb. II. 302; PO. IV. 721. 7, XII. 1434. Cf. Rostovtzeff, op. cit., chapter vii, note 44.

3. Cf. Rostovtzeff, ibid.; P. Bouriant 42 introd.; P. Thunell, pp. 72 ff. and 87; P. Kalén, pp. 67 ff.

4. PO. XII. 1434. 16. f. and Rostovtzeff's conjecture in *Soc. and Ec. Hist.*, chapter vii, note 44.

5. The estate of Antonia must have enjoyed ἀτέλεια, since an impost called ἀτέλεια τελωνική was exacted in connexion with property which had formerly belonged to that estate (P. Fay. 40. SB. 4226 gives the statement: Ἀγρειππιανῆς καὶ Ῥουτιλλιανῆς οὐσίας τοῦ κυρίου Αὐτοκράτορος ἀτέλην καὶ ἀνενγάρευτον), and these same privileges may have belonged to the estate before it reverted to the *patrimonium* of the emperor, but there is no proof of this. In P. Bouriant 42 it may be observed that land which had been sold from the οὐσία Ἀντωνίας paid καθήκοντα at the rate of 1 artaba an arura. I believe that the impost ἀτέλεια τελωνική was exacted upon land which had come into the οὐσιακὸς λόγος (by inheritance or by confiscation) but which was sold outright or leased at a rental comparable to the καθήκοντα on private property; such land did not pay τέλη (= ἐκφόρια), and the ἀτέλεια τελωνική was exacted to recompense, in part at least, the government's loss of revenue which would have come to it by leasing the land at ordinary charges for ἐκφόρια. The land had been brought εἰς ἀπαίτησιν in the nineteenth year of an emperor; if that emperor was Antoninus, the payment of taxes following the sale of parts of the estate of Antonia had begun but a few years before the dates of P. Fay. 40 and P. Bouriant 42. But cf. P. Kalén, pp. 62 and 324.

6. I believe that P. Fay. 82. 13–16 should be read as Grenfell and Hunt first published them rather than following the *Berichtigungsliste*, I, except that μισθ( ) should be expanded as suggested μισθ(ωθείσης). For the ἀτέλεια of philosophers see Chapter VIII, p. 120.

7. Cf. Rostovtzeff, *Soc. and Ec. Hist.*, chapter vii, note 44.

8. Cf. P. Lond. II. 195 (p. 127 f.) republished in P. Ryl. II, pp. 254 ff.

9. Cf. Rostovtzeff, cited in note 7 above.

10. The διχοινικία, sometimes called (εἰκοστή), and usually designated by κ, has been very fully discussed by Kalén (P. Kalén, pp. 256 f. and 305 ff.). He points out that the presence of this tax is often concealed by employees of the sitologi, who included it in the totals of receipts without mentioning it by name. The tax was not ordinarily collected, in case of a payment on one arura or less, in an amount below $\frac{1}{12}$ artaba. The payments for διχοινικία are so nearly universal that any land which was exempt from the tax owed its immunity to circumstances of which we have no accurate knowledge. Kalén also conjectures that the tax had its origin in payments in kind for the tax called στέφανος in the Ptolemaic period and collected in connexion with the transfer of cleruchic land.

11. We have many references to catoecic land in the tax-documents and leases from the Arsinoite nome, but there are very few references to cleruchic land other than catoecic. Practically all of the private land in the great register of P. Bour. 42 pays at 1 artaba to the arura, and the same circumstance could be multiplied by analysis of P. Brux. 1, &c. This fact points to the catoecic origin of the land, for no other class of land in Roman Egypt, except ἱερὰ γῆ ἐπὶ καθήκουσι, consistently paid at the rate of 1 artaba to the arura.

12. P. Ryl. II. 202; cf. P. Lond. II. 194. 36 (p. 124) and Berichtigungsliste, II. 2, which does not give the rate. If P. Lond. II. 193 (p. 120 = SP. XVII, pp. 49 ff.) comes from the Fayûm, we have an example of a tax on the κλῆροι of the μάχιμοι at $\frac{3}{4}$ artaba to the arura (which is found elsewhere in Egypt; cf. Martin, SP. XVII, p. 42 f.) combined with an impost of $\frac{1}{2}$ artaba to make a total tax of $1\frac{1}{4}$ artabae to the arura. It is quite probable, however, that P. Lond. II. 193 does not come from the Arsinoite nome.

13. The editors point out that if the διχοινικία is a tax of 2 choenices or $\frac{1}{20}$ artaba to the arura, it ought to be possible to ascertain from amounts paid for that tax the approximate area of the land subject to tax and hence the approximate rate of the main tax. This has been accepted by Kalén, op. cit.

14. The only examples, so far as I know, are P. Flor. III. 331. 16, which is discussed on p. 16, and P. Giss. 60 (cf. P. Kalén, pp. 308 ff.).

15. Cf. Martin, op. cit., note 12; Lesquier, Les Institutions militaires, p. 221. The μάχιμοι ἱππεῖς τριακοντάρουροι, however, paid at 1 artaba to the arura (P. Teb. 98. 41, 58, and Lesquier, op. cit., pp. 178, 221, 310 f.), and the high rate on the μάχιμοι here may point to this class of cleruchus as the original owners.

16. Cf. Lesquier, ibid.

17. The tax at 2 artabae to the arura was also found in the Ptolemaic period: P. Teb. I. 5. 15, 99. 21 ff.; BGU. VI. 1238. Grenfell and Hunt's note upon P. Teb. II. 346. 14 is, I think, wrong: Cronion is paying land-taxes on different categories of land which include $5\frac{5}{8}$ arurae at

2 artabae and approximately $114\frac{2}{3}$ arurae at $\frac{3}{4}$ artaba (if the restoration of line 14 is correct).

18. The rate for λααρχία in P. Lond. II. 193, (p. 120 = SP. XVII, pp. 49 ff.) is $\frac{1}{2}$ artaba to the arura, but in that document it is combined with the tax on the κλῆροι of μάχιμοι κληροῦχοι at $\frac{3}{4}$ artaba as noted above.

19. P. Teb. II. 453. 2; BGU. I. 139 (on ἰδιόκτητος γῆ).

20. P. Teb. II, pp. 339 ff. (line 24).

21. Cf. Martin in SP. XVII, p. 37 and note 48; P. Ryl. II. 202. 1 note; P. Kalén 3. ii. 11 note.

22. If P. Lond. II. 193 (p. 120 f. = SP. XVII, pp. 49 ff.) is from the Fayûm, we have evidence for γῆ ἀμπελῖτις at $1\frac{1}{2}$ artabae to the arura in the Arsinoite nome. The provenience of this document is, however, uncertain (Martin assigns it to Middle Egypt). If it does not come from the Fayûm our only evidence for the rate on this type of land in the Arsinoite nome must be deduced from P. Ryl. II. 202. 1, 6. In line 6 the amount of the main tax on a parcel of γῆ ἀμπελῖτις is $3\frac{5}{12}$ artabae, and the charge for διχοινικία is $\frac{1}{8}$ artaba (implying an area greater than $1\frac{2}{3}$ arurae and not over $3\frac{1}{3}$ arurae); hence a rate of $1\frac{1}{2}$ artabae an arura would be perfectly possible. But in line 1 the amount of the main tax is $3\frac{3}{4}$ artabae, and the charge for διχοινικία is $\frac{1}{4}$ artabae (implying an area greater than $3\frac{1}{3}$ arurae and not over 5 arurae); consequently a rate of $1\frac{1}{2}$ artabae is impossible, but a rate of one artaba would be satisfactory. It is possible that the parcel of land paying $3\frac{5}{12}$ artabae in line 6 consisted of $3\frac{25}{64}$ arurae (since the arura was not divided into fractions whose denominator was not two or a power thereof). The διχοινικία at $\frac{1}{20}$ on $3\frac{25}{64}$ arurae would be $\frac{1}{8}$ plus $\frac{1}{320}$ artaba, and it is possible that the latter fraction was neglected. If that is true, then a rate of one artaba to the arura is possible for γῆ ἀμπελῖτις in the Arsinoite nome. If, on the contrary, the rate was uniformly $1\frac{1}{2}$ artabae to the arura, it is necessary to assume that an exceptional remission of half of the usual land-tax was allowed to the parcel of land in line 1 or that the scribe made an error. The former is not likely, although P. Grenf. II. 56 is an ἀπογραφή of γῆ ἀμπελῖτις which was uninundated.

23. This remark, of course, applies only to ἱερὰ γῆ ἐπὶ καθήκουσι. The exception is considered on page 17 of this chapter.

24. Cf. P. Teb. II, p. 343, note 30. This may be a category of land somewhat like $I(=\delta\epsilon\kappa)\epsilon\tau\eta\rho\iota\tau\hat{\omega}\nu$ in SP. XVII, p. 42.

25. Cf. PO. VII. 1044, XII. 1434, 1445, 1459, 1534, 1535, 1549, XVII. 2143 introd.

26. The editors call PO. XII. 1445 a report of unproductive land. Is it possible that a κουφοτέλεια had reduced the revenue to the state?

27. P. Amh. II. 85; cf. P. Amh. 86. SB. 5673 is an offer to buy from the state δημόσιος ἀνυπόλογος ἄφορος χέρσος εἰς σιτοφόρον; the bidder promises to pay the ἀρταβεία.

28. Cf. P. Teb. I. 5. 15 note, 56 note.

29. Cf. notes 21–2 above.

30. Cf. note 10 above.

31. The editors of P. Lond. II. 604 (pp. 70 ff.), p. 79, line 69 note, restore πόλ(εως). Wilcken, *Chrest.* p. 403, suggests πολ(ιτῶν) or πολ(ιτική).

32. Cf. P. M. Meyer in P. Giss. III, p. 28, referring to Rostovtzeff, *Kolonat*, p. 103.

33. Cf. Westermann, CP. XVII (1922), pp. 30 ff.; Martin, op. cit., p. 42.

34. Cf. P. M. Meyer, op. cit., p. 29; Rostovtzeff, *Soc. and Ec. Hist.*, chapter ix, note 52, and the material there cited.

35. The rate as stated in the papyrus is $1\frac{1}{12}$ and $1\frac{7}{12}$ artabae to the arura. Kalén, op. cit., pp. 308 ff., points out that the $\frac{1}{12}$ artaba is for διχοινικία.

36. Cf. Wilcken, *Archiv*, IV, pp. 534 ff.; Plaumann, *Ptolemais*, p. 96. The editors had assumed that Crocodilopolis in the Pathyrite nome was the Crocodilopolis of this document.

37. Cf. lines 12 and 122 where ιειˡ may be a peculiar abbreviation indicating temple-land; the rate is $\frac{1}{2}$ artaba, which is lower than that known on private land in the Roman period. Line 44, $a\overline{}_0$ ιε( ), may be temple-land at the usual rate of one artaba to the arura. Otherwise the ἱερὰ γῆ mentioned in line 6 of the document does not appear, so far as I can see, in the body of the document, which, however, is incomplete.

38. P. Teb. I. 98. 27–40.

39. Cf. P. Lond. III. 604, line 69 on p. 79.

40. Cf. 604 B. 255 ff.; 604 A. 105, 106, 111. In line 105 αυˡ (which may be misread; cf. the correction of αυˡ in line 121 given in the *Berichtigungsliste*) must be the abbreviation for the αλλεων of 604 B. 255.

41. The rate on ἰδιόκτητος γῆ, however, is not uniform throughout Egypt. In BGU. I. 139 the rate is $1\frac{1}{2}$ artabae; in P. Lond. II. 193. 19 (p. 120 = SP. XVII. pp. 49 ff.) it is $1\frac{1}{4}$ artabae.

42. Cf. Martin, op. cit., pp. 41 ff.

43. Martin, op. cit., p. 42, thinks Ἰετηριτῶν an ethnic or city name. Rostovtzeff, op. cit., chapter vii, note 47, restores (δεκ)ετηριτῶν and connects the term with grants of land in commemoration of the decennalia of one of the Ptolemies.

44. Cf. Kalén, op. cit., p. 323 f., whose suggestion concerning P. Bouriant 42. 339–61 may be correct. Cf. also note 26 above. Information concerning remissions of rent on domain land has been collected by Westermann, CP. XVII (1922), pp. 30 ff.

45. Cf. Lesquier, op. cit., p. 221.

46. See Chapter V, pp. 55 f., 58.

47. SHA. *Aurelian*, 47.

48. SHA. *Probus*, 9 states that Probus used the labour of the soldiers to open the mouths of the rivers and to drain the marshes, which then became grain-fields. Westermann, *Aegyptus*, I (1920), pp. 297–301,

wishes to connect PO. XII. 1409, a copy of a circular letter from the
Dioecetes of Egypt to the strategi and decemprimi of the Heptanomia
and the Arsinoite nome giving directions as to the building of the
dikes and the cleaning of the irrigation canals, with this activity of
Probus, which would then be dated in A.D. 278 instead of in the reign
of Aurelian. Westermann's argument depends upon the conventional
opinion that the tax called χωματικόν was an optional *adaeratio* of
the corvée of five days of work on the dikes and canals; this opinion
I shall attempt to prove unfounded (see Chapter IX, pp. 141 ff.). Consequently the prescribing of the death penalty for the exaction of
money in place of the prescribed work is simply a measure designed
to end the graft which had become aggravated after Probus had used
the soldiers to improve the irrigation and had then turned that work
over to the civil authorities. It is hard to believe that the increase in
the number of boatmen on the Nile and on the Tiber could alone have
increased the revenues of wheat from Egypt by one-tenth, if the irrigation system was in so bad a state of repair as is suggested by Westermann. Consequently we are obliged to assume an increase in the assessments upon domain land or private land or both in the time of Aurelian,
for which there is no other evidence, or to accept the implication of
Vopiscus that the improvement of the irrigation system by Probus
began in the reign of Aurelian.

49. *History of Egypt under Roman Rule* (vol. v of *History of Egypt*,
ed. by W. Flinders Petrie), 2nd ed., p. 169.

CHAPTER III

1. Documents mentioning the ἐπιβολή are as follows: P. Teb. II.
346; P. Mich. 123 R. xii. 43; PSI. VIII. 906; BGU. III. 830; P. Lond.
II. 175a (p. 119); BGU. IV. 1048; SP. XX. 1; CPR. 1; P. Ryl. II. 202;
CPR. 170; BGU. II. 444 (?); CPR. 188; P. Ryl. II. 202a; P. Fay. 81;
P. Hamb. 62; PSI. X. 1151, 1152; BGU. II. 457; SB. 5168; 5241; O.
Strass. 577; BGU. VII. 1684; SP. XXII. 136; P. Lond. inv. 1911; P.
Fay. 263; P. Lond. II. 311 (p. 219); BGU. I. 282; P. Ryl. II. 388; CPR.
175, 47; SB. 4284; P. Bouriant 37; CPR. 104; PO. X. 1347, XIV. 1633;
O. Mich. 24. Cf. WO. II. 1472, where an ἐπιβολή is paid in money at
Thebes. See also Chapter IX, p. 168.

2. Cf. Martin in SP. XVII, p. 33. Other πλεονασμοί are in PSI. X.
1153; BGU. VII. 1598; WO. II. 777; P. Teb. II. 344.

3. Cf. Wilcken, *Grundz.*, pp. 293 and 295. The following documents
mention ἐπιμερισμοί: P. Ryl. II. 163, 164, 367; P. Amh. II. 99a and
99b (?); P. Ryl. II. 85; P. Amh. II. 106–9; BGU. III. 842; P. Lond.
III. 924 (p. 134 = W. *Chrest.* 355); P. Ryl. II. 341; P. Giss. 51; SB.
4298, 4284; P. Amh. II. 96; PO. XII. 1522 (?); P. Lond. III. 938 (p. 150);
P. Ryl. II. 100; PO. XIV. 1636; PSI. IX. 1070; SP. XX. 63; SP. V. 119
R ii. 20, v. 23, vii. 21; P. Flor. I. 50; P. Strass. 10; PO. XIV. 1638, 1700,

1704, IX. 1208 (this list does not include documents later than the third century).

4. Cf. P. Kalén I R i. 10 note.

5. Cf. Rostovtzeff, *Kolonat*, pp. 53 ff.; Wilcken, *Grundz.*, p. 277; UPZ., p. 477 f.

6. P. Kalén I v i. 10, 4 R v. 15, 25, vi. 21, vii. 5, 12, 21; PO. x. 1304; BGU. II. 381; P. Teb. II. 369, 394; P. Lond. II. 301 (p. 256); PSI. v. 476; PO. XII. 1541, XIV. 1669; P. Grenf. I. 48; P. Goodsp. Cairo 30. xxiii. 3. Cf. O. Strass. 336–7, 349. For a discussion cf. Rostovtzeff in PWRE. VII. Spp. 166 ff.; Wilcken, *Grundz.*, pp. 357, 359 ff.

7. Cf. PSI. v. 476 and introd.

8. The government determined the amount to be levied in an administrative district, and officials (πραγματικοί) distributed the burden among the various villages, and in some cases the village-elders seem to have been responsible for the collection of the grain. This was then delivered to officers of the army, who paid the price fixed by the government, or the money was paid by a commission appointed for that purpose. Cf. BGU. II. 381, III. 807, 842; P. Ryl. II. 85; P. Amh. II. 107–9, 173–8; P. Grenf. I. 48.

9. This view is that commonly accepted by scholars. W. J. Oates, however, cites the πυρὸς συναγοραστικός in Egyptian documents to support his hypothesis that the *canon frumentarius* of Rome referred to the grain which the government purchased at a low price (*Classical Philology*, XXIX (1934), p. 113 and note 37).

10. *L'Armée romaine d'Égypte*, pp. 350 ff.

11. The following documents mention the annona: WO. II. 273; PSI. VI. 683; O. Theb. 102; O. Strass. 161; WO. II. 679, 682, 698, 1479; P. Ryl. II. 341; P. Teb. II. 403; BGU. II. 534, I. 336, II. 529; P. Lond. III. 944 (p. 53); PO. XIV. 1763; WO. II. 1016, 1019; PSI. VII. 795; PO. IX. 1194, XII. 1419; P. Amh. I. 3 a ii. I (?); PO. IX. 1192, VIII. 1115; BGU. I. 94; PO. XVII. 2142; PO. I. 43, iv. 16, XII. 1415; P. Teb. II. 404; PO. XII. 1490, 1573; O. Mich. Car. 131 (a payment of 16 drachmae in A.D. 282 or 285), 132, 149, 586. The annona is mentioned also in many documents of the fourth and later centuries.

12. P. Teb. II. 403; PO. XII. 1573; WO. II. 1479.

13. P. Teb. II. 404.

14. PO. XII. 1573; WO. II. 679, 698, 682. In O. Mich. 16 (from Philadephia) the ἐπιγραφὴ κώμης is 1024 drachmae (ὑπὲρ) τιμῆς οἴνου ἀννων(ικοῦ) in A.D. 290.

15. Τιμὴ πυροῦ is mentioned in the following documents: BGU. VII. 1598; WO. II. 359; O. Strass. 51; O. Tait, p. 106, nos. 195–201; WO. II. 1371, 1388, 1558, 1391, 1325; BGU. VII. 1613; P. Lond. II. 367 a (p. 101); O. Tait, p. 78, no. 91; WO. II. 1535; BGU. II. 414; P. Ryl. II. 186; WO. II. 663, 694; O. Strass. 283; O. Tait, p. 75, no. 70; BGU. I. 223; PO. XII. 1419; and τιμὴ σίτου in P. Ryl. II. 206b. Τιμὴ οἴνου: O. Theb. 88; WO. II. 502, 1574–6; O. Wilb.-Brk. 40–2; BGU. III. 774; SP. xx. 44; WO. II. 1264; O. Theb. 89; WO. II. 662,

691, 697; O. Theb. 90; P. Fay. 63; PO. xii. 1573; in O. Mich. Car.
157 (A.D. 276) 2¾ artabae (of wheat?) are recorded in payment for
τιμὴ οἴνου. Τιμὴ δημοσίου φοί(νικος) from Elephantine-Syene: WO.
II. 84, 93; SB. 7582–3; *Archiv*, v, p. 170, no. 31; WO. II. 111, 126,
159, 161, 172; SB. 4362; O. Strass. 285; WO. II. 227, 232, 243, 254,
255, 257, 266, 281, 288, 1268, 1273, 1609. Τιμὴ φοινίκων from Thebes;
WO. II. 502; O. Tait, p. 94, no. 111; P. Lips. I. 76; WO. II. 692,
693, 697, 1466. Τιμὴ φοι(νίκων) καὶ κούκ(εων) is recorded in O.
Wilb.-Brk. 76, where the tax is collected on date- and nut-palms on
former burial-grounds confiscated by the state; the dates and coco-
nuts sold for 895 drachmae 2½ obols, of which the dates sold at 5
drachmae an artaba (= 55 drachmae), and 56,300 coco-nuts brought
840 drachmae 2½ obols. In WO. II. 1595 the payment in A.D. 258 of
16 drachmae ὑπὲρ τιμῆς ἐλαίου τῶν ἐνταῦθα στρατευμάτων is obviously for the military annona; but cf. WO. II. 659; also P. Iand.
142, where payments of oil are made in kind, and P. Lond. III.
1170 (p. 92).

16. Strabo xvii. 1. 51 (818).

17. Τιμὴ λαχάνου seems to be a tax in O. Tait, p. 97, no. 135 (cf.
SB. 1673). Λάχανον is taxed in kind in BGU. vii. 1636; O. Strass.
450; cf. SB. 2085; SP. xxii. 165. Τιμὴ χλωρῶν is found in P. Lond.
II. 171 a (p. 102); PO. vii. 1046; and P. Lond. inv. 1577. This last
is a most interesting and valuable document, but there are many points
in regard to it which are not clear. Payments for τιμὴ χλ(ωρῶν) over a
period of five years (the first five of the reign of Nero) on two parcels
of land are preserved on the *recto*. The first of these parcels had in the
Ptolemaic period been assigned to one of the ἱππεῖς ἑκατοντάρουροι,
since it was still designated as ἑκατ(ονταρούρων); at the time the document was written the land was in the possession of a certain Olympio-
dorus. This parcel consisted of 23¾ arurae which were assessed at
71¼ artabae (of wheat?). With it was an allotment of 14²⁷₃₂ arurae of
ὑπόλογος (?) land assessed at 1 artaba an arura. The total assessment
in kind was, therefore, 86³₃₂ artabae. The dues exacted in money for
τιμὴ χλ(ωρῶν), however, amounted to 83 drachmae 1 obol. It is
evident that a remission of dues was allowed when the land was put in
rest-crops, since an artaba of wheat was worth more than 1 drachma
even as early as the reign of Nero. The only other possibility is that the
original assessment was not made in wheat, but in some grain less
valuable than wheat, such as barley. The same money-payment was
exacted through the period of five years, except that in the third and
fourth years a πρόστιμον was imposed on account of the ὑπόλογος
land. The πρόστιμον amounted to 34⁵₂₄ artabae or 33 drachmae 2 obols.
In addition, a payment in kind (σιτικῶν) was exacted on the original
23¾ arurae in each of the five years, but it amounted to only 2 artabae
of wheat with an unusually large surcharge, called καθ(ήκοντα), of
¼ artaba 7 choinices (⁴d𝑥̄). The second parcel of land consisted of
48 arurae of land designated by the symbol 𝑥̊ (=χόρτου?) plus

28¼ arurae of ὑπόλογος land. The payments for τιμὴ χλ(ωρῶν) were exacted in precisely the same way as for the preceding parcel, except that instead of an additional payment in kind in each of the five years a single extra payment of 52 drachmae 4 obols was made (apparently in the fifth year). On the *verso* two other parcels of land are recorded, and the payments are quite similar. In the first, however, a charge for καταγώγι(ον) was levied on the πρόστιμον. This document is the most complete account of the payments for τιμὴ χλωρῶν which is preserved, but there is much in it which requires further elucidation. One of its important features is the additional evidence for the *lustrum* of five years in the assessment of taxes.

18. *La Vie municipale*, pp. 387 ff.
19. Cf., however, WO. II. 1431, 1433, 1582.
20. Cf. BGU. III. 760.
21. Cf. O. Theb. 108; WO. II. 901, 905, 927, 936, 1259, 1447.
22. Cf. O. Strass. 445.
23. The receipts for chaff in the Roman period are: WO. II. 765; O. Br.-Berl. 67; SB. 5665; WO. II. 776; O. Mey. 18; O. Theb. 103-4; SB. 4335; P. Bad. IV. 109; SB. 3565; O. Strass. 442; WO. II. 810; O. Tait, p. 75, no. 71; WO. II. 854; O. Tait, p. 105, nos. 185-6, 188; WO. II. 865, 866; PSI. VIII. 996; O. Strass. 446, 445; O. Theb. 105; O. Strass. 447; WO. II. 901, 905, 906, 914; O. Theb. 106-8; WO. II. 927; O. Mey. 19; WO. II. 936, 937; O. Strass. 429; O. Theb. 109; WO. II. 943, 1453; O. Theb. 110; WO. II. 1458, 1010, 1011; O. Br.-Berl. 68; WO. II. 1461, 1464, 1012, 1014, 1015; O. Strass. 438; O. Tait, p. 105, no. 187; O. Strass. 454; O. Theb. 112, 111; WO. II. 1258, 1582, 1431, 1433, 1436, 1259, 1447, 1475, 1476; O. Wilb.-Brk. 71-2.
24. See Jouguet, op. cit., note 18 above.
25. PO. XII. 1543; BGU. IV. 1027.
26. Cf. Rostovtzeff in *Archiv*, V, p. 177.
27. It is sometimes spelled κράστις. Mention is found in WO. II. 760, 761; O. Theb. 113; P. Hamb. 39; *Archiv*, V. 176, no. 27.
28. *Archiv*, V, p. 176, no. 27.
29. BGU. III. 920; PO. XIV. 1628, 1700, IX. 1208, XIV. 1704.
30. Cf. PSI. VIII. 927: τὸ ἐπιβάλλον αὐτοῖς τῶν ἐπιμεριζομένων τῇ κώμῃ κατ' ἔτος σιτικῶν τε καὶ ἀργυρικῶν κεφαλαίοις.
31. PSI. VI. 683; P. Ryl. II. 85.
32. For the ἐπίτριτον paid in money see Chapter XVI, p. 279. Besides the examples in the text the ἐπίτριτον in kind appears in PSI. X. 1133.
33. WO. II. 834, 839, 841, 973; O. Theb. 114; O. Ashm. 178 in WO. I, p. 822 (on p. 289).
34. In *Wörterbuch*, II, s.v.
35. SB. 2088.
36. WO. II. 834 (A.D. 130-1); 839, 841 (A.D. 131-2); 947 (A.D. 190-1); O. Theb. 114 (A.D. 192).
37. P. Kalén, p. 302.

38. See Chapter IX, p. 157 f.

39. Possibly the ἐπιστατικόν is a local variation of the ἐπισπουδασμὸς φορέτρου.

40. Cf. Chapter XIV, pp. 239 ff.

41. P. Fay. 82; P. Kalén 1 R ii. 1, iii. 3.

42. See note 31 above.

43. A payment of ½ artaba of dates is found in O. Strass. 449; but since the payment is made to the ἐπιτηρηταὶ κτημάτων γενη(ματογρα-φηθέντων), it is possible that this is entirely exceptional. WO. II. 35 from Syene attests the payment of bundles of palm-leaves.

44. O. Tait, p. 66, no. 20, and *Archiv*, V, p. 178, no. 32, are receipts for a payment in kind of μυροβάλανοι which may belong to either of two types of receipts for the product of the balsam: ὑπὲρ γ̅ εἰκασμοῦ μυρο-β(αλάνων) found in WO. II. 1460 or ὑπὲρ τρίτου νομ( ) μυροβ(αλάνων) found in WO. II. 296–300. All these receipts are from Syene and date between A.D. 153 and 171.

45. PO. XII. 1414; BGU. VII. 1564. Cf. BGU. II. 655: δέρμα εἰς κατασκευὴν ὅπλων.

CHAPTER IV

1. Philo, *In Flaccum*, § 19.

2. OGI. II. 669. 27–64.

3. It is possible that Ti. Julius Alexander was diplomatically exag-gerating his inability to effect changes demanded by the Egyptian cultivators. It is apparent from PO. XII. 1434, P. Amh. II. 68 *verso*, and P. Lond. III. 921 (p. 133) that the prefect had considerable dis-cretion in regulating abatements of taxation, although it is clear that the emperor alone could effect changes in taxation that applied generally. Cf. Reinmuth, *The Prefect of Egypt from Augustus to Diocletian* (*Klio, Beiträge zur alten Geschichte*, N.F., 21. Beiheft), 1935, pp. 65 ff.

4. Dio Cassius, LVII. 10. 5.

5. Wilcken, *Grundz.*, p. 208.

6. Reinmuth in TAPA. LXV (1934), pp. 248 ff., esp. pp. 256–9.

7. This figure is supported by the statement in the Code of Justinian: Ed. XIII: *de urbe Alexandrinorum et Aegyptiacis provinciis* 8. *felici frumenti missione octogies centena milia complente*. This is the amount of the ἐμβολή diverted from Rome to Constantinople in the first half of the fourth century. It is generally assumed that the measure is the artaba, since that measure is used elsewhere throughout the edict. An artaba of 24 choenices is equal to 2½ modii, so that 8 million artabae were not far from 20 million modii. Cf., however, Schnebel, *Die Landwirtschaft*, &c., p. 1, who cites Rostovtzeff.

8. Cf. Chapter I, p. 8 f.

9. Strabo, XVII. 1. 48 (817).

10. The inundation lasted from about June 22 to November; cf.

E. C. Semple, *The Geography of the Mediterranean Region*, &c., London 1932, p. 158, also pp. 442–4.

11. Cf. K. S. Gapp, *Famine in the Roman World*, unpublished Princeton thesis, 1934; also Rostovtzeff's article 'Frumentum' in PWRE. VII, Spp. 126 ff.

12. On the eclogistes cf. WO. I, pp. 499 ff.; Wilcken, *Grundz.*, pp. 208 ff.; P. Ryl. II. 83. 18, note; P. Giss. 48, introd. The following documents of the Roman period mention the eclogistes: *Archiv*, V, p. 162, no. 9; OGI. 669. 36, 51, 53; PO. XII. 1480; P. Amh. II. 69; BGU. IV. 1033; P. Giss. 10; P. Mey. 3; P. Ryl. II. 83; P. Teb. II. 287; PO. I. 57; SB. 1166; cf. P. Giss. 48; PO. XII. 1436.

13. Philo (*In Flaccum*, § 16) states that the prefect spent the greater part of his time each year in the inspection and audit of the accounts of the nomes. The presence of the eclogistae would have been required in Alexandria during that process.

14. See Chapter I, p. 9; also Rostovtzeff, *Archiv*, III, pp. 201–3; Hohlwein, *Musée Belge*, X (1906), p. 51.

15. Ἀπαιτήσιμα κατ' ἄνδρα are: SP. XXII. 165, 26; BGU. II. 598; P. Bouriant 47 (?); BGU. I. 175; P. Fay. 202; CPR. 33; SP. XXII. 174; BGU. II. 659; P. Fay. 208; SB. 4522; SP. XXII. 88; BGU. II. 457 (a correction of an ἀπαιτήσιμον given by the comogrammateus to the πράκτωρ σιτικῶν). Related documents are BGU. II. 470; P. Ryl. II. 390; PO. XII. 1446; BGU. I. 274, 145, 84; SB. 5272.

16. P. Ryl. II. 83; P. Amh. II. 69; P. Ausonia 2 (ii. 1907, p. 138).

17. OGI. II. 669. 55.

18. BGU. II. 659.

19. Cf. P. Teb. II. 356; P. Kalén 1 R i. 16, iii. 2; 4 R i. 20, iv. 15, 23, v. 4, 6, 23; 5. 3; BGU. III. 921; P. Flor. III. 379; BGU. III. 831; P. Teb. II. 277 introd.; P. Flor. II. 185, III. 364; P. Lond. III. 900 (p. 88); BGU. VII. 1636; O. Mich. 9; the unpublished rolls from Caranis in the collection of the University of Michigan.

20. P. Kalén 5 and introd.

21. In the Ptolemaic period the threshing of the grain was under the superintendence of the γενηματοφύλακες (cf. Rostovtzeff, *Archiv*, III, p. 204 f.; Wilcken, *Grundz.*, p. 181) and probably also the comogrammateus and comarch. Rostovtzeff (*Archiv*, III, p. 214) has conjectured that the πράκτορες σιτικῶν were in charge of the threshing-floor, since they do not seem to have functioned at the granary. This is not impossible, although their chief duty seems to have been the collection of arrears. From PO. x. 1255 it is evident that the comarchs were in charge of the grain after the threshing, and they may have been in charge of the actual threshing and division of the grain. Ἁλωνοφύλακες (which should be read instead of the editors' ἀγωνοφύλακες), guards of the threshing-floor, are mentioned in P. Ryl. II. 90 (third century) together with an official whose duty was to watch over the purity and cleanliness of the grain.

22. PO. X. 1255 (A.D. 292). This was the practice in the Ptolemaic

period, and Rostovtzeff conjectured that the same procedure was followed in Roman times throughout Egypt. But it is difficult to account for the accumulation of arrears in the taxes in kind attested throughout the Roman period, if the cultivator had always to pay his dues to the government before he took any grain for himself. The practice may have been revived in the time of Diocletian as an emergency measure.

23. Cf. BGU. I. 85. For the Ptolemaic period cf. P. Teb. I. 43, 48, 128; cited by Rostovtzeff, *Archiv*, III, p. 204, note 5.

24. P. Teb. II. 346. 6.

25. Ἀλόητρα (in PO. II. 277. 7; BGU. IV. 1031. 11; P. Oslo 33; P. Flor. III. 379. 18) may be payments of a fee for the use of the threshing-floor, but they are more likely to be payments for the expense of labour. A payment for winnowing (λίκμητρα) also occurs in P. Oslo 33. Cf. SB. 7373.

26. P. Teb. II. 356, 375; P. Kalén 1 R i. 16, iii. 2; 4 R i. 20, iv. 15, 23, v. 4, 6, 23; 5. 3; P. Teb. II. 277 introd.; BGU. VII. 1636; O. Mich. 9.

27. Cf. P. Kalén 5, introd. Kalén (p. 57 f.) believes that the series of ostraca from the Fayûm (O. Fay. 24–40; SB. 1492–1517; O. Mey. 51–5; O. Br.-Berl. 81–94; BGU. VII. 1697–1704), which record the use of donkeys in some phase of transportation of government grain and which were issued at the granary, illustrate the σακκηγία, i.e. transportation from the threshing-floor to the granary. Amundsen (O. Oslo, p. 40), however, who examined additional examples (O. Oslo 17–21; O. Mich. Car. 360–562) states: 'There can hardly be any doubt that the texts have some bearing or other upon the καταγωγὴ σίτου from the θησαυρός to the harbour, as supposed in the earlier attempts at interpretation.' It is difficult to see, however, how these ostraca are to be related to receipts for payments by the state bank for services of κτηνοτρόφοι, φύλακες of various kinds, &c., engaged in transport of grain from the granary to the harbour (φόρετρον), e.g. P. Bankakten 1 plus P. Col. 1 R 4; P. Kalén 2.

28. Cf. Calderini, ΘΗΣΑΥΡΟΙ, *Studi della scuola papirologica* IV, pp. 102–4; the subject is treated in the second chapter of the unpublished doctoral dissertation (U. of Michigan) of H. A. Thompson, *The Transport of Government Grain in Graeco-Roman Egypt*.

29. This may be inferred from the frequency of the appearance of the granaries of these towns in the papyri; cf. Calderini, op. cit., pp. 28 ff.

30. The granaries in the metropolis are attested for the Arsinoite, Hermopolite, Antinoöpolite, Hermonthite, and Peritheban nomes; cf. Calderini, op. cit., pp. 27–40.

31. Cf. Calderini, op. cit., pp. 35–40, 103.

32. No attempt is made to collect here the hundreds of receipts for grain paid for rent or taxes. Great numbers of those which yield any information concerning the administration of the revenue in kind have

been cited by Calderini, op. cit. On the question as to whom the receipts were issued by the sitologi cf. P. Fay., pp. 208–11; Preisigke, *Girowesen im griechischen Ägypten*, Strassburg 1910, pp. 89. ff., 154 ff.; Rostovtzeff, *Kolonat*, p. 404; Wilcken, *Grundz.*, p. 216. The payments ὑπὲρ θησαυροῦ in WO. II. 503, 918, 993, have not been satisfactorily explained.

33. E.g. the grammateus gives the receipt in O. Theb. 115; the assistant (βοηθός) in WO. II. 867. For other examples cf. Calderini, op. cit., 82–4.

34. Cf. P. Fay., pp. 208–11; O. Tait, p. 110, no. 219.

35. Calderini, op. cit., pp. 58–81, 103–4.

36. Ibid., pp. 82–4.

37. Ibid., p. 82.

38. Ibid., p. 86 f.

39. Ibid., pp. 86–8.

40. P. Kalén, p. 276; cf. Calderini, op. cit., pp. 88–90; Preisigke, WB. II, s.v.

41. P. Amh. II. 79.

42. Cf. Calderini, op. cit., pp. 95–8.

43. Day-books: P. Kalén 3, 4 *verso*; P. Lond. II. 194 (p. 124); P. Fay. 340 *verso* (?); P. Bad. II. 20 is perhaps an elaborate day-book consisting of copies of the receipts issued by sitologi. Monthly reports: P. Kalén 1, 4 *recto*; P. Fay. 86; P. Lond. inv. 1581 *verso*; PO. III. 595; P. Flor. III. 330; BGU. I. 64, II. 534, III. 835, II. 529; P. Teb. II. 339; PO. XII. 1443 (for two months). P. Fay. 86 (a) is a report covering ten days; P. Giss. 63 and P. Kalén 11 cover five days; P. Bouriant 40 is a special report covering intervals of six days. BGU. III. 905, 976 ff. refer to σω(ματισμός); the reports are from Mendes (A.D. 173) and cover the period from Τῦβι to Μεχείρ.

44. P. Amh. II. 69 (= W. *Chrest.* 190); cf. P. Ryl. II. 83 introd.

45. Detailed reports are: P. Ryl. II. 203; P. Bouriant 33; P. Fay. 263; BGU. II. 561 (?), 585; P. Cornell 37 (?); PO. XII. 1444; P. Lond. III. 1239 (p. 52) (this and the preceding document were issued by decemprimi). The monthly summaries have been cited in note 43 above; summaries of longer periods are: BGU. III. 976–8, 905, I. 188; SP. XXII. 182; P. Iand. 57. Reports for several granaries prepared by a central bureau are: P. Cairo Preisigke 29; P. Flor. III. 386–8; BGU. VII. 1626.

46. Cf. P. Kalén 1 *recto*, 4 *recto*; P. Lond. III. 900 (p. 88); P. Fay. 86; BGU. VII. 1636.

47. A complaint against the πράκτωρ σιτικῶν is found in BGU. II. 515; against the sitologi in BGU. III. 908. The πράκτορες σιτικῶν are connected with arrears in P. Teb. II. 336; P. Ryl. II. 421 (?).

48. The προσμετρούμενα are discussed by Kalén in P. Kalén, pp. 231 ff., especially pp. 231–71, where the references are cited (except where the amount of the surtax is not given). To his lists may therefore be added P. Iand. VII. 135 (a); PSI. X. 1144; P. Fay. 81; P. Oslo

II. 28; BGU. III. 755; PSI. X. 1113; SP. XXII. 158; P. Fay. 84, 83; P. Cairo Preisigke 28; P. Lond. inv. 1911.

49. Cf. P. Teb. I. 61 (b). 317–19 note, and 93 introd.

50. P. Kalén, pp. 261–7.

51. Ibid., pp. 249–55.

52. Ibid., pp. 250–4.

53. This ½ per cent. may represent the ἐνοίκιον θησαυροῦ.

54. In O. Strass. 48 and 313 payments are made without surtax (ἄνευ προσμετρουμένων) apparently indicating that the surtax was normally included in the payment. This would account for the lack of reference to προσμετρούμενα in the many receipts for grain from Upper Egypt.

55. Cf. P. Kalén, pp. 255 ff.

56. Ibid., pp. 267 ff.

57. Cf. SB. 5230; PO. VII. 1031, 1040; P. Hamb. 19; P. Lond. III. 1215 (p. 122).

58. O. Strass. 354, 435 (with πρα(κτορεία) ⅟ L); PO. XII. 1445. κο( ) αρ( ) appears in WO. II. 1317, but it is perhaps a place-name.

59. P. Kalén, pp. 278–86.

60. PO. XII. 1443. 10.

61. P. Teb. II. 339. In P. Teb. II. 538, however, so far as the mutilated condition of the document permits one to judge, the method of calculation seems to be that employed at Theadelphia; cf. P. Kalén, pp. 294 ff.

62. P. Kalén 1 R iii. 12, v. 18; 4 R vi. 23.

63. Cf. ibid, p. 274.

64. BGU. II. 552, 557, III. 743, 744. These charges may have been for φιλάνθρωπον rather than for πόδωμα. Kalén regards the ½-artaba tax in P. Giss. 60 as an example of πόδωμα and suggests that the charge is concealed in the payments in BGU. I. 64, II. 534, III. 835 (cf. P. Kalén, pp. 293 ff.). P. Iand. 137 shows a deduction of 1% on wheat.

65. P. Teb. II, App. I, line 28, where the reading should be ἑκατο-σ[τῆς α L] to agree with the new reading of P. Ghent in SB. 6951, ii. 39. Cf. P. Kalén, pp. 293 ff.

66. P. Kalén 1 R i. 15, ii. 21, iii. 8; 4 R ii. 19, iv. 1, 10, 22, v. 22; P. Giss. 60; PO. XII. 1445; BGU. VII. 1636.

67. Cf. P. Kalén, pp. 299–301.

68. OGI. II. 669. 45–54.

69. P. Kalén 1 R i. 16, note; P. Kalén 5 introd. Actual accounts of φόρετρον are rare: P. Kalén 1 R i. 16, iii. 2; 4 R i. 20, iv. 15, 23, v. 4, 6, 23; 5. 3; P. Fay. 338; P. Flor. III. 388. 104; P. Lond. inv. 1911; P. Amh. II. 69; Archiv, v, p. 386, no. 188 a; P. Fay. 86, 86 a; P. Grenf. II. 44; P. Teb. II. 363, 365, 526; PSI. X. 1177. Orders for payment by the sitologi to the transporters and the latter's receipts are: P. Fay. 18b, 146, 148 (all of which may be Ptolemaic); P. Lond. II. 295 (p. 99); P. Teb. II. 470; P. Genf. 42 (?). Contracts with the trans-

porters: BGU. II. 607, 638. A complaint of a transporter which mentions φόρετρον is BGU. I. 242. Private documents which mention φόρετρον, which in some cases may be paid for the transport of revenue grain, are: PSI. VI. 688 (a payment of money); BGU. IV. 1195; P. Fay. 101; BGU. II. 597, I. 200; P. Oslo. 57; P. Flor. III. 379 (a payment of money); P. Lond. III. 1165 (p. 191) (a payment of money). Official accounts giving money payments for φόρετρον: P. Teb. II. 364, 615; P. Flor. I. 7; P. Teb. II. 347. PO. IV. 740 gives a payment of money for φόρετρον of grain shipped by boat. P. Lond. II. 322 (p. 159) is an order for an assessment in kind to pay φόρετρον, but it does not seem to be transportation of revenue grain; but cf. P. Kalén, p. 111. Leases mention the φόρετρον frequently in order to determine the responsibility of lessor and lessee in regard to these charges which were usually, though not always, paid by the latter: BGU. II. 640; P. Lond. III. 1225 (p. 138); P. Amh. II. 91; BGU. I. 227, III. 918; P. Teb. II. 373, 375; CPR. 47; P. Amh. II. 90; P. Teb. II. 311, 377; P. Lond. II. 314 (p. 189), III. 1223 (p. 139); P. Teb. II. 375; BGU. IV. 1018; PSI. I. 31; BGU. I. 166; SB. 7373; P. Oslo. 33, 34; P. Kalén 19; P. Hamb. 64; PSI. X. 1124, 1134. An enigmatic receipt from the Fayûm (O. Tait, p. 180, H.) may perhaps be connected with the φόρετρον. A payment of ⅛ artaba of wheat was collected (apparently as a surtax) in connexion with a payment of 16½ artabae of seed corn in a receipt issued by a sitologus in A.D. 16 (WO. II. 1546); the payment of ⅛ artaba is designated φορικ(οῦ?) according to Wilcken's reading, but perhaps it should be read φορέτρ(ου) and is simply a charge for transportation.

70. P. Kalén 5 and introd.

71. Ibid., p. 276.

72. P. Teb. II. 520. Cf., however, PO. IV. 740, which the editors consider a private account of an official.

73. Cf. the documents cited in notes 43 and 69 above.

74. Cf. PSI. I. 31 where, however, the φόρετρα ὄνων seem to be distinguished from the φόρετρα νομαρχίας.

75. Cf. Frisk, *Bankakten aus dem Faijûm, etc.*, Göteborg (1931) (*Göteborgs Kungl. Vetenskaps = och Vitterhets = Samhälles Handlingar*, Femte Följden, Ser. A, Band 2, No. 2), 1; also P. Columbia 1 R. 4 and 5.

76. P. Kalén, p. 116 (on P. Flor. I. 7. 9).

77. Ibid. 1 R. i. 10 note.

78. See Chapter III, p. 21.

79. Cf. Kalén's tables, P. Kalén, pp. 49 ff.

80. Cf. Wilcken, *Grundz.*, pp. 378 ff.; Rostovtzeff in *Archiv*, III, pp. 220 ff.

81. P. Thead. 26, 27; PSI. IX. 1048 (ὀβολισμὸς ποταμίων πλοίων); P. Teb. II. 368; BGU. VII. 1613.

82. Cf. P. Cairo Preisigke 33; P. Lips. 64; SP. XX. 93; O. Strass. 172.

83. PO. III. 522; P. Teb. II. 486; PO. X. 1259, XVII. 2125; SP. XX. 32; SB. 7534.

84. SP. XX. 32 is from the Heracleopolite nome.

85. P. Kalén, p. 299.

CHAPTER V

1. See pp. 59 ff. and notes.

2. Payments in money ὑπὲρ τιμῆς οἴνου or φοινίκων at Thebes may sometimes have been made in connexion with exactions for the *annona militaris* in Egypt; cf. Chapter III, p. 24 f. In her introduction to O. Wilb.-Brk. 40–2 Miss Préaux has stated that Wilcken has returned to his first reading of WO. II. 1264: ἔσχ(ομεν) παρὰ σο(ῦ) ὑπ(ὲρ) τι(μῆς) οἴν(ου) γενήματος κβ᾿ εἰς ἀπόμοι(ραν). It is probable, therefore, that the majority of these receipts refer to the ἀπόμοιρα.

3. Cf. P. Teb. II. 343. In the Ptolemaic period special concessions in regard to taxation were made during the first few years after vines had been planted in order to encourage viticulture. No satisfactory evidence of such concessions is available for the Roman period, but they may have existed, although the Roman government was not anxious to encourage viticulture.

4. The ratio of copper drachmae to silver drachmae of 300 : 1 is given by P. Lond. II. 372 (= P. Teb. II, Appendix I) and by SB. 6951, the gnomon dealing with the rates on garden- and vine-land; cf. P. Ryl. II, pp. 246 ff. The actual value of copper in private transactions was much less.

5. In *Social and Economic History of the Roman Empire* (Oxford 1926), pp. 439, 440, 576, 623, 627.

6. WO. I, pp. 173 ff.; also pp. 147 ff. and 313 ff.

7. Ibid. I, p. 193.

8. The editors of P. Ryl. II, p. 249, were unable to account for the apparent halving of the 25 drachmae rate of the γεωμετρία on garden-land, since it followed no logical principles. It now appears that the rate was not halved, but the full rate was being paid in two instalments. Cf. SP. XX. 44; BGU. VII. 1607, III. 915.

9. O. Tait, p. 6, no. 33 note. Cf. O. Strass. 8, 19.

10. Cf. the reference in Milne, JEA. XI (1925), pp. 270 ff., and Preisigke, *Wörterbuch*, III Abschn. 11 sub ἀμπελικά, ἐπαρούριον, and ἀπόμοιρα.

11. See below, p. 58.

12. Cf. SB. 6951 and below, p. 56 f.

13. P. Teb. II. 482.

14. WO. II. 356, 1543. The following examples of payments for γεωμετρία are arranged chronologically under the place of origin: Elephantine-Syene: WO. II. 13–15, 17, 22, 88, 157; O. Br.-Berl. 37; WO. II. 184, 210, 238, 267, 268, 275, 284, 1610; O. Strass. 286; O.

Wilb.-Brk. 36. Upper Egypt: O. Strass. 297, 104. Thebes: WO. II.
407; O. Strass. 78; O. Theb. 71; WO. II. 1561, 1406; O. Tait, p. 90,
no. 88; O. Strass. 204, 191; WO. II. 513; O. Strass. 198; P. Lips.
I. 67; WO. II. 1572, 1423, 1579, 1427; O. Wilb.-Brk. 35; WO. II. 576,
580; O. Theb. 40; WO. II. 587, 593, 594, 595, 599, 1581, 1434, 1435;
O. Br.-Berl. 43; Wo. II. 1292, 1448; O. Theb. 72; O. Tait, p. 71, no.
47; p. 93, no. 108; p. 178, E. 2; O. Wilb.-Brk. 37, 38; O. Tait, p. 71,
no. 48; p. 96, nos. 128-9; O. Wilb.-Brk. 39; O. Strass. 145, 160; WO.
II. 677, 685, 699; O. Strass. 148, 149, 150, 151, 153; WO. II. 1470;
O. Strass. 155; O. Theb. 79. Arsinoite nome: P. Ryl. II, p. 255 (= P.
Lond. II. 195 (p. 127)); P. Ryl. II. p. 253 (= P. Teb. II. 478). P. Ryl.
II, p. 253 (= P. Fay. 55); SP. XXII. 134; BGU. III. 915; SP. XX. 44;
BGU. VII. 1607, II. 563; P. Fay. 218 (in line 9 there should be restored
after γεωμετ(ρίας): (δραχμαὶ) (δύο) (ὄβολος) &c.); P. Iand. 141 and
the unpublished rolls from Caranis in the collection of the University
of Michigan; P. Ryl. II. 192 b; P. Hamb. 82; SP. XXII. 132; P. Lond.
II. 451 (p. 109); BGU. II. 572-4, III. 779. Oxyrhynchite nome: PO.
X. 1308.

The following payments for vine-land include receipts obviously for
γεωμετρία, but may also include payments for other money-taxes
on vine-land: Thebes: WO. II. 1574, 375, 397, 404; O. Strass. 63, 254.
Oxyrhynchite nome: PO. XII. 1473, XVII. 2129 Arsinoite nome: P.
Fay. 42 a; P. Ryl. 186 (probably an official tax-account (according to
the editors) of a high official at Alexandria).

The following are payments for palm-groves: Thebes: O. Tait,
p. 156, no. 29; WO. II. 356, 1364; O. Tait, p. 172, no. 139; O. Strass.
63; WO. II. 1554; SB. 3564; WO. II. 1382, 1383, 1385, 396, 407;
P. Berl. 4434 (cited in WO. I, p. 316); O. Strass. 78; WO. II. 1389,
1398, 1326; O. Strass. 87; WO. II. 1327, 540, 649; O. Strass. 449,
162. Arsinoite nome: BGU. II. 657, VII. 1607, 1587. An interesting
ostracon from Elephantine dated in the late Ptolemaic period (BGU.
VI. 1459) records a payment in kind of $\frac{1}{63}$ (or $\frac{7}{20}$) of the produce in
dates due to 'the god'. Whether such payments were continued in
the Roman period, and so may have been included in receipts ὑπὲρ
φοινίκων, is not known.

The following are payments for ἀκρόδρυα (fruit trees): Elephantine-
Syene: WO. II. 2; SB. 7584. Thebes: O. Br.-Berl. 21. Hermopolis (?):
SB. 5677.

The following are payments for olive-groves: BGU. II. 657, 572-4.
References to ἐλαϊκά (or ἐλαϊκή) are given in connexion with the tax
on olive-oil, where some of them certainly belong, although the word
could refer to a tax on olive-trees and hence on the land producing
olives.

The following are payments for μυροβάλανοι: Syene: WO. II. 296-
300; Archiv, v, p. 178, no. 32; O. Tait, p. 66, no. 20; WO. II. 1460.
These payments are apparently all in kind.

P. Lond. I. 119 and 109 (pp. 140 ff.) which contains all of the classifications cited above is discussed in the text of this chapter. The following readings are suggested:

Lines 44, 55, &c., $\pi\eta\chi(\iota\sigma\mu\dot{o}s)$ $\pi\epsilon\rho\iota\sigma\tau(\epsilon\rho\epsilon\acute{\omega}\nu\omega\nu)$ should be read instead of $\pi\eta\chi(\epsilon\hat{\iota}s)$ $\pi\epsilon\rho\iota\sigma\tau(\alpha\tau\iota\kappa o\acute{\iota})$ suggested by Preisigke in BL. I, pp. 219 ff.

In line 81, 4 obols is the tax on $\frac{1}{8}$ ell, as indicated in the interlinear annotation, instead of $\frac{1}{16}$ as read by the editors or $\frac{1}{12}$ as read by Wilcken (BL. I).

In line 110 the fraction of an ell should be read $\overline{\beta\iota\lambda}$, i.e. $\frac{2}{3}, \frac{1}{10}, \frac{1}{30}$.

In line 127 read $\pi\eta\chi($) $\beta\iota\xi\rho\kappa$, i.e. $\frac{2}{3}, \frac{1}{10}, \frac{1}{60}, \frac{1}{120}$.

In line 133 Wilcken's reading (BL. I, p. 222) $\pi\eta\chi($) $\beta\overline{\gamma\theta}$ is somewhat doubtful because 11 drachmae 4 obols is exactly the tax on $2\frac{1}{3}$ ells, but the editors have noted an error in the copying or the calculation of the scribe.

In line 6 of 109 A (p. 150) the amount of the $o\check{\iota}\nu o\nu$ $\tau\acute{\epsilon}\lambda os$ should be $[\int\eta]$ $\int$ $o^- \chi^o$, since 8 drachmae $3\frac{1}{2}$ obols 2 chalci is the amount of the tax on $1\frac{5}{64}$ arurae of vine-land (in lines 2–3).

In line 13 the taxed land is $\frac{67}{256}$ arurae of vine-land at 350 drachmae an arura, and the amount is 91 drachmae $3\frac{1}{2}$ obols 2 chalci instead of 1 drachma $3\frac{1}{2}$ obols 2 chalci. On the facsimile (vol. I, plate 91) the top and bottom of the ς are preserved, and probably also the top of the sign for drachmae ($\int$) further to the left. The rate of the tax is the same as that of the parcel of land following.

15. In TAPA. LXV (1934), pp. 256 ff.

16. Cf. Milne, *Annals of Archaeology and Anthropology*, VII, pp. 61 ff.; O. Tait, p. 87, no. 79 note; above, note 4. The various rates for $\pi\rho o\sigma\delta\iota\alpha\gamma\rho\alpha\phi\acute{o}\mu\epsilon\nu\alpha$ are discussed in connexion with the various taxes.

17. The parcel at 20 drachmae may have been palm-land, which was normally assessed at 20 drachmae to the arura, or $\lambda\alpha\chi\alpha\nu\acute{\iota}\alpha$ at 20 drachmae to the arura, or $\grave{\alpha}\kappa\rho\acute{o}\delta\rho\nu\alpha$ at the same rate. It is not wholly impossible that a rate of 20 drachmae was allowed for newly planted vineyards ($\nu\epsilon\acute{o}\phi\upsilon\tau\alpha$), but there is no evidence for this in the text.

18. Cf. Reil, *Beiträge zur Kenntnis des Gewerbes im hellenistischen Ägypten* (Borna-Leipzig, 1913), p. 164, and the references there cited.

19. P. Lond. I. 119 (pp. 142 ff.), lines 57, 60, 73.

20. Cf. WO. I, pp. 315 ff.; also O. Wilb.-Brk. 37.

21. P. Lond. I. 119 (pp. 142 ff.), line 70. A $\tau\acute{\epsilon}(\lambda os)$ $\lambda\alpha\chi\alpha\nu\acute{\iota}\alpha s$ is found in WO. II. 787, where it is collected by $\tau\epsilon\lambda(\hat{\omega}\nu\alpha\iota)$, but nothing is stated concerning the rate of payment, so that it is uncertain whether the tax is the $\gamma\epsilon\omega\mu\epsilon\tau\rho\acute{\iota}\alpha$ or some other tax collected on vegetable-gardens. For WO. II. 1075 see the BL. II. I. Wilcken considers the 3 drachmae 4 obols paid in equal shares by two men in the Berlin ostracon 4620 (quoted on p. 250 of WO. I. = SB. 2085) as an *adaeratio* of an impost in kind; if Wilcken is correct the impost was probably in connexion with the military annona.

22. P. Lond. I. 119 (pp. 142 ff.), lines 42, 53, 102. Cf. P. Lond. I. 109 A (pp. 150 ff.), line 5.

23. On the date cf. Wilcken in GGA. 1894, p. 737.

24. See Chapter VIII.

25. These taxes are discussed in the sections immediately following in this chapter.

26. Cf. Otto, *Priester u. Tempel im hellenistischen Ägypten* (Leipzig and Berlin, 1905–8), I, p. 341.

27. For a clear statement of the opposing views of scholars in regard to the significance of the use of the revenue from the ἀπόμοιρα for the cult of Arsinoë Philadelphus see Bevan, *A History of Egypt, The Ptolemaic Period*, pp. 184 ff. The bibliography to 1905 is given by Otto, *Priester u. Tempel*, I, pp. 340 ff., especially p. 343, note 2. Cf. also Rostovtzeff, GGA. 1909, pp. 628 ff.; Bouché-Leclercq, *Histoire des Lagides* (Paris, 1906), III, pp. 194 ff.; Wilcken, *Grundz.*, pp. 94 ff.; Préaux in O. Wilb.-Brk. 4 introd.

28. OGI. 90 and P. Teb. I. 5. 52 and *adn. ad. loc.*

29. Cf. P. Teb. I. 5. 52 note and Bevan, op. cit., pp. 184 ff.

30. In P. Ryl. II. 213 from the Mendesian nome the ἀπόμοιρα is ordinarily assigned to the ἱερατικά division of the treasury; but land in the classification λιμνιτικά pays the ἀπόμοιρα to the διοίκησις. In PO. XII. 1437 the ἀπόμοιρα is probably to be understood as a part of the revenues of the ἱερατικά division, since it is associated with the revenues from ἱερὰ γῆ. In P. Fay. 41 the ἀπόμοιρα is listed under διοίκησις. In P. Bouriant 30 the total distinguishes between διοικήσεως and ἱερᾶς after the epithet ἱερά has just been applied to ἀπόμοιρα.

31. In *Priester u. Tempel*, I, p. 342, note 2, based on *Revenue Laws*, col. 36. 7–8.

32. Cf. e.g. O. Tait, p. 12 f., nos. 69–74. Rostovtzeff, GGA. 1909, pp. 628 ff., considered ἱερὰ γῆ under perpetual lease as liable to the ἀπόμοιρα.

33. *Revenue Laws*, cols. 24. 5; 29. 10, 17; 33. 21 *bis*; 36. 9, 18; 37. 7, 16.

34. *Revenue Laws*, col. 24. 4–13; cf. P. Petrie, III. 57 (b); PSI. VIII. 976.

35. Cf. for the Ptolemaic period BGU. VII. 1561–2; for the Roman period P. Teb. II. 343. 69; P. Lond. II. 195 (p. 127 = P. Ryl. II, p. 255); PO. VI. 917, X. 1283. The difference in the rates of παραγωγὴ ἐλαίας (cf. below) on ἐν κλήρῳ ἐλαιῶν and ἐν ἑκτη(λογουμένῃ τάξει) ἐλαιῶν shows that the distinction between ἕκτη and δεκάτη had not lost all significance.

36. OGI. I. 90. 14–15; P. Teb. I. 5. 52. Cf. O. Theb. D 5, note.

37. *Revenue Laws*, col. 24. 4–13, note, p. 95; WO. I, p. 159.

38. *Revenue Laws*, p. 121.

39. O. Tait, p. 7, no. 43. In his note Tait observes that although 'the ἀπόμοιρα is here paid in χαλκὸς ἰσονόμος it is otherwise in the Revenue Papyrus' (col. 24. 13). I do not know why Milne (JEA. XI (1925), p. 277) states that the ἀπόμοιρα was originally farmed πρὸς χαλκόν.

40. PO. XII. 1437.

41. Cf. P. Ryl. II, p. 249 f. on P. Hamb. 40–1, 46–51.

The following payments are for ἀπόμοιρα: Thebes: WO. II. 355; O. Theb. D 5, D 37, D 52 (other payments are doubtless represented by the receipts issued by the ἐπιτηρηταὶ τιμῆς οἴνου καὶ φοινίκων; cf. note 2 above). Arsinoite nome: P. Ryl. II, p. 255 (= P. Lond. II. 195 (p. 127)); P. Fay. 190; P. Lond. inv. 1581 recto, iii; P. Bouriant 30; BGU. III. 915; P. Iand. 141, and the unpublished rolls from Caranis in the collection of the University of Michigan; P. Hamb. 82; P. Fay. 41; P. Grenf. II. 65; P. Teb. II. 478; P. Ryl. II. 412 (?), 376 (?). Oxyrhynchite nome: PO. III. 653, XII. 1437, VII. 1046.

The following payments for vine-land are evidently for ἀπόμοιρα: Arsinoite nome: P. Fay. 192, 341; P. Ryl. II, p. 254 (= P. Lond. III. 917 (p. xlv)); BGU. II. 572–4; P. Hamb. 40–1 (?), 46–51. Oxyrhynchite nome: possibly PO. XVII. 2129. 73 (cf. adn. ad loc.).

The following documents from the Oxyrhynchite nome record payments for ἕκτη which is equivalent to ἀπόμοιρα: PO. VI. 915, X. 1283. Cf. also P. Ryl. II, p. 255 (= P. Lond. II. 195 (p. 127)), line 16; P. Teb. II. 343. 69; Archiv, v, p. 392, no. 303.

42. Cf. P. Ryl. II, pp. 252 ff., where the editors discuss the significance of the term εἴδη. The word was probably used to indicate those taxes which were originally paid in kind.

43. Cf. note 4 above.

44. In JEA. XI (1925), pp. 269 ff., Milne shows that the charge of 20 per cent. consisted of two charges, one originally set at 10 per cent., and another which gradually increased until it reached 10 per cent.

45. Cf. P. Ryl. II. 192. 10, note.

46. PO. XII. 1437 and introd.

47. The editors of PO. XII. 1437 (introd.) wrongly state that the difference was only 6 per cent.

48. Cf. Milne, JEA. XI (1925), pp. 269 ff.; P. Hib. 67. 15, note.

49. See PO. XII. 1437. 8, note.

50. See the discussion of the ἐπαρούριον in the section immediately following in this chapter.

51. Cf. Rostovtzeff, Soc. and Ec. Hist., pp. 94 and 187 ff., and the references given by him in chapter vi, note 11.

52. Cf. the gnomon in SB. 6951.

53. Milne assumes that the payment designated ἱερᾶς Ἀμμῶ(νος) is for ἐπαρούριον, and the preceding payment for ἀπόμοιρα.

54. The editors of P. Hib. 112. 13, note, suggest that the rate of the ἐπαρούριον in that document (dated c. 260 B.C.) may be 8 obols per arura. They suggest also that in P. Petrie III. 70 (a), i 'the tax of 8 drachmae per aroura on, apparently, vine-land may well be the ἐπαρούριον'. But the tax of 8 drachmae is probably to be connected with the ὀκτάδραχμος or οἴνου τέλος at 8 drachmae to the arura found in the Roman period.

The following are payments for ἐπαρούριον in the Roman period:

Arsinoite nome: P. Teb. II. 345 (? see introd.); P. Ryl. II, p. 255
(= P. Lond. II. 195 (p. 127)); P. Fay. 226; P. Lond. inv. 1581 *recto*, iii;
BGU. III. 776; PSI. VIII. 885, IX. 1059; P. Fay. 190; P. Ryl. II, p. 253
(= P. Teb. II. 478); P. Fay. 55; P. Fay. 341 (= SP. IV, p. 118); P. Fay
218; P. Teb. II. 500; P. Ryl. II. 192 b; P. Hamb. 82; P. Ryl. II,
p. 254 (= P. Lond. III. 917 (p. xlv)); P. Fay. 41; P. Grenf. II. 65; EGU.
VII. 1606; P. Iand. 141, and the unpublished documents from Caranis
in the collection of the University of Michigan; P. Hamb. 46, 41, 40.
Oxyrhynchite nome: PO. XII. 1436, III. 653, VI. 917, 981, 982, X. 1283.
Mendesian nome: P. Ryl. II. 427.

55. P. Ryl. II, p. 248, note 1.

56. See the section later in this chapter on the παραγωγή ἐλαίας.

57. See note 41 above.

58. What the editors of BGU. VII. 1606 have expanded as ἐπ(αρού-
ριον) in line 9 is probably ἐλ(αίας), i.e. παραγωγή ἐλαίας, which occurs
in this position in other receipts, e.g. P. Fay. 55 (= P. Ryl. II, p. 353);
P. Lond. III. 917 (p. xlv = P. Ryl. II, p. 254); P. Fay. 218; P. Iand.
141, where ελ( ) should be expanded ἐλ(αίας παραγωγῆς) instead of
ἐλ(λείματος) as given by Curschmann. In BGU. VII. 1606. 10 ἐπ( )
is doubtless to be expanded ἐπ(αρουρίου), since the amount given, 6
talents, is correct for the ἐπαρούριον on garden-land paying 9 talents
for ἀπόμοιρα, whereas 1 talent 106 drachmae (copper) are not in the
correct ratio to the 9 talents. The 106 drachmae given in line 9 is
probably incorrect, since copper drachmae are ordinarily calculated
in units of 5. Another reason for assuming that the ε . ( ) of line 9
is ἐλ(αίας) is that the προσδιαγραφόμενα on παραγωγή ἐλαίας were
calculated at the rate of $\frac{1}{5}$, whereas the προσδιαγραφόμενα on ἐπαρούριον were $\frac{1}{13}$ and were ordinarily calculated separately in the receipts; but the προσδιαγραφόμενα on πα(ραδείσου), ε . ( ) and
ν(αυβίου) are here calculated together. The amount of προσδιαγραφόμενα given in line 10 is too large; at $\frac{1}{5}$ it requires an amount of 2
talents 5,220 drachmae in excess of 9 talents (for ἀπόμοιρα) plus 4,830
drachmae (for ναύβιον). If the ἐπ( ) be expanded ἐπ(αρουρίου) in
line 10, the προσδιαγραφόμενα at $\frac{1}{13}$ on 6 talents would be 2,770 drachmae, and προσδ( ) Β'ψο would fill the lacuna in line 11. The κόλλυβος, at the rate of $\frac{1}{60}$, demands a total of 39 talents 4,200 drachmae,
which would have to include γεωμετρία ordinarily paid in silver. If
the ναύβιον is the ναύβιον ἐναφεσίων at 150 drachmae to the arura
(as the editors suggest in their note on line 10), there were c. 32$\frac{1}{5}$
arurae on which the ναύβιον was paid. This would mean that the
9 talents for ἀπόμοιρα was not paid on 36 arurae at 1,500 drachmae to
the arura (as the editors state in their note on line 9), but perhaps on
14$\frac{2}{5}$ arurae at 3,750 drachmae, the rate in the third century after Christ.
Since BGU. VII. 1606 records a payment for A.D. 200-1, the year
after Severus made important changes in the financial organization
of the province of Egypt, the change in the rates of taxes on vine- and
garden-land may well date from the first year of the third century (PO.

xII. 1437, dated A.D. 208, is otherwise the earliest published example of the increased rates on vine- or garden-land). But the rate of παραγωγή ἐλαίας must have been greatly increased in the third century, if the taxes in BGU. vII. 1606 are to be calculated on 14⅖ arurae, perhaps double the rate in the second century on an ἐν ἐκτηλογουμένῃ τάξει ἐλαιῶν, i.e. 560 drachmae. On 14⅖ arurae this would amount to 8,080 drachmae, which would be written {α Β΄π. If we assume that the προσδιαγραφόμενα on γεωμετρία when paid in copper were at the rate of $\frac{1}{10}$, the receipt might be restored as follows: (beginning with line 8) Λογγιν[α γεω( ) χ( ) {ιη] προσ[δ( ) {α Δ΄ω] πα( ) θ∫ Φιλαδελ( ) χ( ) {θ ελ( ) {α Β΄π ν( ) Δ΄ωλ πρ( ) {β Α΄τξε (or Α΄το) επ( ) {ϛ [προσδ( ) Β΄ψο] κολ( ) Γ΄το. But payment of γεωμετρία in copper is not attested. In any case such a restoration is entirely hypothetical and is intended merely to show the necessity of a re-examination of the readings of the receipt. If the document can be satisfactorily deciphered it should be possible to determine whether or not the rise in the rates of taxes on vine- and garden-land was a part of the changes introduced by Septimius Severus.

59. The gnomon was first published by J. Persyn, *Revue de l'instruction publique en Belgique*, LVI (1913), pp. 306 ff.; it was again published in part (columns ii and iii of the *verso*) by Johnson, Martin, and Hunt, who gave conjectural emendations in P. Ryl. II, pp. 420 ff.; new readings of the entire text were published by M. Hombert, *Revue belge de Philologie et d'Histoire*, IV (1925), pp. 634 ff., no. 1, and his readings were accepted for SB. 6951.

60. On the ἀναβολή χωμάτων cf. Oertel, *Die Liturgie* (Leipzig 1917), pp. 74 ff.

61. Cf. Jouguet, P. Lille 1 introd., p. 15; P. M. Meyer, P. Giss. 1. 42 introd., p. 51 and p. 53; Wilcken, *Grundz.*, pp. lxxii, 330 (note 5), 334; Smyly, P. Petrie, III, pp. 339 and 345.

62. See P. Hib. 112. 13, note, with references there cited.

63. SB. 6951. 28–31; P. Teb. II, Appendix I. The following are payments for ναύβιον: Thebes: O. Tait, p. 89, no. 84 (cf. note); WO. II. 1396. Arsinoite nome: SB. 5102; PSI. VIII. 905, 906; P. Ryl. II, p. 255 (= P. Lond. ii. 195 (p. 127)); P. Fay. 226; BGU. VII. 1613; P. Fay. 191; SP. xx. 1; P. Fay. 56; PSI. IX. 1059; P. Ryl. II. 188; P. Fay. 190; P. Hamb. 62; P. Lond. II. 201 a (p. 79); P. Ryl. II, p. 253 (= P. Teb. II. 478); P. Fay. 192; P. Ryl. II, p. 253 (= P. Fay. 55); P. Ryl. II. 192; P. Teb. II. 549; P. Fay. 341 (= SP. IV, p. 118); P. Teb. II. 610; P. Ryl. II. 195; BGU. III. 883; P. Fay. 193; P. Teb. II. 500; P. Fay. 194, 218; P. Ryl. II. 192 a, 192 b; P. Hamb. 83; P. Teb. II. 352; P. Fay. 99, 57; P. Ryl. II, p. 254 (= P. Lond. III. 917 (p.xlv)); P. Amh. II. 118; P. Fay. 41; SP. XXII. 147; P. Lond. inv. 1581 recto, iii; BGU. II. 662; SP. XXII. 111–13; P. Fay. 42 a; P. Iand. 141, and the unpublished documents from Caranis in the collection of the University of Michigan; P. Lond. II. 451 (p. 109); BGU. III. 790; P. Grenf. II. 65; BGU. II. 572–4, III. 819, VII. 1606; P. Hamb. 46–51, 40,

41. Oxyrhynchite nome: PSI. x. 1097; PO. ii. 296, xii. 1434, iii.
530, 469 introd., xvii. 2129, 11, xii. 1436, iii. 653 (a), vi. 917, xii.
1546. Mendesian nome: PSI. iii. 233, i. 106. Hermopolite nome: P.
Amh. ii. 85 (a lease); P. Lips. 93–6; P. Lond. iii. 1157 (p. 61), 1217 a
(p. 61). Antinoöpolite nome: P. Lond. ii. 383 (p. 117). Unknown provenience. P. Lond. ii. 193 (p. 122 = SP. xvii, p. 49); P. Ryl. ii. 78,
186; P. Oslo ii. 57.

64. e.g. P. Fay. 57, 191.

65. e.g. P. Fay. 41.

66. Cf. note 63 above; P. Ryl. ii, pp. 239 ff. and 243 ff.

67. Cf. P. Lond. ii. 193 R (pp. 122 ff. = SP. xvii, pp. 49 ff.).

68. Cf. Milne, JEA. xi (1925), pp. 269 ff.

69. P. Ryl. ii, p. 250.

70. O. Tait, p. 89, no. 84 and note.

71. The ἱερὰ γῆ in P. Ryl. ii. 188. 11 pays no ναύβιον.

72. Cf. Oertel, *Liturgie*, p. 392, note 3.

73. P. Ryl. ii. 192.

74. Cf. P. Ryl. ii, p. 252.

75. Cf. P. Ryl. ii. 213 introd.; cf. PSI. i. 106, iii. 233.

76. Cf. Wilcken *Grundz.*, pp. 332 ff.; Oertel, op. cit., p. 429 f.

77. The editors of P. Ryl. ii (p. 248, note 1) think it probable that
ἐν κλήρῳ = κατοικικός and ἐν κατοικικῇ τάξει, but they point out
that in that case the land, although κατοικικός, would pay the ναύβιον
at the ἐναφεσίων rate. The payment for ἐλ(αίας παραγωγή) in P.
Iand. 141 has been noted above; similar payments are to be found in
the tax-rolls from Caranis in the collection of the University of
Michigan. The payments were first correctly identified in the discussions in P. Ryl. ii of P. Lond. ii. 195 (p. 127) (= P. Ryl. ii, p. 255);
P. Fay. 55 (= P. Ryl. ii, p. 253); P. Lond. iii. 917 (p. xlv) (= P. Ryl.
ii, p. 254); cf. P. Ryl. ii, p. 249, note 3; p. 346, note 1; P. Lond. inv.
1581 *recto*, iii. In O. Mey. 43; O. Oslo 16; and WO. ii. 687 payments
are made ὑπὲρ ἐλαιο(ῦ), but this may not be the same tax. Ἐλαικῆς
is found in P. Ryl. ii. 213 and 215; PSI. i. 106; BGU. iii. 753 v.
Ἐλαικῶν εἰδῶν is found in P. Fay. 64 and an ἐπιτηρητ[ὴς ......]
ἐλαικῆς καὶ ἄλλων πρ[οσοδικῶν] in P. Teb. ii. 539.

78. See note 59 above.

79. Cf. P. Ryl. ii, Appendix II, line 20, note; P. Ryl. ii. 216. 128,
note. The following are payments for the 8-drachma tax, some of
which, at least, are probably equivalent to the (ὀκταδραχμὸς) σπονδὴ
Διονύσου: P. Teb. ii. 500; BGU. ii. 572–4; PO. x. 1340 (?), xii. 1436,
iii. 653 (a), vi. 917, x. 1283, xiv. 1744 (?); P. Bouriant 29; PO. vi.
916 (= W. *Chrest.* 185); PO. ix. 1185, xii. 1473, xvii. 2129 (?), x.
1283; P. Ryl. ii. 213, 216. 128, 427. 47; P. Bouriant 37 (?); P. Ryl.
ii. 186; O. Strass. 10, 11, 87; P. Goodsp. Cairo 30, col. xxix (?);
SP. xxii. 67 (*verso*); PO. iv. 788; P. Lond. i. 119 and 109 (pp. 140 ff.).

80. WO. ii. 397, 404. From the Ptolemaic period, O. Strass. 10,
11; WO. ii. 327.

81. Cf. PO. XVII. 2129. 74, note. It is possible, however, to explain the 53 drachmae at the end of the line otherwise, using only the taxes attested elsewhere in the document:

8 arurae at 2 drachmae ($\beta\backslash$)	.	.	.	16 drachmae
,, ,, $\phi \acute{o}(\rho o \varsigma ?)$ (of 2 drachmae)	.	.	.	16 ,,
3½ ,, at 4 drachmae	.	.	.	14 ,,
,, ,, $\phi \acute{o}(\rho o \varsigma ?)$ (of 2 drachmae)	.	.	.	7 ,,
		Total	.	53 ,,

82. e.g. P. Lond. III. 1157 (pp. 61 ff.).

83. *Archiv*, v, pp. 381 ff. (P. Hawara 56).

84. The editors of P. Ryl. II. 216 have discussed the problem in the introduction to that document (p. 329 f.) without coming to a satisfactory conclusion. Confusion has been added by their assumption that the system of assessment must have been uniform in Middle and Lower Egypt, because the ὀκτάδραχμος is found in documents of the Oxyrhynchite and Arsinoite nomes (and possibly the τρίδραχμος in the Arsinoite nome). As noted, the decree of Aemilius Saturninus making the tax of 8 drachmae incident upon the arura probably referred to the crown-tax and not to the (ὀκτάδραχμος) σπονδὴ Διονύσου, consequently the case for identification of the 8 drachmae rate of the tax on land in the Mendesian nome with the ὀκτάδραχμος of the Arsinoite and Oxyrhynchite nomes is irreparably damaged.

85. PO. VI. 916.

86. Cf. the introduction to P. Ryl. II. 216.

87. See Chapters VII and VIII.

88. Cf. the introduction.

89. A φόρος was not ordinarily laid on private property, so that the expansion φό(ρετρον) is possible, although we do not know of any other example of φόρετρον at 2 drachmae an arura. If φόρος is correct, it probably indicates a change in method of collecting taxes and dues or a change in their nomenclature.

90. Cf. the introduction and Chapter XIII.

91. Cf. the introduction to P. Lond. III. 1217 B (p. 61).

92. See the discussion of these taxes in earlier sections of this chapter

93. See Chapter I.

94. Cf. the introduction to PO. XVII. 2129.

95. According to the *Berichtigungsliste*, II. 1 on WO. II. 1301, the expansion πηχ(ισμὸς) περιστ(ερεώνων) is established by O: Bodl. 2238 (unpublished).

96. I assume that the area occupied by the pigeon-house was taxed. The tax is mentioned in P. Lond. I. 119, 109 A (pp. 140 ff.), III. 1171. 73 (?) (p. 177); WO. II. 1301; PO. VI. 981.

97. Cf. O. Tait, p. 14, no. 84, note; Milne in JEA. XI (1925), p. 273.

98. P. Teb. II. 571 (107–106 B.C.).

99. The λειτουργικόν was probably collected in connexion with the

tenure of land when it was credited to the διοίκησις just as when credited to the λιμνιτικά.

100. For ἐπικλασμοί cf. PSI. I. 105; P. Teb. II. 373, 391; PO. VI. 899, IX. 1208, XIV. 1638, 1700, 1704.

101. e.g. BGU. II. 476, 487; P. Lond. III. 1227 (p. 143); P. Teb. II. 494; PO. VI. 899; O. Strass. 271.

102. e.g. P. Iand. 28; P. Ryl. II. 367.

103. e.g. P. Ryl. II. 206, 221.

104. BGU. II. 569–71; cf. P. Teb. II. 325; BGU. II. 487 at 1 drachma an arura. Φόρος ὑπολόγου (γῆς) is mentioned in PO. XII. 1436; a φόρος θησαυρικός in P. Bouriant 42. Payments of φόρος on domain and imperial lands are mentioned in the following documents: P. Teb. II. 477; BGU. I. 277; SP. XXII. 120; BGU. IV. 1091, II. 569–71; SB. 5670; P. Amh. 94; BGU. I. 8. ii; III. 743–4; P. Teb. II. 368; P. Iand. 28; BGU. I. 84 recto, i. 5; PO. XII. 1436; W. Chrest. 176; P. Iand. 26; O. Mey. 59; BGU. II. 476, 487, 567, i. 10, 569–71; unpublished tax rolls from Caranis in the collection of the University of Michigan; P. Fay. 42 a, ii. 9; P. Fay. 87; P. Lond. III. 1227 (p. 143); PO. III. 653, x. 1279; O. Mich. Car. 126; PSI. v. 458 (for hunting and fishing rights); P. Teb. II. 325; P. Flor. III. 340; P. Giss. 50 (for capsarium); P. Hamb. 12; P. Lips. 83; P. Teb. II. 494; P. Ryl. II. 99, 100, 123, 206, 221; O. Strass. 271; P. Bouriant 42 (?); WO. II. 657; O. Tait, p. 98, no. 138 (?); O. Mich. 54(?). There is a προσοδικὸς φόρος in the tax-rolls from Caranis in the collection of the University of Michigan. Φόρος ἐδαφῶν is in P. Lond. inv. 1581 recto, iii.

105. Leases of vine- and garden-land owned by private persons are not satisfactory for comparison with leases of domain land; and furthermore in private leases it is difficult to determine the terms of the lease in money, because the rent often includes payments in kind or the number of arurae is not given. Perhaps the most satisfactory for comparison are P. Flor. I. 16, a lease of a vegetable-garden of 1 arura for 100 drachmae per annum (but the presence of a well (φρέαρ) and a pump (μηχανή) on the property may have increased its value), and PSI. I. 33, where 7 arurae of vineyard and olive-orchard were leased for 1,700 drachmae (plus certain perquisites) per annum (but the depreciation of the currency in the second half of the third century may have raised the rent of this land).

106. The tax is recorded for the Arsinoite nome in O. Fay. 13; P. Ryl. II. 195. 10; P. Fay. 42, 190. In the last example (badly mutilated) the payments in the other lines are for taxes on garden-land. WO. I, p. 403 cites P. Berl. 1394 (unpublished) which has a rubric τελεσμάτων φυτῶν ὄντων ἐν σιτικ[. . .], which may indicate taxes paid in money on certain trees growing in grain-fields. This is confirmed by payments for δραγματηγία listed with payments of taxes on vine- and garden-lands in the unpublished rolls from Caranis.

107. BGU. II. 652. Van Herwerden, Lexicon Graecum Suppl. et Dialect., s.v., states 'nescio quid tributum'.

108. See Chapter III.

109. Cf. P. Ryl. II. 98 (a), 2–3, note.

110. Cf. P. Ryl. II. 213. 9, note.

111. P. Ryl. II. 98 (a), 2–3, note.

112. Cf. ibid. introd.; PSI. v. 458.

113. See Chapter I.

114. An ἀμπέλου πρόσοδος occurs in PO. XII. 1473, VII. 1046; πρόσοδοι φοινίκ(ων) in WO. II. 276.

115. The earliest example known to me is PSI. x. 1144 from Tebtynis, dated A.D. 100; the latest, P. Strass. 61, from Polydeucia, dated A.D. 228. Payments for μονοδεσμίαι are as follows: PSI. x. 1144; P. Teb. II. 373; P. Flor. I. 18; BGU. VII. 1706–7; SB. 5982; BGU. II. 528; P. Fay. 34; P. Teb. II. 572; P. Lond. III. 847 (p. 54); BGU. III. 880; PSI. VI. 693; BGU. I. 334, III. 711; SB. 7166; P. Teb. II. 423; O. Mich. 10; P. Strass. 61, 60; BGU. III. 753, II. 431; P. Amh. II. 121; cf. also BGU. I. 345; P. Strass. 63–4.

116. The assessment *ad aruram* is also suggested by O. Mich. Car. 154 (see note 119 below).

117. On the nomarch see Chapter XVII, p. 333 f.

118. e.g. SB. 5982, 7166; P. Strass. 61; P. Amh. II. 121; O. Mich. 14 where a τέκτων pays 8 drachmae ἐπὶ λόγου; O. Mich. 15.

119. e.g. BGU. VII. 1706. In O. Mich. Car. 154, dated second century, a payment of 2½ artabae of wheat is made on an item Κερκ(εσούχων) κατοίκ(ων) ϛ κα(τοικικῆς) μονο(δεσμίας) and 3¼ artabae of wheat on ἕκτου βασι(λικῆς) μονο(δεσμίας); the significance of ἕκτου in this connexion is to me quite obscure.

120. Cf. P. Strass. 64, where the reading is given as χόρτου ἐν γεν(ήματι) ι̅ διὰ πρεσβυτερῶν. Perhaps it should be read ἐν γέν‹ε›ι διὰ πρεσβυτερῶν.

121. Cf. P. Teb. II. 346. 4, note.

122. Cf. Lesquier, *L'Armée Romaine d'Égypte* (Mémoires, &c., de l'Institut Fr. d'arch. or. du Caire, vol. XLIII), Cairo 1918, pp. 248 ff.

123. Ibid., p. 23.

124. See Chapter III.

125. Cf. *Archiv*, v, p. 176, no. 27; P. Lond. II. 171 (a) (p. 102). Spelled κράστις in P. Hamb. 39, where it is paid to ἱππεῖς εἴλης. Cf. also O. Theb. 102, 113; O. Strass. 255; WO. II, 1134 (?) and perhaps WO. II. 760, although BL. II. 1 calls them memoranda rather than receipts. In the Roman period collections seem to be largely in connexion with supplies for the army. For references to the impost in the Ptolemaic period cf. Preisigke-Kiessling, *Wörterbuch*, III, Abt. II sub γράστις and χλωρά.

126. WO. I, p. 192; also p. 390 f. Examples, besides those in WO. II cited by Wilcken in WO. I, are: P. Fay. 26, 42 a; BGU. I. 216, 41, II. 485, III. 652–3, 761; P. Teb. II. 337; PO. VI. 986; *Archiv*, v, p. 117, no. 30; the unpublished documents from Caranis in the collection of the University of Michigan. In BGU. I. 41 πρόσοδος οἰκίας is

100 drachmae per month and perhaps is the rent (ἐνοίκιον) for the use of government stables, since it is collected with the tax on flocks.

127. To the examples cited by Wilcken (see note 125 above) add: O. Strass. 213; P. Lips. I. 73; *Archiv*, v, p. 177, no. 29; O. Strass. 293; O. Tait, p. 66, no. 22; BGU. IV. 1117, I. 293; PO. XII. 1519; O. Tait, p. 66, no. 22; BGU. I. 293.

128. Cf. the numerous examples of sub-leases of domain and imperial land: e.g., PO. IV. 730; CPR. 243.

129. The phrase is τὸ ὑπὲρ τοῦ ἐργαστηρίου διδόμενον ἐνοίκιον. Does the διδόμενον refer to the 2 obols *per diem* given as the rent in line 13 or to a rate of taxation established by the government?

CHAPTER VI

1. Cf. G. Steindorff, *Das Grab des Ti* (volume II of *Veröffentlichungen der Ernst von Sieglin Expedition*), Leipzig 1913, plate 3. There is also a line-drawing of a portion of the relief in Erman, *Life in Ancient Egypt* (English translation), London 1894, p. 99, taken from Bädeker, *Lower Egypt*, p. 411; cf. Bädeker, *Egypt*, Leipzig 1908 (the latest edition available to me), p. 154.

2. New York 1905, pp. 237 ff.

3. See Chapter I.

4. Cf. P. Teb. III. 703. 63–70, note; Rostovtzeff, JEA. VI (1920), pp. 174 ff.; Schnebel, *Landwirtschaft*, pp. 317 ff.

5. Cf. Oertel, *Die Liturgie*, pp. 116 ff.; PO. XVII. 2131, especially line 12.

6. Cf. Reil, *Beiträge zur Kenntnis des Gewerbes im hellenistischen Ägypten*, Borna-Leipzig 1913, pp. 93 ff.; Chwostow, *Textile Industry in Graeco-Roman Egypt* (in Russian), Kazan 1914.

7. The taxes on animals have recently been discussed by Sandra Avogadro in *Aegyptus*, XIV (1934), pp. 293–7. This study distinguishes the φόρος προβάτων from the ἐννόμιον (which Rostovtzeff had apparently identified), but persists in regarding the φόρος προβάτων as a tax, although it had been recognized as a rent by Preisigke (P. Strass. I. 28 introd.) and Wilcken (*Archiv*, IV. 533; *Chrest.* 272 introd.) and the editors of P. Ryl. II. 213. 9, note. Since the ἐννόμιον is a licence-tax on sheep and goats which involves the privilege of pasturing the animals on unleased public lands throughout the nome, the author of the article maintains that the φόρος προβάτων must be the property-tax assessed on (privately-owned) sheep, because otherwise there is no property-tax attested. Miss Avogadro neglected to prove, however, that the Egyptian system of taxation ever contemplated a property-tax in the sense which she assumes. Even if such a conception of taxation were granted, it is necessary for her to prove that the term φόρος was ever applied to such a tax.

8. The organization of the προβατοκτηνοτρόφοι was probably less elaborate than that of the δημόσιοι γεωργοί, because there were far

fewer of the former, and it is for that reason also that there is much less information about their guild. Cf. San Nicolò, *Ägyptisches Vereinswesen*, Munich 1913, pp. 190 ff.; Schnebel, *Landwirtschaft*, p. 325; Olsson, *Papyrusbriefe*, p. 81, note 4.

9. P. Mich. II. 121 R IV. xii.

10. Cf. P. Cairo Zen. 59394 (where the assessment of 2 drachmae a head on sheep leased by the crown is to be identified with the φόρος προβάτων, and the assessment of ½ drachma a head on sheep owned by the peasants and landholders with the ἐννόμιον); P. Teb. III. 701. 190, I. 72. 232; PO. IV. 807 (*Archiv*, VI, p. 134, no. 13, and WO. II. 1369 record payment for προβάτων, but are probably not φόρος); P. Lond. II. 255 (p. 117) (= W. *Chrest.* 272); SP. XXII. 129; P. Lond. II. 312 (p. 80); PSI. VII. 817; P. Lond. II. 254 (p. 230) (?); BGU. I. 102, 199, 41, 292, 63, II. 382, III. 810; P. Hamb., p. 183, note 6 (Meyer may well be right in referring it rather to the τέλος (cf. his Index VII)); BGU. III. 788; P. Lond. III. 851 (p. 49); P. Strass. 67–9; BGU. VII. 1712; P. Strass. 6–8, 28; SP. XIII, p. 8, no. 1 (from Apollonopolis Magna); the tax-rolls from Caranis in the collection of the University of Michigan.

11. If the sheep were not leased at a uniform rate, this might account for the ½ obol included in the total paid for the φόρος προβάτων in this document. The average rent, however, is quite reasonable. A rough proportion may be established between the average ἐκφόρια and καθήκοντα paid in kind on grain-land and the rates of φόρος προβάτων, and ἐννόμιον assumed in this chapter to be typical, i.e. (ἐκφόρια at) *c*. 5 art. per arura : (καθήκοντα at) 1 to 1½ art. per arura : (φόρος προβάτων at) 5¼ drachmae a head : (ἐννόμιον at) 1⅓ drachmae a head. Another interesting proportion, which is almost exact, may be made between the rates of the assessments on sheep belonging to the crown and those privately owned in P. Cairo Zen. 59394 and the rates of φόρος προβάτων and of ἐννόμιον in the Roman period, i.e. 2 drachmae : ½ drachmae : : 5¼ drachmae : 1⅓ drachmae.

12. In PSI. VII. 817 the προσδιαγραφόμενα on 42 drachmae ½ obol consist of two items, 1 drachma 4½ obols and 1 drachma. This division of the προσδιαγραφόμενα into items of 4 per cent. and 2¼ per cent. is discussed in Chapter XIV, note 53. The surtax of 4 per cent. (ρ ſδ) is found on the ἐννόμιον in BGU. II. 485; presumably the second item of 2¼ per cent. is to be supplied in the lacuna.

13. The rate of 2 drachmae a head in the third century B.C. and that of 5¼ drachmae in the second century of the Roman period illustrate this variation, caused in part, at least, by the difference in the value of the drachma. The payment for προβάτων in *Archiv*, VI, p. 134, no. 13, from Denderah, was made in wheat, but the payment is probably for the tax corresponding to the ἐννόμιον in the Arsinoite nome, since $\frac{1}{12}$ of an artaba of wheat seems too small a rent for even a single sheep, for the price of grain was probably quite low in A.D. 29; cf. the table in Segré, *Circolazione Monetaria*, Rome 1922, pp. 102 ff.; also note 54 below.

14. Cf. especially P. Strass. 6–8; perhaps P. Lond. III. 851 (p. 49); P. Strass. 28.

15. The φόρος ἵππων and φόρος βασιλικῶν ἱερείων ὑικῶν and the like are attested only in the Ptolemaic period; cf. Preisigke WB. III, Abt. 11 sub φόρος.

16. P. Strass. 1. 67–9.

17. See Chapter XVII, p. 312.

18. Cf. San Nicolò, op. cit., pp. 188 ff.

19. Cf. for the φόρος χηνῶν P. Petrie III, p. 282. 7 et passim; for the φόρος χηνῶν τοκάδων P. Petrie III. 112 (c). 12; (d). 9; (g). 4, 24.

20. The object of the φόρος is spelled βωῶν, which is corrected by the editor to βοῶν. It is not impossible that a μ has been omitted, and that the payment is actually for φόρος βωμῶν, on which see Chapter XIV, note 53.

21. See Chapter XIII, p. 222 f.

22. There are also no leases of domestic animals extant from the Ptolemaic period, although we know that the government leased such animals to its subjects.

23. This explanation is quoted from the editors' introduction to PO. IV. 807 and is, I believe, substantially correct. Schnebel (Landwirt-schaft, p. 324) points out that φόρος implies a lease (Pacht), which he feels is incompatible with the editors' term 'impost', although the editors stated that the sheep declared to be Ἀρσινοῆς φορικά were contrasted with those that were private property. Schnebel suggests that the sheep had formerly belonged to an estate, owned by one Arsinoë, which had been confiscated by the government and so were leased from the latter; but the sheep had probably always been Ἀρσινοῆς φορικά in the Ptolemaic period and, like the fish of Lake Moeris, had at one time been granted to Arsinoë (Philadelphus) for pin-money, or perhaps were granted as an endowment for her cult after her death. As both the editors and Schnebel point out, the cult was not continued in the Roman period, so that the revenue from the lease of the sheep devolved to the state.

24. The 240 animals subject to the Ἀρσινοῆς φόρος seem to have been sheep only, for there is no indication in the evidence for the φόρος προβάτων that goats were leased from the government in Roman times, although there is no real reason why the government should not have owned and leased goats.

25. The ἀπογραφαὶ προβάτων have been listed by Miss Avogadro in Aegyptus, XV (1935), pp. 133 ff. Her P. Berl. Möller 7 is SB. 7344. Her elaborate article (ibid., pp. 131–206) should be consulted in regard to returns of all types of property.

26. The difference of 3 lambs in the two summaries is explained by the losses suffered by the herd and recounted in the body of the return.

27. See on the ἐννόμιον, p. 86 f.

28. Cf., e.g., SB. 7344, a return found in the Hermopolite nome, which states that sheep and goats belonging to more than nine individual

owners in the Oxyrhynchite nome were under the charge of a shepherd from the Heracleopolite nome; cf. also PO. II. 245.

29. This definitely does not support Miss Avogadro's view (see note 7 above) of two taxes, a licence-tax, and a property-tax, collected on sheep.

30. On the oath in such documents cf. *Münchener Beiträge zur Papyrusforschung und antiken Rechtsgeschichte* XVII, Seidl, *Der Eid im römisch-ägyptischen Provinzialrecht* (Munich 1933), especially p. 64.

31. See p. 88 f.

32. Cf. P. Lond. II. 376 (p. 77).

33. PO. XVII. 2118; P. Lond. II. 376 (p. 77); PO. XVII. 2117. The ἐξαρίθμησις θρεμμάτων is mentioned in P. Gron. 3, an interesting but very fragmentary document dated second or third century after Christ.

34. PO. XVII. 2117.

35. PO. XVII. 2118.

36. Cf. the representatives of the strategus designated by the term αἱρηθέντων in P. Lond. II. 376 (p. 77).

37. This document is called by the editor a certificate issued by the commission to an individual owner of livestock, but the use of the phrase ἐστι δέ, followed by the name of an owner and the number of foals (πῶλοι), indicates that this is an official's report rather than a certificate. The lack of an address at the beginning of the document is not uncommon in reports to high officials, and this document, like PO. XVII. 2118, may be the draft of a report rather than the official copy transmitted to the higher official.

38. By a slip of the editors Antonia is called the daughter, instead of the wife, of Drusus.

39. Cf. Rostovtzeff, *Soc. and Ec. Hist.*, p. 573; German ed. II, p. 294.

40. Cf. *Aegyptus*, XIV (1934), p. 297.

41. Presumably the lessees of sheep owned by the state enjoyed the same privilege. In P. Teb. I. 72. 232, 236–45 (114–113 B.C.), one Orses became liable to the state for the φόρος προβάτων, and his property was κατόχιμος to the extent of a year's rent πρὸς διαφόρησιν προβάτων. It is probable that a lessee of sheep owned by the government interpreted his privilege of pasturing his sheep 'throughout the nome' too literally and permitted his sheep to stray on the land belonging to the cleruchy of Orses who indignantly killed or appropriated the sheep. The cleruchy of Orses became κατόχιμος because he had thereby injured the revenue of the state from the φόρος προβάτων.

42. Arsinoite nome: BGU. VII. 1599, II. 485; P. Fay. 42 (a); P. Hamb. 42, 40 (?). Hermopolite nome: P. Amh. II. 73. Mendesian nome: PSI. I. 106; P. Ryl. II. 213.

43. BGU. VI. 1351–3. The provenience of 1353 is unknown; 1351–2 are from Elephantine. From Thebes or Upper Egypt: O. Tait, p. 8, no. 49; p. 20, no. 116; p. 21, no. 119; p. 153, no. 4; O. Strass. 177; O. Tait, p. 20, no. 115; SB. 1093, 4326 (Crocodilopolis).

44. Cf. BL. II. 1. If the rate of 1 drachma 2 obols applied to the ἐννόμιον in the Arsinoite nome, the rate of the ἐννόμιον and the

rate of the τέλεσμα καμήλων (10 drachmae a head) are roughly proportional to the value of sheep and camels. This is to be expected, but it does not mean that these taxes are to be regarded as 'property-taxes' assessed on the value of the animals, but the owner of a camel could be made to pay a higher licence-tax for his valuable animal. Similarly there was no 'income-tax' in Roman Egypt, yet in order to exact the maximum revenue from the trade-taxes the rates were fixed with regard to the normal income to be expected from the exercise of each trade.

45. There is a mysterious item for καθήκοντα at 68 drachmae. If that figure could be substituted for the 66 drachmae (paid for ἀριθμητικόν), it would give the desired total of 788 drachmae for the sum of the tax of 1 drachma 2 obols each on the 591 sheep and goats. Such a mistake of the scribe is not impossible, but it is unsafe to base a theory upon the assumption of such a mistake. It would still be necessary to explain an item of 66 drachmae for καθήκοντα.

46. With the ἐννόμιον in PSI. v. 509 (Philadelphia, 256–255 B.C.) is combined a tax called φυλακιτικὸν τῶν κτηνῶν.

47. One drachma is a reasonable amount for the payment for receipt in this document, since in P. Lond. II. 312 (p. 80) one drachma is the payment for the receipt recording the payment of 27 drachmae 5 obols 6 chalci for φόρος προβάτων.

48. In P. Hamb. 42, if we assume that the amount of the προσδιαγραφόμενα and the σύμβολον was not recorded or included in the total paid, 80 drachmae would be the sum of the ἐννόμιον on 60 sheep, and, in P. Hamb. 40. 20 drachmae the ἐννόμιον on 15 sheep. But I am unable to explain the omission of the προσδιαγραφόμενα and σύμβολον.

49. See also note 7 above.

50. Some looseness in terminology must be recognized. In BGU. VI. 1351 and 1353 (Ptolemaic) the tax on camels is called καμήλων ἐννόμιον merely from analogy with the ἐννόμιον on sheep and goats. The privilege of pasture was of no great importance to the owners of camels, for those animals are not turned out to graze like sheep, because the camel, in order to be profitable, must be kept working in transport. Camels too young for service in transport may, however, have sometimes been turned out to graze, and the καμήλων ἐννόμιον may have been a tax applied to foals only. For the *scriptura*, the pasture-fee collected in Italy under the Roman Republic, but which was abolished under the Empire, cf. PWRE. II. 2, Sp. 904; the tax is attested also for Sicily, Africa, Asia, Cilicia, and Cyrene.

51. It is the failure to realize that the ἐννόμιον may have originally been assessed as a general licence-tax that leads Miss Avogadro to seek a property-tax; see above, note 7.

52. O. Tait, p. 20, no. 114; cf. no. 117.

53. WO. I, p. 286.

54. See note 11 above. If $\frac{7}{12}$ artaba of wheat were equivalent to $5\frac{1}{4}$ drachmae (the rent of one sheep in PSI. VII. 817), this would mean that the price of wheat was 9 drachmae an artaba, a famine price, whereas

there is no evidence for famine in A.D. 29. It is also not very likely that the government would lease a single sheep to an individual.

55. BGU. VI. 1351, 1353.

56. In P. Hamb. 40 there is recorded payment of 20 drachmae for the tax on (two) camels, designated merely by καμήλ(ων) κδ ʃ Καρανίδος. At the same time 20 drachmae were paid for ἐννο(μίου) κδ ʃ. As has been stated above (note 48), this would be the tax on 15 sheep. There would be no reason to suppose that this payment of ἐννόμιον was for camels (cf. Aegyptus, XIV (1934), p. 296) instead of sheep, were it not that the payment of the tax on sheep in P. Hamb. 42 is specifically designated by the term ἐννόμιον προβάτων, but such a variation in terms is rather to be explained as idiosyncracies of two scribes. If my whole theory of the nature of the taxes on sheep and camels is wrong, and the ἐννόμιον in P. Hamb. 40 was assessed on camels, the rate was the same as that of the τέλεσμα καμήλων, namely 10 drachmae a head, as Miss Avogadro has suggested.

57. Miss Avogadro has identified BGU. III. 785 as an ἀπογραφή καμήλων in her list of such ἀπογραφαί on p. 133 of Aegyptus, XV (1935). This identification is probably correct, although only the introductory portion of the document is preserved and camels are not mentioned in the extant portion. The document is dated by the editor in the first century after Christ, and Martin thinks that BGU. II. 640, which mentions the same basilico-grammateus, may be dated in the reign of Vespasian (cf. Archiv, VI, p. 164, note 1). If both the identification and suggested date are correct, BGU. III. 785 is the earliest extant ἀπογραφή καμήλων. P. Grenf. II. 45 is the ἀπογραφή καμήλων dated in A.D. 136.

58. The extant ἀπογραφαὶ καμήλων are listed by Miss Avogadro (see note 57 above).

59. See Chapter IV, p. 42.

60. It is difficult to account, on any other theory, for the presence of the docket of the commissioner παρὰ ξένου in P. Lond. II. 328 (p. 75).

61. Ἀπογράφομαι πρώτως occurs in SP. XXII. 15. Reports of final disposal of animals are: SP. XXII. 90; P. Lond. II. 304 (p. 71); BGU. I. 89; SP. XXII. 28.

62. The government seems to have maintained a system of transport on the caravan-route between Coptos and Berenice, although transport seems to have been in private hands in the first century after Christ; see Chapter XV, p. 273 f.

63. P. Grenf. II. 48; P. Lond. II. 468 (p. 81), II. 319 (p. 80), 323 (p. 81); BGU. II. 654, I. 219, II. 521, 461, III. 770; the tax-rolls from Caranis in the collection of the University of Michigan; P. Basel 12; SP. XXII. 108; BGU. I. 199 verso, 41; P. Hamb. 40; SP. XXII. 155; perhaps SP. XXII. 145 should be included; but if Wessely's reading is correct, this is a payment of the μερισμός for the deficiency in the collection of the τέλεσμα καμήλων.

64. Cf. Aegyptus, XIV (1934), p. 295 f., where is corrected Meyer's

erroneous supposition that the rate of the tax on each camel was 2 drachmae a month.

65. The only possible exception is in SP. XXII. 28, where Wessely read $\pi\hat{\omega}\lambda os$ $\lambda[\epsilon\iota\pi]\epsilon\iota$, and no camel is left to be reported. If $\lambda\epsilon\acute{\iota}\pi\epsilon\iota$ means that the foal ran away, then of course there was no camel to report, since the adult camel reported in the previous year had been sold. If, however, $\lambda\epsilon\acute{\iota}\pi\epsilon\iota$ was written for $\lambda\epsilon\acute{\iota}\pi\epsilon\tau\alpha\iota$, and the foal was the only animal left, then it was more than a year old, since it had been reported in the previous year. It is unprofitable to attempt to decide between those alternatives, however, for it is quite probable that Wessely's reading is incorrect, and that we should read $\delta[\iota\epsilon\phi]\theta(\acute{\alpha}\rho\eta)$, the term familiar in other reports.

66. Cf. Segré, *Circolazione Monetaria* (Rome 1922), pp. 128 ff.

67. Cf. Kenyon in the introduction to P. Lond. II. 323 (p. 81).

68. Cf. BL. I.

69. Cf. Preisgike's WB. II, sub $\H{o}vos$.

70. It is not impossible that the tax had the same name as in PO. XII. 1457, and that the title of the officials should be restored $o\acute{\iota}$ $[\acute{\epsilon}\xi\epsilon\iota\lambda\eta$-$\phi(\acute{o}\tau\epsilon s)$ $\tau\grave{\eta}(\nu)$ $\acute{\epsilon}\xi\alpha\delta\rho\alpha\chi\mu\acute{\iota}\alpha\nu$ $\tau\hat{\omega}(\nu)]$ $\H{o}\nu\omega(\nu)$. In P. Lond. II. 305 (p. 79) the $\tau\acute{\epsilon}\lambda os$ $\H{o}\nu ov$ is a sales-tax.

71. Possibly the address of the $\dot{\alpha}\pi o\gamma\rho\alpha\phi\alpha\grave{\iota}$ $\H{o}\nu\omega\nu$ to the collectors of the tax on donkeys rather than to the officials of the financial administration of the nome was caused by the limited incidence of that tax, that is, the officials of the nome did not wish to keep the records for so (apparently) insignificant a tax.

72. P. Ryl. II. 194. P. Ryl. II. 195, perhaps from the Arsinoite nome and dated second century, gives a payment of 8 drachmae for $\pi\epsilon\nu\theta\eta\mu(\acute{\epsilon}\rho ov)$ $\H{o}\nu\omega\nu$; this is discussed in the text of this chapter.

73. On the $\delta\acute{\iota}\pi\lambda\omega\mu\alpha$ $\H{\iota}\pi\pi\omega\nu$ see Chapter XI, p. 186 f.

74. The term $(\acute{\epsilon}\xi\alpha\delta\rho\alpha\chi\mu\acute{\iota}\alpha)$ $\H{o}\nu\omega\nu$ is found in a list of arrears in PO. XII. 1438, from Nebo and dated late in the second century after Christ. The terms $\H{\epsilon}\kappa\tau\eta$ and $\delta\epsilon\kappa\acute{\alpha}\tau\eta$ continued in use as designations for the $\dot{\alpha}\pi\acute{o}\mu o\iota\rho\alpha$ long after that tax was assessed in money at a uniform rate on the arura, so that the terms which indicated a tithe of the yield of the vines was no longer strictly applicable (cf. Chapter V, p. 54). Similarly the rate of the $\acute{\epsilon}\xi\alpha\delta\rho\alpha\chi\mu\acute{\iota}\alpha$ $\H{o}\nu\omega\nu$ may not have been the same for the Oxyrhynchite nome in the second century as it had been in the first century (when the amount recorded is not 6 drachmae, but 5 drachmae 1 obol), but it may have been as high as the rate of $\delta\acute{\iota}\pi\lambda\omega\mu\alpha$ $\H{o}\nu\omega\nu$ in the Arsinoite nome.

75. See note 72 above. Cf. also the requisition of camels by the state mentioned in the $\dot{\alpha}\pi o\gamma\rho\alpha\phi\alpha\grave{\iota}$ $\kappa\alpha\mu\acute{\eta}\lambda\omega\nu$ in BGU. III. 762; P. Lond. II. 328 (p. 75); BGU. I. 266 (= W. *Chrest.* I. 245).

76. P. Ryl. II. 213; PSI. I. 106, 101, 105; O. Strass. 227; possibly in P. Teb. II. 358 ($\tau o\kappa($) $\tau v($)) and in PO. VII. 1046 ($\tau o\kappa($) $\delta\iota o\iota$-$\kappa(\acute{\eta}\sigma\epsilon\omega s)$), but a more probable expansion is $\tau\acute{o}\kappa(os)$ $\delta\iota o\iota\kappa(\acute{\eta}\sigma\epsilon\omega s)$, which would denote interest on sums due to the government.

77. Cf. Table II of the introduction to P. Ryl. II. 213 and the note on line 9.

78. Cf. Preisigke WB. II, s.v.

79. Cf. P. Ryl. II. 213. 9, note.

80. BPW. XXXIII, pp. 870–1.

81. On the possible inference that the ὑική in the Mendesian nome was a capitation-tax, see Chapter IX, p. 145.

82. WO. I, p. 310.

83. BGU. I. 92, II. 649, III. 730.

84. Possibly the payment in WO. II. 265 ὑπὲρ τροφῆς δελφάκων καὶ ἄλλων ἀγέλων is for the rent on pigs leased from the government. The term τροφή suggests an analogy with the lessees of sheep owned by the government who were called προβατοκτηνοτρόφοι; but such an analogy is too slight to serve as a basis for the assumption that this is a receipt for payment of φόρος. A baffling reference to an assessment on pigs and perhaps also on sheep appears in O. Tait, p. 160, no. 52 (dated in A.D. 29–30): χοι( ) τρο( ) οβ . .( ). Cf. also P. Ross.-Georg. IV. 19.

CHAPTER VII

1. See my article on "Census and Poll-tax in Ptolemaic Egypt."

2. Wilcken, *Hermes*, XXVIII (1893), pp. 244 ff.; Viereck, *Philologus*, LII (1893), pp. 243 ff.; Kenyon, *Classical Review*, VII (1893), p. 110; recognized the existence of the fourteeen years' cycle of the census and published their discoveries almost simultaneously.

3. Although lists of published ἀπογραφαί and similar documents have been compiled from time to time, it seems best to list here all the ἀπογραφαὶ κατ' οἰκίαν known to me in order to avoid the complication of references to several lists and to the scattered notes which have attempted to bring the lists up to date. The following ἀπογραφαὶ κατ' οἰκίαν are grouped according to provenience and dating:

Arsinoite Nome

Arsinoe:

A.D. 104, P. Lond. III. 1119 a (p. 25); PSI. IX. 1062.

118, P. Cornell I. 16. ii. 1–22.

132, P. Cornell I. 16. ii. 23–iii. 38; BGU. I. 182.

146, P. Cornell I. 16. iii. 39–48; P. Mey. 9; BGU. I. 137; P. Teb. II. 321; BGU. VII. 1581.

160, P. Ryl. II. 111, 111 a; BGU. I. 57.

174, BGU. I. 123, 298.

188, BGU. I. 115, 116, 117, 118, 120, 126, 128, 129, 138.

Second century: BGU. I. 122.

Second or third century: BGU. I. 125, 131.

A.D. 244, P. Flor. I. 5; SB. 4299; BGU. IV. 1069.

258, SP. II, p. 32.

Theadelphia:
A.D. 20 or 34, P. Mil. 3.
104, P. Lond. III. 1221 (p. 24).
Philadelphia:
A.D. 34, SB. 5661.
104, BGU. VII. 1579.
118, BGU. VII. 1580.
Tebtynis:
A.D. 104, PSI. X. 1136.
Dionysias:
A.D. 132, BGU. I. 53.
Apias:
Uncertain: BGU. I. 130.
Heraclia:
Second century: BGU. I. 158.
Socnopaei Nesus:
A.D. 104, SP. XXII. 32.
118, BGU. III. 706.
146, P. Amh. II. 74.
160, BGU. I. 224 } duplicates
    BGU. II. 410
    P. Grenf. II. 55   Copies of the same return
    BGU. I. 225   addressed to various officials.
    BGU. I. 90 } duplicates
    BGU. II. 537
174, P. Flor. III. 301.
188, P. Flor. I. 102; SB. 6696; P. Rein. 46.
216, SP. II, pp. 29 ff.
Caranis:
A.D. 146, BGU. I. 95.
160, BGU. I. 54, 154, II. 524.
174, BGU. I. 59, II. 447 (= I. 26).
188, BGU. I. 60.
202, BGU. I. 97, II. 577.
216, P. Oslo II 25.
Uncertain:
A.D. 132, BGU. I. 132.
174, BGU. I. 119, 127, 302.
188, BGU. I. 129.

Oxyrhynchite Nome (Oxyrhynchus)

A.D. 6 or 20 or 34, PO. II. 256.
20, PO. II. 254.
48, PO. II. 255.
76, PO. II. 361.
118, PO. IV. 686; XII. 1547.
132, PO. III. 480; PSI. I. 53, VIII 874.

146, PO. I. 171 (= II, p. 208).

202, PO. VIII. 1111 (village of Mermertha), XII. 1548.

230, PSI. X. 1112.

244, P. Flor. I. 4.

Third century: PO. VI. 970.

Memphite Nome (*Memphis*)

A.D. 146, BGU. III. 777.

160, P. Lond. III. 915 (p. 26).

174, BGU. III. 833; SP. XX. 11 (village of Moithymis); P. Lond. III. 919 b (p. 28) (for provenience cf. Meyer in P. Giss II, p. 56).

Hermopolite Nome (*Hermopolis Magna*)

A.D. 90, P. Hamb. I. 60.

216, P. Lond. III. 935 (p. 30), 936 (p. 31).

230, P. Lond. III. 946 (p. 31).

Heracleopolite Nome

Heracleopolis:

A.D. 216, SP. II, p. 27.

230, SP. II, p. 31. (A supplementary return to correct an error in the ἀπογραφὴ κατ᾽ οἰκίαν.)

Ancyra:

A.D. 132, P. Bad. IV. 75 a.

146, P. Bad. IV. 75 b; P. Cornell I. 17.

216, SP. II, p. 28.

Antinoite Nome (*Antinoöpolis*)

A.D. 188, PO. VIII. 1110.

216, P. Rein. 49.

Oasis (*Trimeïthis*)

A.D. 146, PSI. X. 1111 (the editor suggests that the village of Trimeïthis was in the Heracleopolite nome, but cf. P. Lips. I. 64. 20 (= W. *Chrest.* 281) and Wilcken in *Archiv*, IV, p. 478).

Apollonopolite Nome

Heptacomia:

A.D. 118, P. Giss. 44.

Tanyathis:

A.D. 118, P. Giss. 43.

Berenice Trogodytice (*Peptaucha*)

A.D. 132, P. Hamb. 7.

Prosopite Nome (*Thelbonthon Siphtha*)

A.D. 174, SB. 7460.

Uncertain Provenience

A.D. 104, P. Lond. II. 476 (a) (p. 61).
        160, P. Lond. III. 843 (p. 28).

4. Cf. PO. II. 254 introd.

5. There is no reason to suppose that the custom of making the census return in the year following the 'year of the census' as set in the decree of the prefect was ever universal throughout Egypt. The following year became customary in the Oxyrhynchite and Arsinoite nomes. In the other nomes of Egypt the practice varied. The following documents from the Memphite nome were filed in the same year as the year set by the decree of the prefect: BGU. III. 777; P. Lond. III. 915 (p. 26); SP. xx. 11; in the following year: BGU. III. 833; P. Lond. III. 919 b (p. 28). Hermopolis Magna: same year: P. Lond. III. 935 (p. 30); following year: P. Hamb. 60; P. Lond. III. 936 (p. 31); perhaps P. Lond. III. 946 (p. 31). Heracleopolite nome: same year: SP. II, pp. 27, 28, 31; following year: P. Bad. IV. 75 a; P. Cornell I. 17; uncertain: P. Bad. IV. 75 b. Antinoöpolis: same year: PO. VIII. 1110; P. Rein. 49. Trimeithis: same year: PSI. X. 1111. Apollonopolite nome: same year: P. Giss. II. 43-4. Peptaucha: same year: P. Hamb. 7. Thelbonthon Siphtha: same year: SB. 7460. The date of the other extant returns is not preserved. Of the three early census returns from Oxyrhynchus, PO. II. 255 does not refer to the census of the preceding year, but it is dated in Phaophi of A.D. 48, the year after the census-year; PO. II. 254 and 256 have lost their beginnings and the date of filing is uncertain, but they may have been similar to PO. II. 255. SB. 5661 from Philadelphia, the only early return from the Arsinoite nome which affords evidence on this point, is expressly stated to be a return of the same year as the official census-year.

6. Cf. note 78 below. The applications for epicrisis for entrance into the gymnasium continue after A.D. 250, but they have no bearing on this problem.

7. Cf. Kase, TAPA. LXII (1931), p. xli.

8. Cf. Wilcken, *Grundz.*, p. 193.

9. Suetonius, *div. Jul.* 41; *Augustus*, 40.

10. Ἀπογραφαί and the corresponding verb ἀπογράφομαι used in the returns denote the report made by the tax-payers to the officials; ἀναγραφή attested by Diodorus XVII. 52. 6 and the participle ἀναγεγραμμένος used in the returns denote the registration of the tax-payer which was made by the officials.

11. Of the ἀπογραφαὶ κατ' οἰκίαν listed in note 3 the following are landlords' reports of tenants: BGU. I. 182; P. Ryl. II. 111 a; BGU. I. 116 i, 123, 138; SB. 4299; P. Teb. II. 321; P. Lond. III. 1119a (p. 25); PO. II. 254, 255, 256. Cf. also P. Ryl. II. 285 which is a list of lodgers with a statement of their paternity, occupations, and ages; the document is complete, but its purpose is uncertain.

12. Returns sent in by tenants are: Memphis: P. Lond. III. 915

(p. 26), 919 b (p. 28); BGU. iii. 833. Heptacomia: P. Giss. 43. Cf. P. Goodspeed, Cairo 10 (A.D. 189), where a citizen of Memphis pays 400 drachmae for λαογραφία and φύλακτρον, and the payment is designated as ὑπὲρ ἐνοίκων ἀναγραφομένων εἰς αὐτόν.

13. Cf. Oertel, *Die Liturgie*, pp. 179 ff. The evidence that λαογρά-φοι engaged in the collection of taxes is doubtful; cf. WO. ii. 1052; *Archiv*, v, p. 172, no. 10; BGU. vii. 1617. Cf. also WO. i, p. 441, and the references cited there. In Arsinoë there was usually one λαογράφος assigned to each amphodon, although P. Mey. 9 from Arsinoë is addressed to three λαογράφοι. In the villages the number addressed varies from two in PSI. x. 1136, from Tebtynis, to six (or possibly five) in P. Lond. iii. 1221 (p. 24), from Theadelphia. The earliest mention of λαογράφοι occurs in SB. 5661, from Philadelphia and dated A.D. 34. These officials took their name from λαογραφία which, in the Ptolemaic period as late as 94 B.C., was the name of the census (cf. my article on ' Census and Poll-tax in the Ptolemaic Period ' and Chapter VIII, p. 117). Unless the λαογράφοι were employed to check up the returns sent in by the owners of the houses, it is difficult to see what absolutely essential function they performed in taking the census, since returns were filed directly with the comogrammateus or the amphodarch. It is, moreover, hardly credible that the government of Egypt would trust implicitly in the returns sent in by the house-holders, despite the solemn oath and the stringent penalties provided against making false returns. Surely the Roman officials did not rely merely on the chance that some slip or some inconsistency between successive returns would betray a false statement to the watchful clerks in the bureaux. Lack of evidence prevents even a conjecture as to how the λαογράφοι would go about making such a check-up. It is not im-possible that the terms ἀπαράστατοι and ὕστερον εἰκονισθέντες, applied to various ones of the boys and men in SP. iv, pp. 62 ff., refer to an individual interview with the λαογράφοι who had to verify the identification of every boy and man returned in the ἀπογραφαὶ κατ' οἰκίαν before official registration was complete.

14. The amphodogrammateus appears in the returns from Hermo-polis Magna, P. Lond. iii. 935 (p. 30), 936 (p. 31), both from A.D. 216. Elsewhere also the amphodogrammateus appears only in documents from the third century. BGU. iv. 1125. 14, cited by Preisigke's *Wörter-buch* iii, Abschn. 8, s.v., is not a sure testimony for the amphodogram-mateus because of the mutilation of line 14; the document is dated in the reign of Augustus.

15. The extant returns (cited in note 3) from Socnopaei Nesus and dated in A.D. 160 indicate that the owner of a house had to present a a separate copy to each of the bureaux concerned with the census. Duplicates of the copies addressed to the strategus and to the como-grammateus are preserved, and since none of these bears dockets of the officials to whom they were addressed, it is possible that copies in duplicate always were required to be presented to officials. The fact

that many returns are addressed to the officials of more than one bureau does not remove that possibility; it may have been simpler to duplicate a long address several times than to address each copy separately. On the other hand, the number of copies required by the bureaux may have varied at different times and in different places in Egypt. PO. XII. 1547, addressed to the στρατηγῷ καὶ οἷς ἄλλοις καθήκει, and census returns without any address (e.g. PO. VIII. 1111), may indicate that the bureaux undertook the production of copies for distribution to the various officials concerned with the census; but the evidence of these documents does not demand such an interpretation.

16. This view as to the purpose of the docketed copies is that of Martin, SP. XVII, p. 35. Meyer (P. Mey., p. 56) denies that the docketed copy was intended for the person making the declaration, but decides that a copy docketed by the strategus was intended for the officials of the amphodon (or the corresponding officials in a village). The two views are not irreconcilable, if we imagine that the owner of a house, after filing a copy of his return with the strategus, was obliged to present the copy bearing the docket of that official to the amphodarch who noted the docket of the strategus in his own records and then permitted the householder to keep the copy; cf. the records of the date of filing returns with strategus, basilico-grammateus, and the comogrammateus, in SP. II, pp. 29 ff., columns ii, iii, and v.

17. Not only is it reasonable to suppose that the officials of the nome made such a circuit for the purpose of receiving census returns, but it is difficult to see how otherwise the returns from Socnopaei Nesus in SP. II, pp. 29 ff., could have been filed with the strategus and basilico-grammateus and with the comogrammateus on the same day, since Socnopaei Nesus lay at least fifteen miles from the capital of the nome. P. Amh. II. 74, from Socnopaei Nesus, and BGU. I. 95, from Caranis, are both dated on the 30th of Epeiph, A.D. 147. This would be but natural if the strategus and basilico-grammateus were making a circuit, since the two towns are not far apart, and property-owners in both towns would begin to make out their returns at about the same time in preparation for the arrival of these officials. Deputies sign the docket for the strategus or the basilico-grammateus in the following census returns: P. Lond. III. 915 (p. 26); P. Hamb. 60; perhaps SB. 7460.

18. The ἀπογραφαὶ κατ᾽ οἰκίαν have been analysed by Wilcken and Viereck in their articles cited in note 2 and also by Wilcken in WO. I, pp. 440–51. Cf. also Bickermann, *Archiv*, IX, pp. 24 ff.

19. Cf. PO. II. 254, 255. The topogrammateus had been an important official in the Ptolemaic period, but seems to have yielded many of his functions to the comogrammateus in the Roman period, except perhaps in the Oxyrhynchite nome.

20. PSI. VIII. 874.

21. P. Lond. III. 946 (p. 31).

22. P. Mey. 9.

23. Cf. note 14 above.

24. Cf. note 3 above.

25. e.g. BGU. III. 706.

26. e.g. P. Rein. 49.

27. e.g. P. Mey. 9; BGU. VII. 1581; II. 493. ii. 5; 447. 18 ff.

28. e.g. BGU. I. 53, 302. In the returns of late date from Arsinoë reports are made by women χωρὶς κυρίου: cf. BGU. IV. 1069; SP. II, p. 32; BGU. I. 131.

29. Cf. note 5 above. Unfortunately none of the decrees of the prefect authorizing the census have been preserved. Consequently it is impossible to know what the formula of the decree was. Rostovt-zeff, *Kolonat*, pp. 209 ff. (followed by Wilcken, *Grundz.*, p. 193), maintained that a decree of the prefect, directing all persons absent from their place of origin (ἰδία), i.e. who were ἐπὶ ξένης, to return to their ἰδία, always accompanied the decree authorizing the taking of the census. Reinmuth has discussed this question in *The Prefect of Egypt from Augustus to Diocletian* (*Klio, Beiträge z. alten Geschichte*, N.F. 21, Beiheft), and has shown that the evidence does not warrant such a con-clusion. The prefect seems rather to have ordered a return to the ἰδία because of disturbances in the province and to check the urban move-ment of cultivators, and to have utilized the approaching census as an expedient occasion to promulgate the order. Persons with legitimate business requiring their presence at some place other than their ἰδία were not required to return (cf. the decree of Vibius Maximus, W. *Chrest.* 202. 28 ff.). The rigor with which the provisions for return to the ἰδία at the time of the census were enforced doubtless varied, since the inhabitants of Egypt were in doubt as to the necessity for return; cf. PO. VIII. 1157, dated by the editors in the late third century, which is a letter from a man requesting his sister to find out whether or not he could be registered in his absence.

30. *In Flacc.* 16.

31. e.g. P. Ryl. II. 111 b; BGU. II. 447. 14 ff.; I. 130; 115. ii. 7. The description of the house seems to be omitted in P. Ryl. II. 111.

32. e.g. ibid. II. 111 a.

33. e.g. P. Cornell 1. 16. iii.

34. In the returns from Memphis wives and slaves are not men-tioned. The number of extant returns from Memphis is small, and consequently it is difficult to be sure of the procedure followed in the Memphite nome. It is possible, though not probable, that the men making the returns from Memphis had no slaves and that their wives were dead. On the other hand, Memphis was different from most of the rest of Egypt in that tenants made their own census returns. It is better to suppose that wives were not mentioned in the ἀπογραφαί be-cause they did not pay poll-tax, and that slaves were reported separately.

35. The description concerned itself with the presence or absence of distinguishing marks such as moles or scars, the complexion, the height, and any peculiarities of the person such as lameness.

36. Cf., e.g., BGU. I. 115. The profession was added in order to

identify the persons returned rather than to collect the names of those liable to payment of taxes on trades. But just as the ἀπογραφαὶ κατ' οἰκίαν were used to check up the property returns (cf. Eger, *Grundbuchwesen*, pp. 181 ff.), so they could be used to verify the lists submitted by the guilds which controlled the various trades.

37. Cf. BGU. I. 137; P. Flor. I. 5 (man had been ἐπὶ ξένης at the time of the previous census); BGU. IV. 1069, &c. Cf. also PO. III. 479.

38. e.g. P. Ryl. II. 111; P. Cornell 16. iii. 33.

39. e.g. P. Ryl. II. 111. The birth or purchase of a slave was not, so far as is known, reported directly to the officials concerned with the census, but the information was doubtless forwarded to them. See Chapter XIII, p. 230.

40. Cf. note 3 above.

41. e.g. SB. 6696.

42. Ibid. 7460.

43. P. Lond. III. 843 (p. 28).

44. PO. II. 255.

45. Cf. Chapter VIII, p. 119.

46. BGU. v. §§ 58–63. The presence in the Gnomon of these regulations covering penalties for falsification of census returns indicates that the Idiologus collected the fines.

47. It is not clear what the difference is between the penalty for failure to make a return in one census and that for failure in two successive censuses. In the first case the Greek word is τεταρτολογοῦνται; in the second case it is expressed by [ἐν] τέταρτ[ο]ν ⟦ἀναλα⟧ [κατακ]-ρίνονται; that is, the scribe had started to write ἀναλαμβάνεται, erased it, and substituted the stronger word κατακρίνονται. Th. Reinach, *N.R. Hist.* XLIII (1919), p. 613, suggests (with a question mark) that a second quarter of the property is to be confiscated. The difficulty lies in the verb τεταρτολογοῦνται, which, taken with the provision for remission of penalty in section 63, may mean that the one-fourth of the property is not confiscated outright, but is to be sequestrated, worked by the owner, but the income for a period of years is to revert to the state.

48. e.g. SP. II, p. 32.

49. Cf. BGU. I. 116. Almost all returns from the Arsinoite nome were sent in during the last quarter of the year. Cf. Aristotle, Ἀθ. πολ. 40: ἀναβαλλομένων δὲ τὴν ἀναγραφὴν (ἀπογραφὴν?) εἰς τὰς ἐσχάτας ἡμέρας, ὅπερ εἰώθασιν ποιεῖν πάντες.

50. Cf. note 16 above.

51. Cf. P. Cornell I. 16; P. Flor. I. 5; PSI. I. 53; P. Ross.-Georg. II. 12.

52. Cf. P. Petrie III. 59 (d); P. Ross.-Georg. II. 12; BGU. II. 493–510; PO. VI. 984.

53. Cf. P. Lond. II. 324 (p. 63).

54. Cf. PSI. x. 1109, the report to the strategus from a φροντιστής who had searched the records to certify that his client was descended from μητροπολῖται on both sides of his family; PO. IV. 714, XII. 1452, &c.

55. See pp. 109 ff. In WO. II. 52, from Elephantine-Syene and dated A.D. 98, a lad under age (ἀφῆλιξ) pays for λαογραφία 8 drachmae on account (ἐπὶ λόγου). I do not know why he should have made a payment at a time when he could still be designated as ἀφῆλιξ.

56. Cf. P. Ryl. II. 111, 7–8 note.

57. Cf. P. Cornell I. 16. iii. 33.

58. The notices of birth have been analysed by Teresa Grassi in *Aegyptus*, III (1922), pp. 206 ff. The extant notices are:

Arsinoite Nome

Arsinoë:
    A.D. 138–9, BGU. I. 110, 111.
        150–1, P. Fay. 28.
        156, P. Genf. 33 (= W. *Chrest.* 211).

Socnopaei Nesus:
    A.D. 148–9, SP. XXII. 18.
        155, SP. 38.
        183, BGU. I. 28.
        184, SP. XXII. 37.

Tebtynis:
    c. A.D. 50, P. Teb. II. 299.

Coptos-Thebes

A.D. 38–9 or 42–3, O. Br.-Berl. 14. The census is called ἐπίκρισις; cf. P. Hamb. 60, which has ἐπίκρισις κατ᾽ οἰκίαν instead of ἀπογραφὴ κατ᾽ οἰκίαν.

Oxyrhynchite Nome

The notices from this nome are not so much notices of birth as registration of children of privileged classes while they were still under age (ἀφήλικες):

    A.D. 209, PO. X. 1267.
        214–15, PO. XII. 1552.
        287, PSI. III. 164.
        291, P. Cornell 18.

59. Cf. PO. II. 251, 252, 253. 253 and 252 are written in successive years and refer to the removal of the same person. In the introduction to 252 Grenfell and Hunt state that 'it is impossible that these notices had to be sent in annually. Perhaps the fact that his departure took place about the same time as the census (A.D. 19–20) has something to do with it; perhaps 253 was not addressed to the same officials as 252' (but that would not account for the fact that the reports were sent in during successive years).

60. For the μερισμὸς ἀνακεχωρηκότων cf. Chapter IX, pp. 137 ff.

61. Cf. note 59 above.

62. Cf. note 29 above and the statement in the oath of an ἀπογραφὴ κατ᾽ οἰκίαν (PO. II. 255) that no ἐπίξενος lives in the house.

63. Cf. PO. IX. 1210.
64. Cf. Pliny, *Ep.* X. 5-7.
65. Cf. P. Princeton I. 8. iv. 12; 9. iv. 10; P. Ross.-Georg. II. 12. ii. 14; P. Columbia, index, s.v. τελευτᾶν.
66. The notices of death have been analysed by Teresa Grassi in *Aegyptus*, III (1922), pp. 208 ff. The extant notices are:

Arsinoite Nome

Arsinoë:
    A.D. 129, PSI. IX. 1064. Two different notices are preserved in successive columns indicating that notices were joined together to form a roll in the same way as ἀπογραφαὶ κατ᾽ οἰκίαν and so kept in the archives of the nome.
        138, P. Lond. II. 208 a (p. 67).
        140, PSI. X. 1141.
        160, BGU. I. 254.
        158, P. Ryl. II. 106.
        173, P. Fay. 30 (= W. *Chrest.* 214).
        175-6, BGU. I. 79.
Socnopaei Nesus:
    A.D. 66, P. Lond. II. 281 (p. 65).
        101-2, BGU. III. 773.
        170, P. Lond. II. 338 (p. 68).
    Date undetermined: SB. 5176.
Caranis:
    A.D. 101, P. Lond. II. 173 (p. 66).
        112, SB. 7359.
        153, SB. 5138.
        176-7, SP. xx. 8.
Theadelphia:
    A.D. 138, P. Strass. 70.
    Second century: P. Iand. 31.
Euhemeria:
    A.D. 37, P. Fay. 29.
    Second or third century: P. Fay. 237.
Tebtynis:
    A.D. 151, P. Teb. II. 300.
        190, P. Teb. 301.
Bacchias:
    Before A.D. 76, BGU. II. 583.
Apollonias:
    A.D. 101, BGU. IV. 1068 (= W. *Chrest.* 62).
Sentrepaei:
    A.D. 136, P. Ryl. II. 105.
Philopator:
    A.D. 142, BGU. I. 17.

Oxyrhynchite Nome

Oxyrhynchus:
A.D.   3, PO. IV. 826.
        61, PO. II. 262.
       102, PSI. VIII. 952.
       156, PO. XII. 1550.
       174, PO. I. 173.
       212, PO. VII. 1030.
       304, PO. XII. 1551.
Sephtha:
A.D. 181–92, PO. I. 79.
Tëis:
A.D. 150, PO. IX. 1198.

Heracleopolite Nome

Ancyra:
A.D. 20, P. Ross.-Georg. II. 11.
Mouchennomthou:
A.D. 237, SB. 5136.

Hermopolite Nome

A.D. 203, P. Flor. III. 308.

Provenience Unknown

A.D. 176, PSI. VI. 691.

67. A register of deaths is preserved in P. Hawara, *Archiv*, v, pp. 395 ff.

68. e.g. P. Flor. III. 308.

69. Cf. PO. II. 262; P. Lond. II. 281 (p. 65).

70. e.g. P. Lond. II. 173 (p. 66).

71. Op. cit., pp. 242 ff. Cf. *Hermes*, XXVIII (1893), p. 248.

72. *Dig.* 50, 15. 3.

73. BGU. IV. 1140; cf. Schubart's translation in his note, ad loc.: τὸ τῶν ἑξήκοντα = das privileg der 60-Jahre.

74. Wilcken, *Ostraka*, I, p. 238, gives a table showing how the poll-tax was slightly raised in Elephantine–Syene, Charax, and Ophi (all in Upper Egypt) during the course of the first and second centuries. There is no indication that there was any corresponding rise in the rate of poll-tax in Lower Egypt. It is possible that raising the age exemption in Lower Egypt was preferred as a means of increasing the revenue brought in by the poll-tax. It is possible that a corresponding increase in the age of exemption had taken place in Syria between the reign of Augustus and that of Caracalla, since Ulpian's testimony may have applied only to his own time.

75. Since the Jewess in SP. IV, p. 71, line 463 (183), had to have an

epicrisis before she could be listed as ὑπερετής, it is logical to assume that men could not be listed as ὑπερετεῖς in respect to the poll-tax without a similar epicrisis. Cf. P. Mey., p. 59. The old men listed in lines 550 to 566 of SP. IV, pp. 62 ff., are all listed as ἐπικεκριμένοι, but since they are all listed as having undergone epicrisis in the 'first year' and most of the other inhabitants of the amphodon are designated in the same way, no conclusion can be drawn from this passage in regard to an epicrisis for entering the ranks of the ὑπερετεῖς.

76. Cf. Kenyon, P. Lond. II, pp. 42 ff. (260, 261), who first recognized a non-military epicrisis; Grenfell-Hunt, PO. II. 257, 258, III. 478; P. M. Meyer, *Das Heerwesen der Ptolemäer und Römer in Ägypten*, 1900, pp. 109 ff., 229 ff.; BPW. XXI (1901), Spp. 242 ff.; P. Mey., p. 58 f.; C. Wessely, *Epikrisis*, Sitz.-Ber. Wien. Akad. phil.-hist. Kl. 142, 9 (1900); SP. I, pp. 9 ff., IV, pp. 58 ff.; W. Schubart, *Archiv*, II. 155 ff.; J. Lesquier, 'Le recrutement de l'armée Rom. d'Egypte,' *Rev. de Phil.* XXVIII (1904), pp. 22 ff.; P. Jouguet, 'Chronique d. Papyrus II' (*Rev. d. Étud. Anc.* VII (1905)), pp. 59 ff.; *Bull. Soc. arch. d'Alexandrie*, XIV (1912), pp. 203 ff.; Wilcken, *Ostraka*, I, p. 448; *Archiv*, III, pp. 504 f., 556 f., V, p. 237; *Grundz.*, pp. 196 ff.; Bickermann, *Archiv*, IX, pp. 30 ff.

77. Cf. Reinmuth, op. cit. (note 29 above), p. 74 and notes.

78. The epicrisis of youths applying for admission into the privileged class of tax-payers must be distinguished from the epicrisis of youths applying for admission into the class of οἱ ἀπὸ γυμνασίου, as is indicated by the separate applications sent in on behalf of one youth (PO. XII. 1452); the two classes were not mutually inclusive. Cf. Bickermann, *Archiv*, IX, pp. 30 ff. Because it was not at first recognized that these two classes were distinct, it will be necessary to list applications of both classes, in order that the bibliography may be complete; the applications listed below will be distinguished by the abbreviations met. and gym.

Arsinoë (all are met.)

A.D. 121, BGU. I. 109 (re-edited in Preisigke, BL. I, p. 20 f.).

134, P. Ryl. II. 103.

138-61, P. Cairo Preis. 10. (This is called an Arsinoite application by Bickermann, but there is no proof that it is from the Arsinoite nome. Grenfell and Hunt and Preisigke also believed it to be an application for epicrisis.)

138-61, P. Ryl. II. 279.

141, P. Grenf. II. 49.

148, P. Genf. 19.

152-3, P. Ryl. II. 280.

161-9, P. Hawara 401, *Archiv*, V, p. 395.

166-7, BGU. I. 324 (= W. *Chrest.* 219).

175, P. Fay. 27. (One or both parents were descendants of catoeci, but since the father is careful to say that he had

been officially registered as a resident of the metropolis, it
is possible that the statement that the mother of the boy was
the daughter of a catoecus was simply an argument *a fortiori*
for the admission of the boy into the class of οἱ ἀπὸ τῆς
μητροπόλεως. There is no good evidence for the statement
of the editors of this document that descent from catoeci was
ultimately necessary for admission into the privileged class
of tax-payers. It is possible that this application, which is
badly mutilated, was a request for admission into the
class of the catoeci who may have occupied a position in the
Arsinoite nome analogous to that of οἱ ἀπὸ γυμνασίου in the
Oxyrhynchite and Hermopolite nomes.)

181, P. Teb. II. 320, P. Genf. 18.

195-6, BGU. III. 971.

Oxyrhynchus

A.D. 11-12, PO. II. 288. An extract at the end of a tax account dated
A.D. 22-5. PO. II. 314 is a similar extract, but for the following year. Both are probably met.

67-79, P. Ryl. II. 278 (met.). The editors suggest that this
application for admission into the class paying a poll-tax of
12 drachmae is from the Hermopolite nome, but SB. 7440
shows that the privileged class at Hermopolis paid only
8 drachmae. Bickermann, op. cit., assigns this application
to the group from Arsinoë, but there is no evidence for
a class paying 12 drachmae anywhere except at Oxyrhynchus.

86, PO. VII. 1028 (met.).

86-7, PO. II. 258 (met.).

93-4, PSI. X. 1109. Report to the strategus from a φροντιστής
ordered to search the records to certify that a client was of
the 12-drachmae class on both sides of the family. Reference
is made to an epicrisis in the ninth year of Domitian.

94-5, PO. II. 257 (gym.).

98, PO. X. 1266 (gym.).

End of the first or beginning of the second century: PSI. VII.
731 (gym.).

A.D. 122, PO. IV. 714 (met.).

127-8, PO. XII. 1452, col. i (met.); col. ii (gym.).

132, PO. III. 478 (= W. *Chrest*. I. 218) (met.).

153-4, PSI. VII. 732 (met.).

160-1, PO. VIII. 1109 (met.).

172-3, W. *Chrest*. 217 (met.).

214-15 (?), PO. X. 1306 (met.).

Third century, *Aegyptus*, XV (1935), p. 213, no. 3 (met. and gym.).

A.D. 222, ibid., p. 209, no. 2 (met. and gym.).

276, PSI. V. 457 (gym.).

287, PSI. III. 164. A fourteen-year-old youth, whose father submits an application for his enrolment in the τάξις τῶν ὁμηλικῶν, is designated as a δωδεκάδραχμος and ἀπὸ γυμνασίου. It is possible that δωδεκάδραχμος is at this date a social distinction rather than an indication of privilege in regard to the poll-tax.

Hermopolis Magna

A.D. 132, SB. 7440. *a.* (gym. and probably met.). *b.* (met.). 161-8; P. Amh. II. 75 (gym.). Second century. P. Ryl. II. 102 (gym.).

79. See Chapter VIII.

80. Cf. my article on 'Census and Poll-tax in Ptolemaic Egypt'.

81. Cf. Kenyon, P. Lond. II, p. 44, whose arguments have been accepted by later writers. But see Chapter VIII, pp. 117 ff.

82. Cf. the documents cited in note 78 above, and see also Chapter VIII, pp. 118 f., 121, 126 f.

83. See p. 105 of this chapter.

84. Cf. PSI. V. 457. 22 ff.

85. Λαογραφούμενοι and ἐπικεκριμένοι are apparently relative terms. The residents of the metropolis of the Arsinoite nome who paid poll-tax at a rate just half that paid by the rest of the inhabitants of the nome seem to be called λαογραφούμενοι in SP. IV, pp. 62 ff. In many of the ἀπογραφαὶ κατ' οἰκίαν a man is designated as λαογραφούμενος ἰδιώτης ἐπικεκριμένος, the meaning of which has not yet been satisfactorily explained (cf. Kenyon, P. Lond. II, p. 45; P. Mey., p. 58 f.; see Chapter VIII, p. 117 f.).

86. This was true of applicants for admission into the class of οἱ ἀπὸ γυμνασίου; cf. PO. II. 257.

87. BGU. II. 562 (= W. *Chrest.* 220).

88. Cf. Chapter VIII, p. 121.

89. Cf. BGU. I. 324 (= W. *Chrest.* 219); PO. IV. 714; PSI. VII. 732; W. *Chrest.* 217.

90. Cf. PO. III. 478 (= W. *Chrest.* 218).

91. Cf. Wessely, SP. I, pp. 9 ff., IV, p. 59 f.

92. Cf. SP. IV, pp. 58 ff.

93. SP. IV, pp. 62 ff., lines 27, 376 f., 430 f., 488.

94. See Chapter X, p. 171.

95. Perhaps the ἀσθενεῖς, the sick and crippled, enjoyed some exemption from poll-tax, which may have been made up by the μερισμὸς ἀπόρων paid by the rest of the tax-payers; see Chapter IX, pp. 137 ff.

96. SP. IV, pp. 62 ff., lines 646 ff. It is also possible that the victory of Vespasian is meant, and that the new catoecus had served in the victor's army.

CHAPTER VIII

1. Cf. Matt. xvii. 25, xxii. 17, 19; Mark xii. 14; Luke xx. 22.

2. Cf. my article 'Census and Poll-tax in Ptolemaic Egypt'.

3. See Chapter VII, note 3.

4. Cf. my article cited in note 2 above; see also Chapter VII, p. 97. The earliest example of the tax λαογραφία is O. Strass. 38.

5. Wilcken suggested this distinction in *Hermes*, xxviii (1893), p. 249.

6. Cf. Wilcken, *Grundz.*, p. 189, and the notes in the publications of receipts for poll-tax cited below.

7. In *Aegyptus*, vi (1925), p. 332 f. If the census period of fourteen years was in use in the Ptolemaic period, the extract from the census published by Henne cannot be dated in the reign of Augustus or in the reign of one of the late Ptolemies, but it must be dated in the reign of Nero, which is the date preferred by Henne.

8. See Chapter VII, pp. 109 ff.

9. Cf. lines 9–14 in SP. iv. 62 ff., where Wessely has republished P. Lond. ii. 259–60 together with the Rainer papyrus that forms a part of the same report. Hereafter in this chapter reference will be to the continuous numbering of the lines in Wessely's publication. Cf. also Wilcken, *Grundz.*, p. 189, note 6.

10. In BGU. i. 115 there is a man who is ἀπὸ τῆς μητροπόλεως who is λαογραφούμενος. Cf., however, the explanations of the phrases cited given by Kenyon, op. cit., p. 45, and by P. M. Meyer in P. Mey., p. 58 f.

11. *Archiv*, ix, pp. 24 ff., especially p. 42 f.

12. Cf. Wilcken, *Grundz.*, pp. 140 ff.

13. The possession of catoecic land did not necessarily make a person a catoecus, as Tait has pointed out (O. Tait, p. 67, no. 24, note). In SB. 4415 the ἀριθμητικὸν κατοίκων is obviously a tax paid by the owner of catoecic land, a woman in this case, and has nothing to do with the social or civic status of the landowner; this tax is, however, paid as a capitation tax by the owners of catoecic land, and is apparently called ἐπικεφάλαιον in SP. xx. 67 *verso* (see Chapter X, pp. 176 ff.). In BGU. ii. 562 (= W. *Chrest.* 220) a son of a catoecus, who had not yet received epicrisis, was nevertheless put in the class of the λαογραφούμενοι; after his protest he submitted to an examination (ἐξέτασις) in order to establish his rights as a catoecus (σώζειν τὰ πρὸς τοὺς κατοίκ(ους) δίκαια). There is no indication in the document as to the interpretation of δίκαια, and they may well have been limited to his right to share in the ἐφηβεία.

14. Wessely wrongly restores β̄ (two) as the number of Alexandrian citizens in line 338 of SP. iv, pp. 62 ff. The total number of tax-exempt in line 375 is six, of whom two are Romans and three are the slaves of the Alexandrian women, which leaves but one to be accounted for, and he is Nicanor, the Alexandrian.

15. Cf. lines 564 ff.

16. Cf. lines 369 ff.

17. Lines 397–408 give the clue to the meaning of ἐλάσσωμα. There the ἐλάσσωμα is the reduction in the amount of trade-tax (χειρωνάξιον) owed by the potters and weavers of the district, because of the death of one of the potters, half of whose tax was remitted and the other half added to the gnomon of the potter who was admitted into the guild to take his place. The assessment was evidently made by a central bureau; any claim for remittance of any part of the assessment, which had been based upon the number of names upon the records of the central bureau, had to be proved by the local official. If the claim was sustained, the name of the person affected was placed in an ἐλάσσωμα. There it remained until the end of the year, when an adjustment was made in the records of the central bureau, so that the new assessment would no longer include the name of the person who by reason of death or changed civic status was no longer liable to taxation.

18. Cf. lines 179 ff.

19. Cf. the epicrisis of slaves into the class of μητροπολῖται in Chapter VII, p. 111. PSI. x. 1146 is an extract from a census list and contains the phrase ἀπ[ο]λυόμ(ενοι) τῆς λαογρα(φίας) καὶ τῶ[ν] ἄλλω[ν] ἐπιμερισμῶν οἷς ἀπολύονται κατὰ συνήθ[ειαν] ἄνδρες ν̄, ὧν οἱ δοῦλοι λαογραφοῦνται ὡς δεσπόται.

20. Cf. Suetonius, *Aug.* 93; Dio Cassius, LI. 16. 5; Zonaras, x. 31. Augustus' neglect of the Egyptian religion was an indication of the attitude which he would take towards the privileges of the priests.

21. Cf. my article 'Census and Poll-tax in Ptolemaic Egypt'.

22. Cf. Otto, *Priester und Tempel*, II, pp. 247 ff. The number of priests exempt in the large temples seems to have been fifty. In order to maintain their privileges the temples were obliged to provide special reports (ἀπογραφαί), notices of death, &c., to the officials of the nome; cf. PSI. x. 1146; BGU. IV. 1199; PO. x. 1256; P. Lond. II. 345 (p. 113) (= W. *Chrest.* 102), 353 (p. 112); PSI. x. 1147.

23. Cf. O. Strass. 39; P. Teb. II. 306; P. Lond. II. 347 (p. 70).

24. Josephus, *Bell. Jud.* II. 16 (385), implies that Alexandria was free from poll-tax. 3 Maccabees ii. 30 states that in the time of the 'persecutions' of Philopator the Jews could become ἰσοπολῖται Ἀλεξανδρεῦσιν if they would be initiated into the mysteries; since the 'persecution' consisted of enrollment in the census (λαογραφία) for the payment of poll-tax, the implication is again that Alexandrian citizens were exempt from poll-tax. In SP. IV. 62 ff., lines 331 ff., Alexandrian citizens and Romans are listed together, as in the Gnomon of the Idiologus (BGU. v), § 59.

25. Cf. Dio Cassius, LXXVII. 22; SHA. *Caracalla*, 6.

26. BGU. IV. 1073; Viereck, *Klio*, VIII (1908), pp. 424 ff.

27. P. Teb. II. 286, dated in the reign of Hadrian shows that the exemption of victors in games goes back to the first half of the second

century; cf. line 13, Ἰούλι[ο]ς Θέων τῶν ἱερονικῶν καὶ ἀτελῶν. Cf. P. Ross.-Georg. II. 18 (A.D. 140).

28. Cf. P. Ryl. II. 143. 3; BGU. I. 73. 4, 136. 23, 231. 4, III. 729. 3; CIG. III. 4724; P. Flor. I. 68. 6; P. Mey. 6. 8; OGI. 714.

29. Cf. Wessely's remark on p. 59 (SP. IV).

30. L. 6. i. 2 D. *de excus.* (27. 1) fragm. Vatic. 149 Kuhn, I. 83 ff.

31. The method of collection of the poll-tax will be taken up in Chapter XVII.

32. The problems raised by extra charges will likewise be treated in Chapter XVII. Cf. Tait's note (O. Tait, p. 87, no. 79) which summarizes the conclusions of Milne, *Annals of Archaeology and Anthropology*, VII, p. 61.

33. Cf. P. Fay. 50, note 5; P. Teb. II. 617-37.

34. Cf. P. Teb. II. 625 and 627; perhaps SP. XXII. 124; perhaps P. Fay. 196, 197, 198, 282, 284, 350-3, 356-8. Until the Fayûm receipts are fully published it will be impossible to know whether they ever bore local place-names.

35. P. Cornell I. 22 is a list of persons enrolled in other villages who were residing in Philadelphia. There are one hundred and twenty-five names on the list, which seems to be complete. One man was from a village in another nome.

36. In P. Teb. II. 391 there is an agreement between four collectors of the poll-tax at Tebtynis for the division of their duties. Two of them undertook the collection at the village, while the other two contracted to collect from the persons registered at Tebtynis who were away from home in the other villages or in the metropolis. Cf. also P. Princeton I. 8.

37. The applications for epicrisis state that the parents of the applicant are registered in some one of the amphoda of Arsinoë, but it is not impossible that the registration was merely formal. P. Cornell I. 23 is a register for tax or census purposes from Philadelphia. After a list of weavers there is a list of 160 men; before the names of the first six appears the abbreviation μη( ); before most of the rest of the names appears κω( ); before the others appears ἀπε( ). The editors suggest that these are book-keeping terms, and that μη( ) is for μη(νιαίου), a monthly register, κω( ) might stand for a list in the office of the comogrammateus, ἀπε( ) might be expanded as ἀπε(ληλυθό-των) and would indicate that the name belonged to one who had died during the year. I am inclined to think that μη( ) should be expanded μη(τροπολιτικά) or the like, and indicates that the person so designated was a μητροπολίτης and that his poll-tax was paid to the account of the collectors of the metropolis; κω( ) would accordingly be expanded κω(μητικά) and refers to the accounts of the collectors of the village. Ἀπε( ) is more difficult; the suggestion of the editors may be correct, although the term usually employed is some form of τελευτᾶν. Ἀπε(ληλυθότων) might as well be a synonym for ἀνακεχω-ρηκότων. In any case the distinction between the group marked by

μη( ) and that marked by κω( ) is probably connected with the poll-tax, since, as the editors remark, col. ii (b) seems undoubtedly to be connected with the λαογραφία.

38. The men marked by the note μη( ) in the document cited in note 37 above might be such favoured inhabitants of the village rather than citizens of the metropolis.

39. Cf. Wilcken, *Grundz.*, p. 189.

40. Cf. Milne, *Theban Ostraca*, p. 119 f.; Grenfell and Hunt, P. Teb. II, p. 99; P. Ryl. II, p. 258, note 3. It cannot be proved that any of the receipts which purport to show a rate for the Arsinoite nome other than 20 or 40 drachmae is actually a payment made in the Arsinoite nome and not a receipt for poll-tax paid elsewhere and later brought into the Fayûm. I do not know what is the significance of the δεκάδραχμος in BGU. I. 118. ii. 9, but there is certainly no indication of a 10 drachmae rate of poll-tax in the Arsinoite nome.

41. AJP. LII (1931), pp. 263–9. This is the most complete study of the συντάξιμον to date. To Keyes's list of documents dealing with the syntaximon should be added PSI. x. 1133; perhaps P. Lond. III. 1235 (p. 35)—cf. the 6 chalci in line 12; SB. 7608. There is a (joint ?) payment of 60 drachmae 2 obols 2 chalci made by two persons for χειρωνάξιον and συντάξιμον in A.M. 8916 (in the collection in the Library of Princeton University); Dr. Kase informs me that the document is from Philadelphia and is dated A.D. 50. In the same collection Garrett Deposit 7649 (Fayûm, A.D. 141) is a receipt for 12 drachmae 1 obol 6 chalci paid for συντάξιμον, ὑική, and μερισμοί.

42. The ὁμόλογοι were the unprivileged who paid poll-tax at the maximum rate. Cf. WO. I, pp. 253 ff.; Preisigke's *Wörterbuch*, III, Abschn. 15, sub ὁμόλογος.

43. In P. Princeton I. 8 and P. Col. I R 2 the sum above 44 drachmae is sometimes 6 chalci and sometimes 2 chalci, more often the latter. Where the chalci appear on receipts, however, the amount is always 44 drachmae 6 chalci. P. Milan I. 9 and P. Giss. 94, which give a total of 44 drachmae *five* chalci are wrongly read, because their editors misinterpreted the symbol χ (cf. P. Princeton I, p. xix).

44. Wilcken, *Archiv*, II, p. 396; Kenyon in P. Lond. III, p. vii, correction to p. 54.

45. Cf. the discussions in P. Milan I, pp. 45 ff.; P. Princeton I, pp. xx ff.

46. The fact that 44 drachmae often appears as the total amount paid for syntaximon in the receipts need not be disturbing. P. Princeton I. 1 shows that 6 chalci (and the pig-tax) were the amount most frequently left in arrears at the end of the year.

47. The total paid for ἁλική and συμβολικά is 4½ obols in SP. xx. 62, lines 8–9, but since the end of line 8 is lost (cf. also line 4, where the same tax is recorded) it is impossible to determine whether there were also προσδιαγραφόμενα, as is suggested by line 2 of SP. xx. 49, a somewhat similar document.

48. Cf. Keyes, op. cit., p. 268.

49. We do not know precisely what was done with the revenue accruing from the collection of the poll-tax during the period of Roman rule, but it is probable that no small part of it was forwarded to the imperial treasury. Most of the capitation taxes known as μερισμοί were designated for specific purposes in the local administration of Egypt, such as the dike-tax, guard-tax, &c. The ἁλική was an inheritance from the Ptolemaic régime and in the Roman period seems to be found in the Arsinoite nome only (cf. Chapter XI, p. 184). The ἱερ( ) γεφ( ) is a mysterious tax whose nature is unknown. Neither of these taxes ever appear on receipts (except possibly P. Lond. III. 1235 (p. 35), line 12, where the *Berichtigungsliste* reads ἁλικ(ῆς), but this is a very doubtful reading), but the salt-tax appears in the reports of collectors of taxes and so was probably always collected in connexion with the syntaximon.

50. Cf. my article 'Census and Poll-tax in Ptolemaic Egypt'.

51. There are but few extant receipts for syntaximon (cf. Keyes's list, op. cit., pp. 264 ff.) in comparison with the great number of people paying the tax as indicated by the ledgers. Many more receipts for λαογραφία at the 20 drachmae rate have been found, but this may be only an accident.

52. See Chapter IX, p. 144.

53. Two chalci is too small a sum for a fine for arrears, so that its addition to the sum of syntaximon and pig-tax cannot be accounted for in that way. Moreover, no penalties for arrears ever appear in the receipts for taxes.

54. The additional charge for receipt (συμβολικά) was included in the total of the amount owed to the central government, although the charge for receipt was perhaps not forwarded to Alexandria, but kept in the bureau to defray the expenses of issuing the receipt.

55. Cf. SP. xx. 49, line 3; ὑικῶν should be restored in line 9 or 10 of SP. xx. 62 after εἰ[δῶν].

56. Cf. the elaborate tables in the introduction.

57. Cf. P. Princeton I. 8. ii. 21–2; iii. 24–5; vi. 3–5; viii. 7–8.

58. But cf. Keyes, AJP. LII (1931), p. 266.

59. Cf. P. Columbia I, p. 82 f. and the references cited there, especially P. Princeton I. 9.

60. P. Teb. II. 638 (described).

61. P. Bouriant 32; P. Ross.-Georg. III. 24.

62. O. Oslo 10 is not necessarily a payment for the 19th year of Septimius Severus, for in that ostracon the date is not given.

63. Cf. PSI. VII. 739; PO. VII. 1046; P. Ross.-Georg. III. 26.

64. See Chapter XVI, pp. 281 ff.

65. There are no records of epicrisis from Memphis to support the theory of two rates of poll-tax in the Memphite nome, but there is no other reason for thinking that it differed from other nomes of Lower Egypt in this respect.

66. See Chapter VII, p. 110.

67. If the payment of 12 drachmae for λαογραφία in the Hermopolite nome was a part payment on a rate of 16 drachmae, it is possible,
although it cannot be proved, that the normal rate for poll-tax in all
Egypt, with the exception of Thebes and the Arsinoite nome, was
16 drachmae a year. The rate was slightly raised at Elephantine-Syene
at the end of the first century and again at the beginning of the second
century, but the early rate there was 16 drachmae, and the first higher
rate probably merely included surtaxes.

68. See Chapter VII, p. 110.

69. Cf. the extract from an epicrisis given at the end of PO. II.
288; it is for the same family.

70. Ἐπικεφάλαια or ἐπικεφάλια are capitation taxes. In BGU. I.
1 (= W. Chrest. 92. ii) ἐπικεφάλαιον is certainly equivalent to λαογραφία.
It was therefore supposed that ἐπικεφάλαιον was always equivalent to
λαογραφία until Milne (Theban Ostraca, pp. 153 ff.) showed that it
was probably equivalent to χειρωνάξιον in O. Theb. 136. PO. XII.
1438 proves that ἐπικεφάλια might include λαογραφία, μερισμοί, and
various other taxes. Grenfell and Hunt, therefore, tried to distinguish
between ἐπικεφάλια and ἐπικεφάλαιον, reserving the latter for poll-
tax, but PO. XVII. 2131 proves that such a distinction cannot be made,
as the editor admits. In SP. XX. 67 verso ἐπικεφάλαιον probably is to
be identified with the ἀριθμητικὸν κατοίκων. It is frequently impossible to tell what tax is meant by ἐπικεφάλαιον; the word occurs in:
(from Thebes) O. Tait, p. 21, no. 122; O. Strass. 107; WO. II. 533;
O. Theb. 136 ff., 73; WO. II. 676, 681, 686, 696, 1457; O. Tait, p. 71,
no. 49; (Hermopolite nome ?) P. Ryl. II. 185; (Thmuis) P. Ryl. II.
214; (Mendesian nome) PSI. III. 235; (Arsinoite nome) BGU. III. 983;
PSI. VIII. 927; P. Hamb. 85; P. Ryl. II. 191; BGU. III. 881; P. Ryl. II.
106; P. Flor. III. 350; (Memphis) BGU. III. 833; (Oxyrhynchite nome)
PO. IV. 832, II. 311, 288, XVII. 2112, XII. 1438, VIII. 1157; (Antinoë)
W. Chrest. 28. References to an ἐπικεφάλαιον πόλεως in Oxyrhynchus
are found in papyri of the fourth century: PSI. III. 163, VII. 780, IV.
302, V. 462. If the συντάξιμον and the λαογραφία are the same, the
ἐπικεφάλαιον in P. Ryl. II. 191 cannot be the poll-tax, as the editors
take it, but it must have its meaning of χειρωνάξιον or one of its other
undetermined meanings; cf. BGU. III. 881. See also note 13 above.

71. Cf. PO. XII. 1520, 1521, IV. 733, XII. 1436; and also II. 296, IX.
1210, XII. 1516.

72. P. Ryl. II. 213 and PSI. I. 106.

73. Cf. my article on 'Census and Poll-tax in Ptolemaic Egypt'.

74. Cf. PO. II. 288, 289; P. Flor. I. 12.

75. Milne, Theban Ostraca, p. 119 f., attempted to prove the
existence of two or more rates of poll-tax for Memnonia, but the rate
was probably uniformly 24 drachmae in that locality, with smaller
payments to be regarded as instalments and higher payments as including arrears. There is one notice of birth from Upper Egypt (O.

Br.-Berl. 14), but the peculiarity of the name of the sender as read by
the editor prevents a definite conclusion as to the status of the sender
and consequently as to the purpose of the notice; it is hardly sufficient
in itself to prove the existence of a privileged class (other than priests,
officials, Romans, &c.) in Upper Egypt.

76. It is not necessary in these notes to repeat the numbers of the
ostraca in Wilcken's collection which refer to the λαογραφία. The
numbers are given on p. 230 f. of volume I of *Griechische Ostraka*;
to his list should be added from the *Berichtigungsliste*, II. 1: nos. 43,
500, 535. Ostraca from Elephantine-Syene published since Wilcken's
collection was made are (in chronological order): O. Wilb.-Brk. 5; O.
Br.-Berl. 22; SB. 7589; O. Br.-Berl. 23, 24; SB. 1097; *Archiv*, v, pp.
170 ff., no. 1; SB. 1929, 1930, 1931, 1927, 1924; O. Strass. 120; *Archiv*,
v, pp. 170 ff., no. 2; SB. 1925; *Archiv*, v, pp. 170 ff., no. 3; SB. 1926,
1922; O. Strass. 124; SB. 1923; O. Br.-Berl. 30; *Archiv*, v, pp. 170
ff., no. 4; O. Strass. 125, 127; O. Wilb.-Brk. 6-7; SB. 1086, 7590,
7591, 1928; O. Tait, p. 65, no. 15; O. Mey. 28; SB. 4352; O. Br.-Berl.
34; SB. 7592; O. Wilb.-Brk. 8-9; O. Tait, p. 65, no. 17; O. Strass.
284, 136; *Archiv*, v, pp. 170 ff., no. 5; SB. 4360, 4365; O. Tait, p.
175 f., nos. C. 1-2; O. Br.-Berl. 45; *Archiv*, v, pp. 170 ff., no. 6; O.
Tait, p. 66, no. 21; O. Wilb.-Brk. 12-13.

77. Cf. O. Br.-Berl. 31; O. Strass. 116 has a payment of 10 drachmae
(cf. BL. II. 1) for poll-tax and is dated by the editor in the second
century. The receipts from Charax are: O. Strass. 38-43, 53, 59, 62,
64, 65, 66, 68, 69, 72, 74, 76; O. Br.-Berl. 26; O. Strass. 81, 82; *Archiv*,
v, pp. 170 ff., no. 9; O. Br.-Berl. 31; O. Strass. 116; O. Theb. 81; O.
Br.-Berl. 3; O. Strass. 210, 211, 218; O. Tait, p. 93, no. 103; O.
Strass. 223, 228; O. Tait, p. 93, no. 104; p. 69, no. 36; O. Mey. 27;
SB. 6821; O. Tait, p. 71, no. 46; p. 93, no. 105; O. Wilb.-Brk. 10 (A.D.
131), 11 (A.D. 134).

78. WO. I, p. 235.

79. PSI. VIII. 993 is the only new receipt for poll-tax from Ophi.

80. The additional receipts from the North Market Quarter are:
O. Strass. 94; O. Theb. 45, 47, 49; O. Strass. 93, 95, 96, 109, 186, 187,
193, 196; O. Mey. 26.

81. Cf. O. Strass. 109.

82. Cf. the receipts from Charax.

83. *Theban Ostraca*, pp. 119 ff.

84. Receipts for poll-tax from Memnonia are: SB. 4342; O. Tait,
p. 88, no. 81; O. Theb. 97; SB. 4344; O. Mey. 21, 22; O. Strass. 85;
Archiv, v, pp. 170 ff., no. 8; O. Theb. 32; O. Tait, p. 90, no. 87;
p. 156, no. 31; p. 90, no. 91 plus 97; p. 91, nos. 94 and 93; O. Strass.
103, 105, 282, 275; O. Theb. 34; O. Strass. 276; O. Theb. 35; O. Tait,
p. 156, no. 33; O. Strass. 185, 278; O. Mey. 30a; O. Theb. 36, 37, 38,
82, 39; PSI. III. 266; O. Tait, p. 157, no. 38; p. 158, no. 39; PSI. III.
269; O. Theb. 53; O. Tait, p. 158, no. 43; O. Strass. 118.

85. Rabel, in the notes to P. Basel 8, attempted to establish the rule

that all payments for λαογραφία made in the first five months of the year are for arrears. P. Columbia 1 R 1 a–b shows that this is not true for Theadelphia. The rule holds for a majority of the receipts for poll-tax at the rate of 20 drachmae in the Fayûm and also for the receipts from Upper Egypt, but there are enough exceptions to make the application of the rule very hazardous; cf. P. Fay. 352, 356; O. Mey. 28; O. Strass. 210, 105, 103; O. Tait, p. 90, no. 91 plus 97; O. Strass. 118 (?).

86. The difficulty with Tait's dating of O. Stras. 118 is that the μερισμὸς ἀνδριάντος is not elsewhere found after the year A.D. 162. Yet the presence of Aurelii in this ostracon and in O. Theb. 86 seems to prevent an earlier dating. SB. 5677 proves that the poll-tax was collected after A.D. 212, the date of the *constitutio Antoniniana*.

87. Cf. O. Tait, p. 88, no. 83; p. 89, no. 86; SB. 4334; O. Tait, p. 91, no. 95.

88. This would violate Rabel's rule; cf. note 85 above.

89. O. Tait, p. 159, no. 47; O. Strass. 146, 147.

90. The receipts are: O. Tait, p. 88, no. 80; O. Mey. 23, 24, 25.

91. O. Theb. 33.

92. O. Theb. 86 is the only receipt from *Tαυρ*( ).

93. O. Theb. 80; O. Strass. 50; O. Theb. demotic 16; demotic 29; PSI. III. 261; O. Strass. 61; *Archiv*, V, pp. 170 ff., no. 7; O. Theb. demotic 5; demotic 37; O. Strass. 119; SB. 4330, 4332, 4347 (the three preceding are in AJP. XXV (1904), pp. 47 ff., 52); O. Tait, p. 175, B. 1 p. 67, no. 25; O. Strass. 84, 88, 100; O. Tait, p. 86, no. 76; p. 91, no. 92; O. Strass. 106; *Archiv*, VI, p. 220, no. 6; SB. 7400, 4348; O. Strass. 205, 206; O. Theb. 84, 85; O. Tait, p. 158, no. 44; p. 94, no. 109; O. Strass. 117.

94. SB. 4330, 4332, 4347.

95. This again violates Rabel's rule; cf. note 85 above.

96. O. Strass. 780.

97. O. Mey. 20; O. Theb. 83; O. Br.-Berl. 44; *Archiv*, V, pp. 170 ff., no. 10.

98. O. Tait, p. 107, nos. 202–4; p. 108, nos. 208–9.

99. SP. XIII, p. 8, nos. 7 and 9; *Archiv*, V, pp. 170 ff., no. 11; SP. XIII, p. 8, no. 12; O. Mey. 30, 29; SP. XIII, p. 8, no. 3.

100. SB. 1085.

101. *Archiv*, VI, pp. 125 ff.

102. AJP. LII (1931), p. 267.

103. O. Theb. 86, from *Tαυρ*( ) and dated A.D. 213; SB. 5677 from Hermopolis Magna and dated A.D. 222; O. Strass. 118 from Memnonia and dated A.D. 243 (but cf. note 86 above).

104. SP. V. 101.

APPENDIX TO THE NOTES OF CHAPTER VIII

This study of the amounts of the poll-tax in Lower Egypt is too long to be included in the notes. The documents attesting the syntaximon are listed in Keyes's article cited in note 41 above; no attempt is made in this appendix to list them again.

The receipts for λαογραφία at 20 drachmae with προσδιαγραφόμενα of 10 obols are: P. Lond. II. 170 (p. 69), 340 (p. 70), III. 909 b (p. 32), 912 a (p. 33), 1234 (p. 33), 845 a (p. 33), 834 b (p. 34); P. Ryl. II. 360–5; SP. XXII. 124; P. Basel 8; PSI. VII. 924, X. 1138; P. Fay. 50, 52, 196–9, 279–84, 349–58; P. Teb. II. 617–34, 636–7; two papyri in the collection in the Library of Princeton University (Garrett Deposit 7648 (A.D. 174) and 7615 (A.D. 141)). The majority of these receipts refer to amphoda in the metropolis of the Arsinoite nome. I assume that those which do not have place-names also refer to Arsinoë or are receipts given to persons with metropolitan rights. P. Fay. 49 is a payment of 16 drachmae for λαογραφία and 8 obols for προσδιαγραφόμενα; this, however, is a matter of arrears of three years' standing; I assume that 4 drachmae 2 obols had been paid previously.

The list of arrears of λαογραφία in P. Teb. II. 520, where one man owes 90 drachmae 4 obols (for two years) and nine men each owe 45 drachmae 2 obols indicates that the syntaximon was collected at Tebtynis. In P. Teb. 552 there is a list of persons with amounts in drachmae, generally 4, 8, 12, or 16 drachmae, but 22 drachmae 4 obols, and 45 drachmae 2 obols are also found. In P. Teb. II. 306 a priest pays 22 drachmae 4 obols, just half of the full λαογραφία at the high rate including extra charges and all minor taxes; this may have been a half payment for one who had died in the first half of the year. P. Teb. II. 638 has instalments for λαογραφία totalling c. 40 drachmae, but this is perhaps after the abandonment of the collection of the syntaximon with the accompanying minor taxes. O. Oslo 8–11 present a series of receipts from Tebtynis for poll-tax (λαογραφία); all except no. 10 are definitely dated in the 19th year of Septimius Severus (A.D. 210–11), and it is probable that no. 10 is also to be dated in that year. The total amount paid in the four ostraca is 48 drachmae, which may include arrears, although there is no definite indication of this in the receipts. P. Teb. II. 348 (A.D. 23) records two payments of 12 drachmae each, but the fact that the payer is called a βοηθός and that there is a reference to the issuance of a preliminary or provisional receipt in the use of the verb προ[εσυ]μβόλ(ησε?) makes it certain that this is no ordinary receipt for poll-tax. Hence no conclusion as to the rate of poll-tax at Tebtynis can be drawn from this document. P. Teb. II. 627 is a receipt for 20 drachmae for λαογραφία signed by the collectors of Tebtynis; it lacks the additional charge of 10 obols which ordinarily accompanies the payments at the rate of 20 drachmae. It may be a part payment on the rate of 40 drachmae, or it may be a payment by a resident of Tebtynis favoured by a special rate, but until the papyrus is fully published it will be impossible to determine its true significance. P. Teb. II. 595 is a receipt for one hundred drachmae; it is not certain, however, that λαογραφία is to be restored; it might be a receipt for collections such as are credited to collectors in (e.g.) BGU. VII. 1617 P. Teb. II. 353 is concerned with arrears paid by a man returning after several years' absence; he pays arrears of poll-tax at the rate of 16 drachmae for successive years; the place-name is not Tebtynis but Πεενσάκοι, and it is possible that this town is not in the Arsinoite nome, but in a nome where the annual rate of poll-tax was 16 drachmae (such as the Oxyrhynchite nome). P. Lond. inv. 1581 *recto* is an account of payments of λαογραφία during one month of the 19th year of an unnamed emperor. The only thing to connect this account with Tebtynis is a report on the *verso* issued by the sitologi of Tebtynis. Most of the payments for λαογραφία are 4 drachmae; the rest are multiples of 4 drachmae, except that in two cases an extra obol is paid; the highest amount recorded is 32 drachmae.

From Socnopaei Nesus there is little evidence in regard to the λαογραφία, apart from the syntaximon. SP. XXII. 124 is a receipt for 20 drachmae 10 obols, and it may have been issued to a resident citizen of the metropolis, although no amphodon is given. SP. XXII. 123 is a part payment of 8 drachmae 4 obols, but is otherwise similar to SP. XXII. 124. BGU. I. 41 is a report from the collectors ·of Socnopaei Nesus to the strategus recording 100 drachmae paid into the bank for poll-tax in A.D. 199. Such reports are usually of sums in round numbers (cf. SP. XXII. 103), and it is frequently impossible to deduce rates from them.

From Philadelphia come lists of arrears, or of total amounts due, of λαογραφία published in P. Princeton I. 11, 12, 14; P. Cornell I. 24; in all of which the amounts are 45 drachmae and 2 obols. P. Princeton I. 10 probably contains payments for poll-tax, but gives no useful information concerning rates. On the *verso* of P. Cornell I. 21 (cf. P. Princeton I, p. xxi) there is a note to the effect that a certain person in Babylon had paid (or was in arrears) 45 drachmae 2 obols for each of two years; the same person in P. Princeton I. 10. iii. 1 had paid an instalment of 4 drachmae on the syntaximon in Tybi of one of those two years (A.D. 34). The editors of the Princeton Papyri thought that this was evidence of the distinct difference between syntaximon and λαογραφία. Bell, however, suggested that the first payment had been made while the man was still residing in Philadelphia, and that he later went to Babylon where the remainder of his tax was collected. This is, I think, a satisfactory explanation, since what else was a receipt for, if not to prove partial or complete payment of a tax? A receipt for partial payment could easily have been taken along to Babylon. It is not necessary to suppose that the payment in money was forwarded from Babylon to Philadelphia, but the collectors of Philadelphia may have received credit for payment through the memoranda of the state banks. BGU. VII. 1613 contains a list of arrears for various taxes, including both syntaximon and λαογραφία; Keyes has suggested that λαογραφία here is used to distinguish the lower rate of poll-tax from the 40 drachmae rate paid in the syntaximon. BGU. VII. 1617 is a list of payments, including several from collectors of λαογραφία; none of the amounts (except those from the collectors) exceed 40 drachmae, except one receipt from the heirs of a chief priest, but we do not know that all of these payments were necessarily for poll-tax.

From Theadelphia come P. Columbia I R I a–b, 2, 3. These are reports of the collections of λαογραφία (and other capitation taxes) which show the same rates as the syntaximon. P. Fay. 51 (A.D. 186) shows payments for λαογραφία and ἐπιστατικὸν ἱερέων of 16 drachmae; the editors suggested that this was a matter of partial payments. In P. Lond. III. 1235 (p. 35) a person, presumably a priest, pays instalments of 12 and also 16 drachmae for an unnamed tax, which the editors supposed was the λαογραφία, but which may have been the syntaximon, since 6 chalci appear in line 12; the payments are not complete for any year. P. Ross.-Georg. III. 24 is a receipt probably from the beginning of the third century for 40 drachmae.

From Dionysias come two receipts, PSI. VIII. 925 and 926, dated A.D. 191. It is not possible to deduce the rate for λαογραφία, since the payments of 58 and 74 drachmae include payments for φ. ι or φι νι Θεαδελ( ), yet the sums are large enough to include 40 drachmae for λαογραφία.

The only receipt from Theogonis is P. Teb. II. 625, unpublished, which shows a payment for 20 drachmae without an additional payment for προσδιαγραφόμενα. It is apparently exactly similar to the receipt from Tebtynis cited above.

Two great tax-rolls from Caranis in the collection at the University of Michigan show payments for λαογραφία (or syntaximon) made in instalments. When these payments are (apparently) complete, payments designated for χ( ) begin. The totals of these instalments differ among various individuals, although they are multiples of 4 drachmae. This might be understood as indicating a great variety of rates of poll-tax at Caranis; but such cannot be proved because neither of the rolls is complete, and furthermore the totals for the same individuals are not the same in successive years.

The poll-tax is merely attested for Nablas in P. Lond. II. 345 (p. 113).

The poll-tax is attested for Heraclia in P. Fay. 239, a report of the collectors to the strategus.

The collectors of Archelais in P. Fay. 42 report collections of 120 drachmae for the month of Tybi.

P. Bouriant 32 gives a total of 40 drachmae for poll-tax in Apias.

P. Goodspeed Cairo 30, according to the editor (and also Grenfell and Hunt) may contain payments for poll-tax to the collectors of Bacchias and Hephaestias.

SP. IV, p. 118 (= P. Fay. 229) from Euhemeria is perhaps for poll-tax and includes certain other taxes, but it is impossible to determine the rate. P. Fay. 278 found at Euhemeria is for 16 drachmae on account, which yields no information as to the rate, except that it must have been more than 16 drachmae; P. Fay. 303 found at Philoteris was issued by the same scribe of collectors, and is also a receipt for poll-tax. P. Fay. 293 found at Euhemeria is a report of collectors to the strategus concerning poll-tax and other taxes.

The receipt found in Tebtynis, but with the place-name Πεενσάκοι, yields a poll-tax rate of 16 drachmae (P. Teb. II. 353 cited above). P. Teb. II. 354 with a payment of 8 drachmae for poll-tax may be from the same nome (the place-name is mutilated), since the pig-tax in each is 1 drachmae and 4 obols, which is 3 obols higher than the rate known in the Arsinoite nome. Cf. also P. Cairo Preisigke 36, where λαογραφία seems to be paid at a rate of 8 drachmae a year.

P. Goodspeed Cairo 10 is an interesting receipt from Memphis, dated in A.D. 180. In it a man pays 400 drachmae on behalf of his tenants (ὑπὲρ ἐνοίκων ἀναγραφουμένων εἰς αὐτόν) for poll-tax and police-tax. This immediately suggests the provision in the ἀπογραφαί made by tenants in the Memphite nome in which the landlord guaranteed the payment of his tenants' ἐπικεφάλια (capitation taxes of all kinds); see Chapter VII, p. 102. The police-tax is called φύλακτρον. This tax (the name is rare; φυλακία is more common) is also found on the receipts in P. Flor. I. 12, where the amount paid is 3 drachmae 2 obols a year from A.D. 186–7 to 189. In P. Lond. III. 1216, p. 34, dated A.D. 192, I believe that φυλ(άκτρου) should be read rather than ἄλλ(ας), since the amount is but 1 obol higher than payment for φύλακτρον three years before. Therefore I have considered P. Lond. III. 1216 (p. 34) as coming from Memphis in the Memphite nome, since it conforms to the rate for both poll- and police-tax there, rather than from Memphis in the Arsinoite nome, as the editors supposed, comparing P. Lond. III. 845 b (p. 34).

The payment of a landlord on behalf of the residents in his house is perhaps to be remotely connected with the much later ἐξηκοντάδραχμος μερισμὸς εἰς τὸ κατ' οἰκίαν τῆς πόλεως in Hermopolis, cited in Chapter VIII, p. 134.

It seems not improbable that the landlord in the Arsinoite nome was required to make good the poll-tax of his tenants, if they failed to pay, since in many contracts of sale of houses a clause appears guaranteeing that the property is free from various taxes and from λαογραφίαι of those who are registered at that address; the guarantee of freedom from λαογραφίαι is made valid up to the next census. Apparently a clear title could not be had so long as any of the poll-tax assessed against any resident of the house remained unpaid. Cf. CPR. 187, 206, 223; P. Hamb. 15; which are from the metropolis of the Arsinoite nome; also P. Ryl. II. 161; BGU. I. 350; from Socnopaei Nesus; BGU. II. 667 from [Φυ]λακιτικὴ Νῆσος. These documents range in date from A.D. 71 to 221–2.

I agree with Wilcken (*Grundz.*, p. 189) that there was not a τεσσαρακαιεικοσίδραχμος class at Hermopolis, which he had previously suggested as the solution of κδϛ in P. Lond. III. 955 (p. 127). Bell's note (*Archiv*, VI, pp. 107 ff.) on the existence of ιαϛ, ιδϛ, and δϛ in P. Amh.

11. 75 shows that if Wilcken's earlier explanation of $\overline{\kappa\delta}\vert$ be accepted, it would mean that there were at least five classes of citizens paying poll-tax at annual rates of 4 drachmae, 8 drachmae, 11 drachmae, 14 drachmae, and 24 drachmae, and possibly another at 12 drachmae (cf. SB. 5677 and Chapter VIII, p. 118). Despite Bell's belief that so many classes of tax-payers might exist as the result of successive rises of the poll-tax, this seems too many classes. The complication of census and assessment would have been too great. The explanation of the $\overline{\kappa\delta}\vert$ as a topographical designation is supported by Bell's supplementary note (op. cit., p. 113) that $\overline{\iota\delta}\vert$ (cf. Wilcken's note, ibid.) occurs in P. Lond. III. 935 (p. 30), line 7, where it may be topographical; cf. also P. Lond. III. 936 (p. 31), line 8. Wilcken interpreted the symbol $\vert$ as ἀ(μφοδαρχία).

CHAPTER IX

1. For other meanings of μερισμός cf. Preisigke, *Wörterbuch*, II, s.v.
2. The term μερισμός is sometimes applied to taxes on land; this meaning of the term is discussed in the chapter on land-taxes.
3. Cf. Preisigke, *Fachwörter*, s.v.
4. In P. Teb. I. 29. 15 πυρινὸς μερισμός seems to be used to denote the corn-dues in general; cf. note 2 above. In P. Teb. I. 58. 38 the word means 'division' (made by an official) of a large amount of land apparently for the purpose of collection of taxes in kind. Similarly in P. Ryl. II. 70. 11 the 'division' is of the total amount of bath-tax to be collected.
5. Cf. my article 'Census and Poll-tax in Ptolemaic Egypt'.
6. WO. I, pp. 256 ff.; cf. P. Columbia I R I a–b, introd., pp. 11 ff.; cf. also PSI. x. 1146; O. Br.-Berl. 34 (Wilcken in *Archiv*, x, p. 271).
7. Cf. Chapter VII.
8. Cf. Chapter VIII; also O. Osol. 8–11.
9. Cf. Strabo XVII. 1, 3 (788).
10. Cf. SB. 7462; also SB. 8 from the second century.
11. See Chapter XVII, p. 290 f.
12. Cf. SB. 7462.
13. Cf. BL. II. 1, on WO. II. 135; O. Tait, p. 69, nos. 36–7.
14.

				A.D.	
WO. II. 556	.	.	.	132–3	1 (billon) dr. 1 ob.
564	.	.	.	133–4	1 (billon) dr. 4 ob.
579	.	.	.	136–7	4 (billon) dr.
O. Tait, p. 69, no. 36		.		136–7	4 (billon) dr. 3 ob.
no. 37		.		136–7	8 (billon) dr.
WO. II. 585	.	.	.	137–8	6 dr. (total)
610 (?)	.	.	.	141–2	1 dr. 6 ob.
612	.	.	.	141–2	1 (billon) dr. 6 ob.
614	.	.	.	142–3	7 (billon) dr. 2 ob.
1437	.	.	.	143–4	6 dr. 4 ob.

WO. II. 620	.	.	.	A.D. 144–5	6 (billon) dr. 3½ obols.
627	.	.	.	145–6	5 (billon) dr. 4 ob.
630	.	.	.	146–7	3 (billon) *obols*.
631	.	.	.	146–7	3 (billon) *obols*.
635	.	.	.	147–8	1 (billon) dr.
O. Str. 236	.	.	.	147–8	1 (billon) dr.
WO. II. 642	.	.	.	149–50	2 (billon) dr.

It will be noted that amounts paid for the tax in the year A.D. 136–7 in O. Tait, p. 69, nos. 36 and 37, do not agree with the amount of WO. II. 579 for the same year which is 4 (billon) drachmae. O. Tait, p. 69, no. 36, however, is dated A.D. 142, four or five years after the payment was due, and it is not impossible that the payment of 4 drachmae 3 obols includes a penalty for late payment. The payment of 8 (billon) drachmae in O. Tait, p. 69, no. 37, is so large that it is possible that payment made in A.D. 142 included some other tax not mentioned by name, or possibly the payment, although stated to be for the μερισμός ἀνακ(εχωρηκότων) of the twenty-first year (of Hadrian), actually included arrears of another year. Other receipts for μερισμός ἀνακ(εχωρηκότων) are: WO. II. 101, 135; O. Strass. 284; possibly also WO. II. 151, 152, 154, 155, 156, 171, 182, 183, 201, 261, 1272; O. Tait, p. 66, no. 21; all from Elephantine-Syene. From Thebes: WO. II. 601, 602, 606, 651, 1290, 1583; O. Strass. 212, 219; PSI. III. 271; P. Lips. 74. From Upper Egypt: O. Strass. 194; SB. 4338. For the list of ostraca suggested as possibly for this tax but usually associated with the tax for statues cf. the discussion of the latter tax.

In WO. II. 1290 the original reading of φα after ἀνακ( ) has been changed in the *Berichtigungsliste*, II. 1, to καὶ ἄ(λλων). If the original reading is correct, φα is probably the number of men who had fled. If the μερισμός ἀνακ(εχωρηκότων) was, as has been suggested in the text, designed to cover the deficit in the dike-tax as well as the poll-tax (24 drachmae in the South-west Quarter), the number of men liable to taxation remaining in the quarter was nearly 700, so that the normal number of male tax-payers there in about A.D. 140 would have been about 790.

A payment of 1 drachma 2¾ obols for πρόσθεμα ὑπὲρ λαογραφίας (perhaps in the reign of Marcus Aurelius) in O. Zereteli 10 (*Archiv*, v, pp. 170 ff.) is similar to, if not identical with, the μερισμός ἀνακ(εχωρηκότων).

15. P. Bouriant 21.

16. Some economic change or perhaps even a chance to lease land on especially favourable terms may have checked the drift to the cities early in the reign of Antoninus Pius, but there is no other evidence for this.

17. Arrears of the μερισμός ἀνακ(εχωρηκότων) were collected four

or five years after the tax was due in O. Tait, p. 69, nos. 36 and 37; collectors sometimes succeeded in obtaining payment of other taxes which had been in arrears for a number of years; see Chapter XVII, p. 321.

18. In WO. II. 585 two letter of ἀνακ( ) in line 7 are indicated as doubtful.

19. In SP. IV, pp. 62 ff., lines 490 ff., the ἀσθενεῖς are included with the ὑπερετεῖς in the list of those who paid no poll-tax. Such persons may in other documents have been called ἄποροι.

20. As a mere possibility one might suggest a μερισμὸς ἀσθενῶν as the third division of the tax; cf. note 19 above.

21. SB. 7462; BGU. I. 159; PO. IV. 705; PSI. I. 101, 102, 105, III. 232; SB. I. 8; P. Ryl. II. 78. 4 (Busirite nome). Cf. P. Princeton I. 9. v. 7 and vii. 8.

22. P. Fay. 53, 54; P. Lond. III. 844 (p. 54); P. Columbia I R I a; P. Fay. 256, 316; SP. XXII. 117; P. Teb. II. 544, 545; P. Ryl. II. 366. In P. Fay. 54 the μερισμὸς ἀπόρων and the ἐπιμερισμὸς ἀπόρων both appear.

The 'curve' observed in the rate of assessment of the μερισμὸς ἀνακεχωρηκότων at Charax (cf. note 14 above) makes possible a conjectural dating of some of the receipts for μερισμὸς ἀπόρων which give the year of the assessment but which have lost the name of the emperor. If the assessment is very small it may be assumed that the document is to be dated soon after a census had been taken; it is simply necessary to find an emperor whose given regnal year occurs within the first five years after a census-year. Conversely, if the assessment is large it is probable that the document is to be dated shortly before a census year. Accordingly P. Fay. 256 is probably to be dated in the seventeenth year of Hadrian (A.D. 133) rather than of Trajan, for the amount of the receipt is small (1 dr. 2½ ob.) which would be natural after the census of A.D. 132. Similarly P. Teb. II. 545 is probably to be dated in A.D. 120–1 and P. Ryl. II. 366 in A.D. 141–2.

23. Cf. Chapter VIII.

24. Preisigke, Fachwörter and Wörterbuch, s.v., defines διάχωμα as a tax for a Querdamm, a cross-dike.

25. Cf. P. Hib. 112. 13, note, and the references there cited.

26. Receipts for the capitation tax are not found after the third century A.D.

27. There is no indication in the receipts that the μητροπολῖται of Arsinoë paid the χωματικόν. A fortiori Roman citizens and the citizens of Alexandria were doubtless similarly exempted from the payment of the dike-tax.

28. P. Princeton I. 11.

29. O. Tait, p. 92, no. 99 (A.D. 107); O. Theb. 98 (A.D. 111), 36 (A.D. 113), 99 (A.D. 116); BL. II. 1 declares χω(ματικοῦ) to be a misreading in line 3 of O. Theb. 81, where Milne thought 10 drachmae were paid for the tax.

30. Cf. the famous *mot* attributed to Tiberius by Cassius Dio LVII. 10. 5, cited Chapter IV, p. 31.

31. P. Lond. II, p. 103. On the πενθήμερος see Oertel, *Die Liturgie*, pp. 63 ff.

32. Cf. Oertel, op. cit., p. 71.

33. Cf. A. C. Johnson, *Roman Egypt*, p. 303.

34. Cf. Grenfell and Hunt in PO. II. 288 introd.

35. Cf. Oertel, loc. cit.

36. See the discussion of the ναύβιον in Chapter V, pp. 59 ff.

37. Suetonius, *Augustus*, 18; also CIL. III. 6627; CIG. III. 4716^{d}15; Dio Cassius, LI. 18. 7.

38. The receipts for χωματικόν are: From the Arsinoite nome: BGU. II. 391; P. Princeton I. 11; BGU. VII. 1614; P. Columbia I R 1 a–b; the tax-rolls from Caranis in the collection of the University of Michigan; P. Teb. II. 353; P. Reinach 45; P. Cornell 42; P. Genf. 40; BGU. III. 704; P. Lond. II. 296 (p. 107); P. Basel 10–11; BGU. I. 99; P. Lond. II. 337 (p. 107), III. 844 (p. 54). From the Oxyrhynchite nome: PO. II. 389, 313, 289, 311, 309, 308, 288. From Thebes: O. Tait, p. 87, no. 77; SB. 1637, 2133, 4255, 4343; O. Wilb.-Brk. 19; O. Br.-Berl. 2; O. Tait, p. 67, no. 26; O. Mey. 25, 35; O. Strass. 75, 71, 99, 60, 55, 83; O. Tait, p. 87, no. 79; p. 67, no. 27; O. Strass. 92, 102; O. Tait, p. 86, no. 75; O. Theb. 50, 48, 43; O. Strass. 89, 90, 122, 121, 120; SP. XIII, p. 8, no. 11; O. Tait, p. 106, no. 193; *Archiv*, VI, p. 129 (demotic); O. Theb. 98, 36, 99; O. Tait, p. 92, no. 99; also the ostraca listed in WO. I, p. 333 (§ 136). The following were collected at Thebes together with the bath-tax: SB. 1669; O. Tait, p. 68, nos. 28, 32, 33; P. Lips. 69, 72; O. Strass. 80, 79, 77, 203, 197, 195, 188, 184, 220, 217; O. Tait, p. 157, no. 36; p. 92, no. 100; O. Theb. 34, 51, 100 (?); O. Wilb.-Brk. 14–18; O. Oslo. 7. With which cf. the following from the Fayûm: BGU. I. 359; SP. XXII. 102; P. Ryl. II. 194; P. Teb. II. 354 (which is probably not from the Arsinoite nome). The following represent payments of instalments of the dike-tax at Thebes: O. Theb. 35, 33, 32, 97; SB. 3563, 4342; O. Tait, p. 88, no. 83; p. 69, no. 35; O. Mey. 30 a, 37; P. Bad. IV. 103; O. Mey. 23, 36 a; O. Tait, p. 88, no. 81; p. 90, no. 90; p. 69, no. 38; O. Mey. 21; O. Strass. 67, 85, 91, 115, 112, 111, 118, 144, 140, 135, 192, 185, 208, 202, 201, 230, 229, 235, 281, 279; O. Tait, p. 180 G.; p. 156, no. 33; p. 157, no. 37; p. 159, no. 45; p. 108, no. 205; p. 92, no. 101; *Archiv*. V, pp. 170 ff., no. 8; with which cf. from the Oxyrhynchite nome PO. II. 312. The amounts paid in the following are unknown: from Thebes: O. Tait, p. 86, no. 74; O. Strass. 296; SB. 4336; O. Tait, p. 91, no. 94; O. Strass. 100; O. Tait, p. 159, no. 46; O. Strass. 225; O. Theb. 73. From Papa in the Coptite nome: O. Strass. 780. From the Arsinoite nome: BGU. VII. 1596–7, II. 485; references to the tax in SB. 4355 and O. Strass. 131 from Elephantine-Syene are doubtful (cf. BL. II. 1 on SB. 4355). There are references to the dike-tax in the following documents: from the Arsinoite nome: A.M. 8915

in the Library of Princeton University, an account of a bank from Philadelphia and dated A.D. 56(?); P. Cornell 24; BGU. VII. 1613, I. 214; P. Columbia I R I a–b; P. Fay. 42 a; P. Lond. II. 349 (p. 115). Heracleopolite nome (?): BGU. IV. 1198. Oxyrhynchite nome: PO. XII. 1438; Garret Deposit 7687 b in the Library of Princeton University, a tax account. Mendesian nome: PSI. I. 106. From Thebes (?): O. Tait, p. 169, no. 102.

In the introduction to O. Wilb.-Brk. 14–19 (p. 44) Miss Préaux rejects the suggestion that the πενθήμερος (corvée) was waived if the χωματικόν was paid.

39. For references to the pig-tax in the Ptolemaic period cf. Preisigke, *Wörterbuch*, III. 11 sub ὑική.

40. Schwahn in PWRE. A 9, Sp. 289; Comfort, AJA. XXXVII (1933), p. 644. For arguments that the ὑική was a property-tax cf. P. Ryl. II. 193. 4, note.

41. P. Teb. II. 354.

42. P. Teb. II. 353.

43. Receipts for ὑική are as follows: Oxyrhynchite nome: PO. II. 311, 288, 389, 308, 313, 289, XII. 1520, IV. 733, XII. 1436, III. 574, XII. 1516, 1518. Arsinoite nome: P. Fay. 230, 42 (a); P. Princeton I. 1, 4, 8; BGU VII, 1613; P. Fay. 53–4, 316, 317; P. Columbia I R 2; I R I a–b; I R 3. Hermopolite nome: P. Ryl. II. 185, 193. Mendesian nome: PSI. I. 106. Uncertain: P. Teb. II. 353, 354. Thebes: WO. II. 1031.

44. Reil (*Beiträge zur Kenntnis des Gewerbes im hellenistischen Ägypten*, Borna-Leipzig 1913, p. 112) is wrong in supposing that payments of ὑική by a weaver, in PO. II. 288; 311, indicate that he was engaged in agriculture. It is unnecessary to suppose that all the barbers and locksmiths who paid the μερισμὸς ὑικῆς in PO. XII. 1518 were farmers on the side.

45. Cf. Cicero, *de deorum Natura*, II. 64, 160.

46. Cf. Oertel, *Die Liturgie*, pp. 112–15, 157–85, 195–260.

47. See Chapter XVII.

48. References to φυλακιτικά of the Ptolemaic period may be found in Preisigke, *Wörterbuch*, III. 11, s.v.

49. References to the tax ὑπὲρ φυλάκων may be found in the following documents: Elephantine-Syene: O. Strass. 130(?). Coptos: O. Tait, p. 109, no. 211. Apollonopolis Magna: O. Tait, p. 106, no. 192; SP. XIII, p. 8, no. 8. Upper Egypt: O. Strass. 113. Thebes: P. Bad. IV. 108, 107; O. Mey. 39, 25; WO. II. 422, 427, 428, 430, 433, 435, 441, 442, 445, 447, 449, 1281, 451, 455, 1283, 460, 461, 463, 465, 467, 1284, 472, 1285, 478, 480, 529; O. Strass. 207, 221; WO. II. 1477, 1429, 581; PSI. III. 271; WO. II. 616; O. Strass. 234; O. Wilb.-Brk. 25.

50. P. Teb. II. 545; P. Fay. 53; P. Ryl. II. 191; SP. XXII. 117; P. Columbia I R I a–b; I R 3; P. Ryl. II. 194; P. Teb. II. 544, 355; BGU. III. 881; P. Teb. II. 638; P. Ryl. II. 373; BGU. VII. 1625; P. Hamb.

85. At Caranis, according to the tax-rolls in the collection of the University of Michigan, the φυλακία seems to have been paid by only 10 men who were over 65 years of age; perhaps this payment had been assigned to them as a liturgy after they had become exempt from paying capitation taxes.

51. Memphis: P. Flor. I. 12; P. Lond. III. 1216 (p. 34); P. Goodspeed Cairo, 10. Oxyrhynchus: PO. III. 502, which, however, may be a property-tax.

52. P. Columbia, p. 38, equates στατίωνος with φυλ(άκων); cf. Wilcken, *Grundz.*, pp. 413–15.

Receipts from Elephantine are: O. Wilb.-Brk. 20; WO. II. 145, 146, 147, 169(?); SB. 4361; WO. II. 273, 278, 287, 293. The payments for στατίων found at Elephantine are always (except in WO. II. 273) connected in the receipts with the tax for the river-guards (ποταμοφυλακίς), and they may have been μερισμοί for the building of a 'station' for the river-patrol; WO. II. 278, dated A.D. 190, which records the payment of 2 drachmae 1 obol for the στατίωνος ποταμοφυλακ(ίδος) καὶ ἄλλων ἔργων seems clearly an assessment for construction. It is not certain, however, that all payments ὑπὲρ στατίωνος were limited to such a purpose. It seems that at Philadelphia such a term is but an alternate expression for ὑπὲρ φυλάκων.

53. Receipts for the tax ὑπὲρ σκοπ(έλων) are: Apollonopolis Magna: O. Tait, p. 106, nos. 192–3; SP. XIII, p. 8, no. 8. Elephantine-Syene: O. Strass. 126, 128, 130, 129; WO. II. 249, 254, 278, 286. Thebes: WO. II. 495, 497, 499; O. Strass. 189; WO. II. 505, 506; O. Theb. 93; O. Strass. 190; WO. II. 509, 1286, 511; O. Strass. 231; WO. II. 514, 515; O. Theb. 94; WO. II. 1287, 520–4; O. Strass. 200; WO. II. 1570, 529; P. Lips. 68; O. Strass. 207; WO. II. 541, 1422; P. Lips. 70; WO. II. 1424, 545, 547, 551; O. Strass. 221; WO. II. 566, 571, 1477, 1429, 581, 585; SB. 1669; O. Tait, p. 69, no. 34; PSI. III. 271; WO. II. 610, 616, 618, 625; O. Tait, p. 93, no. 106; WO. II. 629, 632; O. Strass. 234; WO. II. 640; O. Strass. 237–9; O. Tait, p. 93, no. 105; WO. II, 678 (?); O. Wilb.-Brk. 25.

54. WO. I, p. 293.

55. Cf. Preisigke, *Wörterbuch*, III. 11, sub μαγδωλοφυλακία, and also BL. II. 1 on O. Theb. 34 and WO. II. 1284, 1285. Receipts for μαγδωλοφυλακία are: from Thebes: WO. II. 1284, 1285; O. Mey. 40; PSI. VIII. 992 (?); O. Tait, p. 90, nos. 91 and 97; p. 91, no. 94; O. Theb. 34; O. Mey. 30 a; O. Tait, p. 157, no. 38. From Coptos: O. Tait, p. 109, no. 214. From the Arsinoite nome: P. Ryl. II. 191; P. Fay. 54, 316, 317; SP. XXII, 117; P. Columbia I R 2; I R 3; I R I a–b; BGU. III. 881; P. Lond. III. 844 (p. 54), 1235 (p. 35); P. Fay. 239, 42 a; P. Bouriant 32; the tax-rolls from Caranis in the collection of the University of Michigan; P. Flor. III. 375 probably refers to private watch-towers. From Peënsaci: P. Teb. II. 353.

56. BL. II. 1 on WO. II. 1284–5.

57. If Viereck's reading is accepted, and the payment of 1 obol is

correct for the μαγδωλοφυλακία, perhaps [μαγδωλ]ο(φυλακίας) should be read in PSI. VIII. 992, where a payment of 2 obols is recorded for A.D. 92.

58. O. Tait, p. 109, no. 214.

59. See Chapter VIII, appendix to notes.

60. P. Teb. II. 353.

61. O. Tait, p. 91, no. 94, note.

62. e.g. P. Lond. III. 844 (p. 54).

63. WO. I, p. 177 f.

64. Cf. WO. I, p. 178.

65. Receipts from Elephantine-Syene for δεσμοφυλακία are: WO. II. 104; O. Br.-Berl. 34; WO. II. 106, 114–19, 121, 123, 125, 128–30, 140, 141, 144, 148; O. Tait, p. 65, no. 17; WO. II. 151, 152; O. Strass. 284; WO. II. 154–6, 158; *Archiv*, V, p. 170 f., no. 5; WO. II. 165, 201; O. Tait, p. 66, no. 19 (?).

66. O. Tait, p. 109, no. 214.

67. Δεσμοφυλακία is found in the following: Arsinoite nome: P. Fay. 53; P. Ryl. II. 191; P. Fay. 54, 317; SP. XXII. 117 (?); P. Columbia I R I a–b, I R 2, I R 3; P. Teb. II. 355; BGU. III. 881; P. Lond. III. 844 (p. 54); SP. IV, p. 118 (=P. Fay. 229); P. Teb. II. 638; P. Ryl. II. 194 (?). From the Oxyrhynchite nome: PO. III. 574, XII. 1438. From the Hermopolite nome: P. Ryl. II. 193, 185. From Memphis or Hermopolis (probably): P. Teb. II. 354.

68. Suggested by Preisigke in BL. I, p. 441.

69. See Chapter VIII, p. 128. Receipts for ποταμοφυλακίς are: from Elephantine-Syene: WO. II. 48; O. Tait, p. 65, no. 18; WO. II. 87, 89–92, 104; O. Br.-Berl. 34; O. Tait, p. 65, no. 16; WO. II. 108, 112; O. Tait, p. 105, no. 191; WO. II. 120, 122, 124, 127, 131, 132, 134, 139, 142, 143, 145–6, 162; O. Wilb.-Brk. 20–3; O. Mey. 41; WO. II. 169, 287, 293, 1274, 1573. From Thebes: WO. II. 439, 440, 507; O. Theb. 93, 36; SB. 4354, 4356, 4357; WO. II. 1241, 1408, 1413; O. Strass. 222; O. Tait, p. 70, no. 41; O. Wilb.-Brk. 25; SB. 4361. From the Arsinoite nome: P. Ryl. II. 191; P. Fay. 54, 317; P. Columbia I R 2, I R 3, I R I a–b; P. Teb. II. 355; BGU. III. 881; P. Lond. III. 844 (p. 54); P. Bouriant 32 (?).

70. On the δέκανοι see Chapter XIII, p. 219 f.

71. P. Bouriant 32.

72. Possibly also in P. Ryl. II. 215. 49.

73. BGU. II. 372.

74. This revolt was dated in A.D. 153–4 by P. M. Meyer in *Klio*, VII (1907), p. 123 f., and he was followed by Wilcken, *Chrest.* 19, introd., and by Lesquier, *L'armée romaine d'Égypte*, p. 27 f. This dating has been questioned by Schehl in *Hermes*, LXV (1930), pp. 197 ff., whose conclusions are approved by Stauffenberg, *Römische Kaisergeschichte bei Malalas*, Stuttgart 1931, p. 308, note 43 f. Meyer based his arguments upon SHA. *Anton.* 5. 5 and Malalas, *Chron.* XI, p. 280; Lesquier cited also Jean de Nikiou, 74; there is a reference to the

revolt in Aristides, *Or.* xiv, vol. i. 351 (Dindorf); coins are cited by Vogt, *Die Alexandrinischen Münzen*, Stuttgart 1924, I, p. 129.

75. Receipts for μερισμὸς διπλῶν are: from Elephantine-Syene: SB. 4352; WO. II. 85, 163, 164; SB. 4359, 4358; O. Wilb.-Brk. 22–3; O. Br.-Berl. 38; SB. 4361. From Coptos: O. Tait, p. 109, no. 214. From Thebes: WO. II. 1429, 578, 600, 605, 613, 622, 625, 1291, 633, 637, 678, 1477. From the Arsinoite nome: P. Fay. 53; P. Lond. III. 844 (p. 54), III. 1235 (p. 35); SP. xxii, 117; P. Teb. II. 355, 638. From the Oxyrhynchite nome: PO. xii. 1438.

76. P. Lond. III. 1171 *verso* c (p. 107) (= W. *Chrest.* 439).

77. OGI. II. 665, a decree of the prefect Cn. Vergilius Capito.

78. From this expression (ἄνευ διπλῶν) instead of ἄνευ διπλωμάτων comes the explanation of the tax μερισμὸς διπλῶν.

79. Cf. Wilcken, *Grundz.*, pp. 360 ff.; Lesquier, *L'Armée Romaine d'Égypte*, pp. 350 ff.

80. Cf., however, O. Tait, p. 70, no. 42, a μερισμός which is possibly connected with the *annona militaris* and which is apparently assessed κατ' ἄρουραν.

81. There is dittography of ἀννώ(νης) according to the editor's note.

82. But cf. Lesquier, op. cit., p. 354, note 4.

83. The payment in column i was credited to a πράκτωρ β(αλανείου) Φιλ[αγρίδος].

84. P. Fay. Ostraca 2–6; O. Mich. Car. 120.

85. P. Mil. 12.

86. PSI. viii. 902. Cf. O. Mey. 75 from the Fayûm, A.D. 4–5, where τελ( ) βαλ( ) might be either τρίτη or μερισμός.

87. WO. II. 1368.

88. Φόρος βαλ( ). Φόρος is rent; see Chapter V, p. 71. But cf. τελ( ) βαλ( ) from the same period cited in note 86 above. Cf. also O. Strass. 259; O. Br.-Berl. 1; WO. II. 1370; SB. 4519; O. Tait, p. 94, no. 114; WO. II. 1263. It is probable that a great deal of confusion and inconsistency existed in the assessment and collection of bath-taxes when the state-owned baths were first introduced by the Romans.

89. Cf. O. Tait, p. 87 f., no. 79, note, which is condensed from Milne, *Annals of Archaeology and Anthropology*, VII, pp. 61 ff.

90. Two tetradrachms would give an overpayment of ½ obol.

91. Cf. O. Tait, p. 92, no. 99.

92. Receipts for the bath-tax are: WO. II. 366–8, 370, 373, 374, 376–8, 384, 386, 387, 389–91, 398, 401, 403, 405, 406, 411, 424, 425, 429, 436, 443, 453, 456, 462, 463, 469, 470, 474, 481, 483, 486, 488, 492, 501, 516, 518–20, 525, 526, 532, 534, 536, 538, 539, 542–4, 546, 548, 555, 565–7 (?), 569, 570, 573, 582–4, 586, 591, 598, 617, 619, 623, 626, 634, 636, 641, 645, 651, 666, 667; O. Tait, p. 94, no. 114; WO. II. 780, 781, 782, 784–6, 789, 795–8, 807, 812, 815, 818, 819, 835, 842–6, 849, 853, 857, 862, 863, 871, 875, 877, 882, 885, 916, 919, 924, 928, 932, 955, 1020, 1032, 1033, 1035, 1036, 1037, 1061, 1243,

1251, 1252, 1287, 1289, 1321, 1368, 1370, 1373–5, 1378, 1380, 1392, 1393, 1400, 1402–4, 1409, 1414, 1415, 1417, 1425, 1426, 1428, 1429, 1452, 1549, 1552, 1562, 1566, 1587, 365, 1263, 457, 460, 508, 527, 535, 585, 1288; O. Theb. 51; O. Tait, p. 68, no. 33; O. Strass. 229, 215, 217, 201, 193; O. Theb. 48; O. Strass. 143; O. Theb. 50, 49, 47, 43, 45; *Archiv*, v, pp. 170 ff., no. 8; O. Tait, p. 88, no. 81; O. Theb. 34; SB. 4342; O. Tait, p. 90, no. 87; O. Strass. 275; O. Theb. 53; *Archiv*, v, pp. 170 ff., no. 9; O. Strass. 199, 235, 223, 228, 230, 218, 220, 102; O. Tait, p. 69, no. 36, no. 38; O. Strass. 208, 65, 82, 62; O. Tait, p. 86, no. 75; p. 93, no. 104, no. 103; O. Br.-Berl. 31, 26; O. Tait, p. 67, no. 27; O. Strass. 81, 74; O. Tait, p. 94, no. 114; O. Theb. 52; D 5; SB. 4519; O. Tait, p. 94, no. 109; no. 115; O. Strass. 180, 206, 211, 96, 61; O. Mey. 27; SB. 4348; O. Tait, p. 175, B. 1, p. 67, no. 25; p. 86, no. 76; *Archiv*, v, pp. 170 ff., no. 7; SB. 1669; O. Strass. 203, 60, 71; O. Tait, p. 69, no. 35; O. Strass. 75; O. Mey. 35; O. Br.-Berl. 2; SB. 4255, 2133; O. Tait, p. 87, no. 77; p. 95, no. 116; O. Strass. 440, 477; O. Mey. 86; SB. 1088; O. Theb. 54, 55; O. Strass. 480–2; O. Theb. 44, 46; O. Strass. 479; O. Tait, p. 161, nos. 60–2; p. 174, no. 3; O. Strass. 260, 264, 267, 269; SB. 4328, 4333, 3562; O. Mey. 11; *Archiv*, VI, pp. 125 ff.; O. Mey. 13, 14; O. Strass. 120, 123, 132, 134; SP. XIII, p. 8, no. 11; O. Tait, p. 106, nos. 192, 193; O. Strass. 263, 262 (cf. 616, 617); O. Br.-Berl 1; O. Strass. 259, 179, 214, 181, 113, 270, 273, 478, 483, 485–90; O. Tait, p. 95, no. 117; O. Strass. 484, 261, 265, 266, 268, 272; O. Wilb.-Brk. 14–18.

93. The receipts are listed by Calderini, *ΘΗΣΑΥΡΟΙ*, p. 36, to which may be added O. Tait, p. 95, nos. 116–17; p. 161, nos. 60–2; p. 174, no. 3; O. Wilb.-Brk. 44–8.

94. BGU. II. 362. i. 24. Miss Préaux (O. Wilb.-Brk., p. 78) has observed that the same person may pay both types of βαλανευτικόν at Thebes.

95. Cf. O. Mey. 13–14.

96. O. Strass. 120, 123, 132, 134.

97. Cf. BL. II. 1 on WO. II. 501.

98. Receipts for the tax to provide statues of the emperors: from Thebes: WO. II. 559, 603, 604; O. Strass. 108, 118, 159; O. Theb. 42. From Elephantine: WO. II. 71–3, 94, 100; P. Bad. IV. 101; WO. II. 105; *Archiv*, VI, p. 219, no. 4; O. Br.-Berl. 36; WO. II. 149, 151–2 (?), 154–6 (?), 1272 (?), 171 (?), 178–80, 182 (?), 183 (?), 201 (?), 249, 254, 261 (?), 270 (?), 285; O. Tait, p. 66, no. 21; p. 70, no. 42 (? cf. WO. II. 603, which is also very doubtful).

99. WO. I, p. 152. He noted that WO. II. 603 has a payment of 5½ obols on 30$\frac{15}{16}$ arurae. Perhaps O. Tait, p. 70, no. 42 μερισμὸς . . αν . . . at 4 obols an arura is similar.

100. Cf. BL. II. 1 on WO. II. 270.

101. Cf. Westermann's discussion in JEA. XI (1925), pp. 165 ff.

102. O. Theb. p. 99.

103. It is not impossible, however, to imagine that the city was a little slow in paying the unfortunate sculptor.

104. O. Theb., p. 99.

105. Cf. BL. II. 1 on O. Strass. 118, where Tait dates the ostracon in the reign of Gordian. Professor A. C. Johnson dates the ostracon in the reign of Hadrian, since contributions for statues are common in that reign and are otherwise unattested in receipts from the third century. If an Aurelius is not impossible so early, Τραιανοῦ would fill the lacuna. See Chapter VIII, note 86.

106. O. Strass. 108; cf. O. Strass. 118.

107. Milne, *History of Egypt under Roman Rule*, rev. ed. 1924, pp. 38 ff.

108. O. Strass. 245.

109. The receipts for μερισμὸς πλινθευομένης are: from Thebes: O. Theb. 92; WO. II. 512, 572, 592, 1421. From the Oxyrhynchite nome: PO. III. 502, 574.

110. PO. III. 502. 43, note.

111. The manufacture of bricks was apparently a government monopoly in the Arsinoite nome; cf. P. Fay. 36 introd. See also Chapter XI, p. 188 f.

112. Cf. WO. I, p. 280; PO. III. 502. 43, note; BL. II. 1 on WO. II. 1421.

113. SP. XXII. 128; SB. 5102; P. Hamb. 83.

114. It might be possible to interpret the μερισμὸς Δρόμου Γυμνασίου and μερισμὸς Δρόμου Θοηρίδος in PO. XII. 1516 as a tax for the construction or repair of a street, but Grenfell and Hunt (*ad loc.*) say that the inhabitants were listed according to μερισμοί of their amphoda.

115. WO. II. 259, 577, 628, 673, 1440.

116. The receipts from Thebes which mention the μερισμὸς τελωνικῶν ὠνίων are: O. Str. 249; O. Tait, p. 70, no. 39; O. Strass. 243; WO. II. 553, 554, 562, 560, 558; O. Strass. 244; O. Tait, p. 94, no. 110; WO. II. 568, 1250, 589, 590, 1249; O. Strass. 246; WO. II. 596, 597, 1329, 670 (?), 607, 608, 611; O. Strass. 247; O. Theb. 101; WO. II. 1438, 1439, 1442; O. Strass. 248; WO. II. 646, 643; O. Tait, p. 70, no. 40; PSI. III. 278; WO. II. 1586, 1445; SB. 1090; O. Strass. 244, 246; O. Wilb.-Brk. 21.

117. P. Ryl. II. 214. 23, note.

118. Cf. WO. II. 1056, 1076.

119. WO. I, pp. 342 ff.

120. The πεντηκοστὴ ὠνίων probably is connected with the τέλος ἀγορανομίας ὠνίων which was collected by a τελώνης; cf. O. Tait, p. 92, no. 102.

121. It is probable that the μερισμὸς τελ( ) ὠνίων (cf. Wilcken's list) is always to be expanded μερισμὸς τελ(ωνικῶν) rather than μερισμὸς τέλ(ους) ὠνίων, since ἐνλ(είμματος) does not always appear with the μερισμός of τελωνικά (WO. II. 554; O. Tait, p. 94, no. 110; contrast e.g. WO. II. 590).

122. O. Tait, p. 92, no. 102.

123. P. Fay. 62.

124. See Chapter XV.

125. P. Ryl. II. 214. 23 and note.

126. Possibly, however, it may be the 'share' of the διοίκησις in some fund which would be a less common meaning of the word μερισμός. The isolated character of the example makes a decision difficult.

127. The meaning of ἀπὸ προχρείας as applied to taxation is not altogether clear.

128. Cf., however, P. Bad. IV. 102.

129. Receipts for μερισμοί from Elephantine-Syene: WO. II. 95-9, 102; O. Strass. 138; WO. II. 170, 173, 174, 178-80, 186, 196-8, 200, 202, 205; P. Bad. IV. 102; O. Br.-Berl. 42; WO. II. 203, 204, 208, 209, 212-15; SB. 4363; WO. II. 218, 228, 219; O. Br.-Berl. 5; WO. II. 221; Archiv, v, pp. 170 ff., no. 26; WO. II. 220, 222, 224, 228, 235, 241, 242, 246-8, 253, 256, 258; O. Tait, p. 66, no. 19 (?); WO. II. 271 (?), 283, 289; SB. 7593-5; O. Wilb.-Brk. 24, 26-8. From Thebes: SB. 1668; O. Strass. 253; O. Tait, p. 91, no. 95; WO. II. 545, 550, 552, 561; SB. 1669; WO. II. 615; O. Strass. 233; WO. II. 637; O. Strass. 253; WO. II. 1443, 652; O. Strass. 111; WO. II. 655; O. Tait, p. 131, no. 341; with these μερισμοί should be compared WO. II. 408, which records the payment by a man and his son of 2 drachmae ὑπ(ὲρ) δραχ(μῆς) Μεμνο(νείων). From Apollonopolis Magna: O. Tait, p. 106, no. 194; Archiv, v, pp. 170 ff., nos. 24-5. From Coptos: O. Tait, p. 109, nos. 214 (?) and 215; p. 162, no. 63; p. 109, no. 216.

130. See Chapter VIII, p. 134.

CHAPTER X

1. SP. XIII, pp. 8 ff., nos. 4, 6, 20, 10, 13, 13 b, 15, 14, 16, 17, 18; O. Mey. 33; W. Chrest. 295; SP. IV, p. 71 f., columns xi–xiii; cf. SP. I, pp. 9 ff.

2. SP. IV, loc. cit. (= W. Chrest. 61).

3. See Chapter VII, p. 107 f. Wessely (SP. IV, p. 60) supposes that Tryphaena, who is stated to have been examined, at the epicrisis of the fourth year of Vespasian, among the ὑπερετεῖς (ἐτῶν) ξ̄α, that is, tax-exempt because 'over sixty-one years old' (i.e. sixty-two years old), is wrongly made to pay the tax on Jews. He mistakenly supposed the age of exemption to be sixty years. Tryphaena had been fifty-nine years old at the time of the epicrisis in the previous year, so that it is possible that she was not even sixty years of age when Heraclides the amphodarch made up his tax-list.

4. Cf. SP. XIII, p. 8 f., nos. 10, 13, 16, 17, 18; O. Mey. 33.

5. SP. XIII, p. 8 f., no. 20.

6. SP. XIII, p. 8 f., nos. 4, 6; W. Chrest. 295.

7. Taxes are computed in *denarii* instead of drachmae in the document published by Norsa and Vitelli in *Studi e Testi* 53, a land-register from Marmarica.

8. Josephus, *Bell. Jud.* VII. 6, 6; Dio Cass. LXV. 7.

9. SP. IV, p. 60.

10. O. Mey. 33, introd.

11. *Geschichte des jüdischen Volkes*, III⁴, p. 117.

12. *Chrest.* 61, introd.

13. *Domitian*, 12.

14. *Chrest*, loc. cit. His exact words are: 'Das letztere trifft nicht zu.' Yet he goes on to say, 'Trotzdem wird Wessely recht haben, denn sonst müszten wir annehmen, dasz die Juden in Ägypten auszer dem alten Didrachmon noch ein Didrachmon bezahlt hätten.' See note 24 below.

15. See Chapter VII, p. 105. For Syria cf. Ulpian, *Dig.* 50, 15, 3.

16. LXVI. 10.

17. *Historiae*, IV. 53.

18. Hieronymus (Schoene), p. 159; (Helm), p. 188. The Armenian version of Eusebius places the beginning of the restoration in the third year of Vespasian's reign according to the edition of Schoene, or the fourth year (apparently) according to Karst's edition. If it should prove that the Armenian version of Eusebius is here more accurate than Hieronymus, the argument presented in the text of this chapter would require but slight modification, since the work of rebuilding the temple on the Capitoline might have been begun in earnest as soon as the income from the Jewish tax was assured.

19. Josephus, *Bell. Jud.* V. 3 and 9; VI. 2 and 6.

20. *Shekalim*, VIII, quoted by Schürer, op. cit. II⁴, p. 315, note 57.

21. Chambalu, in *Philologus*, XLIV (1885), pp. 507 ff., places the date of the triumph about the end of June, A.D. 71.

22. Schürer, op. cit. II⁴, p. 315.

23. The Egyptian calendar did not coincide with the Roman calendar. Although the elevation of Vespasian to the principate had occurred but a month before, in Egypt the second year of his reign was reckoned as beginning on August 29, A.D. 69. The fourth year of Vespasian began in Egypt on August 29, A.D. 71, about two months after the triumph over the Jews. If the δίδραχμον was not confiscated until after the triumph, this would allow but scant time to prepare tax-lists for the collection in the year A.D. 71-2 in Egypt, but the elaborate records of the census were available for the purpose.

24. For the privileges of the Jews in Egypt cf. Josephus, *Antiq.* XIV. 7, 2; XIX. 5, 2; Philo, *leg. ad Gaium*, 10. For a discussion of the subject cf. H. I. Bell, *Jews and Christians in Egypt*, London, 1924, pp. 10-21, and the bibliography cited in his notes, especially note 1 on p. 10. Wilcken's criticism (quoted in note 14 above) seems to me to recognize that the Jews in Egypt paid the δίδραχμον to the temple of Onias instead of to the temple in Jerusalem. But Wilcken failed to

realize that Vespasian's confiscation of the δίδραχμον included that paid to the temple of Onias. If that is what Wessely meant, then his statement is irreproachable, for it is unnecessary to assume that the Jews paid two δίδραχμα either before or after the collection of the Ἰουδαίων τέλεσμα in Egypt.

25. *Bell. Jud.* VII. 10.

26. PO. X. 1266.

27. Cantarelli (*La serie dei prefetti di Egitto*, I, p. 35 (R. Accad. d. Lincei, 1906)) attempted to date the στάσις at Alexandria in the second half of the year A.D. 73, but since Q. Paulinus was in office as the successor to Ti. Julius Lupus in the year 72–3, it is impossible to restrict even the events described by Josephus (including the pursuit of the σικάριοι into the Thebaïd) between July 1, 73 and the date of the accession of Paulinus to the prefecture, even if he became prefect only in the last days of the year 72–3. Although Josephus describes the στάσις at Alexandria after his description of the siege and fall of Masada, it is his intention to picture the events at Alexandria as one of the effects of the Jewish War, of which the capture of Masada was merely a belated ending.

28. Cf. J. Strahan in Hastings, *Encyclopaedia of Religion and Ethics*, VI, pp. 46 ff., and the literature there cited.

29. Quoted from J. Strahan, loc. cit., p. 47.

30. O. Tait, p. 67, no. 24; P. Fay. 330; SP. XXII. 135; BGU. III. 817, I. 342; SP. XXII. 106, 111–13, 144; P. Lond. II. 451 (p. 109), 380 (p. 110); PSI. VIII. 905, 906; SP. XX. 1; CPR. 240. 30; P. Teb. II. 361, 347 (?); SB. 4415; BGU. I. 330; CPR. 175. 19; BGU. I. 236, III. 883; P. Ryl. II. 194; BGU. VII. 1584, 1585, 1613; the tax-rolls from Caranis in the collection of the University of Michigan have payments at the rate of 17 drachmae 1 obol 6 chalci.

31. P. Teb. II. 361 introd.

32. There is no reason to believe that the owners of catoecic land were ever exempt from this charge, since it was paid by a Roman Statia Petronia. Schwahn in PWRE. A 9, Sp. 299, supposed that the guarantee-clause in transfers of catoecic property stating that the parcel is free from ἀριθμητικόν (&c.) meant exemption from the ἀριθμητικὸν κατοίκων, but it is much more likely that the guarantee is against arrears of unpaid taxes which would have to be assumed by the new owner of the catoecic land. In P. Mich. II. 121 *recto* the lessor assumes responsibility for the payment of ἀριθμητικόν on catoecic land, while the lessee assumes liability for the rest of the taxes.

33. A payment of 66 drachmae for ἀριθμητικόν is recorded in P. Lond. III. 1171 (p. 177), an agricultural account of unknown provenience, dated 8 B.C., where it follows a payment of 720 drachmae for [ἐ]νόμιον προβ(άτων) καὶ [α]ἰγῶ(ν); it is unlikely, in my opinion, that this is the same as the tax paid by the catoeci in the second half of the second century after Christ, since it is included among the δαπανήματα, whereas in the accounts of the following year the taxes (δημόσια) are

reckoned separate from the δαπανήματα. P. Princeton 13, xvi. 1, dated A.D. 35, is a heading of an account of payments: καὶ πρὸ τ(ῆς) ἀπητή(σεως) ἐνεστ( ) ἀριθμη( ); the editors expand ἐνεστ(ῶτος) ἀριθμη(τικοῦ) and regard the following payments of 8, 9, and 20 obols, 5½, 10, 15½ obols or drachmae, 2 and 4 drachmae, as all payments for the ἀριθμητικόν; it is possible, however, to expand ἀριθμή(σεως), and even if the editors' expansion is correct it is far from certain or likely that the ἀριθμητικὸν κατοίκων is meant. In P. Lond. II. 349 (p. 115) ἀριθ(μήσεως) is more probable than ἀριθ(μητικόν), as the editor pointed out. Garret Deposit 7676 (in the collection in the Library of Princeton University) is a tax account dated in the third century after Christ; it contains a payment which is doubtfully read as ἀριθμητικόν.

34. The first receipt in BGU. I. 342 is dated in the 21st year, and the payment is said to be for the previous (20th) year. The second receipt on the papyrus is dated in the 25th year; the year for which the payment was made comes in the lacuna. The editors have restored κδ ϛ (on the basis of the reading in the first receipt), but it is entirely possible that the payment was for the 25th year instead. If the payment in A.D. 184 was made for the current year, the interval between the assessments would have been five instead of four years.

35. WO. I, p. 351.

36. Cf. Schwahn in PWRE. A 9, Sp. 299, who has taken Wilcken's suggestions too literally. He limits the activity of the ἀριθμηταί to verification of ἀπογραφαί of cattle. The editors of P. Ryl. (II. 213. 22, note) had warned that the presence of ἀριθμητικόν after ἐννόμιον προβάτων καὶ αἰγῶν in P. Lond. III. 1171 (p. 177) might be purely fortuitous. Schwahn's reference to the Ptolemaic δοκιμαστικόν paid to δοκιμασταί is not very cogent, because the three references to δοκιμαστικόν (cf. Preisigke, Wörterbuch, III, Abt. 11, s.v.) are very uncertain.

37. P. Teb. II. 361 introd.

38. Münch. Beitr. VI, pp. 91 ff.

39. Cf. Rostovtzeff, Soc. and Ec. Hist. of the Roman Empire, chapter vii, note 35 and the literature there cited.

40. It has long been maintained that catoeci were exempt from the payment of the λαογραφία. Although this is unlikely for the Roman period, it may well have been true of the Ptolemaic period. See Chapter VII, p. 109, and Chapter VIII, pp. 117 ff.

41. Cf. my article, 'Census and Poll-tax in Roman Egypt'.

42. See Chapter VIII, pp. 117 ff.

CHAPTER XI

1. The monopolies in Egypt have been treated by Heichelheim in PWRE. XXXI, Spp. 158–97.

2. Cf. San Nicolò, Ägyptisches Vereinswesen, Munich 1913, pp. 66–142.

3. Op. cit., Spp. 158–86: Ptolemaic period. Spp. 192–7: Roman period.

4. It is doubtful whether documents dealing with the monopolies of the Roman period similar to the great Revenue Papyrus and P. Teb. III. 703 will ever be found; such elaborate formulations of policy were unnecessary in the Roman period, because the Romans merely modified practices well established in the Ptolemaic period.

5. On the salt-monopoly see Heichelheim, loc. cit.; Amundsen, *Ostraca Osloënsia*, Avhandl. utgitt av D. Norske Videnskaps-Akademi i Oslo II. Hist.-Filos. Klasse, 1933, No. 2, pp. 1 ff.

6. According to P. Hal. 1 260–4, there were exempted from the salt-tax by order of the king, besides young children, teachers of letters and of gymnastics, actors, and victors in the three important athletic festivals at Alexandria; the descendants of these were also exempted from the tax. The Dioicete could grant special exemption to others (cf. P. Cairo Zen. 59130). Cf. also the exemptions from the poll-tax in the Roman period, Chapter VIII, pp. 117 ff.

7. O. Theb. 41, listed by Amundsen, op. cit., p. 6, note 4, does not refer to the salt-tax according to BL. II. 1.

8. P. Fay. 192, listed by Amundsen as a receipt, has been corrected by BL. I, and does not refer to the salt-tax.

9. P. Lond. III, p. vii.

10. If the reading ἁλική is correct, it is impossible to explain the total payment for the συντάξιμον of 44 drachmae 6 chalci as Tait did (O. Tait, p. 88 (note on p. 87, no. 79)); cf. Chapter VIII, pp. 121 ff.

11. SP. xx. 62 is unfortunately mutilated, but the reading at the end of line 8 is ἁλι[κῆς . . . . .], and line 9 gives σ(υμβολικά) ₀—/β = . This total is the payment of two men, and it should include salt-tax (ἁλική), surcharge (προσδιαγραφόμενα), and charge for receipt (συμβολικά). The charge for συμβολικά is stated to be ½ obol for two men, and since the προσδιαγραφόμενα on 1 drachma 2 obols would be exactly ½ obol, it is almost certain that the payment for one man would be ἁλική 4 obols; προσδιαγραφόμενα 2 chalci; συμβολικά 2 chalci. Amundsen's note (op. cit., p. 7) on this document is incorrect: the number of ὁμόλογοι in line 3 is 144, not 141; five of the 144, however, had not paid the salt-tax, so that line 4 should be restored: ἁλικῆς ʃ ϛβ[ϝ πρ(οσδιαγραφόμενα) ʃ εϝ₀—χᵇ], which will give the total of 104 drachmae 1½ obols of line 5. The payment for συμβολ(ικά) on the λαογραφία of 144 men would be 60 drachmae; consequently the 64 drachmae recorded in line 4 either is an overcharge or includes payment of 4 drachmae of arrears. In line 5 (presumably the same) five men had not paid the tax called ἱερ( ) γεφ( ). On the payment of the pig-tax in line 6, however, cf. Chapter IX, pp. 143 ff.

12. O. Tait, p. 87, no. 79, note.

13. See Amundsen, op. cit., p. 37, note 4, who points out that although the monopoly of retail sale (κοτυλίζειν) was leased by the government to an individual, it is not clear whether the ἐλαιουργεῖον was also rented from the state.

14. The references have been listed by Amundsen, op. cit., p. 36:

P. Teb. II. 539; P. Fay. 64; BGU. VII. 1618; P. Ryl. II. 215; PSI. I. 106 and P. Ryl. II. 213; BGU. III. 753. This impost is regarded as a consumers' tax by Heichelheim (PWRE. XXXI, Sp. 168) at least in the Ptolemaic period; by Reil (*Beiträge zur Kenntnis des Gewerbes im hellenistischen Ägypten*, p. 143) in the Roman as well as in the Ptolemaic period; by Wachsmuth (*Jahrbb. für Nationalökonomie und Statistik*, III, Folge XIX (1900), p. 801) for the Ptolemaic period; by Rostovtzeff (*Wochenschr. f. klass. Phil.*, 1900, Sp. 116) for the Ptolemaic period; Wilcken (*Schmollers Jahrb.* XLV (1921), p. 402) for the Ptolemaic period. It is assumed that this consumers' tax was a capitation tax. The only *receipt* for the tax in the Roman period is P. Fay. 64 which records the payment of 7 drachmae for ἐλαικῆς καὶ ἄλλων πρ[οσοδικῶν], and there is no indication in such a phrase that the tax was assessed *per capita*; the payment of 56 drachmae for εἴδη ἐλαικά (only or in connexion with some other tax?) is too large for a consumers' capitation tax. Until a document analogous to SP. xx. 62 is found giving a *per capita* rate for the ἐλαική, the existence of a consumers' capitation tax on oil must be regarded as absolutely unproved for the Roman period; the survival of the ἁλική as a capitation tax in the Arsinoite nome does not prove it.

15. The examples have been collected by Amundsen, ibid.: O. Mey. 43; O. Strass. 255; WO. 687. The payments of 4 drachmae in the first two examples might be taken as a rate for a capitation tax at Thebes. If, however, a similar rate prevailed in the Arsinoite nome, it would be difficult to explain the small total of the tax for that nome in BGU. III. 753 (dated third century A.D.), viz. 1 talent 1,096 drachmae; for if the rate was 4 drachmae per man, this would mean that only 1,774 men had paid the tax in a year, an absurdly low figure for the Arsinoite nome.

16. Cf. Chapter III, note 15.

17. PSI. I. 106. 14; III. 232. 21; 235. 11.

18. The tax on the mortars of oil-mills is mentioned in the following documents: P. Amh. II. 93, 118; BGU. I. 199 *verso*; P. Fay. 42 a; SP. XXII. 183; BGU. I. 337; P. Lond. II. 347 (p. 71). For a discussion of this tax cf. Otto, *Priester u. Tempel*, I, pp. 296 ff. It is not impossible that the τέλος θυιῶν in the Arsinoite nome was equivalent to the τέλος ἐλαιουργικῶν ὀργάνων in the Mendesian nome.

19. The second word was restored as ἱπ[πων] by Radermacher in *Rh. Mus.* LVII (1920), p. 48, and this is regarded by Schönbauer (*Zeitschr. d. Savigny-Stift. Röm. Abt.* N.S. XLVI (1926), p. 202) as more likely than ὑπὲρ διπλώματος ἱπωτ(ηρίου) suggested by Reil (*Beiträge*, &c., p. 17, note 1), although Reil's suggestion has been adopted by the BL. I. (p. 432) Nachtrag zu P. Amh. II. 92 in preference to Radermacher's restoration.

20. Loc. cit., Sp. 196.

21. References to payment of φόρος by ζυτοποιοί in the Ptolemaic period have been collected by Heichelheim, loc. cit., Sp. 170 f. For the Roman period cf. P. Fay. 42 a. ii. 9, and note.

22. *Beiträge*, pp. 167 ff.

23. Loc. cit., Sp. 171 f.

24. Ibid., Sp. 196.

25. O. Oslo 12 (p. 32). On the beer-tax cf. P. Oslo 29 and notes; O. Strass. 165; PO. XII. 1433. 52, note; Reil (see note 22 above); Preisigke's *WB.* III, Abt. 11 s.v. ζυτηρά.

26. See Chapter XII, p. 209.

27. Cf. Chwostow, *Textile Industry in Graeco-Roman Egypt* (Russian), Kazan 1914, pp. 221 ff., who attempted to prove that the monopoly was entirely abandoned in the Roman period. Although, as Chwostow showed, P. Lond. II. 286 (p. 183 = W. *Chrest.* 315) does not absolutely prove the existence of a monopoly of the industry by the state in certain villages of the Arsinoite nome, yet it is unsafe to assume, as Chwostow did, that the absence of a trade- or license-tax proved that a monopoly had been abandoned throughout all Egypt.

28. See Chapter XII, pp. 193 ff.

29. Cf. Heichelheim, loc. cit., Sp. 196, who cites W. *Chrest.* 392; BGU. IV. 1188; 1208. iii. 41. Cf. also PO. IV. 732.

30. See Chapter XV, note 21. Cf. PO. XVII. 2116.

31. For the Ptolemaic period cf. P. Petrie III. 115; P. Teb. I. 140. For the Roman period cf. P. Strass. I. 59; P. Mich. II. 123. See Chapter XIII, p. 237.

32. See Chapter XVII, p. 323.

33. XVII. 1, 13 (p. 798).

CHAPTER XII

1. WO. I, pp. 321 ff.

2. Cf. Milne's discussion of the term in O. Theb. p. 153 ff.; see also Chapter VIII, note 70.

3. e.g. in P. Lond. II. 203 (p. 248): ὑπὲρ γερδίων. The phrase παρὰ γερδίων is used in BGU. II. 471. Τέλος and δημόσια are also used to refer to taxes on trades, as well as to other types of taxes.

4. Cf. the report of the amphodarch in SP. IV, pp. 70 ff., columns vii–x. Cf. also the list of weavers of Philadelphia, who were listed in groups of three for the purpose of assigning some liturgical service, in BGU. VII. 1615.

5. Cf. BGU. VII. 1615.

6. On the organization of the guilds cf. San Nicolò, *Ägyptisches Vereinswesen zur Zeit der Ptolemäer und Römer*, Munich 1913, pp. 66–206. For the statement of the occupation of men in the ἀπογραφαὶ κατ' οἰκίαν see Chapter VII, p. 102. In PO. II. 262 notice of the death of a weaver (a slave) is sent to the ἐγλήμπτωρ γερδ(ιακοῦ).

7. The weaving industry was exhaustively studied by Chwostow in the first volume of projected *Studies in the Organization of Industry and of Commerce in Graeco-Roman Egypt*. The first volume entitled *The Textile Industry in Graeco-Roman Egypt* has been cited above

(Chapter XI, note 27). The taxation of the industry is treated in pp. 203 ff. Cf. WO. I, pp. 322 ff.; O. Theb. p. 106; Otto, *Priester und Tempel*, I, pp. 301 ff.; II, pp. 67, note 3, 331 ff., 341; Schwahn in PWRE. A 9, Sp. 285; Reil, *Beiträge zur Kenntnis des Gewerbes im hellenistischen Ägypten*, Borna-Leipzig 1913, pp. 95 ff., 107.

8. See p. 212 of this chapter.

9. WO. II. 23, 27; discussed in WO. I, pp. 322 ff.

10. WO. II. 45, 50, 66, 67.

11. On the monopoly of this class of weaving in the Ptolemaic period cf. Heichelheim, PWRE. XXXI, Sp. 179, and the authorities cited in Sp. 181; cf. also Otto, op. cit. I, pp. 300 ff.; II. 331; Chwostow, op. cit., pp. 69 ff.

12. Op. cit., p. 212.

13. WO. I, p. 324, note 1, suggested that WO. II. 16 was more likely to have come from Thebes than from Elephantine, but Tait is quoted in BL. II. 1 as conjecturing the provenience as Elephantine because of the use of διαγεγράφηκεν and χειρωνάξιον in the formula of the receipt.

14. The provenience is doubtful. Viereck states that the ostracon is probably from Elephantine-Syene, presumably because of the nature of the sherd ('mit weisser oberfläche'). The tax-payer, however, seems to be the same as in O. Strass. 43 and 48 from Thebes, but dated some twenty years earlier. Possibly he had changed his residence; cf. Viereck's note on O. Strass. 43.

15. Milne (Annals of Archaeology and Anthropology VII, p. 51) has attempted to show that payments of 1 or 3 chalci were never made, because there were no such coins.

16. *Archiv*, VI, p. 131, no. 166.

17. SP. XIII, p. 8, no. 2.

18. SB. 676.

19. WO. I, pp. 238 f.; *Archiv*, V, pp. 274 ff. Receipts from Thebes are: O. Tait, p. 95, no. 119; WO. II. 1551; SB. 4327; WO. II. 1040, 476, 1416, 1077, 1059, 1060; O. Strass. 252; WO. II. 574; O. Theb. 56; O. Tait, p. 174, A. 4; p. 160, no. 55; WO. II. 1063, 1064; O. Theb. 57; WO. II. 650, 680; O. Theb. 58; WO. II. 1067, 660; O. Theb. 59; O. Tait, p. 70, no. 43; WO. II, 664; O. Theb. 60–4; WO. II, 1073; O. Tait, p. 71, no. 44; O. Theb. 65–9; WO. II. 1332; *Archiv*, V, p. 176, no. 23; O. Theb. 70.

20. O. Theb., p. 106.

21. In PO. II. 275, P. Teb. II. 384, and PSI. III. 241 the apprenticeship is for a term of one year; in BGU. III. 855 for one year and six months; in PO. II. 322 and PSI. VIII. 902 for two years; in PO. XIV. 1647 for four years; in PO. IV. 725 for five years.

22. See WO. II. 680 and *Nachträge*, p. 436. The restoration is questioned by Viereck in BL. II. 1.

23. Like the theory of multiple rates of the poll-tax once assumed for the Arsinoite and Hermopolite nomes (see Chapter VIII, appendix to notes) it falls of its own weight. There is no evidence from

Lower Egypt, where the contracts for apprenticeship for varying lengths of time are found, for so rigid a control of the weaving industry by the ἱστωνάρχης as is attested for Thebes in WO. II. 1154–6. If such rigid control over the weaving industry was exercised throughout Egypt, perhaps the various classes of weavers could have been sufficiently distinguished in official records to insure collection of the proper tax from weavers of seven or more classes.

24. Cf. the rise in the rate of the χειρωνάξιον at 20 drachmae to 20 drachmae 2 obols at Elephantine-Syene, which occurred between A.D. 68 and 83–4. The receipts for the tax on weavers in the Arsinoite nome are: at 38 drachmae, P. Fay. 48; P. Lond. II. 203 (p. 248); at 38 drachmae 2 obols, P. Teb. II. 602–4; PSI. X. 1139. Cf. also P. Teb. II. 384; PSI. VIII. 902; P. Teb. II. 298; BGU. VII. 1616, 1602, 1591; PSI. IX. 1060; P. Grenf. II. 60; BGU. IV. 1040; PSI. X. 1154; BGU. III. 753; P. Genf. 71; BGU. II. 471 (from the Arsinoite nome according to Grenfell and Hunt in P. Teb. II, Appendix II, § 5, p. 376).

25. Lines 2 ff. read γέρδιός εἰμι τελῶν κατ᾽ ἔτος εἰς τὸ δημόσιο(ν) εἰς λόγον (δραχμὰς) ος.

26. W. Chrest. 325, note on line 4.

27. Cf. the remarks of the editors of BGU. VII. 1616, especially in regard to the diagonal check-marks omitted at the beginning of certain lines. Cf. also the payment in P. Grenf. I. 50, dated A.D. 260, of 76 drachmae to the ἀπαιτη(ταὶ) διδρ(άχμου) γερδίων; the last word is the reading of Wilcken (Archiv, III, p. 120) which is accepted by the BL. I, but was rejected by Grenfell and Hunt in P. Teb. II, p. 98. It is tempting, but hazardous, to identify this payment of 76 drachmae for δίδραχμον γερδίων with the higher rate of γερδιακόν at 76 drachmae attested in BGU. VII. 1616. If the identification should prove correct, it would mean that the depreciation of the currency of Egypt in the third century had not affected the assessment of the tax on weaving until after A.D. 260. There are in the great tax-rolls from Caranis in the collection of the University of Michigan payments for χ( ). Instalments for this tax are credited after the payments for poll-tax are complete. The amount of the tax is 16 drachmae, but there is a λο(ιπόν?) of 20 obols paid by ordinary tax-payers and of 12 obols paid by priests. If this abbreviation is expanded to χ(ειρωνάξιον), as seems possible, the only trade tax which could have been paid by so many people would be the weavers' tax. A payment of 16 drachmae is the same as that of one of the weavers recorded in BGU. VII. 1616, but it will not fit into a scheme of only two rates for the weavers' tax in the Fayûm.

28. PO. II. 309, 310; also ibid. II. 288, 308, 284, 285, XIV. 1647.

29. See Chapter VIII, pp. 129 ff.

30. Cf. Peripl. mar. Erythr. 6, 8; also Archiv, V, p. 389, no. 208; Reil, op. cit., p. 115.

31. See p. 196 and note 27 above.

32. This is the objection raised by Milne (O. Theb., p. 106) against

Wilcken's theory of monthly payments for γερδιακόν at Thebes at a uniform rate, of which my suggestion is a modification. If, however, Chwostow's practice of regarding payments other than 4 or 8 drachmae as irregular instalments on account (despite the statement of the ostraca that 2 drachmae, 6 drachmae, or 10 drachmae are the τέλος of a particular month) is allowed, we can as easily regard a statement that 10 drachmae is the τέλος μηνὸς Θώθ as meaning that previously unpaid instalments totalling 10 drachmae had been due by the month Thoth, when they were paid. In the earlier receipts for γερδιακόν the amount of the tax due in a given month is generally omitted because the amount of the normal instalment was well known to collector and tax-payer; the amount of the instalment is omitted as late as A.D. 193 in O. Theb. 64. Possibly the inclusion of the names of the months is a rather awkward inheritance from the formula of the earlier receipts when the amount of the instalment was ordinarily omitted. Such an awkward use of formulae is not unknown in other types of receipts: cf. SP. XXII. 62, a customs receipt from Socnopaei Nesus dated A.D. 163, which states that 1 drachma was paid as τέλος for ἐπὶ ὄνου ἑνὸς ὄνον ἕνα, although the writer of the receipt obviously meant that the tax was paid for the passage through the toll-gate of one unloaded donkey! It would be surprising, however, if the misleading naming of the months had been continued through so many years, unless we are to regard all receipts giving the amount of the payment in drachmae as exceptional, which is unlikely.

33. O. Strass. 280, which records a payment by two men of 40 drachmae ὑπὲρ τέλ(ους) λινο(ύφων) ἀριθ(μήσεως) μη(νός) ʼΕπείφ. The payment for the ἀρίθμησις of a particular month does not indicate a monthly rate of 20 drachmae, for 240 drachmae a year is an impossibly high annual tax in the first half of the second century. We might, therefore, assume that in many of the receipts, which give a trouble-some amount as the τέλος of a particular month, ἀριθμήσεως should be supplied before μηνός. This, however, would not satisfactorily explain statements that a payment is the τέλος of two or three months.

34. These instalments of 2 drachmae a month were met by payments of 2 drachmae ½ obol 2 chalci, i.e. ʃβ—0 χβ αἰ κ(αἰ) ʃβ. The use of the formula with αἰ κ(αἰ) is unusual in the case of payments for χειρωνάξιον; προσδιαγραφόμενα are seldom recorded in connexion with such payments (cf. Chapter XVII, p. 326). In PO. II. 288 the payments toward the total of 36 drachmae for the annual assessment of the γερδιακὸν ʻΙπποδρόμου are generally made in instalments of 7 drachmae 3 obols or 3 drachmae 4½ obols. The payments cover four years: the payments of Tryphon for the 8th, 9th, and 10th years of the reign of Tiberius, and the payments of Tryphon's father, Dionysius, for the 11th year. The payments of Dionysius for the 11th year and of Tryphon for the 9th year total, respectively, 36 drachmae, the rate of the γερδιακόν attested also in PO. II. 310 and 309. In the 8th year, however, Tryphon is credited with only one payment of 7 drachmae

3 obols, and the editors suggest that he may have paid only part of the weavers' tax in that year because he became fourteen years of age and hence liable to payment of taxes during the course of that year, but they also suggest that the account for that year may be incomplete. The payments of Tryphon in the 10th year are more puzzling, for in lines 11–15 he is credited with instalments totalling 32 drachmae 1½ obols, but in lines 31–4 he is credited for the same year with two payments totalling 7 drachmae 3 obols; the total for the year would, therefore, be 39 drachmae 4½ obols, or 3 drachmae 1½ obols higher than the ordinary assessment. Although Tryphon became fourteen years old only during the 8th year of Tiberius, as is evident from the statement that at the time of the epicrisis in the 41st year of Augustus he was only three years of age, it is rather improbable that the 7 drachmae 3 obols, recorded in lines 29–31, satisfied the assessment upon his trade for that year. That payment is recorded to have been made in Φαμενώθ, the seventh month of the year, so that he must have been engaged in his trade for at least half of the 8th year, and therefore responsible for the tax during that time. He is not credited with any payment of poll-tax for the 8th year, probably because he was not fourteen until after the date when the poll-tax was officially due. The whole document is a copy (ἀντίγραφον) of official receipts, and since a copy of an abstract from the epicrisis is subtended I am inclined to think that the document was prepared in connexion with some dispute over the payment of alleged arrears of taxes, and that it had been necessary to refer to the official records in an effort to disprove the claims of the collectors of arrears. Therefore I believe that the account for the 8th year is incomplete, but that the extra payment in the 10th year was made on account of arrears of the 8th year, especially since the two payments of 3 drachmae 4½ obols each are separated from the rest of the account for that year (although they were made before the rest of the payments for that year), and follow immediately after the account of the payment in the 8th year. I assume, therefore, that Tryphon had paid in the 10th year at the same rate as in the 9th year, that is, at the rate of 36 drachmae a year. It is probable that amounts credited in the account as 7 drachmae 3 obols represent payments of two tetradrachms, and similarly a credit of 3 drachmae 4½ obols represents a payment of one tetradrachm Ordinarily the government charged 1½ obols to the tetradrachm for προσδιαγραφόμενα; on 8 drachmae that would amount to 3 obols. In this document from the Oxyrhynchite nome, however, instead of requiring payment of the surcharge of $\frac{1}{16}$, i.e. requiring payment of 8 drachmae 3 obols or of 4 drachmae 1½ obols, the so-called bankers' discount was used, whereby credit was allowed for but $\frac{15}{16}$ of the total paid in tetradrachms. Eight tetradrachms, therefore, when paid were credited as only 30 drachmae. The final payment in lines 15 and 24 is consequently given as 6 drachmae. There is no indication in the text of any discount or προσδιαγραφόμενα upon the final payment of 6 drachmae. If the 6 drachmae in lines 15 and 24 were actually accepted

at full value, the total actually paid in coin was (8 tetradrachms =
32 drachmae plus 6 drachmae) 38 drachmae, which was the assessment of the tax on weavers in the Arsinoite nome according to
the earlier receipts. If the rates of the γερδιακόν were actually
the same in the Oxyrhynchite and Arsinoite nomes, the later rise
of the rate in the Arsinoite nome to 38 drachmae 2 obols would
merely indicate that προσδιαγραφόμενα were being collected on the
full assessment of 36 drachmae *per annum*; in fact an excess of $\frac{1}{2}$ obol
was being collected, since $\frac{1}{16}$ of 36 drachmae is 2 drachmae $1\frac{1}{2}$ obols;
but if the payments had been calculated upon a bankers' discount, as
they apparently had been in the Oxyrhynchite nome, the additional
2 obols would have represented a slight underpayment, since $\frac{15}{16}$ of
38 drachmae 2 obols is slightly less than 36 drachmae. It is not certain,
however, that the credit of 6 drachmae in lines 15 and 24 of PO. II.
288 had not been subjected to discount for προσδιαγραφόμενα. In the
corresponding payment of lines 5 and 6, the total of 6 drachmae is
obtained by adding two payments (made on the same day) of 3 drach-
mae $4\frac{1}{2}$ obols and 2 drachmae $1\frac{1}{2}$ obols, respectively. If this 3 drachmae
$4\frac{1}{2}$ obols represents the payment of a tetradrachm, then the total paid
in coin was 38 drachmae $1\frac{1}{2}$ obols, if we assume that the credit of 2
drachmae $1\frac{1}{2}$ obols represented the actual amount paid. 38 drachmae
$1\frac{1}{2}$ obols is exactly equal to 36 drachmae plus προσδιαγραφόμενα at
$1\frac{1}{2}$ obols to the tetradrachm. If this, however, is the correct interpretation of the payments in lines 5–6, and similarly of lines 15 and 24,
it is hard to see why the rate of the γερδιακόν in the earlier receipts
from the Arsinoite nome should have been only 38 drachmae, although
it is easy to see why it was raised to 38 drachmae 2 obols. If the rise
in the rate of the γερδιακόν in the Arsinoite nome in the second
century A.D. is correctly explained in this way, the increase of 2 obols
can have no apparent relation to the supposed increase of the χειρωνάξιον at Elephantine-Syene from the rate of 20 drachmae to 20
drachmae 2 obols which had occurred about the middle of the second
half of the first century A.D. There is no evidence in the Arsinoite
nome, however, for an increase of the higher rate of γερδιακόν to 76
drachmae 4 obols, although such a rise may have occurred, especially
if P. Grenf. I. 50 really has nothing to do with the γερδιακόν (cf. note
25, above).

35. Wilcken doubtfully suggested this expansion in WO. II. Zusätze,
p. 441. In the text he had expanded δαπ(ανήματος), and the BL. II.
1 suggests δαπ(ανῆς). P. Hib. 112. 76, dated in the third century B.C.,
records payment of a tax on ταπιδυφάντων.

36. The document is dated by the editors from the character of the
writing. I am not sure that the date in the second century should be
accepted, however, since the much higher rate in this document may
have been caused by depreciation of the currency in the third century
A.D.

37. It is probable that these amounts are incomplete payments on

account rather than different rates of taxation on this particular branch of the weaving industry. The payments are recorded in fragment γ, line 2, and fragment η, lines 2–3.

38. Reil, op. cit., p. 107 and note 10; Chwostow, op. cit., p. 212.

39. The new Liddell and Scott *Greek Lexicon* cites BGU. III. 753. iv. 4 for ἰστωναρχία; ἰστωναρχικόν is not given. Perhaps BGU. III. 753 iv. 1 should be restored Κερ[κε]ήσεως ∫λ[η], the payment of one weaver for a year, and line 2, Λυσιμαχίδος ∫[ρι]δ, the tax of three weavers. The total ∫τξδ (364 drachmae) cannot be divided evenly by 38, but the total may include 22 drachmae for arrears, or some of the payments from villages in the lost portion of column iii may have been incomplete.

40. WO. II. 1154–6.

41. BGU. I. I. 3 (= W. *Chrest.* 92. ii. 3); cf. Chwostow, op. cit., p. 226. Cf. P. Lond. II. 478 (p. 111); P. Teb. II. 305; P. Amh. II. 119; cf. Otto, op. cit. I, pp. 304 ff.; WO. I, p. 616 f. For infrequent (in the Roman period) ὀθονιηρά cf. ibid. I, pp. 266 ff.; P. Ryl. II. 214, 374.

42. Chwostow, op. cit., p. 226; cf. Rostovtzeff in GGA. CLXXI (1909), pp. 615 f., 619, 626 f., 639 ff.

43. Cf. Heichelheim in PWRE. XXXI, Sp. 195; cf. also WO. II. 1487 and WO. I, p. 226.

44. Cf. Chwostow, op. cit., pp. 96 ff., 225.

45. BGU. I. 337. 18 ff. (= W. *Chrest.* 92 i. 18); SP. XXII. 183. 23, 25 ; cf. also P. Lond. II. 286 (p. 184); Wessely, *Karanis und Soknopaiou Nesos*, p. 71.

46. *Archiv*, v, p. 274.

47. Op. cit., p. 219.

48. The guild of potters in the amphodon of ᾿Απολλωνίου παρεμβολή at Arsinoë was required to keep up the amount paid annually despite the death of one of its members who had, therefore, to be replaced, and the absconding of another whose annual tax could not be remitted. Consequently it is probable that the sum paid by the fullers and dyers remained constant from year to year in spite of temporary changes in the number actively engaged in business. For the guild of potters see p. 203 f.

49. W. *Chrest.* 251 introd.

50. *Archiv*, v, p. 273 f. Wilcken was followed by Chwostow, op. cit., p. 218.

51. Op. cit., p. 14, note 8.

52. WO. I, p. 327 f.

53. I do know how Wilcken would reconcile a rate of 24 drachmae a year for the fullers' tax at Thebes in the late second century with his supposed rate of 192 drachmae a year at Tebtynis in the reign of Marcus Aurelius.

54. BGU. IV. 1087. i.

55. SP. IV, p. 70, lines 410–17; P. Teb. II. 305. 5.

56. P. Fay. 58-9; P. Teb. II. 455; P. Grenf. II. 60; P. Amh. II. 119; P. Lond. II. 478 (p. 111); BGU. II. 617. Cf. Otto, op. cit. I, p. 302.

57. Unless, of course, Wilcken should prove to be correct in his interpretation of P. Teb. II. 287.

58. Op. cit., p. 213 and the references there cited.

59. WO. II. 464, 1039, 1069-72, 1282; O. Theb. 75; O. Tait, p. 95, no. 120; all from Thebes. The amounts paid in WO. II. 1282 have been disputed by BL. II. 1.

60. WO. II. 658, 1062, 1065, 1462, 1585, 1591. In O. Tait, p. 71, no. 45, the τελ(ῶναι) θησ( ) ἱερῶν collect one drachma ὑπὲρ τελ( ) ταφῆς μιᾶς; this is perhaps a variation of the same tax received by different collectors, but why the rate should be only one-half that in the receipts in WO. II, is not clear.

61. WO. I, pp. 304 ff.

62. So I interpret the phrases in SP. IV, p. 70 f., lines 391 f., 404 f., 425 f.

63. Ibid., line 391.

64. Ibid., lines 391-3, 403-6, 425-7.

65. Cf. τὸ αἱροῦν in P. Ryl. II. 167. 25.

66. SP. IV, p. 70, line 396 lists the total payments of all the potters in the fourth year (A.D. 71-2) as τῶν δι(ὰ) προσγ(ράφου or -ων).

67. See Chapter XIII, p. 224 f.

68. WO. II. 385; Archiv, IV, p. 146, no. 6 (= O. Strass. 54).

69. BL. I, p. 454.

70. P. Fay. 36; Aegyptus XIV (1933), p. 430.

71. The word is spelled κασιδηραταις in the text of BGU. IV. 1087. iv.

72. Schwahn (PWRE. A 9, SP. 286) states that κασσιτεροποιοί paid a tax of 36 drachmae annually, but his reference to WO. II. 672 is wrong, and I do not know of any evidence for such a rate.

73. P. Lond. inv. 1562 verso.

74. Cf. WO. I, pp. 227 ff.

75. In the gnomon for the market at the Serapeum in Oxyrhynchus all the rates of trade-taxes (except for the κοινωνεῖα and, of course, for the sales-taxes) were based on an annual assessment. No barbers, however, are included in this gnomon, and it is possible that this particular market was under special regulations which did not apply to other markets or business-establishments in the city. But until evidence to the contrary is presented it seems best to regard the 6 drachmae assessed upon barbers as an annual rate.

76. BGU. I. 337. 21; SP. XXII. 183. C. J. Kraemer, Jr., and F. A. Spencer, 'New Light on the Ταριχευτής in Augustan Egypt', in TAPA. LXV (1934), p. xlv.

77. Τέλος ὀνηλατῶν: WO. II. 392, 395, 684, 1054, all from Thebes. Τέλος ἁμαξῶν: ibid. II. 392, 395, 1054, 1057, 1261, all from Thebes.

78. Ibid. I, p. 292.

79. BGU. IV. 1087. v.

80. P. Teb. II. 612.

81. P. Lond. inv. 1562 *verso*: πα(ρὰ) καθαρουργ(είου ?) ἑκα(στοῦ) ἐργ(άτου)∫ κδ.

82. *Archiv*, v, p. 274. On the monopoly see Chapter XI, pp. 184 ff.

83. The meaning of λάχανον is uncertain, although it is usually supposed that it refers to vegetables in general.

84. PWRE. A 9, Sp. 285. 18.

85. See Chapter XIII, p. 224.

86. BGU. I. 9. i.

87. Ibid. IV. 1087. ii. The word for beer-sellers is restored as ζ[υτᾶτα]ις by Wilcken in *Archiv*, v, p. 275, instead of the ζ[υτοπώλα]ις of the text.

88. WO. I, p. 136, followed by Schwahn, PWRE. A 9, Sp. 286. Cf. WO. II. 1330 (from Thebes and dated A.D. 160) in which a total of 6 drachmae ὑπὲρ τέλο‹υ›ς μεταβολ(ῆς) ἁλιε‹ί›ων is paid to the ἐπιτηρητ(αὶ) τέλους ἀγορανομ(ίας); WO. II. 1331 is similar.

89. P. Ryl. II. 196. The tax was paid διὰ Σοκμήνεως καὶ τῶν λοιπῶν ἡγου(μένων); cf. San Nicolò, *Vereinswesen*, pp. 95 and 135; also WO. I, p. 136.

90. See Chapter XIII, p. 219 f.

91. PWRE. A 9, Sp. 386. 48; cf. WO. I, p. 400.

92. WO. I, p. 218, and note 1.

93. *Archiv*, VI, p. 219, no. 5.

94. The supposed example of a tax called ἐτα‹ι›ρίσματα in P. Grenf. II. 41 (cited by WO. I, p. 219) has been otherwise restored by Mitteis in his *Chrestomathie* (II), 183, introd.

95. Suetonius, *Gaius*, 40; cf. also the references collected in WO. I, p. 217, note 2.

96. WO. I, p. 217, note 3.

97. The evidence from Thebes and from Oxyrhynchus seems to confirm Wilcken's contention that the assessment of the tax was on a monthly basis. Perhaps the evidence of WO. II. 83 from Elephantine contradicts this only because the ἑταῖραι of that village could offer no such variety of quality as Wilcken has shown to have been available at Athens and Palmyra (cf. ibid. I, p. 217, note 3).

98. The κακιοπώλης sold, I believe, the κάκεις mentioned by Strabo (XVII, 2. 5 (824)) as a peculiar kind of bread. The only other possibility, so far as I can see, is that κακιοπώλης was miswritten for κικιοπώλης, sellers of *kiki*. The use of *kiki*-oil was widespread in Egypt, according to Strabo (loc. cit.), and the plant is frequently mentioned in the papyri, so that it would not be unnatural to find a seller of *kiki* at the market at the Serapeum. But the scribe of P. Lond. inv. 1562 *verso* seems very careful, and it is more likely that the reading κακιοπ(ῶλαι) is correct.

99. Καρπῶ(ναι) means literally *buyers* of fruit.

100. It does not seem possible to restore σκυτοποιοί from Mr. Skeat's reading, but I can think of no other trade which bears any

relationship to the reading. A tax on shoemakers (τέλος σκυτέων) is attested for the Ptolemaic period in WO. II. 334 and 1359.

101. At the present time alum is peddled in the streets and from door to door in the towns of Egypt. It is used in an incense to ward off the evil eye, and it is probable that this custom is connected with the practical use of alum in the treatment of trachoma. The alum used for incense is now peddled by women; and, on the assumption that such customs have not essentially changed since the writing of our document, I would expand πολο(υσῶν) rather than πολο(ύντων); the following word should perhaps be expanded ἰδιω(τικῶς). It may be noted that in this same document the salt is peddled by women.

102. The meaning of κωδᾶς was doubtfully suggested by the editors of PO. XII. 1519.

103. Cf. note 102 above.

104. There is some doubt that this document is a list of payments for trade-tax, because a payment in line 6 could be interpreted as for oil, and the editors suggested that the document might be an official record of sales of oil by the state-monopoly, which would thus have continued to a late date. I do not believe that this explanation of the document is so likely as its interpretation as a list of payments for χειρωνάξιον. With this interpretation, the ἑρμηνεὺς ἐλαίου may be compared with the ἑρμηνία ἀλοπωλῶν in P. Fay. 23. If, then, the payments are for χειρωνάξιον, the rates should be compared with those of BGU. I. 9, and IV. 1087 and Archiv, v, p. 273 f., for PO. XII. 1517 is dated in A.D. 272 or 278, and therefore is about contemporary with those documents from the Arsinoite nome. The rates of the Arsinoite documents have been collected by Wilcken in Archiv, v, p. 274, as follows:

ἐλαιοπῶλαι	.	.	.	.	(annually)	96	drachmae
ἀρτοκόπαι	.	.	.	.	,,	96	,,
στιβεῖς	.	.	.	.	,,	96	,,
γρυτοπῶλαι	.	.	.	.	,,	144	,,
ζυτοπῶλαι	.	.	.	.	,,	192	,,
γναφεῖς	.	.	.	.	,,	192	,,
βαφεῖς	.	.	.	.	,,	288	,,
ἀρτυματᾶτες	.	.	.	.	,,	432	,,
κασσιτερᾶτες	.	.	.	.	,,	432	,,
μυροπῶλαι	.	.	.	.	,,	720	,,
φακινᾶς	.	.	.	.	,,	1,200	,,

105. WO. I, pp. 321 ff. and the references there cited; SB. 1932; O. Br.-Berl. 28, 29; SB. 4353; Archiv v, p. 170, nos. 21, 22; O. Br.-Berl. 39; O. Tait, p. 176, C. 2; O. Br.-Berl. 46; O. Tait, p. 67, no. 23; cf. also O. Tait, p. 160, no. 56; PO. XII. 1436; P. Teb. II. 579.

106. Perhaps στουππτηρίου was written for στυπτηρίου, or στουπ-πούργου for στιππούργου.

CHAPTER XIII

1. See Chapter III, p. 23 f.; also Lesquier, *L'Armée Romaine d'Égypte*, pp. 350 ff. Some of these contributions were more in the nature of liturgies than of taxes in kind; cf. BGU. VII. 1564.

2. Cf. Rostovtzeff, *Röm. Mitt.* XI (1896), pp. 317 ff.; Wochenschr. f. kl. Phil. XVII (1900), Sp. 115; *Catalogue des plombes de la Bibl. Nationale*, p. 10; *Social and Economic History*, pp. 379, 536, 611 f., 618; also Zucker, *Philol.* LXX (1911), pp. 79 ff.; Reil, *Beiträge*, pp. 9, 17, note 7; Jouguet, *P. Thead.*, p. 184, note on line 25 of no. 34; Persson, *Staat u. Manufaktur im Röm. Reich*, Lund 1923, p. 35; Chwostow, *Textile Industry in Graeco-Roman Egypt*, Kazan 1914, pp. 214 ff.; Lewis, *L'Industrie du Papyrus dans l'Égypte Gréco-Romaine*, Paris 1934, pp. 140 ff. For other views cf. Mommsen, *Ann. d. Inst.* XXI (1849), p. 214, followed by Marquardt, *St.-V.* II², p. 234, note 4; Kubitschek in PWRE. I. 2, Sp. 2016; Humbert in D.-S. Dict. d. Ant. I, p. 259; also Cantarelli in *Bull. com.* XVI (1888), pp. 366 ff.; followed by Ruggiero, *Dizionario Epigrafico*, I, p. 463; also Borghesi, *Œuvres*, III, p. 132.

3. SHA. *Aurelian*, 45.

4. There was probably a partial monopoly of the papyrus industry in the Roman period; see Chapter XI, p. 189. On pp. 611 ff. of the *Social and Economic History* Rostovtzeff states that the manufacture of the articles comprised in the *anabolicae species* was monopolized by the state in the Ptolemaic period. Perhaps this limitation in period was in answer to Reil's objection cited in the text of this chapter. There is no evidence, however, that the manufacture of glass was monopolized by the state in the Ptolemaic period; and it is unlikely, since that industry was of no consequence until the discovery of the process of blowing glass in the reign of Augustus.

5. Rostovtzeff, *Röm. Mitt.* XI (1896), pp. 320 ff., derived *anabolicum* from ἀναβάλλειν which he explained as meaning 'to load a ship'. Wilcken, *Grundz.*, p. 249, pointed out that the term for loading a ship was not ἀναβάλλειν but ἐμβάλλειν; he did not, however, offer any suggestion as to the correct explanation of ἀναβολικόν. Persson, op. cit., p. 36, contrasts *anabolicae species* with *annonariae species*; the latter term he refers to such products as grain and wine and oil, which were used, as a rule, when not older than one year; therefore he regarded the former as including products which could be stored ('thrown up') for an indefinite length of time and withdrawn from storage whenever need arose. Rostovtzeff now in *Social and Economic Hist.*, p. 611 f., derives ἀναβολικόν from ἀναβάλλειν meaning 'to deal out' (a portion of a certain kind of goods for export to Rome).

6. OGI. II. 669. 21.

7. Cf., however, the editors of the document and also the new Liddell and Scott, where ἀναβολικόν is cited from this papyrus as meaning a 'deferred payment', from the common meaning of ἀναβάλλειν,

'to put off'. Lewis, op. cit., p. 140, note 2, suggests that the writer of the letter in P. Amh. II. 131 was a farmer of the ἀναβολικόν.

8. *Social and Ec. Hist.*, p. 611 f.

9. Cf. A. C. Johnson, AJA. xxxviii (1934), p. 53 f.

10. See Chapter XII, p. 213.

11. See Chapter III, p. 23 f.

12. Cf. D.-S., *Dict. d. Ant.* I, p. 259, sub *Anabolicae species*, note 2, where, however, the reference is wrong.

13. Tacitus, *Annales*, II. 56–7; cf. Marsh, *The Reign of Tiberius*, London 1931, pp. 90 ff.

14. Cf. Furneaux's edition of Tacitus, *Annales*, Appendix II to Book II.

15. The army of 50,000, to the command of which Vespasian was appointed, would have required extensive preparations for its support, and the campaign lasted until after the fall of Jerusalem in A.D. 70. It is quite improbable that the ἀναβολικά mentioned by Ti. Julius Alexander could have been intended for the use of the Rhine army during the revolt of Vindex, for that event did not take place until too near the date of Ti. Julius Alexander's decree.

16. Cf. Westermann in JEA. XI (1925), pp. 165 ff.

17. Cf. Heichelheim in PWRE. xxxi, Sp. 187, and the references there cited.

18. Cf. WO. II. 326, 337, 339, 340, 346, 349, 1029, 1233, 1347, 1348, 1522; BGU. VI. 1312–18; W. *Chrest.* 167; P. Paris, 67. 15; O. Tait, p. 13, nos. 76, 79; p. 14, no. 80; p. 19, no. 108; WO. II. 331; O. Tait, p. 6, no. 38.

19. Grenfell and Hunt (P. Teb. II. 347. 23, note) suggested that the τέλος ἰχθυηρᾶς δρυμῶν and a tax paid by ἁλιεῖς on Lake Moeris (BGU. I. 220–1, III. 756) both correspond to the Ptolemaic τετάρτη ἁλιέων; but cf. Heichelheim, PWRE. xxxi, Sp. 187. 31.

20. BGU. I. 337 (= W. *Chrest.* 92).

21. SP. xxii. 183. 35.

22. The term ἐναποσημαιομένων, referring to some seal set upon boats which had fishing privileges, might apply equally well to boats leased from the state or to boats owned by the temple which received a seal as a mark of the concession of rights to fish on the waterways of the state. The concession was sublet by the temple; cf. Wessely, *Karanis und Soknopaiu Nesos* (Denkschr. Akad. Wien, XLVII (1902)), p. 72; also P. Teb. II. 298. 33 and note.

23. BGU. II. 653: Ἀντω( ) ουσ( ) φο( ) πλο( ); cf. ibid. I. 212.

24. Cf. O. Mey. 84. 2; 4 drachmae are recorded as the payment for πλι^a which was unintelligible to Meyer. It may, however, have been written for πλοια( ) = πλοια(ρίων), or possibly πλοίο(υ) or πλοίω(ν) should be read. If one of these readings is correct, and the boats were used for fishing, this would be the only case of a tax on fishing from Upper Egypt as yet attested for the Roman period. Cf. also BGU. I. 199 *verso*.

25. Cf. ὠνή in line 15.

26. Cf. P. Teb. II. 308. 4, note, and the reference to Pliny, *N. H.* XXV. 74 there cited. It is not entirely certain whether the μισθωταὶ δρυμῶν καὶ ἐρήμου αἰγιαλοῦ Πολέμωνος μερίδος, who in P. Teb. II. 308 give a receipt to a priest for the price of 20,000 papyrus stalks at Ibion Argaei, are to be identified with the μισθωταὶ ἰχθυηρᾶς δρυμῶν of BGU. II. 485. It is not impossible that the leases of these μισθωταί of government marshes may have differed in their terms from time to time or in different places. The comprehensive title of the collectors (μισθωταί) in P. Teb. II. 308 may be misleading.

27. The report also mentions ὑποδόχια at Hephaestias, but the ἐπιτηρητής states that nothing had been received on account of them from the θηρᾶς ἰχθυίας up to the end of the year. These reservoirs had, however, been used by οἱ ἀπὸ κώμης who had paid the ἀπότακτος φόρος demanded by the strategus. It is possible, therefore, that the ὑποδόχια had originally been intended for the catch of fish belonging to the state-monopoly.

28. P. Teb. II, Appendix II, sub. Καινὴ κώμη.

29. BGU. I. 221; cf. also BGU. I. 220 of uncertain provenience.

30. Cf. Mau, *Pompeii*, Engl. transl., New York 1904, pp. 388 ff.

31. BGU. IV. 1062. 3 (= W. *Chrest.* 276); P. Lond. III. 856. 17 (p. 91); P. Fay. 42 (a). iii. 10; P. Amh. II. 56. 7 (?); PO. XVII. 2128. 10 and note; P. Ryl. II. 167. 20 and note.

32. According to the note of the editors on line 16 of PSI. VII. 787, Rostovtzeff proposed to read [πάσης τῆς ἀρτο]ποιίας because the plural διπλωμάτων would thus be justified by the various kinds of ἀρτοποιία. Perhaps, however, we may restore [καὶ δ' τῆς ἀρτο]ποιίας, if it is possible to equate ἀρτοποιία with the profession of the ἀρτοπώλης.

33. Cf. P. Fay. 15; P. Petrie III. 58 (c); 117 (h).

34. PO. XVII. 2128.

35. See Chapter XII, p. 207.

36. WO. I, p. 373.

37. The editors of P. Fay. 23 a (introd.) suggested that γυψική was a plasterers' tax; this is accepted by the new Liddell and Scott, *Greek Lexicon*.

38. The προσδιαγραφόμενα are stated to be 1 obol 1 chalcus on 8 drachmae, a strangely low rate (see Chapter XVII, pp. 324 ff.).

39. WO. II. 1363.

40. Cf. the citations collected in Preisigke-Kiessling WB. III, Abschn. II, p. 251, sub τετάρτη for the τετάρτη τῶν ἁλιειῶν, τετάρτη ἀρτοπωλῶν, (τετάρτη) ὑπὲρ φόρου γενῶν ζωγραφικῶν, τετάρτη σίτου, τετάρτη σιτοποιῶν, τετάρτη τοῦ ταρίχους.

41. See Chapter IX, p. 155 f.

42. Cf. P. Hib. 116. 1, and note.

43. PO. XII. 1436. 2, 20, 39; P. Ryl. II. 213. 474. Cf. also the leases of a bath in P. Mich. II. 121 *verso*, VII. 12; also 123 *recto*, XIII. 27.

44. P. Lond. III. 1171. 72 (p. 177); the provenience of this document is uncertain.

45. Meyer stated that a land-tax was indicated by the phrase καθήκοντα τέλη in εἰς τὰ καθ(ήκοντα) περιγι(νομένων) ὑπ( ) Θεαδελ( ), since that phrase is used of land-taxes. Καθήκοντα τέλη, however, is also used of other kinds of taxes: in PO. II. 245. 21 τὸ καθῆκον τέλος refers to a tax on sheep; O. Br.-Berl. 47 is a receipt for τὸ κ(αθῆκον) τέλ(ος) issued for the month Μεσορή by the ἐπιτ(ηρηταὶ) ἀγορα(νομίας), which doubtless refers to a trade-tax, although probably of the capitation type.

46. These articles are designated in the document as ἐλά(ας), φοί-(νικας) σικ(ύας) καὶ κολοκύνθ(ας) καὶ λάχ(ανα). The phrase used for the dealers is τῶ(ν) ει . σατο( ) κ(αὶ) πω[λ]ο(ύντων). Although εἰσα-γο(ύντων) does not fit the reading of the mutilated second word as given by Mr. Skeat, some special classification was applied to these articles which made this rate of 2 obols a package applicable to their sale, since later in the document a rate is given for the tax on the sale of dates (φοίν(ικες)) at 6 drachmae (?) per palm-leaf basket; further a capitation tax was assessed upon the ordinary seller of λάχανα in line 13. I can see no reason for this differentiation, except a preferential tariff collected through this sales-tax.

47. The symbol in the papyrus interpreted as 2 obols by Mr. Skeat is Ƶ.

48. It is not easy to see why beans and condiments were distinguished from the olives, dates, cucumbers, pumpkins, and vegetables, since they were both assessed at the same rate. Possibly the unit of measure for beans and condiments was different, although it is not given in the text of the document.

49. In Egypt at the present day salt is sold by women in the streets of the towns and villages. This salt is in large lumps as it comes from the mines in the mountains, and is highly prized by the modern Egyptians. Πλ(άκους) is the only expansion of a Greek word known to me which gives any sense in this passage, but it is rather doubtful whether πλάκους can bear the meaning of 'large lump'. Πλ( ) might easily be the abbreviation of some hitherto unattested designation of weight or measure.

50. Λ[ατό]μ(ων) seems to be the only attested Greek word which will fit the lacuna. It is rather difficult to see, however, why a quarry-man appears in a classification consisting of purveyors of fertilizer. Λατόμος may, perhaps, have been a popular designation for a digger of sebakh which was probably used in Roman times as well as to-day for fertilizer.

51. See Chapter XII, p. 204.

52. The jars purchased for the waterworks of the metropolis (in P. Lond. III. 1177 (p. 180), lines 158–63) at 6 drachmae per hundred might well have been taxed at 1 drachma a cart-load or donkey-load

53. See Chapter III, p. 23 f.

54. Cf. the καρπῶναι of P. Lond. inv. 1562 *verso* cited in Chapter XII, p. 211.

55. The phrase is τέλ(ος) παγης (?) βοὸς λ [. . . .]. Παγης, if correctly read, may mean a fastening of some kind; it may, on the other hand, be a hitherto unknown adjective whose meaning in this phrase is not clear.

56. See Chapter IX, pp. 164 ff.

57. P. Fay. 62. See Chapter XVII, note 265, end.

58. Cf. Revillout in *Proceed. Soc. Bibl. Arch.* XIV (1892), pp. 120 ff.

59. Cf. Westermann, *Upon Slavery in Ptolemaic Egypt*, London 1929, pp. 43 ff.; also P. Teb. II. 350, introd.

60. This is the conventional statement; cf. Westermann, op. cit., p. 45; P. Teb. II. 350, introd.; PO. X. 1284, introd. The statement rests, however, on rather slight evidence. In extant published documents the amount paid for the tax is $\frac{1}{10}$ of the amount recorded as the sale-price of the property in only three documents: PO. I. 99; II. 242, 333. All of these documents are from the Oxyrhynchite nome and all are dated in the first century after Christ. In PO. II. 242 and 333 the tax is $\frac{1}{10}$ of the principal, only if the editors are correct in regarding the sums recorded in silver drachmae as equivalent to those given in copper drachmae at a ratio of 1 : 450. In P. Teb. II. 580 the amount of the ἐγκύκλιον is given as 160 drachmae, but the selling price is restored by the editors as 2 talents 400 drachmae. Were this correct the rate of the tax would be scarcely more than 1 per cent. The document, however, is concerned with the sale of a fourth interest in the house, which probably indicates that the house was a part of an estate which had not been settled by the heirs before this sale; and if 1 talent is restored instead of 2 talents in the selling price, the price of the whole house would have been 6,400 drachmae, $\frac{1}{4}$ of which is 1,600 drachmae upon which a tax of 160 drachmae, that is $\frac{1}{10}$, is recorded in this document. In all other documents from Lower Egypt which deal with the ἐγκύκλιον the rate is not given, or is lost because the document is incomplete, or is larger than 10 per cent. as indicated in the text of this chapter. In addition to the four documents mentioned above, the ἐγκύκλιον is mentioned in the following papyri from Lower Egypt: P. Ryl. II. 118; P. Teb. II. 587; BGU. III. 748. ii; P. Teb. II. 350; BGU. III. 914; P. Lond. II. 297 b (p. 110); P. Teb. II. 351; P. Lond. III. 933 (p. 69) (= W. *Chrest.* 294); PO. II. 238 (= M. *Chrest.* (II.) 213), XII. 1462, XVII. 2129, X. 1284; P. Ryl. II. 215; P. Teb. II. 508; P. Lond. III. 1217 (p. 61); PO. II. 238; W. *Chrest.* 392; P. Flor. I. I. 6; P. Lond. III. 1158 (p. 151) (= M. *Chrest.* (II.) 256); SB. 7173. 11.

61. WO. II. 473, 1378, 1599; O. Tait, p. 88, no. 81; p. 158, nos. 40-1; O. Mey. 23. 6; O. Theb. 40 (?).

62. Cf. Westermann, op. cit., p. 41.

63. Ibid.

64. Ibid.; also p. 45.

65. Ibid. with reference to P. Columbia inv. 480, paragraph 2, line 11.

66. Cf. also BL. I on line 19 of PO. I. 99. Cf. the title of a collector in P. 8953 quoted by WO. I, p. 575 : ἐγλ(ήμπτωρ) . . . . ϊ ἀγορα(νομίας); since the assessment of the ἐγκύκλιον was under the superintendence of the ἀγορανομία perhaps the title should be restored ἐγλ(ήμπτωρ) [ὅ καὶ] ϊ ἀγορα(νομίας); cf. the τελ(ώνης) ῥ καὶ ικ in O. Mey. 77 and see the discussion in note 91 below.

67. Quoted in the note on line 21 of P. Lond. III. 933 (p. 69).

68. In PO. XIV 1697, a sale of a courtyard in A.D. 242, the provision is recorded that the καταγραφῆς τέλη and the γραμματικά are to be paid by the vendor of the property. Such charges added to the ἐγκύκλιον may have increased the τέλη διαγραφῆς to the figure in PO. X. 1284.

69. The sum is so large that the fee must have been exceptional; it could hardly have been collected, in addition to the ἐγκύκλιον, on every sale.

70. P. Lond. II. 305 (p. 79): ἐπιτη(ρη)τ(αῖς) ἐκ‹σ›τάσ(εως) καὶ δεκ(άτης). It is not known whether this tax was paid by Roman citizens in Egypt. Similarly it is not known whether the Greek and native inhabitants of Egypt paid the same inheritance-tax as the resident Roman citizens; see p. 234 of this chapter.

71. PO. II. 243.

72. PO. II. 274 (= M. Chrest. (II.) 193 = Meyer, J.P. 60); PO. VIII. 1105.

73. PO. III. 510. 20; II. 348.

74. Cf. WO. I, p. 190.

75. PO. I. 96, introd.; cf., however, Westermann, op. cit., p. 45; cf. SB. 7533.

76. Cf. P. Strass. 79 and the remarks thereon in PO. XII. 1523, introd.

77. Partsch, Sitzungsber. Akad. Heidelberg, VII (1916), Abh. 10, p. 41, note 1, states that ἐγκυκλεῖον, a bureau concerned with the tax on sales, is to be distinguished from ἐγκύκλιον, the tax; he therefore corrected the accent of ἐγκύκλιον in PO. I. 95. 26 to ἐγκυκλῖον which was accepted by the BL. I, and by Meyer, J. P. 34 (cf. ibid. 7. 6, note). PO. I. 95 has been republished by Hunt and Edgar in Select Papyri (Loeb Edition), I. 32, where the accent as marked in the original publication has been retained.

78. BGU. I. 96. 8.

79. Cf. note 70 above.

80. Elephantine: WO. II. 1051 (see BL. II. 1); cf. also P. Paris 17. 22, which mentions a μισθωτὴς εἴδους ἐγκυκλίου καὶ ὑποκειμένων βασιλικῷ γραμματεῖ. Thebes: WO. II. 1066, 1454.

81. Cf. the ἀπόμοιρα in Chapter V, p. 54, especially note 35.

82. Following Wilcken, introd. to Chrest. 175.

83. Cf. Westermann, op. cit., pp. 45 ff.

84. See Chapter X, p. 179 f.

85. SP. XXII. 50; cf. P. Fay. 65. 5; BGU. VII. 1588. Grenfell and Hunt (P. Teb. II. 357. 3, note) have pointed out that the τέλος

καταλοχισμῶν on an original grant of catoecic land from the government would be parallel to the fees exacted in the Ptolemaic period in the shape of the προσλήψεως στέφανος.

86. See p. 234 f. of this chapter.

87. e.g. P. Teb. I. 113.

88. P. Hamb. 84; BGU. I. 328, II. 622. The editors of PO. XVII. 2129 in the introduction note that the τέλος καταλοχισμῶν there is generally, but not invariably, about ⅙ of the ἐγκύκλιον on the same transaction in that document. If the τέλη καταλοχισμῶν in the Oxyrhynchite nome were assessed in the manner indicated by the gnomon (P. Iand. 137) for the Arsinoite nome, that proportion is but a coincidence, since the ἐγκύκλιον was an ad valorem tax, whereas the τέλη καταλοχισμῶν were assessed at fixed rates κατ' ἄρουραν.

89. See Chapter I, p. 2, and Chapter X, pp. 176 ff.

90. PO. VIII. 1114; cf. the references cited in the introd.; also BGU. I. 240. 10, 326. ii. 10.

91. O. Mey. 77 from Thebes (?) and dated A.D. 92, is a receipt: Ἀπέχω τὸ ι κλ τοῦ ιαˡ. This is apparently a tax assessed at 10 per cent. For the expansion of the abbreviation κλ Meyer suggested κλ(ηρούχων) or κλ(ηρονομιῶν); but since the formula seems to indicate that the receipt is for an annual tax, he regarded the latter expansion as impossible. The collector is called the τελ(ώνης) ρ κ̣α̣ὶ̣(?) ιˡ. It will be remembered that the tax of 10 per cent. on the sale of property in PO. I. 99 was followed by an ἐπιδέκατον, and that in P. Teb. II. 351 the τέλος on a sale of property was exactly 11 per cent. Consequently it is tempting to see in this τελώνης a collector of the ἐγκύκλιον, especially since in O. Theb. 40 we find a receipt ὑπ(ὲρ) ἐνκ(υκλίου) κλ( ) αϛ. In the latter case, too, the apparent designation of the tax as annual is against the expansion κλ(ηρονομιῶν). Possibly the abbreviation should be expanded κλ(ηρουχιῶν) on the assumption that κληροῦχοι held the only private land around Thebes, so that the ἐγκύκλιον on cessions of land was paid only by them; or if there was private land other than cleruchic land the latter paid a special rate of ἐγκύκλιον on transfers. If, in spite of the objection to the apparently annual character of these payments, κλ(ηρονομιῶν) is the correct expansion of the abbreviation, we have 11 per cent. (or 10 per cent.) as the rate of the inheritance-tax paid by the native inhabitants of Egypt.

92. In Recherches, pp. 307 ff.

93. P. Lips. 10. ii. 20–1; cf. introd. and references there cited.

94. Cf. PO. XII. 1475. 42, note.

95. e.g. PO. IV. 719. 29–31.

96. Cf. διανομὴ ἀρουρῶν in PO. XII. 1490 introd.

97. PO. I. 56. 22, XII. 1473. 30.

98. PO. II. 274; Meyer, J. P. 60.

99. Meyer, J. P. 60.

100. P. Teb. II. 397, 399; BGU. III. 825.

101. Cf. P. Teb. I. 61 (b). 342 note.

102. P. Teb. II. 345; BGU. III. 820; PO. XIV. 1650, 1650 (a), XII. 1473, XIV. 1697, 1651; P. Fay. 42 (a): (γραμματ(ικοῦ) φυλ(άκων)); P. Lond. I. 131. 131 (p. 166).

103. P. Michigan II. 123 recto I. (a). 16; (b). 23; (d). 7, 8, 17; verso II. 12; IV. 8; V. 7, 22, 28; X. 6; XI. 3; 128, II. 36. Cf. Boak's remarks on p. 100. Cf. also P. Strass. 59. 15; BGU. I. 277. ii. 11.

104. WO. I. 403 (cf. Archiv, I, p. 552). Zucker (Philologus, LXX (1911), p. 97) maintained that the χαρτηρά was a tax on the manufacture of papyrus for writing purposes, which he considered a private industry under state control; but as Boak points out, the fact that the χαρτηρά was collected by those in charge of the γραφεῖον does not support Zucker's view. Lewis (L'Industrie du papyrus de l'Égypte gr.-rom., Paris 1934, pp. 145 ff.) suggests that the χαρτηρά was a tax which served to legalize a document (and he compares 'le timbre fiscal d'aujourd'hui').

105. Cf. P. Mich. II, p. 101.

106. In Yale Classical Studies, IV (1934), pp. 229 ff.

CHAPTER XIV

1. On the priests and temples under the New Empire and down to the Persian conquest cf. Breasted, History of Egypt, chapter xiii and pp. 489–528, 574–6. The confiscation of a portion of the temples' wealth by Amasis (mentioned by Breasted, p. 592) was but one of the temporary checks which the priesthood suffered and from which it recovered rapidly because of its control over the sources of wealth. For the Ptolemaic period cf. Bevan, History of Egypt (ed. by W. Flinders Petrie), IV[2], pp. 80, 177–88, 204–14, 262–8, 316–17, 322–3, 346–9, 388–92, where the important documents are translated or analysed. See also Bell in CAH. x, p. 290. Cleopatra, like Amasis, temporarily injured the wealth of the temples by confiscating τὰ ἐκ τῶν ἁγιωτάτων ἱερῶν ἀναθήματα (Dio Cassius, LI. 17. 6; cf. LI. 5. 4–5), but this hardly affected the sources of the temples' wealth.

2. Cf. Bell in CAH. x, p. 291; Otto, Priester u. Tempel, pp. 58 ff.; P. M. Meyer, Festschr. f. Hirschfeld, pp. 157 ff., and H. S. Jones, Fresh Light on Roman Bureaucracy (Oxford, 1920), pp. 22 ff., pointed out that the offices of High-Priest of All Egypt and of Idiologus were probably not held by one man before the end of the second century after Christ. This is disputed, however, by Th. Reinach, in Rev. de l'histoire des religions, LXXXV (1929), p. 17, and by Reinmuth, The Prefect of Egypt from Augustus to Diocletian (Klio, Beiheft 34), pp. 28 ff., referring to Otto, Priester u. Tempel, I, pp. 66 ff.; but there is no actual evidence for their contention that the offices were united by Hadrian.

3. In the second century after Christ the financial administration of the temples was controlled by the department of the treasury called

ἴδιος λόγος, to which were assigned the revenues from φόρος βωμῶν, ἐπιστατικὸν ἱερέων, εἰσκριτικόν; on these taxes see pp. 248 ff. of this chapter; cf. also Meyer, op. cit., p. 159. There is no evidence that the department of the Idiologus was in charge of the priestly revenues before the
reign of Hadrian, and Reinmuth (op. cit., pp. 28 ff.) argues that this step
was taken by Hadrian, since the priests seem to have appealed directly to
the prefect concerning the administration of their property and finances
during the first century after Christ.

4. *Priester u. Tempel*, pp. 261–403.

5. See Chapter I, p. 4; Chapter VIII, p. 119.

6. Revillout in *Rev. ég.* I, p. 82, argued that the σύνταξις was introduced by the Ptolemies because the word is merely transliterated in
the demotic version of the Rosetta Stone; cf. Otto, op. cit., pp. 370 ff.
The argument was accepted by Bevan, *Hist. of Egypt*, IV², p. 188.

7. For a payment in money cf. BGU. III. 707; payments in kind,
Archiv, V, p. 287 (188 R). On the syntaxis in general cf. Otto, op. cit.,
pp. 366 ff.

8. In CAH. X, p. 291.

9. BGU. IV. 1197, 1200; *Archiv*, V, p. 387 (188 R); P. Lond. II. 359
(p. 150); P. Teb. II. 298. 58, 302 *passim*; BGU. III. 707; SP. XXII. 184.
94; PO. VII. 1046; P. Ross.-Georg. III. 26 (cf. W. *Chrest.* 82).

10. Cf. Index in WO. II, pp. 448 ff.; also Calderini, pp. 119 ff. and
pp. 36, 39, 45.

11. See Chapter IX, p. 157 f.

12. e.g. a μέτρον τετραχοίνικον θησαυροῦ θεοῦ at Tebtynis (P. Teb.
II. 445); a θησαυρὸς "Αμμωνος in the Hermopolite (?) nome (P. Cairo
Preis. 29. 28; cf. P. Amh. II. 41, 56, 57). Cf. the mention of a μέτρον
τέταρτον θεοῦ Σοκνοπαίου in P. Lond. II. 216 (p. 186).

13. This is accepted by Preisigke WB. II, s.v.

14. Cf. P. Kalén 1; PO. XII. 1443; P. Flor. III. 387. 49; SB. 5101;
also O. Tait, p. 110, no. 219.

15. PSI. I. 106.

16. See Chapter V, pp. 53 ff.

17. P. Ryl. II. 213, where the ἀπόμοιρα belongs to the ἱερατικά
division of the treasury (see the editors' Table II on p. 294), except
for that assigned to the subdivision under Διοίκησις (see Table I); if
the λιμνιτικά designates revenue from land recovered by reclamation
projects, the ἀπόμοιρα of such land had never belonged to the temples
and naturally was assigned to the Διοίκησις. In P. Fay. 41. i the
ἀπόμοιρα is listed under διοίκησις. In P. Bour. 30 (from the Arsinoite
nome) the ἀπόμοιρα is called ἱερά, which probably indicates that it was
assigned to the ἱερατικά, and possibly the term ἱερα was used to distinguish this tax from an ἀπόμοιρα which belonged to the διοίκησις
like the example in P. Fay. 41. i from the same nome. The ἀπόμοιρα
in the latter document may have been collected on newly developed
land and so assigned to the διοίκησις.

18. It does not necessarily follow that all the revenue assigned to

the division ἱερατικά was annually expended for the benefit of the priests and temples. As time went on more and more of that income was probably appropriated by the Roman government for its own purposes. The (ἑξάδραχμος) Φιλαδελφοῦ, mentioned in line 354 of P. Ryl. II. 213, which had probably been assigned to the support of the cult of Arsinoë Philadelphus in the Mendesian nome (so the editors in note *ad loc*.), was not assigned to the ἱερατικά but to the διοίκησις; why this tax should have been treated differently from the ἀπόμοιρα is not evident; cf. Chapter V, p. 64.

19. The διδραχμία Σούχου is known from P. Teb. II. 281 (dated 125 B.C.) to have been a tax of 10 per cent. on the sale of real property, collected in addition to the ἐγκύκλιον of 10 per cent., and assigned to the temple of Suchus, the most important deity of the Arsinoite nome. From BGU. III. 748 it is known that this double tax on sales was continued as late as the reign of Nero, although it is not certain that the διδραχμία Σούχου continued at the rate of 10 per cent.

20. On the difficulty of explaining the charge for θησαυρικόν see the introduction to P. Ryl. II. 213, pp. 295 ff. The editors note that the θησαυρικόν on γῆ λιμνιτική was assigned to the διοίκησις, probably for the same reason that the ἀπόμοιρα on that class of land was similarly assigned. The θησαυρικόν is mentioned also in the related PSI. I. 106.

21. For the sacred goats of Mendes cf. Herodotus II. 42; Strabo XVII. 1, 19 (802), 40 (812); cited by the editors of P. Ryl. II. 213. 164, note, who remark: 'Such a charge (λύτρωσις αἰγῶν) would be intelligible if by a legal fiction all goats were regarded as the property of the priests, and a redemption fee was payable in acknowledgement of this, or if a relaxation of the law of abstinence from goats' flesh (Herodotus, loc. cit.). were involved. In PO. IV. 784 the expression [λ]ύτρα ἱερῶν occurs in a private account.'

22. P. Lond. inv. 1562; the same term is used of the ἐπιτηρηταί who collect the weavers' tax in P. Teb. II. 305, 601, 602; PSI. X. 1139; and apparently in connexion with the lease of fishing and grazing rights in PSI. III. 160.

23. It appears also in an early receipt (WO. II. 359) together with a payment for τιμὴ πυροῦ, but the amount is lost.

24. Tait (O. Tait, p. 87, no. 79, note) believed ιερ( ) γεφ( ) to be one of the charges comprised in the συντάξιμον of 44 drachmae 6 chalci; see Chapter VIII, p. 123.

25. Perhaps the large payment in O. Strass. 52 was for building. Inasmuch as statues of the emperors were set up in the Egyptian temples, those temples could not be allowed to fall into ruin, and so the government was willing to allow taxes to be collected for building and maintenance; cf. A. D. Nock in *Harvard Studies in Classical Philology*, XLI (1930), p. 18.

26. P. Fay. 42 (a). A payment for ἱερατικά is included also in the report of a tax-collector (P. Oslo 46 *recto* (p. 110)), but because of the

mutilation of the document it is impossible to be certain that this tax was collected in money, for arurae are mentioned in a previous line of the report.

27. P. Fay., p. 155.

28. In *Priester u. Tempel*, I, p. 364.

29. P. Fay. 39. 15, note.

30. The editors (ibid.) also suggest that, 'If ἀπαιτεῖται has no reference to arrears, we may perhaps compare the present document with the ἀπαιτήσιμα sent to the πράκτορες by government officials.'

31. Cf. the θεορικόν, called a tax by Schwahn in PWRE. v, Sp. 2237, who refers to the documents quoted in WO. I, p. 373 f. The meaning of these documents is ambiguous, and the θεορικόν is not listed as a tax in Preisigke WB. III, Abschn. 11. In PO. x θεορικόν is listed among the taxes in the index, although PO. x. 1333 does not prove that it was a tax. It is not a tax, although conceivably the funds supplied by a tax, in PO. III. 473. 4.

32. In BL. II. 1, p. 21.

33. WO. II. 402, 412–18, 420–1; Spiegelberg, *Ztschr. f. aeg. Sprache*, LIV (1918), pp. 116 ff.; cf. Otto, op. cit. I, pp. 359 ff.

34. WO. I, p. 253, distinguishes the office of προστάτης θεοῦ from that of φέννησις, which Wilcken (WO. II. 413, note) with Revillout's help had explained as equivalent to the Egyptian *p ḥn n ēse*, 'the Priest of Isis'. This was accepted by Otto, op. cit. i, p. 361 f., and by Spiegelberg, loc. cit. The terms are regarded as equivalent in Preisigke WB. III. Abschn. 20, s.v. φέννησις.

35. Why the drachma should have been indicated in demotic by a term 'stater-kite' is far from obvious. The stater was equivalent to the tetradrachm, and the demotic kite was usually equivalent to 2 drachmae. See the remarks of Spiegelberg, *Ztschr. f. Aeg. Sprache*, LIV (1918), p. 120.

36. It is so understood in WO. I, p. 255. The term ἱερατικῶν δη(μοσίων) occurs in P. Fay. 42 (a), apparently as a tax in a collectors' report of arrears.

37. WO. I, pp. 253 ff.; Otto, *Priester u. Tempel*, I, p. 361; Spiegelberg, *Ztschr. f. Aeg. Sprache*, LIV (1918), p. 116 and note 4, following Preisigke, varies from Wilcken's view only in making the attachment to the land the result of contract or lease; cf. also Deissmann, *Licht vom Osten*⁴, p. 84, note 8. The meanings of the term ὁμόλογος are well discussed in P. Ryl. II, p. 287 f.

38. Cf. the use of the term ὁμόλογοι as applied to men liable to the payment of the high rate of poll-tax in the Arsinoite nome.

39. Otto, op. cit. I, p. 359, believed that the λογεία had originally been a free-will offering of the people which had in the course of time become obligatory. This is probably correct, but there is still no evidence that the Roman government consistently recognized that obligation, much less aided in the collection.

40. This seems to have been the usual practice. The payment in

Garret Deposit 7630 (in the Library of Princeton University) may have been made on the day preceding the sacrifice.

41. WO. I, pp. 384-5, explained the τέλος μόσχου θυομένου as an impost paid by the officiating priest upon the profits of the sacrifice; this was accepted by Otto, op. cit. II, p. 173 f. The editors of P. Teb. II. 307 (introd.) have argued effectively against this view.

42. Garret Deposit 7630 (cited in note 40 above) comes from the Fayúm and probably from Socnopaei Nesus; it is dated A.D. 206.

43. Other examples, besides those cited in the text, are: P. Fay. 244 (A.D. 161-9); P. Lond. II. 472 (p. 82) (A.D. 188); BGU. II. 383 (second or third century).

44. For such official reports of the μοσχοσφραγισταί cf. W. Chrest. 89; SP. XXII. 138; P. Genf. 32; P. Grenf. II. 64.

45. The collection of this tax by the keeper of the toll-gate at Philadelphia is not inconsistent with the theory that it was the same tax as the τέλος μόσχου θυομένου. The latter, as I have attempted to show (pp. 246 ff. of this chapter), is probably, like the δεκάτη μόσχων, an outgrowth of the ἐγκύκλιον or sales-tax. The ordinary sales-tax on the sale of a cow was 2 per cent., but perhaps the tax on a sacrificed animal was higher because that transaction was so final that it precluded the possibility of the collection of a sales-tax on subsequent transfers of the same property. In Chapter XV I shall try to show that the customs-tax collected at the town-gate (at the boundary of the nome) was closely connected with the sales-tax collected on transactions in the market-place.

46. Only on the assumption that the payment of 14 obols was an instalment or a payment of arrears could that sum be compared with the 24 drachmae paid in BGU. II. 463; but see Chapter XV, note 79.

47. The reading 1½ obols 3 chalci is marked doubtful in line 60 of P. Ryl. II. 213.

48. In BGU. III. 986 the amount is read as ἀργυρίου δραχμὰς τριακοσίας . . . . κοντα. Segré, Circolazione monetaria, p. 130 f., gives this amount as 310 drachmae, which is obviously an error.

49. The only time the amount of the τέλος μόσχου θυομένου at Socnopaei Nesus is specified it is 24 drachmae (unless the 20 drachmae in Garret Deposit 7630 is correct, and that document really comes from Socnopaei Nesus). It is not impossible that the conventional price of a μόσχος was 200 drachmae, and that the tax in consequence was ordinarily 20 drachmae and so was not stated in the receipt. If this suggestion is correct, the tax at Socnopaei Nesus is more closely related to the δεκάτη μόσχων than the editors of P. Teb. II. 307 were willing to admit. The total of 84 drachmae paid for the latter tax ὑπὲρ διετίας, in P. Teb. II. 572, might then be explained as 60 drachmae for three ordinary μόσχοι plus 24 drachmae for a more valuable animal.

50. See note 21 above.

51. But cf. Archiv, VI, p. 297.

52. Namely, BGU. I. 337 (= W. Chrest. 92); P. Lond. III. 1235

(p. 35), but this is very doubtful, since what the editors read as φόρρυ [βωμῶν] in lines 11 ff. is now read as Φαμε[νώθ] (BL. 1. p. 275), and the φō [βω]⁻ in line 6 should probably be restored as the name of a month, since it is immediately followed by the word ἀριθμ[ ]; P. Lond. 11. 460 (p. 70); BGU. 1. 199; SP. xxii. 176; BGU. 1. 292, 337. Payments for θυσία and τέμ(ενος) are found in a tax-list of 223–222 B.C. (SB. 6279), but the connexion between these payments and the Roman exaction of a φόρος βωμῶν may be slight indeed.

53. In SP. xxii. 183 the amount of the φόρος βωμῶν is 2100 drachmae, and the προσδιαγραφόμενα are 131 drachmae 4½ obols; $\frac{1}{16}$ of 2,100 drachmae is exactly 131 drachmae 1½ obols, so that the προσδια-γραφόμενα of 131 drachmae 4½ obols may include a charge of 3 obols for σύμβολον. In W. Chrest. 92 the φόρος βωμῶν is again 2100 drach-mae, but the προσδιαγραφόμενα are given are 131 drachmae 4 obols; I am unable to account for the missing ½ obol—possibly it should be restored. In SP. xxii. 176 the φόρος βωμῶν is 320 drachmae, and the προσδιαγραφόμενα are given by Wessely as 2 drachmae and the συμβολικόν as 3 obols; but 2 drachmae is an impossible rate of προσ-διαγραφόμενα on a principal of 320 drachmae, and it should un-doubtedly be corrected to 20 drachmae ($\frac{1}{16}$ of 320 drachmae), since β is easily misread for κ. In BGU. 1. 199 there is apparently no state-ment of the προσδιαγραφόμενα. Unusual supplementary charges appear in P. Lond. 11. 460 (p. 70) and BGU. 1. 292. In both of these receipts the principal of the φόρος βωμῶν is 500 drachmae. The BL. 1, p. 246, gives the reading of the supplementary charges of line 3 of P. Lond. 11. 460 (p. 70) as follows: ϟφ ρϟ δ (= ἑκατοσταὶ τέσσαρες) ϟκ βο∠(= βοῶν?) ϟια–ο⁻ συ(μβολικοῦ) ϝ. The explanation of the symbol ρϟ δ is certainly correct; a supplementary charge of 4 per cent. is found, in BGU. 1. 156. 8, made on the price of land purchased from the state by a soldier. The doubtful suggestion of βοῶν as the explanation of βο∠ is certainly to be rejected. The amount which follows the βο∠ is 11 drachmae 1½ obols, which is exactly 2¼ per cent. of the principal of 500 drachmae; the ρϟ should be supplied from the preceding symbol (ρϟ δ), and the βο∠ should be read as βδ' and means simply 2¼ per cent. (2¼ drachmae per hundred). The same in-terpretation applies to the payment of 300 drachmae for φόρος βωμῶν in line 5 of the same document: φόρου βωμῶν ϟτ ρϟ <δ> ϟιβ βο∠ ϟϛϝό συ(μβολικοῦ) ϝ. In BGU. 1. 292 the reading of the BL. 1, p. 36, is φόρου βωμῶν γ̄ (ἔτους) (δραχμαὶ) φ ριδ' κ[.]φ (or β[.]φ) (δραχμαὶ) ιαϝ κ.τ.λ. It seems obvious that the κ following the symbol ρϟ δ' (the correct reading of ριδ') represents 20 drachmae, which is 4 per cent. of 500 drachmae. The next amount, 11 drachmae 3 obols, is more difficult, for it is exactly 2·3 per cent. of 500 drachmae; there is not room for a symbol representing 2·3 per cent. (i.e. β ē ι), and it is un-likely that such a symbol should be restored, as will be demonstrated presently. According to note 15 on p. 36 of BL. 1, Otto suggested the restoration β[ο(ῶν)], but Plaumann and Schubart denied that it would

suit the traces visible on the papyrus. Otto misunderstood the symbol βο∠, as is evident from the discussion above; but that symbol is, nevertheless, what is wanted in this passage in place of [.]φ, which is wholly unintelligible. It may be observed that 4 per cent. plus 2¼ per cent. equal 6¼ per cent. or 1⁄16, the normal amount of the προσδιαγραφόμενα. In BGU. I. 292 the second item of the supplementary charges (11 drachmae 3 obols) apparently includes 1½ obols for σύμβολον which is omitted from the list of charges in this document. Why the προσδιαγραφόμενα on the φόρος βωμῶν in these two documents should have been divided into two separate charges is not at all clear: it merely complicates the problem of explaining the προσδιαγραφόμενα; see Chapter XVII, p. 325 f. The same division of προσδιαγραφόμενα may be observed in a payment for ⟨φόρος⟩ προβάτων and in another for ἐννόμιον; cf. Chapter VI, note 12.

54. O. Tait, p. 88, no. 82; O. Mey. 38.

55. Otto, *Priester u. Tempel*, II, p. 182 f., attempted to distinguish between payments ὑπὲρ εἰσκρίσεως made by the higher priests yearly (for the right of choosing members of their own order) and the payments of εἰσκριτικόν which he identified with the Ptolemaic τελεστικόν, as meaning the sum paid by priests upon entering the sacred office. The editors of P. Teb. II. 294. 20, note, have refuted Otto's theory, and have correctly identified the two payments.

56. Cf. Otto, op. cit. I, pp. 203 ff.; P. Teb. II. 292, introd.

57. Cf. WO. I, pp. 397 ff.; Otto, op. cit. II, p. 182.

58. See note 2 above.

59. WO. II. 136, 137. The sum paid in each case is 8 drachmae 3 obols, but the 3 obols undoubtedly represent the προσδιαγραφόμενα. In PO. XII. 1435 the payment of 8 drachmae by a *pastophorus* is accompanied by a charge of 3 obols for προσδιαγραφόμενα.

60. Cf. Otto, op. cit. I, pp. 244 ff.; Gnomon of the Idiologus (BGU. v. 2, edited by Uxkull-Gyllenband), §§ 82, 83, 94, 95 (and note, pp. 89 ff.).

61. *Archiv*, III, p. 239, note 1. On the basis of this document Wilcken corrected his earlier reading (in P. Lond. II. 329 (p. 113)) ἰσκρίσεω(ς) ἱερέων to ἱερῶν. In SP. XXII. 171, however, Wessely read ἰσκ[ρί]σεως ἱερ(έων), and in SP. XXII. 143 εἰσκριτικοῦ ἱερέων.

62. P. Lond. II. 329 (p. 113) with BL. I, p. 253; SP. XXII. 171, 143, where the amount of the εἰσκριτικοῦ ἱερέων [Σοκνοπ(αίου)] Νήσο[ο]υ should be corrected from 2 drachmae to 20 drachmae (cf. note 53 above for a similar correction of SP. XXII. 176), and πρ(οσδιαγραφομένων) ∫α—ὁ σ(υμβολικοῦ) Γ should be restored at the beginning of line 10; while Wessely's reading of ∫Α′ ὁμοῦ ∫η immediately after the lacuna at the beginning of line 10 should be corrected to ῾Ερμοῦ ∫η. In SP. XXII. 171 as in 143 the προσδιαγραφόμενα on the payment of 20 drachmae should be 1 drachma 1½ obols (instead of 1 drachma 1 obol), and perhaps it should be so restored in the text.

63. BGU. I. 162. 15-17 (= W. *Chrest*. 91).

64. See note 60 above.

65. P. Teb. II. 298. 14 *et passim*.

66. P. Teb. II. 298. 21. Cf. the payment of 70 drachmae in the Ptolemaic period by two ἰβιοβοσκοὶ εἰς τιμὴν ἰβιοβοσκείου καὶ τῆς προφητείας καὶ τοῦ ἡμίσους τῆς δωρείας γῆς (SB. 1178 a–b).

67. P. Teb. II. 298. 14–20.

68. P. Achmim 8 (= *Bulletin de l'Institut français d'archéologie orientale*, XXXI (1930), pp. 75 ff.). For the auction of the office of στολιστής cf. BGU. v, 1–2, § 80, where the auction of the office is not specified, but it is not forbidden as in the case of the office of prophet (§ 78).

69. P. Achmim 8. 16–19: κἂν μηδεὶς πλέον δῷ, παραδοῦναι αὐτοῖς μ[ὴ] μέντοι ἐλλάτονος [τ]ῆς συντιμήσεως.

70. P. Teb. II. 294.

71. BGU. v. 1–2, § 79.

72. According to BGU. v. 1–2, § 78, the office of prophet was to be sold outright without bids, but this provision was disregarded in P. Teb. II. 294, 295, and perhaps 296.

73. That is, the *pastophoria* (but see note 60 above) or the initiation into the higher order of priests which was marked by the rite of circumcision.

74. As in P. Teb. II. 294–6; in the last the post of prophet was purchased for a talent of silver.

75. Following Wilcken, UPZ. p. 44 f. Cf. Otto, *Priester u. Tempel*, I, p. 239, who believed that the ἐπιστάτης ἱεροῦ was identical with the ἀρχιερεύς, and that the temples paid the ἐπιστατικόν to the government for the priests' privilege of electing their own ἐπιστάται; refuted by Rostovtzeff in GGA. 1909, pp. 611 ff. There is a curious parallel between the status of land and other common forms of property and the status of the priesthoods. The hereditary priesthoods, entrance upon which required merely the payment of the εἰσκριτικόν at a fixed rate, correspond to the land leased in perpetuity upon which the holders paid δημόσια καθήκοντα at a fixed annual rate. The priesthoods sold at auction correspond to the domain land leased periodically for the highest rate it would bring (the annual ἐκφόρια). In the case of the priesthoods, however, the payments were, so far as we know, made but once, whereas the payments on land were annual.

76. P. Teb. I. 5. 62–4 and note; 97 and introd.

77. P. Teb. II. 298.

78. This would explain the remission of the ἐπιστατικά to the ἐπιστάται τῶν ἱερῶν (as well as to the ἀρχιερεῖς καὶ ἱερεῖς) which troubled the editors of P. Teb. I. 5 (cf. their note on lines 62–4).

79. SP. XXII. 183; BGU. I. 337 (= W. *Chrest.* 92); probably also P. Lond. II. 347 (p. 71) (restore ἐ[πισ]τ( ) ἱερέω(ν) in line 15). Although the official of the Ptolemaic period was called ἐπιστάτης ἱεροῦ or τῶν ἱερῶν, the tax of the Roman period was called ἐπιστατικὸν ἱερέων. This is a natural change, however, since the salient feature of the tax is the fact that it is an annual assessment upon the priests,

especially after the office of ἐπιστάτης ἱεροῦ (or ἱερῶν) was abolished. In SP. XXII. 183. 13, however, the ε apparently is restored in [ἐπισ]τατικο(ῦ) [ἱ]ερ(έ)ω(ν).

80. The item of payment for the three priesthoods at Nilopolis is separated from the payment for ἐπιστατικὸν ἱερέων by ten lines in BGU. I. 337 (= W. Chrest. 92), yet I am inclined to think that the two items represent payments for the same type of exaction. The amount of the payment for the three offices, 64 drachmae, seems too small for the purchase (or εἰσκριτικόν) of such offices, even in a subsidiary shrine; cf. the payment of 28 drachmae for προσδιαγραφόμενα for the λεσωνεία at Apias, which implies a principal of 448 drachmae (if Wessely's dubious readings of SP. XXII. 114 are really correct), a sum so large that it must represent the purchase-price of the office. The item of 64 drachmae for the three priesthoods at Nilopolis does not appear in the similar account of the finances of the temple at Socnopaei Nesus found in SP. XXII. 183. The payment cannot be for the salary of these offices, since payments for such purposes are not designated ὑπὲρ προφητείας, &c., but are indicated by the dative case, e.g. προφήτῃ Σούχου θεοῦ μεγάλου [μεγάλου] ∫τμδ (BGU. I. 337 (= W. Chrest. 92. 16)).

81. Cf. BGU. II. 471; P. Teb. II. 306; P. Lond. III. 1235 (p. 35); P. Fay. 51, 42 a; P. Lond. II. 352 (p. 114). But some of these may represent individual instalments of the priests.

82. These rolls are the unpublished P. Mich. inv. 4171, 4172; and a third roll designated as the Cairo roll, but whose inventory number is not yet available.

83. Line 1250 f. of the Cairo roll (see note 82 above): ἱερεὺς Πετεσούχο(υ) θεοῦ μεγάλ(ου) μεγάλ(ου) ἐπιστατ(ικοῦ) ἱερέων ιβ (ἔτους) Καράνο(υ) ∫πζϛ προ(σδιαγραφόμενα) ∫ιβϛ/∫ρ. The designation of the god as μεγάλου μεγάλου probably indicates that his temple belonged to the first class temples; cf. Otto, Priester u. Tempel, I, pp. 18 ff.

84. The προσδιαγραφόμενα are high on the 24 drachmae rate of ἐπιστατικόν as well as on the rate at 87 drachmae 3 obols.

85. It is odd that the totals of the payments of the priests should be exactly 100 drachmae or 32 drachmae. In P. Teb. II. 298 the payments (apparently of εἰσκριτικόν) for the office of στολιστής are stated to be 100 drachmae, and the payments for the 'priesthood' (ἱερετία) 52 drachmae. There is probably no important conclusion to be drawn from the similarity of these amounts, however, for in P. Achmim 8 the purchase-price of the στολιστεία is given as 100 drachmae plus προσδιαγραφόμενα.

86. P. Teb. I. 5. 65, 79–80; 6. 21, 34. In P. Teb. I. 189 there is a tax-list headed . . . . λαογρ(αφία) Θεογο(νίδος) τῶν τε[τελη]κότων τὴν σύντα[ξιν κ]αὶ τὸ{ν} ἐπιστατικ(όν), &c. There follows a list of names concluding οἱ πάν(τες) ἄνδ(ρες) Σοβ. The next column is headed ἀφ' ὧν τελ(οῦσιν) Σξγ ἀν(ὰ) τ (τάλαντα) λθ 'βψ. Καὶ τῶν ἀνὰ ψν

followed by the names of eight persons, thus accounting for 271. It
is not impossible that the persons paying the lower rate are priests
(eight would be about the right number of priests for a village whose
adult males totalled 271 or 272), and that the rate of 750 drachmae
annually represents their ἐπιστατικόν. At the conventional conversion
ratio of 300 to 1, the rate of 750 copper drachmae would be 2½ drachmae of silver. This was probably a monthly rather than an annual
rate (cf. my article *Census and Poll-Tax in Ptolemaic Egypt*), so that the
annual total would be 30 drachmae, which is not far from the total of
32 drachmae paid for ἐπιστατικόν and γέρα and supplementary charges
by the priests at Caranis in the Roman period (note 85 above).

87. On the προσδιαγραφόμενα and the κόλλυβος see Chapter XVII,
p. 324 f..

88. P. Fay. 51.

89. See Chapter VIII, p. 126.

90. The payment of λαογραφία is suggested by the editors in the
introduction to P. Lond. III. 1235 (p. 35).

91. This is demonstrated by the fact that the poor were forced to
flee, because of their inability to meet the exactions of the state, and that
the government was therefore forced to make up the deficit by further
exactions made upon the well-to-do, i.e. the μερισμὸς ἀπόρων and μερισμὸς ἀνακ(εχωρηκότων); see Chapter IX, pp. 137 ff.

92. Dio Cassius 71, 4; SHA. *Aurelius*, 21; also Milne in *Hist. of
Egypt*, IV², p. 52, and Lesquier, *L'Armée romaine d'Égypt*, pp. 29, 70.

CHAPTER XV

1. Cf. especially E. H. Warmington, *The Commerce between the
Roman Empire and India*, Cambridge 1928, pp. 6–17; also M. P.
Charlesworth, *Trade-Routes and Commerce of the Roman Empire*, Cam-
bridge 1924, Chapters II and IV; Chwostow, *History of the Oriental
Trade of Graeco-Roman Egypt*, Kazan 1907, *passim*; Schur, *Klio*,
Beiheft 15 (1923), pp. 49 ff.; Kornemann, *Festschrift f. Lehmann-
Haupt* (Janus I) (1921), pp. 69 ff.; Kortenbeutel, *Der ägyptische Süd- u.
Osthandel*, &c., Berlin-Charlottenburg 1931; A. Sarasin, *Der Handel
zw. Indien u. Rom*, &c., Basel 1930.

2. N.H. XII. 84.

3. Pliny, as a member of the equestrian order and a high official
under Vespasian, undoubtedly had access to accurate information about
the contracts for customs at Red Sea ports, and probably of the customs
of Syria as well, for he speaks (XII. 64–5) of the dues collected at Gaza.

4. N.H. XIX. 7.

5. The *Periplus Maris Erythraei* lists commodities acceptable at
Eastern ports. Cf. Warmington, op. cit., pp. 261 ff.

6. N.H. VI. 101. The suggestion seems probable because the figure
of 50 million sesterces for the trade with India is included in a discussion of the commerce of Egypt.

7. XVII. I. 13 (798).

8. Ibid.

9. P. Cairo Zen. 59015 R.

10. § 19.

11. For the attempts to date the *Periplus* see the edition of Fabricius, Leipzig (1883), Introd., pp. 23 ff., and Kortenbeutel, op. cit., pp. 11 (and note 12) and 63, who accepts A.D. 70 as the date of its composition.

12. *Periplus*, § 19: Διὸ καὶ εἰς αὐτὴν παραλήπτης τῆς τετάρτης τῶν εἰσφερομένων φορτίων καὶ παραφυλακῆς χάριν [καὶ] ἑκατοντάρχης μετὰ στρατεύματος ἀποστέλλεται.

13. *Die kaiserlichen Verwaltungsbeamten bis auf Diocletian*[1], p. 20, note 2; cf. second edition, p. 81 f.

14. *Archiv*, IV, pp. 306–7. Wilcken and some others have held the toll at Leuce Come to be purely Nabataean. For a summary of the opinions, cf. Warmington, op. cit., p. 335 f., note 35, who gives his own opinion on p. 16.

15. § 19.

16. XVI. 4. 23 (780).

17. *Trade Routes*, &c., p. 64.

18. N.H VI. 101.

19. According to Pliny, N.H. VI. 84, Annius Plocamus had leased the *maris rubri vectigal* from the *fiscus*. Those who are inclined to see in the 25 per cent. toll at Leuce Come a Nabataean tax perhaps have forgotten that Pliny states that the *libertus* of Annius Plocamus was sailing *circa Arabiam*.

20. OGI. I. 202.

21. BGU. III. 697 (= W. *Chrest.* 321) from Socnopaei Nesus, dated A.D. 145. Alum was subject to a government monopoly (cf. Chapter XI, p. 189). This document records payment to the camel-driver who had transported the alum from the Little Oasis. Included in the amount is reimbursement for 45 drachmae paid at the toll-gate of Nynpou (which is not otherwise attested). The fee is so low that it may have been a nominal charge for inspection. There is a reference to the 'customary $6\frac{1}{2}$ per cent.', but this is unlike any other surcharge. The government in some cases deducted $6\frac{1}{2}$ per cent. for payments in advance (BGU. VI. 1564; P. Columbia I R 4. 10), but there seems no relation to the payment in BGU. III. 697. 19.

22. XVII. I. 41 (813).

23. In *Geog. Gr. Min.* I, p. 122.

24. Both Strabo and Agatharchides refer only to traffic down the river as paying the tax at Hermopolis Magna. The analogy with the tax for the Harbour of Memphis, however, suggest that any cargoes travelling up the Nile to the Thebaid were also subject to the tax.

25. This is a deduction from the tax for the Harbour of Memphis collected at the toll-stations on the northern boundary of the Fayûm. The documents from the Oxyrhynchite nome undoubtedly refer to exports.

26. If the receipts for λιμένος Μέμφεως were presented to the Harbour-Master at Memphis, the camel- and donkey-drivers must have retained possession of them, for they have all been found in the Arsinoite nome. Most of the drivers were illiterate, and would have desired to retain the receipts only for protection 'against sycophants' (see p. 267).

27. The receipts for λιμένος Μέμφεως are arranged approximately in chronological order as follows: P. Lond. iii. 1265 (b) (p. 36); ii. 206 (c) (p. 85); SP. xxii. 11, 13, 149; P. Lond. iii. 1266 (d) (p. 38); ii. 469 (b) (p. 86); P. Ryl. ii. 370, 197 (c); P. Str. ii. 124, i. 12; P. Lond. iii. 1266 (e) (p. 38); P. Hamb. 77; P. Grenf. ii. 50 (d); P. Amh. ii. 116; P. Grenf. ii. 50 (e); SP. xxii. 153; P. Grenf. ii. 50 (k), (1); P. Fay. 69; P. Ryl. ii. 368,369; P. Fay. 74, 72, 164–76 (described, but not published); BGU. vii. 1594, 1592; P. Hamb. 78; SB. 7566; AM. 8953 in Princeton U. Lib. (from Philadelphia). Of the foregoing only P. Ryl. ii. 197 (c); P. Fay. 74; P. Lond. iii. 1266 (d) (p. 38) are for imports. P. Fay. 76 (a) may also be a receipt for λιμένος Μέμφεως, although the toll is not so designated; the tax of ½ obol an artaba is, however, the same as the rate found in SB. 7365. The type of toll is not specified in SP. xxii. 104 and 105, but there is no similar reason for assigning them to the tax for the Harbour of Memphis rather than to the ρ καὶ ν́ or the ἐρημοφυλακία.

The overland transport from the Fayûm to Memphis was profitable because the bountiful products of the Arsinoite nome could not all be carried with sufficient speed by boat through the canals and the Nile to Memphis; it is probable that private commerce had to yield right of way to carriers of government grain in the transport on the canals.

28. P. Lond. iii. 1169 (p. 43); SB. 7365. P. Amh. ii. 77. 36–83 does not give rates. P. Lond. iii. 929 (p. 40); SP. xxii. 63–5 also do not give rates. Neither does P. Lond. iii. 964 (p. 211), but a reference to the μισθωτὴς ἐρημοφυλακίας may, as the editors suggested, indicate that it was a report of the collection of the ἐρημοφυλακία. Similarly the reference to the Harbour-Master in SB. 7365 seems to mark that as a report of the λιμένος Μέμφεως, and the similarity of the rates in P. Lond. iii. 1169 (p. 43) may well indicate that it too was a report of the same toll. The other reports listed above may have been for the collection of any of the three types of tolls.

The rates in SB. 7365 are as follows:

1 artaba of wheat, lentils, barley, orobus, or aracus				½ obol.
1 „ „ black beans				1½ obols.
1 „ „ green dates				2 „
1 „ „ fine salt				3 „
1 „ „ λάχανος-seed, green olives, or pressed dates			1 drachma	1½ obols
1 chlibion of leeks			1 „	1½ „

1 donkey-load of fish (νεάρα ἰχθύς) .   .   2 drachmae
1 chlibion of pickled fish   7   ,,
1 ceramion of sour wine .   .   .   .   1 drachma   1½ obols
1 metretes of olive oil   .   .   .   .   5 drachmae
Leather chairs, each   2   ,,
Iron, &c., 24 (plus) minae   .   .   .   3   ,,   1½ ,,
Copper 72 (plus) minae   3   ,,
Donkey-load of wood or white leaves   .   1 drachma
Oxen, each   .   .   .   .   .   .   2 drachmae
Horses (exported), each   13   ,,   1 obol.
Donkeys (imported), each   .   .   .   13   ,,   2 obols.

On wool a fee of 10 obols an 'angion' is designated as ἐραυνητικόν
(examination-dues).

The rates in P. Lond. 1169 (p. 43) are as follows:

1 metretes of olive oil   .   .   .   .   4 drachmae 1 obol.
1 camel load of fine salt   4   ,,
1 ceramion of olives   .   .   .   .   4 obols.
1 donkey-load of pressed dates .   .   .   2   ,,   4   ,,

For an attempt to convert the camel- and donkey-loads into measures
comparable with those in SB. 7365 cf. Clauson's discussion in *Aegyptus*,
IX (1928), p. 257.

29. In *Nachrichten der Gesellschaft der Wissenschaften zu Göttingen*,
Philol.-Hist. Klasse 1925–6, pp. 57 ff., especially pp. 77–9.

30. Fiesel's assumption, that in SP. XXII. 140 the payment of 4
drachmae included ῥ καὶ ν̓ and ἐρημοφυλακία, and that, since the
ἐρημοφυλακία on a camel was 2 drachmae, the ῥ καὶ ν̓ must also have
been 2 drachmae, led him to the absurd conclusion that 4 drachmae
represented a toll of 6 per cent. on the value of the exported or imported camel, and that 2 drachmae similarly represented a toll of
6 per cent. on a donkey. A glance at Grenfell and Hunt's argument
against regarding the 1 per cent. of the ῥ καὶ ν̓ as a tax on the value of
the beast of burden would have saved Fiesel from such an error.
According to Fiesel the value of a camel would have been reckoned at
66 drachmae and that of a donkey at 33 drachmae. Segré's tables
(*Circolazione Monetaria*, pp. 126–9) prove the impossibility of such
prices. Since Fiesel regarded the tax for the Harbour of Memphis as a
surtax at the same rate as the ἐρημοφυλακία, 3 per cent. is also an impossible rate for the λιμένος Μέμφεως. The rates in SB. 7365, which
was not available to Fiesel, show that the tax (probably for the Harbour
of Memphis) on a donkey was 13 drachmae 2 obols. Fiesel's calculations on pp. 88 ff. are similarly worthless, as has been demonstrated by
SB. 7365, because he made no allowance for changing prices on various
products at different periods of time, and he wrongly equated the price
of green dates with that of fresh dates.

31. The toll on cereals was uniformly ½ obol an artaba, although
the prices of wheat and barley, for example, were quite unequal. In

P. Ryl. II. 197 (a) the ρ καὶ ν́ on wheat was 1½ obols an artaba. It is possible, therefore, that the rate of ½ obol an artaba in SB. 7365 was intended to represent 1 per cent. of the value of wheat. A glance at Segré's table (pp. 138 ff.) shows that the highest price recorded for a ceramion of wine during the second century after Christ was 20 drachmae, and the lowest price 7 drachmae 2 obols. If the price of sour wine was not much higher or lower, a toll of 1 drachma 1½ obols per ceramion represents a rate between 6¼ per cent. and 17 per cent. It is obvious, therefore, that the toll in SB. 7365 was not assessed at a uniform rate upon all articles.

32. Cf. Clauson's discussion in *Aegyptus*, IX (1928), p. 257 f.

33. There is no record of surcharges on the individual payments in the day by day record. Extra charges for χειριστικόν and ἀλλαγή appear also in the λόγος Μέμφεως in PO. XIV. 1650 and 1650 (a), but in PO. XIV. 1650 at a higher rate (i.e. approximately 10 per cent.) than the 8½ per cent. specified in SB. 7365. 150. The higher rate in PO. XIV. 1650 may have resulted from the collection of χειριστικόν and ἀλλαγή there in round sums, viz. 5 drachmae for χειριστικόν and 1 drachma for ἀλλαγή.

34. Cf. Clauson in *Aegyptus*, IX (1928), pp. 273–6. Previous editors had supposed that Hermes was the name of one of the officials in charge of the toll-station.

35. In P. Grenf. II. 50 (b) the ρ καὶ ν́ has the additional designation νομ(αρχίας) Ἀρσινο(ΐτου).

36. *Les Épistratèges*, Geneva 1911, p. 159.

37. The difficulty with this suggestion lies in the comparative uniformity of the payments accredited to various towns. The boats used on the canals of the Fayûm could not have been very large, and perhaps the amount given in P. Lond. III. 1107 (p. 47) for each of the villages represents the toll upon more than one shipload. A further difficulty lies in the fact that it is impossible to determine the length of time that is included in the report: even if μηνιαῖον (which the editors declare impossible) could be read in line 26, there would be no proof that the report covers the period of a month. Professor A. C. Johnson has suggested that the sums in the report represent the salary paid to the officials charged with the collection of the tax for the Harbour of Memphis and stationed at those villages and at Arsinoë, but I do not see how the surtax of 20 per cent. (πέμπτη) is to be explained on such an hypothesis.

38. One may compare the provision for confiscation of undeclared merchandise in the νόμος τελωνικός in PO. I. 36. ii.

39. It is unfortunate that P. Fay. 104 is so mutilated that it is impossible to determine whether the ἐραυνηταί in lines 14 and 32 had special designations like those in lines 18 and 19. In line 18 appear ἐραυνηταὶ εὐθεν[ίας], and in line 19 ἐραυνηταὶ ἀνα . [ ] which, since the document is dated late third century, perhaps should be restored as ἐραυνηταὶ ἀνα[βολικοῦ].

40. Payments for σχεδία and ἐπιστατία appear also in P. Flor. III. 335.

41. It is slightly less than ½ obol an artaba, the rate of the tax on wheat found in SB. 7365, which as suggested above may have been intended to represent a tax of 1 per cent. But compare the prices for wheat listed in Segré's *Circolazione Monetaria*, pp. 102 ff., where in the second century after Christ the prices range from $5\frac{6}{10}$ to 20 drachmae an artaba.

42. The editors thought that the charge πηδαλίου was payment for a new rudder, and they connected it with νέων which they translated 'repairs'. It is impossible, however, that every ship putting out of Oxyrhynchus for Memphis should have required a new rudder, yet πηδαλίου appears in all the accounts of this type (PO. XIV. 1650-1), comprising four ships.

43. The payments for φύλαξ ἀπὸ γ(ῆς) καὶ κυδ(άρῳ) and for ἐραυνητικ(οῦ) εἰς λ(όγον) σπονδ(ῆς) appear only in the first column of PO. XIV. 1650, although the document lists the fees for two ships. These payments, therefore, are probably not for duly authorized government charges. This is perhaps confirmed by the fact that the *pour-boire* in this document is just twice the additional payment to the ἐραυνητής in PO. XIV. 1651, which is concerned with only one ship.

44. The same objection applies to the editors' interpretation of νέων as 'repairs' as was raised in note 42 above against their explanation of πηδαλίου. In PO. XIV. 1651 the charge for νέων seems to be replaced by a payment designated as ἀναλώματος οἰνηγίας, 'expense of carriage of wine'. The payment of προσδιαγραφόμενα thereon marks the fee for ἀναλώματος οἰνηγίας as a government charge, and perhaps it was collected as payment for stevedores working under the control of the government.

45. For the meaning of ἑρμηνεύς (translated by the editors as 'interpreter') cf. Preisigke WB. I, s.v. ἑρμηνεύς (3).

46. On Artemis as a goddess of shipping cf. PWRE. II, Sp. 1349. 15. It is probable that in Egypt Artemis or Artemis-Hecate was identified with Isis, who was also the goddess of streams and rivers (particularly the Nile) and the patroness of sailors and merchants. Cf. the Invocation of Isis in PO. XI. 1380, with the introduction and notes, especially lines 61, 69, 15 and 74, 84, 91, 113, 121-6. A three-faced goddess (Artemis-Hecate?) is figured on the leaden tokens of Memphis (cf. PO. XI. 1380. 84, note).

47. Cf. PO. XIV. 1650 (a). 7, note.

48. See note 31 above. The rate of the toll on wine is two-fifths less than on sour wine in SB. 7365, but even if this cargo were valued at 20 drachmae per ceramion, the toll would amount to 3·75 per cent.

49. See note 44 above.

50. Cf. PO. XIV. 1650. 5, note; 1651. 4, note.

51. See note 33 above.

52. The same charge appears in P. Fay. 104. 20.

53. Cf. the editors' note on line 19 of PO. XIV. 1651.

54. Perhaps the charge for ἀναλώματος πλοίου represents a payment for lighterage when the river was low.

55. The editors read [χρω]μάτων, which was corrected by Grenfell and Hunt (cf. BL. I, p. 288) to [ ]ιμάτων. The correct reading is [χρι]σμάτων or the older form [χρ]ιμάτων. Λείρινον χρῖσμα, for example, is found in Dioscorides, III. 116.

56. The toll on [χρυ]σολίθου (or [ ]ος λίθου) was 9 drachmae 1 obol a xestes. White lead and ochre and perhaps oil of cedar are also mentioned.

57. *Archiv*, III, pp. 185 ff. Cf. also Dirksen in *Abh. d. K. Akad. Wiss. Berlin*, 1843, pp. 80 ff.

58. *Archiv*, IV, pp. 310 ff.

59. NH. XII. 109. Arabia is not mentioned among the sources of the fragrant oil. Although Pliny mentions the banks of the Nile at Canopus as the best source of the oil, it is quite probable that it was produced elsewhere in Egypt.

60. Wilcken identified the ὑκσιωτικὴ ἄμμος as aloes from Arabia, but a tax of 22 drachmae a shipload seems too low for such an article. Professor Johnson has suggested that a special form of sand used in the manufacture of the famous Egyptian glass is meant. The epithet ὑκσιωτική is not yet satisfactorily explained.

61. Cf. the payments for χειρογραφία in PO. XIV. 1650–1. Cf. also Rostovtzeff in *Archiv*, IV, pp. 312 ff.

62. W. *Chrest.* 463. 14. Cf. Schehl, *Aegyptus*, XIII (1933), pp. 137 ff., who gives a bibliography.

63. Cf. Grenfell and Hunt in P. Grenf. II. 50 introd. and P. Fay. pp. 196 ff.; WO. I, pp. 359 ff.; Preisigke in P. Strass. I. 12 introd.; Jouguet in *La Vie municipale dans l'Égypte romaine*, Paris 1911, p. 436; Fiesel, op. cit.

64. Cf. Strabo XVII. 1. 16 (800) on the name of Schedia above Alexandria.

65. In D.-S., *Dict. d. Ant.*, s.v. *Portorium* (9° Égypte).

66. Strabo was in Egypt in 27 B.C. The date of the creation of the ἐπιστρατηγία of the Heptanomia is disputed (cf. Martin, *Les Épistratèges*, pp. 86 ff.). The oldest receipt for λιμένος Μέμφεως dates from A.D. 83; the latest from late in the third century after Christ.

67. For other taxes belonging to the νομαρχία see Chapter XVII, p. 333 f. The receipts for ῥ καὶ ὔ are: P. Lond. III. 1265 (a) (p. 36) (?); SP. XXII. 150–2; P. Grenf. II. 50 (b); P. Lond. II. 307 (p. 84), III. 1265 (c) and (d) (p. 36); SP. XXII. 148; P. Iand. 59; BGU. III. 724; P. Strass. II. 123; P. Ryl. II. 197 (a); P. Lond. II. 206 (d) (p. 86), III. 1265 (e); P. Hamb. 76; P. Lond. III. 1265 (f); P. Grenf. II. 50 (f); P. Lond. III. 1266 (b) (p. 38), (a), (c); P. Grenf. II. 50 (g), (h); P. Cairo Preisigke 25 (= P. Fay. 185 (a)); P. Fay. 70, 71, 73, 76, 177–85; P. Teb. II. 362, 461, 557; BGU. VII. 1593, 1595, III. 803; P. Lips. 81; BGU. III. 766, 767, 804, 724; SP. XXII. 9, 10.

68. Cf. Clauson's discussion in *Aegyptus*, IX (1928), pp. 258–60.

69. WO. I, p. 360.

70. P. Fay., pp. 197–200. Cf. P. Bouriant 31.

71. In the introduction to PO. XII. 1439 the editors expressed the opinion that the 1 per cent. toll on barley and garlic was paid at a station in the Little Oasis. It is somewhat doubtful, however, whether barley was exported from the Oasis. Perhaps the πύλη Ὀάσ[εως] was the designation of a toll-station in the Oxyrhynchite nome and situated on a road that led to the Oasis.

72. W. *Chrest*. 292; WO. II. 806, 1569; O. Theb. 91; O. Tait, p. 172, no. 140.

73. WO. II. 43 (= *Chrest*. 291), 150. In O. Strass. 250 the collectors are called ἐπιτηρηταὶ πεντηκ(οστῆς λιμένος), according to the editor. Cf. SB. 7579–80, 7526.

74. See note 62 above.

75. VII. 20. 2.

76. In BL. I, p. 278, the reading πελωχικοῦ, suggested by the editors of P. Ryl. II. 167. 20, note, has the support of Bell. It is difficult to see why the πελωχικόν should have been distinguished from the ἀγορανομίας ὠνίων (see Chapter XIII, p. 227).

77. Perhaps the other taxes (μνημονείου καὶ τῶν ἄλλων εἰδῶν καὶ γραφείου ὅρμου μητροπόλεως) were somewhat analogous to the ἐπιστατεία καὶ ἔ in the Arsinoite nome and the fees for scribes and official paper in the accounts from the Oxyrhynchite nome (PO. XIV. 1650–1).

78. If the restoration of [Βουβ]άστεως is possible at the beginning of line 8, there is further evidence of the origin of the document in the Delta.

79. See Chapter XIV, pp. 246 ff. A tax of 4 drachmae 4 obols is 2 per cent. of 233 drachmae, which is not an unreasonable price for a μόσχος (especially if the payment of 24 drachmae for τέλος μόσχου θυομένου in BGU. II. 436 represents a tax of 10 per cent.). In P. Ryl. II. 193. 20 the payment of 14 obols would be 1 per cent. of 233 drachmae, it would be 2 per cent. of 116½ drachmae, a low but not impossible price for a μόσχος.

80. *Archiv*, VI, p. 130, where Milne calls the Dromos-tax a market-tax. See also Chapter XIII, p. 226 f.

81. Various provisions for restricting importation of oil through Alexandria into the χώρά are found in the famous Revenue papyrus (especially col. 52) which suggest the possibility of a toll-station between Alexandria and the χώρά, but it is possible to explain col. 52 as meaning payment of toll at the point of entry into Alexandria (and Pelusium) by sea.

82. The ἐρημοφυλακία is sometimes called ἴχνος ἐρημοφυλακίας or simply ἴχνος. The receipts for ἐρημοφυλακία are: BGU. IV. 1088; P. Lond. II. 316 (c) (p. 84); P. Grenf. II. 50 (c); SP. XXII. 12; P. Ryl. II. 197 (b); P. Lond. II. 316 (b) (p. 86), 469 (a) (p. 85); SP. XXII. 140;

P. Fay. 68; SP. xxii. 62; P. Lond. iii. 922 (a) (p. 40), 1266 (g) (p. 39); P. Grenf. ii. 50 (i), (m); P. Fay. 75, 76, 186–9; P. Lond. iii. 1266 (f) (p. 39); P. Amh. ii. 117; P. Lips. 82; P. Teb. ii. 461; BGU. iii. 867. PO. xiv. 1652, dated in the third century after Christ, is an account of transport on land and river or canal. Each item of expense is followed by a surcharge of approximately 10 per cent. designated ἐρήμων; this suggests some relationship to the ἐρημοφυλακία, but the relationship cannot be definitely established because no similar surcharges have been found.

83. P. Grenf. ii. 50 (a) and BGU. iv. 1088 are for the same article of import, a camel. In P. Fay. 76 and P. Teb. ii. 461 both ῥ καὶ ν̄ and ἐρημοφυλακία are recorded on the same receipt. Similarly receipts have been found where ῥ καὶ ν̄ and the tax for the Harbour of Memphis have been exacted upon the same article: SP. xxii. 13 and P. Lond. iii. 1265 (c) (p. 36); SP. xxii. 148 and 149; P. Hamb. 76 and 77; P. Fay. 73 and 74.

84. *Nachrichten der Gesellsch. der Wissensch. zu Göttingen*, Phil.-Hist. Kl. 1925–6, pp. 76–9.

85. In P. Fay. 68 the export, upon which ἐρημοφυλακία was collected, is definitely stated to be to the Oasis (BL. i, p. 130).

86. See note 30 above.

87. The tax for the Harbour of Memphis seems to have been collected on imported asses and horses in SB. 7365.

88. SP. xxii. 62 gives 1 drachma as the toll for one donkey carrying only a pack-saddle without load. P. Fay. 68 gives 8 drachmae for 4 camels.

89. The camel-receipts are: P. Rein. 42; P. Lond. ii. 318 (p. 87), 330 (p. 88); P. Grenf. ii. 58.

90. In P. Grenf. ii. 58 the μισθωτής seems to have been replaced by a [πραγ]ματευτής. In P. Lond. ii. 330 (p. 88) ἐρη[μοτ]ελω[ν]ίας is given as an alternate name for ἐρημοφυλακίας.

91. The name of the toll merely suggests that it was a transit-toll. Fiesel's hypothesis that it was identical with the ῥ καὶ ν̄ was based on false premises (cf. note 30 above and Fiesel, op. cit., pp. 94 ff.).

92. ii. 3, 5 (101.) Cf. Uxkull-Gyllenband's discussion in BGU. v, 2 Heft, pp. 63 ff.

93. BGU. v, § 68.

94. On the date of the Gnomon of the Idiologus cf. the discussion in BGU. v, 2 Heft, p. 3 f.

95. BGU. v, §§ 64–9.

96. Cf. note 92. For the earlier treatments cf. Hogarth in Flinders Petrie's *Koptos*, London 1896, pp. 27 ff.; Rostovtzeff in *Röm. Mitt.* xii (1897), pp. 70 ff., and *Archiv*, iv, p. 309; WO. i, pp. 347–51; Lesquier in *L'Armée romaine d'Égypte*, Cairo 1918, pp. 423 ff.; OGI. ii. 674; *Archiv*, ii, p. 437; IGRR. i. 1183; Fiesel in *Nachr. d. Gesellsch. d. Wissensch. zu Göttingen*, Phil.-Hist. Kl. 1925–6, pp. 95–103.

97. N.H. vi, 102–3; cf. Fiesel, op. cit., pp. 102 ff.

98. τοῦ ἀνδρὸς ἀναβαίνοντος is taken by Dittenberger (OGI. II. 674) to mark the time of the payment for the πιττάκιον, but the phrase was probably used only to distinguish travellers from donkey-men and camel-drivers who were not required to purchase πιττάκια.

99. The phrase γυναικῶν πασῶν means merely that the rate was uniform for women of every description (although the rates for the principal charge varied); Hogarth took it as evidence of polygamy!

100. This was the interpretation of Hogarth.

101. τοῦ ἐν Κόπτωι ὑποπείπτοντος τῆι Ἀραβαρχίᾳ ἀποστολίου.

102. Hogarth and Rostovtzeff and others have regarded the extraordinarily high rate of 108 drachmae exacted from prostitutes as an attempt of the government to prohibit the entry of such women into the province. Lesquier pointed out that such paternalistic care for morals was not characteristic of the Roman government in the provinces. He rightly understood the fees to be exacted upon travellers leaving Coptos for the seaports, and properly remarked that preventing the emigration of prostitutes from Egypt hardly protected the morals of the province. It is unnecessary, however, to emend δραχμὰς ἑκατὸν ὀκτώι to δραχμὰς δέκα ὀκτώι, as Lesquier proposed, although the suggestion is ingenious. Enlisted men could not contract legal marriage, yet the γυναῖκες στρατιωτῶν are among those listed, and it is probable that γυναικῶν εἰσπλεουσῶν should be emended to γυναικῶν εἰσπλεούντων and understood as referring to the concubines of the marines of the Red Sea fleet. The prostitute was better able to pay a large fee than such women, and consequently a higher assessment was made. The higher fee set for sea-captains was not intended to discourage them from using the road, nor was the lower rate for sailors intended to encourage them.

103. Cf., however, Fiesel, op. cit., p. 100, whose suggestions I cannot accept.

104. WO. II. 262, 263, 274, 277, 302-4, 1276; O. Strass. 274; O. Br.-Berl. 4, 32; Archiv, v, p. 177, no. 28. Antonius Malchaeus, a Jew of Roman citizenship held the office of collector in the time of Trajan.

105. Cf. WO. I, p. 273.

106. Op. cit., p. 97.

107. P. Hib. 80 (250 B.C.) gives the assessment upon wine exported from the Heracleopolite nome to Hiera Nesus as $\frac{1}{24}$. No exactly similar rate for internal customs has been found in the Roman period, and the natural conclusion is that the assessment was changed. This is not a necessary conclusion, however, for there is no similar document from the Heracleopolite nome dated in the Roman period, and it is necessary to remember that the internal customs were not uniform throughout all the nomes.

108. It is not impossible that the various internal customs-dues may date from the Pharaonic period, when they would doubtless have been collected in kind; but since the duties of the internal customs in the extant documents are collected in money, the full development of the

system was certainly carried out under the administration of the Ptolemies.

109. Cf. the authorities cited in note 1 above; also Rostovtzeff, *Soc. and Ec. Hist.*, chapter iii, note 18.

CHAPTER XVI

1. See Chapter XIII, p. 234, for the inheritance tax; Chapter X for the ἀπαρχή paid by Jews. For another use of ἀπαρχή cf. BGU. IV. 1150.

2. Cf. P. Teb. I. 61 (b). 342–5, 81, 89, 91, 93, 94, 97, 98; P. Hib. 110. 23–4.

3. P. Fay. 42 (a); P. Ryl. II. 213.

4. See Chapter X, pp. 176 ff.

5. *Archiv*, I, p. 153 (O. Gizeh, no. 9632); O. Strass. 182; O. Theb. 87; P. Bouriant 31; and the three ostraca mentioned in the text are examples of the τέλος ἐπιξένων. Cf. the references to ἐπίξενοι in P. Princeton 13; P. Cornell 22; and the documents listed in Preisigke WB. I, s.v.

6. See Chapter III, p. 27 f.

7. Cf. P. Teb. II, Ostraca 6, 7, 8 (?); PSI. x. 1137.

8. P. Teb. II. 384; PSI. VIII. 902.

9. O. Strass. 44; cf. P. Gnomon (BGU. v); § 55, and P. Grenf. II. 80.

10. See Chapter IX, p. 164.

11. P. Fay. 47; P. Mil. 11, 12.

12. Cf. P. Berl. Bibl. no. 21, lines 7–8 (edited by G. Parthey in *Nuove Memorie d. Instituto Arch.* II, pp. 440 ff., and quoted by WO. I, p. 300): Στεφάνου τοῦ ἔνπρ[οσ]θεν βα[σιλικοῦ, νυνὶ δὲ εἰς] τὸν φίσκον ἀν[αλα]μβ(ανομένου). Cf. Rostovtzeff *Soc. and Ec. Hist.*, pp. 317, 368, 379, 403, 462, 466, and 611 (chapter ix, note 56) where a bibliography is given.

13. WO. II. 1376, 1556.

14. *Archiv*, VI, p. 131, nos. 30, 168, 31, 25.

15. P. Strass. 23. 82.

16. The definitely dated examples are (besides those listed in notes 13 and 14 above): WO. II. 1298 (A.D. 171), 1334 (A.D. 220 (?)—cf. BL. 2. 1 *ad loc.*); O. Strass. 142 (A.D. 157 or 180 or 212); O. Br.-Berl. 48 (A.D. 237); O. Tait, p. 97, no. 136 (A.D. 232); P. Hamb. 81 (A.D. 188); P. Teb. II. 353 (A.D. 192); P. Lond. II. 474 (p. 108) (A.D. 199); BGU. I. 62 (A.D. 199); P. Teb. II. 640 (A.D. 181–2 or 213–14); P. Ross.-Georg. III. 25 (A.D. 212); BGU. II. 458 (A.D. 220), 518 (A.D. 219); P. Lond. II. 477 (p. 109) (A.D. 220–1); BGU. II. 452 (A.D. 220–2); PO. XII. 1441 (A.D. 197–200), XIV. 1659 (218–21), XII. 1522 (A.D. 220–2); PSI. VII. 733 (A.D. 235). Examples not definitely dated are: O. Theb. 95; WO. II. 675, 683, 690; O. Fay. 46; BGU. II. 535; P. Iand. 56; SB. 4418;

BGU. I. 268; P. Hamb. 80; PO. XII. 1413; BGU. IV. 1185 (?); P. Strass. 23. 82; P. Ryl. II. 213. 352; 91; P. Fay. 20; SP. XXII. 67. 312, 56. 26; SB. 5224. 45 (but this payment of 2 obols in an account is probably not for the tax). In BGU. IV. 1123 (from Abusir, dated in the reign of Augustus) three heirs make an agreement to pay a στέφανος of 1,000 drachmae to the πράκτωρ προσόδων; this was a payment familiar in the Ptolemaic period when a grant of land was obtained from the state, and Kalén believes that in the Roman period it was transformed into the διχοινικία (P. Kalén, pp. 313–17).

17. In the introduction to PO. XIV. 1659 Grenfell and Hunt suggested that, since PO. XII. 1522 and BGU. II. 518 indicate that payments for crown-tax were made at intervals throughout the year, it was possible to infer that 12 talents 5,890 drachmae 4⅛ obols, the amount of the assessment for Hathyr 10–14, represent $\frac{1}{73}$ of the whole annual amount due from the Oxyrhynchite nome for that impost, i.e. nearly 950 talents. This is, however, very uncertain, for it is hardly likely that uniform amounts were collected every five days throughout the year. In P. Lond. inv. 1938 there are two columns containing names of tax-payers and their payments of στεφανικά; the payments were made in the months Pachon, Payni, Epiph, Mesore, and the intercalary days of one year and in Thoth and Hathyr of the following year (in the third century). The total of the payments in the first column is 2,674 drachmae, in the second column is 1,499 drachmae. At the end of the second column is a total which seems to be 7 talents 4,684 drachmae, which, if it is correct (Mr. Skeat regards it as an impossibly large sum), must include payments from a large district. P. Lond. inv. 1939 gives the total amounts collected from the persons mentioned in P. Lond. inv. 1938; the largest amount, 1206 drachmae, was collected from Julius Serenus a gymnasiarch, and the next largest, 580 drachmae, was collected from Nilus (son of Mysthus) a high-priest; other large payments were 520 drachmae from Salvius Justus, 432 drachmae from Thermutharion, and 492 drachmae from Apollonius a former exegete. The smallest payment recorded is 12 drachmae from Heron an exegete. It is unfortunate that the district covered by P. Lond. inv. 1938 and 1939 is not indicated in the documents.

18. P. Fay. 20 (A.D. 222—the date, which was disputed, has been definitely established by Wilcken in Zschr. f. Rechtsgesch. XLII (1921), pp. 150 ff.).

19. O. Tait, p. 97, no. 136; PSI. VII. 733.

20. Tait (see note 19 above) has suggested that, 'The aurum coronarium may have been decreed to Alexander on the occasion of his (alleged) victory over the Persians'.

21. PO. XII. 1441; O. Theb. 96.

22. PO. VI. 916. See also Chapter V, p. 65.

23. In O. Theb. 96 four drachmae are paid for στεφ(ανικοῦ) on ⅙ arura; it is possible, however, that 4 drachmae was the minimum payment permitted for a tax assessed at 8 drachmae an arura. Most of the

accounts of the crown-tax give payments of 4 drachmae or multiples thereof. The rate at Thebes, therefore, may have been the same as at Oxyrhynchus.

24. It is impossible to distinguish the accounts for the crown-tax collected *ad aruram* from that levied as a special tax. The Oxyrhynchite payment for the land-tax is dated A.D. 197–200, while the Theban receipt is dated A.D. 222, so that they might represent special (i.e. not annual) assessments. O. Tait, p. 104, no. 181, recording a payment (in *c.* A.D. 240–2) ὑπὲρ ʽƷ ⸗ may have been for στεφανικόν.

25. PO. XII, 1413.

26. It is probable that the ἐπικλασμοί ordered by the prefect Aemilius Saturninus (PO. VI. 899) refer to the crown-tax (which he first seems to have made incident upon land). If this is correct, the petition of Apollonarion illustrates how burdensome the crown-tax had become; she alleges that to meet the exactions she had been obliged to sacrifice her household possessions, private ornaments, and various other property.

27. See Chapter II, p. 19.

28. Cf. WO. I, p. 304.

29. See Chapter XII, p. 202 f.

30. Cf. Spiegelberg in *Ztschr. f. Ägypt. Sprache*, LIII (1917), pp. 120–2. A payment of ½ or 1 (or perhaps more) silver kite were made to the superintendent of the necropolis 'in the name of' the mummy which was brought into the necropolis.

CHAPTER XVII

1. Cf. WO. I, pp. 511–55; Wilcken, *Grundz.*, p. 182; Bouché-Leclercq, *Histoire des Lagides*, III, pp. 343–59; Rostovtzeff in CAH VII, p. 129 f. The principal sources are the *Revenue Papyrus* published by Grenfell and Hunt, P. Paris 62 republished by Wilcken with valuable commentary in UPZ. 112, and P. Hib. 29.

2. OGI. ii. 669.

3. In *Staatspacht*, pp. 464 ff; cf. *Wochenschr. f. klass. Phil.*, 1900, Sp. 122.

4. In *Grundz.*, p. 212 f.

5. In *Römische Staatsrecht*, II³, p. 1017.

6. *Grundz.*, p. 213.

7. WO. I, p. 633, cites A. Peyron (P. Tur. I, p. 147), J. G. Droysen (*Klein. Schrift.* I, pp. 10 ff.), C. Leemans (P. Leid. I, p. 57), and K. Wessely (*Bericht. Sächs. Ges. Wiss.* 1885, p. 244; *Die griech. Pap. der kais. Samml. Wiens*, 1885, p. 16). Rostovtzeff, in CAH. VII, p. 124, describes the Ptolemaic τραπεζῖται as 'the directors of the local branches of the treasury, half-officials, half tax-farmers'.

8. It is not necessary to give a complete list of such receipts. Suffi-

cient examples may be found by referring to the list of τραπεζῖται in WO. II, Indices, pp. 446–8; other examples from the Ptolemaic period may be found in BGU. VI and VII, pp. 14–64, and O. Tait, particularly Part I; further examples will be cited below in notes.

9. In *Grundz.*, p. 152 f. and WO. I, pp. 633 ff., where he refers to Franz (CIG. III, p. 298) and Lumbroso (*Recherches*, p. 333). Cf. WO. I, pp. 65–9.

10. BGU. VII. 1617 is perhaps the best example. It is a list of payments for an unknown tax—the editors suggest the tax on catoecic land, but it is probably the crown-tax assessed on land—made by 41 persons. The payments range from 4 to 52 drachmae, with the exception of two payments made by Paesis, practor of the poll-tax, who once turned in 168 drachmae and again 72 drachmae. It is unlikely that Paesis made those payments on his own account, for he surely did not have so much more property than any of the others in the list which included gymnasiarchs, a centurion, even a strategus, and other officials. Therefore it is most probable that Paesis brought to the bank the collections which he had lifted, while the others named were tax-payers who had made their payments directly to the bank. In P. Princeton I. 8, a ledger made up from entries in a day-book and from payments turned in by χειρισταί at various villages around Philadelphia, the latter appear to have turned in their collections in a lump sum at specified intervals, for no dates accompany items marked χιριστ(ῶν). In this case, however, the practor may have remained at the bank in the town of Philadelphia, while his assistants lifted the taxes from Philadelphians temporarily domiciled in surrounding villages.

11. WO. I, pp. 572 ff.

12. Ibid., p. 575.

13. In *Staatspacht*, p. 473 f.

14. Cf. note 1 above and M. Harper in *Aegyptus* XIV (1934), pp. 49 ff., 269 ff.

15. Cf. the edict of Ti. Julius Alexander, OGI. II. 669; Hadrian's rescript in Dig. 49, 14, 3, 6.

16. Cf. P. Teb. II. 484; P. Lond. II. 213 *verso* (p. 160 = W. *Chrest.* 267).

17. P. Graux 1 (= SB. 7461), 2 (= SB. 7462); P. Teb. II. 391; PO. II. 285; W. *Chrest.* I. 28. The πράκτωρ κατακριμάτων evidently performed an invidious duty continued from the Ptolemaic period.

18. P. Graux 2 (= SB. 7462).

19. *De spec. leg.* III. 159 ff.

20. Extortionate exactions of the tax-collectors were not the only factor in the depopulation of the villages during the reign of Claudius and of Nero. Poor harvests probably drove the peasants from their holdings, for an abnormally high Nile occurred during the reign of Claudius, and there is evidence for abnormal flood conditions in A.D. 42 and 45–6 and 46–7; cf. the references cited by A. C. Johnson, *Roman Egypt*, pp. 17 ff. The attractions of the cities have been mentioned

above; Alexandria in particular became a hive of industry as commerce with East and West developed. The prefects were obliged from time to time to issue special edicts requiring the return to the country of the peasants who had flocked to the cities (cf. Reinmuth, *The Prefect of Egypt*, pp. 67–71). Later on it was flight from liturgies that caused the desertion of farms and villages (Reinmuth, l.c.), and this factor may have been effective in the first century as well.

21. References are given in the text and notes below. It may be noted that after the introduction of the πράκτορες ἀργυρικῶν the banks were less active in collecting taxes, or at least issued fewer receipts.

22. See Chapter IX, pp. 137 ff.

23. Ibid., pp. 164 ff.

24. See above, note 13, and pp. 288, 299.

25. Cf. PO. XII. 1405 and introduction. For the earlier practice cf. P. Lond. III. 1220 (p. 114) where the names of two 'candidates' for the office of πράκτωρ ἀργυρικῶν of Socnopaei Nesus are submitted by the comarch to the prefect, although the document belongs to the period at the beginning of the third century (the prefecture of Subatianus Aquila, A.D. 202–7). Cf. BGU. I. 194, 235; P. Amh. 139; P. Flor. I. 2; WO. I, pp. 601 ff.; Oertel, *Die Liturgie*, pp. 198 ff. *et passim*.

26. P. Lond. II. 213 *verso* (p. 160 = W. *Chrest.* 267) with BL. I, p. 256.

27. BGU. I. 8.

28. The charges, for which the village elders and citizens were held responsible, are unfortunately in the mutilated portion of the account. But they were several, for the statement in regard to the responsibility of the elders and the citizens is thrice repeated. One item is restored [γερ]δίων. The first part of the document lists payments in money; the second part has payments in grain. The editors date the document in the second century, and it is possible that the village elders became responsible for tax-collections before senates were established in the municipalities; but the document may belong to the third century.

29. For a more complete discussion of the financial administration of the prefect cf. Reinmuth, *The Prefect of Egypt*, chapter viii.

30. *In Flaccum* 16, and 1.

31. Cf. WO. I, p. 492; Bouché-Leclercq, *Histoire des Lagides*, III, pp. 381 ff.

32. Cf. Reinmuth, op. cit., p. 65 f.; for exemption from payments of the poll-tax see Chapter VIII, pp. 116 ff.

33. Cf. Hohlwein, *L'Égypte Romaine*, Brussels 1912, p. 249.

34. Ibid., pp. 250, 285 f.

35. Ibid., p. 202 f.

36. Ibid., pp. 275–9; P. M. Meyer, *Festschrift f. O. Hirschfeld*, pp. 131–63; BGU. v (volumes I–II).

37. Cf. Otto, *Priester und Tempel*, p. 62 f.; Reinmuth, op. cit., p. 28.

38. Cf. Martin, *Les Épistratèges*, pp. 132–57; but see Chapter XV, p. 260 f.

39. PO. VI. 895; P. Teb. II. 239, 336; cf. PO. VIII. 1115.

40. Cf. BGU. III. 747 (= W. *Chrest.* 35), lines 19–23.

41. Cf. PO. I. 44 (= W. *Chrest.* 275); P. Paris 69 (= W. *Chrest.* 41), lines 39 ff. in column iii; cf. PO. XII. 1405 and the references cited in the introduction; the epistrategus in the second century frequently chose practors by lot from the lists furnished to the strategus by the comarchs or other village officials.

42. See p. 320.

43. See p. 334.

44. K. Wessely, *Zythos u. Zythera*, p. 43.

45. P. Teb. II. 239. See pp. 321, 333 f.

46. See Chapter IV, p. 31 f.

47. Cf. Reinmuth in TAPA. LXV (1934), pp. 256 ff.

48. Cf. the edict of Ti. Julius Alexander, OGI. II. 669; also Reinmuth, op. cit., pp. 65 ff.

49. OGI. II. 669, lines 6, 47 ff.

50. BGU. III. 903; cf. Reinmuth, op. cit., p. 62.

51. See p. 32 f.

52. Cf. WO. I, p. 504; for the activity of the strategus in the *logisterium* cf. P. Paris 69 (= W. *Chrest.* 41).

53. Op. cit., p. 62.

54. This is inferred from the fact that the prefect commanded the publication of the Coptos Tariff.

55. See Chapter V, note 59. A similar gnomon is found in P. Teb. II, Appendix I.

56. The following seem to be ἀπαιτήσιμα: P. Fay. 40; P. Lond. I. 119, 109 A, 109 B (pp. 140 ff.); BGU. II. 657; SP. XX. 40, XXII. 167; SB. 5118; P. Fay. 226 (?); P. Ryl. II. 217, 373; BGU. VII. 1620; P. Fay. 193, 194.

57. See Chapter X, pp. 171 ff., 179 f.

58. The first column of SB. 7365, originally published by N. Y. Clauson, is missing from the papyrus roll in the collection of the University of Wisconsin. The missing column is in the British Museum, and a photograph sent to Mr. Clauson is in the possession of Professor A. G. Laird. The first column contains the formal introduction of the report sent by the ἐπιτηρητής of the toll-gate at Bacchias to the strategus of the Heraclides division, and the collector states that his collections have been made in accordance with the gnomon (κατὰ τὸν γνώμονα).

59. In Upper Egypt the payment for bath-tax was frequently included with the poll-tax, or the bath-tax was paid in two instalments, one with the poll-tax and the other with the dike-tax; see Chapter IX, p. 156 f. The unpublished Michigan papyri from Caranis, of which P. Iand. 141 is a column, show that tetradrachms were accepted by the tax-collectors at the usual rate of 24 obols, but payments in units less

than a tetradrachm required an additional fee; cf. A. C. Johnson, *Roman Egypt*, p. 429, note 49.

60. See p. 318 f.

61. See pp. 287 f., 297, 300 f., 304 ff., 313, 316, 319 f. Preisigke (*Girowesen*, p. 38) maintained that the state-banks were to be found only in the metropoleis of the nomes, while private banks served the towns and villages.

62. Cf. WO. I, p. 69, for the Ptolemaic period. In the villages of the Fayûm in the Roman period it may be observed that payments of taxes in money (such as the poll-tax and the various assessments) were made in great numbers on certain days of certain months. H. C. Comfort has collected instances in his review (in AJA. xxxvii (1933), p. 643) showing that in P. Princeton 1. 9 the payments are concentrated on the 16th of Mechir and the 14th of Pachon, and that neither P. Princeton I, 8 nor 9 show any payment before the 6th of any month. The editors of P. Columbia had observed that most of the collections in their registers of syntaximon were made during the first nineteen days of the month; but Comfort pointed out that in one month the collections did not begin until the 10th. Comfort further noted that P. Fay. 153 and P. Columbia 2 show no payments in Thoth, and that P. Princeton I.9 shows nothing before Hathyr 23 and P. Princeton I.8 shows nothing before Choiak 9 and nothing in Mesore. He suggested that the practors, despite the titles which connect them with a definite village, moved about from place to place, or else oddly limited their collections to certain days of the month and to certain months. Comfort wondered what the practors did with the rest of their time, if the latter alternative were correct. I would suggest that the practors appeared at the local branch of the state bank on specified days to receive collections, and that the remainder of their time was spent in running down reluctant tax-payers and in the preparation of their periodic reports to the strategus. This suggestion does not eliminate the possibility that the collectors made a circuit of several towns, but this cannot be proved. I can offer nothing toward the solution of the problem of double-dating and the receipts with the phrases μετὰ λόγον, μετ( ), and εντ( ), which are discussed by Comfort with references to the previous discussions; the addition of the receipt in PSI. x. 1133 further complicates the problem.

63. This is Viereck's formula 1. 9. It is similar to the formula of ostraca from Edfu (O. Tait, p. 106, nos. 192–4).

64. WO. II. 32, 34, 36–40.

65. Cf. WO. II, index, p. 466.

66. Ibid.

67. WO. II, index, pp. 458 ff. To this may be added the following (dated from A.D. 83 to 139): O. Bruss.-Berl. 30; SB. 1086; O. Mey. 28; *Archiv*, v, pp. 170 ff., nos. 22, 31; SB. 4354, 4356; O. Tait, p. 65, no. 16; *Archiv*, vi, p. 219, no. 4; O. Tait, p. 105, no. 191; SB. 4357; *Archiv*, v, pp. 170 ff., no. 20; O. Bruss.-Berl. 35, 36, 38;

SB. 4358, 4359; O. Mey. 41; SB. 4361; O. Wilb-Brk. 6 (?), 7, 20, 22, 23.

68. WO. II. 128; λαο(γραφίας) is conjecturally restored in WO. II. 117 (dated A.D. 120).

69. WO. II. 135; cf. the correction on p. 431 and the index on p. 455.

70. To the list of πράκτορες ἀργυρικῶν to be found in WO. II, index, pp. 459–61, may be added O. Tait, p. 65, no. 18; P. Bad. IV. 101; SB. 4362; O. Bruss.-Berl. 40, 41, 42; P. Bad. IV. 102; SB. 4363; O. Strass. 285; *Archiv*, V, pp. 170 ff., no. 26; O. Bruss.-Berl. 5; SB. 7394; O. Tait, p. 66, no. 22; O. Wilb.-Brk. 26–8.

71. WO. II. 294, 293. The πράκτορες ἀργυρικῶν Σοήνης are found in WO. II. 89, 90, 93, 95-8, 276, 285, 288.

72. For references see note 70 above.

73. To the list of ἐπιτηρηταὶ ἱερᾶς πύλης Σοήνης in WO. II, index, pp. 454–6 may be added O. Tait, p. 65, no. 17; O. Strass. 284; O. Bruss.-Berl. 37; *Archiv*, V, pp. 170 ff., no. 5; O. Bruss.-Berl. 39; SB. 4360; *Archiv*, V, pp. 170 ff., no. 30, no. 6; O. Tait, p. 66, no. 21, p. 67, no. 23; O. Wilb.-Brk. 8–9. To the list of μισθωταὶ ἱερᾶς πύλης Σοήνης in WO. II, index, pp. 463–4, may be added *Archiv*, pp. 170 ff., no. 21; O. Tait, p. 180, no. F 1; SB. 4365; O. Tait, p. 175, no. C 1–2; O. Bruss.-Berl. 46, 45; O. Tait, p. 66, no. 20; *Archiv*, V, pp. 170 ff., no. 32; O. Strass. 286; O. Wilb.-Brk. 12, 13, 36, 32 (?).

74. WO. II. 140, 141, 194.

75. See Chapter III, p. 29.

76. For references see note 73 above. The receipts issued by practors were sometimes signed by assistants (βοηθοί) or by clerks (γραμματεῖς); for references see notes 67 and 70 above.

77. *Archiv*, V, pp. 170 ff., no. 30.

78. WO. II. 262, 263, 274, 277; O. Strass. 274.

79. WO. II. 302-4, 1276; O. Bruss.-Berl. 4; *Archiv*, V, pp. 170 ff., no. 28.

80. WO. II. 43, 150. There are also ἐπιτηρηταὶ πεντηκοστῆς λιμένος Σοήνης in O. Strass. 250. A τελώνης κλεινεντ( ) is found in WO. II. 185 and 187, but the nature of the tax is unknown.

81. WO. II. 83; cf. SB. 7399 and *Archiv*, VI, p. 219, no. 5. The same collector whose title appears as μισθωτὴς χειρωναξίου μηνιαίου καὶ ἑταιρικοῦ in O. Wilb.-Brk. 33 has his title shortened to μισθωτὴς χειρωναξίου μηνιαίου in O. Wilb.-Brk. 34.

82. WO. II. 298, 299, 1460.

83. Goodspeed read ['Ιο]ύλιος Μάξιμος καὶ μέτοχ(οι) [. . . .] . πραισιδ(ίου) Σοή(νης), but added that the last word might be σοκ( ) or τοκ( ).

84. Cf. WO. II, index, pp. 447 ff.; O. Strass. 38–44, 141–64; O. Tait, p. 71, no. 49; pp. 86 ff., nos. 75–98; p. 156, nos. 30–1; p. 174 f., nos. A 1, B 1; p. 67 f., nos. 24–30; O. Wilb.-Brk. 14, 15, 19, 43, 38–9 (?); W. *Chrest*. 413; PSI. III. 261; O. Bruss.-Berl. 21 ; O. Mey. 36; SB. 2133.

85. The miscellaneous receipts include: διώρυγος, κυνηγίδος, ποταμοφυλ(ακίας), ἐπικαρπίας, ἐννόμιον προβάτων, τιμὴ θρεμμάτων, φόρος Ἀντω( ) νεᾱ( ), ἐνοίκιον, στεφανικόν, ἐπιβολή, μερισμὸς ἀννώνη, ἐπικεφάλαιον.

86. O. Strass. 146–8.

87. For practors at Thebes cf. WO. II, index, pp. 461–3. To this may be added: O. Strass. 282, 186, 187, 188; O. Tait, p. 92, no. 100; O. Strass. 190, 281; PSI. VIII. 993; SB. 4348; O. Strass. 225, 202, 214; SB. 5352; O. Tait, p. 93, no. 107; p. 68, no. 31; O. Theb. 83; O. Bruss.-Berl. 44; O. Theb. 85, 86; O. Tait, p. 157, no. 34; O. Strass. 192, 203; P. Lips. 68; O. Strass. 206, 207, 213, 280; O. Theb. 84; O. Strass. 198; P. Lips. 69; O. Theb. 94; O. Strass. 200; O. Tait, p. 92, no. 102; O. Strass. 209; P. Bad. IV. 103; O. Strass. 189, 184, 195, 196, 197; O. Mey. 26; O. Strass. 201, 212, 215, 216, 217, 219, 229, 234, 231; O. Theb. 81; O. Tait, p. 68, no. 32; p. 157, no. 36; O. Strass. 199, 228, 210, 208, 211, 222, 220, 218, 221; O. Tait, p. 93, no. 103; O. Strass. 223, 224; P. Lips. 73; O. Strass. 226; O. Tait, p. 93, no. 104; p. 69, nos. 34–7; O. Mey. 27; O. Strass. 230; O. Tait, p. 93, no. 106; O. Strass. 235, 236; O. Bruss.-Berl. 43; O. Tait, p. 69, no. 38; O. Strass. 238, 239; O. Theb. 34, 35; O. Strass. 276; O. Tait, p. 156, no. 33; O. Strass. 277, 278; O. Mey. 30 a; O. Theb. 36, 37, 38; O. Tait, p. 92, no. 101; O. Theb. 82; O. Strass. 279; O. Theb. 99; O. Tait, p. 159, no. 46; O. Theb. 39; O. Tait, p. 157, no. 37; PSI. III. 266; O. Tait, p. 157, no. 38; PSI. VIII. 995; O. Tait, p. 158, nos. 39–41; O. Theb. 40; PSI. III. 269; Archiv, V, pp. 170 ff., no. 29; O. Tait, p. 158, no. 43; O. Strass. 240; O. Theb. 53; O. Tait, p. 93, no. 108; O. Theb. 79, 51; O. Tait, p. 68, no. 33; PSI. III. 271; P. Lips. 74; O. Tait, p. 180, no. G; O. Strass. 233, 237; O. Tait, p. 92, no. 99; SB. 1669; O. Strass. 283; O. Wilb.-Brk. 10, 16, 17, 11, 18, 35, 24, 25.

88. The miscellaneous taxes include: θησ( ) ἱερῶν, ἐνοίκιον, ὑπολ( ) Νησ( ), κυνηγ( ) δορ( ), λογι(. . .).

89. For the πράκτωρ βαλανείου see WO. II. 1032, 1033, 1552, 1035, 1036, 390, 1037. The πράκτωρ τοκ( ) is found in O. Strass. 227. The πράκτορες Θεαγῶν are found in O. Strass. 262–3.

90. Cf. WO. II. 1009, 763, 716, 1321, 365, 1030, 1372, 376, 1386, 396, 402, 1038, 1041, 1394, 1395.

91. WO. II, index, p. 456; SB. 4353; O. Theb. 56, 59, 60; O. Tait, p. 70, no. 43; O. Theb. 61, 62, 63; O. Tait, p. 71, no. 44; O. Theb. 65, 66, 67, 68, 69, 70; O. Tait, p. 95, no. 120; O. Theb. 75, 76, 87; O. Tait, p. 94, no. 113; O. Theb. 89; O. Tait, p. 94, no. 111; O. Strass. 449; P. Lips. 76; O. Tait, p. 164, no. 75; O. Bruss.-Berl. 47; O. Tait, p. 161, no. 57.

92. WO. II. 1449.

93. O. Tait, p. 94, no. 113; O. Theb. 87; WO. II. 1454.

94. WO. II. 1574–6, 1264, 662; O. Theb. 89; O. Tait, p. 94, no. 111; O. Strass. 449; P. Lips. 76; O. Tait, p. 164, no. 75; O. Wilb.-Brk. 40–2.

95. WO. II. 1587.

96. WO. ii, index, p. 457; O. Tait, p. 95, no. 119; SB. 4327; O. Strass. 252; O. Tait, p. 174, no. A 4; SB. 4364; O. Tait, p. 161, no. 58; *Archiv*, v, pp. 170 ff., no. 23; O. Theb. 57, 58, 64; O. Tait, p. 95, no. 118; O. Mey. 34; SB. 1675; O. Tait, p. 172, no. 140; O. Theb. 91; O. Mey. 77; O. Tait, p. 96, no. 122; SB. 4519.

97. O. Strass. 477; see above, p. 287. For the τελῶναι θησαυροῦ ἱερῶν cf. WO. ii, index, pp. 457 ff.; SB. 4520, 1088; O. Theb. 44, 46; O. Strass. 479-82; O. Tait, p. 161, nos. 60, 61; p. 174, no. A 3; O. Strass. 483-90; O. Tait, p. 71, no. 45; O. Strass. 440; O. Tait, p. 95, no. 116, no. 117; O. Wilb.-Brk. 44-8. For ἐπιτηρηταὶ θησαυροῦ ἱερῶν cf. WO. ii, index, p. 457; O. Strass. 270, 273; O. Tait, p. 161, no. 62; O. Theb. 54, 55; O. Wilb.-Brk. 46.

98. SB. 4519 (dated A.D. 14).

99. WO. ii. 1056, 1569; SB. 1675; O. Tait, p. 172, no. 140; O. Theb. 91; WO. ii. 1076.

100. WO. ii. 1056, 1053, 1419, 1031, 410, 787, 1057, 1054; O. Mey. 77.

101. WO. ii, index, p. 464 f.; O. Strass. 241-4; O. Theb. 42; O. Tait, p. 70, no. 39; p. 94, no. 110; p. 70, no. 41; O. Strass. 245, 246; O. Theb. 52, 92, 101; O. Strass. 247, 248, 249; O. Tait, p. 70, no. 40; PSI. iii. 278; O. Theb. 90. Cf. also O. Tait, p. 74, no. 68, and O. Strass. 450 for ἀπαιτηταί of taxes in kind.

102. For the μερισμὸς ἐνλείμματος ὠνίων see pp. 164 ff.

103. For these μερισμοί see pp. 159 ff.

104. WO. ii. 549, 551, 1577.

105. WO. ii. 1066, 538, 539.

106. O. Theb. 90; WO. ii. 973.

107. O. Bruss.-Berl. 44.

108. *Archiv*, v, pp. 170 ff., no. 10.

109. WO. ii. 801, 806.

110. Apollonius is the most probable expansion of Ἀπολ( ), although it might be one of the other names beginning with those four letters (cf. Preisigke, *Namenbuch*, pp. 41 ff.).

111. O. Tait, pp. 106 ff., nos. 195-212.

112. O. Tait, p. 109, no. 214.

113. O. Tait, p. 109, no. 213.

114. Cf. O. Mey. 31 introd. The receipts are: SP. xiii, p. 9, no. 19; p. 8, nos. 4-7; O. Tait, p. 106, no. 192; SP. xiii, p. 9, no. 20; O. Tait, p. 106, no. 193; SP. xiii, p. 8, nos. 8-12; p. 9, nos. 13-18; O. Mey. 30, 33; O. Tait, p. 106, no. 194; O. Mey. 33; *Archiv*, v, pp. 170 ff., nos. 24, 25; SP. xiii, p. 8, no. 1; *Archiv*, v, pp. 170 ff., no. 11; SP. xiii, p. 8, no. 3; O. Mey. 29.

115. It is possible that the following receipts, which are dated later than the introduction of πράκτορες ἀργυρικῶν elsewhere in Egypt and which include payments for λαογραφία, μερισμός, and Ἰουδαίων τέλεσμα, were collected by practors: O. Mey. 30; O. Tait, p. 106, no. 194; *Archiv*, v, pp. 170 ff., nos. 24, 25, 11; O. Mey. 29.

116. *Archiv*, VI, pp. 125 ff., no. G 2. The other receipts are included in Milne's article in *Archiv*, VI, pp. 125 ff. and include payments for poll-tax, bath-tax, dike-tax, dromos-tax; *vicesima*, crown-tax, weavers' tax, ferry-tax, transport-tax; SB. 7381-7.

117. WO. II. 1138.

118. O. Tait, p. 172, no. 140.

119. SB. 676.

120. SB. 1085.

121. O. Strass. 183.

122. O. Bruss.-Berl. 47; O. Strass. 251.

123. O. Strass. 243; 241.

124. O. Strass. 44, 77, 73, 112, 84, 99, 113, 110, 117, 142, 111, 158, 161, 162, 164.

125. O. Strass. 259, 261, 265, 266, 181, 182, 268, 271, 272, 297, 194.

126. P. Columbia 1 R.; P. Princeton 1. 1-12, 14; cf. P. Cornell 21.

127. Cf. P. Fay. 291.

128. P. Teb. II. 350, 580, 587; BGU. III. 914.

129. BGU. III. 882 (?), 812.

130. See pp. 319, 334.

131. The assistants collected taxes in the villages near Philadelphia; a list of the villages is found on p. 28 of P. Princeton 1; cf. P. Princeton I. 13 (A.D. 35) and the introduction. Cf. P. Genf. 17.

132. BGU. III. 830.

133. Receipts signed by practors (without further title) are: P. Fay. 56, 53; PSI. VIII. 885; P. Fay. 47 (a), 54; BGU. III. 761; P. Teb. II. 361; P. Fay. 55; P. Teb. II. 544; P. Lond. III. 909 (b) (p. 32); BGU. I. 273; P. Fay. 293; P. Lond. II. 367 (a) (p. 101); P. Ryl. II. 192 (b); P. Lond. II. 319 (p. 80), 340 (p. 69); P. Teb. II. 352; BGU. I. 212; P. Lond. II. 323 (p. 81); BGU. I. 219, 66, III. 704; P. Lond. III. 1234 (p. 33), III. 845 (a) (p. 33); P. Goodspeed Cairo 30 (col. xxxix); BGU. I. 270; P. Lond. II. 451 (p. 109); P. Fay. 42; P. Teb. II. 615; BGU. I. 61, 65; P. Bouriant 33; BGU. II. 362; P. Genf. 40; BGU. VII. 1711; SB. 7244; SP. XXII. 155; O. Mich. 6 (a receipt issued by a βοηθὸς τῶν πρακτόρων in A.D. 29-30).

134. Πράκτορες ἀργυρικῶν are found in the following receipts and documents from the Arsinoite nome: P. Iand. 29; PSI. IX. 1059; P. Ryl. II. 194; P. Fay. 64; BGU. IV. 1046, iii, 7, I. 134, 256; P. Lond. III. 1235 (p. 35); BGU. II. 662, III. 784, I. 15. i. 13; P. Fay. 42 (a); BGU. III. 779; P. Hamb. 44; BGU. I. 194 (= W. *Chrest.* 84), I. 49; P. Lond. III. 845 (b) (p. 34), 1216 (p. 34); P. Amh. II. 114; P Fay. 61; *Archiv*, V, p. 388 (P. Hawara 188 *verso*); P. Teb. II. 579, 355, 306, 638, 354, 353 (= W. *Chrest.* 269); P. Fay. 41; P. Lond. III. 925; P. Hamb. 45; P. Ryl. II. 192; P. Lond. II. 306 (p. 118) (= W. *Chrest.* 263); SP. XXII. 134, 135; P. Fay. 239; P. Amh. II. 118; SP. XXII. 145, 132, 144; BGU. III. 790, I. 61, 215, III. 817; P. Columbia 1 a-b; P. Oslo II. 29; P. Ryl. II. 192 (a); P. Ryl. II, p. 254 (= P. Lond. III. 917); P. Ross.-Georg. III. 24; P. Ryl. II. 191; SP. XXII. 129, 1; P.

Grenf. II. 62 (a); BGU. I. 214, III. 881; P. Lond. II. 296 (p. 107); P. Basel, 10; BGU. I. 99; SP. XXII. 139; P. Lond. II. 337 (p. 107); SP. XXII. 109; P. Cornell 42; P. Lond. III. 844 (p. 54), 919 (a) (p. 56); BGU. I. 359; SP. XXII. 102 verso, 108, 120; BGU. I. 199, 41; SP. XXII. 128, 67 verso (col. v); BGU. I. 25; SP. XXII. 103; BGU. II. 653; P. Lond. III. 1220 (p. 114); SP. XXII. 6; BGU. II. 652, 392, 639; P. Lond. III. 1232–3 (p. 57), II. 349 (p. 115); BGU. I. 42; P. Genf. 17; P. Hamb. 83; BGU. VII. 1584, 1585; P. Hamb. 81; BGU. VII. 1586; P.Grenf. II. 52; BGU. I. 330, II. 391, I. 342, III. 791, I. 222; P. Hamb. 42; P. Oslo, II. 20; P. Fay. 57; P. Preisigke 24 (= P. Fay. 200); P. Lond. II. 166 (a) (p. 116); SP. XXII. 106; SB. 5102; BGU. III. 817; SP. XXII. 147, 111–13; P. Lond. II. 380 (p. 110); O. Oslo 8, 10; O. Mich. 7, 126.

135. These miscellaneous taxes include: δαπανὴ κρίου, ἁλική, ναῦλον, ἐπίτιμον παραχειρογραφούντων, ἐπιστ(ολ . . .), θη(ρίων), στεφανικόν, ἐπικεφάλαιον, τιμὴ θυρῶν.

136. SB. 7462.

137. P. Teb. II. 391.

138. BGU. VII. 1617.

139. The fact that ια (ἔτους) [Τε]πτύνεως immediately follows λα[ογ(ραφίας?)] may indicate that the latter word is not to be understood as a part of the collector's title, but is the name of the tax. So far as we know, however, there was no poll-tax collected at the rate of 100 drachmae a year.

140. P. Teb. II. 640; P. Lond. II. 474 (p. 108); BGU. I. 62; SP. XXII. 67 verso (col. v); P. Hamb. 80; P. Ryl. II. 91; BGU. II. 458; P. Lond. II. 477 (p. 109); BGU. II. 452; cf. BGU. II. 518.

141. SB. 5982. A πράκ(τωρ) μον(οδεσμίας) χόρτ(ου) is found in O. Mich. 10.

142. BGU. II. 655.

143. BGU. II. 382. In BGU. I. 72 a πράκτωρ δημοσίας κώμης complains that persons unknown had ruined his wheat-fields, but the competence of the official is obscure (the document is dated A.D. 191).

144. BGU. I. 342.

145. P. Teb. II. 305; BGU. VII. 1602; SP. XXII. 114; P. Teb. II. 455, 539 (?), 287; BGU. I. 10, 199 verso; P. Amh. II. 119.

146. P. Teb. II. 359; PSI. III. 160; P. Ryl. II. 98 (a); PSI. v. 458; P. Fay. 42 (a).

147. P. Ryl. II. 98.

148. BGU. I. 293.

149. BGU. III. 697 (= W. Chrest. 321).

150. BGU. VII. 1607.

151. SB. 4416; BGU. III. 851, I. 49, P. Fay. 23 and introd.

152. BGU. VII. 1591.

153. P. Fay. 58, 59; P. Grenf. II. 60.

154. P. Hamb. 9.

155. PSI. v. 459.

156. SB. 7365, with the first column (unpublished) in the collection of the British Museum gives the title of the collector at Bacchias as ἐπιτηρο(ῦντος) τῆς πύλης Βακχιάδος ὑποπιπτούσης τῶ(ι) τῆς Μέμφεως λιμένι; in P. Amh. ii. 77 Polydeuces is referred to as ἐπιτηροῦντος τὴν προκειμένην πύλην (at Socnopaei Nesus), and Harpagathes may have been his grammateus; in P. Lond. iii. 1169 (p. 43) also from Socnopaei Nesus there was but one collector, whose title is not indicated, but his report was prepared by a grammateus.

157. Ibid.

158. P. Lond. ii. 478 (p. 111).

159. P. Lond. ii. 318 (p. 87), 330 (p. 88); SP. xxii. 122.

160. BGU. i. 213.

161. P. Fay. 39.

162. P. Strass. 66.

163. O. Mey. 74.

164. The phrase with ἀπό suggests that the sale of myrrh was merely the source of the money for the payment of a tax, rather than the name of the tax.

165. P. Teb. ii. 357; SP. xxii. 50; P. Hamb. 84.

166. P. Ryl. ii. 118; P. Teb. ii. 350, 580.

167. P. Ryl. ii. 188; for χειρισταί collecting syntaximon cf. P. Princeton i. 8, 10, 13; P. Lond. ii. 181 (p. 146); PSI. x. 1133.

168. P. Ryl. ii. 196.

169. BGU. iii. 882. Perhaps πέζης should be restored ⟨τρα⟩πέζης, as the editor suggested.

170. BGU. vii. 1590; P. Fay. 244.

171. For the νομογράφος cf. BGU. vii. 1589. For the οἰκονόμος οὐικάριος cf. BGU. i. 102.

172. Cf. BGU. vii. 1587 (a–b).

173. BGU. iii. 756, i. 221.

174. BGU. ii. 392, 639.

175. The editors note that the scribe first wrote πρεσβ(υτέρων) and then erased it and wrote ἡγου(μένων).

176. BGU. ii. 382; cf. BGU. i. 63, 102; P. Genf. 42.

177. P. Bouriant 27.

178. BGU. vii. 1707; P. Lond. iii. 847 (p. 54); PSI. vi. 693; BGU. i. 334, 345, iii. 711 (from Bacchias and Hephaestias).

179. BGU. i. 214.

180. P. Teb. ii. 364.

181. PO. i. 96, ii. 288, 289, 312, vi. 916, vii. 1046, x. 1283, 1284, xii. 1435; xiv. 1659.

182. The πράκτορες ξενικῶν found in SB. 7339 and PO. ix. 1203 apparently did not collect taxes.

183. PO. x. 1258.

184. PO. ii. 284.

185. PO. ii. 393.

186. PO. xii. 1520.

187. PO. XII. 1521, IV. 733, III. 597, VI. 981-2, VI. 917, XVII. 2141, X. 1283, XII. 1538, 1433, 1419, 1436.

188. The taxes include: λαογραφία, ὑική, μερισμὸς ἐρημοφυλακίας, γερδιακόν, ὀθωνιηρά, τρίτη βαλανείου, ἐπαρούριον, ἀπόμοιρα, σπονδὴ Διονύσου, ναύβιον, οὐσιακὸς φόρος παραδείσων and other φόροι, πηχισμὸς περιστερεώνων, ναῦλον.

189. PO. XVII. 2141.

190. Cf. PO. XII. 1419. 4 note.

191. PO. IV. 734.

192. PO. XII. 1441, 1522; PSI. VII. 733.

193. PO. XIV. 1659. An official designated as ὁ πρὸς παραδοχῇ is found in PO. XIV. 1659 in connexion with the collection of the crown-tax.

194. PO. I. 96, XII. 1523.

195. P. Lond. inv. 1562 verso.

196. PO. III. 580.

197. P. Ryl. II. 95.

198. SB. 5678.

199. PO. IV. 732, XII. 1440.

200. PO. XII. 1457.

201. PSI. VI. 692; PO. XII. 1562, IX. 1208, 1209, I. 185.

202. PO. I. 44 (= W. Chrest. 275).

203. PO. XII. 1413.

204. PO. X. 1257.

205. PO. IX. 1194; cf. PO. XVII. 2142.

206. Cf. PO. XII. 1418, 1417.

207. PO. I. 186.

208. P. Ryl. II. 99, 185.

209. PSI. I. 56; SB. 5677.

210. P. Lond. III. 944 (p. 53); for χειρισταί cf. P. Lond. III. 1157 (p. 62), line 25, note.

211. P. Goodspeed Cairo 10; cf. P. Flor. I. 12; SP. XXII. 130. Cf. P. Ross.-Georg. II. 24.

212. P. Ryl. II. 83; P. Bad. IV. 76, 81; P. Giss. 58; BGU. II. 434; P. Ryl. II. 78; P. Hamb. 13; BGU. II. 425, 429; P. Lond. II. 166 (a) (p. 116).

213. P. Strass. 23. 82.

214. PO. IV. 712 (= M. Chrest. 231).

215. P. Lond. II. 305 (p. 79); SB. 7342.

216. PSI. III. 222.

217. PSI. VII. 785.

218. P. Lond. III. 1157 (p. 61).

219. PSI. VI. 688.

220. PSI. VII. 798; SB. 4516, 7366.

221. Cf. W. Grundz., p. 218; PO. XII. 1410.

222. See p. 113. A practor is mentioned in SB. 7448 concerning an embassy sent to Augustus by the Alexandrians, and the τέλος ὄνου in P. Lond. II. 305 (p. 79) was paid to ἐπιτηρηταὶ ἐκστάσεως καὶ δεκάτης ἀγορᾶς at Alexandria.

223. It is pointless to attempt to list here all the receipts issued by collectors to individual tax-payers. Examples of receipts issued to representatives of corporations are: PSI. IX. 1060; BGU. VII. 1591; P. Ryl. II. 196; BGU. I. 63. Examples of receipts issued by collectors to other collectors (their subordinates) are: BGU. III. 991, I. 49; P. Lond. III. 1232–3 (p. 57 f.).

224. Cf. P. Princeton I. 9 and introduction; P. Columbia I R 2. 2. 19, 8. 18; cf. also BGU. I. 340.

225. Ibid. Cf. BGU. VII. 1616; C. W. Keyes in AJP. (1931), pp. 288 ff.

226. P. Fay. 21, especially note on lines 12–14. Cf. Reinmuth, *The Prefect of Egypt from Augustus to Diocletian*, pp. 64 ff.; A. C Johnson, *Roman Egypt*, p. 583 (no. 334 introd.).

227. Cf. WO. I, chapter iii; O. Strass., p. viii.

228. All the daybooks and registers listed above in the text are for poll-tax and other capitation taxes. The great Michigan tax-rolls (of which P. I and 141 is a column) show extensive payments of land-taxes as well. A day-book of receipts of the weavers' tax is found in PSI. X. 1154. An account of the camel-tax is found in P. Lond. II. 468 (p. 81), and an account of the naubion and μερισμός Ἀδριανείου is found in P. Lips. 93–6. Cf. P. Lond. III. 1157 (p. 61); P. Ryl. II. 185; P. Teb. II. 347; P. Cornell 36. Like the day-books of the sitologi, BGU. VII. 1617 shows that in collecting taxes in money the bank's day-book of tax-collections was sometimes divided into periods of five days; cf. P. Lond. II. 254 *verso* (p. 230). On the half-week of five days and the week of ten days cf. P. Giss. 63 introd. and the references there cited.

229. Cf. P. Ryl. II. 187; P. Ross.-Georg. II. 34; BGU. VII. 1625; P. Iand. 58; P. Ryl. II. 195; SP. XXII. 179, 180, 67 *recto*, XX. 49, 62; P. Bouriant 31; SP. XXII. 67 *verso*; BGU. I. 343, 271, II. 572–4, VII. 1627; PO. II. 389, XII. 1437; SP. XX. 68; P. Ryl. II. 374–6, 417, 427, 431; SB. 3575.

230. Detailed reports (κατ' ἄνδρα) are: BGU. I. 134, 199, II. 392, 639, I. 42, 141; PO. XII. 1433. Monthly summaries (usually called διαστολαί) are: P. Fay. 230, 293; BGU. I. 273; P. Fay. 42; BGU. I. 41, 25 (= W. *Chrest.* 270), II. 652, 653; PO. XII. 1435, X. 1283. Cf. PO. XII. 1432 and BGU. I. 121 (= W. *Chrest.* 184).

231. P. Fay. 41; P. Lond. II. 460 (p. 70).

232. P. Fay. 42 (a).

233. PO. XII. 1432; cf. PO. XII. 1435 with introd.

234. Cf. P. Lond. III. 1169 (p. 43); P. Amh. II. 77.

235. P. Ryl. II. 83; see also Chapter IV, p. 33.

236. *Archiv*, IV, pp. 122 ff.

237. Wilcken (ibid.) thinks that the dioecetes (in PO. I. 61) acted as the representative of the procurator of Neapolis. The editors of PO. I. 61 had considered him head of the financial administration as in the Ptolemaic period. Probably, however, he assessed the fine merely in his judicial capacity.

238. PO. II. 298.

239. P. Teb. II. 353 is a receipt for four years' taxes paid after a return from an absence during that period. Accounts of arrears are found in the following documents: P. Princeton I. 11, 12; SB. 7462; BGU. VII. 1614; P. Hamb. 3; BGU. II. 474; P. Fay. 42 (a); SP. XXII. 67 *verso*, col. i; BGU. I. 7; P. Ross.-Georg. II. 24; SB. 8; PSI. I. 101, 102, 105; P. Ryl. II. 213 (?); PO. II. 291, XII. 1438, X. 1257, XII. 1519, 1527, 1517; P. Cornell 47 (?); P. Iand. 32; SB. 1089.

240. OGI. II. 669. 16.

241. P. Amh. II. 114; BGU. VII. 1613. In BGU. II. 486 there is a statement that arrears of taxes in kind may be remitted if a πρόστιμον (penalty) is paid.

242. *Archiv*, III, p. 542.

243. Quoted from Reinmuth, *The Prefect of Egypt*, p. 81.

244. Cf. Reinmuth, op. cit., pp. 81-4.

245. See Chapter IV, p. 31.

246. OGI. II. 669.

247. Philo, *In Flacc.* 131-4.

248. OGI. II. 669.

249. PO. I. 57 is a letter from Aurelius Apolinarius, strategus of the Oxyrhynchite nome, to Apion, ex-strategus of the Antaeopolite nome, written at the instigation of Dioscorus, the successor to Apion, and requesting the immediate payment of the sum which the former eclogistes had failed to pay over to the treasury at the proper time. It is not entirely clear what the strategus of the Oxyrhynchite nome had to do with the matter. If the eclogistes actually embezzled the money, it was his superior, the strategus, who was held responsible for its repayment.

250. PO. III. 474. 1-20; cf. *Archiv*, VIII, p. 84; Reinmuth, *The Prefect of Egypt*, p. 84.

251. PO. II. 284, 285, 393, 394; P. Teb. II. 287.

252. Reinmuth, *The Prefect of Egypt*, p. 83.

253. P. Amh. II. 77; see Chapter XV, p. 260 f.

254. P. Giss. 61; cf. PO. III. 488; P. Iand. 53; P. Reinach, 47; PO. XII. 1460; P. Teb. II. 288 (= W. *Chrest.* 266).

255. Cf. Reinmuth, *The Prefect of Egypt*, pp. 83 ff.; see also Chapter IX, p. 153 f.

256. PO. III. 474. 20-30.

257. Cf. P. Hamb. 3; PO. XIV. 1650 (a); P. Fay. 56; PSI. VIII. 885; P. Fay. 190; P. Lond. II. 201 (a) (p. 79); P. Teb. II. 478 (= P. Ryl. II, p. 253); P. Teb. II. 361; P. Columbia 1 a-b; P. Fay 55 (= P. Ryl. II, p. 253); P. Teb. II. 295, 305; P. Ryl. II. 192; P. Lond. II. 312 (p. 80); P. Fay. 60, 193; P. Teb. II. 500, 298; P. Fay. 341 (= SP. IV, p. 118); P. Teb. II, Appendix 1; BGU. II. 471; P. Fay. 218; PO. XII. 1436; P. Ryl. II, p. 254 (= P. Lond. III. 917); P. Ryl. II. 192 a-b; SP. XXII. 171; BGU. I. 102, 219, III. 704; P. Lond. II. 329 (p. 113); P. Hamb. 82; BGU. I. 99; P. Basel 10-12, BGU. VII. 1605; P. Fay. 41; P. Lond. II. 460 (p. 70); P. Goodspeed Cairo 30; P. Lond. II. 451 (p. 109); SP. XXII.

176, xx. 49, 62 *recto*, xxii. 143; P. Bouriant 32; BGU. iii. 1010 (?), iv. 1089.

258. P. Teb. ii. 345, 298. 63; BGU. ii. 471; SB. 7379; P. Teb. ii. 338; P. Flor. i. 56.

259. Cf. J. G. Milne in JEA. xi (1925), pp. 269–83.

260. Extra charges, although not found in the receipts for internal customs-dues, are found in SB. 7365, a customs-register, and are discussed on p. 325.

261. O. Tait, p. 87, no. 79 note, citing PSI. iii. 261. In the Fayûm the surtax was introduced before the thirty-ninth year of Augustus, if the προσδιαγραφόμενα were included in the charge of 44 drachmae 6 chalci for syntaximon (cf. P. Fay. 45). Προσδιαγραφόμενα are mentioned in BGU. iv. 1189, dated 1 B.C. or A.D.

262. O. Strass. 48, which is, however, a receipt for the *adaeratio* of a payment of wheat.

263. Cf. J. G. Milne in *Annals of Archaeology and Anthropology*, vii, pp. 61 ff., summarized in O. Tait, p. 87, no. 79 note.

264. Ibid. The uniform rate of $\frac{1}{16}$ applies only to Thebes. The majority of receipts from Lower Egypt show the same rate of surtax, but there are many exceptional rates which are considered below. A. C. Johnson (*Roman Egypt*, p. 429 with note 48) believes that the receipts with the formula αἴ κ(αί) represent exactions for a premium charged when payments were not made in even tetradrachms. But I cannot follow his arithmetic in note 48, and consequently I prefer Tait's explanation of the apparent exceptions as resulting from the neglect of fractional amounts and the practice of 'subtracting $\frac{1}{16}$ from the amount paid'. It seems to me that the matter is settled by the curious rate of surtax on the dike-tax in the Arsinoite nome which is discussed above on p. 327 f.

265. In addition to the receipts from Upper Egypt found in WO. ii (which are too numerous to list) the following receipts from Thebes mention the προσδιαγραφόμενα: O. Strass. 48, 54, 55, 60; O. Mey. 36; SB. 4255; O. Strass. 61; *Archiv*, v, pp. 170 ff., no. 7; O. Strass. 62, 63; O. Tait, p. 172, no. 139; O. Strass. 64, 65, 66; O. Tait, p. 87, no. 77; O. Strass. 67, 68; O. Mey. 35; SB. 3564; O. Strass. 69; SB. 4343; O. Strass. 70, 72, 76; SB. 2133; O. Strass. 112; SB. 4330; O. Tait, p. 86, no. 76; O. Strass. 73, 74, 75, 78, 79; SB. 4332; O. Strass. 80; O. Br.-Berl. 26; SB. 4347; O. Tait, p. 175, no. B 1; p. 67, no. 26, no. 25; O. Strass. 83; O. Mey. 36 a; O. Theb. 71; O. Br.-Berl. 2; SB. 3563; O. Strass. 90, 95, 91, 92; O. Theb. 43; O. Strass. 94; O. Tait, p. 86, no. 74; O. Theb. 45; O. Tait, p. 86, no. 75; O. Theb. 48, 47; O. Strass. 96; O. Theb. 49, 50; SB. 4336; O. Tait, p. 67, no. 27; O. Br.-Berl. 31; O. Strass. 102; O. Tait, p. 156, no. 32; SB. 1637; O. Theb. 94; O. Strass. 115. To the list of receipts with αἴ κ(αί) listed in WO. i, p. 132, may be added: O. Theb. 32, 37, 38, 39, 33; O. Mey. 43, 44; O. Tait, p. 156, no. 33; O. Theb. 36. 35; O. Tait, p. 157, no. 37; p. 87, no. 79; p. 89, no. 84; p. 90, no. 90; p. 89, nos. 83, 85; p. 159, no.

45; p. 90, nos. 89, 88; p. 92, no. 99; *Archiv*, v, pp. 170 ff., no. 8; in
PSI. I. 102-3 αἱ κ(αί) seems to have another meaning. I have not
collected the references to ῥυπαραὶ δραχμαί; they require further
study; cf. J. G. Milne in *Annals of Archaeology and Anthropology*, VII,
pp. 61 ff., and A. C. Johnson, *Roman Egypt*, pp. 424-38. The following
documents from Lower Egypt show προσδιαγραφόμενα apparently at
the usual rate of $\frac{1}{16}$: P. Fay. 36; P. Teb. II. 296, 295, 579, 361; P.
Grenf. II. 48, 52; P. Lond. II. 312 (p. 80); SB. 5670; BGU. III. 889,
890; P. Lond. II. 319 (p. 80); SP. XXII. 171; P. Lond. II. 323 (p. 81),
296 (p. 107); BGU. II. 654, I. 219, III. 704; P. Lond. II. 329 (p. 113);
BGU. I. 99; P. Basel 10-12; P. Lond. II. 337 (p. 107); SP. XXII. 139,
183; P. Reinach 45; SP. XXII. 108, 176, 143; P. Genf. 40; P. Bouriant
31; P. Ryl. II. 187; SP. XX. 62 *recto*; PO. XII.1435, III. 574, 513 (= W.
Chrest. I. 183), VIII. 1112; P. Ryl. II. 215, 213; PSI. I. 101, 105; SB.
8; P. Ryl. II. 216; BGU. IV. 1189; P. Ryl. II. 225; P. Iand. 53; P. Oslo
II, p. 110. In the following receipts from the Fayûm the προσδιαγραφόμενα at 10 obols, on poll-tax at 20 drachmae, are supposed by Tait
(O. Tait, p. 87, no. 79 note) to contain 2½ obols for συμβολικά: P. Fay.
198 (= P. Cairo Preisigke 22); PSI. X. 1138; P. Fay. 350-8, 349, 49; P.
Lond. III. 909 (b), p. 32; SP. XXII. 124; P. Lond. III. 912 (a), p. 33;
PSI. VIII. 924; P. Fay. 279-84; P. Ryl. II. 360-5; P. Fay. 199 (= P.
Cairo Preisigke 21); SP. XXII. 141, 123; P. Basel 8; P. Fay. 50,
279 (= P. Cairo Preisigke 23), 197, 196, 52; P. Teb. II. 617-37. The
following documents contain προσδιαγραφόμενα at the rates char-
acteristic of garden-land in Lower Egypt: P. Lond. II. 193 (p. 122); P.
Fay. 56; P. Ryl. II. 188; PSI. VIII. 885, IX. 1059; P. Fay. 190; P. Lond.
II. 201 (p. 79); P. Teb. II. 478 (= P. Ryl. II, p. 253); P. Fay. 192, 55 (=
P. Ryl. II, p. 253); P. Ryl. II. 192; P. Fay. 341 (= SP. IV, p. 118), 193,
194, 218; P. Teb. II, Appendix I (= P. Lond. 372); P. Teb. II. 500,
549; SB. 6951; P. Ryl. II. 192 (a), 192 (b); P. Teb. II. 352; P.
Fay. 57; P. Hamb. 82; P. Ryl. II, p. 254 (= P. Lond. III. 917); P. Fay.
41; SP. XXII. 147, 111-13; P. Lond. II. 451 (p. 109); P. Grenf. II. 65;
BGU. VII. 1606; P. Hamb. 46-51, 41, 40; PO. XII. 1436, 1437. The
following documents from Lower Egypt show some pecularity in the
rate of προσδιαγραφόμενα: BGU. II. 391; P. Lond. III. 844 (p. 54); P.
Cornell 42; PSI. VII. 817; BGU. II. 471; P. Teb. II. 298; P. Hamb. 3;
PSI. IX. 1060; P. Teb. II. 306; SP. XX. 62 *recto*; P. Iand. 141 and the
great tax-rolls from Caranis in the University of Michigan library where
(in addition to unusual rates noted above in the text) the payment by
potters of προσδιαγραφόμενα of 2 drachmae on a tax of 30 drachmae
probably indicates a rate of 6½ per cent.; PO. III. 574; P. Iand. 143; PO.
XIV. 1651; P. Amh. II. 115; PSI. I. 103.

In P. Bouriant 31 what Collart read as (ἑκατοστῆς) is probably ρ =
προσδιαγραφόμενα; consequently the πεντηκοστή in this document
(which mentions also τέλος ἐπιξένων and χειρω(νάξιον) τε[κτόν]ων (?)),
may be the 2 per cent. market-tax in the Arsinoite nome.

266. P. Ryl. II. 213. 45 note. It is possible that the increase of the

poll-tax from 16 to 17 drachmae at Elephantine-Syene (see Chapter VIII, p. 128) represents the inclusion of the surtax at $\frac{1}{16}$.

267. For another expansion of $\kappa($) or $\kappa\alpha($) see p. 330.

268. P. Lond. II. 460 (p. 70); BGU. II. 485; PSI. VII. 817; see Chapter VI, note 12, and Chapter XIV, note 53. Cf. P. Fay. 57.

269. O. Tait, p. 87, no. 79 note. It is not known whether there is any connexion between the item of 4 per cent. in the προσδιαγραφόμενα and the deduction of 4 per cent. from a sum received by priests from the δημόσιοι τραπεζῖται in P. Ross.-Georg. IV. 15 : ἀργ(υρίου) ʃ χβϛ Ϝ ἐξ ὧν ὑπολ(ογοῦνται) ὑπὲρ ρ ʃ δ̄ ʃ κζϜ. A deduction of 6½ per cent. (one of the rates of προσδιαγραφόμενα) is found in a ship-captain's account in P. Columbia 1 R 4. 10. 18 (cf. BGU. VII. 1564, where the deduction is probably 6[⅓] per cent. and BGU. III. 697).

270. O. Strass. 54; WO. II. 380-2, 385 (?), 1377, 1555. Cf. P. Teb. II. 579, where the χειρωνάξιον is collected by practors.

271. Tait (O. Tait, p. 87, no. 79) assumed that the surtax was not collected on μερισμοί because they were used for purely local purposes.

272. Except in PSI. IX. 1059; cf. PO. XII. 1436 and P. Teb. II. 500.

273. J. G. Milne in JEA. XI (1925), pp. 269-83.

274. Cf. P. Ryl. II. 192. 10 note. Examples of payments of κόλλυβος in the Roman period are from the Fayûm: P. Fay. 56; PSI. VIII. 885, IX. 1059; P. Fay. 190; P. Lond. II. 201 (p. 79); P. Teb. II. 478 (= P. Ryl. II, p. 253); P. Fay. 55 (= P. Ryl. II, p. 253); P. Ryl. II. 192; P. Teb. II. 549; P. Fay. 193, 194, 218, 341 (= SP. IV, p. 108); P. Teb. II, Appendix 1 (= P. Lond. II. 372); SB. 6951; P. Bouriant 30; P. Ryl. II. 192 (a), 192 (b); P. Teb. II. 352; P. Fay. 57; P. Hamb. 82; P. Lond. III. 917 (= P. Ryl. II, p. 254); SP. XXII. 147; P. Fay. 41; SP. XXII. 111-13; P. Lond. II. 451 (p. 109); P. Grenf. II. 65; BGU. VII. 1606; P. Hamb. 46-51, 40-1.

275. Cf. P. Ryl. II, p. 246 f.

276. In P. Teb. II. 306 the rate of προσδιαγραφόμενα on five monthly payments varies slightly on four and is omitted on one. On the three payments the rate is 8½ per cent., while on the payment of 275 drachmae in line 11 the surtax of 24 drachmae 3 obols gives a rate of $8\frac{10}{11}$ per cent.; perhaps κδ (τριώβολον?) should be κγ (τριώβολον), which would give a uniform rate of 8½ per cent. In P. Teb. II. 298, lines 61 ff., the προσδιαγραφόμενα on a payment (perhaps for ἐπιστατικὸν ἱερέων, as suggested by the editors) amount to 127 drachmae 3 obols. The amount of the principal is lost, but the rate of surtax is more than $\frac{1}{16}$, because at $\frac{1}{16}$ the principal would be 2040 drachmae, whereas the total amount paid for the principal, προσδιαγραφόμενα, πρακτορικόν, [. . . . .], and συμβολικόν is less than 2,000 drachmae.

277. P. Lond. II. 329 (p. 113); SP. XXII. 171, 143; PO. XII. 1435; P. Teb. II. 295 (cf. P. Teb. II. 296).

278. BGU. II. 391; P. Cornell 42; P. Lond. III. 844 (p. 54).

279. It may be noted that a payment 100 drachmae higher, that is

of 581 drachmae 3 obols, would have yielded a surtax, at $\frac{2}{21}$, of 55 drachmae 2 obols 2 chalci.

280. A. C. Johnson, *Roman Egypt*, p. 574.

281. In PO. xiv. 1650 the ἀλλαγή is 1 drachma while the χειριστικόν is 5 drachmae; in PO. xiv. 1650 (a) the ἀλλαγή is 2 drachmae whereas the χειριστικόν is 14 drachmae; in PO. xiv. 1651 the ἀλλαγή is 2 drachmae 1 obol, but the amount for προσδιαγραφόμενα is 30 drachmae.

282. In P. Hamb. 3 (B) an amount for τιμὴ πυροῦ is recorded as 195 drachmae 3 obols with προσδ(ιαγραφόμενα) 1 drachma and συμβολικά 3½ obols; the total is given as 197 drachmae; there seems to be no explanation of such a rate of προσδιαγραφόμενα. In PSI. ix. 1060 a payment of 200 drachmae made by the ἡγούμενος γερδίων is followed by ō ʃα, which the editors suggest is προσδιαγραφόμενα of 1 drachma; again the rate is inexplicable. In O. Mey. 35 a payment of 6 drachmae 4 obols for dike-tax and 4½ obols for bath-tax is followed by προσδιαγραφόμενα of 2 obols; if the reading is correct an item of ½ obol (or of 6 chalci) has been omitted from the προσδιαγραφόμενα. In SP. xxii. 183 the amount for τέλος θυιῶν is given as 42 drachmae 2 obols with προσδιαγραφόμενα of 9 drachmae ½ obol; the principal should be read 142 drachmae 2 obols, for the total is correctly read 151 drachmae 3½ obols, which means that the surtax was calculated at the rate of 6½ per cent. and should be read 9 drachmae 1½ obols. The similar payment in W. *Chrest.* 92. 11–12 should be restored (δρ.) ρμβ (διωβ.) [προσδ(ιαγρ.) (δρ.) θ (ὄβολος ἡμιωβ.)]. In SP. xxii. 171. 7 it is probable that ½ obol has inadvertently been omitted from the amount of προσδιαγραφόμενα on the principal of 20 drachmae; similarly in SP. xxii. 143. 9–10 the amount of the principal should be 20 drachmae (ʃκ instead of ʃβ) with προσδιαγραφόμενα of 1 drachma 1½ obols, and the προσδιαγραφόμενα on 8 drachmae in line 10 should be 3 obols instead of 4 obols. In SP. xxii. 112 the amount of ναύβιον κατοίκων should be read φ (500 drachmae) instead of ρ (100 drachmae), since the προσδιαγραφόμενα are ʃν (50 drachmae). In PSI. viii. 885 line 6 should be read ναύβ(ιον) ἑνα(φεσίων) τεσσαρακαιδεκ(άτου) (ἔτους) Θεαδελ(φείας) and line 7 should continue χα(λκοῦ δραχμὰς) ʃκε προ(σδ.) χα(λκοῦ δραχμὰς) με ἐπαρο(ύριον) χα(λκοῦ δραχμὰς) τρισχ(ιλίας) | [. . .]. In P. Teb. ii. 549 the editors point out that the sum of 3,700 drachmae (ʃ Γ Ψ) should be 4,300 drachmae, the amount demanded by the προσδιαγραφόμενα and by the subsequent total; possibly 600 drachmae had been paid previously. In P. Teb. ii. 478 the προσδιαγραφόμενα should be 1 drachmae 4 obols (ʃ α ϝ) instead of 1 drachmae 3 obols (ʃ α ϝ). On BGU. vii. 1606 see Chapter V note 58. In SP. xxii. 176 the surtax on 320 drachmae for φόρος βωμῶν should be read 20 drachmae (ʃκ).

283. PO. i. 99; see also Chapter XIII, p. 228.

284. P. Lond. iii. 856 (p. 91 = W. *Chrest.* 274). This is a gnomon for customs-tolls and market-tax.

285. In the Michigan tax-rolls.

286. Cf. also PO. XII. 1434. 25.

287. Cf. J. G. Milne, JEA. XI (1925), pp. 269–83.

288. Cf. P. M. Meyer, *Festschr. f. O. Hirschfeld*, pp. 157 ff.; BGU. v (2. Heft), p. 5 f. and the references there cited.

289. Cf. O. Hirschfeld, *Die kaiserlichen Verwaltungsbeamten*, pp. 343 ff.; Reinmuth, *The Prefect of Egypt*, p. 26 and pp. 59–84.

290. See Chapter XIV, p. 250.

291. Cf., e.g., P. Kalén I R, 2 R, 4 R; SP. XXII. 120.

292. See Chapter X, p. 179.

293. Cf. A. C. Johnson, *Roman Egypt*, p. 559; P. Ryl. II. 213. 9, note.

294. It is possible that taxes called εἴδη were ear-marked for some particular fund, or perhaps they were not forwarded to Alexandria but kept for some purpose in the nomes where they were collected.

295. i.e. the item called τιμὴ θρεμμάτων which Wilcken, quoted by the editors of P. Ryl. II. 213. 69 note, thought to be an *adaeratio* of a tax in kind.

296. For a complete list consult the introduction to P. Ryl. II. 213. The τριτὴ περιστερεώνων and ὑποκείμενον ἐννομίου were not included among the εἴδη; but why these taxes on animals should not have been so included is not evident; it is obvious that the τριτὴ περιστερεώνων was once collected in kind.

297. Γῆ λιμνιτική forms a special category in P. Mend. Genev. published by Martin in SP. XVII, pp. 9 ff. Beach-land seems to form a special category in the great tax-rolls from Caranis in the University of Michigan library.

298. See Chapter V, p. 53.

299. Tables III–IV in the introduction to P. Ryl. II. 213 list the taxes to which the θησαυρικόν was added; the editors note that when the θησαυρικόν was collected on taxes belonging to the λιμνιτικά division it was not assigned to the ἱερατικά.

300. Cf. PSI. I. 101–6; SB. 8; all from the Mendesian nome.

301. Martin, *Les Épistratèges*, pp. 137–57; cf. P. Ryl. II. 213. 46 note.

302. Cf. W. *Chrest.* 92 (= BGU. I. 337 and I); SP. XXII. 183; O. Strass. 158; P. Fay. 42 (a); P. Lond. II. 447 (p. 71); BGU. I. 199; PSI. I. 101–6; SB. 8; P. Ryl. II. 213; P. Princeton 13; PO. XII. 1436; P. Paris 17; P. Flor. III. 375 (?); P. Grenf. II. 54 (?); the tax-rolls from Caranis at the University of Michigan.

303. BGU. I. 220, 221; P. Teb. II. 329, 307, 360; PSI. IX. 1055; P. Teb. II. 350, 580; P. Lond. II. 297 *verso* (p. 110); SP. XXII. 177; BGU. I. 356, IV. 1072 *verso*; P. Grenf. II. 50 (a); P. Amh. 77; PSI. I. 30, IX. 1043; P. Grenf. II. 44; P. Teb. II. 356, 605–7; P. Fay. 34; BGU. VII. 1604, 1605; PSI. VII. 787; P. Strass. 59–64. Cf. BGU. I. 8, III. 753, 733, 748, 756.

304. O. Mey. 42 introd.

305. Cf. A. C. Johnson, *Roman Egypt*, p. 569. The total in BGU. I. 8 may be near the end of the fiscal year.

306. Cf. A. C. Johnson, op. cit., pp. 439, 443 f., and in AJA. xxxviii (1934), pp. 52 ff.; Heichelheim, *Klio*, xxv (1932), pp. 124-31.

307. Velleius, II. 39; cf. Tenney Frank, JRS. xxiii (1933), pp. 143 ff.

308. Cf. Hirschfeld, *Die kaiserlichen Verwaltungsbeamten*, p. 369; Rostovtzeff, articles 'Fiscus' in PWRE. vi, Sp. 2402 f., and in De Ruggiero's *Diz. Epigr.* iii, p. 125 f.

309. Cf. Rostovtzeff, ibid.

CHAPTER XVIII

1. Epitome, 1, 6.
2. *Bellum Judaicum*, ii. 385 f.
3. *Ad Dan.* xi. 5, p. 1122 (Bened.).
4. WO. i, p. 412.
5. In *The Transport of Government Grain in Graeco-Roman Egypt*, Chapter I, an unpublished doctoral dissertation in the library of the University of Michigan.
6. In JRS. xxxiii (1933), p. 148.
7. Strabo, xvii. i. 3 (788).
8. Op. cit. (note 5 above). Thompson uses the evidence of P. Petrie iii. 76; he compares BGU. vi. 1217, which perhaps comes from the Hermopolite nome and is dated in the second century B.C.
9. Justinian, *Edict* 13, c. 8. The conversion to *modii* is reckoned with an artaba of 32 choenices; with an artaba of 24 choenices, which is less likely, the 'embole' diverted to Alexandria would have amounted to 20 million *modii* annually.
10. In *Roman Egypt*, p. 483, note 2; cf. p. 481, note 1.
11. Ibid., pp. 17-19.
12. Ibid., p. 483, note 2.
13. See Chapter XIII, pp. 216 ff.
14. Cf. A. C. Johnson, op. cit. (note 10 above), p. 246; Reinmuth, *The Prefect of Egypt from Augustus to Diocletian* (*Klio*, N.F., 21 beiheft), p. 67 f.
15. *De spec. leg.* iii. 159 ff. Cf. Rostovtzeff in *Jour. Econ. and Bus. Hist.* i (1929), pp. 337 ff., who makes no allowance for Philo's rhetorical exaggeration.
16. SB. 6944; discussed by Westermann in JEA. xi (1925), pp. 165 ff.
17. In *Festschr. f. O. Hirschfeld*, p. 129.
18. SHA, *Commodus*, 17.
19. Cf. A. C. Johnson, op. cit. (note 10 above), pp. 482 ff., citing PO. i. 58. The πράκτωρ οὐσίας appears in the third century.
20. SHA, *Aurelian*, 47.
21. See Chapter II, note 48.

22. *Ad Dan.* XI. 5, p. 1122 (Bened.).

23. *History*, II. 39.

24. Plutarch, *Pompey*, 45, states that the total tribute of the empire after Pompey's conquests was 85 million drachmae (or 340 million sesterces); this was before the conquest of Gaul. In the reign of Tiberius the total revenues of the empire, excluding Gaul, must have been much greater, for they included the tribute of Egypt which had been added by Augustus and which, as Strabo's testimony indicates, had been increased by the end of his reign. Hirtius (*Bell. Gall.* VIII. 49) states that Caesar imposed no new burdens upon Gaul, but that is no proof that Augustus did not do so later.

25. Strabo, XVII. i. 13 (798). Diodorus (XVII. 52), however, says that the king of Egypt, by whom he probably meant Ptolemy Auletes, had an income of 6,000 talents.

26. It may be possible to reconcile Strabo's statement of an income of 12,500 talents with Diodorus' 6,000 talents (see the preceding note), if we assume that Diodorus was using a figure based on the standard Attic drachma, whereas Strabo quoted Cicero who obtained his figure from Rabirius who was familiar with the accounts of Auletes based on the depreciated Egyptian drachma. Thus the income of Auletes would have amounted to 144 million sesterces, and the income from Egypt at the end of the reign of Augustus to a little more.

27. Strabo, XVII. i. 53 (819).

28. In JRS. XVII (1927), pp. 1 ff.

29. Dio, 51. 5, 17. 6.

30. In JRS. XXIII (1933), pp. 145 ff.

31. The increase in bureaucratic officials in Egypt occurred in such sorry days as those preceding and during the reign of Diocletian; cf. PO. I. 58.

32. Dessau 1431, 1433; CIL. III. 682.

33. A. C. Johnson, op. cit. (note 10 above), p. 671 f.

34. P. Bad. IV. 107–8, ostraca from Thebes.

35. A. C. Johnson, op. cit. (note 10 above), p. 487.

36. PO. II. 252 (A.D. 19–20) is the report of the flight of a weaver. Cf. Rostovtzeff in *Jour. Econ. and Bus. Hist.* I. (1929), p. 350; cf. also PO. II. 253.

37. See Chapter XVII, p. 291.

38. Dio, LXV. 8; SP. IV, p. 68 f., lines 331–68, 564–8; see above, Chapter VIII, p. 118 f. Rostovtzeff, in PWRE. 6, Sp. 2403 f. (cf. his article 'Fiscus' in De Ruggiero, *Diz. Epig.* III, pp. 125 ff.), believes that Vespasian exacted the poll-tax from the Alexandrians, but he is unable to explain the passages here cited.

39. SP. XIII, p. 8, no. 5.

40. Philo, *In Flacc.*, § 6 (M. II. 523); cf. J. Juster, *Les Juifs dans l'empire romain*, vol. I, p. 209, note 9.

41. P. Fay. 67; the variety of customs-due is not specified, but it was probably ρ καὶ ύ.

42. O. Mey. 40.

43. O. Strass. 130.

44. See Chapter VIII, p. 128. At Thebes the poll-tax paid at the rate of 10 drachmae a year was increased to 10 drachmae 4 obols, but this again may mean merely that the προσδιαγραφόμενα at $\frac{1}{16}$ ($=$ exactly 3 obols 6 chalci, which is likely to have been reckoned roughly at 4 obols) was included in the main sum, as has been suggested above for the increase of 1 drachma in the poll-tax at Elephantine-Syene in A.D. 96–7. It is not so simple to explain why the poll-tax at Elephantine-Syene in the reign of Trajan was advanced again from 17 drachmae to 17½ drachmae, unless we assume that the additional 3 obols represent the inclusion of a charge for receipt (συμβολικά). It is impossible, however, to account for the rise in the rate of 20 drachmae for χειρω-νάξιον at Elephantine-Syene to 20 drachmae 2 obols about A.D. 83–4 by any such assumption, for the προσδιαγραφόμενα on 20 drachmae would total 1 drachma 1½ obols.

45. See Chapter XVI, p. 283.

46. See Chapter IX, p. 168, and Chapter VIII, pp. 118 f., 131.

47. In the Roman period even the dues paid by priests for advances in the hierarchy show the same relation to ἐκφόρια and καθήκοντα; see Chapter XIV, note 75.

48. Milne, 'The Ruin of Egypt by Roman Mismanagement', in J.R.S. XVII (1927), pp. 1 ff.; Rostovtzeff, 'Roman Exploitation of Egypt in the First Century', in *Jour. Econ. and Bus. Hist.* I (1929), pp. 337 ff.; Bell, 'The Decay of a Civilization', JEA. X (1924), pp. 207 ff.

49. PO. VI. 899.

50. Zosimus, I. 20.

51. Cf. Milne, *History of Egypt under Roman Rule*, New York 1898, pp. 77–81.

52. Cf. PSI. V. 476 and introduction.

INDEX

In the Greek Index are included references to the pages where the Greek name of a tax or of a collector has been replaced by the English translation.

A

α . . . 353.

ἄβροχος γῆ 8, 9, 13, 32, 33, 358.

ἀγορανομεῖον 165, 288, 315.

ἀγορανομία 208, 317, 449. ἀ. ὠνίων 270, 467.

ἀγορανόμοι 208.

ἄγραφος 235.

ἀθηροπώλης 207.

αἱ κ(αί) 324, 437, 486.

αἰγιαλοί 72.

αἰτήσεως τέλος 235.

ακκ( ) 353.

ἀκρόδρυα 52, 375, 376.

ἀληθικ( ) μυομ(εν) 353.

ἁλιεύς 209, 212, 334, 445. ἀ. ἀπὸ ποδός 221.

ἁλιευτικά 221. ἀ. πλοῖα 219, 220, 334, 445.

ἁλική 123, 124, 184, 188, 409, 410, 432, 433, 481.

ἀλλαγή 55–7, 59, 60, 259, 263, 264, 325, 329, 330, 464, 489.

αλλεων or αλτεων 17, 363.

ἀλόητρα 370.

ἁλωνία 34.

ἁλωνοφύλακες 369.

ἅμαξα 206, 281, 301.

Ἄμμων θεὸς μέγιστος 244. ἱερᾶς Ἄμμωνος 378.

ἀμπελικά 49, 374.

ἀμπελῖτις 14, 15, 19.

ἀμφοδάρχης 99, 100, 112, 113, 114, 115, 170, 171, 173, 174, 192.

ἀμφοδαρχία 418.

ἀμφοδογραμματεύς 99, 100, 106, 289, 396.

ἀναβολὴ χωμάτων 142, 380.

ἀναβολικόν 214–19, 339, 349, 444, 445, 464.

ἀναγραφή 235, 395.

ἀνακεχωρηκότες 105, 106, 137–140, 161, 164, 203, 204, 291, 292, 298, 302, 307, 420, 491, 492.

ἀνάλωμα οἰνηγίας 264, 328, 465. ἀ. πλοίου 265, 466. ἀ. χρόνων . . ακ( ) 353.

ἀναμέτρησις 28.

ἀναπόγραφος 114.

ἀνδριάς or ἀνδ( ) 159–62.

ἀνεπίκριτος 114, 314.

ἀνιερωμένη γῆ 4, 356, 357.

ἀννώνη 23, 24, 29, 154, 155, 216, 299, 305, 315, 365, 425.

ἀντιγραφεύς 286, 288.

απαι( ) 353.

ἀπαιτήσιμον 9, 33, 295, 296, 359, 369, 454, 475.

ἀπαίτησις 34, 204.

ἀπαιτητής 164, 165, 288, 300, 303, 305, 308, 316, 331, 479. ἀ. ἀννώνης 23, 316. ἀ. ἀχύρου 25. ἀ. γράστεως 26. ἀ. διδράχμου γερδίων 436. ἀ. ἱεροῦ ἀναβολικοῦ 215, 316. ἀ. κριθῆς κυριακῆς 23. ἀ. κυάμων 303. ἀ. μερισμοῦ βαλ( ) 159. ἀ. μερισμοῦ πλινθευομένης 163. ἀ. μερισμοῦ πρακτορίου 166. ἀ. τέλους ἐγκυκλίου 303. ἀ. τιμῆς πυροῦ 316.

ἀπαράστατος 114.
ἀπαρχή 170, 176, 234, 277, 470.
ἀπεύθυνοι 292.
ἀπογραφή 8, 10, 13, 83, 84, 86, 89–91, 94, 98, 100, 103, 104, 179, 235, 295, 358, 362, 390, 392, 395, 407, 417, 431. ἀ. δευτέρα 81, 82. ἀ. καμήλων 84, 88, 89, 390, 391. ἀ. κατ᾽ οἰκίαν 10, 96–111, 116, 117, 359, 392–401, 434. ἀ. ὄνων 90–3, 315, 317, 391. ἀ. προβάτων 81–2, 86, 88, 387.
ἀποδέκτης 36. ἀ. λίνου τοῦ ἀναβολικοῦ 216.
ἀπολογισμός 321. ἀ.τοῦἐδάφους 6.
ἀπόμοιρα 24, 48, 49, 53–9, 61, 62, 65, 68, 231, 241, 286, 313, 326, 330, 332, 348, 353, 374, 377–80, 449, 452, 483.
ἀπομ( ) πολ( ) 353.
ἄποροι ἀνεύρετοι 137, 321.
ἀποστόλιον 274, 469.
ἀπόστολος 273, 274.
ἀπότακτον τῶν ἐναποσημαιομένων ἁλιευτικῶν πλοίων 219, 445.
ἀποχ( ) 353.
Ἀραβάρχης 274.
ἀραβοτοξότης 259–61, 323.
ἀργυρικὰ τελέσματα τῶν σιτικῶν 47.
ἀργυρικὸς φόρος 71.
ἀργυρίου μερισμός 168.
ἀρίθμησις 67, 195, 313, 431, 437.
ἀριθμητής 179, 431.
ἀριθμητικόν 86, 87, 179, 180, 280, 330, 389, 430, 431. ἀ. κατοικικῆς γῆς 176. ἀ. κατοίκων 127, 176–80, 278, 295, 307, 308, 327, 331, 406, 411, 430, 431. ἀ. τέλειον 177–9. ἀ. φυλακιτῶν 180, 331.

ἄρουρα 64, 142.
αρ . . . ρ 353.
Ἀρσινόης φορικά 81, 387.
ἀρταβία 15, 362.
Ἄρτεμις 263, 465.
ἀρτοκόπος 207, 208, 443.
ἀρτοποιία 222, 446.
ἀρτοπῶλαι 222, 446.
ἀρτοστάσιον 207.
ἀρτυμᾶτες 208, 212, 443.
ἀρχιερεὺς Ἀλεξανδρείας καὶ Αἰγύπτου πάσης 238, 250–2, 293, 331, 451.
ἀρώματα 188, 208, 209.
ἀσχολούμενος, ὁ, 288, 315. ἀ. τὴν ὁρμοφυλακίαν 275, 300. ἀ. τὴν παντοπωλικήν 208, 315.
ἀτέλεια 12, 29, 117–20, 239, 281, 282, 293, 294, 318, 346, 360, 407, 408, 432.
ἀτελεῖς 113, 118.
α . τ( ) λημμάτων 353.
ἀφ( ) 353. ἀφ( ) σ( ) 353.
ἀφῆλιξ 193, 400.
ἀχυρικά 25, 367.
ἀχυραιοί 25.
ἀχυροπράκτορες 25.

B

βα( ) 353.
βαλανεύς 304.
βαλανευτής 156.
βαλανευτικόν 28, 130, 132, 155–9, 167, 188, 223, 240, 287, 301–6, 327, 345, 351, 418, 425, 426, 475, 480, 489.
βασιλικός. β. γεωργός 3. β. γῆ 2, 3, 5, 11, 14, 16, 17, 21, 55, 59, 61. β. γραμματεύς 7, 8, 33, 37, 42, 82–4, 89, 90, 99, 111–14, 120, 165, 192, 288, 294, 311, 315, 320–3, 333, 397, 449. β. κτήνη 78. β. μονοδε-

σμία 384. β. τράπεζαι 287, 304.
βαφεύς 200, 201, 212, 443.
βαφική 199.
βεβαιωτικόν 229.
βενεφικιάριος 265.
βιβλιοθήκη ἐγκτήσεων 10, 237, 359. β. τῶν δημοσίων λόγων 10, 105.
βιβλιοφύλακες 9, 10, 84, 110, 113.
βικάριος 277.
βοηθός 33, 36, 85, 221, 300, 304, 311, 371, 414, 477, 480. β. ἁλιέων 311. β. γεωργῶν 73, 289.
βολβιτοπῶλαι 225.
βουλευτής 313.
βουλή 29, 100, 168, 292, 334, 339, 349.
β . . το( ) 353.
βύσσος 199.
βυσσουργός 193.

Γ

γενηματογραφούμενα ὑπάρχοντα 5, 309.
γενηματοφύλακες 369.
γένος 263, 264. γ. ζωγραφικά 222.
γέρα 253, 327, 460.
γερδίαινα 192.
γερδιακόν 194-9, 302, 436-9, 453, 480, 483, 484.
γερδικὸν τέλος 194, 297.
γερδιοραβδιστής 202, 308.
γέρδιος 193-9, 212, 309, 327, 434, 436.
γεωμετρία 28, 47-55, 63, 179, 296, 297, 299, 301, 302, 306, 374-6, 379, 380.
γῆ ἀμπελῖτις 14, 15, 362. γ. ἔμβροχος 8. γ. ἐν ἄμμῳ 8. γ. ἐν ἀφέσει 2, 60, 61, 142. γ.

ἰδιωτική 283. γ. καθ᾽ ὕδατος 8, 32, 33. γ. λιμνιτική 332, 453. γ. ὕφαμμος 8. γ. ὑφ᾽ ὕδωρ 8. γ. φυλακιτῶν 278.
γλυ( ) 353.
γναφεύς 200-2, 327, 443.
γνώμων 40, 58-62, 192, 200, 205, 224, 225, 232, 265-7, 273-4, 293, 295, 296, 380, 399, 468, 475, 489.
γνωστήρ 110.
γραμματεία φυλακιτῶν 278, 279.
γραμματεύς 33, 36, 83, 259, 263-5, 304, 333, 371, 477, 482. γ. θησαυροῦ 304. γ. μητροπόλεως 99, 100, 106, 112, 114. γ. πέζης Ἀνουβίου 311. γ. πόλεως 9, 100. γ. πρακτόρων ἀργυρικῶν 353. γ. πρεσβυτέρων καὶ οἱ μέτοχοι 313. γ. τοπαρχίας 353.
γραμματικόν 70, 236, 237, 277, 449. γ. φυλακιτῶν 277, 278. γ. φυλάκων 451.
γράστις 25, 74, 384.
γραφεῖον 71, 236, 237, 270, 323, 467.
γραφὴ ἐνοικίων 99. γ. καταλοχισμῶν 179, 180. γ. λειτουργῶν 307.
γράφοντες τὸν νόμον, οἱ, 82.
γρ( ) τ( ) 353.
γρυτοπώλης 208, 443.
γυμνασιάρχης 25, 110.
γυμνασίου, οἱ ἀπὸ, 118, 119, 403-5.
γυψική 223, 327, 446.

Δ

δ( ) or δα( ) 353.
δαπάνη 439. δ. διπλῶν 153. δ. κρίου 481.
δαπιδύφων 198.
δ[. .]ασ κορακ 354.

δασμ( ) 353.
δεκάδραχμος 65, 409.
δεκανικόν 70, 209, 219. δ. ἰχθυο-
μεταβολῶν 249.
δέκανοι 151, 219, 424.
δεκαπεντάρουροι 18.
δεκάπρωτοι 27, 37, 244, 317,
371.
δεκάρουροι 18.
δεκάτη 54, 227, 377. δ. ἀγορᾶς
226, 317, 449. δ. κλ 450. δ.
μόσχων 247, 248, 455.
δέρμα εἰς κατασκευὴν ὅπλων 368.
δεσμοφυλακία 128, 150, 299, 304,
310, 353, 354, 424.
δημόσιον 259, 436.
δημόσιος. δ. (τελέσματα) 205,
222, 223, 299, 308, 321, 430,
434. δ. βιβλιοθήκη 105, 111.
δ. βιβλιοφύλαξ 113. δ. γεωργός
3, 4, 21, 26, 49, 61, 72, 74, 79,
306, 357, 385. δ. γῆ 3, 55, 357.
δ. καμῆλοι 88. δ. κτήνη 78, 80.
δ. ὄνοι 78. δ. τῆς Φεννησίας
245. δ. τοῦ μυλαίου 222. δ.
τράπεζα 312, 324. δ. τραπεζῖται 241.
δημοσιώνης 165, 287, 305, 315.
δ. τέλους καταλοχισμῶν 232,
233, 310.
δημοσίωσις 234, 235.
διαγραφή 228, 229, 353, 449.
διαίρεσις 236.
διανομή 235. δ. ἀρουρῶν 450.
διαπύλιον 269, 270.
διαρταβία 40, 356, 361.
διαστολή 484.
διάφορα 56. δ. φορέτρου 21, 43.
διάχωμα 140, 420.
διδάσκαλος 193.
διδραχμία 67, 68. δ. Σούχου 242,
453.
δίδραχμον 170, 171, 173, 174,

176, 353, 429, 430. δ. γερδίων
308, 436. δ. τριόβολοι 65, 66.
δίκαια 120, 406.
διλ( ) 305, 347, 353.
διογ[ ] 353.
διοίκησις 50, 52, 53, 61, 63, 64,
66, 67, 70, 135, 144, 166, 223,
242, 284, 331, 332, 377, 382,
428, 452, 453.
διοικητής 293, 321, 484.
διπλῆ 153, 154, 298, 299, 302,
304, 425.
δίπλωμα 92, 153, 187, 425, 446.
δ. . . . . ἀρτοποιίας 222. δ. εἱε-
ρῶν 186. δ. ιπ[. . .] 186. δ.
ἵππων 391, 433. δ. ἱπωτηρίου
433. δ. λαχανοπωλῶν 207. δ.
ὄνων 91, 92, 309, 391.
διχοινικία 12, 16, 40, 361, 362,
363.
διῶρυξ 477.
δο( ) 354.
δοκιμασταί 431.
δοκιμαστικόν 431.
δόσις χόρτου 74.
δραγματηγία 34, 35, 42, 334,
383.
δραχμή 68. δ. Μεμνονείων 428.
δρόμος 226, 242, 271, 467, 480.
δρύμοι 72, 220.
δωδεκάδραχμος 110.
δω( ) ἱερευτικῶν 243.
δωρεαί 1.

E

ε( ) 354.
ἑβδομή 224.
ἐγκύκλιον 67, 75, 165, 226–31,
234, 237, 246, 288, 302, 303,
306, 310, 313–15, 317, 324,
329, 334, 344, 448–50, 453,
455. ἐ. κλ( ) 450.
ἐγλήμπτωρ 288, 309, 317. ἐ. β̄

ἀγορανομίας καὶ ἑτέρων εἰδῶν 208, 317. ἐ. γερδιακοῦ 315, 434. ἐ. γερδίων καὶ ἄλλων 309. ἐ. διπλώματος ὄνων νόμου καὶ ἄλλων ὠνῶν 309. ἐ. ζυγοστασίου μητροπόλεως καὶ νόμων καὶ ἄλλων ὠνῶν 309. ἐ. . . . . ï ἀγορανομίας 449. ἐ. μέλιτος καὶ κηροῦ 280. ἐ. ὄνων νόμου καὶ ἄλλων ὠνῶν 91. ἐ. χειρωναξίου κοπῆς καὶ τριχός 309.

ἐγμετρητής 37.

εδ( ) 354.

εἶδος 55, 61, 73, 74, 93, 124, 208, 270, 317, 326–8, 332, 354, 378, 391, 467, 490. ε. ἀννώνης 155. ε. γενῶν ζωγραφικῶν 308. ε. ἐγκυκλίου 310, 449. ε. ἐλαϊκά 186, 433. ε. ὄνων 91, 317. ε. ὁρμοφυλακίας 275, 300. ε. ὑικῆς 94, 322, 410.

εἰκοσίδραχμος 73, 74.

εἰκοστή 75, 231, 241, 332, 333. ε. ἐλευθεριῶν 230.

εἰληφότες, οἱ, 215.

εἰσαγώγιον 271.

εἰσιτήριον 278, 281.

εἰσκριτικόν or ὑπὲρ εἰσκρίσεως 249–51, 298, 299, 452, 457–9.

ἑκατοστή 39, 228, 231, 232, 260, 268–70, 278, 372, 487.

ἐκδόσεων τελέσματα 279.

ἐκλογιστής 32, 33, 200, 201, 295, 322, 333, 369, 485.

ἔκστασις (καὶ δεκάτη ἀγορᾶς) 226, 229, 317, 449.

ἕκτη 54, 231, 377, 378. ἑ. τεμάχων 223.

ἐκτηλογουμένη τάξις 58, 59, 62, 377, 380.

ἕκτον 28. ἑ. βασιλικῆς μονοδεσμίας 384.

ἐκφόρια 10, 49, 71, 72, 76, 95, 338, 350, 356, 360, 386, 458, 493.

ἐλαϊκά 375, 381.

ἐλαϊκή 186, 308, 375, 381, 433.

ἐλαιοκάπηλος 185.

ἔλαιον 29, 186.

ἐλαιοπώλης 207, 443.

ἐλαιουργεῖον 185.

ἐλάσσωμα 107, 118, 203, 407.

ἐλευθέρωσις 230.

ἐμβαδεία 230, 317.

ἐμβολή 368, 491.

ἔμπορος 207, 212, 266.

ἐννόμιον 72, 83, 86, 87, 93, 297, 325, 330, 332, 333, 350, 385–90, 457, 478, 490. ἐ. καμήλων 88, 389. ἐ. προβάτων καὶ αἰγῶν 430, 431.

ἐνοίκιον 75, 76, 308, 354, 385, 478. ἐ. ἀνακ(εχωρηκότων) 76. ἐ. θησαυροῦ 40, 41, 45, 372. ἐ. οἰκίας 299. ἐ. οἰκοπέδων 75.

ἐνόρμιον 275, 300.

εξ( ) 354.

ἐξαγώγιον 271.

ἐξαδραχμία τῶν ὄνων 90–2, 315, 328, 391.

ἐξάδραχμος Φιλαδέλφου 64, 453.

ἐξαρίθμησις 84, 87. ἐ. θρεμμάτων 388. ἐ. καμήλων 84. ἐ. προβάτων καὶ αἰγῶν καὶ καμήλων καὶ ἄλλων 84.

ἐξειληφότες, οἱ, 91, 288. ἐ. τὴν ἐξαδραχμίαν τῶν ὄνων 90, 94, 315. ἐ. τὸ τέλος τῶν ὄνων 90, 317.

ἐξέτασις 8, 111, 359, 406.

ἐξεταστὴς τέλους χειρωναξίου 309, 322.

ἐξηκοντάδραχμος μερισμὸς εἰς τὸ κατ' οἰκίαν τῆς πόλεως 134, 417.

επ( ) 354.

ἐπαρούριον 48, 49, 53, 56–62, 64, 68, 326, 374, 378–80, 483, 489.
ἐπεικτής 315. ἐ. χρυσοῦ στεφάνου καὶ Νίκης 315.
ἐπιβολή 20, 21, 51, 168, 349, 364, 478. ἐ. κώμης 20, 21. ἐ. πηχισμοῦ 76.
ἐπιγραφή 50. ἐ. κώμης 365.
ἐπιδέκατον 228, 329, 450.
ἐπίθεμα 26.
ἐπικαρπίᾳ 478.
ἐπικαρσίου 354.
ἐπικαταβολῆς ὑποθήκης 236.
ἐπικεκριμένοι, οἱ, 110, 114, 117, 118, 403, 405.
ἐπικεφάλαιον 126, 127, 191, 325, 406, 411, 417, 478, 481.
ἐπικλασμός 26, 70, 71, 290, 307, 351, 383, 472.
ἐπίκρισις 10, 98, 105, 109–19, 126, 171, 172, 400, 403, 404, 407–11, 428. ἐ. κατ᾽ οἰκίαν 400.
ἐπικριταί 110.
ἐπιμελητής 23. ἐ. ἀννώνης 315. ἐ. λιμνασμοῦ κώμης 359.
ἐπιμερισμός 20, 21, 27, 29, 43, 364, 367, 407. ἐ. ἀπόρων 139, 420.
ἐπινέμησις 27.
ἐπίξενοι 121, 278, 470.
ἐπίπλοος 264.
ἐπίσκεψις 6–9, 359, 360.
ἐπισπουδασμὸς φορέτρου 42, 368.
ἐπίσταλμα ὡρισμένον 236.
ἐπιστατεία (καὶ πέμπτη) 261, 262, 265, 465, 467. ἐ. φυλακιτῶν 279.
ἐπιστάτης 261, 333. ἐ. ἱεροῦ 252, 457, 459. ἐ. ἱερῶν 252, 457, 459. ἐ. φυλακιτῶν 279.
ἐπιστατικόν 28, 70, 354, 368, 459, 460. ἐ. ἱερέων 223, 252,

253, 327, 416, 452, 458, 459, 488.
ἐπιστολικόν 279, 481.
ἐπιστρατηγία 255, 267, 268, 273, 275, 347, 466.
ἐπιστρατηγός 23, 33, 200, 260, 261, 293, 310, 322, 333, 475.
ἐπισφραγισταί 36.
ἐπιτήρησις ὠνῆς πελωχικοῦ 289.
ἐπιτηρητής 24, 224, 288, 296, 298–300, 302, 303, 308, 309, 315–17, 326, 446, 453. ἐ. ἀγορανομίας 305, 447. ἐ. γενηματογραφουμένων ὑπαρχόντων 309. ἐ. γερδίων or γερδιακοῦ 195, 308. ἐ. γραφείου μητροπόλεως 309. ἐ. ἐγκυκλίου 229, 314. ἐ. εἴδους ὁρμοφυλακίας 300. ἐ. ἐκστάσεως καὶ δεκάτης ἀγορᾶς 226, 317, 449, 483. ἐ. . . . . ἐλαϊκῆς καὶ ἄλλων προσόδων 308, 381. ἐ. ἑρμηνίας 309. ἐ. ἑρμηνίας ἁλοπωλῶν 183. ἐ. θησαυροῦ ἱερῶν 157, 158, 240, 302, 303, 479. ἐ. ἱερᾶς πύλης Σοήνης 288, 292, 299, 300, 477. ἐ. ἱερατικῶν ὠνῶν 308. ἐ. ἰχθυηρᾶς δρύμων 220. ἐ. κατακ( ) 302. ἐ. κοπῆς καὶ τριχός 308. ἐ. κπ[ησ . . .] 205, 308. ἐ. κτημάτων γενηματογραφουμένων 302, 368. ἐ. λεσωνείας 308. ἐ. μισθοῦ βαφικῆς 199, 308. ἐ. νεᾶς ἀμπελίτιδος 302. ἐ. νόμων 72. ἐ. ξενικῆς πρακτορίας 316. ἐ. οἴνου καὶ φοινίκων 302. ἐ. οὐσιακῶν 309. ἐ. πεντηκοστῆς λιμένος 300, 467, 477. ἐ. πορθμίου 302. ἐ. προσόδων Ἀλεξανδρείας 293. ἐ. σταθμοῦ Πτολεμαΐδος Ὅρμου 309. ἐ. στεφανικῶν 282, 316. ἐ. τέλους ἀγορανομίας 302, 442.

ἐ. τέλους γερδίων 195, 302.
ἐ. τέλους ἐγκυκλίου ἀνδραπόδων καὶ πλοίων 230, 302. ἐ. τέλους ἐπιξένων 278, 302. ἐ. τέλους ἱματιοπωλῶν 202, 284. ἐ. τέλους μεταβολῶν ἁλιέων 209, 302. ἐ. τέλους χειρωναξίου 201, 309, 322. ἐ. τελωνικῶν 220, 222, 308. ἐ. τῆς νομαρχίας 260, 323. ἐ. τῆς πύλης 259, 260, 320, 323, 475, 482. ἐ. τιμῆς οἴνου 302. ἐ. τιμῆς οἴνου καὶ φοινίκων 302, 378. ἐ. τῶν ἐπιστολῶν 321. ἐ. ὑπὲρ καταπομπῆς μηνιαίου 320. ἐ. φόρου φράγμου 315. ἐ. ...... ων καὶ δρύμου 220.
ἐπίτιμον παραχειρογραφούντων 481.
ἐπίτριτον 27, 28, 279, 311, 367.
ἐπίτροπος Νέας πόλεως 321, 484.
ἐ. οὐσιακός 8, 293, 331, 333.
ἑπόμενα, τά, 38, 39, 329.
ἑπτάρουροι μάχιμοι 14, 18.
επ( ) χ( ) 354.
ἐραυνητής 262, 264, 464, 465.
ἐραυνητικόν 263, 264, 465.
ἐργαστήριον 35.
ἐρετικόν 279.
ἐρημοτελωνία 468.
ἐρημοφυλακία 151, 152, 155, 268, 272–4, 462, 463, 467, 468.
ἐρήμων 329, 468.
ἐριοκάπηλος 211.
ἐριοκάρτης 211.
ἐριοπώλης 211.
ἐριοραβδιστής 202.
ἑρμηνεύς 263, 465. ἐ. ἐλαίου 207, 212, 443.
ἑρμηνία ἁλοπωλῶν 183, 443.
ἑταιρικόν 193, 209–11, 300, 442.
εὐθηνία 94, 464.
εὐσχήμονες 8.

ἐφηβεία 406.
ε . ( ) . . ω( ) 354.
ἐωνημένη γῆ 3, 5, 16.

Z

ζευγματικόν 280.
ζυτηρὰ κατ' ἄνδρα 73, 187, 188, 249, 312, 334, 434.
ζυτοποιία κατ' ἄνδρα 187.
ζυτοποιός 187, 433.
ζυτοπώλης 209, 443.

H

ἡγούμενοι, οἱ, 311, 312, 442, 482.
ἡ. γερδίων 489. ἡ. ἱερέων 106, 249, 311.
ἡμιαρταβία ποδώματος 40.
ἡμιόλια 39.
ἡμιτέλειον ἀριθμητικόν 177, 178.
ἠπητής 202, 212.

Θ

θεορικόν (θεωρικόν) 454.
θηρᾶς ἰχθυίας 446.
θηρατικοὶ φόροι 317.
θηρία 481.
θησαυρικόν 241, 242, 332, 453, 490.
θησαυρός 35–7, 45, 370, 371. θ. τῶν ἱερῶν 35, 240, 449, 478.
θησαυροφύλακες 36.
θησαυροφυλακικόν 39.
θησο( ) 354.
θρυοπώλης 211.
θυσία 456.
θωνειτικὰ καὶ λιμνιτικά 70.

I

ἰδίᾳ 106, 121, 278, 398.
ἴδια κτήνη 78.
ἰδιόκτητος γῆ 3, 5, 15, 16, 362, 363.

ἴδιος λόγος 3, 33, 239, 246, 250, 252, 273, 278, 284, 293, 316, 320, 331, 334, 399, 451, 452, 468.

ἰδιω( ) 354.

ἰδιωτικὴ γῆ 3–5, 9, 13–17, 27, 283.

ἱερά or ἱερατικά (department of the treasury of the province) 51, 53, 63, 66, 157, 240–3, 247, 331, 332, 334, 377, 452–4, 490.

ἱερατικὴ γῆ 2–4, 11, 35, 363. ἱ. ὠνή 242.

ἱερατικόν 242, 243.

ἱερ( ) γεφ( ) 123, 124, 243, 410, 432, 453.

ἱερεῖς 333. ἱ. Δήμητρος 327.

ἱερευτικόν 243.

ἱερόν 250. ἱ. Βουκόλων 243, 244.

ἱερός. ἱ. ἀννώνη 24. ἱ. γῆ 4, 12, 14, 16, 17, 28, 53, 61, 239–41, 377, 381. ἱ. γῆ ἐν ἐκφορίῳ 4, 14, 51. ἱ. γῆ ἐπὶ καθήκουσι 4, 12, 13, 17, 18, 361. ἱ. ἐπιβολή 20.

Ἰετηρίτεις 18, 362, 363.

. ικουγ( ) [.]οργ( ) 354.

ιλ( ) 354.

ἱματιοπωλικόν 202.

Ἰουδαίων τέλεσμα 111, 114, 170–6, 296, 305, 325, 335, 347, 348, 428, 430, 479.

ἱππεῖς 54.

ἰσονόμος 54, 57, 58, 60, 330, 377.

ἱστωνάρχης 436.

ἱστωναρχία 199, 308, 440.

ἰχθυηρὰ δρύμων 220, 289.

ἰχθυΐας θηρᾶς 221.

ἰχθυομεταβολοί 209.

ἰχθυοπώλης 209.

ἴχνος ἐρημοφυλακίας 467.

Κ

κ( ) 325, 330, 354, 488.
.... κ( ) 354.

κα( ) 325, 330, 354, 488.

καθαρουργεῖον 207, 222, 442.

καθαρουργία 222.

κάθαρσις. ὁ ἐπὶ τῆς καθάρσεως τοῦ δημοσίου πυροῦ 40.

καθήκοντα, τὰ, 4, 11, 14, 17, 18, 78, 95, 202, 271, 329, 330, 338, 350, 353, 354, 356, 360, 366, 386, 389, 447, 458, 493. τὸ καθῆκον τέλος 83, 86.

καθόλικος 293.

κακιοπώλης 211, 442.

καμηλοτρόφοι 78.

κάπηλοι 209.

καρπῶναι 211, 442.

κασσιτερᾶτες 205, 443.

κασσοποιοί 199.

καταγραφῆς τέλη 234, 449.

καταγωγὴ σίτου 370.

καταγώγιον 43, 62, 325, 330, 367.

κατακρίματα 29, 37, 114, 204, 249, 321, 399, 473.

καταλοχισμοί 66–8, 232, 233, 310, 313, 355, 449, 450.

καταφυτεία 71.

καταχωρισμός 237.

κατοικικός 381. κ. γῆ 2–4, 13, 15–17, 19, 26, 35, 40, 42, 60, 61, 67, 68, 78, 95, 142, 176–80, 232, 233, 310, 355, 406, 430, 473. κ. γραφή 178, 179. κ. μονοδεσμία 384.

κάτοικος 13, 54, 109, 111, 113–21, 176–80, 316, 351, 384, 404–6, 431. ὑπὲρ κατοίκων 233. κατοίκων ἐπικεφάλαιον 127.

κεραμοποιοί 203, 204, 224.

κῆνσος 116.

κηποῦροι 211.
κηριοελκός 207.
κηρός. μέλι καὶ κηρός 280.
κηρυκεῖον 232.
κηρυκικά 231, 232.
κιθ( ) 354. κιθ( ) ἀργυρίου Σε( ) 305.
κλειδοποιοί 206.
κλεινεντ( ) 354.
κλῆρος 2, 3, 12, 13, 16, 361, 362, 377, 381.
κληρουκικὴ γῆ 1–5, 12–14, 18, 19, 35, 39, 42, 61, 74, 78.
κλήρουχοι 14, 15.
κναφική 201.
κο( ) 40. κο( ) αρ( ) 372.
κοινεία 210.
κοιτή 357.
κολλυβιστής 56.
κολλυβιστικὴ τράπεζα 304.
κόλλυβος 56, 60, 253, 324, 327, 379, 380, 460, 488.
κολωνία 16.
κομακτορία 230.
κοπὴ καὶ θρίξ 202.
κοπροπῶλαι 225.
κορμός 280.
κορσᾶτες 206.
κοσκινευτικόν 40.
κοσμητὴς φόρου κήπων Σαραπείου 316.
κουρεῖς 206.
κοτυλίζειν 186.
κουφοτέλεια 12, 281, 282, 293, 362.
κράστις 367, 384.
κριοτάφοι 248.
κτηνοτρόφοι 370.
κύδαρος 263–5, 465.
κυνηγίς 151, 477, 478.
κυριακὴ κριθή 23.
κωδᾶς 212, 443.
κωμάρχης 369, 474, 475.

κωμογραμματεία 333.
κωμογραμματεύς 6–10, 33, 99, 100, 104, 106, 112, 120, 192, 295, 311, 323, 333, 397.
κωπηλασία 280.

Λ

λααρχία 14, 15, 362.
λαξικά 205.
λαογραφία 70, 96–9, 105, 107–13, 116–40, 144, 150, 156, 157, 172, 180, 184, 193, 197, 253, 280, 284, 290, 291, 295, 297–9, 301, 302, 304–7, 310, 314, 316, 318, 321, 332, 343, 344, 346–51, 355, 396, 400, 402, 404–19, 431, 435, 438, 459, 460, 475–7, 479–81, 483, 487, 488, 492, 493.
λαογράφος 99, 100, 110, 304, 396.
λαογραφούμενοι,οἱ, 110, 111,113, 114, 117, 119, 405, 406.
λαχανία 376.
λαχανοπώλης 207.
λειτουργία 12, 20, 22, 29, 70, 78, 115, 136, 138, 141, 142, 146, 203, 286, 290, 294, 323, 474.
λειτουργικόν 70, 382.
λειτουργός 70.
λελμ( ) 354.
λεσωνεία 459.
λήμματα 168.
ληναῖον 75.
λιθικόν 280.
λίθινον ὅφριον 280, 304.
λίθος 167.
λίκμητρα 370.
λιμενάρχης 259, 320.
λιμὴν Μέμφεως 258–69, 272, 347, 461–3, 466, 468.
λιμιντικά 66, 70, 277, 332, 377, 383, 452, 490.

λιμνιτικὴ γῆ 5, 6, 332, 490.
λινική 198.
λῖνον 216.
λινοπλόκοι 198.
λινοπῶλαι 193, 198, 212.
λινοϋφικόν 198.
λινόϋφοι 193, 194, 198, 212. λ.
βυσσουργοί 193.
λογ( ) 354.
λογεία 244, 245, 454.
λογευτής 311. λ. λαογραφίας
321.
λογι( ) 478.
λογιστήριον 33, 295, 296, 475.
λόγος ἀρχικυνηγῶν 167. λ.
καυ . [. .] 354. λ. Μέμφεως
263, 274, 464. λ. προσθήκης
354.
λου( ) 354.
λύτρωσις αἰγῶν 241, 242, 248,
453.
λυχνίτιδος θρυίτιδος 220.

M

μαγδωλοφυλακία or ὑπὲρ μαγδώλων 149, 150, 304, 333, 347,
423, 424.
μαγειρῶν κοινόν 211.
μαχαιροφόρος 290.
μάχιμοι 2, 13–15, 361, 362.
μέλι καὶ κηρός 280.
μεριδάρχης 294, 333.
μερίς 357.
μερισμός 94, 96, 99, 102, 103,
105, 106, 128, 134–80, 193,
285, 291, 295, 297–9, 302,
305, 307, 310, 314, 316, 326,
333, 345–7, 349, 350, 352,
409–11, 418, 423, 425, 428,
476, 479, 480. μ. Ἀδριανείου
162, 163, 484. μ. . . αυ . . . 426.
μ. ἀνακεχωρηκότων 105, 106,
137–40, 161, 164, 165, 168,

292, 298, 306, 354, 400, 419,
420, 460. μ. ἀνδριάντος 159–
62, 413, 426. μ. ἀνδριάντος
καὶ προτομῆς 160. μ. ἀννώνης
154, 155, 305, 478. μ. ἀπόρων
137–40, 151, 292, 405, 420,
460. μ. ἀσθενῶν 420. μ. α. ᵀ( )
λη(μμήτων) 305. μ. βαλ( )
159. μ. διθ( ) 167. μ. διοικήσεως 166. μ. διπλῶν 153, 154,
304, 425. μ. διώρυγος 164. μ.
Δρόμου Γυμνασίου 427. μ.
Δρόμου Θοηρίδος 427. μ. ἐνδεήματος τελωνικῶν 166. μ.
ἐνλείμματος ὠνίων 164, 479.
μ. ἐπιβολῆς 168. μ. ἐπικεφα-
λίου ἀνδ( ) ἀνακεχ( ) 160,
161. μ. ἔργων Κρίου 163, 164.
μ. ἐρημοφυλακίας 151, 152,
155, 483. μ. Ζοίλου 164. μ.
θηρίων 167. μ. Κάμπωνος 164.
μ. κρίθης 28. μ. κυνηγετικῶν
δοράτων 167. μ. λαχάνου 28.
μ. μαγδώλων 150. μ. μη( )
καὶ Σύρεως 167. μ. να( ) 167.
μ. οἰκοδομίας σκοπέλων 148.
μ. πεντηκοστῆς 164. μ. πλινθευομένης 163, 427. μ. ποταμοφυλακίδος 298. μ. πρακτορίου 166. μ. πρεσιδίου 166.
μ. προχρείας 167, 303. μ.
τέλους 355. μ. τελωνικῶν 165,
427. μ. τελ( ) ὠνίων 164.
μ. σκοπέλων 148–50. μ. στόλου
στρατιωτῶν 166. μ. τελέ-
σματος καμήλων 155, 166, 390.
μ. ὑικῆς 145, 422. μ. ὑπὲρ
προυρίου περὶ Φοινίκην καλού-
μενον Σανδάντην 166, 298. μ
ὠνίων 164, 165, 305. μ. ὠνίων
ἐνλείμματος τελωνικῶν 164–6,
226, 292, 303, 427.
μερισ . . . Φιλ. τοπ( ) 167.

]μερῶ Σουχ( ) 354.
μετεπιγραφή 233.
μέτοχοι 298, 301, 313.
μηνιαῖος 193, 194, 408, 464.
μ. ἐν κεφαλαίῳ 37, 320.
μητροπολῖται or οἱ ἀπὸ τῆς μητροπόλεως 109-11, 118, 119, 121, 126-8, 134, 242, 399, 403, 404, 406-8, 414, 420. μ. δωδεκάδραχμοι 110, 118, 119, 126, 404, 405. μ. ὀκτάδραχμοι 110, 118, 126.
μίσθωσις 220, 227. μ. ποταμοφυλακίδος 299.
μισθωτής 220, 243, 274, 288, 303, 310, 324, 446. μ. ἀγριῶν θηρᾶς ζωῶν καὶ ὀρνέων 317. μ. διπλώματος ὄνων 310. μ. δρυμῶν καὶ ἐρήμου αἰγιαλοῦ Πολέμωνος μερίδος 446. μ. εἴδους ἐγκυκλίου καὶ ὑποκειμένων βασιλικῷ γραμματεῖ 310, 449. μ. εἴδους ὁρμοφυλακίας 175, 300. μ. ἐρημοφυλακίας 462, 468. μ. ἐρημοφυλακίας καὶ παροδίου Προσοπίτου καὶ Λητοπολίτου 272. μ. ἱερᾶς πύλης Σοήνης 288, 292, 299, 300, 477. μ. ἰχθυηρᾶς δρυμῶν 446. μ. κοπῆς καὶ χειρωναξίου 309. μ. ξενικῆς πρακτορίας 317. μ. πλείθου νόμου 281. μ. τέλους ἀγορανομίας ὠνίων 303, 305. μ. τέλους ἱεροῦ Βουκόλων 310. μ. χειρωναξίου μηνιαίου 477. μ. χειρωναξίου καὶ ἑταιρικοῦ 193, 300, 477.
μνημονεῖον 270, 467.
μολυβάτης 212.
μοναρταβία 13, 18, 19, 356.
μονοδεσμία 72, 73, 384. μ. ἀργυρικῶν 73, 74. μ. εργ( ) 73, 74. μ. χόρτου 72-4, 289, 334.

μονόδραχμος 67, 68. μ. ζευγματικῶν 67-9.
μοσχοσφραγιστής 246, 455.
μόσχου τέλος 241, 242, 247, 333.
μυρ( ) 354.
μυροβάλανοι 29, 299, 300, 305, 368, 375.
μυροπῶλαι 443.
μυρρῶν τιμή 310.

N

ναύβιον 13, 47, 59-61, 67-9, 142, 143, 162-4, 278, 301, 379-81, 421, 483, 484. ν. ἐναφεσίων 15, 60, 142, 326, 379, 381, 489. ν. κατοίκων 60, 142, 177, 233, 326, 489.
ναυκληρία 62.
ναύκληροι 44.
ναυλοδόκοι 153.
ναῦλον 44, 481, 483. ν. φορέτρου 62.
ναυπηγοί 205.
νε[ ] 354.
νεόφυτα 376.
νέων 263, 465. νέου 264.
νομάρχης 43, 73, 167, 192, 219, 221, 247, 268, 292, 294, 306, 334.
νομαρχία 260, 268, 289, 464, 466.
νομαρχικὰ ἀσχολήματα 71, 73, 307, 312, 333, 334, 352. ν. πάντα 222.
νομογράφος 311, 482.
ὑπὲρ νομῶν 86, 87.
νόμος τελωνικός 266, 267, 296, 315, 464.
νομοφύλαξ 315.

Ξ

ξενικὴ πρακτορία 316, 317.
ξυληγοί 224.

ξυλικόν 262, 264.
ξυλοπῶλαι 211.

O

ὁ πρὸς παραδοχῇ 283, 483. οἱ ἐπὶ τοῦ καθ( ) 304. οἱ ἐπὶ τῶν παρακαταθηκῶν 304.
ὀβολισμὸς ποταμίων πλοίων 373.
ὄβολοι 44.
ὀθονιηρά 440, 483.
οἰκοδόμων, ὑπέρ, 204, 205.
οἰκονόμος 231, 251. ο. οὐικάριος 311, 312, 482.
οἰκόπεδον 29.
οἶκος πόλεως 5.
οἰνηγίας ἀνάλωμα 264.
οἰνοπράται 209.
οἰνοπώλης 209, 212, 225.
οἴνου καινοῦ καὶ κάρρου 310. οἴνου τέλος 51, 63–5, 376, 378.
ὀκτάδραχμος 63, 65, 71, 110, 312, 378, 381, 382. ὀ. σπονδὴ Διονύσου 62, 63, 65, 381, 382.
ὁμόλογος 8, 9, 122, 123, 134, 140, 144, 184, 245, 409, 432, 454.
ὀνηλασία 78.
ὀνηλάτης 206, 212.
ὀρβιοπῶλαι 207.
ὀρβιοπωλία 207.
ὀργάνων τελουμένων, ὑπὲρ τῶν, 186.
ὁριοδείκτης 359.
ὅρκος 102, 103.
ὁρμοφυλακία 275.
ὀρυζιοπωλική 208.
οὐσία 1, 3, 5, 11–13, 85, 220, 360, 445.
οὐσιακά 309. οὐσιακοὶ γεωργοί 4. οὐσιακὴ γῆ 3, 4, 11, 12, 39, 41, 331, 341, 354. οὐσιακὸς λόγος 338, 339. οὐσιακὸς φόρος παραδείσων 483.

ὀψολογία 270.
ὀψώνιον 148. ὀ. μαγδώλων φυλάκων 150. ὀ. σκοπέλων 149. ὀ. φυλάκων 146, 147.

Π

π⁻( ) 354.
παικίσων 300, 354.
[. . .] πανηγύρεως 241, 242.
παντοπωλική 208.
παραγωγὴ ἐλαίας 58, 59, 61, 62, 326, 377, 379–81.
παραζυγὴ ζυγῶν 280.
παραλήμπται ἀχύρου 25. π. τῆς Ἐρυθρᾶς θαλάσσης 257. π. τῆς τετάρτης 461.
παρατομή 358.
παρόδιον 272, 274.
πατ( ) 355.
πέδια 72.
πεδιακὴ ἐπίκρισις 10.
πελωχικόν 222, 270, 289, 355, 467.
πε( ) μηχ( ) 355.
πέμπτη 261, 262, 265, 464, 467.
πενθήμερος 141–3, 421, 422. π. ὄνων 92, 391.
πεντάδραχμος 65. (πενταδραχμία) ὄνων . . . ἀπεργασίας 92.
πενταρταβία 41.
πεντεφυλία 249.
πεντηκοστή 260, 268–71, 278, 300, 315, 487. π. λιμένος Σοήνης 269, 300. π. ὠνίων 164, 165, 225, 270, 271, 427.
πεντηκοστῶναι λιμένος Σοήνης 269, 300.
πηδάλιον 263, 264, 275, 465.
πηχισμός 305. ἐπιβολὴ πηχισμοῦ οἰκοπέδων 76. πηχισμὸς περιστερεώνων 69, 376, 382, 483.
πιττάκιον 262–4, 273, 274.
πλεῖθος 281, 310.

πλεονασμός 21, 364.
πλινθευομένη 163, 189, 302, 427.
πλινθευτική 205.
πλοῖα Θεαγῶν 249. πλοῖον πραιτωρίου 298.
πο( ) 40.
πόδωμα 40, 45, 372.
ποικιλτής 199.
.... ποιμένων 241, 242.
πολ( ) 16, 17.
πόρθμιον 302. ὑπὲρ πορθμίδων 189, 480.
πορθμοφυλακία 152.
πορτᾶς 212.
ποταμοφυλακίς 151, 297, 301, 423, 424, 478.
πραγματευόμενοι, οἱ, 310.
πραγματευτής 288, 310, 317. π. ἐρημοφυλακίας 310, 468. π. πύλης Φιλαδελφίας 247.
πραγματικοί 365.
πρακτορία 290, 301, 316, 317, 331, 332, 372. π. νομαρχικῶν ἀσχολημάτων ζυτηρᾶς καὶ μονοδεσμιῶν 73, 294, 307.
πρακτορικόν 166, 324, 327, 488.
πράκτωρ 132, 166, 248, 286–8, 290, 294, 297, 298, 301, 305, 306, 311, 313, 314, 316, 317, 319, 320, 321, 333, 334, 345, 454, 475, 476, 478, 480, 483, 488. π. ἀργυρικῶν 24, 83, 157, 184, 198, 291, 298, 299, 301, 302, 304–8, 314, 316, 319, 320, 324, 474, 476, 479, 480. π. ἀργυρικῶν καὶ σιτικῶν 298. π. βαλ( ) 157, 302, 303, 425, 478. π. δερμάτων χορούντων εἰς κατασκευὴν ὅπλων 308. π. δημοσίας κώμης 481. π. δημοσίων 313. π. Θεαγῶν 158, 302, 478. π. κατακριμάτων 290, 473. π. κατοίκων 233.

π. λαογραφίας 70, 290, 291, 307, 314, 473. π. μονοδεσμίας χόρτου 481. π. νομαρχικῶν 308. π. ξενικῶν 482. π. οὐσίας 308, 491. π. πολιτικῶν 314. π. σιτικῶν 37, 38, 369. π. στεφανικῶν 307, 314. π. τοκ( ) 302, 478. π. τῶν προσόδων 307. π. χειρωναξίου 313, 322. π. χειρωναξίου γερδίων 290.
.. πραμ Διὸς πόλεως 355.
π[. .] ρ( ) εἰδῶν 354.
πρεσβύτερος 8, 25, 34, 72, 304, 311, 312, 359, 384, 482. π. κώμης 292, 310–14, 365, 474. π. παστοφόρων 311. π. προβατοκτηνοτρόφων 80.
προβάτων, ὑπὲρ, 87, 386.
προβατοκτηνοτρόφοι 79, 80, 385, 392.
προπρατικόν 228.
προπωλητικόν 228.
πρόσγραφον 204.
προσδιαγραφόμενα 50, 52, 55, 56, 58–60, 62, 69, 79, 87, 89, 121, 123, 132, 145, 177, 178, 180, 204, 206, 213, 228, 248, 249, 251, 253, 264, 324–30, 345, 347, 354, 376, 379, 380, 386, 389, 409, 414, 416, 432, 437–9, 446, 456, 457, 459, 460, 465, 486–9, 493.
πρόσθεμα 28, 419.
προσλήψεως στεφανός 449.
προσμετρούμενα 28, 29, 35, 38–41, 358, 371, 372.
προσοδικός. π. γεωργοί 3. π. γῆ 55. π. φόρος 383.
πρόσοδος 32, 72, 241, 251, 384.
προσόδου γῆ 3–5. πρόσοδος οἰκίας 384. π. οἰκοπέδων 29, 75. π. ὑδατική 72. π. ὑπαρχόντων 72. π. φοινίκων 299.

πρόσταγμα 273.
προστάτης 281. π. τοῦ θεοῦ 245, 304, 454.
προστατικόν 281.
πρόστιμον 10, 76, 281, 366, 367, 485.
προφητεία καὶ λεσωνεία καὶ θεαγεία 252.
προφήτης 244, 458, 459.
προχρεία 167, 353, 428.
πρύτανις 292, 334.
πυλωνικόν 270.
πυρινὸς μερισμός 418.

Ρ

ῥ καὶ ικ 303, 449, 450.
ῥ καὶ ύ 260, 268–70, 272, 273, 334, 347, 462–4, 466, 468, 492.
ῥαβδοφόροι 18.
ῥυπαραὶ δραχμαί 324, 327, 487.

Σ

σ( ) 355.
σακκηγία 34, 42, 370.
σακκο( ) 206.
σακκοποιοί 206.
σακκοφόρος 37, 206.
σεβεννία 29.
σιδηρουργός 205, 212.
σιτικὸν τέλεσμα 222.
σιτοκάπηλοι 211.
σιτόλογος 24, 35–8, 40–5, 320, 371, 373, 484. σ. ἱερατικῶν 240.
σιτομέτραι 37.
σιτομετρικόν 42.
σιτοπαραλημπταί 36.
σκόπελοι 148, 149, 305, 347, 423.
σκυ[.]ποιμ( ) κοινόν 211.
σκυτοποιοί 442.
σλ( ) 355. σλ( ) κατοίκων 355.
σο( ) 284.

σπονδή 62, 63, 228, 236, 263, 465. σ. Διονύσου 62–5, 483.
στατίων 148, 298, 423.
στατιωνάριος 264.
στεπτικόν 281.
στεφανικόν 26, 126, 281–4, 305, 312, 314, 316, 332, 345, 348, 349, 351, 352, 355, 470, 471, 473, 478, 480, 481.
στεφανοπλόκοι 211.
στέφανος 308, 315, 361, 470.
στημονοποιεῖον 211.
στιβεῖς 202, 443.
στιππουργός 206, 443.
στιχάρια 216.
στοίχημα 355.
στολιστεία 459.
στρατηγός 8, 23, 33, 37, 42, 44, 82–5, 89, 90, 94, 99, 165, 246, 252, 257, 288–90, 292–5, 313–15, 319–23, 397, 399, 404, 475, 485.
στρατιώτης 264, 304, 313.
στυπτηρία 189, 211, 309, 443, 461.
συ(˙) 355.
συμβολικά or σύμβολον 62, 87, 89, 123, 134, 262, 264, 318, 323, 327, 328, 389, 409, 410, 432, 456, 457, 487, 488, 493. σύμβολον καμήλων 272, 274, 310, 468.
συναγοραστικὸς πυρός 22, 365.
συνεισφορὰ ἀνδριάντος χαλκοῦ καὶ προτομῆς ἀργυρᾶς Ἀδριανοῦ τοῦ κυρίου 160.
συντάξιμον 108, 122–5, 133, 140, 184, 306, 311, 319, 321, 326, 409–11, 413–16, 432, 453, 476, 482, 486.
σύνταξις 29, 116, 123, 125, 187, 239–41, 307, 316, 353, 452, 459.

σφραγίς 357. σφραγισμός 247, 273, 274.
σχεδία 258, 262, 268, 271, 465, 466.
σωματικόν 284.
σωματισμός 371.

T

ταβουλάριος 317.
ταπιδύφαντες 439.
ταπιτᾶς 198, 212.
ταριχευταί 206, 441.
τέκτονες 205, 213.
τέλεσμα ἀμπέλου and παραδείσου 64, 67, 69. ἀργυρικὰ τ. τῶν σιτεικῶν 47. δημόσια τ. 50. τ. ἐκδόσεων 279. τ. καμήλων 89, 90, 93, 155, 166, 350, 389, 390, 484. τ. κεραμέων 204. τ. κοτυλισμοῦ 187. τ. τῶν ὀργάνων 186. τ. φυτῶν ὄντων ἐν σιτικ[ ] 383.
τελεστικόν 250, 457.
τέλος or τέλη 76, 151, 195, 197, 199, 202, 215, 222, 226–8, 234, 243, 264, 316, 317, 355, 360, 386, 434, 437, 447, 450. τ. ἀγορανομίας ὠνίων 165, 227, 302, 427. τ. ἀγορασμοῦ 229. αἰτήσεως τέλος 235. τ. ἀληθικ( ) μυομ(εν) 353. τ. ἁμαξῶν 281, 441. τ. βαλ( ) 425. τ. βαλανευτικόν 158. τ. βοός 226, 271. τ. γερδικόν 194, 297. τ. γερδίων 302. γνήσια τέλη 67–9. τ. γνωστείας 232, 313. τ. δελφακίδος 94. τ. διαγραφῆς 449. τ. διαιρέσεως 236. τ. δούλου 230. τ. εἰκοστόν 231. τ. ἐκστάσεως 229, 306. τ. ἐλαιουργικῶν ὀργάνων 186, 433. τ. ἐμβαδικόν 230. τ. ἐνκυκλίου 230, 302, 303. τ.

ἐπικαταβολῆς ὑποθήκης 236. τ. ἐπιξένων 278, 302, 306, 470, 487. τ. ἠπητῶν 302. τ. θησαυροῦ ἱερῶν 302. τ. ἱεροῦ Βουκόλων 243, 244, 310. τ. ἱματιοπωλῶν 202, 284. τ. ἰχθυηρᾶς δρύμων 220, 445. τ. θυιῶν 186, 327, 433, 489. τ. καμήλων 90. καταγραφῆς τ. 234, 449. τ. καταλοχισμῶν 66, 67, 232, 233, 310, 355, 449, 450. τ. κορμῶν τριῶν 280. τ. λαχανίας 376. τ. λινοπλόκων 198, 302. τ. λίνου 198. τ. λινύφων 302, 437. τ. λυχνίτιδος θρυίτιδος 220. τ. Μέμφεως 262. τ. μεταβολῶν ἁλιέων 209, 442. τ. μισθώσεως 227. μόσχου τέλος 241, 242, 247. τ. μόσχου θυομένου 242, 246–8, 310, 311, 455, 467. τ. ναυπηγῶν 302. τ. νεκροτάφων 284, 289, 315. οἴνου τ. 51, 63–5. τ. ὀνηλατῶν 441. τ. ὄνου 391, 483. τ. πάγης βοός 448. τ. προβάτων 87. τ. σκυτέων 443. τ. ταφῆς 203, 284, 303, 441. τ. τάφου καὶ ψιλῶν τόπων 229. τ. τῆς ἐλευθερώσεως 230. τ. τῆς τετάρτης 223. τ. τῆς τρυγῆς 64. τὸ καθῆκον τ. 83, 86, 447. τ. τῶν ὄνων 91, 93, 317. τ. χειρωναξίου 201, 309.
τελῶναι 158, 164, 165, 189, 266, 287, 288, 303, 305, 310, 314, 315, 317, 323, 324, 326, 376. τ. ἀγορανομίας 303. τ. ἀγορανομίας ὠνίων 226, 227. τ. ἁμαξικοῦ 303. τ. βαλανείου 303. τ. γερδίων or γερδιακοῦ 195, 198, 303, 304. τ. εἴδους ὄνων 91, 317. τ. ἑταιρικοῦ 210, 300. τ. ἠπητῶν 202, 303. τ. θησαυροῦ ἱερῶν 157, 240, 302,

303, 441, 479. τ. ἱματιοπωλῶν
202, 302, 303. τ. κλεινεντ( )
477. τ. λαχανικοῦ 303. τ.
νήσου 303. τ. ὀνηλατικοῦ 303.
τ. (πεντηκοστῆς) 164, 165,
169, 303-5. τ. πεντηκοστῆς
λιμένος Σοήνης 269, 300. τ.
πεντηκοστῆς ὠνίων ὑποτελῶν
225. τ. ρ̅ καὶ ι̅ᴷ 303, 449, 450.
τ. ὑικῆς 94, 144, 303. τ. χειρωναξίου 315. τ. ὠνίων ὑποτελῶν 303.
τελωνικά 164, 165, 220, 222,
314. τελωνικὴ ἀτέλεια 29, 360.
τελώνιον 75.
τέμενος 455.
τεσσαρακαιεικοσίδραχμος 417.
τεσσαρακοστή 256.
τετάρτη 219, 222, 223, 256, 257,
446, 461. τ. ἁλιέων 219, 445,
446. τ. ἀρτοπωλῶν 222, 446.
τ. σιτοποιῶν 222, 446. τ. σίτου
446. τ. τοῦ ταρίχους 446. τ.
ὑπὲρ φόρου γενῶν ζωγραφικῶν
222.
τετράδραχμος 66.
τιμὴ ἀναβολικοῦ 215. τ. ἐλαίου
186. τ. θυρῶν 164, 481. τ. καὶ
δαπάνημα ἀνδριάντος Τραιανοῦ
159. τ. οἴνου κ.τ.λ. 24, 25, 43,
225, 298, 299, 301-4, 365-7,
374, 378, 453, 477, 489, 490.
τ. στολιστείας 251, 459. τιμήματος τ. 234.
τοκ( ) τυ( ) 355, 391.
τοκαδεία 93, 94, 329, 332.
τόκος διοικήσεως 284, 355, 391.
τοπάρχης 84, 294, 321, 333.
τοπογραμματεύς 100, 120, 192,
333, 397.
τόπος 358.
τρ( ) 355.
τράπεζα 43, 146, 287, 288, 296,

304-6, 312-14, 316, 319-21,
324, 334, 370, 415, 473, 476,
482, 484. τ. νομαρχίας 306.
τραπεζίτης 209, 241, 263, 264,
287, 297, 300, 301, 472, 473,
488.
τραπεζιτικόν 285, 355.
τρίδραχμος 66, 67, 241, 242, 332,
382. τ. μητροπολιτῶν 65, 66.
τρίτη 425. τ. βαλανείου 155, 223,
425, 483. τ. διοικ( ) 67. τ.
εἰκ( ) μυροβαλάνων 299, 368. τ.
νομ( ) μυροβαλάνων 299, 300,
368. τ. περιστερεώνων 69, 490.
τριχοινικόν 39.
τροφὴ δελφάκων καὶ ἄλλων ἀγέλων 392.
τυραννικὰ ἐδάφη 3.

Υ

..υ 355. .... υ 355. . [.]υ ......
355.
ὑελουργός 207.
ὑική 93, 94, 123, 124, 128, 143-
5, 314, 328, 332, 351, 392,
409, 410, 422, 483.
ὑπερετής 107-9, 111, 114, 118,
138, 170, 403, 420, 428. ὑ.
ἐποχῆς ἐμβαδείας 317.
ὑποκείμενα, τὰ, 211, 279, 310,
314, 327, 332, 333, 449, 490.
ὑπολ( ) Νησ( ) 478.
ὑπόλογος γῆ 5, 28, 68, 71, 366,
367, 383.
ὑπόμνημα ἐπιγεννήσεως 105, 112,
400, 411.
ὑποσχεσάριος ὠνῆς ἀθηροπωλῶν
καὶ ὀρβιοπωλῶν 315.

Φ

φ( ) 355. φ . . Θεαδελ( ) 355,
416. φῑ( ) νῑ( ) Θεαδ( )
355, 416.

φακινᾶς 208, 443.
Φέννησις 245, 304, 454.
φιλάνθρωπον 41, 372.
φοίνικες 375, 376.
φόρετρον 21, 26, 28, 42–4, 62, 67, 70, 312, 370, 372, 373, 382. ἐλαίων φ. 62. φ. νομαρχίας 373. φ. ὄνων 373.
φορικ( ) 43, 373. Ἀρσινοῆς φορικά 81, 387.
φόριμος γῆ 47, 56, 76.
φόρος 41, 67, 68, 71, 72, 76, 78–81, 95, 116, 183, 186, 187, 189, 219, 222, 227, 248, 249, 306, 307, 310, 316, 317, 332, 346, 348, 350, 382, 383, 387, 392, 433, 446, 483. φ. ἀμπέλου 71. φ. Ἀντω( ) νεᾱ( ) 478. φ. ἀρνίων 79. φ. βαλ( ) 425. φ. βαλανείου 156. βαλανικὸς φ. 305. φ. βασιλικῶν ἱερείων ὑικῶν 387. φ. βοῶν 80, 387, 456. φ. βωμῶν 248, 249, 325, 387, 452, 456, 457, 489. φ. γένων ζωγραφικῶν 80, 222, 308, 446. φ. δεύτερος 90. φ. διώρυγος 299. φ. ἐδάφων 314, 383. φ. θησαυρικός 383. φ. ἵππων 387. φ. κήπων Σαραπείου 316. φ. νομαρχικῶν ἀσχολημάτων 71. φ. νόμων 72, 312, 329, 334. φ. ὀρνίθων 80, 93. φ. οὐσιακός 333. φ. πλοίων ἁλιευτικῶν 308. φ. παραδείσου 71. φ. πλεονασμῶν 72. φ. πορθμειός 315. φ. προβάτων 79–81, 86, 87, 93, 305, 308, 311, 312, 385–9, 457. φ. τελέσματος 222. φ. ὑποδοχίου 72. φ. ὑπολόγου γῆς 383. φ. ὑῶν 94. φ. φοινίκων 71. φ. φράγμου 72. φ. φυτῶν 71 (φυῆς 71, ἐλαίνου φύτωνος 71). φ.

χεσον( ) 72. φ. χηνῶν 80, 387. φ. ψίλου τόπου ἐν κώμῃ 72.
φροντιστής 36, 101, 110, 399, 404.
Φυλακή 258, 268.
φυλακία, φυλακή, or φύλακες 146–9, 151, 153, 168, 298, 301, 302, 304, 305, 307, 316, 345–7, 370, 410, 417, 422, 423.
φυλακῖται 14, 180, 277–9.
φυλακιτικόν 128, 146, 422. φ. τῶν κτηνῶν 389.
φύλακτρον 147, 189, 396, 417. φ. ἀπόρων 150, 151.
φύλαξ ἀπὸ γῆς 263, 264, 465.

X

χ( ) 355, 416, 436.
χάλασμα 21.
χάλκινα 355.
χαλκὸς ἰσονόμος 54, 377.
χαρτηρά 237, 334, 451.
χειρήτης 213.
χειριστής 306, 309–11, 314, 473, 482, 483. χ. κώμης 310.
χειριστικόν 259, 263, 264, 325, 328–30, 464, 489.
χειρογραφία 262–4, 267, 466.
χειρονάξιον 114, 191–4, 201–5, 207, 211–13, 227, 291, 296–303, 307, 309, 314, 326, 332, 334, 344, 346, 350, 355, 407, 409, 411, 435–7, 439, 443, 487, 488, 493.
χερσάμπελος 16, 18.
χερσονομαί 79.
χλωρά 74, 384.
χλωραγωγοί 224.
χο( ) 74, 355, 366.
χοι( ) τρο( ) οβ . .( ) 392.
χόρτος ἐν γένει 74. χ. ἐν γενήματι 384.
χρηματισμός 234, 235.

χρυ( ) 355.
χρυσοχοική 189.
χω( ) ὀψώνιον 300, 355.
χωματικόν 60, 61, 127, 128, 132, 140–3, 156, 157, 167, 301–5, 307, 321, 327, 328, 332, 343, 344, 351, 364, 410, 420–2, 475, 480, 486, 489.

Ψ
ψυγμοῦ καὶ διαψειλῶν 354.

Ω
ὠνή 309, 315. ἱερατικὴ ὠνή 242. ὠ. πελωχικοῦ 289. πρὸς ἀργύριον ὠνή 54, 91. ὑπὲρ ὠνίων 165.

ENGLISH AND LATIN

adaeratio 28, 54, 55, 57, 74, 141–3, 154, 158, 281, 364, 376, 486, 490.
anabolicae species 444, 445.
annona civilis 13, 32, 46, 337, 341. annona militaris 74, 301, 303, 304, 339, 374, 376, 425.
annonariae species 444.
arrears 22, 29, 37, 124–7, 130, 132, 136–8, 159, 164, 215, 216, 286, 297, 314, 321, 332, 349, 370, 371, 410, 411, 413–15, 438, 455, 485.
capsarium 383.
classis Augusta Alexandrina 46.
portoria 270, 287.
praefectus annonae 32.
Prefect of Egypt 8, 24, 26, 31, 32, 41, 101, 200, 238–40, 273, 274, 286, 289, 292–5, 317, 320–2, 335, 343, 368, 369, 398, 473.
Procurators 45, 238, 293.
scriptura 389.
vectigal 266. v. Maris Rubri 257, 265, 461.
vicesima 234, 480.